METHODOLOGIES
in CARIBBEAN RESEARCH
on Gender and Sexuality

Notes

1. Future references to Cather's preface are to the 1938 Cassell edition, which incorporates the author's 1937 revisions to the novel. My quotations from the novel itself throughout this essay are from the original 1915 version.
2. See, for example, Carlin's *Cather, Canon, and the Politics of Reading*, Stout's *Strategies of Reticence*, and Skaggs' *After the World Broke in Two*.
3. See O'Brien, *The Emerging Voice*, and Lee, *Willa Cather*.
4. Cather reviewed performances by contraltos such as Clara Butt, Louise Homer, Helena von Doenhoff, Jessie Bartlett Davis, Ernestine Schumann-Heink, and Marie Tempest, the latter as Francesca in De Koven's *The Fencing Master* (1892). 'who as usual spent most of her time masquerading as a boy' (Traubner 361). According to Cather, Lempest's form 'is exquisitely moulded and her tights become her wondrous well, so well that she ought never to appear in skirts in the last act' (*World and the Parish* 1: 170). Schumann-Heink may have been the inspiration for the character of the contralto Wilhelmina Schroeder-Schatz in Cather's novel *One of Ours* (1922).
5. According to Fremstad's secretary/companion Mary Watkins Cushing, Octavian 'would indeed have been a superb role for her. It was cast in her best vocal range; and with her fine legs and lean haunches, she would have made a handsome boy. She was well aware of this and told me that she had often sung male parts in Munich and had been much admired in them; that even in *Carmen* she sometimes wore breeches for mountain climbing in Act III' (56).
6. In her essay '148 Charles Street,' Cather recounts how Annie Adams Fields regaled her with accounts of Viardot-Garcia's performance—'my hostess gave me such an account of hearing Viardot sing Gluck's *Orpheus* that I felt I had heard it myself'—and of Chorley's impressions as well (61–62).
7. Because Cather's will prohibits direct quotation of her letters, I can only summarise the text of the *serenata*. It contains three stanzas of eight lines each with a rhyme scheme of *ababcdcd*. The first stanza makes a comparison between the rose of night that has bloomed and the availability of the singer to her lover; the second compares the dry winds of day with the singer's thirsty lips at night; and the third speaks of how the tired eyes of the singer that fade to dreams of the lover resemble the fading stars. At the end of each stanza is an exhortation to the lover to accept the respective invitations to love (Letter, 15 June 1912).
8. Cather's attraction to Julio lends weight to the argument that her later friendships with androgynous young men such as Stephen Tennant and Truman Capote were not as uncharacteristic as some biographical accounts indicate (Woodress 385).
9. See Heilbrun pages 14 and 43 for a discussion of how Cather resisted writing about events from her own life that could have compromised her reputation.
10. It is interesting that Beethoven's song, like Schumann's and Gluck's, documents the woman's absence, again highlighting the important role played by gender divisions in Thea's growth to musical maturity and the consequences of seeing herself as a female 'other.'
11. According to Rosowski, Cather's novel tells the story of 'Thea's liberation from a modern sense of linear time and into an older, cyclic one. . . . We are interested not in what happens to Thea in a worldly sense but in the new order she will imagine or create' ('Subverted Endings' 77).
12. Hermione Lee notes that, even though Cather omitted most (but not all) references to Kronborg's marriage to Ottenburg when she revised the novel in 1937, she also 'moderated Thea's masculine qualities' in order to maintain a balance between 'images of domineering male heroes' and Thea's intense femininity (126).

METHODOLOGIES
in CARIBBEAN RESEARCH
on Gender and Sexuality

*Kamala Kempadoo and
Halimah A. F. DeShong*

IAN RANDLE PUBLISHERS
Kingston • Miami

First published in Jamaica, 2021 by
Ian Randle Publishers
16 Herb McKenley Drive
Box 686
Kingston 6
www.ianrandlepublishers.com

© 2021 Kamala Kempadoo and Halimah A. F. DeShong
ISBN: 978-976-637-989-6

National Library of Jamaica Cataloguing-in-Publication Data

Names: Kempadoo, Kamala, editor. | DeShong, Halimah A. F., editor.
Title: Methodologies in Caribbean research on gender and sexuality / Kamala Kempadoo and Halimah A. F. DeShong, editors.
Description: Kingston : Ian Randle Publishers, 2021 | Includes bibliographical references and index.
Identifiers: ISBN 9789766379896 (pbk) | ISBN 9789768286345 (epub).
Subjects: LCSH: Gender identity – Research – Methodology – Caribbean Area. | Feminism - Caribbean Area. | Sexualities – Research – Methodology - Caribbean Area.
Classification: DDC 305.3 -- dc23.

All rights reserved. While copyright in the selection and editorial material is vested in Kamala Kempadoo and Halimah A. F. DeShong, copyright in individual chapters belongs to their respective authors and publishers and no part of this publication may be reproduced, stored in a retrieval system or transmitted in any form or by any means electronic, photocopying, recording or otherwise, without the prior express permission of the author and publisher.

Cover and book design by Ian Randle Publishers

Cover image *Paper Queen Suri* (2010) © Brianna McCarthy.
Used with permission of the artist.

Printed and bound in the United States of America

Contents

Introduction

1. Locating Methodologies in Research on Gender and Sexuality in the Caribbean 1
   Halimah A. F. DeShong and Kamala Kempadoo

HISTORY AND HISTORIOGRAPHY

2. Recollections into a Journey of a Rebel Past 29
   Lucille Mathurin Mair

3. Gender and Memory: Oral History and Women's History 41
   Mary Chamberlain

4. Women and Gender in Caribbean (English-speaking) Historiography: Sources and Methods 60
   Bridget Brereton

METHODOLOGIES FOR FEMINIST ORGANIZING AND ACTION RESEARCH

5. Feminist Action and Research in Haiti 87
   Carolle Charles

6. Feminist Research and Action Methodology: The Experiences of the Caribbean Association of Feminist Research and Action 97
   Frederica M. Deare

7. Red Thread's Research: An Interview with Andaiye 119
   Kamala Kempadoo

8. A Method of Decolonial Arts Practice 141
   Honor Ford Smith

RESEARCHING GENDER

9. Women in the Caribbean Project: An Overview 153
   Joycelin Massiah

10. Learning to be a Man 179
    Barry Chevannes

11. Gender Studies in Cuba: Methodological Approaches, 1974–2001 187
    Marta Núñez Sarmiento

12. Feminist and Quantitative: Measuring the Extent
    of Domestic Violence in Georgetown, Guyana   211
    Linda Peake

13. Interdisciplinary Feminist Research, Environment,
    and Community: The Nariva Swamp Case Study   225
    Rhoda Reddock and Grace Sirju-Charran

SEXUALITIES RESEARCH

14. No Tide, No Tamara/Not Today, Not Tomorrow   249
    Gloria Wekker

15. Embodied Theories: Local Knowledge(s), Community
    Organizing, and Feminist Methodologies in Caribbean
    Sexuality Studies   269
    Angelique V. Nixon and Rosamond S. King

16. Researching Caribbean Sexual Labour   289
    Kamala Kempadoo

17. Caribbean Sexualities and Ethnographic
    Research Methods   307
    David A. B. Murray

18. Subjective Mapping: A Brief Introduction   325
    Krystal Nandini Ghisyawan

RESEARCHING THE VISUAL AND CULTURAL

19. Defining Women Subjects: Photographs in Trinidad
    (1860s–1960s)   351
    Roshini Kempadoo

20. Feminist Witnessing: Creating Visual Media through
    Ethnographic Research   370
    Deborah A. Thomas

21. Decoding the Image as Method for Researching Culture 392
    Patricia Mohammed

METHODS FOR ANALYSING TALK AND TEXT

22. Reconceptualizing Voice: The Role of Matrifocality
    in Shaping Theories and Caribbean Voices   411
    Michelle V. Rowley

23. Studying Religious Mobilizations in the Anglophone
    Caribbean: A Feminist Critical Reading of Discourse   419
    Latoya Lazarus

24. Caribbean/Anticolonial Feminist Methods for Analysing Talk and Text in Research on Gender-Based Violence   *449*
   Halimah A. F. DeShong

REFLECTIONS ON POSITIONALITY: LESSONS FROM THE FIELD

25. Toward a Native Anthropology: Methodological Notes on the Study of Successful Caribbean Women by an Insider   *465*
   Nesha Z. Haniff

26. Anthropological Research Methods for the Study of Black Women in the Caribbean   *480*
   A. Lynn Bolles

27. Downtown Ladies: Informal Commercial Importers, a Haitian Anthropologist, and Self-making in Jamaica   *493*
   Gina A. Ulysse

28. "Insider" Experiences and Ethnographic Knowledge: Reflections from Trinidad and Tobago   *513*
   Gabrielle Hosein

29. 'You is One of We': Positionality in the Field   *532*
   Tami Navarro

List of Figures

Chapter 18

Figure 1:	Scan of N'Dare's map.	345
Figure 2:	Scan of Ariel's map (name removed).	345
Figure 3:	Photo of Jean's map alongside a digital reproduction.	346
Figure 4:	Scan of Jean's map of Chaguanas.	346
Figure 5:	Jane's maps.	347

Chapter 19

Illustration 1:	Anon. (unknown). *Untitled (Standing on either side)*	358
Illustration 2:	Kempadoo, Roshini. (2006). *Mrs Procope's family photographs*	359
Illustration 3:	Anon. (unknown). *Untitled 3.*	361

Chapter 21

Figure 1:	'Flagellation of a Female Samboe Slave' William Blake c. 1791	393
Figure 2:	Agostino Brunias: *A Negro Festival in the Island of St Vincent.* Lithograph of Original Oil on Canvas, (painted between 1773 and 1796).	397
Figure 3:	*The Barbados Mulatto Girl*, Agostino Brunias.	401
Figure 4:	*The West India Serving Woman*, Agostino Brunias.	402
Figure 5:	Hand Coloured Postcard Trinidad, East Indian Women, circa 1890.	403
Figure 6:	Two Women Seated in Hammock in Trinidad, circa 2003.	405

List of Tables

Chapter 12

Table 1:   Defining Legitimate Knowledge for Positivist and Feminist
           Philosophies of Knowledge   213

Table 2:   Main Findings on Domestic Violence Survey   220

Introduction

1. Locating Methodologies in Research on Gender and Sexuality in the Caribbean

Halimah A. F. DeShong and Kamala Kempadoo

> *Many Caribbean women writers today, also engaged in their acts of conscious self-affirmation, explore history, myth and memory, seeking cultural continuities. Refusing to pursue futility, they seldom lament the absence of ruins. On the contrary they celebrate their presence, not the presence of fragmented, desolate remnants that signify nothing, but the valued monuments, human artefacts ready to receive vibrant new forms through the genius of those pens which are busily creating praise songs for Caribbean women. And here, of course, is where the journey has brought me.*
>
> Lucille Mathurin Mair
> 'Recollections into a Journey of a Rebel Past' (2006, 328)

The journey to which Lucille Mathurin Mair refers in the opening quotation has long been regarded as a site for critical engagement by feminists, and other social researchers in the Caribbean concerned about the processes by which knowledge is created and legitimised. Writing in the mid to late 20th century, the contributions to Caribbean feminist research practice and methodology made by scholars like Mathurin Mair undermined a colonialist project of constructing a Caribbean, which in many instances, invalidated, distorted, and silenced the experiences of large groups of people. Like Caribbean historian Elsa Goveia before her, Mathurin Mair broke new ground and ruptured a particular kind of orthodox Eurocentric masculinist historiography, and she is described as engaging a process of decoding the archival texts (Beckles and Shepherd 2006). In particular, Mathurin Mair exposed the value of myth, memory, and other cultural artefacts to the process of what she called 'excavating women from layers of distortion and obscurity'. Her work, which interrogated how women in Jamaica were implicated in various relations of power under the systems of slavery, racism, and the colonial project, and how agency and resistance were indeed enacted as women navigated these processes, represents an epistemic shift in Caribbean historiography. Her contribution extends well beyond writing women into history. Mathurin Mair's historical method and focus serve as an important point of departure for those who succeeded her.

Inspired by these earlier developments in Caribbean historiography, and a desire to examine what Alison Jagger refers to as 'knowledge-generating strategies' (2008, vii), this collection traces the often-overlooked contribution to critical discussions of methodology undertaken by feminists, and other gender and sexuality studies scholars, in the Caribbean. Even before the existence of entire collections devoted to reflections on feminist and other critical research practice, Caribbeanist scholars have consistently expressed concerns about the processes and conditions under which knowledge is created, given a history replete with examples of hegemonic ideologies masquerading as objective research.

This volume, *Methodologies in Caribbean Research on Gender and Sexuality*, traces and examines knowledge-generation strategies offered by feminist and other researchers studying gender and sexuality in the Caribbean, with an emphasis on the English-speaking countries. It not only archives foundational texts on methodologies for doing research in the region but also provides a range of new critical perspectives on feminist methodologies in the Caribbean. It adds to the already robust body of work that exists globally on feminist methodologies and furthers the conversation about decolonizing feminisms more generally, from a Caribbean vantage point.

Caribbeanist researchers of gender and sexuality have written about methods in a variety of places, including peer reviewed journal articles, short sections of their single authored books, and/or as essays in anthologies about gender and/or sexuality. In our ongoing effort to make this methodology explicit and visible (see Kempadoo, DeShong and Crawford 2013), we have brought together here complete essays and articles as well as excerpts from these writings. As opposed to focusing exclusively on either data collection or analysis, or on either quantitative or qualitative methods, we trace the methodological concerns of the researchers at various stages of the knowledge generation enterprise. In addition, methodological and epistemological concerns are not discussed in abstraction. We include the actual experiences and insights from empirical studies of gender and/or sexuality in the Caribbean since the 1960s. Due to language limitations, we present here texts that were previously published in English, and/or have been written by scholars working in English, although we were able to include chapters that reflect on work in Haiti, Cuba, and Suriname, and one that is pan-Caribbean in scope. This necessarily means that scholarship from the non-English-speaking Caribbean, in particular the Spanish-speaking countries – especially the Dominican Republic and Puerto Rico – which have rich and deep histories of feminist organizing, research, and theorizing, are not well represented and which could, if fully explored, bring other dimensions to this conversation.

This collection reveals both the embrace of multiple methods by researchers of the Caribbean and the limitations that the need to produce detailed and comprehensive knowledge about gender and sexuality imposes on the research process. Thus, although Caribbean(ist) feminist research has been characterized as peacefully co-existing between, or as a blending of, qualitative and quantitative research methods, the former method is overrepresented in the collection. This follows the trend common in much feminist research around the world since the 1980s, where qualitative research is more readily undertaken in order to bring depth and richness to understandings and meanings of gendered and sexualized lives and subjectivities. We also recognize a greater tendency, among feminist anthropologists and anthropologists researching gender and sexuality in the Caribbean, for their published work to include more extensive discussions of methodology when compared with research emerging from other disciplines or even in some interdisciplinary research. This might be partly explained by the extensive use of ethnography among anthropologists, which is often presented with extensive reflections on epistemic claims, methodology and data analysis as indivisible. This collection features contributions from nine anthropologists, three of which are new works written specifically for this collection, related especially to research into discourse, culture, texts, and the visual arts.

Nevertheless, we cannot dismiss the significance of quantitative research methods in research endeavours as even within a field skewed toward the qualitative there is much evidence that the use of quantitative methods has played an important role. So, for example in this collection, in research conducted by Red Thread in Guyana, (featured in the interview with Andaiye on 'The Red Thread Method', and also discussed by Linda Peake in 'Feminist and Quantitative?'), surveys about the extent of domestic violence and the statistical counting of women's work have been critical to building knowledge about working women's lives. As well (and also featured in this collection) the regional Women in the Caribbean Project (WICP), research by Barry Chevannes in *Learning to Be a Man*, the interdisciplinary research on the Nariva Swamp project in Trinidad by Rhoda Reddock and Grace Sirju-Charran, and gender studies research in Cuba, described by Marta Núñez Sarmiento, all relied on or reflected on the combined use of quantitative and qualitative methods. Other studies, such as by Patricia Mohammed and Althea Perkins in their study of motherhood in Barbados, Dominica, and St Lucia (1999), have also made full use of surveys and other such methods. This type of quantitative research is typically large-scale, requiring an extensive period of time and multiple researchers, characteristics that are often in short supply in academic, research and policy worlds that privilege short time-frames and immediate outputs. Yet, as Linda Peake reminds us, there is no method that is inherently feminist. Rather, as for other researchers, Caribbeanist feminists rely on a range of data collection tools to address key questions and to provide an empirical basis from which to make claims about relations of power and possibilities for change.

In putting together this collection, we reviewed a large number of writings and texts and solicited a number of new or revised pieces to bring depth to some areas, then organized them through a number of themes that link them together: historiography, feminist organizing, gender, sexualities, the visual and cultural, text and talk, and researcher positionality in the research process. Within each of the themes, the texts are presented in chronological order so that we gain a sense of the historical depth in methodological approaches and can appreciate temporal shifts and changes.

A few trends are discernible in the approaches to research that this collection represents. First, and predominant, is that the research focus is on women, which by the 1990s had shifted to a focus on gender, from the analysis of unequal gendered relations of power. For example, the WICP project, an empirical project, was one of the first to centre women's concerns in research across several countries of the Anglophone Caribbean and even while not articulating an explicit feminist perspective, examined the working of gendered relations of power in women's lives. This women/gender-focus led to increasingly sophisticated examinations of constructions of femininity, and gender relations more generally (see also Shepherd, Brereton and Bailey 1995; Barrow 1998; Barriteau 2003; Bailey and Rynie 2004), and to research into masculinity, by scholars such Barry Chevannes (2001), Linden Lewis (2003) and Rhoda Reddock (2004).

This methodology challenged earlier research of Caribbean women, men and family that was reductionist, racist, pathologizing, and patriarchal. While addressing occlusions and distortions of the lives of Caribbean women, it has also been argued by scholars such as Michelle Rowley and Rosanne Kanhai, that the conflation of Black and Caribbean, in some of the early Caribbean feminist work, produced a specific image that works against both Black and non-Black women in the region (Haynes 2017). Drawing from such insights, Tonya Haynes (2017) shows how a prototypical Afro-maternal, working-class Caribbean woman, as the subject of much of the earlier Caribbean women/gender research, homogenises notions of race and gender, and fails to acknowledge that Caribbean feminism emerges from knowledge produced in and through ethnic and religious diversity.

Attention to axes of power around race, ethnicity, sexuality, and class, and a methodology that produces knowledge about intersected lives has, however, also been evident in Caribbeanist feminist research, (see for example, Lopez Springfield 1997; Mohammed 1998; and Reddock 2007 about the theorizing of difference in Caribbean feminisms). In this collection, such an approach is key in Andaiye's account of the Red Thread method, Barry Chevannes' research on learning to be a man in three Caribbean countries, research in Suriname into *mati* by Gloria Wekker, Kamala Kempadoo's research on sexual labour, and Patricia Mohammed's method for reading images of the Caribbean. Related is an explicit anti-colonial/decolonial feminist approach that draws from analysis of both colonial (neocolonial and postcolonial) and gendered relations of power. So, while Mathurin Mair in the 1960s laid the foundations for a Caribbean feminist methodology that disrupted Eurocentric patriarchal knowledge, it is scholars such as Nesha Haniff in 'Toward a Native Anthropology' (see chapter 25) who have explicitly argued for a paradigmatic shift.

Haniff draws from the work of scholars such as Frantz Fanon and Paolo Freire, as well as the earlier Caribbean women/gender analysis such as found in the WICP, in order to read against the grain of standard social scientific knowledge and to generate an anti/decolonial feminist paradigm. Such an approach shares with those utilizing intersectional analyses, an acknowledgement of racialized-ethnicized, classed, gendered, and sexualized ways of knowing and strategies of knowledge that underpin research and analysis, yet pushes this to new depths. Similarly, in chapter 15, Angelique Nixon and Rosamond King introduce the notion of 'embodied theory' that pays particular attention to the centrality of the material reality of the body in decision-making and other processes of knowledge production; Honor Ford Smith reflects, in chapter 8, on Sistren Theatre Collective's performance, participatory drama workshops and overall feminist organizing, through popular theatre, as a decolonial arts practice; and elsewhere, Gabrielle Hosein and Lisa Outar (2017) elaborate on Indo-Caribbean feminist epistemology that is grounded in specific histories, subjectivities, and praxis. Such research takes into account the ways that ethnicity and racialization produce specific languages, ontologies, and knowledge-generating strategies about gender and sexuality, and this is further reflected in this collection in the work of scholars such as Deborah Thomas, Roshini Kempadoo, and Gina Ulysse. But also, some Caribbean(ist) feminists are asking us to think explicitly about the location of gender within Western/European colonial and colonizing epistemologies, thus calling for a rethinking of the categories of gender and sexuality themselves. For instance, scholars such as Tonya Haynes (2012; 2016) take up Sylvia Wynter's challenge of not only looking at the entanglement of relations of power that produce specific intersectional subject categories, ontologies and knowledges, but about how the ethno-racial ordering of humanity is foundational to and generative of gender. In this same vein, Halimah DeShong (2018) performs a decolonial feminist analysis of intimate partner violence (IPV) in the Caribbean. In a new essay for this collection, she addresses the possibility of analysing text and talk produced from interviews about IPV, grounded in feminist anti/decolonial readings of broader histories of violence. Intersectional and anti/decolonial Caribbean feminist concerns about processes and conditions under which knowledge is created, thus emerge as ever more critical for research on Caribbean gender and sexuality.

In the following we take a closer look at the specific sections contained in this volume and discuss these and other trends in further detail.

History and Historiography

Caribbean historiography has, for several decades, explicitly included women and been 'engendered' (Shepherd, Brereton and Bailey 1995), producing re-interpretations and re-investigations into past social, cultural, and economic life in the region. As pointed out at the start of this introduction, Lucille Mathurin Mair pioneered a Caribbean feminist historical method through her doctoral research in the 1960s, and we start this collection with her reflections on that method in 'Recollections into a Journey of a Rebel Past'. This essay was initially presented at the first international conference of Caribbean women writers held at Wellesley College in 1988 and published in the resulting volume (Cudjoe 1990). It traces how Mathurin Mair went about reconstructing a history in the absence of recorded enslaved women's narratives that could provide insight into their inner lives. Using official archival texts, traditionally held up as one of the most treasured sources of data among historians, as well as diaries, wills, and other legal documents, Mathurin Mair examined a range of gendered relations within which women were engaged between 1655 and 1844 in Jamaica. Her investigation touches on the problematic that is central to the three chapters in this section on methods for researching women and gender in Caribbean history, namely, how to bring into view and make meaning of histories of social groups that have left few conventional sources. As all three authors point out, such research moves historiography out of its traditional realm and shifts it towards interdisciplinarity (Mathurin Mair), 'oral ethnography' (Chamberlain), and 'cultural studies' (Brereton). They underscore that this methodology requires not just a counter reading of conventional archives and recorded sources such as wills, land deeds, tax records, census, and court records but also investigation into unofficial and non-traditional sources. Mathurin Mair notes that she had to probe deeply into conventional sources, reading against colonial, Eurocentric, and patriarchal interpretations and ideologies in order to bring enslaved women's lives out of the shadows of the archives. Bridget Brereton's comprehensive review of Caribbeanist feminist historiography reveals that key non-traditional written sources have included newspapers, church records and correspondence, travel books and narratives, plantation reports, as well women's journals, memoires, autobiographies, and diaries, and family letters. But also, she points out, gender research in the English-speaking Caribbean has heavily relied on oral history as well as visual sources and oral traditions such as folktales, proverbs, and songs due to the lack of written documents to draw upon. Mary Chamberlain's chapter takes up in greater detail the oral history method based on her research with migrant Barbadian women to Britain, providing guidelines for performing a feminist gendered analysis that takes into account memory, language, and subjectivity. She advances that such a methodology enables the researcher to approach history 'from the inside out', through which the public and formal can be read in tandem with the intimate and private, whereby the personal appears as a 'central, unifying feature of human life'.

As importantly, the three essays included in this first section highlight how methods for researching women's and gender history and historical memory throw light on women's resistance, passion, and persistence in the making of the Caribbean and in constructing gendered selves and collective identities, and can lead to a chronicling of the gendered ways Caribbean people cope but also change or subvert meanings and their circumstances. In this regard, these historians point to ontological foundations of gender in the Caribbean, while offering sound guidelines for conducting historical research.

Methodologies for Feminist Organizing and Action Research

Feminist research praxis, in the form of action research, is critical to Caribbean feminist organizing. In this section, we document how research has served the political agenda for change among groups organizing around a feminist consciousness and/or women organizing for social justice in the region. In this regard, and through the writings of Carolle Charles, Honor Ford Smith, Fredericka Deare, and in an interview with Andaiye, the purpose and reach of research for social change are examined in the organizing of groups such as Sistren Theatre Collective of Jamaica, the Caribbean Association of Feminist Research and Action (CAFRA) (Pan-Caribbean), Red Thread of Guyana, Centre Haitien de Recherche pour la Promotion Feminine (CHREPROF) and KAY FANM in Haiti, and

Centro de Investigacion Para Acción Feminista (CIPAF) of the Dominican Republic.

Carolle Charles traces the emergence of women's organizations in Haiti from the mid to late twentieth century and their use of feminist participatory action research approaches from the 1970s to the mid-1990s. She distinguishes between those that engage in organizing to improve the lives of the most disadvantaged women and those that use research as part of their work to improve the lives of the most dispossessed women. A further distinction is made between participatory action research employed by these groups and research done by international development agencies in Haiti. The development agency, externally-driven process, Charles argues, ends up alienating the very women for whom development planning is targeted, in contrast to feminist participatory action research.

Charles identifies a number of ways in which feminists approach the process and subject of research differently. Dialogic research, she explains, emphasizes the relationship between participants and researchers. In addition, individuals may study groups with which they are allied. There is also the use of the methodologies of participatory research and it is here that Charles situates feminist action research. Moreover, she notes, feminists and other critical social researchers have reshaped the ways in which we think about the promise and possibilities of conducting empirical analyses.

In the interview conducted by Kamala Kempadoo, Andaiye maintains that Red Thread's research and organizing are inextricably linked. She identifies and describes three phases of the organisation's development and the evolution and use of research for action: income-generation focused, survey and other types of research for describing specific issues, such as domestic violence, HIV and sex work, and research through grassroots organizing. She cites the research conducted in phase three as the most useful for Red Thread's organizing. Women from similar socio-economic backgrounds diarized their lives as part of a time use survey, the purpose of which was the counting and valuing of women's work. According to Andaiye, the data generated gave women important insights into their own lives and those of women from other ethnoracial communities and continues to support Red Thread's programming and advocacy.

From its inception the Caribbean Association of Feminist Research and Action (CAFRA), according to Fredericka Deare, set as its mandate the intent 'to bridge the gap between research and action and to provide a continuum between research activities and the activities of organizations working with women in the region', which they argued could 'only be effective if there was the strong involvement of women whose life issues are at stake'. Thus, CAFRA trained women activists to conduct and produce research about women. CAFRA's analysis challenged the dichotomy between researchers and participants; valued orally produced data; featured research conducted by coordinators and members who were also historically involved in feminist movements; included women who were part of community organizing at various stages of the research; and produced reports in accessible ways in the form of videos, pamphlets, drama, inter alia. In short, actions and interventions were undertaken based on the various research products of both Red Thread and CAFRA.

In 'Method of Decolonial Arts Practice', Honor Ford Smith defines the cultural work of Sistren Theatre Collective as part of the 1970s women's organizing in the region, with the explicit purpose of using popular theatre to demonstrate the complexities of working-class, Afro-Jamaican women's lives and communities. For Ford Smith, Sistren's work, as part of Caribbean feminist research and arts praxis, simultaneously prefigures and emerges alongside Black feminist scholarship that explicitly refers to intersectionality. Using Sylvia Wynter's theorizing of embodied knowledge as mobilized by those existing at the margins, Ford Smith tells of how the women of Sistren set out to reframe colonialist representations that tend to caricature, pathologize and generally flatten their experiences. The complex autobiographies of Sistren women are storied as multi-layered and enfleshed; making possible, alternative and more authentic visions of identity for those existing at the 'margins'. Ford Smith concludes that defining Sistren as 'a Black feminist, decolonial act', opens up other possible usages of 'embodied decolonizing pedagogy' in areas of critical concern, such as food, land, sexuality, and sports, all of which serve to sustain the body and physical environment we inhabit.

Distinctive about the research approaches described in this section is that the women for whom change is sought are actively engaged in the creation and implementation of research projects and programmes with the expressed intention of changing unequal relations of power in communities, and that the research is located within the broader context of the women's movement in the region. Attention to the materiality of difference, as raised by Andaiye in the context of Red Thread, also recognizes relations of power inherent in research and in research for organizing, and the means by which this can be addressed. This remains important in reflections on the experiences of groups involved in feminist action research throughout the region. Nevertheless, according to Andaiye, Charles, Ford Smith and Deare, essential to Caribbean feminist action research are those networks and programmes created for women, as well as opportunities for women to become aware of what are shared experiences across difference.

Researching Gender in the Caribbean

The approaches deployed for conducting multidisciplinary and interdisciplinary research on gender in the Caribbean is the central focus of the works collected in this section. Starting with research that began in the 1970s and culminating with contemporary reflections on late twentieth century multi-method feminist participatory research for action, this section is indicative of the multiple and complex ways in which concepts and terms such as gender, women, men, boys and girls are mobilized in Caribbean research on gender and sexuality. The contributions include an overview of the work of the multidisciplinary team of researchers convened to produce interdisciplinary work for the Women in the Caribbean Project (WICP) by project leader Jocelyn Massiah; the critical reflections by anthropologist, Barry Chevannes on conducting ethnography within Caribbean communities about masculinity; qualitative interviews conducted by Martha Núñez Sarmiento with Cuban academics on the methodologies employed in producing knowledge under the rubric of gender studies; a discussion and example of the use of quantitative methods in feminist research as conducted by Red Thread in Guyana, presented by Linda Peake; and the interdisciplinary, multimethod research on gender and the environment by Rhoda Reddock and Grace Sirju-Charran.

Much of this work on gender identity construction and expression reinforced a normativity of both gender and sexuality that begins to be challenged in later research on gender and sexuality in the region.

However, they provide key methodological insights for the production of both single and multi-method research on Caribbean gender relations.

The section opens with Massiah's discussion of the methodology employed in WICP, which was one of the first to centre women's concerns in research across several countries of the Anglophone Caribbean. As earlier indicated, WICP researchers never articulated an explicit feminist perspective at the time of the study and although it has been criticized for narrowly focusing on the experiences of working-class women, for reproducing particular heteronormative scripting of women's positionalities and for avoiding an explicit discussion of the theoretical insights informing the project, this work has been acclaimed as a key contribution to Caribbean feminist knowledge production, given the emphasis on women's experiences across a variety of themes. Massiah provides a detailed overview of the multiple methods undertaken in WICP – national surveys, life histories, and sector specific studies – that facilitated data collection for comparison across countries, but more importantly to present the multi-dimensionality of women's lives. The WICP prefigures much of the empirical interdisciplinary research on women and gender in the Anglophone Caribbean.

Ethnography as methodology for studying gender identity construction and expression among boys in six communities across Jamaica, Guyana, and Dominica is the focus of the piece included by Barry Chevannes here. Conceptually, Chevannes uses the term manhood to signal a set of practices, ideologies, and institutions to which boys are encouraged to aspire. Male ethnographers, who produced fieldnotes based on observations and interviews, were trained to oversee the research in each community, and they each worked alongside a female and male animator. Chevannes discusses the application of the animation technique as supplementing the ethnographers' fieldnotes through the use of games, drama, and other performances to analyse the patterns of normative behaviour among participants. He makes a connection between the use of animation among the research team with similar approaches applied in the work of Sistren Theatre Collective and in research on fathers in Jamaica. Moreover, the operation and framing of gender as oppositionally derived and produced, underpins both the approach to fieldwork and the overall knowledge creation enterprise. This can be observed in the selection of fieldwork teams to observe both boys and girls, the assumptions which inhere about gender in the framing of the project, and the analysis of the data produced about the study.

The use of survey research by Red Thread in Guyana to investigate domestic violence in women's lives is chronicled in this section by Linda Peake. Before outlining the process by which this work was conducted, Peake addresses a retreat from survey research by feminist geographers in North America, who appear to eschew the use of quantitative methods. In so doing she addresses a tendency in feminist critiques from the 1980s and 1990s to conflate quantitative methods and positivist-masculinist epistemologies. In the research in Guyana, the extremely high response rate of participants who were asked to disclose experiences of domestic violence was largely due, according to Peake, to the expertise of Red Thread's members who were trained in survey research methods to facilitate data collection, entry and analysis. She points to Red Thread's ability to generate high quality data that they would later use as a means through which to fund raise for interventions to support women affected by domestic violence in Guyana.

Gender is more centrally named as a tool of analysis for framing both the methodological and conceptual approach to studying the use and governance of natural resources in the Nariva Swamp in Trinidad and Tobago. Rhoda Reddock and Grace Sirju-Charran discuss the use of multi-method research for conducting a gender analysis of the ecosystem; its governance at the household, community and national levels; as well as the changing nature of state policy regarding the Swamp. They outline the possibility of producing multi-method, interdisciplinary feminist research to secure environmental sustainability and social transformation. Working across the natural and social sciences, and using key Caribbean feminist approaches to knowledge creation, Reddock and Sirju-Charran provide important methodological insights for performing Participatory Rural Appraisal (PRA) methods for accessing, not only community knowledge but, more importantly, for deploying necessary local insights for transforming communities and securing environmental sustainability. Finally, in this chapter the authors consider the operation of gender in the research process with particular reference to the differential experiences of female and male researchers interviewing men and women respectively.

Gender is presented as a feminist analytical resource, mobilized in study design, and data collection and analysis.

Finally, in this section, Marta Núñez Sarmiento reflects on interviews with 24 Cuban academics working in the field of gender studies in Havana, to outline the methodological approaches they deployed in their research. Based on the interviews, she emphasizes methodology as opposed to the thematic focus of the works of these scholars and provides a discussion of the socio-political and historical context out of which gender studies emerged in Cuba in the 1980s. She foregrounds the importance of empathy when conducting research interviews with one's peers and provides insights on how the interview event itself becomes a space for the shaping and reshaping of the subject matter and form of the research instrument. Her positionality as the professional equal of her participants also caused her to reflect on her own role in the research process, describing her movement between interviewer and interviewee. She observes that researchers, regardless of their disciplinary location, situated themselves within the field of gender studies both intellectually and politically as they defined their work and research as serving to secure social justice in the areas of gender and sexuality. Her participants also advocated the use of multi-method research within gender studies as a means through which to access non-traditional sources of data and challenge the orthodoxy of mainstream approaches to research. Although Sarmiento did not begin with a concrete conceptualisation of gender and its significance to her research, she concludes with key insights offered by Cuban academics working out of Havana about how gender might serve as a feminist conceptual, analytic and political resource for conducting social research which not only exposes but seeks to undermine uneven relations of power.

Sexualities Research

Similar to the previous section, reflections on approaches for conducting research emerge from both multi- and inter-disciplinary studies. Much of the early research reproduced a normativity of both gender and sexuality, as can be observed in mid-twentieth century family studies and research on sexual and reproductive health. The contributions featured in this section trace the processes for and conditions under which feminist/gender/ sexuality-focused research on the erotic, sexual economic relations, and sexual citizenship is produced in the Caribbean. Negotiating research relationships as ethical practice is a recurrent feature of the contributions in this section.

The opening chapter is excerpted from Gloria Wekker's 2006 *Politics of Passion: Women's Sexual Culture in the Afro-Surinamese Diaspora*. Wekker provides a reflexive engagement on performing ethnographic research focused on sexuality among Black working-class women in Suriname. She addresses the tensions inherent in doing this work against histories of racist pathologies of Black women's sexuality as excessive and animalistic. Wekker confronts the various axes of difference and power inherent in the research process, and, more specifically, what it means to tell Juliette's story; a woman with whom she shared both a friendship and intimate relationship. She exposes the often-neglected issues of intimacy and love in research relationships when conducting ethnographic research that involves long periods of immersion within communities; an issue she engages as central to the knowledge emerging from her study. Wekker invites researchers to confront the responsibility of speaking for others – in her case producing oral history accounts – while also reminding us that research is conducted and produced at the intersections of various categories of difference and forms of power.

In many ways, Nixon and King's reflections on conducting interdisciplinary (bridging the social sciences and the humanities) sexualities studies as diasporic researchers, extends Wekker's reflections on the salience of positionality in producing knowledge claims in sexualities studies. First pointing to the epistemic dangers of conducting disembodied studies of sexuality – as is the case in much of the sexual health research in the region – Nixon and King situate embodied theories and methodologies as that which emerge from a Caribbean feminist intellectual tradition. In particular, the authors are inspired by aspects of Caribbean, Black and women of colour feminism in which the material needs of the body are taken up as a critical site of analysis of research relationships. They join Wekker in a shared commitment to locating 'embodied' research relationships as key sites of analysis for the production of knowledge. Their focus extends to the co-production of knowledge with communities and groups in the Caribbean that organize around the issue of sexual citizenship; acknowledging such work as complex, pleasurable, and embodied.

The continuities of colonial and racialized relations of power in framing sexual economic relations (sex work in particular) is addressed in the chapter by Kamala Kempadoo, as she outlines the evolution of her methodology for performing sexuality research, which started in the early 1990s. She also provides critical insights on her own research into sexual labour in the Caribbean. Acknowledging the largely tabooized nature of the study of sex work, sex tourism, and sexual economic relations in general, her transnational/intersectional feminist methodology is equally grounded in what she refers to as 'social praxeology' (a theory of social praxis). K. Kempadoo delineates the process by which she not only refines her methodological approach, but disrupts dominant conceptualizations of women's sexual labour away from framings which centre violence, disease, and victimization. The guiding frameworks situate her collaborative, participant-centred ground-up approach to researching sexual labour. A key contribution made by K. Kempadoo is the value of research for making the kinds of ontological and conceptual shifts necessary to reflect the lives of women in more expansive ways. Utilizing interviews, analysis of documents and some observation, K. Kempadoo shows how her approach to researching sexual labour has reoriented knowledge away from a narrow focus on prostitution to sex work; from sexual exploitation to sexual agency. Her work displaces dominant knowledge about prostitution, migration for sex work, and HIV and AIDS; thus, rewriting colonialist scriptings of sexual labour in the Caribbean. In the process, K. Kempadoo offers insights into building ethical research relationships and working within research teams of feminist organizers-scholars, and sex workers, for producing knowledge on sexual economic relations in the Caribbean and beyond. A key organizing feature of the contributions of Nixon and King, Wekker, and K. Kempadoo, in this section, is a shared commitment to intersectional, embodied, transnational and anti/decolonial methodologies and analysis in the production of knowledge.

Subjective mapping as a method for studying the experience of same-sex desiring/loving women in Trinidad and Tobago is the focus of the chapter authored by Krystal Ghisyawan, newly written for this collection. This novel interdisciplinary approach to data collection and analysis in Caribbean sexualities studies is inspired by mapping methodologies and logics drawn from the fields of education, geography, planning, agriculture, epidemiology, international development, anthropology and sociology. Ghisyawan defines subjective mapping as the processes by which the production of identity, relations of power and agency are graphically represented by participants. In particular, Ghisyawan used subjective mapping for an understanding of how same-sex loving women negotiate space, safety, and sexuality in their everyday lives. Data collected from this procedure took the form of individualized images and text that not only revealed specific experiences but also broader patterns of power and agency.

In keeping with the approach to writing about research by the anthropologists featured in this collection, David Murray, in this new essay, offers a reflexive narrative on his methodological choices for doing research on sexual identity politics/relations in Barbados. Murray demonstrates how his motivation for and approach to conducting sexualities research were shaped by affective personal ties and intimacies, as well as a desire to unpack the operation of identity politics in Barbados, against a backdrop of the dominance of a global North nomenclature and conceptualization of sexual identity. In so doing, he outlines the multiple methods used in ethnographic research (observations, document analysis, interviews, etc.) of this kind, building on relationships in the fieldwork setting, and, more centrally, the place of positionality as key to the generation of knowledge. The chapter closes with a discussion of the ethical issues that must be confronted in performing and reporting on research which relies on the development of close ties with research participants. Even as Murray extols the value of ethnographic research for capturing the complexity of sexual identity relations, he advocates the need for researchers to remain cognizant of navigating multiple identity relations, relationships, and friendship in producing ethical research on sexuality.

Researching the Visual and Cultural

While the production of images and other cultural products are key to signifying what it means to be Caribbean (as is the case for other regions of the world), methodologies for making and reading said products are rarely articulated. This section features three chapters, two of which were specifically written for this collection by Deborah Thomas and Patricia Mohammed and a third by Roshini Kempadoo, which was previously published. All three authors outline Caribbean and anti/decolonial feminist methodologies for producing and analysing still and moving images in the Caribbean. From Thomas' discussion of visual ethnography as a feminist methodology that facilitates increased access to research products, to Mohammed's and R. Kempadoo's methodologies for reading colonial and contemporary images, the chapters in this section are important to extending the small body of work in the Caribbean for analysing and creating visual and cultural products.

The case for visual ethnography as feminist resource is well made by Thomas as she defines its collaborative and interdisciplinary orientation. Visual ethnography, she tells, places individuals and communities, about whom the output is based, at the centre of its making. Thomas outlines approaches to film-making grounded in both feminist and anticolonial praxis. Juxtaposing the process by which contemporary films are produced as a form of counter-archive – when compared to traditional reliance on official documents – these visual ethnographies trace the continuities of race, class and violence, thus functioning as a kind of anticolonial knowledge product. The chapter is at once explicitly epistemological, conceptual and methodological, as she defines the transformative possibility of producing visual ethnographies in the form of film as a kind of awakening/re-awakening. Feminist witnessing or the creation of visual archives, in the form of film, provides a space, Thomas argues, for simultaneously naming violent continuities, addressing questions of accountability and pursuing liberatory possibilities.

In outlining a methodology for the study of colonial images of Trinidadian women, Roshini Kempadoo locates these photographs within their socio-historical context, analysing the 'visualizing practices' out of which these images were produced. She suggests a reading of colonial photographs that extends beyond a focus on aesthetics, to not only expose the racialized and gendered storying of women lives, but to one which includes how these images are read. For example, she incorporates fieldnotes of her response to illustrations and photography, featured in textbooks, as a student in secondary school, as indicative of the evolution of her own anticolonial political investments and how these shape the analysis she performs. In addition, she provides specific guidelines about the selection of images as part of a larger set of knowledge-making practices to expose photography as a key instantiation of colonization.

Mohammed is specifically focused on the socio-historical and cultural making, production and reading of images as a set of visual codes. In other words, she is concerned about the spatiotemporal production and reception of images, whether painted, sketched, printed, sculpted or digitized. Both R. Kempadoo and Mohammed share a commitment to historicizing the emergence of the image as well as accounting for the positionality of the reader studying the image, as central to the analyses they perform. Learning to read images (moving or still) is essential work that must be appreciated, according to Mohammed, in much the same way the researcher is trained to read text. She explains that as a major site of cultural formation, the production and reading of images are key to the making of Caribbean identity at various stages in the history of the region. In particular, reading images exposes the racialized, gendered, and classed relations at work at any given moment in the history of the Caribbean.

Methods for Analysing Talk and Text

Beginning with a short excerpt from Michelle Rowley's essay that was first published in *Gendered Realities* (Mohammed 2002) and continuing with two newly written, original essays by Latoya Lazarus and Halimah A.F. DeShong, this section foregrounds methods for making visible unnamed voices, subjectivities and materialities though analysis of discourses, represented especially by talk, speech, and written scripts. The authors stress the importance of locating discourse and textual analysis within relations of power in the given cultural, socioeconomic and geographic context while being mindful of political, transformative, and empowering agendas. In many ways these essays echo and update some of the early oral ethnography guidelines offered by Mary Chamberlain in chapter 3, for examining not only language but also paralanguage, such as intonations, silences, and the unsaid, which, when read intertextually, can alert the researcher to gendered constructions of self and collective identities and to the subversions held within them. They also closely dovetail with the methodologies presented in the previous section on researching the visual and cultural, as described by Deborah Thomas, Roshini Kempadoo, and Patricia Mohammed.

Rowley focuses on 'voicing' by Afro-Tobagonian mothers – 'matrifolk': women who are central to the Caribbean family and domestic realm – as a form of speech and an act of naming and representation. This talk, she proposes, is a bridge 'between the conceptual and operational, the experiential and material' – between theory and method – while representing women's political and agentive processes that signal alternate worldviews and ontologies. Her methodology draws inspiration from Caribbean feminist theory from the 1980s and 90s, operationalizing the call issued through the Women in the Caribbean Project for Caribbean women 'to speak for themselves', while extending that theorizing to embrace matrifocality as grounds for transformative Caribbean feminist knowledge.

Lazarus offers advice and guidelines on how to analyse dominant discourses as these are reproduced, challenged, and transmitted through written texts, visual representations, interviews, and speeches. Drawing from her doctoral research about the ways conservative and evangelical Christian groups control and access the content of public discourse about gender, sexuality, human rights and citizenship, she reviews key theories about discourse analysis. Noting the limitations of earlier Foucauldian ideas, she argues for a critical discourse analysis (CDA) approach such as developed by Teun van Dijk and Stuart Hall, due to its attention to both power structures and relations, and transformations of that power, and argues for a marrying of CDA with feminist and feminist post-structuralist critical discourse analysis. The combination of these frameworks, she finds, creates a methodology that enables the research to give voice to those who have been traditionally marginalized or silenced while also explicitly and unapologetically taking a political stance – in her case 'a feminist political agenda'. Lazarus also offers valuable details on specific methods and techniques in the research process such as interviewing and data coding, while discussing how critical self-reflexivity about her positionality as an 'insider/outside/returnee' Caribbean researcher can work as a specific research instrument.

Furthering this work, DeShong presents a methodology for reading text and talk that is feminist *and* anticolonial, drawing directly from her Caribbean research on gender-based violence. She argues that the gender binary around which much of the Caribbean feminist analysis of intimate partner violence centres needs to be displaced through a framework that locates Caribbean gender within European colonial racial categorizations and epistemologies, in order to take into account material, racialized histories of gendered violence in the region. DeShong goes on to demonstrate how a close reading of talk and text, as evidenced in interview scripts, case files, print media, policy documents, legislation, popular culture, etc, enables us to revisit the ways in which gender has to date been deployed in Caribbean feminist research, and performs a twenty-first century anti/decolonial feminist theory and praxis. This chapter offers a bold methodology that is at once attentive to the discursive colonial and postcolonial construction of the Caribbean and to new transformative feminist possibilities.

Reflections on Positionality: Lessons from the Field

The final section comprises five chapters that reflect on ethnographic research and discuss positionality, subjectivity, and knowledge production in light of the 'native anthropologist'. The writings span a time frame of over 30 years, providing a sense of change but also continuity in the ways Black and Caribbean feminist anthropologists have situated themselves and their research in the field and constructed a reflexive practice. Despite their own self-identification as Black and/or Caribbean women, all authors take up questions about their insider/outsider positions and how to negotiate the distance from their research participants or community that results from holding an academic status, being from another Caribbean country or another part of the country, being culturally and economically from another ethnicized/racialized or class group, and/or from coming from the US. The reflections here pick up from and extend insights offered in various earlier chapters by other Caribbeanist ethnographers and anthropologists on positionality, such as Gloria Wekker, regarding participant observation with 'mati' in Suriname in the 1990s, and David Murray, with respect to his 'outsider' subject position in research on gay men's sexuality in Barbados, but also by researchers such as Latoya Lazarus, on the idea of being an insider/outsider/returnee' while researching gender, sexuality, human rights, and citizenship in Jamaica in 2013. The authors here also discuss positionality in relation to other aspects of their methodology, such as their theoretical frameworks, their selection of research topics, the ethics of doing research as a 'native', gaining entry to and acceptance by the communities, their selection of data collection methods and techniques, and relations of power in the field and in the production of knowledge. Together they provide us with further insights into what it can mean to be reflexively engaged as an ethnographer in the Caribbean.

Nesha Haniff, writing at a time when scholarship on women in the global south was almost completely dominated by the Eurocentric and masculine perspectives, argues for the critical embrace of a 'native' position and identity by Caribbean and other Third World feminist researchers to make visible Third World women's lives, meanings, voices, and experiences. She moreover favours a dialogical approach in order to diminish distance between the researcher and researched. In her own quest to research successful Caribbean women, she notes that the methodology must also attend to class dimensions of knowledge production, given that most existing definitions and concepts of 'success' render invisible contributions by women, especially in societies such as the Caribbean that are predominantly working class. Despite her insistence that a native/insider perspective is preferred to those generated externally, she recognizes that the question of what constitutes native knowledge is complicated, given, as she puts it, that the colonized/the native is often trained in Western science and ideas, and may continue their/our own ideological domination through uncritical application of the ideas. She thus urges the insider/native researcher to remain critical and to take methodological implications of that position and perspective seriously and consciously.

Also writing in the 1980s, Lynn Bolles reflects on her role as an African American anthropologist conducting ethnographic research about the experiences of urban working-class women factory workers in Jamaica. In so doing, she addresses how access needed to be negotiated across various axes of difference and power, beyond notions of insider/outsider, and raises questions about the kind of challenges and possibilities that arise when a Black woman studies another Black culture. The chapter begins with a critique of anthropology's imperialist history, as a means through which to foreground the research as not only transcending this history but framed within the interdisciplinary approach taken in late twentieth century studies of women. Moreover, Bolles situates her research as drawing on key principles of anthropology and social science research, and reflects on the practice of 'responsible research', based on notions of equality and exchange, increased accuracy, mutual respect, and a sharing of civic responsibility. Such reflexive 'native anthropology' she demonstrates, can counter a top-down/external approach and can generate materials that are of significance to Black women's empowerment in their workplaces and everyday life.

In excerpts from two chapters, Gina Ulysse, like Haniff and Bolles, critiques Western social and political science and production of knowledge for its homogenization of the native woman and for treating her as a non-interlocuter, and similarly, takes a dialogical approach. Using autoethnography, Ulysse substantially deepens the interrogation started by Bolles, on what it means to be Black feminist anthropologist and an insider and outsider in research about a community of working-class women in Jamaica. She takes up the significance of colour, race, and class in the field, and describes how she negotiated the complexity of identity – at times conforming and at other times, rebelling to the conventions and norms. Explaining how, through her appearance, she navigated various sites and spheres, Ulysse emphasizes the ways 'cross-dressing across class' and 'code-switching' confounds and disrupts existing orders and categories. Being both 'out of place' and a Black Caribbean 'native', and managing successfully to gain the trust and support of the informal commercial importers, she questions the idea of insider/native knowledge as superior. Thus, unlike Haniff and Bolles, Ulysse does not privilege the position and perspective of 'the native anthropologist', due to what she sees as unfixed qualities of the subject, yet like them, she recognizes the complications of the subject and reiterates the call to locate Caribbeanist feminist research in political agendas and activism in order to contribute on various fronts to redressing past injustices for Caribbean women.

Gabrielle Hosein, in her chapter that reflects on her doctoral research on gender and politics in South Trinidad, echoes ideas advanced by the other scholars in this section, that reflexivity in feminist research is more than looking at identities and positionalities, and requires thinking about where, how, and why knowledge is produced and the relationship of the researcher to the production of that knowledge. She describes how she gained access to a community located in her country yet unfamiliar to her, identifying herself in that context as an insider/outsider. And as with Ulysse, she writes about the significance of 'crossing' and 'enacting hybridity' for navigating the field successfully, especially when her appearance did not conform to the norms and expectations of her class, ethnicity, religion, gender, age, or marital status. Hosein further provides concrete tips for gathering data through participant observation, about the time and sense one needs to successfully research sensitive issues around family, livelihood, religion, culture, and gendered relations of power, and on questions about building trust, using connections, negotiating power, and ensuring reciprocity. Ultimately, the essay is a call for greater awareness of how we research 'home'/our native place that is at once known and unknown.

The final chapter in this section and book is by Tami Navarro, who explains that self-reflexivity is, today, an integral part of the training of anthropologists, particularly of feminist and non-white/western anthropologists. This chapter, written specifically for this collection, thus gestures towards what the future holds for Caribbeanist feminist ethnography – i.e., a greater interrogation into the impacts, positionality and implication in structures of power of the researcher, and into the production of knowledge, and less on the Other. Navarro's own study, like that of Ulysse and Hosein, began in the context of her doctoral dissertation. She explains how she was able to use her age and class to gain access to her research population and collect insights into the femininization of labour in information and management sectors and service industries in St Croix. Both belonging and being an outsider to the community of employees, she discusses the significance of appearance and 'fitting in' to expectations and ideals of feminine respectability and appropriate behaviour. Despite Navarro's acute awareness of her difference and transgression of the norms and ideals, she documents that she was read and viewed as 'one of we', leading her to question whether, as a native of St Croix, she could ever be seen as an 'impartial' academic researcher on the island. In raising this question, she returns us to a recurring theme in this section, and indeed throughout the entire volume, that Caribbeanist feminist methodology is, at heart, a political practice that is grounded in a sense of a shared struggle from a perspective that centres 'the native' gendered subject.

Concluding Thoughts

Through this collection, we foreground some main trends in research and methods for researching Caribbean gender and sexuality over the span of some 50-odd years. The collection is by no means exhaustive. There are very many gaps, elisions, and areas to be filled in, and many pieces that have not made it into this collection. Still, what we have tried to do here is to demonstrate the critical and vast contributions to the methodological literature made by researchers of gender and sexuality in the Caribbean, in support of ongoing work in the field. Our aim is to showcase the scope and care with which the subject of researching the Caribbean has been taken up and reflected upon by scholars who have paid attention to gender and sexuality, and the relations of power through which they are structured. We hope that this collection can serve as an important resource for students, researchers and practitioners studying gender and sexuality in the Caribbean and beyond, and that the collection encourages greater engagement with and scholarship on feminist methodologies and research methods. Even with the tremendous amount of existing scholarship, we hope that by bringing these works together, as we have in this collection, the contributions will generate even greater conversations and further research on gender and sexuality in the Caribbean. It is also our hope that this collection contributes Caribbean content to wider feminist discussions of methodology and to the ongoing conversations about the production of anti/decolonial feminist methodologies.

References

Bailey, Barbara, and Elsa Leo-Rhynie, eds. 2004. *Gender in the 21st Century: Caribbean Perspectives, Visions and Possibilities*. Kingston: Ian Randle Publishers.

Barrow, Christine, ed. 1998. *Caribbean Portraits: Essays on Gender Ideologies and Identities*. Kingston: Ian Randle Publishers.

Chevannes, Barry. 2001. *Learning to Be a Man: Culture, Socialization and Gender Identity in Five Caribbean Communities*. Kingston: The University of the West Indies Press.

DeShong, Halimah A.F. 2018. 'The Language of Violence in the Caribbean: A Decolonial Feminist Analysis.' In *Caribbean Crime & Criminal Justice: Impacts of Post-Colonialism and Gender on Crime*, ed. Katharina J. Joosen and Corin Bailey, 123–38. London: Routledge.

Haynes, Tonya. 2012. 'The Divine and the Demonic: Sylvia Wynter and Caribbean Feminist Thought Revisited.' In *Love and Power: Caribbean Discourses on*

Gender, ed. Eudine Barriteau, 54–71. Kingston: University of the West Indies Press.

———. 2016. 'Sylvia Wynter's Theory of the Human and the Crisis School of Caribbean Heteromasculinity Studies.' *Small Axe: A Caribbean Journal of Criticism* 20, no. 49: 92–112.

———. 2017. 'Interrogating Approaches to Caribbean Feminist Thought.' *Journal of Eastern Caribbean Studies* 42, no. 3: 26–58.

Hosein, Gabrielle J., and Lisa Outar, eds. 2017. *Indo-Caribbean Feminist Thought: Genealogies, Theories, Enactments*. New York: Palgrave Macmillan.

Kempadoo, Kamala, Halimah DeShong, and Charmaine Crawford, eds. 2013. 'Caribbean Feminist Research Methods.' Special Issue of *Caribbean Review of Gender Studies* 7: 1–6.

Jaggar, Alison M., ed. 2008. *Just Methods: An Interdisciplinary Feminist Reader*. Boulder: Paradigm Publishers.

Lewis, Linden, ed. 2003. *The Culture of Gender and Sexuality in the Caribbean*. Gainesville: University of Florida Press.

Mair, Lucille Mathurin. 2006. *A Historical Study of Women in Jamaica: 1655–1844*. Edited by Hilary Beckles and Verene Shepherd. Kingston: University of West Indies Press.

Mohammed, Patricia, ed. 2002. *Gendered Realities: Essays in Caribbean Feminist Thought*. Kingston: University of the West Indies Press.

———, ed. 1998. 'Rethinking Caribbean 'Difference': Special Issue of *Feminist Review*, no. 59.

Mohammed, Patricia, and Althea Perkins. 1999. *Caribbean Women at the Crossroads: The Paradox of Motherhood Among Women of Barbados, St. Lucia and Dominica*. Kingston: Canoe Press.

Reddock, Rhoda E., ed. 2004. *Interrogating Caribbean Masculinities*. Kingston: University of the West Indies Press.

Shepherd, Verene, Bridget Brereton, and Barbara Bailey, eds. 1995. *Engendering History: Caribbean Women in Historical Perspective*. New York: St. Martin's Press.

Springfield, Consuelo Lopez, ed. 1997. *Daughters of Caliban: Caribbean Women in the Twentieth Century*. Bloomington and Indianapolis: Indiana University Press.

History and Historiography

2. Recollections into a Journey of a Rebel Past*

Lucille Mathurin Mair

In the early 1960s I started to seek out the women of Jamaica's past during the period of slavery, women of all classes and of all colors – black, brown, white. I had no feminist motivation, or at least none that I recognized. I was motivated mainly by intellectual inquisitiveness, the usual ambition of the doctoral candidate to investigate virgin territory, which it was at that time. There was almost nothing to guide such a search. There was, in fact, nothing in modern historical scholarship about the women who came before me. But this was not surprising, for historiography, which has for centuries been a male academic preserve, has been stunningly devoid of a consciousness of women as significant beings.

So feminist historians have been faced with the methodological challenge of excavating women from layers of distortion and obscurity; of getting beyond and behind the formal roles conventional history has accorded them and in the process, perhaps, even transforming the discipline of history.

Digging into the lives of the small minority of free white women in Jamaican slave society takes one along a relatively straightforward route. There is a substantial body of data to be found in contemporary histories and accounts by residents and travelers. There is even more valuable material in legal documents, in wills, in diaries, and in the volume of transatlantic and inter-American correspondence that has been preserved in the papers of planter families. Letters and diaries of women of this class reveal some of the personal and domestic implications of absentee proprietorship, an alienating phenomenon

---

* Reprinted with permission from *Caribbean Women Writers: Essays from the First International Conference*, ed. Selwyn R. Cudjoe. Wellesley, Mass.: Calaloux Publications, 1990, 51–60.

that has been distinguished throughout most of Jamaica's history by the nostalgia of its white elite for all things English, an intensely female nostalgia that is communicated through the pens of women with perturbing immediacy.

Other approaches are required to recover the feelings of brown and black women and to gain insight into the multidimensional nature of their lives. Until the very recent development of indigenous scholarship, the Caribbean researcher's main reference point was the Eurocentric, ethnocentric historiography of the colonizer and the slaveholder, which is incapable of addressing the humanity of transplanted Africans labelled chattel, identified for the historical record in an entry on a bill of lading or an estate inventory, and rendered voiceless. The state of slavery further compounds the methodological challenge in that women and slaves, as oppressed groups, themselves frequently suppress their objective reality. Their words, if we could only hear them, may have been designed not to reveal but to conceal, not to inform but to misinform.

In attempting to decode the mysteries of the black female condition the Caribbean scholar is at greater risk than her Afro-American counterpart, who can study collections of slave narratives, with opportunities for testing their authenticity. Nothing has surfaced to date in the Jamaican records comparable to the statements of a Sojourner Truth or a Harriet Tubman, or the remarkable testimony of the slave woman Harriet Jacobs, whose autobiography has only recently come to light.

Only one woman of color has left a strong imprint on the pages of Jamaica's past, leaving literary evidence of her lively existence: this was Mary Seacole. Her autobiography, a classic of its kind, entitled *Wonderful Adventures of Mrs. Seacole in Many Lands*, was first published in England in 1857. It is a vivid, witty account of a life of a spunky mulatto woman who labelled herself a "female Ulysses". Her ambition and wanderlust took her as an innkeeper, huckster, and nurse to Haiti, Cuba, The Bahamas, Panama, England, and the battlefield of the Crimea, where she became celebrated as the "brown Florence Nightingale". Her portrait dominated the platform of the Hall at the University of the West Indies in Jamaica, where I lived and worked during the years of my research.

Mary Seacole's "wonderful adventures" occurred during the post-emancipation period and, therefore, fell for the most part outside of my research time-frame, but I expected to meet her on my journey. I did, and certainly she came alive through the picture she drew of *herself*. Today's Caribbean women writers will be intrigued to explore the value of her contribution to our literary heritage, for her autobiography is both a historical document and a creative work, a unique expression of the female mulatto syndrome.

Nanny of the Maroons was more enigmatic. For as long as I can remember, she has been somewhere in the Jamaican consciousness but without acquiring solid flesh and blood. Was she an Ashanti chieftainess who wielded power over her people in the Portland mountains of eastern Jamaica and kept the establishment at bay for years as she led the war of black liberation, frustrating colonial designs to make the island free for King Sugar? Or was she a creature of legend, summoned up by the Maroons from the spirit world to sustain their struggle for freedom?' The supernatural powers attributed to her in popular sayings seemed so bizarre as to produce skepticism about her humanness. I did not know precisely how much I would discover about this heroic but insubstantial figure; and if one rejected the folk memory as a valid base for scholarly theses, was there any certainty of finding incontestable evidence that she had really lived?

The twilight zone Nanny inhabited symbolized the hazy state of our knowledge about our black foremothers. Records existed, most of them the result of the very nature of the slave society and economy. Estate papers and slave registration returns are rich in the demographic data compiled by proprietors and managers to keep account of the size, age, physical condition, occupation, and other attributes of their human property. Colonial Office and parliamentary reports provide prime evidence of the strategic and commercial interests of imperialism, which shaped the island polity and made precise prescriptions for the functioning of each racial group and, above all, of each unit of the work force. There are data in abundance, but there is very little about the inner lives of slaves.

Clearly, one must probe deeply into the conventional sources of Caribbean history to find those missing women, to attempt new interpretations, and imaginatively to bring new insights to the task of opening up the slaves' private world, where black women lived in cultural antithesis to the white plantation. The historical, sociological and creative writings of Orlando Patterson and Edward Kamau Brathwaite in the 1960s and early 1970s indicated how and where one might find that Afro-Caribbean world. As Brathwaite expressed it, "history becomes anthropology and sociology, psychology and literature and archaeology, and whatever else is needed to make the fragments whole". In the 1960s, however, we were a long distance away from refining multidisciplinary scholarship.

Understandably, I was nervous about embarking on my venture with such undeveloped professional tools. But I was inspired and supported by a friend and teacher, that great woman, Elsa Goveia; and there could be no more appropriate occasion than this historical gathering of Caribbean women writers at which to pay tribute to her shining spirit and towering intellect: she was a native of Guyana, the first female professor and the first professor of West Indian History at the University of the West Indies. Sadly, she died too soon, at the age of fifty-five. But what a legacy she has left us! Her first major publication in 1956 was a study of the historiography of the British West Indies. In it she dissected with a cool and devastating critique the racialist and authoritarian ideologies of those historians who, under the guise of academic objectivity and humanist values, previously attempted to record the Caribbean past.

Nine years later, she produced her landmark history, *Slave Society in the British Leeward Islands at the End of the Eighteenth Century.* In his annual lecture in her memory at the University of the West Indies, Professor Franklin Knight aptly described that work as "magisterial".

Professor Goveia's piercing vision and rigorous scholarship brought fresh understanding of the complex historical forces that have shaped our island societies. Brilliantly, meticulously, she analyzed the decisive force of race and color in constructing Leeward Islands society, demonstrating how "the social order of the whole community hung upon the distinctions established between the constituent races". Simultaneously, she identified the propensity of those same constituents to destabilize the social order. Her thesis tempted me with prospects of an exciting dialectical exploration to illuminate the buried lives of women: if the fact that she was black or white or brown ascribed to a woman her status, her functions and her subversive potential, would her being female make a difference? In short, how far would her sexual identity diminish or enhance her capacity to conform or to resist?

It took time, of course, to find answers, and a great deal of patience, like that of the gold prospector, sifting through tons of material in search of the occasional nugget of enlightenment. But fragments of women's lives came to light increasingly out of the shadows of the archives, and the contours of black, brown, and white women's stories took shape.

The combined ideologies of white supremacy and patriarchalism laid down clear guidelines for the status and functioning of white women in a plantation colony. The majority, conditioned to accept such concepts, performed accordingly, but not all did. Some proved capable of flouting convention, of engaging in economic activities that did not fit the white female stereotype, of indulging in unbecoming social conduct, of violating interracial sexual taboos. Women of the plantocracy struck out with even more spirit, in some ways, than did women of lesser classes, making definitive statements of white female distaste for Creole norms. Many came, saw, and fled, leaving behind awkward social and domestic gaps that threatened to undermine the nice designs of the establishment.

Colored women had their allotted place, initially a marginal one. But selective co-option carried some to the status of surrogate whites, who served partially to defuse the racial imbalance, ten blacks to one white, the highest in the transatlantic plantations and a terrifying specter to the white establishment. Numbers of brown women exploited openings in creole society, carving out for themselves significant roles that had not been previously prescribed, virtually inverting the social order. Such processes, within the context of Jamaica's sexual and racial demography, have important implications for brown women's assertive capacity to influence the shaping of a society. But under the close scrutiny of research, the black slave woman emerged as the most aggressive of women: she took center stage as rebel.

Rebels on the run are usually the first to catch posterity's eye, for as valuable property that had to be recovered when they fled their estates, the made copy in the local press. That liberating act of "pulling foot" gave them names, faces and identities. They became conspicuous in the fugitive population, confounding customary perceptions of the passive sex, whose physical mobility is constrained by motherhood. The female runaway often made sure her children joined her escape from bondage in what was one of the most threatening forms of protest, for each missing person, man, woman or child, jolted the system. A family, such as that of Margaret, alias Amy, stands out in the rogues' gallery. She was a "slender black woman, with a large eye, prominent forehead and straight nose, and marked CH or MH"; her daughter Eliza Arnold was also "slender, with very large eyes, and a thin visage"; and her son Richard McLeod, aged eighteen, accompanied them. Described in the advertisement for their capture as a "plausible trio", they had crossed the length of the island from the north-western parish of Hanover and were hiding somewhere in the city of Kingston in the southeast. They and others like them moved through a black underground that sustained fugitives for long periods, over long distances, in the countryside or in the busy subculture of the island's growing towns.

Women featured prominently among the "incorrigible" slaves who ran away again and again, risking recapture and punishment, which increased in severity for each repeated offence. When caught and returned to me plantation, they made common cause with an equally "incorrigible" band of rebels: the industrial saboteurs. Women had the power and the will to destabilize the plantation's labor productivity through a variety of single or collective acts, some blatant, some devious, but all ultimately damaging to the economic enterprise. I developed a special feeling for one such subversive activist, a slave woman of Port Royal, whose owner was so misguided as to name her "Industry". She could not resist that challenge: "For refusing to work and setting a bad example to other negroes on the property by her contumacious conduct", Industry was sentenced by the magistrate to two weeks' hard labor.

Women were highly visible in the go-slows and work stoppages that were endemic on the plantations; for example, a "petticoat" rebellion of those assigned to carry cane trash halted the operations of the sugar mill at Matthew Lewis's Cornwall estate in the parish of Westmoreland during the early nineteenth century. Such open sabotage was frequently supplemented by more equivocal strategies such as pretending illness. When admitted to the hospital, the malingerers would settle in for a long stay, to the detriment of the estate's output.

Women often used their reproductive power to erode the productive functions demanded of them. The plantation looked to them increasingly after the abolition of the slave trade in 1807 not only to provide massive inputs of labor but also to replenish the labor force. But slave birth rates declined steadily in the later years of slavery until emancipation in 1834, partly because of the arduous tasks and the physical and sexual abuse to which slave women were often subject, but partly also because women willed it so. They aborted regularly with the expertise of that formidable figure of the slave community, the midwife, who was knowledgeable in the use of folk medicine and who projected an image of having almost supernatural gifts. When they did give birth, slave women exercised their maternal prerogatives to the maximum. Few female acts provoked more frustration and rage in estate managers than women's insistence on nursing their infants for as long as they could and too often for the estate's liking, often for as long as two years. It was an effective strategy because slave laws provided nursing mothers with time off and special allowances, all charged to the estate's accounts.

Women were clearly determined to retain control over their reproductive and maternal rights. During the last years of slavery and the interim period of apprenticeship preparatory to full emancipation, when the fear of labor shortage haunted the plantocracy, women's withdrawal of that labor and that of their children seriously threatened the viability of sugar plantations. One official report gave evidence: "Negro mothers have been known to say, pressing their children to their bosoms, we would rather see them die than become apprentices." During the four years of apprenticeship, from 1834 to 1838, of the thousands of slave children who were eligible, only nine were released by their mothers for recruitment into the estate workforce.

The other side of such reluctant and minimal effort for the plantation was the remarkable industry and productivity of women and their families on their provision grounds. There they labored long, hard hours, traveled miles weekly to nearby towns to sell their crops and made themselves indispensable to the domestic economy. The profits from such enterprise provided them with the means to acquire possessions for home and person, including the colourful clothes in which women took pride. Personal property represented a degree of economic autonomy which slaves jealously guarded and defended in courts, where they pressed their legal rights to their own time for cultivating their plots. And there another band of determined rebels made their presence felt, the habitual litigants, among whom women were conspicuous. They stormed the courts claiming their maternal privileges, and they protested excessive physical abuse and punishments, raising their voices loud and clear, displaying black verbal skills to great effect.

Women's voices, clamorous and ceaseless, were a marvelous medium for affirming their identity and for expressing their "magnificent discontent". Words are tools to which everyone has access. They can be explicit or insidiously shrouded in double entendre. Exasperated whites described woman's tongue as a "powerful instrument of attack and defence, exerted in insufferable insult. With malice and artistry their work songs in the field explored Buckra's frailties, which many women had reason to know well. The use or misuse of the master's language developed into sharp and enduring weapons for resistance which received added force from the mystique that surrounded African cultural perceptions of language and the word.

Far more than the written word, the spoken word established Nanny's awesome reality. Close examination of the official records verifies her status as the civic, military and religious leader of a free community in the mountains of eastern Jamaica during the period of the first Maroon war of the 1730s. The records also show how false was an often-quoted allegation that she died in 1733 at the hand of Cuffee, "a very good party negro". It is not clear whether this was a mistake or misinformation, but she certainly lived and continued to defy the colonial establishment until 1740, when she reluctantly accepted a truce. The land patent she received from the British Crown in 1741 can be found today in the National Archives in Spanish Town. It granted to her and her people 500 acres in the parish of Portland, land they still inhabit.

Such documents are invaluable for the reconstruction of Jamaica's history. Of equal value are the oral traditions of the Maroons. Like other Afro-Caribbean groups, they carry their past in their heads. Their storytellers are charged with the sacred and professional responsibility of preserving the historical narrative intact. They have done so with such seriousness and consistency from generation to generation that modern scholarship increasingly acknowledges the ability of the folk memory to validate the authority of the printed page. To do justice to the actual and symbolic presence of a Nanny, as Brathwaite has stated, implies "the commitment of the researcher to undertake an investment in the veracity of our oral traditions and enlist those traditions in the reconstruction of a broken legacy". It is a broken but hardy legacy, not easily lost by the millions of young female adults who for nearly two centuries crossed the Atlantic carrying, if nothing else, their certainty of being African and being women. The majority, before enslavement, had undergone the rites of passage their societies required of them, which ceremonially expressed a civilization's clear perceptions of the truths and joys as well as the mysteries and dangers of existence. Each new and potentially frightening phase of the life-cycle was realistically confronted and exorcized, in the process invoking ordeals that tested physical and spiritual resources to the ultimate and challenged the human will to address, survive and transcend pain, always seeking and drawing strength from a pantheon of deities whose power and wisdom resided with the ancestors – the guarantors of society's integrity.

Female status within such cultures was clearly articulated and structured to ensure respect and self-respect. Motherhood, sisterhood, age and healing gifts assumed supreme significance in African women's world view. It was a view perpetuated through chant and drum and dance, languages virtually impenetrable to the outsider or slaveholder but full of meaning for generations of the enslaved, and increasingly for the musicologists, linguists and other cultural explorers of today, without whom that world view could not be reconstructed. Among its main references is a history of regal women, not unlike Nanny of the Maroons.

Wonderful things happened on the journey into that rebel past, of which Nanny became the permanent, powerful icon. I can here only briefly indicate the personal process of self-growth it meant. No one could spend so many years in the company of such women and remain the same. The expansion of one's emotional and intellectual resources and the deepened pride in one's inheritance and in one's womanhood were inevitable, and are subjects for another article.

More relevant was the great occasion when a personal conviction about Nanny's profound significance to the Jamaican psyche became a public reality. I advanced it as an opinion and a recommendation, and in 1975 the Jamaican government proclaimed her Right Excellency and thereby enshrined her among the galaxy of national heroes: Paul Bogle, George William Gordon, Marcus Garvey, William Bustamante and Norman Manley.

Somewhere along the way, I noted that Brathwaite's great verse trilogy of the African diaspora, *The Arrivants*, is inspired by the almost exclusive assumption of a "poor, pathless, harborless spade", who is male. The next epic creation of this historian-poet-visionary was his *Mother Poem*, which met the challenge splendidly. Brathwaite also invited me to join him in filling a vacuum in the existing literature by editing a special volume of the journal of the Caribbean Artists Movement, *Savacou*, on Caribbean women's writing, and for the first time, such a collection appeared in 1977. It contained contributions, among others, by participants of this conference such as Merle Hodge, Lorna Goodison and Opal Palmer. It also contained Maureen Lewis's article "The Nkuyu: Spirit Messengers of the Kumina", an essay of seminal importance in the growing body of Caribbean literature that acknowledges the integrity of the oral tradition and finds a respected place for "groups like Queenie's Kumina bands which today attempt to preserve a sense of historical continuity through spiritual and cultural means". This pioneer publication was dedicated to the memory of the Jamaican poet and playwright Una Marson, another precious and precocious spirit. She would have been at home with her wayward ancestors, those fractious females who ridiculed their masters, downed their tools, harassed the courts, placed themselves between their children and the slave driver, refused to give birth on order, planted their food crops, walked ten miles to market, flaunted their bright finery, and disappeared in the melting pot of towns, where they joined the men in plotting poison, arson, and rebellion.

One might ask, where on earth did such women, the "subordinate" sex, get this nerve? Perhaps it came from their very subordination – the moral force of the powerless confronting the powerful – and also from their ability to draw strength from that inheritance of ancestral spirits from the other side of the ocean.

The militant acts and words of Afro-Jamaican women were neither isolated nor inadvertent. They constituted a political strategy that took different forms at different times but at all times expressed the conscious resolve of the African enslaved to confront the New World plantation's assault on their person and their culture. "Victimization", as Herbert Aptheker has written, "does not simply make victims: it also produces heroes." We might add, "and heroines too". Women expressed the will to resist with an intensity fueled by their outrage at the sexual violence in their lives. The passion and persistence of their heroic acts of self-affirmation and rebellion rescued them from silence and invisibility, and embedded the meaning of those acts in a people's memory.

Many Caribbean women writers today, also engaged in their acts of conscious self-affirmation, explore history, myth and memory, seeking cultural continuities. Refusing to pursue futility, they seldom lament the absence of ruins. On the contrary, they celebrate their presence, not the presence of fragmented, desolate remnants that signify nothing, but valued monuments, human artefacts, ready to receive vibrant new forms through the genius of those pens which are today busily creating praise songs for Caribbean women. And here, of course, is where the journey has brought me.

References

Aptheker, Herbert. 1974. *American Negro Slave Revolts.* New York: International Publishers.

Brathwaite, Edward Kamau. 1967. *The Arrivants: A New World Trilogy: Rights of Passage.* Oxford: Oxford University Press.

———. 1968. *Masks.* Oxford: Oxford University Press.

———. 1969. *Islands.* Oxford: Oxford University Press.

———. 1971. *The Development of Creole Society in Jamaica, 1779–1820.* Oxford: Clarendon Press.

———. 1972. *Mother Poem.* Oxford: Oxford University Press.

———. 1977. *Wars of Respect: Nanny, Sam Sharpe and the Struggles for People's Liberation.* Kingston: Agency for Public Information.

Goveia, Elsa. 1965. *Slave Society in the British Leeward Islands at the End of the Eighteenth Century.* New Haven: Yale University Press.

———. 1980. *A Study on the Historiography of the British West Indies to the End of the Nineteenth Century.* Washington DC: Howard University Press.

Jacobs, Harriet. 1965. *Incidents in the Life of a Slave Girl, Written by Herself,* ed. L. Maria Child. Cambridge, Mass.: Harvard University Press.

Mathurin Mair, Lucille. 1975. The Arrivals of Black Women. *Jamaica Journal: Quarterly of the Institute of Jamaica.*

———, Edward Brathwaite, ed. 1977. Caribbean Women. *Savacou.*

———. 1971. Creole Authenticity. Review article on Edward Brathwaite's *The Development of Creole Society in Jamaica, 1779–1820. Savacou.*

———. 1978. Erotic Expediency: The Early Growth of the Mulatto Group in West Africa. *Caribbean Journal of African Studies.*

———. 1974. A Historical Study of Women in Jamaica, 1655-1844. PhD dissertation, University of the West Indies.

———. 1975. *The Rebel Woman in the British West Indies During Slavery.* Kingston: Institute of Jamaica.

———. 1987. Women Field Workers in Jamaica During Slavery. The 1986 Elsa Goveia Memorial Lecture, Department of History, University of the West Indies.

Patterson, Orlando. 1972. *Die the Long Day.* New York: Morrow.

———. 1967. *The Sociology of Slavery.* London: MacGibbon and Kee.

Seacole, Mary. 1857. *The Wonderful Adventures of Mary Seacole in Many Lands.* London: James Blackwood.

3. Gender and Memory: Oral History and Women's History*

Mary Chamberlain

Introduction

Precisely because memory is malleable, is susceptible to confusion and conflation, to lapses and lying, to suggestion and sensation, and always to the role of the imagination, oral sources have been dismissed by many traditional historians as untrustworthy, or relegated to the periphery of historical enquiry. 'For some areas of historical study,' Arthur Marwick reluctantly conceded in the 1989 edition of his student primer, *The Nature of History*, 'relating to the poor and the underprivileged, this kind of source may be the main one available...for Black Americans in the Deep South, working class wives in Edwardian Britain, Italian peasants in the First World War, and for much recent Third World history'.[1]

This is the only reference Marwick makes to oral history, black history or women's history. In some ways his assessment is correct. Oral testimonies have been used as a prime, or supplementary, source in constructing histories of certain social groups who, by reason of gender, class, education, race or culture, have left few other, if any, conventional sources. Unless engaged in contemporary political history (where their informants are likely to be key political players), historians who use oral sources have been forced to argue not only for the value and validity of their *sources* but equally the value and validity of their *subjects* within the historiographic taxonomy. The task of the academic historian has not been made easier by the association of 'oral history' with both political and consumer populism. 'Oral history' 'empowers' and, in the right hands, 'sells'.

---

* Reprinted with permission from *Engendering History: Caribbean Women in Historical Perspective*, ed. Verene Shepherd, Bridget Brereton and Barbara Bailey. Kingston: Ian Randle Publishers, 1995, 94–110.

The issue, however, is not to do with whether oral sources are good or bad, true or false, or whether they enhance the supply side or empirical research, or offer an antidote to historical elitism.[2] It rests in what Alessandro Portelli identified as the 'peculiarities' of oral history.[3] In his view, oral sources tell us less about events as such than about their meaning, and their value lies in the areas of language, narrative and subjectivity. Oral sources are different from conventional sources, precisely because they deal with perception and subjectivity. But if those differences and problems are recognised not as limitations, but as representative of a 'different credibility', then their evidential value takes second place to their potential value of signification. I wish here to use Portelli's argument and insights, but to focus on some of the characteristics of oral sources which offer particular insights into the history of gender.

Memory and Culture

The first, obvious and most vital feature of oral sources is that they rely on memory. The relationship between memory and the imagination has been a constant feature in the history of both rationalist philosophy and romanticism, in which memory plays a non-rational role as inferior image, or subconscious prompt, to the imagination.[4] At the same time, memory and the imagination have been perceived as unique to the individual. Indeed, what constitutes the 'individual' has been defined by the specific properties of memory. Memory and the individual are indivisible. This notion, central to much Western philosophy since the eighteenth century, was given added impetus by psychoanalysis in the nineteenth century, which highlighted the role of memory in the construction of individuality. Yet obvious though it may seem, the synonymity between memory and individuality is an epistemological, and therefore cultural, construct. Many of the criticism of oral sources *qua* sources rest on this notion. Memory, as a function of the imagination, is both volatile and inferior; at the same time, the individual, peculiarly identified by memory, cannot speak for the collective.

Yet the language, images, priorities and expectations, which shape memory and give it structure and meaning derive from shared, that is social, languages, images, priorities and expectations. In this sense, although the *voice* may be individual, and differs from one to another, the form memory assumes, the ways in which it is collated and expressed, is collective. It is culturally and socially determined.

If we recognise that memory rather than being confined to, and by the individual, manifests elements of a shared consciousness and is part of the process of social production, then oral sources offer the potential for entering into a wider cultural milieu. In that sense, the individual voice may be representative of the collective voice and provide evidence of broader attitudes, values and patterns of behaviour. Several such voices may confirm cultural practices. They become objectively self-validating and are the stock-in-trade of ethnographic studies in which comparative research argues forcefully that what appear to be universal principles of human behaviour are always culturally determined. In this sense, the historian who uses oral sources enters the terrain of what may be termed 'historical ethnography'. What may appear to be an individual and fragmented account, is representative of the totality and it is the totality which provides, through affirmation or denial, meaning.

Memory, Language and Gender

The second obvious, and related, feature of oral evidence is that it is spoken evidence. The form of medium for expressing memory is language. Historians cannot study the substance of their oral evidence without taking account of the form on which it is structured, and the ways in which language itself structures meaning. Again, the relationship of language to meaning has been one of the predominant concerns of Western philosophy, although it is only relatively recently that gender has entered into the philosophical debate. Language[5] itself is gendered. The internal categories employed to structure perception are man-made. Women's experience, in that sense, is already alienated. Moreover, the broader socialisation of men and women encourages them to use language in particular ways. For women, this stresses personal, rather than public, categories. 'Men talk but women gossip' may be a stereotype, but evidence for gendered linguistic subcultures has been supported by research in both the social and behavioural sciences and noted by educationalists.

The first task, therefore, for the feminist historian using oral sources is to enter into this gendered subculture by acknowledging its linguistic roles and its subtexts; and by recognising that women are, as it were, culturally bilingual, that they inhabit simultaneously, not sequentially, a domestic and a public world, and it is this which shapes their experience, the language which expresses it and the priorities allocated within. In dealing with memory and language, one must deal with gender. Compare, for instance, these narrative extracts from recent interviews with Barbadians. They are responses to the question, 'tell me about your mother'. I have deleted references to names, but the extracts are otherwise unedited.

> Mrs. A., born Barbados, 1908: *My mother, my grandmother, we live together... My grandmother, when she took sick in 1921, hair, enough hair pretty white hair like silk cotton, and me and my sister would pick her hair, and we did fair size children at the time, so my mother had the last baby she had born, and my grandmother took sick so. After she took sick, we had to go and pick porn grass and let my mother stay at her mother, that is how it was. Yes, we had to went and pick porn grass and then my mother stay with my grandmother.*[6]

> Mr. B, born Barbados, 1906: *I came along and find my mother... had five children when I made six, and she had one more after me then, seven. That was all she had did then. Well, them all, [she] do different work coming on, cor[because] it was for people, do enough field work and about servants and so on, from time to time . . . do while for do, you see time it didn't use a lot of money.*[7]

The respondents were a married couple. The wife's response was badly ordered. It jumped erratically between six subject categories within short narrative space. Alternatively, her narrative may be interpreted not as a catalogue of subject areas ('indirect-style' or 'topic-associating' response) but in terms of a single unitary vision, as a graphic, textual and sensual description of her grandmother and mother within the totality of their relationship.[8] By contrast, her husband's response listed sequentially the functions performed by his mother. It had segregated, selected and ordered data. In that sense, it could be perceived as the more logical response. Yet to my mind, there is no question that the woman's response expressed an integrated, holistic description of the context in which her mother lived and the context in which, as children, they went out to work. Her husband, on the other hand while perceiving the integrative world inhabited by his mother, had difficulty expressing it, preferring instead to list methodically two functions performed by his mother and measuring her role against outside referents of class with which, as historians, we are already familiar.

His mother worked 'for people'; her earnings 'didn't use a lot of money'. For his wife, the reference points are internal to the family. Her narrative conveys the meaning of her mother's life, implicitly acknowledging the relationship across the generations, the values and attitudes inherent within it, and the emotions generated by it. Her grandmother's 'pretty white hair' privileges us to this. For the historian, the husband's response may offer the most useful evidence, for his wife's response appears too confused and illogical to be of any (conventional) empirical value.

Contrast these two accounts also.

> Mr. B, born Barbados, 1917: *She was a very hard working peasant of Barbados. Very poor, but very honest. She worked at various estate plantation, work in St Joseph, St Andrew, St Lucy. And agriculture. Heading cane, working, the dumping, cutting grass, cutting bush, is to make, doing the cane that they make, dung, you know, nutritious dead or the soil.*[8] *(emphasis added)*

> Mrs. B, born Barbados, 1919: *My mother was a very hard working woman. She had thirteen children, but only six of us live. I was the eldest of them all... So she married, but not to my father, so I, her husband die only, then the last boy was four months old and she had to work, go out to work, hard and hard and I was the only one to help her. I has to go out early and work, in the third class and when I work, I gets twenty cents a day, then it raise to twenty four cent. I used to try to do the same work as the older women that older than I, so to help her and I would bring all my money and give her. So she used to say I was her husband, yes.*[10] *(emphasis added)*

Again, the first response contains external reference points. His mother he describes as a gender-neutral 'peasant,' her ascribed role. He offers a sequential and compartmentalised description of her work. His wife's response foregrounds gender. Her mother was a woman. Mrs B. does not distinguish between her mother's domestic and public roles and her own position within the family. Clearly, in all these narratives, class and education enter into the nature of the language. This is 'working-class' speech. Yet all informants had attained the same educational level at school (standard four). In theory, the gender differences cannot be accounted for by differing access to education, although there may have been (though this is beyond the scope of this article) different and perhaps unconscious emphasis on gender attainment in the education process.

In addition to structure, language also contains what Portelli labels 'orality', which embraces not merely the linguistic framework, but such para-linguistic features as timbre, volume, rhythm and velocity, which equally convey meaning. Such 'meanings' often provide a subtext, a set of aural symbols which can convey obvious clues to class or emotion, but also less obvious ones to identity and perception. The 'subject' is lost in the process of transcription, but can contribute significantly to interpretation.

Let me offer another example, from a non-Caribbean context. A poor London woman in the 1920s pawned her wedding ring in order to make ends meet. To prevent her husband finding out, she replaced the gold wedding ring with a brass one from Woolworth's.

Eventually, she was able to redeem the original ring, but, as her daughters recalled:

> *We couldn't get the Woolworth's ring off…she was saying 'Your father'll kill me, your father'll kill me.' And she had a big red finger, because it was her paralysed hand, you see. And every time you pulled the finger out (straight), after a while it would take your hand and close up with your hand on it…*[11]

They eventually succeeded in removing the ring. It is a story of urban poverty, within a context of domestic violence. In many ways it is sufficient. Yet this story was told not 'straight' by her two daughters, but within a context of laughter. They could barely talk. They repeated themselves, emphasising and illustrating the narrative by mimicking the movements of their mother's paralysed hand. What meaning does this subtext of mirth and mimicry offer? First, it signalled collusion, a recognition that the act of pawning the wedding ring was an implicit subversion not only of male authority in the home but in the broader society, which defined working-class women as feckless and fecund. Second, it signalled judgement, an indication that they had evaluated the road they had travelled from childhood to the present and were able to measure the distance and locate it within its historical context. This subtext signalled a gap between the available codes and conventions of description, and the meaning which these women ascribed to their behaviour. As Anderson and Jack suggested:

> *A woman's discussion of her life may combine two separate, often conflicting perspectives: one framed in concepts and values that reflect men's dominant position in the culture, and one informed by the more immediate realities of a woman's personal experience. Where experience does not 'fit' dominant meanings, alternative concepts may not readily be available.*

As a result, they argue, 'To hear women's perspectives accurately, we have to listen in stereo.'[12]

Historians, like informants, are required to exercise distance and objectivity. Logicality and rationality are the required hallmarks of the historian's trade. Historians are trained to investigate what is explicit, either 'wittingly' or 'unwittingly'; any other 'readings' lead to conjecture only. Nevertheless, although this aural 'para-language' may not exist in literary communication, it does in oral communication. The meanings suggested are implicit. They are not articulated. My understanding of the 'subtext,' of which this is one example, alerted me to how a 'para-language' can offer a contradictory meaning, and/or suggest a position of unarticulated dissonance, or discomfort, with prevailing norms and values. Further questioning on the theme of subversion confirmed my initial hunch. But it was the para-language, not the language, which alerted me to this, and led, finally to a wider interpretation of the culture of working-class women in London, which emphasised the role of deception and subversion in the construction of self and collective identity.

If one looks at language, as these small examples show, gendered language – both women' s and men's – needs to be understood precisely because it is gendered and therefore makes different connections and priorities. This does not invalidate either 'language'; but it does recognise that the memories of men and women provide different insights, motivations, and reference points which must be accommodated within an interviewer's framework and should not be dismissed when they fail to do so. Historians have been trained in the positivism of their profession. Looking at language and gender may require skills and insights which take them beyond the limits of their profession, limits which are, arguably, gendered themselves, but which may offer valuable insight into how identities and memories are constructed, and the role these play in the process of historical socialisation and social change.

Memory and Subjectivity

And yet oral evidence is also subjective evidence. Oral sources are first-hand, personal accounts. However much one may wish to 'read' them as assertions of a wider set of social relations, it flies in the face of 'common sense'. Memory is autobiographical. It remains doggedly 'individual'. In the historian's pursuit of objectivity, the value of oral evidence can, it is assumed, be upheld only when it can be corroborated with evidence from other sources, or by accounts of analogous similar experiences. Oral history offers facts. In the examples quoted above, the man's evidence is easy to comprehend and to corroborate: the primary emphasis is on their mother's working lives outside the home, defined by familiar social and economic reference points and confirmed by analogy. The women also refer to their mother's work beyond the home, but their descriptions interweave their mother's workplace role with her domestic role, and their own place and role within the family. It is difficult to disentangle the subject-ordering from the content. All that can be validated by analogy is evidence of 'muddled thinking', an apparent confusion and conflation within the text, a chaos, substantiating a broader mythology that women are overlaid with what appears extraneous information. How do phrases such as 'pretty white hair' (Mrs A), or 'she called me her husband' (Mrs B), offer insight into the material structures which provide the context for these women's lives, other than as thicker, more flowery description? This evidence is impressionistic. It lies within the imaginative. It is, above all, subjective. It belongs more appropriately within the realms of fiction and romanticism than a rationalist, positivist tradition.

Should one then dismiss subjectivity when it intrudes into the collective memory, for diminishing the value of 'hard' empirical evidence? What use can it be to the historian? Subjectivity, as the Italian historian, Luisa Passerini, summarised it, is: 'both the aspects of spontaneous subjective being contained and represented by *attitude, behaviour and language* as well as other forms of awareness such as the sense of identity, *consciousness of oneself* and more considered forms of intellectual identity.'[13] (emphasis added)

Memory is both collective and subjective. Thus, what is said can be taken as representative of a culture, but this culture is reflected not only in its material world of artifacts and spatial arrangements, and in its ordered world of social relations and shared structures, including language, but also in the symbols and myths, the dreams which reflect and reproduce that culture and which give expression to otherwise abstract values of hopes and desires, failure and envy. These values are socially (and therefore historically) constructed; they all play a role in the shaping of identity and behaviour; they are, however, gendered in that they are the product of particular sets of relationships and ascribed behaviour.

In order to understand society, it is essential to understand first the construction and operation of gender as acted out in the relations (attitudes and behaviour) between men and women, and in the cracks and niches within those relationships, in the subversions and deceptions; and second, how gender is represented in consciousness and expressed in notions of identity. Men and women's narratives are constructed differently. This is reflected in their use of language and para-language and the intrusion of seemingly irrelevant information. But if the premise of a gendered subculture is extended, such extraneous detail may offer further clues into this subculture. Rather than dismiss what appear to be frivolous and subjective embellishments, one should perhaps look at them as the mechanisms by which the individual negotiated with the social, although always within the categories of the latter. Indeed, they may offer vital clues into an historical understanding of gender.

Precisely because one listens to memories in their oral expression (for otherwise one shares no access to it) one should, therefore, mark out the points of subjectivity, in the extraneous detail, in the flights of imaginative fancy, that the often inarticulate world of the senses, of passions and dreams, of disappointments, discordancies, and the restrictions of human life and human identity, as experienced by women, find expression.

Thus the sensual world of hair 'like silk cotton,' suggests intimacy offered, provided and valued. It suggests the importance of hair as a symbol of (female) gender and sexuality. It suggests also a recognition of chronology, of growing up, of getting old. There may be other interpretations. But this is an insight into the world which women value, and is no less important for doing so. Equally, the phrase 'she called me her husband' is not just an indication of the accepted role of the male as provider. It indicates also a broader mythology, accepted by both generations, of the fallibility of all husbands. That her daughter tried to work as hard as the older women is not only a symbol of the daughter's pride in assuming the role of provider but implicit acknowledgement of women's role as providers as well as nurturers.

But there is more to subjectivity. Let me offer another example. In response to the question: 'When you landed in England, what was your first impression?' Mrs C, born in 1930, replied:

> *When I was leaving, I got a tailor to make me a nice jacket, and I made a skirt, so I had a nice outfit. And when I came to Victoria, my brother bought a lovely red coat, fitted one. And I was this pretty young girl, this lovely red coat. Well, I first look at the house, and I wonder, what's these things on the roof for? And I said, 'All these factories!' 'Cos I only knew factories had chimneys, you know, and I said . . . 'they must got a big shortage here for labour, with all these factories.*[14]

Mrs C answered the question by locating herself, as subject, in this new country, by identifying herself in terms of her gender, in the guise by which, perhaps stereotypically or mythically, female gender is most conspicuously identified, in terms of clothes and appearances. The chimneys represented (mistaken) opportunities, of equal importance to her as appearance. Subjectivity and gender awareness were interlaced. Above all, she was 'this pretty young girl, in this lovely red coat.' She was feminine. This was her identity and it demarcated difference. Her (erstwhile) partner (born 1929) on the other hand replied:

> *Gloomy, but that didn't surprise me because I was told about the weather conditions and it was in the season, the cold season, gloomy, gloomy, very gloomy, you walk, you going in, you see the chimneys, every house has a chimney stick up and the smoke going up and smog and what have you.*[15]

It is significant that in his response, England was identified 'objectively'; this world conformed to what he had been told about. His own subjectivity, his sense of self, was missing in this extract, although it emerged in different ways later in his narrative, as he recounted his life story, building up a chronological account of his career. But nowhere was there any overt statement that he was masculine, that his self-identity was linked with gender. It was taken as implicit, in the work he undertook, in the roles he performed. But for his erstwhile partner, her subjectivity, her sense of self was central to being feminine. She was there. Again, should one dismiss this as evidence of frivolity, edit it out of her account, focus instead on her career, force her narrative to conform to a male-ordered world of objectively defined categories and roles? To do so invalidates her perception. If the historian must be true to the sources, then what emerges in oral sources, even if it does not conform to historical categories, must be accounted for.

In these extracts, I am favouring the women's account by suggesting that their potential is richer than that of men's. I do so for two reasons. First, because I understand what women tell me and can relate to it. As a woman, I have no problem with their spiralling descriptions, although as an academic historian I do. There is a temptation to dismiss such memories as too difficult to disentangle, or too frivolous to be of historical value. What does it matter what she wore? Yet as this and the earlier examples show, the problem of compartmentalising women's memories should not invalidate those memories, but alert us to what may be of significance. Equally, when an informant emphasises her subjectivity, her femininity, this should be taken not as an uncomfortable intrusion into the historian's objectivity, but accepted as a vital indicator of the difference in which she lived her life. Second, I think that it is necessary in the spirit of positive discrimination and equal opportunities to investigate these issues. Although many feminist historians have used oral sources, on the whole they use them within masculine academic categories of class, power, and so on. I said in my introduction to *Fenwomen*[16] that 'the women's story must be told, but it must be seen in a perspective of its own.' I believe that oral history should go beyond the story, and explore how those stories are perceived, received and transmitted.

Women's subjectivity, as Sally Alexander reminds us:

> *is only one element in the relation of sexual difference, but one fraught with difficulties of interpretation because it opens up not only behaviour, thought, opinion and family stories to historical enquiry, but also the unconscious mental processes. That is, we listen to fantasies about desire and loss, the compelling inner directives of the structure of sexual difference.*[17]

In this view, sexuality and the politics of gender must be considered a powerful determinant of human behaviour, at least as powerful as the more familiar materialist determinant of class. This requires not only a fresh interrogation of sources, but the courage to argue that subjectivity matters, precisely because it may provide clues to the private, personal and often unconscious 'directives' with which an individual negotiates a life course. This is particularly important in the case of women where the bargaining points are not in her control, when the perceptions of 'logicality' and 'illogicality' are gendered, when the values implicit in her evidence are marginalised in both general and academic convention. If memories contain gender differences in structure and content, then those differences require exposure and explanation. They may contribute to an alternative interpretation of the historical process and present a fundamental challenge to interpretation. Indeed, gender should offer a challenge to the reading not merely of oral sources, but of all sources.

With each generation and with each layer of subjectivity, the past moves on. Memory, too, has a history, but the history it offers is generational history. Nevertheless, it is a vital part of the process of socialisation, for the structures, themes and shifting meanings of memory are inherited, passed down through the generations. Studying memories across generations may be used as an exercise in 'micro-history', to chronicle the ways in which people cope and change, reject and reflect, inherit, and construct their sense of self, and with what effect.

Oral sources provide an opportunity to approach history, in which gender should be a determining characteristic, from the inside out, to recognize that men and women's memories are different, and differently expressed, and that these differences are important agents in historical transmission. This idea is not new. The social and behavioural sciences and the growing field of family therapy all point to the importance of the family, and a family 'ethos' in shaping the life courses of subsequent generations.[18] Historians, however, have been slow to accommodate these insights. But a focus on gender, on questions of subjectivity, necessarily orientates our understanding towards the family, and the ways in which gender is represented and transmitted (or transformed), and with what effect.

Mrs C, this 'pretty young girl in a lovely red coat', signalled her identity through emphasising her femininity. Her daughter was seven when her mother left for England. 'I can remember her going…I can remember my mother had on a white organza blouse on the day she left. And I always remember thinking how pretty she looked. But I was devastated.'[19]

Why should both mother and daughter describe arrival and departure in terms of clothes? Given the trauma of the separation, clothes (say the rationalists) should be the last, not the first, item on the agenda of recall.

Mrs C goes further:

> *My mother was very smart. Half of her money went on clothes… (I was) young, free and happy. I was always a kind of happy woman, you know?…I used to make (my daughter's) clothes and she was happy, she was happy, she*

> was a happy little girl...I used to make her so pretty... and she was a good child. No problems with [her].[20]

A love of clothes may have been inherited from her mother and projected on to her daughter. More particularly, Mrs C emphasises happiness of which clothes were the outward expression. It is a perception corroborated by her daughter:

> One of the memories I have of my mother is a fun person. Nothing seemed to make her cross...I think I was a grandmother child, firstborns in Barbados usually are. So I remember my grandmother being the focal point of my life, and my mother was this woman who wafted in, smelling of perfume, with nail polish, wide skirts, thin waist, made a lot of noise in the house, laughing...

Fun and clothes were part of Mrs C's sense of self and the *persona* was directly perceived and interpreted by her daughter. But there was more. Her daughter recalls her father visiting and taking her:

> to his family in St Lucy, and I used to feel like a little treasure, because my mother was a dressmaker and she, when she knew he was coming, she would dress me up in the prettiest dress...I think she used to show off about me and I think he also is the passion of her life. He was her first lover...both of them are always telling me, and I'm very conscious of it, that I was a love child, and very much a love child for both of them...he would collect me, and carry me down to St Lucy, to my grandmother, who would then parade me through the village...she'd just show me off, she'd take me to the village shop and she'd put me on the counter and my dress would fan out...[21]

Clothes were an expression of her mother's (and her father's) sexuality, of which she, as the daughter, was the living embodiment. Her early sense of self was not only vividly connected with appearances, but also inseparable from her mother's love and sexuality. Throughout her narrative, her mother's clothes are a recurrent theme. When her father left for England,

> I must have been probably five. I remember my stepmother, and my mother and a couple of other girlfriends that my father had...all at the quayside... He was kissing all of them. And they all adored him, although he'd obviously done dirties on most of them...and they started to quarrel...I can remember all of this. I can actually remember the dress my mother had on that day. And she was laughing...[22]

Equally, when her mother re-migrated to Canada,

> I was devastated...she has an old dressing gown that she left in the house the morning she left. And I picked it up, and when I'm upset, I put it on, and I

sleep in it. Sometimes I go and I wrap it round my neck. I can smell her on this dressing gown, which is ridiculous. I am forty two years old.[23]

Far from being a frivolous accessory, in this mother/daughter relationship, clothes were an expression and a symbol of their relationship, with all the complexities of absence, of loss, of sexuality, of happiness, and of love. Clothes, in other words, conveyed a set of meanings which were integral to the various identities of both mother and daughter.

Yet historians are not supposed to view appearances as important. A history of fashion features low on the historian's agenda. Worse, why should feminist historians emphasise appearances, when most of their endeavours have been on denying, personally and politically, the gendered meanings inherent in appearances? What can the historian make of these sources, which are couched in highly subjective terms and which carry a conspicuous amount of emotional weight? First, a recognition that personal relationships are a central and unifying feature of human life. In women's memories, as these testimonies show, the family nexus is prominent. If one is to understand gender historically, then the centrality of passions, of relationships, and their role in directing attitudes and behaviour needs to be accommodated even though the evidence is awkward, charged with emotion and seemingly irrational. If one takes sufficient notice of these subjective sources, emblematic themes may emerge which could illuminate what I described earlier as the cracks and niches in gender relations, the means by which women create, sustain and transmit identity in a culture which daily disadvantages and discredits identity.

As an illustration, I have highlighted how in two (possibly three) generations of one family, clothes are a significant theme for the women. More generally, in the interviews with Barbadian migrants, and over the years in interviews with others, women refer again and again to the clothes they wore. Appearances represent identity; they signal femininity. On a broader level, clothes are part of the iconography of womanhood. But they also indulge the imagination and the senses. Clothes represent a definition or statement of difference, independence and autonomy. They may also signal defiance and deception. 'I ent show poor', another informant told me. Such definitions may be illusory, but dressing well places women in the centre, as creators of the illusion, as appropriating one set of male-derived meanings and investing them with their own. The signal may be subtle, but then the best deceptions are.

The Dialectic of Memory

But, the critics say, memory is multi-layered and multi-faceted. It may be subjective, but it is not pure. Memory contains vicarious as well as experientially derived experience. It is mobile and fluid, and subject to influences which may be traced vertically across the generations and horizontally within the generations. Memories change and distort as other social and cultural influences – film images, song, dance, literature, politics, and so forth, and personal factors, such as the life cycle itself, enter into perception and alter or adjust those memories. Memories, therefore, offer shifting interpretations. People live through and with memories which have already mapped out a territory in the social imagination, in whose paths they walk. At the same time, the form which memory takes, the way people remember, shapes not only the content, but what is revealed to others, and how it is revealed. In addition, in narration, there is always an element of genre and a notion of audience. The mentality or orality of memory is necessarily complex, subject constantly to revision and interpretation.

Rather than this being a limitation, it can be used positively to enrich the analysis. For example, Mrs C.'s daughter was left in Barbados when her mother migrated to England. In this unedited extract she describes how her mother

> *sent me a blonde dolly, which I hated. She sent her sister, who would have been a lot younger than her, a brunette. It was smaller than mine and bit by bit, I couldn't do it for my grandmother to see, but over a period of probably a month, I had completely destroyed this dolly, because I hated the blonde hair. Interestingly, because now I can see it in intellectual terms, the blonde dolly was alien to me, as a black child who had never seen a blonde person. But my mother, thinking I was her little girl, she had sent me the biggest, prettiest doll England had to offer. I hated it. I resented my mother. I was angry with her for sending M. the pretty little brunette, which was more to what I was used to. And I, in turn, resented M. for having this dolly, not parting with it, to let me borrow it. And bit by bit, I used to have accidents with this dolly, the big one. I remember another day hitting it with a stone. Then I remember another time, being extremely angry and I actually took a rock and bashed its face in. By the time I was finished with it, you couldn't recognise it as a dolly. But I hated it. Isn't it strange how you remember!*[24]

Recalling and narrating this event required interpretation and reinterpretation: to make sense of her antagonism to the doll, to account for the anger and resentment towards her mother, to accommodate her mother's motives and exonerate her, to articulate her jealousy of her aunt, and to explain deceiving her grandmother in whose charge she had been left. The story operates on a range of psychological, social, emotional and racial levels. More particularly, it was not mere hindsight which enabled this understanding. The daughter joined her mother in England when she was ten years old, and her interpretation is necessarily overlaid with her subsequent experiences of racism in England and the means she developed to cope with this. Until prompted, she had 'forgotten' the doll; once prompted, that memory was necessarily evaluated and explained. The doll was both a symbol of abandonment and a prefigurement of alienation. This single memory, therefore, was recounted in a multi-layered fashion, mobile, fluid and conveying a complicated arrangement of 'meanings'. It is also reminiscent of Maya Angelou (who received a similar gift of a white doll from her absent mother[25]) and perhaps broader cultural archetypes: the moment of time when the child's sense of abandonment is synchronised and symbolised in a gift which was alien to her experience, understanding, and culture. The doll was an intrusion and an insult. But she cannot be sure. The daughter was a university-educated woman. She was well-read in both Caribbean and black American literature. Its symbolic importance may have been given meaning by external influences.

It does not matter. The individual is not immutable. There is no single, authoritative centre. There is no autonomy. Instead, there are, as Gwendolyn Etter-Lewis described it,'multiple and differing images of a black female self.'[26] And it is these 'multiple and differing images' which need to be reinvestigated in any history of gender.

Oral evidence offers one way forward, by providing a three-dimensional source which can be interrogated at a range of levels, not least of which will be the points at which memory is both revised and/or blends personal experience with the language and images of a more public world. Oral sources cannot be examined as narratives, and can be located within genres, in terms of grammar, structure and theme. For memories are narratives; they are biographical and as such are shaped by particular conventions; they require selection and simplification; there is a constant dialectic between internal experience and external categories, between the personal and the public, between private space and symbolic space and symbols. Even time is constructed not on linear or chronological lines, but in terms of priorities. It is possible to look for archetypes, or for particular recurrent mythologies which contribute towards and shape how a life is interpreted. Such analysis is beyond the ambition of this article; yet the pointers cannot be abandoned. Even within this short piece, the white doll/absent black mother emerges as one possible archetypal theme. Equally, the grammar of memory divides on the faultline of gender. The totality of mothers and grandmothers may be representative of an ideal, rather than a literal, type. Holistic memories, incapable of corroboration or analogy, may reflect in structure and form, a more universal way of perceiving and acting. If one looks at narratives partly through the lens of a cultural fiction, then their force and role in conveying moral values, in ordering forms of heroism or neglect or even brutality, as systems which convey meanings rather than truth, as powerful didactic elements in the historical construction of self and identity may be recognised as central to an understanding of how gender is both determined and acts as a determinant. They may suggest a way in which such seemingly disparate sources can be collectively validated. It may be necessary to look to literary criticism, to folklore, to ethnography, to find paradigms, to be more interdisciplinary in the interpretation of sources. But out of the chaos of gendered memories some order may be found. It may not conform to the more familiar rational conventions, but that could release, rather than inhibit, further insights.

Conclusion

Oral sources are neither true nor false, and to pursue them as either is to pursue a chimera. What is needed is an interrogation of oral sources to arrive at a different set of historical evidence. The language of memory is the means by which tradition is transmitted, the means by which structure and values are internalised, passed on and inherited. Memories are imaginative recounting representative of a set of meanings by which and through which lives are interpreted and transmitted, constructed, and changed. Rather than relegate gender and memory to the edges of history; they should be foregrounded as one of a set of central, interpretative tool for understanding the nature and process of historical change.

Acknowledgments

I am grateful to the Nuffield Foundation whose grant enabled me to undertake research into the social history of migration from Barbados to Britain. This article has drawn on examples from that research.

Notes

1. Arthur Marwick, *The Nature of History*, 3rd ed. (London: Macmillan, 1989; first published 1970).
2. Mike Frisch, *A Shared Autobiography: Essays on the Craft and Meaning of Oral History* (New York: Albany, 1990).
3. Alessandro Portelli, "The Peculiarities of Oral History", *History Workshop Journal*, no. 12 (Autumn 1981).
4. For the relationship between memory and imagination in philosophy, see Mary Warnock, *Imagination* (London: Faber, 1976).
5. Dale Spender, *Man Made Language* (London: Routledge, 1985).
6. Ref: B28. All such references from the Barbados Migration Project (Mary Chamberlain). Tapes and transcripts deposited with the National Life Story Collection of the National Sound Archive of the British Library.
7. I am grateful to Dr Velma Pollard for offering me this insight. See Velma Pollard, "Indirectness in Afro-American Speech Communities: Some Implications for Classroom Practice", Faculty of Education, University of the West Indies, Mona, Jamaica.
8. Ref: B30.
9. Ref: B4.
10. Ref: B10.
11. Mary Chamberlain, *Growing Up in Lambeth* (London: Virago, 1989), p. 117.
12. Kathryn Anderson and Dana Jack, "Learning to Listen: Interview Techniques and Analyses", in *Shema. Berger Gluck and Daphne Patai (eds.), Women's Words: The Feminist Practice of Oral History*, ed. Shema Berger Gluck and Daphne Patai (London and New York Routledge, 1991).
13. Luisa Passerini, "Work Ideology and Consensus under Italian Fascism," Historical *Workshop Journal*, No. 8 (Autumn 1979): 82–108.
14. Ref: BB29.
15. Ref: B34.
16. Mary Chamberlain, *Fenwomen*, 1st ed. (London: Virago, 1975).
17. Sally Alexander, "Becoming a Woman in London in the 1920s and 1930s," in *Metropolis*, ed. D. Feldman and G. Stedman Jones (London: Routledge, 1990).
18. See Mary Chamberlain, "Family and Identity: Barbadian Migrants to Britain," *The Yearbook of Oral History and Life Stories* (Oxford: Oxford University Press, 1994); and 'Motive and Myth in Migration: Barbadians to Britain,' paper presented to 25th Annual Conference of the Association of Caribbean Historians, University of the West Indies, Jamaica, 1993.
19. Ref: BB45.

20. Ref: BB29.
21. Ref: BB45, 31.
22. Ref: BB45, 11–12.
23. *Ibid.*
24. Ref: B45.
25. Maya Angelou, *I Know Why the Caged Bird Sings* (London: Virago, 1984).
26. Gwendolyn Etter-Lewis, "Black Women's Life Stories: Reclaiming Self in Narrative Texts," in *Women's Words*.

4. Women and Gender in Caribbean (English-speaking) Historiography: Sources and Methods*

Bridget Brereton

Introduction

In keeping with international trends, there has been a movement from the 'women's history' approach to that of 'gender history' in this body of work. In the earlier phase, in the Caribbean as elsewhere, the focus was on recovering/retrieving information about women in past societies. The women's history approach concentrates on women's special historical experiences and insists on their centrality to the research: from women without a history to women in history, as Jean Stubbs puts it. The gender history approach, of course, tries to analyse significant differences in the historical experiences of men and women in a given society and chronological period; it concentrates on gender roles and ideologies, how they develop and are transformed over time, and how they help to shape historical change. This approach aims not only to 'put women into history'– though this will always be the foundational spade-work – but also to redefine and reconstruct the historical narratives. In general, the work on the English-speaking Caribbean over the last 40 years has followed this progression from women's to gender history, but in practice, of course, the two approaches are often combined, whereas, the need for the first approach, the 'retrieval and recovery' work, has by no means disappeared (Stubbs 1999, 95–135; Brereton 2002, 129–44).

Both types of historical investigation are embedded in the so-called 'new' social history which has dominated the discipline for many decades. Caribbean historiography has leaned more towards social history over the last 30 years, affecting research on virtually all the themes and periods,

---

* Reprinted with permission from *Caribbean Review of Gender Studies* Issue 7 (December 2013).

in particular, those pertaining to the post-Emancipation nineteenth and twentieth centuries. Many historians have probed the patterns of social formation in the different colonies, trying to tease out the interrelations between ethnicity, class and gender. The turn to social history has led to a focus on themes such as race relations, the construction of 'race' and ethnicity, social stratification, gender ideologies and their repercussions – often in the form of 'micro' studies of specific colonies or (at times) specific groups. More recently, one may detect a 'cultural turn', a focus on cultural history, studying the material and expressive cultures of past societies. Of course, this emerged out of – and is often indistinguishable from – the 'new' social history, and is also closely related to the discipline of 'cultural studies'. Research into women's historical experiences and the construction and significance of gender in the past, in the Caribbean as elsewhere, is part and parcel of the broader work on social and cultural history (Brereton 2006, 187–209).

In general, then, women's and gender history in the English-speaking Caribbean has shared the concerns and forms of social scientific and 'structural' historiography. But one important counter-trend has been the continuing interest in writing the life stories of individual women of the region, especially, though not solely, those of significant leaders in public life. Biography as a historical genre, of course, lies at the opposite pole from 'structural' and 'social-scientific' approaches to the past, but it has always been an important methodology for women's history, and is often more accessible to a non-academic readership. We now have well-researched biographies on, or volumes of essays about, such prominent twentieth-century regional women as Una Marson, Amy Ashwood Garvey, Amy Jacques Garvey, Edna Manley and Mary Seacole of Jamaica; Eugenia Charles and Phyllis Shand Allfrey of Dominica; Nita Barrow of Barbados; and Elma Francois, Claudia Jones, Nesta Patrick and Christina Lewis of Trinidad and Tobago – and this is by no means a complete list (Autobiographies, memoirs and diaries by Caribbean women will be considered as sources later in this article.) (Jarrett-Macauley 1998; Taylor 2002; Martin 2007; Brown 1975; Manley 2008; Robinson 2005; Higbie 1993; Barriteau and Cobley 2006; Paravisini-Gebert 1996; Blackman 1995; Barriteau and Cobley 2001; Reddock 1988; Boyce Davies 2008; Sherwood 1999; Joseph 2004; Cummings 2009).

This article will focus, not on the theoretical contributions or even the empirical findings of the body of work produced on women's and gender history in the English-speaking Caribbean, but on the sources and methods employed. It will argue that historians have used the full range of sources – and therefore of methods – typical of the 'new' social history. They have not, in my view, 'invented' new methodologies or utilized hitherto unknown sources, but they have asked new questions of those sources, brought different perspectives to bear on them, and extracted insights and information from them in which previous historians had shown little interest. In seeking to illustrate this conclusion, I will consider both those works falling explicitly into the category of women's and gender history and those which are more generally about social history but have much to say on women and gender. Needless to say, the examples chosen will reflect my own interests and my own reading, and will by no means adequately represent the full range of relevant published work which has appeared since the early 1970s.

Archival Sources: Official Records

History is an empirical discipline: its findings must be based on primary sources, traces or 'tracks' of past human activities and experiences which have survived to the historian's present. For nearly all studies of the post-Columbian Caribbean, the sources have been mainly written. Whether we like it or not, the document holds a privileged place in the historian's work; the archive largely shapes the scope and success of her investigations. And it has been official records, documents generated by government bodies or persons writing in an official capacity, which have dominated the archive, for the Caribbean as elsewhere. By the eighteenth century, the British and colonial governments had developed fairly efficient record-keeping systems, ensuring the survival and accessibility of a huge amount of official documentation. The sheer abundance, the relative accessibility, and the intrinsic value of all this governmental documentation have ensured the dominance of the official archive as the base for most Caribbean history writing, including social, women's and gender history.

Of course, this presents inevitable problems: the official view; the metropolitan eye; the white, male gaze may dominate the historiography. For all who research women's and gender history – or indeed, social and cultural history more generally – questions of interpretation and standpoint are critical. A conscious effort to decode, deconstruct and read against the grain, to extract usable data about people's real lives and thoughts from the archive, to tease out a subaltern history from perhaps unpromising sources, is always required. As Mathurin Mair wrote in 1974, historians were obliged to revisit the 'conventional sources' in order to open up 'new emphases and new interpretations relating to' the black Jamaican woman, and to decode the real world of enslaved and free women so as, eventually, 'to shift the parameters of traditional historiography' (Mathurin Mair 2006, 234–35).

One category of official documents which has been fruitfully mined in this way, by historians probing women's lives in the English-speaking Caribbean, comprises deeds, land patents, wills, inventories, assessment rolls and levy (tax) records. We can point to examples relating to Jamaica, Barbados and Tobago. Mathurin Mair was able to find the Jamaican Land Patent of 1740 which recorded the government grant of 500 acres to Nanny of the Windward Maroons and her people, establishing the 'historicity' of this famous, legendary personage, the only female National Hero of Jamaica. She used legal inventories in the archives to detail the extent of property ownership by Jamaican free coloured women during slavery, probing how they inherited land, slaves and other property, and how they in turn amassed wealth and bequeathed it to their children; and wills showed how white male Jamaicans disposed of their property among their wives, their legitimate sons and daughters, their non-white mistresses and their illegitimate, mixed-race children. For a later period, Veront Satchell based his detailed study of land transactions between 1866 and 1900 on 12,492 conveyance deeds, allowing him to probe the extent of female participation in Jamaica's land market in this period, and to track changes in that participation as the reviving plantations tried to concentrate land ownership in the hands of fewer people towards the end of the century (Mathurin Mair 2006, 62, 90–97, 152–55, 173–75; Satchell 1990, 3–10, 151–55).

Shifting to Barbados, two recent works have used similar documents to establish property ownership patterns among white and free coloured women during slavery. Pedro Welch considers the Barbados Levy (Tax) Books to be the 'best available source for tracing the fortunes of the coloured people', and he has used them to establish the property holdings of free coloured women, especially during the last decades of slavery, along with other legal documents. For the same period, Cecily Jones used deeds, wills and inventories to examine the extent to which white Barbadian women owned property, including enslaved persons, and actively participated in the property market. She succeeds in showing clearly that they were active participants in the colonial economy, despite the well-known legal restrictions on married women's rights to hold or control property independently of their husbands: single, married and widowed women all carried out property transactions of many different kinds, though widows were especially active (Welch 2000, 13; Jones 2007, chapters 3 and 5).

In her magisterial study of Tobago, Susan Craig-Jones also utilizes wills to probe how free coloured and free black women inherited property and in turn bequeathed it. But especially impressive is her intensive study of the Tobago Assessment Rolls for 1881/82, which provide detailed information on female ownership of taxable property – the Rolls indicate the sex of the owner. (Overall, 30 per cent of all properties were owned by women, but they owned only 19 per cent of properties assessed at over two pounds and ten shillings, and only 16 percent of those assessed at ten pounds or above). Craig-James extracts from this detailed source valuable data about the role of gender in the acquisition and utilization of land in post-Emancipation Tobago, which was becoming a mainly peasant economy by the 1880s (Craig-James 2008, 1, 44–49, 121–31).

Another category of official documents which have always been immensely valuable to demographic and social historians, and of course to those researching women and gender, is the colonial census. In the colonial British Caribbean, governmental censuses began in 1844 or 1851 and continued to be taken, usually every ten years. Again, Craig-James has subjected the Tobago censuses to immensely detailed analysis, yielding a huge body of data about women's occupational and economic situation between 1844 and 1946. Women were well over half of the waged agricultural labourers in the late nineteenth century (58 percent in 1891 and 59 percent in 1901), but only 13 percent of persons recorded as 'skilled' were women in 1901. The census data show, Craig-James concludes, 'the extraordinary importance of low-waged female labour in

Tobago's agrarian production in the century after Emancipation', giving 'major significance to gender as a factor interacting with social class for any meaningful analysis of Tobago society'. In their fine work on Jamaican social history between 1865 and 1920, Brian Moore and Michele Johnson use the censuses and the Registrar-General's Annual Returns to establish the empirical realities with respect to 'legitimate' versus 'illegitimate' births, and legal marriages, in this period (Craig-James 2008, 1, 278; 11, chapter 7, 187–20 2; Moore and Johnson 2004, chapter 4).

When slavery was formally abolished by Britain in 1834, Special Magistrates were appointed throughout the colonies to oversee the transitional 'Apprenticeship' scheme which succeeded slavery; when it in turn was ended in 1838, most continued in office under the designation Stipendiary Magistrates. These men often wrote very detailed, and very frequent, reports on conditions in their districts, most of which have survived, and in many cases these reports continued into the late 1840s. Their reports are probably the best single source for understanding the situation of ex-slave women after the end of slavery, their contestations with the planters, and their 'withdrawal' from plantation wage labour. The reports were indispensable, for example, to the research on these developments by Swithin Wilmot for Jamaica, and by myself on the British Caribbean generally. Mathurin Mair also used the 'SM' reports to probe the treatment of black Jamaican women during the Apprenticeship, concluding that 'the harassment of the black female became one of the most notable features of the first years of a free society'. For the Windward Islands, both Craig-James (Tobago) and Nicole Phillip (Grenada) used these reports to examine the strategies and actions of the freedwomen during and after the Apprenticeship (1834–38). (Brereton 1999, 77–107, 275–81; Wilmot 1995, 279–95; Mathurin Mair 2006, 307–09; Craig-James 2008, 1, 63–64; Phillip 2010, 42–45, 48–50)

In Jamaica and Barbados, where the Anglican Church was firmly established as the 'official church', the Anglican Vestry in each parish carried out many functions of local government. Their records (Minute Books and other papers), going back to the seventeenth century in some cases, can illuminate aspects of women's lives in the early period of colonization, especially white women. In her study of white Barbadian women, Jones used Vestry Minute Books for two parishes to probe how poor relief was administered to indigent white women. She argues that the Vestries, run by propertied white men, manipulated relief in order to regulate the sexual conduct of poor white women, to discourage them from unions with black men (free or enslaved), in the interest of the white patriarchy. Mathurin Mair also found that Jamaican Vestry Minutes and Proceedings shed light on the administration of poor relief to white women, who were the recipients of most of this relief – non-white (free) women rarely benefited from money grants ('outdoor' relief) nor were they admitted to the parish poor houses. Vestry records from St Michael parish, Barbados, in which Bridgetown is situated, were also a useful source for Welch in his examination of free coloured women in pre-emancipation society. (Jones 2007, chapter 1; Mathurin Mair 2006, 140-48; Welch 2000)

For historians in the tradition of the 'new' social history, records of law courts, trial transcripts or reports and related documents have provided a lens into people's actions and beliefs in the past; crime and criminality can open up new insights into social and gender dynamics. David Trotman pioneered this approach for the British Caribbean with his work on post-Emancipation Trinidad; he was especially interested in how both Afro- and Indo-Trinidadian women were victims of crime, and frequently also deemed criminals before the colonial courts, in the second half of the nineteenth century. One historian who followed up this approach, applied to Jamaica both before and after Emancipation, is Jonathan Dalby, who utilized Jamaican Assize Court records as his main source. He considered patterns in the prosecution of sexual offences, and of domestic violence murders and assaults, especially in post-Emancipation Jamaica – clearly highly relevant to any analysis of gender norms in the society. For an earlier period, Mathurin Mair mined the records of the parish Slave Courts in the 1820s and 1830s, and the Kingston Court of Quarter Sessions between 1787 and 1812, for evidence of court-ordered punishments of enslaved women in Jamaica. And Verene Shepherd has used the evidence given to a special Commission of Inquiry, held in Guyana at the end of 1885 to probe the death of a young female Indian immigrant on board ship, apparently as a result of rape by crewmen, to consider the whole issue of Indian immigrant women's exploitation in the nineteenth-century indenture system. Very usefully, she has reproduced most of this evidence as appendices to her book (Trotman 1984, 60–72; Trotman 1986; Dalby

2008, 2011, 2000; Mathurin Mair 2006, 223–25, 23739; Shepherd 2002, appendices, 83153).

Of course, there are several other categories of official or governmental records which have been fruitfully mined by many historians of women and gender in the Caribbean: Colonial Office correspondence, especially between the governors and the Secretary of State; reports from official commissions; official publications like the colonial Blue Books and Handbooks; papers and minutes of the colonial legislatures; laws; British Parliamentary Papers. But I hope I have done enough to show that the 'conventional' sources, the official records in the archives, can yield exciting insights and detailed empirical information about the lives of women in the past and the operation of gender. It is unlikely that the official records will be supplanted as the single most important category of primary sources for the history of the colonial Caribbean. But, as Mathurin Mair wrote so long ago, what matters is the determination of the historian to ask the right questions of the documents and read them against the grain.

Archival Sources: Unofficial Records

Undoubtedly, official or governmental records constitute the mainstream of primary sources for historians of the English-speaking Caribbean, because of their abundance, their relative accessibility, and their immense evidential value. But there are many types of written sources generated by non-official bodies, and of course by private individuals, which are of great value to historians, and have been frequently and fruitfully used by historians of women and gender in the region.

Newspapers are clearly one of the most important types of unofficial written sources excluding here the government Gazettes which were not true newspapers but organs for governmental notices and other publications. The British Caribbean colonies possessed a lively and extensive newspaper press, beginning in the eighteenth century, but especially dynamic in the post-Emancipation period into the twentieth century. Articles, editorials, letters to the editor, advertisements of all kinds, serialized novels, short stories, poetry, and birth, marriage and death notices – these are only some of the material to be found in the colonial newspapers. They have proved to be tremendously valuable for historians of women and gender, especially but not only in the post-Emancipation period.

Moore and Johnson have edited two compilations of articles from the two leading Jamaican newspapers of the day which provide vivid and detailed descriptions of social and economic conditions in the colony as a whole in 1890, and in 'squalid Kingston' between 1890 and 1920. They are an excellent illustration of the value of newspaper sources, and naturally include considerable material on women's lives. But it is their magisterial two-volume study of Jamaican society and culture between 1865 and 1920 which really proves how indispensable this source is for social and cultural historians of all kinds, including those mainly interested in women and gender. To focus on one or two examples out of many, Moore and Johnson describe the lively debate in the *Daily Gleaner* (Jamaica's oldest paper, still going strong) on gender, proper wifehood, the 'new woman', marriage and female independence, which took place in 1904; and more generally, they use the newspapers to show how the 'Victorian gender ideology' was imposed on Jamaica through newspaper letters, articles and reports of speeches. Reports in the papers on court cases involving domestic violence and female misbehaviour like drunkenness, articles and letters describing how people of different classes celebrated births, deaths and marriages, newspaper coverage of Indo-Jamaican culture and life – all this and more, highly relevant to understanding women's historical experiences in Jamaica – illustrate the value of this type of source material (Moore and Johnson 2000a and 2000b; Moore and Johnson 2004, 108–13, 137–40, 159–60; Moore and Johnson 2011, 57–61, 320–22, 375–81).

For the period of slavery, newspapers provide a wealth of material on the lives of enslaved women. Advertisements for runaway slaves have long been recognized as an important source, and Mathurin Mair was able to examine a series from 1791 to 1829 to probe to what extent women ran away, what kinds of women, why, and where they were hoping to go. Hilary Beckles and Barbara Bush also used this source for their studies of women in slave society. Though Tobago's newspaper press was not substantial, Craig-James finds some useful data in the *Tobago News*, which struggled to survive in the last decades of the nineteenth century, about middle-class women's occupations, including running guest houses. They were the pioneers of the island's hospitality industry, she concludes. Melanie Newton studied early nineteenth-century Barbadian newspapers to show how philanthropy and charitable organizations were gendered, and how they contributed to constructing 'proper' gender ideologies in that island before and after Emancipation. For St Vincent, Sheena Boa has probed contesting views of culture and gender in Kingstown, in the post-Emancipation decades, using that island's newspapers (Mathurin Mair 2006, 246–49; Beckles 1989; Bush 1990; Craig-James 2008, 1, 275–77; Newton 2005, 225–46; Boa 2005, 247–66).

The records of the Christian churches which were active in the colonial Caribbean, especially from the late eighteenth century, have been very thoroughly mined by many historians, in particular for the closing decades of slavery and the post-Emancipation nineteenth century. Missionaries and clergymen of all stripes wrote copiously – to each other, to their superiors and the parent bodies in Britain, to their relatives at home – and much has survived in various public and church archives, mostly in Britain. Moreover, they were often close to 'their people' and were capable of shrewd observations, even if these were always coloured by ethnocentric and religious biases and prejudices. Mathurin Mair used these sources extensively; for instance, the records, correspondence and published narratives of the Wesleyan (Methodist) Mission shed light on the roles of free coloured women in the Jamaican congregations of this denomination. They were often lay leaders and significant supporters of the clergymen, but the latter were warned to beware of the temptations they represented, and legal unions between a white minister and even a 'respectable' mixed-race woman were frowned on. The London Missionary Society records for Jamaica in the 1830s also yielded valuable data about the clergy's ideas on gender, the role of the missionary wives and teachers, and attitudes to Afro- Jamaicans' practices relating to sex and marriage (Mathurin Mair 2006, 287–90, 298–303).

Moore and Johnson used a very wide range of church records for their study of Jamaican social and cultural history after the 1860s: they examined those of the Anglicans, Methodists, Moravians, Baptists, Quakers or Friends, Roman Catholics (the Jesuit mission), Presbyterians, Church of Scotland and Congregationals. Evidence from this immensely rich collection on women's lives and on the operation of gender ideologies is to be found all through their two-volume work, especially in their chapter on 'Christianizing Jamaica'. Women were the majority of the church-going population in colonial Jamaica, and the special target both of evangelism, and of the wider moral mission to make them into decent, respectable, God-fearing wives and mothers. Taking a somewhat different line, Mimi Sheller used the reports of meetings, correspondence, and petitions from the records of the Baptist and Methodist Missions to probe the construction of subaltern masculinities in post-Emancipation Jamaica (Moore and Johnson 2004, chapter 6, 167–204; Sheller 2005, 79–98).

Contemporary publications, including travel books, novels, ethnographic descriptions and general works about the islands, have always been recognized as valuable primary sources for social historians. Jamaica is especially rich in this regard, especially for the nineteenth and twentieth centuries, and these sources are often full of insights into gender dynamics and the lives of women, notwithstanding the inevitable Eurocentric and (usually) male biases. Moore and Johnson make full use of this type of source in their social history of Jamaica between 1865 and 1920. One of the publications they cite frequently is *Black Roadways*, the pioneering ethnographic study of Afro-Jamaicans by the American anthropologist Martha Beckwith, published in 1929 – a rare (at that time) academic text by a woman. Other female-authored books, which are especially rich in data about Caribbean women, include Mrs A.C. Carmichael's text on her experiences as a planter's wife in St Vincent and Trinidad in the 1820s, and Frances Lanaghan's interesting study of Antiguan society just after the end of slavery (Moore and Johnson 2004 and 2011; Brereton 1995, 63–93).

One of the most important categories of sources for the history of Caribbean slavery comprises plantation papers, correspondence and accounts. Because so many plantation owners lived in Britain, their agents in the colonies wrote frequent reports about their properties, often including detailed accounts, inventories of assets including enslaved labourers, and similar information. In many cases these documents have survived and are now in various public and private archives in Britain. They yield rich data about enslaved women's lives and work. Mathurin Mair was the first to use these documents specifically to extract material about the enslaved women and the gender dynamics on the Jamaican plantations. It was on the basis of plantation papers that she established that women outnumbered men in the field gangs of Jamaica's sugar estates at least by the 1790s, for instance, and that female slaves endured chronic ill health under the punishing regime of gang labour. To take another example, the Holland House Papers, dealing with the several Jamaican estates owned by the aristocratic family of Lord Holland, were used by Mathurin Mair to probe the behaviour of women during the Apprenticeship scheme between 1834 and 1838. Phillip's study of enslaved women in Grenada utilized plantation papers, and she is unusual in also finding some estate records of the 1950s to 1970s as a source for examining the working lives of Grenadian women field labourers in this period (Mathurin Mair 2006, 198–210, 210–23, 306–07; Phillip 2010, 18–43, 83–87).

In writing women's history, researchers have been especially keen to find personal documents written by women – autobiographies, memoirs, diaries and journals, and family correspondence. Such sources have been central to the reconstruction of women's lives in the past. They are not abundant in the English-speaking Caribbean, certainly not for any period before the mid-twentieth century, but those that do survive are immensely valuable for providing what I have called 'gendered testimony': insights into aspects of female lives which are not generally written about by men, or in the official record. The autobiographical writings of Mary Prince and Mary Seacole have become well known, and so has the diary of Maria Nugent, the wife of the governor of Jamaica in the early 1800s. There are other such works, including unpublished collections of family letters by women, which have been used to provide this kind of testimony on the private and usually hidden aspects of female life, in different social and ethnic groups – though the majority of these letters, memoirs and diaries were, inevitably, written by upper-class, usually white women, or educated mixed-race persons like Seacole. Prince is the exception; her short memoir is the only account we know of written (actually dictated) by a former enslaved woman from the English-speaking Caribbean (Brereton 1998, 143–62).

Mathurin Mair was able to use some of these female-authored personal documents in her pioneering study of women in Jamaican slave society. Family letters by white Jamaican women, both Creole and British, allowed her to reconstruct the lives of upper class females during this period. For instance, a series of letters from an elite woman to her daughter in England, published in 1938 as *Letters to Jane from Jamaica, 1788–1796*, proved to be a valuable source, along with other similar but unpublished collections of letters by women. Family papers, containing letters by men and women, such as the Ricketts Family Papers, shed much light on the gender dynamics of plantation households; and diaries and letters of men were used to illustrate family relationships, conjugal affection, and attitudes to girls and women in this sector of Jamaican society. The diary of J.H. Archer, an early nineteenth-century pimento planter and country doctor, yielded interesting information about his mother's life as an active farmer and estate manager, who sometimes clashed with her son on slave management issues, including how to punish troublesome female slaves. And naturally Mathurin Mair frequently turned to the Nugent diary for insights into the private and domestic lives of white Creole women, including pregnancy and childbirth; Nugent herself provided a lively and much-quoted description of her first 'Creole confinement' (Mathurin Mair 2006, 101–05, 117–19, 127–34, 167–69).

A unique type of personal document, heavily used by Moore and Johnson, is the collection of 312 essays written by Jamaicans from widely different social and ethnic groups. Known as *Jamaican Memories* and housed in the country's National Archives, these were submitted to the *Daily Gleaner*, in 1959. Contributors were asked to write on their memories of life 50 years ago. The essays provide rich data on gender and women's lives at the start of the last century (and, of course, on much else); they are comparable in many ways to transcripts of oral history interviews, except that the authors were all literate men and women (Moore and Johnson 2004 and 2011).

Oral History and Oral Traditions

The most important non-written sources for historians of women and gender in the English-speaking Caribbean have been oral history, and to a lesser extent, oral traditions. (The former refers to interviewing individuals about their personal recollections of the past; the latter to communally held knowledge, handed down orally over at least three generations.) While these historians certainly did not 'invent' the oral history methodology, nor are they by any means the only ones to use it, the oral record has always been especially important to those researching women's lives in the past. The reason is simple: until recently, in virtually all societies, far fewer women than men were literate, so that documents written by them have always been much rarer. Women spoke far more than they wrote. Moreover, the official archive, generated overwhelmingly by men holding positions of authority, usually has little to say about most aspects of women's lives in the past, especially those relating to family life, childbearing and raising, domestic work, and so on. The oral record can capture data on those aspects, and much else. Of course, there is a major limitation: oral history can only be employed when the period being studied is within the living memories of individuals now alive (or alive when the interview was carried out). We cannot interview enslaved women; the last women to come as adults from India as indentured immigrants have gone.

Many Caribbean historians have eloquently written, or spoken, about the need for oral sources to illuminate women's lives in the past. In a 1989 public lecture, Blanca Silvestrini pointed out that women were often ignored in the archival sources and their voices could rarely be heard in the documents. She urged us to utilize the oral history method, not merely to supplement other sources, or to obtain information, but so that the voices and the life histories could help shape the historian's discourse and interpretation. Her own work in interviewing women involved in Puerto Rico's famous needlework industry in the middle decades of the last century was offered as an example. In an important article published in 1995, Mary Chamberlain discussed some of the issues in the use of oral evidence in gender history. She suggested that women's spoken testimony and narratives of their lives may follow distinctly different patterns from those by men, patterns the historian must recognize and respect even if they seem, at times, 'illogical' or preoccupied with 'trivialities' such as feelings, affections or appearances. Chamberlain has followed up these insights with a body of important work based largely on oral history interviews of Barbadians living in Britain and at home (Brereton 2002, 131; Chamberlain 1995, 94–110).

Craig-James is among the many Caribbean social historians who have made the oral history method integral to their work. For her study of Tobago society, she conducted 96 interviews with elderly Tobagonians about their memories of the period 1890 to 1950. As she points out, 'the basic problem with most of the written documents is not simply that they cannot answer the questions we ask, but that the majority of the population were excluded from having a direct input into their creation', a statement even more true for women than for men. Much of the 'significant information on the texture of social and cultural life in Tobago survives only in the oral record', she concludes. Her oral history interviews are rich sources used throughout her two-volume study. Rhoda Reddock, in her pioneering study of women in twentieth-century Trinidad and Tobago, made considerable use of the oral history method. A younger historian who has studied the lives of Indo-Trinidadian women in the first half of the twentieth century, Shaheeda Hosein, makes much the same point as Craig-James when she notes that the rural women she studies appear 'only as statistics' in the official written records. Their 'lived reality remained invisible within the discourse of traditional historiography'. Oral narratives were crucial to gain a rounded picture of the rural Indo-Trinidadian women, secured through conversations with persons who were 80 or older when interviewed in 1997–98, and who 'came of age' in the 1920s. 'Through the use of oral narratives I was able to analyse the historical experiences of the women through their eyes and in their sphere: the private domain', she writes, to show their real lives, previously either taken for granted, or seen as 'not the stuff of which history is made' (Craig-James 2008, 1, 20–22; Reddock 1994; Hosein 2011, 101–02).

Erna Brodber, the Jamaican novelist and historian, has brilliantly illustrated the value of oral interviews for illuminating social and cultural history, and revealing the multi-faceted operations of gender systems in the past. For her 1985 doctoral study on what she called the 'second generation' of free men and women in Jamaica, she conducted 90 interviews of men and women born between 1890 and 1910. The original transcripts are lodged with UWI's Mona (Jamaica) campus, and have been used by historians such as Moore and Johnson. In 2003, Brodber published 24 'self-portraits' of Jamaican men; she chose 24 interviews with men from her 90 accounts and published edited transcripts of them. Much was revealed in these accounts about Jamaican ideas of masculinity, fatherhood and gender in the first half of the last century. In 2004, she published a revised version of the doctoral thesis, based, as noted, mainly on the 90 oral history interviews. A more recent study of the small village where Brodber lives combines archival research with 17 oral history interviews with individuals as well as some group interviews. Her lead has been followed by Craig-James, who, it has been already noted, conducted

96 interviews with Tobagonians about their lives in the early twentieth century. While these interviews enrich the entire work, she devotes a whole long chapter to oral testimonies about peasant agriculture and trading in the first half of the last century. Most of these came from women, and they illustrate female roles in traditional Tobago peasant farming and the operation of gender in this vanished agrarian world. From these testimonies, Craig-James concludes 'there was a clear sexual division of labour in virtually every sphere of activity'. Some of the testimonies describe the unique Tobago system of barter, called 'exchange', which was dominated by the women who did most of this traditional cash-less trade between villages and districts, as well as trafficking in agricultural produce and livestock between Tobago and Trinidad (Brodber 2003 and 2004a and 2004b; Craig-James 2008, 11, chapter 2, 37–72).

The oral history method has been used extensively to research the life of indentured Indo- Caribbean women and their descendants in the post-indenture era. Since indentured immigration only ended in 1917, until fairly recently it has been possible to interview surviving immigrants and their children, the first post-immigration generation. The leader here has been Patricia Mohammed, whose fine book *Gender Negotiations among Indians in Trinidad, 1917–1947* combines archival and newspaper research with over 60 interviews with Indo-Trinidadian men and women, mostly carried out in the early 1990s for her doctoral thesis. (The original transcripts are in UWI's St Augustine, Trinidad, campus library.) Mohammed's work has revealed the value of the oral history method, as well as making important theoretical contributions to gender history in the Caribbean. Younger historians researching Indo-Trinidadian women's history have followed Mohammed's lead. Sherry-Ann Singh, using oral sources, has shown how the *Ramayana* cycle of stories, and the folk theatre based on it, helped to shape the Hindu Trinidadian view of gender roles, especially 'proper' relations between husband (Rama) and wife (Sita). Halima Kassim, in her study of marriage and dowry in the Trinidadian Indian Muslim community, leaned heavily on oral history interviews, especially with women, and included 'conversational narratives' derived from them in her analysis. We've already noted that Hosein found oral interviews to be the most important source for her study of rural Indo-Trinidadian women involved in peasant agriculture and marketing in the early twentieth century. Based mainly on these interviews, her findings countered the traditional view that these women were largely subservient, passive and dependent. Rather, they revealed women who earned their own livelihoods, and often supported whole families, owned land in their own right, and in general exercised considerable independence in their economic, domestic and personal lives (Mohammed 2002; Singh 2011, 21–51; Kassim 2011, 52–97; Hosein 2011, 101–20).

Capturing oral traditions – as opposed to oral history interviews – to research Caribbean women's lives in the past has been more difficult, in practical terms. But two recent works by the anthropologist Jean Besson and the historical linguist Maureen Warner-Lewis tap into Caribbean oral traditions. Besson's book on the 'two histories' of Martha Brae, a village in Jamaica, consolidates and extends her many previously published articles on this area and on the evolution of the 'family land' system. 'Although oral tradition cannot be assumed to be an entirely accurate account of past events', writes Besson, 'combined with historical and anthropological research it can illuminate the past'. She taps into the oral traditions of several of Martha Brae's 'Old Families'; as one of their members told her, 'most of the history of the black people don't come in big logbook. They keep it themselves and grandparents told their children and grandchildren'. Her oral sources yielded rich material on gender within the family land system and on the lives of Jamaican peasant women (Besson 2002, chapter 5, quotations 159, 172).

In her ambitious study of 'Central Africa in the Caribbean', Warner-Lewis utilizes 'oral records' of the descendants of enslaved or indentured Central Africans brought to the Caribbean: folktales, proverbs, songs, language and rituals, captured in Trinidad, Tobago, Jamaica and Guyana. Much of her data retrieved from oral traditions and testimonies illuminate the social, cultural and gender history of African-Caribbean people after slavery ended, and after Africans ceased to arrive in the region. Craig-James also taps into the rich oral traditions of Tobago people, overwhelmingly descended from enslaved Africans. In particular, she heard several very old folk songs, nearly all sung to her by women, who had long lost the context and significance of their words. Her research into the documentary record allowed her to 'explain' the meaning and historical context of some of these songs to the women who had learnt them from older relatives. Several of these songs, which are presented in Craig-James' text, deal with marriage, courtship, and 'proper' behaviour of girls and women (Warner-Lewis 2003; Brereton 2006, 196–97; Craig-James 2008, 1, 20–21, 66–67, 214–15, 282).

Other Non-Written Sources

Visual sources – paintings and drawings, photographs, tombstones and statues, video and film – have long been recognized as valuable, especially for social history. Some historians have utilized them to probe gender history in the Caribbean, especially as they illustrate modes of dress and body and hair ornamentation. A useful article published by Glory Robertson in 1995 points to the importance of pictorial sources for nineteenth-century women's history in Jamaica; dress, she wrote, was 'a mirror of attitudes to women'. Her article includes several very revealing photographs of Jamaican women of different social and ethnic groups and probes what they tell us about changes in gender roles and social expectations of ladies and 'other' women. This lead was taken up by S.O. Buckridge, whose full-length study of 'the language of dress' in Jamaica between 1750 and 1890 depends heavily on photographs, paintings, drawings and postcards of women during that period. He sees the choices Jamaican women made about dress, and hair and body ornamentation, as revealing of their choices between 'resistance' (rejecting European modes) and 'accommodation' (accepting them). While this may be too rigid a dichotomy, his book certainly points to the value of pictorial sources for gender history (Robertson 1995, 111–22; Buckridge 2004, passim but specially 135–64).

Both Moore and Johnson, and Craig-James, respectively, in their fine studies of the social history of Jamaica and Tobago, enriched their work with many fascinating illustrations. In each of her two volumes, Craig-James has many wonderful paintings and photographs of Tobago worthies of the nineteenth and twentieth centuries, including many of her oral informants. Moore and Johnson also include many illustrations, often showing women of different social classes and engaged in different (or no) occupations. Especially fine are the colour plates of Jamaican women painted around 1905 and reproduced from a book published in that year. Many of these illustrations, in both works, can be 'read' like a written document to reveal intricacies of class and gender operations (Craig-

James 2008, passim; Moore and Johnson 2004, plates between 156–57 and passim: Moore and Johnson 2011, 49, 52, 62, 66, 217, 286).

In a recent article, the anthropologist Kenneth Bilby has suggested that when we study Caribbean cultural history, we should 'move beyond one-sided modes of historiography that depend exclusively on written forms of documentation'; we might use 'contemporary ethnography to overcome the limitations of written sources' and thus grasp otherwise inaccessible dimensions of traditional cultural forms (like Junkanu, the subject of his article). By using 'ethnographic methods', he believes he was able to grasp the spiritual foundations of what has become an ostensibly secular performance – something he could not have done if he had relied only on 'historical documents written by uncomprehending European observers' in the past (Bilby 2010, 180, 216–17).

The work by Besson, noted earlier, certainly succeeds in integrating anthropological or ethnographic approaches with those of history. She combines conventional archival research with oral history and oral traditions and her own painstaking, 'insider' ethnography conducted over many decades. Using all these sources and methods she is able to tell the 'two stories' of Martha Brae: the story of the plantation town founded in the eighteenth century, which is well documented in the colonial archive, and the story of the post-Emancipation peasant village, which is not. Also with regard to Jamaica, Diane Austin-Broos bases a book on Pentecostalism in that island on oral history testimonies, newspapers, anthropological fieldwork and participant observation, which she describes as 'ethnographic historical writing'. Her work presents a considerable amount of historical data on the Jamaican indigenous religious tradition from about 1860, and the place of Pentecostalism in that tradition after its introduction from the United States in the early 1900s. Since the great majority of the adherents to Pentecostalism in Jamaica were and are women, her study sheds much light on the intricate connections between gender and religion in Jamaica, and on the role played by these churches in Jamaican women's lives. The work by Warner-Lewis already mentioned combines the methods and approaches of anthropology or ethnography, history, and historical linguistics (Besson 2002; Austin-Broos 1997, chapters 1 to 5; Warner-Lewis 2003).

A recent book on Jamaica by Diana Fox, an anthropologist, seeks to reveal how gender lies at the root of 'everyday life' there, how it is the 'cultural DNA' of Jamaicans' lived reality. In her efforts to understand the cultural history of her chosen fieldwork location (Frankfield in Clarendon), Fox seeks 'stories' about its history, collected from 'folktales', the archives, and 'cultural memory' (such as stories about Nanny, the Maroon leader). She believes that both oral traditions and ethnographic studies can help to write gender into history. Moreover, in her otherwise academic text, she includes 'personal narratives' from her informants. One of the writing strategies and methodological tools of the new 'feminist ethnography', she points out, is to present the stories of 'ordinary' people in their own words, showing how they negotiate gender, revealing the 'lived experiences' of gender. This collaborative process between researcher and researched, so salient in more recent ethnographical work, is usually impossible for the historian, but something like it can be achieved through using oral traditions, oral history interviews and ethnographic fieldwork to illuminate the cultural history of gender in a specific locality (Fox 2010, 1–13, 60–82, 123–37).

Conclusion

As Fox makes clear, more recent anthropology/ethnography has developed distinctive methods or approaches, influenced by feminism and post-colonial guilt about the close links between traditional anthropology and the imperial enterprise. The feminist ethnographer is concerned about self-reflexity and the researcher's 'positionality'. She accepts that all scholarly findings are subjective; she searches for 'empathetic understanding' of her subjects; she aims at participatory and collaborative research with those she is researching. She employs writing strategies like personal narratives and life histories, she embraces multivocality, and she aims at a multi-authored text (ethnographer and research subjects). And these approaches and strategies have been widely adopted by feminist social scientists in general, I believe (Fox 2010, 1–26).

However, the case of the historian is different. Her major sources will always be mainly written and archival. Oral history cannot be used to study periods beyond living memory, and oral traditions are of limited use for most historians, and most fields of investigation. Ethnographic studies can be very useful but will rarely become a major source for historical research. Above all, most historians study people who are no longer alive, and this simple fact makes it difficult to adopt the approaches and strategies outlined briefly in the last paragraph. This of course helps to explain the attraction of the oral history method: it does allow the historian direct, unmediated contact with her subjects, and it does open the possibility of a 'multi-authored' text. But, to repeat: many, perhaps most, historians study periods too remote in time to make oral history feasible. 'Empathetic understanding' with the people she studies is, or should be, a given for all historians, and can hardly be seen as a specially gendered or feminist approach.

In my view, historians of women and gender, in the English-speaking Caribbean as elsewhere, have not developed any unique or special methodologies, nor have they 'discovered' any previously unused sources. Instead, they have utilized the full range of methods and sources typical of social and cultural history as it has developed over the last 50 years. They are particularly drawn to the oral history method, but they are hardly unique in this. What they have done is to ask new questions of the sources, read them consistently against the grain and with critical (feminist) eyes, chosen new areas for investigation, and insisted on different perspectives. In these ways they have changed Caribbean historiography and will continue to do so.

References

Austin-Broos, D. 1997. *Jamaica Genesis: Religion and the Politics of Moral Order.* Chicago and London: University of Chicago Press.

Barriteau, E. and A. Cobley, eds. 2001. *Stronger, Surer, Bolder Ruth Nita Barrow.* Kingston: University of the West Indies Press.

———. 2006. *Enjoying Power: Eugenia Charles and Political Leadership in the Commonwealth Caribbean.* Kingston: University of the West Indies Press.

Beckles, H. 1989. *Natural Rebels: A Social History of Enslaved Black Women in Barbados.* London: Zed Books.

Besson, J. 2002. *Martha Brae's Two Histories: European Expansion and Caribbean Culture-building in Jamaica.* Kingston: Ian Randle Publishers.

Bilby, K. 2010. Surviving Secularization: Masking the Spirit in the Jankunnu (John Canoe) Festivals of the Caribbean. *New West Indian Guide* 84(3,4): 179-223.

Blackman, F. 1995. *Dame Nita: Caribbean Woman, World Citizen.* Kingston: Ian Randle Publishers.

Boa, S. 2005. Young Ladies and Dissolute Women: Conflicting View of Culture and Gender in Public Entertainments in Kingstown, St Vincent, 1838-1888. In *Gender and Slave Emancipation in the Atlantic World*, ed. P. Scully and D. Paton, 247-66. Durham and London: Duke University Press.

Boyce Davies, C. 2008. *Left of Karl Marx: The Political Life of Black Communist Claudia Jones.* Durham and London: Duke University Press.

Brereton, B. 1995. Text, Testimony and Gender: An Examination of some Texts by Women on the English-Speaking Caribbean, 1770s to 1920s. In *Engendering History: Caribbean Women in Historical Perspective*, ed. V. Shepherd, B. Brereton and B. Bailey, 63-93. Kingston: Ian Randle Publishers.

———. 1998. Gendered Testimonies: Autobiographies, Diaries and Letters by Women as Sources for Caribbean History. *Feminist Review* 59: 143-63.

———. 1999. Family Strategies, Gender and the Shift to Wage Labour in the British Caribbean. In *The Colonial Caribbean in Transition*, ed. B. Brereton and K. Yelvington, 77-107, 275-81. Kingston: University of the West Indies Press.

———. 2002. Gender and the Historiography of the English-speaking Caribbean. In *Gendered Realities: Essays in Caribbean Feminist Thought*, ed. P. Mohammed, 129-44. Kingston: University of the West Indies Press.

———. 2006. Recent Developments in the Historiography of the Post-emancipation Anglophone Caribbean. In *Beyond Fragmentation: Perspectives on Caribbean History*, ed. J. De Barros, A. Diptee and D. Trotman, 187-209. Princeton: Markus Wiener.

Brodber, E. 2003. *Standing Tall: Affirmations of the Jamaican Male—24 Self-portraits.* Mona, Jamaica: SALISES, University of the West Indies.

———. 2004a. *The Second Generation of Freemen in Jamaica, 1907-1944.* Gainesville: University Press of Florida.

———. 2004b. *Woodside, Pear Tree Grove P.O.* Kingston: University of the West Indies Press.

Brown, W. 1975. *Edna Manley: The Private Years 1900-1938.* London: Andre Deutsch.

Buckridge, S. 2004. *The Language of Dress Resistance and Accommodation in Jamaica, 1750-1890.* Kingston: University of the West Indies Press.

Bush, B. 1990. *Slave Women in Caribbean Slave Society, 1650-1838.* London: James Currey.

Chamberlain, M. 1995. Gender and Memory Oral History and Women's History. In *Engendering History: Caribbean Women in Historical Perspective*, ed. V. Shepherd, B. Brereton and B. Bailey, 94-110. Kingston: Ian Randle Publishers.

Craig-James, S. 2008. *The Changing Society of Tobago.* 2 Vols. Arima, Trinidad: Cornerstone Press.

Cummings, J. 2009. *Christina Lewis: Her Life and Times.* St Augustine, Trinidad: University of the West Indies Open Campus.

Dalby, J. 2000. *Crime and Punishment in Jamaica, 1756-1856.* Mona, Jamaica: Department of History, University of the West Indies.

———. 2008. 'An Epidemic of Sexual Deviance': Sex Offences and Their Prosecution in Post-emancipation Jamaica. Paper presented at 40th Conference of Caribbean Historians, Suriname.

———. 2011. 'A Hell of a Murderation': Patterns of Homicide in Nineteenth-century Jamaica. Paper presented at 43rd Conference of Caribbean Historians, Puerto Rico.

Fox, D. 2010. *Cultural DNA: Gender at the Root of Everyday Life in Rural Jamaica*. Kingston: University of the West Indies Press.

Higbie, J. 1993. *Eugenia: The Caribbean's Iron Lady*. London: Macmillan.

Hosein, S. 2011. Unlikely Matriarchs: Rural Indo-Trinidadian Women in the Domestic Sphere. In *Bindi: The Multifaceted Lives of Indo-Caribbean Women*, ed. R. Kanhai, 101-20. Kingston: University of the West Indies Press.

Jarrett-Macauley, D. 1998. *The Life of Una Marson, 1905-65*. Kingston: Ian Randle.

Jones, C. 2007. *Engendering Whiteness: White Women and Colonialism in Barbados and North Carolina, 1627-1865*. Manchester and New York: Manchester University Press.

Joseph, F.G. 2004. *The Life of Nesta Bonaparte Patrick: A Truly Caribbean Woman*. St Augustine, Trinidad: University of the West Indies School of Continuing Studies.

Kassim, H. 2011. Rings, Gifts and Shekels. Marriage and Dowry within the Indo-Muslim Community in Trinidad, 1930 to the Globalized Present. In *Bindi: The Multi-Faceted Lives of Indo-Caribbean Women*, ed. R. Kanhai, 52-97. Kingston: University of the West Indies Press.

Manley, R. 2008. *Horses in her Hair: A Granddaughter's Story*. Toronto: Key Porter Books.

Martin, T. 2007. *Amy Ashwood Garvey*. Dover, MA: The Majority Press.

Mathurin Mair, L. 2006. *A Historical Study of Women In Jamaica, 1655-1844*, ed. H. Beckles and V. Shepherd. Kingston: University of the West Indies Press.

Mohammed, P. 2002 *Gender Negotiations Among Indians in Trinidad, 1917-1947*. New York: Palgrave.

Moore, B. and M. Johnson, eds. 2000a. *The Land We Live In: Jamaica in 1890*. Mona, Jamaica: Department of History, University of the West Indies.

———. 2000b. *"Squalid Kingston" 1890-1920*. Mona, Jamaica: Department of History, University of the West Indies.

———. 2004. *Neither Led Nor Driven: Contesting British Cultural Imperialism in Jamaica, 1865-1920*. Kingston: University of the West Indies Press.

———. 2011. *"They Do As They Please": The Jamaican Struggle for Cultural Freedom after Morant Bay*. Kingston: University of the West Indies Press.

Newton, M. 2005. Philanthropy, Gender, and the Production of Public Life in Barbados, ca. 1790- ca. 1850. In *Gender and Slave Emancipation in the Atlantic World*, ed. P. Scully and D. Paton, 225-46. Durham and London: Duke University Press.

Paravisini-Gebert, L. 1996. *Phyllis Shand Allfrey: A Caribbean Life*. New Brunswick, NJ: Rutgers University Press.

Phillip, N. 2010. *Women in Grenadian History, 1783-1983*. Kingston: University of the West Indies Press.

Reddock, R. 1988. *Elma Francois: The NWCSA and the Workers' Struggle for Cange in the Caribbean in the 1930's*. London: New Beacon.
———. 1994. *Women, Labour and Politics in Trinidad and Tobago: A History*. Kingston: Ian Randle Publishers.
Robertson, G. 1995. Pictorial Sources for Nineteenth-century Women's History. In *Engendering History Caribbean Women in Historical Perspective*, ed. V. Shepherd, B. Brereton and B. Bailey, 111-122. Kingston: Ian Randle Rublishers.
Robinson, J. 2005. *Mary Seacole: The Charismatic Black Nurse who Became a Heroine of the Crimea*. London: Constable.
Satchell, V. 1990. *From Plots to Plantations: Land Transactions in Jamaica, 1866-1900*. Mona, Jamaica: ISER, University of the West Indies.
Sheller, M. 2005. Acting as Free Men: Subaltern Masculinities and Citizenship in Postslavery Jamaica. In *Gender and Slave Emancipation in the Atlantic World*, ed. P. Scully and D. Paton, 79-98. Durham and London: Duke University Press.
Shepherd, V., B. Brereton and B. Bailey, eds. 1995. *Engendering History: Caribbean Women in Historical Perspective*. Kingston: Ian Randle Publishers.
Shepherd, V. 2002. *Maharani's Misery: Narratives of a Passage from India to the Caribbean*. Kingston: University of the West Indies Press.
Sherwood, M. 1999. *Claudia Jones: A Life in Exile*. London: Lawrence and Wishart.
Singh, S.A. 2011. Women in the Ramayana Tradition in Trinidad. In *Bindi: The Multi-faceted Lives of Indo-Caribbean Women*, ed. R. Kanhai, 21-51. Kingston: University of the West Indies Press.
Stubbs, J. 1999. Gender in Caribbean History. In *General History of the Caribbean Volume VI: Methodology and Historiography of the Caribbean*, ed. B. H. Higman, 95-135. London and Oxford: UNESCO/Macmillan.
Taylor, U. 2002. *The Veiled Garvey: The Life and Times of Amy Jacques Garvey*. Chapel Hill and London: University of North Carolina Press.
Trotman, D. 1984. Women and Crime in Late Nineteenth-century Trinidad. *Caribbean Quarterly* 30(3,4): 60-72.
———. 1986. *Crime in Trinidad: Conflict and Control in a Plantation Society, 1838-1900*. Knoxville: University of Tennessee Press.
Warner-Lewis, M. 2003. *Central Africa in the Caribbean*. Kingston: University of the West Indies Press.
Welch, P. 2000. *"Red" & Black Over White: Free Coloured Women in Pre-emancipation Barbados*. Bridgetown: Caribbean Research and Publications.
Wilmot, S. 1995. 'Females of Abandoned Character?' Women and Protest in Jamaica, 1838-65. In *Engendering History: Caribbean Women in Historical Perspective*, ed. V. Shepherd, B. Brereton and B. Bailey, 279-295. Kingston: Ian Randle Publishers.

Methodologies for Feminist Organizing and Action Research

5. Feminist Action and Research in Haiti*

Carolle Charles

The development of the women's movement in the 1960's, the establishment of 1975 as International Women's Year and the declaration of the United Nations Decade for Women, not only introduced women's issues to the international agenda but had an important impact on research. Indeed, conducting research about women has become the focus of feminist scholars and activists from the 1960's to the present.

Some Fundamental Premises of Feminist Research

Feminist research builds upon and links two levels of analysis: structure and life experiences (Roberts 1981; Young 1993; Richardson and Taylor 1993; Riano 1994). At the structural level, feminist scholars and activists look at the social institutions and cultural practices which create and sustain gender inequalities and link those inequalities to other systems of oppression. At the biographical level, feminist scholars and activists study individual and collective expressions of women's experiences. Thus feminist research helps us learn how oppressions are structurally arranged and personally experienced.

Feminists are interested in knowing about the rich complexities of women's lives and in discovering ways of knowing these experiences. Also feminists are concerned to offer the prospect of effective and real positive change. Knowing how systems of oppression impinge on women's lives, knowing about the larger social forces that contribute to the multiple sources of oppression, help to understand the shape of one's life and the difference between "suffering and suffering from oppression" (Richardson and Taylor 1993).

---

* Reprinted with permission from *Caribbean Studies* 28, no. 1 (Jan.–Jun. 1995): 61–75. Excerpted.

Feminist research is redefining methodology and reconceptualizing social relations and practices based on these premises:

a. That researchers should acknowledge the pervasive influence of gender. Feminists question how research is done, how it is analyzed, who does it and in what social setting. There is thus a critique of the "scientific" claims about human behavior based on research on men (Richardson and Taylor 1993).

b. Feminist research wants to uncover the links between gender and other systems of inequality; how does one experience gender oppression differently and how does one recognize diversity of responses to oppression?

c. Feminist research focuses on consciousness raising by incorporating cultural understanding about women and operating with a "double vision". This is a vision where women's lives are seen simultaneously through the "old lens of patriarchy and the new lens of feminism". This is a vision that helps understand the contradictions between consciousness and action (Richardson and Taylor 1993).

d. Feminist research rethinks the relationship between the researcher and the researched. In contrast to traditional scientific research that assumes a separation between researchers and researched as the fundamental condition to produce objective and valid knowledge, feminist researchers challenge this tenet that treats women as objects because it contravenes feminist goals for equality. A central concern is how to do research that empowers both the researchers and the researched: how to create social research practices that reduce the power of the researcher to collect, categorize and name the experience of other women (Hill Collins 1993; Young 1993; Riano 1994).

In order to bring solutions to these questions feminists use different methodologies. Some researchers engage in dialogic research in which the interplay between the researchers and the researched is the research topic. Others study the groups with which they are allied. And still others do participatory research where the researchers and the researched determine together the topics, methods, goals and political action to follow from the research. The emphasis is on empowerment and transformation. Feminist action research is one of the methodologies of participatory research.[1]

Feminist action research challenges the notion that oppressed groups are not conscious of their oppression and are somehow less capable of understanding the relations of ruling (Frye [1983], 1993; Hill Collins [1989], 1993; Richardson and Taylor 1993). Thus the logic in using action research is to identify social projects in which social actors seeks to create a new social reality, a new culture, a new understanding for all aspects of life.

Feminist Action Research in the Caribbean

The Caribbean has also experienced such trends. Since the late 1970's many research centers, women's groups and organizations and feminist researchers have integrated this new perspective in their framework. At the regional level, organizations like Caribbean Association for Feminist Research and Action (CAFRA) or the Women and Development Unit (WAND) are doing research about women's lives in order to empower both researchers and researched and to help develop a pan-Caribbean women's movement.

At the local level, research centers like the Centro de Investigación para Acción Feminista (CIPAF) in the Dominican Republic and Collectives like SISTREN in Jamaica are mounting national surveys on Rural Women, exploring women's involvement in national development, or creating a women's media watch in order to highlight the causes of violence and improve women's images in media. Some of the strategies are monitoring media, gathering information, lobbying, and education. Since 1987 CAFRA has been involved in a large-scale agricultural research action project on Women in Caribbean Agriculture (WICA). The main goal is to find out about women's contributions and needs and to empower them. The researchers tend to be primarily activists and not academics because the aim is to strengthen and develop work being done with women at the local level. The findings of this project led to design action programs to respond to the needs. The many action research projects in the area involve the use of popular theater, comic books, videos, production of educational materials; increase public education and outreach, etc.

Such a perspective is also part of the agenda of Sistren Theater Collective of Jamaica, of centers like CIPAF (Centro de Investigación para Acción Feminista) of the Dominican Republic, of other centers like Researchers for Education, Action and Development (READ) in Trinidad; the women Collectives of Centro de Estudios, Recursos y Servicios a la Mujer (CERES) and the Women's Project both in Puerto Rico, to cite a few. Many action research projects in the Caribbean have also a development perspective. Participation of women varies. It can often be seen and used as a form of data gathering. In such projects, the goal is to change a current critical practice, to encourage active support or to mobilize a community. Women constitute only a subject of information and strategies of participation are conceived as a set of techniques used to implement some of the stages of the development program. Many of the projects led by international agencies like UNDP, UNICEF or USAID tend to fall into this framework (Young 1993).

International agencies like UNDP, UNICEF or USAID whose primary goal is to promote economic growth oriented policies in "'developing'" countries of the South are cases in point. Since the adoption of the second development decade of 1970–80 and the adoption by the United Nations of the Decade for Women (1975–85), these agencies have been compelled to take some initiatives in line with a Women in Development (WID) perspective. Women became objects of study and of special attention in order to achieve modernization. Yet as many studies show (Young 1993; Sen and Grown 1987), development programmes led by these agencies, including Haiti, have many limitations; they do not take into account men/women unequal relationships and development is reduced to adding women components to projects. Women's positions are examined as a set of problems that can be resolved through technical means like training and integration to the labor market. Thus, the objective in most of their research studies is to assess the situation of women's needs in order to implement measures. The concern is more about development than gender relations. Development is defined primarily as an economic process. Although access of women to resources of the development of their skills are a necessary step for their empowerment, this does not guarantee changes in forms of gender discrimination and inequalities. A case in point is the document published in 1991, during the military ruling in Haiti, by the United Nations Inter-agencies of Women and Development. The report titled *La Situation des Femmes Haitiennes* consists primarily in a description of women's roles and status in different areas of social life in Haiti.

Another perspective is to view participation as development and as part of the process of social change. Women become participant in a process that enables them to take control of their lives, to develop confidence and information skills. Participation is a way to support social struggles, to advocate and defend rights, to promote group reflections, to awake consciousness and to diffuse new forms or representations. Women constitute in such framework the subjects of struggle and change. Participation is both a dimension and a condition for social change. It has the potential to empower. Women have control over the process and are involved in most stages of the planning, design, production and diffusion of projects. This alternative view is being adopted by many women's organizations like CAFRA and WAND within the Caribbean.

...

Women and Feminist Action Research in Haiti

The 30-year dictatorship left no space for the development of a women's movement in Haiti. Such an absence did not hamper the emergence in the early 1980's of many women's groups and organizations. Indeed, although there was and still is no women's movement in Haiti, there is a history of organizing.

During the years of the first U.S. occupation between 1915 and 1934, the first women's organization, the Ligue Feminine d'Action Sociale was created. This organization, composed primarily of women of the middle class, obtained the vote in 1950 as a result of their struggle. With the increased militarization and policing of the political space under the dictatorship of the Duvalier family the movement rescinded but reemerged in the various communities of immigrants and exiles, particularly in North America (Charles 1995).

Nonetheless, the early 1980's marked the beginning of the emergence of some new political forces. With the return of many women from the diaspora, many groups and feminist organizations reemerged or were newly created. Among them were organizations and women's groups like Centre Haitien de Recherche pour la Promotion Feminine (CHREPROF), created in 1975 and whose main activities are the provision of services of family planning and training of poor women; the Fond Haitien d'Aide a la Femme (FHAF), an organization which since 1983 gives small loans to market women; KAY FANM , created in 1985 as one of the few feminist organizations; the Ligue Feminine d'Action Sociale (1934), the oldest Haitian women's organization; the Centre de Promotion des Femmes Ouvrieres (CPFO) (1985), the Solidarite Fann Aysyen (SOFA), another feminist organization created in 1986, and FANM D'HAITI an organization founded in 1986, but with a short life. The period witnessed also the creation of research centers like the Centre National et International de Documentation et d'Information des Femmes en Haiti (ENFOFANM) in 1988 and the Centre de Recherche et de Formation Economique et Social pour le Developpement (CRESFED) in 1987.

At the same time, as a result of the external flow of funds and the development of NGOs that offered services and resources to urban and rural communities, women's groups or in some cases women's sections were created in order to implement development projects or to offer basic need services. Although many of the newly created women's organizations only experienced a short political life, prior to the September 1991 military coup, a study by ACDI (Agence Canadienne de Developpement) registered at least 76 organizations working with women and women's groups.[2]

Interestingly, what is striking in Haiti, is the absence of a feminist movement and of any women's organization at the national level. The recent creation of the Ministry is in that sense very telling. Most women's groups were clearly opposed to the creation of this state unit, perceiving it as the marginalization of women's issues.[3] Indeed, in the 1995 UNIFEM brief survey of women's groups and organizations, it was evidenced that in spite of the proliferation, these groups vary by their nature, type of services offered, political orientation, access to resources, location, and gender perspectives. Some are part of a national religious network, others receive their funding from an external donor, while others can barely support their costs of maintenance. Most of these groups are not really focusing on gender-specific issues. Yet, all are committed to promote women's rights and wish that the discussion of women's issues be part of a national debate. Moreover, most of these women's groups, organizations and/or sections are weak because of inadequate resources, lack of institutional development base and, more importantly, most of these groups have no clear perspective of gender subordination.

Moreover, the lack of a national platform where women could voice their claims evidences a state of powerlessness that is reinforced with the absence of gender issues and the paucity, if not absence, of research and assessment of the status of women in society. Indeed, for the last 50 years one can only cite no more than a couple of comprehensive studies on Haitian women. Among them, two are worth mentioning. There is the work of Madeleine Sylvain-Bouchereau *Haiti et ses femmes* in 1957 and the more recent study of Mireille Neptune-Anglade *L 'Autre Moitie du Developpement* in 1986. Besides, some women's groups, organizations, research centers and feminist researchers like ENFOFANM, CRESFED, CPFO, TAG, GRAD, CHRAD, CHREPROF, WCAI have either produced a few documents or have published a journal. In addition, some international agencies like UNICEF, UNDP, USAID and FNUAP have published documents on sectorial and/or general conditions of life for women.

Profile of Some Research Action Groups and Organizations on Women

Centre de Promotion des Femmes Ouvrieres, CPFO, was created in 1985 with funding from a US agency OEF international. The center targets primarily women in the assembly industries. It offers services in preventive health care, family planning and legal aid. More importantly, it has produced some sectorial documents related to living conditions, health, education of women workers in that economic sector, among others, "Quelques aspects de la Scolarisation et de la Formation des Ouvriers de la Sous-traitance en Haiti"; "Quelques Aspects de la Sante et de la Nutrition des Ouvriers de la Sous-traitance en Haiti"; "Quelques Aspects de la Fecondite du comportement des ouvrieres de la Soustraitance en Haiti." All these documents published in 1988, are the findings of a survey on the situation of women workers in the offshore production sector located in Port-au-Prince. Women participated mainly as sources of information. They had no input in the design of the research.

Nonetheless, through the publication of its journal FANM OUVRYEZ, CPFO attempts to implement some active participation of women. The journal is published in creole and gives priority to issues of daily life like Violence, AIDS, Human Rights, Inflation, etc., all topics that are parts of their women formation workshops. Moreover, a whole section of the journal is dedicated to voicing the direct experience of women workers.

CHRAD (Centre de Recherche et d'Action pour le development) was founded in 1986 and has close ties with a feminist group SOFA. This center focuses on doing popular education with peasant women and rural communities in different parts of the country. The centre also publishes a newsletter in creole SAK PASE and dedicates itself to formation, and consciousness raising with an objective towards the formulation of demands and protests. Most of the women working with CHRAD come from the peasantries (80%). The center also targets women in the shantytowns of Port-au-Prince (8%) and some professional women (12%) (Tardieu-Bazin, Magloire, Merlet 1991).

KAY FANM is one of the few newly-created feminist groups that has attempted to bring a gender perspective in most of its activities. Founded in 1985 as a woman's house by some feminists, the main goal has been to organize poor women in order that they can improve their situation as people and as women. KAY FANM established four areas of intervention prioritizing research/formation and action. Activities and projects centered around education with a focus on law, health, and leisure time for domestic workers. Through workshops, animation and popular theater, women participated in the making of the programmes. Although KAY FANM has not published any document, one of their most successful areas of intervention was their advocacy programmes. Up until the 1990, the centre had a radio program and a popular theater group where many women intervened and participated actively. KAY FANM was also one of the few groups that made an effort to launch the idea about the needs of a national women's network. The military coup of September 1991 halted this effort. The center became the target of the regime and the site was burned in 1993.

ENFOFANM and CRESFED are the two research and documentation centers that could be classified as two sites where research on women is being done. Such a statement must, however, be qualified. Whereas ENFOFANM focuses all its activities on gender, such is not the case for CRESFED. In the latter, only their collective of women deals with gender issues. Paradoxically, CRESFED has produced more studies on Haitian women, among them a document resulting from a discussion with different women's groups and feminists.

In contrast, ENFOFAM, which was founded in 1988, has not been able as projected to develop its research section. Nonetheless, the center is doing a very important archival work in relocating and reproducing some of the documents of the first Haitian women's organization, the "Ligue Feminine d'Action Sociale". The center also publishes a journal in creole, "FANM AYSYEN."

Notes

1. It is interesting to note that action research methodology began in the United States in the 1940's and was closely related to industrial management concerns. Most projects on action research aimed at increasing productivity of workers in the work place. By the 1960's with the emergence of the Civil Rights Movement that generated demands for equality, many government-led action research projects in order to improve the socio-economic situation of minority groups and at the same time to restrain protests were implemented in the field of education and of community empowerment. For more detailed analyses see Whyte (1991).
2. In 1991 The Canadian Agency for International Development (ACDI) published a listing of about 70 women's groups and organizations. This list, the most complete up to this day, concentrated on organizations, women groups, and NGO's located primarily in Port-au-Prince. It does not mention for example women's groups in the countryside or in other Haitian towns. Two cases in point are the peasant women group, *kombit fanm deside* of Jacmel in Southeast and the largest peasant women groups in Haiti that belongs to the Papaye Peasant Movement (MPP) located in the Central area of the country. Both groups are not even mentioned.
3. See Mones and Charles (1995) and also Castor (1994).

References

CAFRA Newsletter, Vol 3, 4, Dec 1989.
CAFRA Newsletter, Vol 4, 2, June 1990.
CAFRA Newsletter Vol 8, 3, July 1994.
Castor, Suzy. *Les Femmes Haitiennes aux Elections de 1990.* CRESFED Haiti, 1994.
Charles, Carolle. "Gender and Politics in Contemporary Haiti: The Duvalierist State, Transnationalism, and the Emergence of a New Feminism" (1980-1990). *Feminist Studies.* Vol. 21, 1, Spring 1995, pp. 1-39.
―――. "Sexual Politics and the mediation of class, gender and race in Former Slave Plantation Societies: The Case of Haiti" in G. Bond and A. Gilliam, eds. *Social Reconstruction of the Past.* London: Routledge, 1994, pp.44-56.
CRESFED *Theories et Pratiques de la Lutte des Femmes.* Port-au-Prince Haiti, 1988.

CPFO/OEFI. «Laviche» *Jounal Fanm Ouvryez*. No. 34, March-April 1992, Port-au-Prince, Haiti.

———. "Characteristics of Street Food Vending Establishments in the Industrial Area of Port-au- Prince." *Mimeo*. Port-au-Prince, Haiti, October 1989.

———. *Quelques Aspects de la Fecondity et du Comportement Fecond*. Rapport de Recherches. OEFl/CPFO, 1988.

———. *Quelques Aspects de la Scolarisation et de la Formation des Ouvrieres de la SousTraitance en Haiti*. Rapport de Recherche, 1988.

Frye, M. "Oppression" [1983] reproduced in Laurel Richardson and Verta Taylor eds. *Feminist Frontiers III*. McGraw Hill, NY 1993:7-10.

Hill Collins, P. "The Social Construction of Black Feminist Thought" (1989) reproduced in *Feminist Frontiers III*. McGraw Hill, NY 1993:20-30.

Neptune-Anglade, Mireille.*L'Autre Moitie du Developpement*. Port-au-Prince and Montreal: Editions des Alizes & ERCE, 1986.

ONU/UNICEF/COMITE INTER-AGENCES. *La Situation des Femmes Haitiennes*. Port-au Prince, Haiti, 1992.

Riano, P. ed. *Women in Grassroots Communication*. Newbury, California: Sage Publications, 1994.

Richardson. L. and Verta Taylor eds. *Feminist Frontiers Ill*. New York: McGraw Hill, 1993.

Roa, A.M.B. Anderson and Catherine Overholt. *Gender Analysis in Development Planning*. Hartford, Connecticut: Kumaria Press, 1992.

Roberts, H., ed. *Doing Feminist Research*. London: Routledge & Kegan, 1981.

Tardieu-Bazin, D., D. Magloire and M. Merlet. *Femmes/Population/Developpement Organisations Feminines Privees en Haiti*. Tomes I and II, FNUAP, Port-au-Prince, Avril 1991.

Whyte, W.F. *Social Theory for Action*. Newbury, California: Sage Publications, 1991.

Young, K. *Planning Development with Women*. NY: St. Martin Press, 1993.

6. Feminist Research and Action Methodology: The Experiences of the Caribbean Association of Feminist Research and Action*

Frederica M. Deare

Introduction

The emergence of the new women's movement in the 60s and 70s in the Caribbean led to an increased consciousness and understanding of the issues faced by women in the region. During the last twenty five to thirty years, this increased awareness has given rise to hundreds of women's organizations which deal with various issues affecting women's lives. Along with the movement's expansion and the increased lobby for improvement of women's position in society came demands for information and analysis of women's issues within the Caribbean context. Understanding and acquiring knowledge on women's issues could be used by activist groups, non-governmental and governmental agencies as the basis for action to assist in the alleviation of problems affecting women.

The Caribbean Association for Feminist Research and Action (CAFRA) was established to bridge the gap between research and action and to provide a continuum between research activities and the activities of organizations working with women in the region. The founders of the Association envisaged that the women's concerns and needs could be better addressed if planners, researchers and activists alike could explore the conditions and concerns of women in the Caribbean while at the same time becoming involved in the process of change. This process would only be effective if there was a strong involvement of the women whose life issues are at stake.

It was particularly important therefore to ensure the participation of community-based women and the organizations that work among them, given CAFRA's commitment to reflecting the concerns of women at the

---

* Reprinted with permission from *Caribbean Studies* 28, no. 1 (Jan–Jun 1995): 30–60. Excerpted.

grassroots level. Several methods have been used to ensure their active participation: involving grassroots and activist women in data collection; establishing channels for two-way communication and collaboration between project officials and the community; setting up multi-faceted project teams that represent a wide cross section of interest groups or stakeholders; translating findings of research into language that could be understood from the community to regional levels.

CAFRA has implemented two major research and action projects, namely the Women in Caribbean Agriculture Project and the Women and the Law Project. Based on these projects several methodological features have been identified. In order to get a clearer picture of the methodological approach utilized in these projects the paper first examines some of the issues faced by women in the two areas of Caribbean societies which the projects addressed…[then] describes and analyses the methodological aspects of these projects, their differences and constraints to implementation and how they were dealt with.

…

Methodological Approach

When CAFRA was established there was a need for information on the lives and concerns of Caribbean women. In the past, researchers investigating the contribution and concerns of Caribbean peoples used traditional research methodologies which tended to exclude specific analysis on women's roles and issues. These mainstream methodological approaches, based on the principles of objectivity and "neutrality," were androcentric and therefore inappropriate for the study of women or gendered relations. In this context, CAFRA became involved in a new approach to research, which redefines the techniques and methods used. CAFRA founders were able to draw on the experiences and work of philosophers of feminist research methodology (Mies, 1979, 1982; Harding, 1987), adapt them to Caribbean situations, and incorporate them to popular participatory methodologies developed in the third world, including the Caribbean region.

Four features may be identified in CAFRA's research and action methodology which make it distinctive from traditional approaches: a) it is work done on and for women by mainly women researchers and activists; b) it draws upon the experiences of the women being researched and the researchers as part of the analyses; c) it sensitizes and raises the consciousness of researchers and the women being researched to the issues and concerns of women; and d) it capitalizes on Caribbean oral traditions of documentation and expression.

The feminist research and action approach could be seen as "women helping women and themselves", that is, women activists and researchers were not simply helping other women but in the process helping themselves. This new approach not only allowed researchers to gain an understanding of the complexities of Caribbean women's situations but also helped to change the *status quo* of women in Caribbean societies. Apart from utilizing their skills as researchers the women were allowed to use their experiential knowledge as women in the research and action process.

Methodological Process

To date, CAFRA has carried out two major research and action projects in the region, namely the Women in Caribbean Agriculture (WICA) project and the Women and the Law (WAL) project. Through these projects CAFRA has been able to put into practice many of the organization's ideological views on the research and action process. Based on the two projects the methodological approach can be summarized as follows:

1. The process was participatory involving NGOs at the community and national levels and members of governmental agencies. Mechanisms were devised for continued discussions and feedback between the coordinating organization (CAFRA) and the participatory organizations and agencies.

2. The Coordinators and some members of the project staff were feminists, with histories of active involvement in the Caribbean women's movement. They, therefore, were able to bring a wealth of knowledge and practical experience in women's issues as well as skills as researchers into the research process.

3. The process followed the "bottom-to-top" approach, where grassroots women and/ or organizations working with them played an active part (through consultations or working as researchers) in the various stages of the research process.

4. In each target country, the projects were linked with activists to plan and develop follow-up action programmes, ensure that actions were carried out and assist in the project evaluation process.

5. Women at the community level were chosen as researchers. Where necessary they were trained in the principles of feminist theory and methodology. In doing this, these women were able to be actively involved in recording and analyzing women's conditions and concerns in their communities and assist in the formulation of solutions and action, thereby themselves becoming highly conscious of the conditions faced by women.

6. Networking with local agencies working in communities in the subject matter area and among women through:
    i. regular meetings with coordinating project teams;
    ii. meetings/workshops in the communities; and
    iii. meetings of back-up teams and advisory teams.

7. A variety of methods/tools of classical research and participatory methods/techniques were used in the research stage, for example, the use of survey instruments, archival searches, case studies, researcher observation, workshops, etc. These were used in ways which reflected the new methodological context.

8. Documentation was produced on the various stages of the project research and action process: diagnosis, results, evaluation, follow-up action. This also meant ensuring that the research results were simplified into a language and form that could be understood by the researched and other audiences through that the use of videos, pamphlets, drama, etc.

9. Appropriate methods were selected for reaching the various audiences. For example, dissemination of results and conducting follow-up action at community level through traditional and popular methods workshops using role playing, poems; or the presentation of research findings at national, regional and international fora.

There were several differences in the research and action applied in the WICA and WAL projects. In the WICA project there was great emphasis on the research aspects and a number of community-based women were involved in the project as researchers. On the other hand, in the WAL project the research component, though very important, was limited to the consultants who were hired to examine the deficiencies in the law and to make recommendations. In the WICA project, discussions and consultations took place among communities, participating organizations and project teams during the research phase and hence project teams were established at the beginning. In the WAL project, discussion among these groups took place at the end of the research stage and therefore the project team was commissioned at the beginning of the action stage of the project.

Women in the Caribbean Agriculture Project

Women in Caribbean Agriculture (WICA), which was carried out between 1988 and 1990, was CAFRA's first major research and action project. The agricultural sector was chosen as the focus area because of the historical and socio-economic importance of this sector to Caribbean economies. Agriculture has played and continues to play an important role in our socio-economic development in the region and for some territories it is the primary contributor to the gross domestic product, foreign exchange earnings and rural employment. However, sector analyses have not revealed the vital position of women in the agricultural sector and in fact there has been a general lack of gender disaggregated data for many economic and social indicators.

This shortage of information is partly due to the male biases inherent in traditional research methods that makes women's labour and concerns invisible. In early farm-household studies, researchers conceptualized and reported the family and household as the basic unit, assuming a male head of household and breadwinner with a dependent, non-working/non-productive housewife. The fields or areas outside the home were seen as the main area of production and no effort was made to look at the inputs and labour of the individual members of the farm family. As a result, there was no distinction between male or female labour in the fields. Moreover, because the home was not perceived as an area of productivity within the farm-household system, women's work (both reproductive and domestic) went unrecognized and was never quantified. Little data exists on the role of subsistence agriculture in securing national food security and so the important contribution of women in this sector remains hidden. The lack of data was seen as one reason why policymakers found it difficult to address women's concerns.

The WICA project which was seen as an important link between research and agricultural development, attempted to investigate the contribution and needs of women in agriculture and, based on the outcome of the research, developed and implemented action programmes to address their concerns. In an effort to move away from the Caribbean countries which are more researched, CAFRA chose to implement the project in the Commonwealth of Dominica and St Vincent and the Grenadines. Additionally, individual women and organizations in these countries, who were committed to the women's movement, were willing to collaborate with each other and develop and carry out follow-up programmes.

The project aimed to strengthen and develop the work done with women at the grassroots level, by strengthening the organizations who work with these women, and empowering community-based women themselves. With this in mind the project had several short-term and long term objectives, as follows:

Long Term
   i.   to promote a basis for strengthening the economic position of women involved in agricultural production;
   ii. to increase the consciousness of the public in general and the governments in particular to women's contribution in all aspects of agriculture;
   iii. to make women in agriculture more aware of their economic importance and their potential for development;
   iv. to develop parameters for the analysis and quantification of women's work in the sector.

Short Term
   i.   to generate data on the situation of women involved in agricultural production in Dominica and St. Vincent;
   ii. design and develop a participatory framework for the analysis of the current situation of women in agriculture. Intrinsic in this

framework is the active participation of women researchers and local women and organizations.

iii. based on the acquired information formulate programmes of action which would lead to the improvement and strengthening of women's positions in the Agricultural sector.

Theoretical Framework

The nature, extent and location of women's agricultural work are greatly influenced by their domestic and reproductive work and responsibilities. Because of the close relationship between domestic and agricultural work in these women's lives, many activities performed at home may be inaccurately termed as domestic. It is important to examine the sexual division of labour both in the home and on-farm in order to quantify women's work and to examine women's position in the agricultural sector.

Their productive strategies may involve a wide range of activities from farming, providing agricultural labour, to carrying out home-based processing. An examination of women's productive strategies is also needed in order to see how women survive in agricultural households and the type of resources required to meet these needs. It is also important to put an economic value on subsistence production and determine to what extent Caribbean families depend on this type of production for their sustenance. Women face a wide range of problems in the agricultural sector. Determining women's concerns and problems is vital for developing approaches to alleviate their situation.

Methodological Aspects of the Project

The Process

The research and action of the WICA project, which involved several steps, has a number of features which made it a unique process for generating information on women's activities and concerns in the farm-household unit and community, leading to appropriate action, based on the findings. The process could be outlined as follows:

i. choosing target communities within each territory which reflected the major agricultural production activities in the project countries;

ii. linking the project with activist groups within each country;
iii. selecting women researchers from among women active and working in the local women's movement.
iv. training the research teams in feminist theory, research methodology and popular dissemination;
v. conducting workshops in the communities as a means of collecting data, collaboration, education, communication and evaluation;
vi. involving local organizations working with communities, farmers and women as facilitators of the research and follow-up actions in each country;
vii. drawing the project and back up teams from several local agencies;
viii. using a variety of research techniques for data collection in order to enhance the reliability of data and to increase the involvement of community-based women in the project.
ix. designing, developing and implementing action programmes from research findings.

The structure and organization of the project were so designed that information gaps on women's participation in agriculture would be highlighted and so ensure that what was once invisible, would gain recognition. In addition, the involvement of local nongovernmental agencies and feminist groups as facilitating organizations and as members of the research and back-up teams encouraged collaboration, information-sharing among groups at the national level. The agencies represented a range of interests, from women's federations, teachers unions and youth councils to farmers organizations. However, all the organizations had worked at some level with women, either through community work, in agriculture or directly among women.

Perhaps one of the most powerful aspects of the project was the selection of local activists in women's issues as researchers and their subsequent training in research methodologies and feminist theory and practice. By empowering these women with the tools of analysis and their acquired field experience, the project has not only strengthened the local research capabilities of the women's movement but also made it a learning experience for the women and contributed to increasing their self-esteem.

Josephine Dublin (1990) epitomized this empowerment when she wrote, "It was indeed a dream come true: to do research about women's lives, to empower them, to empower me." Josephine Dublin went on to become an opposition senator in the Dominican Parliament and a member of the Dominican National Council of Women.

In each territory, three communities were chosen for the study. In Dominica the communities selected were Giraudel, Grand Bay and Marigot. In St. Vincent the communities of Buccament Valley, Lauders and Orange Hill were chosen. By choosing these districts the researchers were able to obtain information on women in agriculture which was representative of the various agricultural systems in the country. Primarily, land tenure system and crop destination to either local, regional or international markets, and to a lesser extent women's participation, capital investment and level of economic activity within the community were criteria used for selection of the community. To ensure that accurate selection was made, the process was carried out through consultation with the Statistical Department and Agricultural Ministry in each country and by making several exploratory visits to each community.

Selection of households was based mainly on the union status of the women, their age, life cycle and access to land. This ensured that the study represented conditions that reflected most situations of women in such areas, for example single parents, married women, older women, women with no land, etc.

In the research process a variety of methods for data collection, including traditional and participatory popular techniques was used at the community and household levels. This approach sought to increase the reliability of the information as researchers would be able to confirm and double-check information collected by different means. Also, some techniques were more effective in obtaining certain types of information than others. For example, information about time allocation and household dynamics were best obtained through observation over a period of time. Time was needed to build relationships with the women in order to obtain information of a personal nature. Researchers lived in selected households in each community over a period of time and were able to obtain information on areas in which survey instruments would be ineffective and inadequate. Therefore, through participant observation and living within the communities researchers gained knowledge about time women spent on reproductive, domestic and agricultural work, about time spent on various agricultural and household activities. Further, the women and researchers were able to build enough trust in each other to speak on matters such as woman-man relations, rape, incest, sexual harassment, etc. (French, 1988).

At the start of the study, profiles of each community were prepared through archival search and community investigations using a questionnaire guide and observation and interviews with key informants in the community. Through the archival search the researchers become conscious of the lack of sex disaggregated information in population and agricultural records. From the community investigation, information was obtained on general features, infrastructural provisions, social and cultural issues (such as health, education and housing, types of organization and recreation activities), economic and political aspects of women in agriculture in each community.

Women working in agriculture in 10% of the households or a minimum of 30 households from each community were surveyed using the community survey questionnaire. A small sample of men was also interviewed from each country for comparative purposes. From this approach, apart from obtaining demographic information on the communities, data were also collected on women's involvement in agriculture at the community and farm-household levels. Therefore, researchers gathered data on the sexual division of labour, gender differentiation in crops, tasks, type of livestock, control and access to resources (such as land, credit, agricultural inputs), control of income, involvement in non-agricultural income-earning activities. Information was also gathered on women's involvement in social activities such as agricultural, recreational and church organizations, their leisure activities and participation in the electoral process.

In each country, a special area, which was thought to be of relevance and importance to the particular territory, was undertaken. In St. Vincent, the "Questionnaire to 15 year-olds" examined the involvement of younger women in agriculture and interest to continue or to work in the sector. In Dominica, the "Questionnaire to Past and Present Estate Workers" looked at the past and present economic and social status of estate workers.

The researchers also prepared case studies from selected households within each community. The case studies were prepared by interviewing the main woman in each selected household, using the "Questionnaire for Main Woman," preparing time budgets and through observation. To compile the time budgets and make observations, researchers spent long hours in the households. This allowed them to observe and become conscious of the excessive time being spent by women in activities in the home in which men almost always do not participate. This tradition is upheld in the greater time spent by girls in doing housework as compared to boys. In this way researchers also examined the amount of work performed by the women, both in the home and field, and found that some women's work which is usually classified as domestic could be reclassified as agricultural because it consists of income generating or expenditure-saving agricultural activities (French, 1990).

There were also workshops within each community where women and other community members came together. Through this forum a two-way communication channel was established between the researchers and the community. At the workshops the women were able to discuss and be updated about happenings in the project, how women felt about themselves and issues affecting their lives; to verify information gathered through other means and to make recommendations for follow-up action.

The results of the research process were shared and discussed at several fora, in the communities, at the national level, and with regional organizations working with women and/or in agriculture. Such discussions were held in order that recommendations for follow-up action could be as broad based as possible and involve persons and agencies who have an interest in the issues. The recommendations for action which were made at all levels were compiled and developed in programmes of action that could be carried out by organizations within the two project countries. French (1990) identified twelve activities which were in progress as a result of the study. The activities were varied and indicative of the types of action that were likely to result from a project of this nature.

These were as follows:

- Women's farming cooperative, Orange Hill (St. Vincent);
- Women's vegetable production projects (Dominica)

- Land Reform: lobbying and organising for more and better land for women within these programmes
- Building of toilet facilities in Orange Hill (St. Vincent)
- Organization building
- Public education and consciousness-raising on the issues, e.g. Radio Series in Dominica
- Workshops on land rights, inheritance (St. Vincent)
- Use of WICA materials in existing education programmes
- Short stories based on the life stories of women in the communities (St. Vincent)
- Lobbying: for example, to CARICOM Secretariat for improved statistics on women; realistic and equitable credit terms; equitable wages; improved roads and water supply; and recreational facilities
- Further research to support lobbying activities, for example, survey on the effect of aerial spraying of bananas on women's vegetable production in Dominica
- Exchanges between Dominica and St. Vincent to share experiences and strengthen skills
- Production of two videos now used in educational programmes throughout the region.

Also, out of this process, the researchers have been able to share their acquired skills and knowledge and act as an information resource to national organizations, consultations, displays, etc.

Problems and Constraints

In the research stage of the project several methodological limitations were identified, which must be taken into consideration if the process is to be repeated. Firstly, the sample size of men interviewed in the community survey was too small for valid comparison with the female sample and between countries. The findings of the male survey indicated only tendencies and no conclusions could be made. As a result, some of the issues experienced by women may not have been gender specific. For example, the problems of basic amenities and infrastructure such as bad roads, large distances between farm plot and to home, etc. were cited as common to women, but in reality they are problems that are experienced by both sexes.

The complexity of Caribbean households made it difficult to categorize household types and male-female relations. For example, researchers were in a quandary to classify homes where the children had meals at a parent's home and slept elsewhere or the marital status of women who are legally married but do not obtain support from their spouse. There was also no distinction between single-person or single-parent extended families and nuclear extended families. Such differentiation would have led to a better assessment of the situation of female-headed households and determine to what extent women parent children to whom they did not give birth. This phenomenon is important because of its possible historical link to a similar practice during slavery and also its link to migration (French, 1988).

Another issue which was problematic at the onset but led to great rewards was the fact that all the activists did not share a "feminist" philosophy and had to be "convinced" about the question of women's subordination in Caribbean society. Ancelma Morgan (1990) wrote about her resistance to and confusion about feminist concepts at the training course on "Feminist Theory and Research Methodology." Only by conducting the interviews with women and men and finding out about their daily lives and how the issues affected them in different ways, did she come to understand and appreciate the concepts discussed in the training session.

Some of the women and men in particular were also very suspicious of the research team and the collection of the information was not an easy task. Sometimes the researchers were given inaccurate information. This problem was solved when the relationship between researchers and women was established and through the use of several data collection methods.

Women and the Law Project

The Women and the Law (WAL) project (1989–93) emerged during a period of increased awareness of the role of the legal system in the women's struggle against social and economic inequalities. Based on findings from the CAFRA/ILSA Regional Women Rights and the Law project, carried out from 1987 to 1988, it was found that little information existed on women's rights and the law, and that this information was only available to academic audiences (Clarke, 1992). It was felt therefore that a project of this kind which would reach women from all socioeconomic levels was needed.

Although all women were seen as beneficiaries, the project was designed to impact mainly on rural and low-income women. Organizations in the region identified several areas of concern requiring immediate legal attention, including domestic violence, sexual violence, family law and labour law. Under these broad headings several areas were further identified for legal reform and education, including:

- *Violence against women:* incest, domestic violence, sexual assault, and marital rape
- *Labour Law.* occupational health and safety, equal pay for equal work, maternity benefits, collective bargaining, minimum wage rights, child labour, and sexual harassment
- *Family Law.* matrimonial property, common law spouse rights, child maintenance, provision of day care centres, abortion

Project activities focused mainly on education, training, legal reform and the provision of legal services. The project was specifically aimed at:

- creating an awareness and understanding of laws that affect women's daily lives;
- providing information on the law which can be used by women, in particular when making important decisions about key issues in their lives;
- generating a body of knowledge on the ways in which the legal structures (laws, courts, legal aid clinics, etc.) operate;
- identifying specific areas in which action should be undertaken and making recommendations about the types of institutions that might undertake such actions;
- influencing overall legislative policy, the provisions of specific laws and administrative procedures that would benefit women and increase their capacity to deal with socio-legal issues.

In addition, the project focused on strengthening the capacity of local agencies (halfway houses, rape crisis centres, trade unions, etc.) to deal with women who have legal problems and the production of educational materials aimed to conscientize grassroots women about legal issues.

Initially, Antigua, Dominica, Grenada, St. Lucia and Trinidad and Tobago were selected as countries urgently requiring such work. Later, the project was also partially carried out (the research component and legal literacy programmes) in the Dominican Republic, Guyana, Jamaica, Puerto Rico and the Bahamas. In the former countries, many nongovernmental and governmental agencies actively participated in the project Team which was responsible for the monitoring of activities within each country. They also coordinated outreach activities to rural and low-income women.

Theoretical Framework

Law is the body of rules which defines and regulates human behavior within a society. An examination of legislation passed indicates its links to social norms and values reflecting the societal trends of the day, and makes it almost impossible to view the law as an objective and neutral entity. It tends to reflect the dominant vision of a society. Women in recorded legal history were portrayed as lower and inferior beings than men and were thought to be men's property. Classical examples of this vision are manifested through laws in effect up to the turn of the century which prohibited women from voting and holding public office, and stipulated that married women could not hold property in their own right.

Like many societal structures, present laws to a lesser extent continue to promote this inferior image of women. While Caribbean women are guaranteed equal rights under their country's Constitution (for example, the right to vote, to hold public office and the right to work) many laws still encourage and perpetuate female subordination and gender inequality. For instance, in St. Lucia, while the male teacher is free to have as many children as he chooses in and out of wedlock, an unmarried female teacher can be dismissed upon a second pregnancy.

There are few laws that recognize the importance of women as heads of households who may be solely responsible for their family's well-being. As such, in most Caribbean countries, no laws exist granting women the right to paid maternity leave. Women are found in under-unionized and non-unionized sectors of the economy and are vulnerable to poor working conditions and relations. Laws relating to proper health and safety regulations and protecting women against sexual harassment are virtually non-existent.

Because of the prevailing ideology suggesting that matters which occur in the home are private and secluded, women are susceptible to the power of men. Legislation to deal with the perpetrators of domestic violence and marital rape have been noticeably absent in many Caribbean countries and where they do exist they tend to be weak, and provide inadequate protection to abused women and children.

With limited study on the impact of the law on women's lives, it was important to focus on such work with a view to understanding the role that the law plays in the organization and development of society. It is also vital for women to possess the ability to manipulate the legal system in order to make it more responsive to their social and economic needs. This is particularly important for women of lowincome levels who have low educational attainment, as they may be intimidated by the complexities of the system.

Methodological Aspects of the Project

The project sought to generate information on the legal status of women in the countries involved in the project and through various methods/techniques disseminate the acquired information and knowledge to the relevant agencies and women in rural communities.

...

Based on the WAL project, the following methodological features were identified:

1. An initial project (the Women's Rights and Law project) was carried out. The major objective of the study was to generate information about women's rights and the legal system that would improve the effectiveness of the legal system to deal with women's problems and rights. From this study women's organizations identified priority areas for legal reform and education which could be used as guidelines for the WAL project.

2. With the exception of Grenada, the consultants chosen to research and prepare the report on women's legal status were women lawyers, many of whom had experience working in the women's movement in their country or the region. The Grenadian lawyer worked in the

legal-aid clinic in his country and had considerable exposure dealing with women's legal problems.
3. The project was linked to participatory agencies that have outreach programmes with rural and low income women or offered services against sexual abuse and domestic violence or dealt with legal services.
4. The project involved collaboration between NGOs and governmental agencies to ensure that project activities were effectively undertaken.
5. Consultations/workshops were used as mechanisms to ensure two-way communication and feedback.
6. Para-legal training was offered to persons working with women who face legal problems.
7. Education materials as a mean of reaching rural women were developed through a process of dialogue and discussion.

In the initial stages of the project, consultants were employed to research and prepare reports on the legal status of women in the selected countries. The documents examined the following seven areas of concern and gave, where appropriate, relevant legal reforms required for each category: i) Family Law; ii) Labour Law; iii) Property Rights; iv) Constitutional Rights; v) Citizenship and immigration; vi) Sexual offenses, and domestic violence; and vii) Succession Laws.

The action component of the project centred mainly around the participation of persons from the community and organizational levels in consultations and workshops (reform workshops and paralegal training workshops) and the design and production of popular education materials for dissemination.

The consultant's report was used as the basis for the National Consultations held in Antigua, Dominica, Grenada, St. Lucia, and Trinidad and Tobago. These meetings brought together non-governmental and governmental agencies as well as the public to collectively develop a programme of follow-up action in the areas of popular education, paralegal training and legal reform. Additionally, these activities also helped to increase collaboration between NGOs and the governmental sector.

As part of the participatory Consultation process, participants discussed and determined the role of CAFRA in facilitating and coordinating project activities. Consequently, the following structure of the administration system was formulated. Advisory teams were selected from among participants representing governmental and non-governmental sectors. The presence of the project team at the country level ensured that the execution and monitoring of project activities were as decentralized as possible and allowed for the maximum participation of women at the organizational and community levels.

Out of the National Consultations, three country-specific priority areas for legal reform as well as the programmes and strategies to address these issues were identified. As a result, legal reform workshops were held in each country for community-based women and persons who work with legal problems, for example, lawyers and personnel from crisis centres, half-way houses, the protective services (police) and health services.

The para-legal training workshops brought together persons from development NGOs, women's organizations, trade unions and governmental agencies. This training was meant not only to equip individuals from front-line agencies with skills to assist women requiring legal aid but would also increase the number of resource persons knowledgeable on law and magistrate court procedures at the community level who could assist and advise women on their legal rights. This would also make legal services less expensive and more available to community-based women. The workshops included court visits, lectures and discussions, for example, by Attorneys-at-law on various topics such as the Constitution, Family Law, Labour Law, Criminal Law, Property Rights and Elements of Contract and Tort.

The workshop on *Participatory Methodologies for Legal Education* which was conducted in Trinidad and Tobago brought together participants from the five target countries as well as Dominican Republic, Guyana, Jamaica and The Bahamas to develop a legal education programme for reaching community-based women. In formulating this programme, participants were called upon to analyse the different techniques used for teaching women's legal rights concepts, to develop a plan of action for legal education and to design and generate printed educational materials in accordance with Caribbean realities. In this way the participants were able to develop strategies for organising women's rights campaigns and produced several pamphlets on a number of topics which were tested in a rural community in Moruga, Trinidad and Tobago. Out of this meeting and the legal reform workshops, brochures and pamphlets on various issues (for example, domestic violence, property rights, status of the common-in-law spouse, child maintenance) were produced in the project territories.

Problems and Constraints

There were several major constraints that surfaced during the execution of the project which affected its implementation and these may serve as lessons for future undertakings of this kind. Because the research and action approach is participatory and requires collaboration between a wide cross section of groups and individuals, this made the process time consuming and made it sometimes difficult to meet project deadlines. This was further aggravated by the lack of human resources to carry out some of the activities. A. Clarke (1993) made this point in the example on the late production of popular education materials, which involved voluntary participation of persons who were already in other community-based projects. As a result, the production of pamphlets and other factsheets turned out to be a lengthy process. One of the greatest challenges for all involved in the execution of the project was to ensure that proper communication among countries was maintained and decision-making and activities were decentralized as much as possible. CAFRA is committed to collaborating with national organizations throughout the region. However the great distances and high cost of travel between project countries made communication very difficult and led at times to over-centralisation in decision-making at CAFRA headquarters where the Project Coordinator was mainly located. In addition, inadequate personnel to deal with administrative matters and the lack of financial resources sometimes led to inefficiency in implementation once the project was handed over to the local agency. CAFRA had the difficultly of working with some organizations not necessarily committed towards looking at gender and other related issues that contributed to women's subordination, so that many had to be convinced of the problems that women face in the legal system. This problem was lessened to some extent by soliciting the help of persons sensitized to women's issues and, for others, their resistance broke down when faced with glaring facts.

Conclusion

The research and action approach involved the active participation of both researchers and researched women, and brought together a wide cross section of women and organizations into this process. Several features were common to the WICA and WAL projects. Firstly, women researchers and activists carried out activities and studies that examined and affected various aspects of women's lives. Secondly, the women (both the researched and researchers) were able to draw on their experiences as women as part of the research process. This, therefore, influenced the issues examined and the manner in which the activities and studies were undertaken.

All involved in the process (the researched and researchers organizations/agencies alike) were sensitized and conscientised to the issues of Caribbean women. For some, the act of conscientisation was the catalyst and driving force for them to take action to alleviate the plight of community-based women. Apart from influencing the national decision-making process, the information generated from these projects brought issues such as law reform, improved statistics on women, equitable credit terms to the national and regional levels.

In addition, Caribbean oral traditions of documentation and expression were incorporated into the research and action process. Therefore, project staff drew heavily on popular techniques such as drama, poems, songs in workshops and meetings in order to gather and disseminate information.

Apart from the research stages being seen as an avenue for action, it formed the basis to follow-up action. For example, in the WICA project several activities were identified as a direct result of the process, varying from the establishment of a women farming cooperative in St. Vincent to lobbying for women's issues both at the national and regional levels. In the WAL project, follow-up activities also varied widely. For instance, some activities took place at the community level (preparation of educational pamphlets geared at sensitising community-based women to legal issues), while others impacted at the country or regional level (women's and other activists organizations lobbied for law reform).

One of the most challenging aspects of the research and action approach which was common to both projects was the inability of women to "see" the subordination of women and relate this to the feminist philosophy. Some women spoke of their resistance to feminist concepts and their confrontational approach to the whole issue. For the women, understanding came only after being exposed to their own lives on a day-to-day basis and observing for themselves how these issues affected women. What makes the research and action process so powerful and rewarding is perhaps the "clearer vision" that the researcher and activists alike obtained and the motivational force which followed that inspired them to do "something" to alleviate the problems they witnessed.

Finally, by using the research and action approach activists and researchers can ask the right questions, capitalize on women's experiences and knowledge thereby gaining insights into aspects of their lives that usually remained hidden when traditional research approaches are utilized. At the same time, they learn more about the commonality between themselves and the researched. The information gathered during the process can be appropriately used to affect positive change that would lessen the burden faced by Caribbean women.

Notes

My thanks go to Joan French, ex-Coordinator of the WICA project and Roberta Clarke, ex-Coordinator of the WAL project. I drew heavily on reports and other documents written by these women and have benefited tremendously from discussions with them and their review of the paper. I am also grateful to Rhoda Reddock, CAFRA Chairperson and Rawwida Baksh-Soodeen, CAFRA Coordinator for their detailed review of the paper and their discussions on the epistemological and methodological issues raised in the research an action approach as well as CAFRA's vision as seen in the early years.

References

Clarke, A. 1992. "Designing legal literacy to make the law accessible to women in the Caribbean." In *Legal Literacy: A Tool for Women's Empowerment* New York, U.S.A.: UNIFEM, 73-92.

Clarke, A. 1993. Women and the Law Project (1989–1993): End-of-Project Report. Trinidad and Tobago: Caribbean Association for Feminist Research and Action.

Ellis, P. 1986. "Introduction – An overview of women in Caribbean society." In *Women of the Caribbean* P. Ellis (ed.). New Jersey, U.S.A.: Zed Books Ltd, 1-24.

Fletcher-Paul, L.M. Roberts-Nkrumah, L.B. and Johnson, L. 1990. An Assessment of Female U.W.I. Graduates in Agriculture. Proceedings of the Fourth Disciplinary Seminar (Agriculture), Women and Development Studies, The University of the West Indies, held on January 22–26, 1990, St Augustine, Trinidad and Tobago.

French, J. 1988. *Women in Caribbean Agriculture Research and Action Project: Overall Report and Summary of Main Findings.* Trinidad and Tobago: Caribbean Association for Feminist Research and Action.

French, J. 1990. "The Women in Caribbean Agriculture Project: Planned to Empower, An Overall View of the Main Findings." *CAFRA News* Vol. 3 (4) Dec 1989-Feb 1990: 4-17.

French, J. 1990. Gender Issues in Caribbean Agriculture: Methodology and Process in the Movement Towards Change. Proceedings of the Fourth Disciplinary Seminar (Agriculture), Women and Development Studies, The University of the West Indies, held on January 2226, 1990, St Augustine, Trinidad and Tobago.

Harding, S. 1987. "Introduction: Is there a feminist method?" In *Feminism and Methodology: Social Science Issues* S. Harding (ed.) Indiana University Press, Indiana, USA: 1-14.

Mies, M. 1979. Towards a methodology of women's studies. Occasional Paper, The Hague, The Netherlands: Institute of Social Studies.

Mies, M. 1982. "Women's struggles and research: an introductory note." In *Fighting on Two Fronts: Women's Struggles and Research*. M. Mies (ed.) The Hague, Netherlands: Institute of Social Sciences, 5-17.

Morgan, A. 1990. "New knowledge and skills: Burn de Bra?" *CAFRA News* vol. 3 (4) (Dec. 1989–Feb. 1990): 20–21.

Reddock, A. 1989. Organisations and movements in the Commonwealth Caribbean in the context of the World economic crisis of the 1980s. Paper prepared on Research Group, "Women's movement and visions of the future" Development with Women for a New Era (DAWN).

UN/ECLAC. 1988. Women in the Inter-Island Trade in Agricultural Produce in the Eastern Caribbean. Paper prepared for the Fourth Regional Conference on the Integration of Women into Economic and Social Development of Latin America and the Caribbean. Guatemala City, Guatemala, held September 27–30, 1988.

———. 1989. Comparative Status of Women in Selected Caribbean Countries as Indicated by Selected Social, Economic, Demographic and Legal Procedures. Trinidad and Tobago, UNECLAC.

von Braumuhl, 1994. Women in Development Implementation under Lomé IV: Trinidad and Tobago, Grenada, Netherlands Antilles, Barbados, St. Vincent, St. Lucia, Dominica. Mission Report for the Commission of the European Communities Directorate General for Development, June 1994.

7. Red Thread's Research: An Interview with Andaiye*

Kamala Kempadoo

In January 2013, on a visit to Georgetown Guyana, I had a special opportunity to interview Andaiye about research by the women's organization, Red Thread. Andaiye is a co-founder and organizer of Red Thread, as well as an internationally renowned activist for working women's rights. While aspects of her work with Red Thread have been covered in various media, I hoped through the interview to hone in on her perspective of the roles and meanings of research in the organization's activities and to add to the documentation of Red Thread's unique experience with research. During the interview, Andaiye repeatedly stressed that she did not have all the information and that certain details needed verifying by other members of Red Thread. After the interview she filled in and elaborated on the transcript as much as possible. The following, then, is an example of a mixed method for documenting history and practice, incorporating a great deal of reflection and some dialogue, and bringing to light yet another dimension of the Red Thread story.[1]

Red Thread has remarkable experience in doing its own research. You mentioned before there were three different phases in the development of the research. What name do you give those phases, how do you identify them, and what characterizes them?

I think what I really meant was that there've been three phases in the development of Red Thread, and that the kind of research we have done, our reasons for doing it, and how much it's been part of our organizing are inseparable from those phases. The identification of the phases can't be via the research in the first place. Because I believe that our research changed

---

*   Reprinted with permission from *Caribbean Review of Gender Studies* Issue 7 (December 2013).

fundamentally in our third phase, and that doing it changed us, I want to focus on that phase after briefly describing the other two.

The first phase was the income-generating phase...From 1986, when we were formed, all the way through to about 1992–93, our main aim wasn't building an organization; it was to build an income-generation project that could provide reasonable income for a few hundred women. That's what women we were in contact with asked us to do; they said they weren't interested in "politics" (we were all then associated with a political movement, the Working People's Alliance [WPA]);[2] they needed income. But the notion of doing an income-generation project alone drove us crazy. Later on all of us came to have a lot of respect for the income-generating part of our work, but in the beginning some of us were mortified that we were doing this. We had some clear political ideas that we took with us into Red Thread. Since we were all committed to working with women across race, we based ourselves in urban and rural communities that were Indo-Guyanese, Afro-Guyanese, or Indigenous. Also, we all believed that women should not be organized into arms of political parties; that if we organized that way our interests would never be central. Red Thread was therefore independent of the WPA; we never reported to the party on what we were doing. We also never asked any woman what party she supported or if she supported any party at all.

What Red Thread did from the beginning always tended to be creative and innovative. This stage was led, I would say, by four of the founders: Jocelyn Dow, Bonita Harris, Vanda Radzik, and Danuta Radzik.[3] Many women who joined already had embroidery skills, but I remember Red Thread bringing in artists we knew to talk about design and colour. We used the embroidery the women made to sell, and for them to tell the stories of their work and culture. This process was a kind of research which opened up conversations across race/cultural divides; they were what Jocelyn calls "trigger-points". The other research we did in this period, three oral histories of Indo-Guyanese sugar workers – Rookmin, Etwaria and Indra – were recorded in booklets by Danuta and then "translated" into a slideshow by Karen de Souza, another founder and later, coordinator of Red Thread, who had the same aim. These were to be followed by stories of other women. So we never did "only" the income generation, but our perspective on what more we had to do could be described as "consciousness raising", which is the opposite of our perspective now.

Phase 2 began in about 1992–93, and what had brought Phase 1 to an end was that we stopped the income-generating. It wasn't economically sustainable. This changed us in many ways. Naturally, a large number of women moved away [from the organization] since their primary interest had been income, and what remained in Red Thread was a small, hard core of women, one of whom recently told me that she stayed (and she thought the others did too) because she could not bear for Red Thread not to exist for two reasons. One was that she had learned something that she wanted to tell other women, and the second was that when she wasn't at Red Thread she felt she was missing something: Red Thread was a place where you could express what you were thinking and feeling, a place which said you didn't have to follow the tradition of what women were supposed to do and be, and a place where you discussed the why of events and developments in the country that you did not fully understand, the why of your experience – the overwork, the violence, the no money, the family stress and conflict – which she'd never heard explained before except from a religious point of view.

By Phase 2, of the seven co-founders only Karen and Vanda were still active, Vanda running a Red Thread press we'd started. Another founder had migrated, I was away ill for a long time, and the others were doing other work. Each one followed her particular passion, for example, Bonita worked almost completely on ending violence against children. The bond the core developed with Karen in this phase was fundamental to their commitment to Red Thread's survival for years.

In Phase 2, Red Thread did research on domestic violence and reproductive health (two issues but one questionnaire) and sex work, which you (Kamala) were in some way involved in as well. It seems to me that in that phase, the impetus for research came from Karen, or sometimes from somebody else – Linda [Peake], or you – *with* Karen.[4] Linda was doing her own research when she first trained Red Thread and other grassroots women to do fieldwork; the Red Thread women included Karen, Joycelyn Bacchus, Halima Khan, Vanessa Ross, Chandradai Persaud, and Nichola Marcus. They then did some more training and research before embarking on the domestic violence research, which was a Red Thread project. Although it was initiated by Karen, it was pushed by the other women, not least because it contributed to an incredible and far-reaching initiative they'd started – led by one woman, Cora Belle[5] – to buy our own centre. Women gave up their stipends for a year to achieve this! The payment for the domestic violence project was donated to that fund. Linda donated the fee that the funding agency allocated to her as chief researcher, and others gave most of the much smaller amounts that the agency allocated to them. The connection with our other work was that we'd done numerous community workshops on domestic violence and had written, recorded, and aired a radio serial on domestic violence. With the sex workers, we did three pieces of research: one was a sero-prevalence survey which we did for the Caribbean Epidemiology Center, CAREC (which I don't think we should have done), and another was a needs assessment – what problems they were facing from police harassment, robbery and rape, physical and verbal abuse from clients, and pressure from families and religious bodies, and how they could address these problems. Out of this we proposed to them that they form a group, and they did form a group that worked with G+ (Guyanese People Living with HIV and AIDS). But I don't think that we had worked out at that stage how to use research in order to strengthen organizing – women's self-organizing. It is at Phase 3 that it seems to me to change.

I think we can see a line of continuity between the research in Phases 1 and 3 – both were about women telling stories about their lives, but in spite of the similarities, there's also a big difference. It is at Phase 3 that we begin to go for information on "what life is really like for us down here"[6] for grassroots women.

Phase 3 is to me, then, the interesting phase – the phase at which research becomes organizing. But I'm getting ahead of myself, so let me do the politics first. I've heard it suggested that the relation between Red Thread and the Global Women's Strike, which came out of the Wages for Housework Campaign, is limited to me. The reality is quite different. I had met them [the Campaign] ever since. I went on a church occupation in London with them,[7] and we worked together in Beijing.[8] What happened first with Red Thread was that when I told the working-class women – I used the phrase that came from [Selma] James – that housework was the production and reproduction of labour power, I was about to explain what that meant when their faces lit up. And the thing that came to my mind was Walter Rodney once telling me that over and over again he had taught students at university level the Marxist principle that workers produce surplus value, and they would take one month, two months, three months, four to understand this. Then he went to Linden [the bauxite mining town in Guyana] and he said basically, "Yuh'all does produce surplus value" and he said the response was "Yes, right. Next" – meaning that what he had done was to uncover a fundamental truth about their lives, which they therefore "knew" at some deep level – and that's the response I got from Red Thread when I said that they produced and reproduced labour power. They really understood it.

A piece of it was pride that somebody feels that all that stuff which you do is actually work and is not being dismissed. But the thought that this "thing"– I mean capitalism is not a word that Red Thread working-class women would use, but it's thrown around in front of them – the thought that capitalism has at its foundation their work was "empowering"; they liked it. Let me just say that: they liked it. Later they said that it was one of the things they remembered from Phase 1, that occasionally I talked about counting women's work. And at that stage it wasn't connected to a Red Thread politics and we were not in touch with the strike. We just talked about counting women's work, which of course I'd got from the strike.

This was in the income-generating phase?

Yes, and in that phase, another of the founders, Jocelyn (Dow) often did discussions with the women on valuing their labour, although she and I never even talked about where her head was going with that, I just knew it was something she talked about a lot – valuing labour, valuing the resources around you, was her phrase, "the resources around and in you" – the resources in the environment and the resources in your own labour. She was very concerned that when people were pricing things they always started with the point at which something was being produced; for example, in Indigenous communities the women would never count the labour of gathering the materials that were going to be turned into a product. She wanted them to know that they had to put a price on these "free" resources and this "free" labour. So that had been there from the very beginning, but not put forward as "this is going to be THE politics" or anything. Maybe the best way to put it is that the whole question of invisible and unwaged work was a thread in what we were doing and saying but not yet fundamental to it.

But in Phase 3, the time-use survey was seminal; although, of course, we didn't fully understand in advance what we would find and where it would take us. It was seminal, but at the same time, they [Red Thread women] couldn't bear the process of doing it. The four women who did it were all working class, two Indo-Guyanese, two Afro-Guyanese: Nicola, Halima, Jocelyn and Chandradai. It was hard to do…They did the most painstaking thing, which is diaries. First, they did their own for practice, and then they went to other women. In some cases, they felt that the women were able to make their own records, and in other cases they felt they had to make the record. One of the reasons for them sometimes doing the record, apart from the obvious ones like literacy and women forgetting the details of their work, and so on, was that by then we had talked about things such as simultaneous activities – what people call multi-tasking – and "ordinary women" don't know that they do that. So that when they looked back at a diary recorded by somebody who was recording herself, it would not be there – the fact that at the same time she was cooking she was also doing whatever else, minding the child, and so forth. That was one reason. And the other thing they had been very attracted by, which other people were not looking at, was what Selma called emotional housework. And none of that would be recorded by women normally. The Red Thread women were very excited at the notion that one was supposed to count all that worry, they would say, "all dat worrying because de money cyan' do" – all of that – the placating of the man, if there was a man, care of the child, holding the relationship together, and so forth.

They were counting emotional labour too?

Yes. Everything in life that had most burdened them, and they thought burdened just them, was now to be counted. So it was a pain in the ass…

How was it counted, in terms of hours, minutes?

The duration of each task was counted by the minute or by the hour and minute, depending on the task. I know nothing about scientific research. I doubt that we had the skills to do what people would call a scientific piece of research, although all of the core except me had been trained to do research during Phase 2. But there's a woman in the International Women Count network, of which I'm a member – Solveig Francis – who has long been the person that would deal with statistics, and so on, who was becoming experienced in the methods of counting women's work. Along with Selma, she helped design the time-use survey and as it was being administered she helped whenever asked. But this was, without any question, their baby – Joycelyn's, Chandra's, Halima's, Nicola's. You know, Solveig is not here (in Guyana), and this was pre-Skype, 2000 to 2001. Then, they were often out of town, far from where Karen and I were. So they worked problems out as they came up. Until that moment it's theory.

So, the women were very engaged and completely wrapped up in doing this.

I want to be fair to what happened. They got completely wrapped up in and fed up with the entire process, which they found really, really, really hard. Really hard. I mean let's face it, it was a very burdensome thing that they were doing...They were in tears some days, because of all kinds of things: having to babysit and do housework for women whose time use they were doing so the women could be partly freed to do the diary, having to go back to the same house four or five times only to be told in the end that the woman wouldn't do the diary, usually because the man had objected, having to do the diaries hiding from husbands and partners who didn't want the women to do them, the men who shouted at them – I can't remember the stories, they all tended to be so dreadful – having nowhere to sleep, being bitten by swarms of mosquitoes, being bitten by centipedes, they found the thing awful to the point where it was often clear that they had lost sight of what it was about. In some Indo-Guyanese communities people were afraid of the Afro-Guyanese women and even if they did the diaries they were tense and fearful. Who else but grassroots women would have persevered through this whole process!

Who designed this method of doing research?

There were two or three methods that people were developing of how to do time use, and diaries was the one we chose. That's the one that we, not Red Thread alone, but with Solveig and Selma, chose, as making sense. It was also the one that made most sense for grassroots women – both those doing the research and the women whose time use they were researching.

When the diaries were finished, they sent what they had to Solveig, who was beside herself with excitement...

They had recorded everything!

(Laugh) It just became "We did this thing!" Then you're hearing what you had hoped to be hearing all the time, about what it is that they were learning, what they were seeing, how much they were seeing the samenesses of women's lives, how much they were also seeing differences in women's lives depending upon race, depending upon which part of the country you came from, depending upon whether they had electricity or running water – what some might call obvious things. But the point is that nobody told them, they uncovered it for themselves. And they uncovered more than what was already known because they were grassroots women engaging other grassroots women.

One of the striking things in the first phase of Red Thread was how little the women knew of each other. I had not realized that Guyana had grown quite that divided. The difference I'm drawing here between "them" and "me" is generational. I grew up in a Guyana that had not been physically divided by the violence of the early 1960s.[9] I don't mean that there was no racial conflict between Indians and Africans; I mean that we were not ignorant about each other, though we were very ignorant, most of us, about Indigenous peoples. I remember when Red Thread had our first Encounter, which was our notion of an annual general meeting, all the women came in dressed to the nines, the Afro-Guyanese women looking like they were going to a party. And I remember a stiffness on both sides. And later, when there were food shortages and some relationship had grown sufficient for women to be collaborating, "I could buy so and so in Linden if you buy so and so on the West Coast", the women were shopping for each other in that kind of way, and they were beginning to hobnob with each other. I remember the total amazement of Indo-Guyanese women from the West Coast when they went up to Linden. They came back and said "They poor!" People had told them that black people weren't poor, and black people didn't behave as if they were poor... The Afro-Guyanese women had the same response when they went to the homes of Indo-Guyanese women. So they were always full of these discoveries about each other, of what seemed to me to be perfectly normal things. I remember another day that was totally mind-blowing to them was when Sistren brought a video in which the sugar workers were Afro-Jamaican.[10] Oh, they were beside themselves. Never in their life had sugar workers been Afro, anywhere.[11]

So the discoveries via the time-use survey included things of which I would have said "everybody knows that", but everybody didn't know that. I remember when Cora went to the Pomeroon and saw Indigenous people who were, in fact, bonded labourers. She came back and said to black people in town, "Do not ever let me hear you say again that you are the poorest people on the face of the earth. I just see the poorest people on the face of the earth. Just shut up yuh mout' in future." They didn't know that there were so many Amerindian people who had no running water. That they were walking to creeks for water, and so forth. And those who knew never told them. So as I've said, with the survey they saw both the absolute sameness of the housework and the ways in which the intensity of the housework varied because of race, geographic location, and so on. It was a real process of discovery for them, for the women who were the researchers. And, to me, it really changed them. One of them told me that in spite of the frustration they felt doing the survey, even at the time "it brought to life everything about our lives", adding, "Even when we used to have the discussions about counting unwaged work, it was never as real as with the time use". Since they counted everything, including emotional work, they were really, literally counting "everything about our lives".

Clearly the RT women were looking both at their own lives and looking at and helping to document the work and lives of other women. Were those other women who were being researched expressing the same kind of enthusiasm, or curiosity, or awareness? I mean, was there any way to see what kind of impact the time-use survey had on the larger population that was interviewed?

As I remember it, they got different responses from different women. The survey involved 101 women. There were clearly women who were doing it only because we were asking them to do it. But there were others, as I remember from the reports at the time, with whom there were moments of recognition, there were moments of surprise, there were responses from the women in relation to their own lives, as if they were looking at these lives from inside/outside, for the first time. And what certainly happened across the years is that one of the women who'd administered the time use would tell us, "Let's ask so-and-so to do that", and we would ask, "Who is so-and-so?" And they would say "Time use". So that's where they know the woman from and had made sufficient contact with the woman, who was still there to be called on. I think some of those women went into Grassroots Women Across Race.

That's another organization?

We're now thinking for the first time of expanding Red Thread, but we weren't [doing that before] because the one absolute qualification for being in Red Thread from early on was anti-racism. This is not in plentiful supply in Guyana. Not. There would be people who would say publicly they were Red Thread, and then we'd be climbing under a table because they would go somewhere and say, "Oh those *** coolie people" or "These *** blackman" or "These *** buck people…" I'm not saying that everyone else is a racist; I'm saying that not many people are anti-racist. So the first way that we dealt with that after the income-generating phase was over was by keeping Red Thread like it was, a very small but solid and reliable core, and having networks. The first network was Grassroots Women Across Race (GWAR) – across race means that you are willing to work across race. It doesn't mean that your head has reached where it should reach in relation to anti-racism, but that you're open to others. And then we expanded what we wanted – nobody ever discussed anybody's sexuality, but I watched the whole of the Red Thread core become, in addition to being anti-racist, anti-homophobic, and anti-violence. Those three. Of course, we also support the rights of people with disabilities (which is why our centre is wheelchair-accessible), but we're less active on that.

But now we're beginning, just beginning, to say in relation to Red Thread itself, you can be a member if you are either already anti-racist, anti-homophobic, and anti-violent, or really open to these principles, because it's too incestuous just to keep the core – you know, as if "we're the pure ones". I think we've come to this stage because we're all so much more confident in who we are. But GWAR was the first network we created, which at one stage…it had 60-something, 70-something women. Not all over the country – we've always been weak in Berbice[12] – but in parts of the interior, and other parts of Guyana.

Red Thread's Research

And that in part also came out because of the survey?

Yes. So a lot of the other "research", which we in all honesty never thought of as research at all, in Phase 3, was directly connected to the time use... More than once we were planning an action, and it would seem sensible to say "Go do a diary. Let's see what that is." Sometimes it was "Go do a diary for a day", "Go do a diary for a half-day" – it tells you something that you want to know. It became a method that came to make sense to us, as a way of finding out what you couldn't find out any other way. So, directly connected to counting work and the valuing of work, would be, after the time-use survey, the flood research; we counted what the work of coping with the flood was for women. One reason we did it was the amount of racial tension we saw at a post-flood meeting of about 300 Afro- and Indo-women at the centre; the time use uncovered for us and for those women the amount and kind of work they were all doing, across race, for their families and communities to survive.

Another kind of "research" we did after the time-use survey was the price research around the introduction of VAT, showing the effect of VAT on our budgets. We did "case for" research to argue for increases for pensioners and women on public assistance, based on careful recording of their budgets...We could never get a whole large group to do it, right. But we didn't even care about that because by then – we're talking about two or three years ago – by then we knew what it was that we were seeing. We knew what it was we thought. We knew, and we wanted to bring it alive. And in a sense some of the "research" was not to find out anything at all, it was to demonstrate.

After collecting the diaries – the women do the diaries for these various purposes of documenting, making public statements, etc. – how is that information analysed? For the time-use survey, for example, did Solveig analyse it and then bring it back to the organization? And the organization was to carry it forward?

Yes, Solveig analysed it, always consulting us. It was a long back-and-forth process that started with all of us reading all the diaries and Solveig proposing a chart that we worked on and then entered the information into and sent back to her. It went back and forth, but we never really did anything with it outside of using it ourselves. It's down on our work plan every year to publish it, but it never felt like it was important outside of… um… OK, yes, it's important. It's important from the point of view that it was grassroots women who surveyed the time use of other grassroots women, and did it for themselves and other women; it's also important for the findings. As far as we know, it's the first time-use of grassroots women by grassroots women. So it would be valuable to publish it.

But publish how? When I look at the research we did in Phase 2 what I see are reports, and the reports could not have been intended for them [the women who did the research]. So for example, when I look at the bibliography for those reports I laugh out loud, because I don't know what many of the titles mean, so why would anybody else? I'm not saying there was an active hostility to publishing the time-use survey. It's just that we've used it over and over again in all kinds of ways. I wish I could find all the ways in which it's been used, but we're always alluding to it; we're always pulling from it.

It provides a knowledge base for RT?

Yes, I mean we and the women we work with are very happy when [we make things] like leaflets…We really did get into doing things like that, because they would be so accessible to the people whose lives you were talking about, and the other forms like reports were so inaccessible. I'm not saying there's no way of publishing findings in an accessible way, but I don't know what it is. We don't know.

Do the women in RT, who conducted the time-use survey and these other projects around the floods and VAT, and so forth, consider themselves researchers?

They used to. And if they don't now, that would be my "fault". When I came back to Red Thread in about 1992 after I'd been ill the first time, I was pissed because they would describe themselves to me as community facilitators. And it very much expressed an us- and-them relationship with the community that I didn't think was a good relationship….

I don't know if I could put a word to what they are, but they certainly think of themselves now as, and are capable of, finding out whatever they want to find out, and of being able to increasingly record it in some form that can then be taken and made some use of, and so on. So it's a skill and competence they feel good about. They feel what we all feel when we master work, especially work which we're told is beyond us. That feeling had begun with the Phase 2 research and grew with the time-use survey.

Was there any particular kind of training that happened within the organization before doing any of the research?

As I mentioned earlier, in Phase 2 they'd been trained in participatory research methods, qualitative and quantitative research methods, but the main focus was qualitative research. Both before the survey and after, a lot of the work that had to do with counting the work and then counting other things about grassroots women's lives had been done with me… From counting time use we went to counting what money women got or didn't get for their work. Before Red Thread went to other women we would talk about what we wanted, we would talk about where we thought we might get it from, we would talk about how we thought we might get it. Often enough the women doing the research knew more than I did. And often there was a degree of trial and error. They would go and come back and say, well, that didn't work, and so on.

Whomever you are talking about – pensioners, domestic workers – in however small a number, we were always testing to see what is the way we would get it out of them, the "it" being what you had gone to retrieve, because you already knew it was there.

I remember in particular, when they were talking to other women about how they managed their budgets – that was a trip. They were talking to other women just like themselves, and if you are talking to women just like yourself you both know more and you know less. So, you know more because that's your life as well, but you know less because things don't seem surprising. I remember the biggest thing we had to go back and forth on was this: they thought it was completely normal to come back with findings that said that "So-and-so earned or was paid a total of G$30,000 and spent G$100,000." They thought there was nothing weird about that because that's just how they lived themselves. So they would come back to me and I would say, "Whey it (the rest of money) come from?" and we'd play with that and they'd go back and they'd see something else, and so on. And, in fact, in the process we all learned a lot watching them look at themselves, look at all kinds of things, including that when that's the kind of budget you have what slips is food, that's what you spend less on.

So you had a very instrumental role in asking the questions and setting up the time-use survey?

I was a kind of conduit between the women here and Solveig – at the time, I was the person who knew both. So the to-and-fro is, they tell me the piece that they know, which is usually more than I know, and something then occurs to me that I put to them, and so on, so it's a conversation. A conversation that can take a long time, but which I never thought of for one moment as training, except insofar as you hope that you wouldn't have to do that all over again. They do very well for themselves now.

A question in my mind, as I'm listening to you is, how does an organization like RT build upon this experience? I'm seeing the information being collected by "grassroots" women, the analysis happening elsewhere and some of the probing coming from another group of people.

First, the three groups you identify: grassroots women, which you put in quotes but we don't; Solveig, the "elsewhere" where the analysis happened; and me, where "some of the probing [was] coming from ...." Of course, we have different skills, but they're not a hierarchy of skills. I have the skill of probing, but I couldn't have collected the information that Halima, Joycelyn, Nicola, and Chandra did and I couldn't analyse the information as Solveig did in consultation with us. All of it was a collaboration. More generally, the only thing I can tell you is that on the research and analysis skills the need for external help becomes less and less. And that is really just literally true. When we've done the mini time-use and other surveys I mentioned, we analyse them ourselves. So that leads into my response to your question, "how does an organization like Red Thread build upon this experience [of doing the time-use survey]?" The time-use survey changed all of us. It opened the way to what came after. I could show this better if we were better at documenting what we do. That's one of the main things I would like us to do. And it can't be us in Red Thread doing it. We've obviously made a mess of it so far, because we are not a writing unit and we haven't used video systematically either. And we're very pressed for time to get things done.

You mean documenting the organization's work?

Yes, and within the organization's work, very crucially the research. Documenting what we do. Every time I write project proposals, although that's beginning to be done by others as well, every single time, as I'm writing about work we've done, I have to sit people down and say "and then what", "and then what?", and so on.

That's why I am curious about the role that you have, in probing, and asking those questions, and perhaps guiding.

Sometimes I'm only probing for information about what we've all worked on. Sometimes I'm probing for ideas. I am older than all the others, and there is a different experience I have, including more formal education, and I do that – the probing and the sorting and the documenting – better than others in the core do, up to now, yes. That's true. But it's a constantly evolving relationship, and we all are very conscious of that. I don't mean that I am making it evolve, but the way other Red Thread members talk to me now is utterly different from how they spoke to me even two years ago, and what they know and what they're sure they know is different. It's different, and it's good. Not only in relation to research, but generally, I am what you call the prober. I would call it the pusher. As I said, that's in relation to the living income issues. For violence it's Karen, and there, too, the relationship is changing. The they/us is changing. We operate as a collective.

But organizations can sometimes be so determined by the persons within that organization that continuity is hard. People sometimes step out of an organization, and it moves into something completely different, or doesn't have the ability to carry forward what it had before. And, with your role being so central in such a process…?

All of us are central. And all of us are very conscious that we intend to survive. When I got sick last year, another of the Red Thread members said that [because] they have two "sickly" co-ordinators (Karen was also ill), she thought it was time to step up to the plate. And they would survive. If the "sickly co-ordinators" went under, they would survive. This is not a one- or two-woman organization…

The region is full of what we thought were organizations that disappeared because one person left. Peggy Antrobus left WAND[14] and there's no WAND, and so on. That's an oversimplification of what happened, but it's not an oversimplification to say that Peggy's retirement meant that most of what was good in the old WAND died. But Red Thread will make it, and I think some of the things we will do this year will underscore that. We will make it because of internal strengths but also because we are part of an international network that has made and continues to make a lot of difference to our organizing, as we do to the whole network's.

Before we get into the future plans, I want to ask about lessons learned. Is there anything you think you may have done differently—any other way of collecting information, any other kind of method? The diary method is an important one, but is there anything you tried that didn't work so well?

Well, there are some things I can't answer because I literally just don't know. One of the things I do know about is that we tried to do political report cards (that is, reports on what action political parties had taken, planned, or tried to take in relation to their manifesto promises), which were a failure…It was something that we wanted to do, it didn't come up because we wanted to go somewhere for funds, we wanted to do it. But I think by the time we tailored it to suit what we could go to a funder with, we were in trouble.

…As the main person designing the project, I had made a fairly fundamental error to start with, which was not seeing that the (political) parties that would respond to us were the parties that felt weak enough to need friends – that the ruling People's Progressive Party (PPP) certainly wouldn't feel that, but that the main opposition People's National Congress (PNC) would, but only in a half-ass way, and so on.[15] There were ways of getting past that, there were things that we could do, if we were not busy trying to follow step 1, step 2, step 3, and so on, as we'd designed it. Because one of the things about funders, most of them, is that if you tell them in advance that you are going to do 20 steps, then you have to do those 20 steps, regardless of what happens…Funders don't have any room for trial and error, even when they're funding a pilot. So the rigidities of their evaluation, monitoring and reporting requirements, and so forth, throw you out totally...

So that is one project that I think was a failure, beginning with the failure of judgement on our part to start with, but very much because the project was never doable in the way that a funder would want. And so in the end it became not doable at all.

Some of the things we did in Phase 3 as far as I remember were unfunded. And those were the best we did. I don't remember reporting to anybody...except ourselves and other women we organize with. Except for a very few, funders constrain you.

I want to ask you about funding priorities or research priorities from funding organizations. How has RT responded to that?

I come out of a long, left-wing tradition which says be wary of certain institutions – I'm afraid of certain institutions. I no longer belong to the same tradition but I'm very conscious of what's been called the "NGO-ization" of the region: a use of NGOs to carry forward the neo-liberal project. And I'm not always sure that, however good you think you are, you have the capacity to turn their help into your self-interest or the self-interest of the people that you're working with. So, those people frighten me. But it really has not been many [that have funded RT research] – it's been CAREC, the IOM,[16] and UNICEF.

Now with UNICEF – we didn't do the actual research, we facilitated it – it was to get children's experience of violence. And as I remember, that one made sense to me. This was a period not long after Karen did a vigil.[17] She was absolutely hysterical over the state of children, deeply, deeply upset. There was a time when she came and stood up next to me and stared into space, and I said, "What is it this time?" And she said that a mother had just come [to RT] because she thought that her three-month-old child had thrush. And what it was, was dried semen in the child's mouth because some blasted man had worked out that a child's instincts to suck could work to his advantage. She was going berserk. So in a sense, her going on the road with a vigil in 2003, or doing the UNICEF research in 2004/2005 all became part of, "what can I, what can we do about this?" So, responding to a request from a UN agency then made sense for us. The point of the research, like the point of the vigil, was to find a way to force attention to the traumas that were being inflicted on children and demand that government and all of us address them.

Is there anything that RT is thinking about doing at the moment? Any new projects?

We've designed a project, which is the closest we've ever come to designing a project exactly as we would like to do it. Whether anyone will give us the money or not…the project is ours. Now, there's one big piece of research that we did not build into the project because we don't have the capacity to do it – and didn't want to get diverted by it –a profile of domestic workers in Guyana. A group that we're really interested in organizing with is domestic workers. We're on the steering committee of the Caribbean Domestic Workers' Network (CDWN) and through the ILO, they're going to do a profile of domestic workers in Guyana and Antigua.[18] The idea started because I said at a CDWN meeting that I did not recognize the domestic workers of Guyana in anything that we were saying, and that we had to acknowledge that domestic work is not the same thing all over the region: it depends on your economy, it depends on all kinds of things. There's also going to be a difference between domestic workers in what they call sending and receiving countries for migrant domestic workers, and Guyana is one of the sending countries. Another possible difference is that we can find very few domestic workers who only do domestic work. They are sex workers, they are vendors, they are all kinds of workers –they run outside their house and sell two sweeties, come inside and sell beauty services, and so on. They have to do all this for their children to be able to eat and go to school.

We think that is a good thing to know, not for the sake of knowing, but for the sake of understanding what it is we're doing, because there are things people want us to do that sound wrong. But we have to prove them wrong. For example, under the CARICOM Single Market and Economy Free Movement of Persons, to exercise their right to travel around the region for domestic work, women will have to do a Caribbean regional vocational qualification. And we think that this is about policing domestic workers, and not anything to do with facilitating their movement in the region to do domestic work. But we have to show that. Because the women are doing quite a fine job at the moment travelling up and down this region without anybody's permission, and now they want them to show a piece of paper which many will find it difficult or impossible to get. Few domestic workers here can do the kind of course we hear people talking about – they would have to pay for it, take time off work, maybe have pre-qualifications they don't have and show no signs of needing – we need to show that.

Anyhow, that's not built into the proposal but what would be built in would be – and again, we don't think about this as research in the first place – a drop-in centre for domestic workers, because women who are domestic workers don't know if they have any labour rights. All these women are just "unorganized" and the unions don't care about them. So obviously in the process of giving them advice, you yourself are making records out of which you discover things, in the same way as we did and do out of the violence drop-in centre.

The method that we're trying to use with the violence drop-in centre is that you provide a service, that as far as possible you train women so that the service becomes, at least partially, self-help, so people understand the law, and so on. One woman told us one day that she went to court and "The lawyer din come and I just come there and talk for myself because I did know what I was talking". So you do the self-help. But you also are trying in the process to identify, along with the women, changes that we all want and need in policy and law…So that drop-in centre is on violence, and we're going to do a drop-in centre principally for domestic workers. But since there is, as we say, no such thing as a pure domestic worker, it's really for everybody.

It is preferably documentation, as distinct from what you store in your head – documentation from the service – that becomes the source of your advocacy and campaigning…In terms of dissemination, we're going to do a TV talk show and stop the vain attempt to write. We are going to do a TV talk show, and the talk show in part should be fed by that documentation.

We haven't yet talked about the race research, which I don't know if we'll be able to finish, but we could not have done that without Alissa.[19] This is how that research came about. In 2001, when post-electoral violence escalated following a jailbreak of five men who went on a rampage [and] whose motives were at once political, racial and criminal – Alissa wanted to research that with Red Thread.[20] And we could not get people to talk.

We found one person who would talk, and then he died in an accident – one person who was prepared to tell us something that was not widely known, what those men were doing to women in Buxton,[21] which is rape with guns…And, of course, black people around us were getting nervous because you know "We always put our dirty linen outside." But we say "Whether your linen is dirty or not, you have to put it out" – and what we have to try to ensure is that all dirty linen comes out. We have to stop hiding these truths which fester and fester.

The one thing that kept on coming up during discussions about 2001 was something I think we all know, but it was nonetheless startling. It was how alive 1964, which was the height of the violence of the 1960s, is in everybody's consciousness, even if they weren't alive at the time. They might not know the exact year, but they would tell you something about it. And so, eventually, we decided to research 1964, and essentially she (Alissa) is doing the interviews with Joycelyn [Bacchus]. We're in a total dilemma over how to use it, and are in a conversation with a friend about whether there's a way that film can do it. So we haven't dropped it, it's been going on for ages, but I mention it because it's a good example of something where you do need the other skills that you don't have, and it would be stupid to pretend you have them or to try to build them. We don't have them here and we can't have all skills ourselves. But the aspects of interviewing skills that can be passed on, Alissa is passing on to Joycelyn, while at the same time relying on Joycelyn's greater knowledge of Linden, which is where some of the worst violence was in 1964.

To wrap up, RT doesn't really do research as something distinct, although it's an integral part of what it does. Is there a name for what you do?

No. You know when CAFRA[22] started – the very name was research and action – the notion was, you do research and then you do action. That one-step, two-step kind of notion. No, I don't know any kind of name for all we've done, because it is such a gamut. One of the reasons I did the phase explanation is because what we did with sex work or with domestic violence is not similar to what we do now. What we do now are all various forms of organizing at the grassroots, using all the various methods of other sectors. What we do now is far more under our control, in terms of deciding to do it, designing it, and using methods that are manageable by more and more of us. And now the search is for methods for publicizing that are also manageable by us. If that has a name other than organizing, I don't know what it is…It's really that there is a politics which drives your campaigning, and your campaigning includes your research.

Notes

1. There are several publications by and about Red Thread. One of the more comprehensive was written by Andaiye and published as "Red Thread: The Red Thread Story," in *Spitting in the Wind: Lessons in Empowerment from the Caribbean*, ed. Brown, Suzanne Francis (Kingston: Ian Randle Publishers, 2000).
2. The Working People's Alliance (WPA) was a political party, which always functioned more like a movement, launched in 1979 in opposition to an authoritarian regime. It was pro-working class and, in a country with deep racial divisions, especially between Guyanese of Indian and African descent, it was multi-racial. It had a collective leadership, but its popular leader was Walter Rodney until his assassination on June 13, 1980.
3. The other three were Diana Matthews who migrated soon after Red Thread started, Karen de Souza and Andaiye.
4. Linda Peake teaches at York University. The studies referred to here were published as Red Thread Women's Development Programme, "'Givin' Lil' Bit Fuh Lil Bit': Women and Sex Work in Guyana," in *Sun, Sex and Gold: Tourism and Sex Work in the Caribbean*, ed. Kempadoo, Kamala (Boulder: Rowman & Littlefield, 1999) and Red Thread's *Study on Reproductive and Sexual Health and Domestic Violence: Issues of Women in Guyana*, Guyana, 2000.
5. Cora was a founding member of Red Thread in 1986 and remained an active member and a point of reference in Red Thread until her death in 2012 at the age of 62.
6. This is Selma James' explanation of what Marx tried to find out with his 100 Questions.
7. In 1982, the English Collective of Prostitutes (ECP), an autonomous group in the Wages for Housework Campaign, carried out a 12-day occupation of a church in London to demand support for prostitutes in their conflict with the police. The ECP was backed by Women against Rape and Black Women for Wages for Housework, two other groups in the Campaign. In London, as International Secretary of the WPA, Andaiye actively worked in support of the occupation.
8. Before and during Beijing, where Andaiye was a Guyana delegate and a CARICOM-employed adviser to the CARICOM Ministers responsible for Women's Affairs attending the Conference, she worked to get support for the Campaign's lobby to win agreement on the inclusion of counting unwaged work in the Beijing Platform for Action.
9. The early 1960s witnessed some of the worst racial violence in Guyana's history. By the end of it, Guyanese of Indian and African descent had fled and been chased out of their communities and came to live in communities that were racially homogeneous.

10. Sistren Theatre Collective, formed in 1977, is a Jamaican women's organization. The video, *Sweet Sugar Rage* (1985), documents conditions of female sugar workers, including their experiences of sexism in the trade union.
11. In Guyana, after Indian indentured labourers replaced enslaved Africans on the sugar plantations following Emancipation, fieldworkers in sugar have been so overwhelmingly Indo-Guyanese that Guyanese people think of cane cutting as an "Indian" occupation everywhere.
12. Red Thread has done a fair amount of work on the West Coast of Berbice, so this is in reference to the Corentyne, which is the section of Berbice to the east of the Berbice river, stretching all the way to Guyana's border with Suriname. Both the sex work research and the trafficking in persons research were done on the Corentyne, but the main impediment to doing more work there was the same as for other parts of the country – not enough money.
13. The Women and Development Unit of the School of Continuing Studies at the University of the West Indies, Cave Hill campus, Barbados.
14. The People's Progressive Party (PPP) is, since 1992, the ruling party. The People's National Congress (PNC) is the main opposition party.
15. IOM is the International Organization for Migration.
16. In 2003, Karen de Souza led a Red Thread 24-hour vigil from April 17 to April 30 for a schoolboy, Joshua Bell, who was kidnapped and murdered.
17. Since the interview was done, the Government of Antigua and Barbuda decided to do a profile of domestic workers there, so the ILO research is on Guyana alone.
18. Alissa Trotz, who teaches at the University of Toronto, is an overseas member of Red Thread.
19. It became known as the Mash Day jailbreak, given that the escape occurred around the time of the annual Mashramani celebrations in Guyana, a national holiday.
20. The residents of Buxton, like the five men, are Afro-Guyanese. Most of the victims in the post-election violence in 1997 and 2001, as well as during the 2002 rampage were Indo-Guyanese. In what was said to be retaliation, a group that came to be called the Phantom Squad, allegedly financed by businessmen (including those with connections to the transnational drug trafficking trade) and supported from within the highest echelons of government, targeted and executed large numbers (estimated to be in the hundreds) of predominantly Afro-Guyanese men.
21. Caribbean Association for Feminist Research and Action.

8. A Method of Decolonial Arts Practice*

Honor Ford Smith

Sistren began in 1977, mainly on the initiative of a small group of working-class women who had been part of a special make-work program created by the Michael Manley government to remedy women's unemployment. It grew, over time, to become one of a few black feminist performance collectives in the Americas, coming to influence a much larger constellation of what was then called "'third world'" women's organizations emerging in the 1970s and after. It was formed in response to the stated desire of the founding actors to do plays about how men treat women bad.[1] But that is not all there was to the origin story.

Much has been written about Sistren, but these accounts do not deal specifically with Sistren's embodied cultural production or relationship to feminist decolonization.[2] Here, I want to attend specifically to Sistren's existence as a cultural project, legible to a broad public beyond its own local communities and grassroots political groups (to which many of Sistren's members belonged). This was possible, at least in part, because the idea of the cultural agent as envisioned by Nettleford was given institutional meaning through the Cultural Training Centre. This materialization of practice came about because of the demands of social movements of the time for access to institutions and for authorization there. These social movements on the outside impacted what was possible on the inside, changing the terms of cultural access and cultural accountability. The demand for access was graphically dramatized by Stafford Ashani in his play *Masqueraders*, which is about a group of dreadlocked performers who gain access to a formal theater after having been stoned in a performance

---

* Reprinted with permission from 'The Body and Performance in 1970s Jamaica: Toward a Decolonial Cultural Method,' *Small Axe* 58 (March 2019): 150–68. Excerpted.

on the street. State reforms in cultural education were formulated by a committee struck through the Office of the Prime Minister and led by Nettleford, and they were implemented in response to the demands of those largely outside colonial educational institutions.[3] The creation of the schools of the arts around this idea of cultural agency complemented community-based work in other agencies, such as the Social Development Commission, and created an opening through which human subjects could bring their knowledge of sequestered embodied African-diasporic rites, languages, music, orature, and dance into the institution.

The mandate for the cultural agent allowed groups such as Sistren, among others, to find a home at the Cultural Training Centre (opened in 1976). Under Dennis Scott's leadership at the Jamaica School of Drama, the notion of cultural agency allowed the school to include communities of the deaf, disabled, prisoners, teachers, dub poets, and more. It allowed space for Sistren to meet, and from time to time it required faculty members like me and later Hertencer Lindsay to include work with Sistren as part of our directing responsibilities. The educational opening at the center placed the arts in the middle of educational democratization and decolonization. The question of how to bring the "cultural agent" into being was not a closed subject. It was open to interpretation and depended on the formation and artistic commitments of the teacher artists who worked there. The gestural languages of the body could take center stage because it was a way to jettison theatrical glitz and turn scarcity into abundance. At the time, the publishing world was still largely outside the country, and it could not keep up with the immediacy of demands of the time. Course work at the School of Drama—Community Drama (taught by Thom Cross), Caribbean Lab (taught by Jean Small), acting (taught by Scott, Lindsay, and me), directing (taught by Lloyd Reckord and Rawle Gibbons), for example—took place with few published texts. Structures for the voice and body had to be devised then and there because few plays were easily accessible at the time. The dearth of published material led to jazz-like structures, storytelling, movement-based improvisation, and devised work. Sistren's emergence as a collective was both maverick and typical of the time. Sistren founding member Afolashade argues that the 1970s was a period when "anything grassroots was encouraged": "During that time, not just Sistren Theatre Collective emerged as a theatre group but about three other popular theatre groups."[4] What is more, in keeping with the movements outside the school's walls, the space at the school also allowed for new forms of collaboration across differences of skill, class, and race. Although the majority of Sistren members were working class and led from their experience, the directors, students, artists, and others who worked with the collective often had been trained in the United Kingdom or the United States and had to figure out new modes of collaboration beyond the colonial structures we had inherited.

In 1978, we faced the question of how to find a mode of address that could shift the language of performance away from inherited colonial legacies and decolonize stereotypical images of black and Caribbean women. The most obvious way to do this was to turn the stages of the middle-class theater into a forum for the voices of working-class experience, to refuse the confinement of working-class bodies to bracketed-off community spaces and insert their actual and embodied presence into more visible modes of production in the anticolonial nation. Sistren's first plays were determined to create a dramatic forum for working-class women and to build a broad audience for this across the boundaries of class and race. But the questions were how that would actually materialize and how it would change how people saw the challenges facing working women beyond their mere visibility on stage.

The dominant (mis)representations of black women in the region were those of the stereotypical full-bodied masculinized black woman, the Mammy, as she is called in scholarship on African Americans, or the hypersexualized and often brown-skinned Jezebel. These images caricatured black and brown women as hulking, strong, clumsy, strident, ignorant, and grotesquely asexual or as hypersexualized, manipulative, cunning figures who preyed on the sexual frailty of white men in return for material favors. They justified the exploitation of women's labor and sexuality on the plantation and differentiated black and brown women from the idealized white woman (small, leisured, chaste, physically weak). This system of representation lived on through commonplace descriptions of Jamaica as a "matriarchal society." The scholar M.G. Smith gave academic credence to this when he wrote that lower-class families were functionally matriarchal.[5] Female-headed households were equated with poverty and were seen as "backward." Children were described as "fatherless," and there was little sense that these families might have anything positive to offer as alternatives to the Western patriarchal model. As Joan French has argued, colonial policy proposed that overcoming this signifier of backwardness depended on controlling women's sexuality, teaching them to conform to patriarchal models of family and to pursue respectability through the model of the domesticated housewife.[6]

Black middle-class women writers and performers struggled long to evade the reach of these racist discourses. The work of Louise Bennett is a case in point. Her persona as a working-class black woman emerged in the 1930s and became the dominant voice of women in the field of orature and performance. By the 1970s Bennett embodied the role of mother of the nation and as such constantly negotiated the pitfalls of both stereotypes, the masculinized and the oversexed woman. While much has been written about her work, little of it explores how she deployed her body as she literally narrated the nation out of her own physicality, creating a national public, often through flesh-and-blood presence. She wore the bandana for much of her performing life, played the role of a full-bodied peasant/working-class woman, was always good-humored, and out of her mouth came what was then called "dialect." She inhabited the bandana stereotype to flip it, which she did by satirizing pretension and the establishment. But she always downplayed her own sexuality, never speaking about erotics, and the image she portrayed was always respectable.[7] In her solo performances, she was also careful to signal that "dialect" was not the only language she spoke. She moved across the language spectrum, skillfully doubling the image she presented and making it clear that off stage she was, in fact, middle class. She embodied "Tek kin teet kibba heart bun," a proverb she was fond of quoting, and while she was often ironic and sometimes sad, she was rarely, if ever, confrontational or angry. That the stereotypical vulgar black woman cast a long shadow on her work is perhaps borne out by her comment, "Nobody could ever say I was vulgar. I never was."[8]

By the time Sistren emerged, forty years after Bennett had come to voice, the women's movement of the socialist People's National Party and the largely communist Committee of Women for Progress were fighting hard for food justice, maternity leave, labor reforms, minimum wage for domestic workers, equal employment for women, and recourse for families, particularly around childcare. The colonial bastardy laws had been repealed by 1976, and women were demanding the right to have children outside marriage without being stigmatized. Sistren was very much part of this movement for women, though in the 1970s it worked mainly through performance and participatory drama workshops. The structure of feeling of the time had decisively shifted away from the release of social anxiety in laughter, and the tone of the time was activist and uncompromising about naming material injustice.

Sistren's first full-length play, *Bellywoman Bangarang*, negotiated this by moving away from the enduring old stereotypes and placing women's sexed bodies at the center of the narrative, talking about sex and telling the stories of single mothers and daughters from the inside out. The work we created emerged from what the performers wanted to address, but it also began to talk back to the old inaccurate representations of the strong black woman that now seemed pejorative. The plays of the 1970s—*Bellywoman Bangarang, Bandoolu Version,* and *Domestic*, directed by me; *Nana Yah*, directed by Jean Small; and *QPH*, directed by Hertencer Lindsay—proceeded to demonstrate the inaccuracy of this representation, telling another story of women's experience. In Wynter's terms, the performances drew on embodied knowledge from the margins to reframe and challenge the dominant, colonial representations.

Bellywoman is a coming-of-age story of four working-class girls questioning what it means to inherit the identity of the women around them. In 1978, it was controversial precisely because it tackled questions of identity formation, the female body, and sex. It did not romanticize the poverty of the rural and urban working class, and it critiqued the social acceptance of male sexual violence. It showed women on stage laboring, exploring their developing bodies, discussing the emergence of their own sexuality, and holding the world around them accountable for their limited choices. It mocked the tropes of masculinity in cross-dressing. The play demonstrated the vulnerability of women as they attempted to raise their families while negotiating impossible conditions of employment, sexual violence, and other issues. *Bellywoman* also symbolically staged a much-discussed scene of rape by three men in stocking masks—two holding down a girl while the third aims blows between her legs. The scene, choreographed by Pam Reid, portrayed rape as an act of corrective violence aimed at punishing a young woman for her refusal of a young man's advances.

Bellywoman avoided the prevailing tendency to pathologize single mothers and blame them for social problems, drawing attention to how women themselves resisted the conditions that constrained them. The lead character, Didi, is a young girl who desires to emerge from crippling domestic responsibility and limited freedom. This leads her to run away to the city and to a boyfriend and pregnancy. Her story is supplemented by others that demonstrate the denigration of women's public and private labor and sexuality and contrasts these with a nurses' strike for better conditions in the public sphere. At the end of the play, the character Gloria confronts her baby's father, calling for public responsibility for children. She says, "Is not mi one mek dis big belly. It no just come so. It tek work and a whole heap more work haffi do before dis pickney can have a healthy life. And is not mi one gwine do it. Widdout no mi no get some good argument from yuh, mi nah move from here tonight."[9]

Similarly, in the concluding scene of the play, when the women have birthed their own children together by themselves during the nurses' strike, Didi holds out the body of her child to the audience and speaks directly to them: "Is like all di experience dat me pass through, is dem bring mi come. Is dem is mi madda. Now my child is born, Him come off a my navel string but him belongs to all a we. And fi him labour just begin."[10]

The play was devised by refusing existing representations and searching for new ones through the embodied collective life autobiographies of the women of Sistren. These were then contained and contextualized through existing vernacular repertoires introduced by me as the director. *Bellywoman* was structured through traditional Caribbean ring games. These games, which typically involve a circle, action in the middle, and sung choruses, became metaphorical structures within which the scenes from the life histories play out. Members of the group enacted scenes from their life histories for each other in overlapping and competing versions. The ring game was elaborated to symbolize a social obstacle (such as inaccessible education or church authority) that had to be confronted for the young woman to achieve her identity and escape social entrapment. The actors' memories were provoked in song, and they took turns acting out layered interpretations of the original memories. These proposals were recorded and inventoried, and a formal scenic structure was put together by me as director; I also functioned as scribe. A drum score was created by Mackie Burnett and Joy Erskine. Acting strategies left room for improvisation in early performances and depended on role shifts in storytelling, mime, male impersonations, and cross-dressing, as well as sparse use of props and minimal costumes.

In the full version of this article, I argue that cultural work of the 1970s can be read through the theories of Wynter and Nettleford, which I propose offer key methodological principles for future work on performance, decolonization, and the body. Here, I have given an example of how Sistren's work can be read, in reflection, as an example of how this might work in praxis. I hope that this enables a number of claims. The first of these is that there is a profound reason why the embodied performance of humans existing at the margins can be both powerful and productive. Embodied knowledge from the margins of societies of the African diaspora make it possible to challenge dominant representations of experience and envision new forms of human identity and relationships in community. That this contribution emerged in the radical opening of the 1970s in the Caribbean is important, but what is more important is that it does not have to stay there. Perhaps such a method can transcend linear time, and embodied responses to dominant representations can form the basis of inspiring critique in the present. Second, the interventions of the 1970s do not have to be absolute ruptures to enable a path toward a future that realizes the full meaning of emancipation. The imperfect and incomplete radical opening enacted by the Michael Manley government between 1972 and 1980 provided the material and institutional space for embodied decolonial cultural critique, such as that undertaken collectively by the Sistren Theatre Collective and others, to take place. But even when Sistren and other groups faced aggressive censorship, as we did in the first years of the 1980s, and were forced to separate from national institutions, the temporary opening of the 1970s left a legacy that can enable ongoing decolonial cultural work, and inspire possibilities. Telling the stories of what happened back then can be important for empowering new struggles, since struggle cannot take place without drawing on older repertoires of social justice.

Finally, discussing Sistren as a black, feminist, decolonial act is only one example of how a broader method of embodied decolonizing pedagogy opens up many possibilities for future cultural work and has implications for other areas of embodiment. Food, land, sexuality, and sport are the areas that most easily come to mind because they sustain the body and the landscape in which they dwell. How might working from embodied responses to colonial representations of food production and consumption lead to new forms of knowledge? Many questions remain to be answered. What are the pitfalls of embodied knowledge productions when investigated in different contexts? How might such methods avoid an aestheticization of the political that resists dialogical interrogation? Can such a method be transferred across borders to differently raced and gendered bodies in a variety of material contexts? Can it be transferred across spaces and places in which power is configured differently? What happens when this approach is placed outside the context of social movements and struggles for transformation? Do they not depend on prevailing representations even in their opposition? Is such a method ever immune from being domesticated by dominant ideologies and the operations of hegemony? Nettleford never transferred this research enterprise to the University of the West Indies. Could this have to do with the way the body is treated within the epistemologies that the academy reproduced at the time?

"A world ends," García Canclini tells us, "not only when the answers have to be archived but also when the questions that gave rise to them lose their meaning."[11] Perhaps this path of work with the body and its active memories, allusions, and actions can be one way to pose some of the new questions that can lead to the archiving of old colonial questions and the opening up of new ways of being and knowing.

Notes

1. Initially, Sistren worked only in theater and drama, rehearsing and taking special classes at the Jamaica School of Drama, which supported it and many other groups at the time. By 1981, the collective had produced a body of plays performed for broad audiences at venues such as the Barn Theatre, which was at the center of developments in theater. Supported by a growing feminist movement, black women and women of color in diaspora, and women of the global South, Sistren was able to survive and expand, going on to produce more plays, a book of life histories, a small magazine, a collection of screen prints, two films (that survive), research into the history of women's struggles in Jamaica, and a program of popular education. It toured extensively nationally, regionally, and internationally and had an impact far beyond its size. The work privileged the histories and stories of black working-class

women. Gender as a theoretical framework for analysis was just coming into being, and Sistren's work—with its emphasis on cultural work, class, and gender—like some of the other women's organizations in the region, anticipated debates around intersectionality of oppressions, though this term is usually mapped out through discussions of work in North America.

2. Among the many discussions of Sistren's work are Kanika Batra, *Feminist Visions and Queer Futures in Postcolonial Drama: Community, Kinship, and Citizenship* (New York: Routlege 2011); Nicosia Shakes, "Gender, Race, and Performance Space: Women's Activism in Jamaican and South African Theatre" (PhD diss., Brown University, 2017); Honor Ford-Smith, "Ring Ding in a Tight Corner: Sistren, Collective Democracy, and the Organization of Cultural Production," in *Feminist Genealogies, Colonial Legacies, Democratic Futures*, ed. M. Jaqui Alexander and Chandra Mohanty (New York: Routledge 1997), 213–58; and Karina Smith, "Demystifying Reality in Sistren's *Bellywoman Bangarang*," *Kunapipi* 26, no. 1 (2004): 66–77, ro.uow.edu.au/kunapipi/vol26/iss1/8.

3. For a more complete discussion of this process see Rex Nettleford, *Caribbean Cultural Identity—the case of Jamaica: An essay in Cultural Dynamics* (Kingston: Institute of Jamaica, 1978).

4. Maria Di Genzo and Susan Bennett, "Women, Popular Theatre, and Social Action: Interviews with Cynthia Grant and the Sistren Theatre Collective," *Ariel* 23, no. 1 (1992): 84.

5. M.G. Smith, "The Plural Framework of Jamaican Society," *British Journal of Sociology* 12, no. 3 (1961): 249–62, doi:10 .2307/587818.

6. Joan French, "Colonial Policy toward Women after the 1938 Uprising: The Case of Jamaica," *Caribbean Quarterly* 34, nos. 3–4 (1988): 38–61.

7. Louise Bennett, *Selected Poems* (Kingston: Sangsters Book Stores, 1982).

8. Louise Bennett, interview by the author, Toronto, 2004. *Tek kin teet kibba heart bun*, which translates literally as "Take laughter to cover a burning heart," is the Jamaican equivalent of "Laughter is the best medicine."

9. Sistren Theatre Collective, "Bellywoman Bangarang," in *Contemporary Drama of the Caribbean*, Erika J. Waters and David Edgecombe, eds. (St Croix: University of the Virgin Islands, 2001), 126.

10. Ibid., 129–30.

11. García Canclini and David Frye, *Art beyond Itself: Anthropology for a Society without a Story Line* (Durham, NC: Duke University Press, 2014), 12.

Researching Gender

9. Women in the Caribbean Project: An Overview*

Joycelin Massiah

Like women researchers in many regions of the world, WICP researchers were faced with the situation that knowledge of women's experiences in their region has been filtered through studies and methodological tools designed, conducted and interpreted by males. Personal experience and knowledge of their communities persuaded the group that a more accurate picture could be obtained by addressing issues other than the structure and function of family groupings. The major objective of the project was therefore to identify the subjective meaning of the social realities which women face, the way these realities are manifested and the consequences at the individual, community and societal level. We wished to identify the gaps in our knowledge about women's activities, to try to fill these gaps and to identify areas for further research.

The second major objective of the study was to devise a theoretical framework which would integrate the analysis of women's roles as they are affected by processes of social change. Closely related issues included a critical reassessment of concepts such as role, status, family, household, head of household, and work. This objective implied a recognition of the need to examine these issues from the perspective of a variety of disciplines, and in different ecological settings and further, to devise appropriate methodologies which would more adequately reflect how these concepts are operationalized in the daily lives of women. Additionally, the rapidly changing socio-economic environment in the region suggested that the project needed to examine the extent to which these changes affect and are affected by women.

---

* Reprinted with permission from *Social and Economic Studies* 35, no. 2 (June 1986): 1–29.

The third objective related to the stated need of policymakers and Women in Development practitioners in the region for data and/or the research skills necessary to generate data relevant to policymaking for women. The project aimed to use the data collected, to develop guidelines for defining and elaborating a cohesive social policy directed towards women, which could be readily adapted for inclusion in the development programmes of government and non-government organisations.

A fourth objective is related to the identification of appropriate mechanisms for the dissemination of research results and for incorporating those results into ongoing development programmes. The research group felt strongly, that too often, research results remained unread in sophisticated and learned journals or in confidential government files. This luxury, the group felt, could not be afforded in the context of the condition of women.

The final objective of the study was to produce a cadre of women who would be adequately equipped with the necessary research skills to conduct good research in general and good female-centred research in particular; who would have developed a level of professional self-confidence which would permit them to develop their full creative potential and engage in more meaningful participation in their national life, and who would therefore be a powerful resource group on whom the region could rely for future work of this kind.

In summary, the project was conceived as an exploratory attempt to identify the broad spectrum of issues confronting women, as these were defined by women themselves and to utilise the insights gained in the process to help to develop skills, policies and programmes which could impact on the quality of thought and action devoted to the welfare and development of women in the region.

BACKGROUND TO THE PROJECT

The WICP was envisioned at a time of growing expressions of concern by governments and international agencies about the situation of women in the region. Impetus for this concern was given by the declaration of the UN Decade for Women in 1975 and with the call for more female-centred research and data collection.

In the Caribbean, government and non-government organisations looked to the UWI to provide the data which, hopefully, could take some of the guesswork out of policy making, programming, planning and implementation. But within the UWI, data of the kind required were not available. Further, the available methodological and analytical tools appeared to be inappropriate for an adequate understanding of the social and economic experiences of women. On the methodological side, it seemed that purely quantitative techniques provided, at best, only very broad (and rough) indicators of the context in which women were functioning but said little about how, why, when, or even, if they were functioning at all. By contrast, purely qualitative techniques tended to focus at the macro-level on a specific community, often with only broad (or rough) indications of how this relates to the wider society.

On the analytical side, it is evident that social science research in the region has proceeded based on movement from one theoretical model to another, all offering explanations/interpretations at the macro-level, but none of them being particularly suited to explaining gender relations within the region. Thus, *cultural pluralism* - drawing on anthropological techniques as elaborated by its main protagonists - draws attention to the importance of ethnic differentiation and its implications for defining social and political structures in the Caribbean. The *plantation model* of Caribbean society - essentially an economic model - draws parallels between the plantation as a social system and contemporary economic organisation as an explanation for the inability of Caribbean economies to achieve their full capacity. A related model, the *dependency model* - also an economic model - notes that the relationships between developed and underdeveloped countries serve mainly to widen the gap between the two and to increase the dependency of the latter on the former. The other model which attempts to explain Caribbean societies – the *Marxist-Leninist* model - stresses the need for the type of social change which involves realignment of class structure and the replacement of private by state enterprise.

In an illuminating article, Greene (1984) has shown how these various models emerged at specific points in the history of the region and how each was unable to respond to important theoretical issues. This inability, he argues, presaged a shift from theorising to what he calls "middle range" analysis characterised by a concern with testing hypotheses and quantitative verification. Political and economic events at that time had the effect of further shifting the thrust of research from middle-range to micro-level studies which, in turn, was associated with a shift in methodologies from the quantitative sample survey method to the qualitative anthropological method (Green 1984).

More recently, the theoretical concern has focussed on issues of regionalism and ideological pluralism, issues which have not really been formulated in the manner of a model, but which have certainly occupied a central place in the utterances and writings of key regional personnel. Once again, it has been political and economic realities in the region which have forced academics to redefine their parameters.

In all this ferment, the issue of the determinants and nature of gender relations in the region received scant attention. Most of the available knowledge on the subject comes from the anthropological studies of the institutions of kinship and the family undertaken in the 1950s and early 1960s and of socio-demographic studies of patterns of mating and fertility. However, once again, the approach is holistic. Thus, a considerable literature attests to the variety of forms of family union, the relationship of different family types to levels of fertility, the movement between different family forms, but very little is known about the nature of the relationship between the women and men in these family types. We have some knowledge of differential formal and informal socialisation of male and female children. We have some knowledge of the economic role of women, garnered mainly from those early family studies, but also from demographic and labour force studies which highlight women engaged in wage employment.

But, most of this information relates to the structural roles performed by men and women with only hints of the interactions between the sexes and mutual perceptions of each other. For the latter, we must turn to the folk culture – mainly calypsoes - to the novels, poetry, and short stories, to drama, dance, painting, and sculpture. And here, we begin to see changes, e.g., whereas male calypsonians of the 50s and 60s viewed women as devious, manipulative, promiscuous, spendthrifts, now female calypsonians are advising women 'to put some wheels on your heels'.

The response within ISER has been to focus on applied research within a multi-disciplinary framework. This research strategy is guided by four main considerations.

i. the small size and limited resources of the region require that traditional concepts and methodologies be modified, amended or even, abandoned in order to be relevant;

ii. the artificial distinction between qualitative and quantitative data gathering techniques should be discarded in favour of a technique which seeks to blend the two;

iii. comparative analysis - both spatially and temporally should be integral to the methodological designs;

iv. collaboration between researcher and practitioner should be included at every stage of a project.

WICP was therefore conceived in the context of a research agenda which was seeking an appropriate theoretical paradigm for the analysis of Caribbean realities, while at the same time seeking appropriate methodological tools. It was concerned with contributing to this search by focusing on the issue of gender relations.

1. CONCEPTUALISING THE WICP

Intrinsic to the exploratory and innovative nature of the project were the conceptual issues associated with the design of the fieldwork programme. From the outset, a decision was taken to focus the study on 'role', which we believed to portray more effectively the multidimensional character of women's lives, than the more static concept 'status'.[1] The team expressed dissatisfaction with the latter on several grounds. Initially, there was a concern with identifying the determinants of sexual status and secondly, there was a concern with the inability to devise appropriate measures which relate an increase or decrease in 'status' to corresponding increases or decreases in specific areas e.g. employment or fertility. Related to the latter, was the difficulty, if not impossibility, of devising a single index of women's status.[2] In the discussions around these methodological problems, the team eventually agreed that the inability to devise a single index of women's stat us may be attributable to the multiplicity of roles they perform, the differential statuses ascribed to those various roles by the society and the differential statuses which the women themselves may have achieved in respect of their various roles.

Attention then focussed on the complementary concept of role and its associated components – role performance, role relationships, role expectations, role conflict, role strain. The major advantage of this approach was that it permitted the use of the individual as the unit of study. It became possible to place the individual woman in the context not only of a specific structure (household, community, society) but also of a specific and varying set of relationships, e.g., with household members, kin, co-workers, etc. It became possible to document the behaviour expected of women: how they behave, what difficulties they encountered, what strategies they adopted in conforming to the expected patterns of behaviour, what sanctions were encountered by failure to conform, what rewards were achieved by conforming. Further, this could be done for different groups of women at different stages in their lifecycles and thus, at different stages in the historical development of their societies. In short, the application of the concepts of role theory permitted us to address the important issue of changes over time.

i. Qualitative vs. Quantitative Data

From the earliest discussions, there was an expressed need to review available data, however inadequate, in order to place women's issues in specific historical and developmental contexts. This was particularly important in a region where slavery, colonialism and political independence have been crucial in shaping the conditions within which both women and men of the region strive. It was felt that the project ought to provide some understanding of the inter-connections between the economic, the social, the political, and the ideological spheres in order to assess their impact on transforming women's roles. Such interconnections could not be made solely on the basis of the available documentary data.

Accordingly, the study was designed in two phases consisting of a general documentary study at the regional level and a series of micro-studies at the national level.[3] These phases were conceived separately for heuristic purposes but a distinction between the two was not too sharply drawn, since in many respects the activities of the two phases were mutually dependent. The linkage between the two phases was provided in two ways.

> **b. Multi-level Interviewing**: Interviewing was designed to proceed at three levels of specificity: a national study, life histories and sector studies. At the first level of interviews, the aim was to obtain good, descriptive, quantitative data at the national level which would provide indicators of the socio-economic context within which women functioned. Additional aims were to provide standardised data for comparison between project territories and to identify specific problems requiring further analysis at the micro-level. This round of interviewing was envisaged for three territories selected as illustrative of different stages of the development continuum. Using criteria derived from an examination of quantitative socio-economic indicators, literature reviews, survey material and prevailing circumstances, the territories finally selected were Barbados, Antigua and St. Vincent.[4] It was agreed that a study concerned with the CARICOM region could neither be focused on a single territory nor could it be expected to cover the entire region. Restriction to a single territory would mask inter-territorial differentials crucial to a proper understanding of the issues under review. Detailed study of two territories stood in danger of representing two extremes while concealing important variations between the two.
>
> The approach adopted seemed an attainable ideal as it could permit the inclusion of non-campus territories which do not have the research capacity to inform their decision-making and allow them to benefit from access to a valuable source of data. The decision also reflects the team's concern to present findings indicative of the considerable heterogeneity prevailing in the region.
>
> The second level of interviews was directed to small numbers of women from the original sample who fit certain pre-selected criteria, determined by reference to the relevant literatures, who were willing to be re-interviewed and whose original interview suggested that more detailed interviewing would be worthwhile. To these women, life history techniques were applied using data from the quantitative survey to initiate and guide the interview.

These two levels of interviews yielded indications of particular issues and particular groups of women which seemed to merit attention of a more specific and focused character. A third level of interviews was therefore developed around each of these issues/groups with individual researchers being responsible for devising appropriate data gathering techniques. The issues/groups were investigated in several territories and included rural women in Guyana, unemployed women in Barbados, elderly women and their men in Jamaica, women in public life in the Eastern Caribbean, women's networks in Jamaica and men in Barbados.[5]

The particular mix of interviewing techniques was selected to achieve four basic aims:

- to provide a household and community context for the women;
- to achieve the richness of anthropological data without the excessive cost in terms of time;
- to achieve a better understanding of how macro and micro factors interact to affect women's lives;
- to allow a comparative analysis of how differing patterns of socio-economic change impact on women at different stages of their lifecycle in different classes and in different territories of the region.

c. **Thematic Frame of Reference**: The second technique for linking the quantitative and qualitative data was the development of three themes which were to be used, together or separately, as the framework for the data collection and analyses. A review of available material suggests a tendency for women's issues to be studied with reference to a specific institution. However, such an approach tends to mask the linkages between the operation of these various institutions within the lives of individual women.

In much of the literature on Caribbean family systems, for example, much emphasis is given to such issues as the sextyped socialisation of children and young adults, ambiguous male/female relationships, the economic and psychological dependence of women on men, the double standard of morality and, as mentioned earlier, differential family forms and associated levels of fertility. However, few writers attempt to deal with roles women perform beyond the mother, domestic and economic role. Thus, there is little attempt to see how the institutions of law, education, politics, religion, interact with each other to affect and be affected by the institution of the family. Yet, there is an understanding that the effect of their interaction impacts heavily on women. As early as 1957, the eminent Caribbean sociologist, Lloyd Braithwaite had indicated the need for such research: "…in the situation as it exists in the West Indies a heavy burden is placed upon the women, a heavier burden than most people think reasonable and desirable. But for a proper assessment of the situation mere expressed evaluations are not enough." (Braithwaite 1957).

The WICP group therefore devised these three themes:

b. *Sources of Livelihood* which relates to access to social rewards, goods, services, and knowledge and to the institutional options and choices open to female members of society (Durant-Gonzalez 1980). The concern here is to highlight the fact that livelihood for these women refers not merely to income derived from employment, but also to income, in cash or kind, derived from the manipulation of a range of options whether intra or extra domestic. It reflects an understanding that the fragility of Caribbean economies and the precariousness of employment, forces women (and men as well) to seek sources of livelihood other than, or in addition to, conventionally prescribed sources;

c. *Emotional support* which derives from kinship and friendship ties, work situations and participation in formal and informal associations. The concern here is to demonstrate the wide range of systems from which women garner emotional support in order to carry out their responsibilities to self and others;

d. *Power and Authority* which relates to control over social rewards in political and non-political spheres. The concern here is with an examination of the woman's capacity to control events in her life, and to resist control by others.

These three themes or forces were seen as fostering or inhibiting women in carrying out their responsibilities to themselves and others. It was felt that such an approach would lend itself to a more realistic understanding of the lives of women than the compartmentalized approaches of the past have allowed.

ii. Issues of Change

Essentially, this implied a need to provide a historical context to the analysis. This perspective was included in the project in two ways. First, documentary sources were used to provide historical trends in a number of critical areas. This coincided with Phase I of the project which produced material describing the changing position of women in the law, the family, education, politics, work, and development as well as changing perceptions of women.[6] Secondly, data from the first level interviews were analysed in terms of age cohorts and supplemented by appropriate selections of qualitative data gained from the second and third level interviews. When combined with data from retrospective questions, this technique provided a cross-sectional view of a woman's life over a period.

The two approaches were not of course, mutually exclusive. The first level of interviews focussed on women aged 20-64 in 1980, i.e., women who were born between the years 1916 and 1960. By linking their lifecycle experiences to historical changes occurring from 1916 onward, it became possible to situate the women's actual experiences in the appropriate historical context.

iii. Issues of Class

The major concern of the WICP team was to avoid the pitfall of indiscriminately transporting class formulations appropriate to Western European-type societies to a region which is so culturally differentiated. For, in addition to the usual indicators such as income, occupation, education, style of life and heredity, there are additional criteria such as race, ethnicity and colour to be considered (Braithwaite 1957). Several studies have highlighted the difficulties of describing and understanding the multidimensional bases of the social status system prevailing within the region (Smith 1970; Foner 1973; Graham and Gordon 1977). But few of the available studies look specifically at the operation of the class system from the perspective of women.

The WICP concern with issues of class related to three major areas. These were:
  a. the analysis of the origin and operation of the existing class system;
  b. the analysis of how this system impinges on women;
  c. the derivation of indices which would permit the identification of women in different classes.

The study chose to proceed with the latter problem first. The particular procedure chosen was to stratify census enumeration districts into rural and urban districts based on observation of the areas, discussions with the local technical personnel and discussions with local interviewers.[7] Appropriate numbers of enumeration districts were selected from each group, rural and urban, and from these enumeration districts were selected household clusters according to the rural/urban ratio and the population obtaining at the relevant census. This approach provided an initial 'class' division into urban and rural, insofar as residential location may be taken as a valid indicator of social status. A subdivision of urban into lower income, lower-middle and middle-upper income came about with hardly any specific effort on our part to do so, mainly because of the small size of the populations with which we were dealing.

In two project territories, provisions were made to include special interest groups. In Antigua, a particular area was included to accommodate the Syrian/Lebanese community which is locally regarded as a critical component of the middle-upper income group. In St. Vincent, three depressed areas were included to reflect the Black Carib Community in the north east of the island, the 'poor white' community in the Dorsetshire Hills in the South of the island, and the 'East Indians' in Richland Park on the east of the island.

At the individual level, general indicators of the class of respondent were further provided by supplementary data on social amenities in the community of which the survey cluster was a part, by the amenities within the respondent's household and by using the education and job characteristics of the respondent. It was proposed to use these indicators to derive a system of socio-economic groupings which can be used as variables in subsequent analyses.

In the latter regard, preliminary experiments suggest that the level of education, if not the most useful single indicator of status differences between women is certainly the simplest to manipulate.

iv. Unit of Analysis

The major issue here centred on whether the household, the family or the individual should be the conceptual and methodological unit of analysis.

Discussions on using the household as the unit of analysis centred around the available Caribbean literature on the subject and pointed to the frequently cited assertion that the household is not a single bounded unit but is linked to other units by ties of kinship and marriage and by exchanges between core residential groups. Interaction between such groups can only be understood after study of the activities of individuals within the groups. The decision was therefore taken to adopt the individual woman as the basic unit of study, but in order to place that individual within a residential context, minimal information on household composition should be collected. The method of selection of the women is described by Durant-Gonzalez [Part I].

A study concerned with the role of women cannot divorce itself from consideration of the role of men. Experience of the researchers in other work suggested practical problems in ensuring participation, spontaneity and reliability in responses culled from partners even where interviews were conducted separately. Experience from the pilot study suggested that some men were unwilling to be interviewed; some were even antagonistic. On the other hand, some men encouraged their womenfolk to participate and some even requested to be interviewed. Among the women respondents, there was considerable reluctance to encourage the idea of an interview if the partner was present. The decision was taken therefore to interview separate samples of men and women. The results of the male survey are discussed in Barrow [Part II].

v. Type of Information

The generalist bias of the project objectives suggested that a wide range of information should be collected and that, at least in the initial stages, no efforts should be made to establish and test hypotheses.

Initially, there was a need to be able to develop a socio-economic profile of respondents and to locate them in their appropriate household contexts.

In the area of education, we needed a history of their education and training experience; an assessment of that experience in the light of their current situation and their occupational aspirations when they left school; their education preferences for their children (boys and girls, separately). Information of this nature could conceivably assist educational planners in their current search for programmes which are 'more relevant' to the needs of the region. From the perspectives of the themes, such information could provide some insight into the extent to which women perceive that their education and training provided, or did not provide, access to particular opportunities for obtaining some form of livelihood; also, whether their investment in the education of their children could be construed as a particular form of source of livelihood in that it could be assumed to produce some tangible reward in the future. These issues are discussed by McKenzie [Part II].

In the area of family and kin, the group felt that the trends and patterns of pregnancy, family planning, union and partner history were sufficiently well known not to be repeated (Roberts 1978; Roberts and Sinclair 1978; World Fertility Survey 1978 and 1979). The present context seemed to require only general information on these matters but more specific information on women's attitudes to child bearing, their expectations from their present union, their preferences for one or other type of union, their attitude towards men. This section addressed the project themes in several ways. Emotional support was tapped from responses on attitudes to children, child rearing and current male partner; responses about men in general revealed perceptions of men as sources of livelihood as well as perceptions of male/female power and authority within the context of male/female relationships. It was hoped that Women and Development practitioners could use this kind of information in devising programmes aimed at assisting women to function more effectively in their family unions. Various aspects of these issues are discussed in Powell, Barrow, Odie-Ali [Part 1] and Brodber [Part II].

Our main consideration in the context of work was to identify women's perceptions of what constitutes work, to describe that work and the problems women encounter in doing that work; to identify specific skills which women possess and the extent to which they are utilised. This we felt could assist regional statisticians in their quest for appropriate definitions of employment and unemployment. Having identified women's perceptions of work, the next step was to examine, through participant observation, the difference between perceptions and reality, then to apply that reality to the question of appropriate definitions of work, employment and unemployment. Data from this section could assist WID practitioners to develop incomegenerating programmes based on the existing skills of women. These issues are discussed by Massiah [Part I].

This section was also concerned with main sources of income to the women, spending and saving patterns, ownership, child care arrangements, sharing of household tasks and decision-making in the household. These data provided knowledge of how different groups of women manage their households. Data of this kind could inform programme developers of the additional factors which need to be addressed when devising programmes for women. This section addressed the theme of sources of livelihood specifically in terms of sources of income; emotional support derived from satisfaction with job or own business venture; and property ownership; power and authority from management of own business, management of household expenditure and participation in household decision-making. These issues are variously discussed by Massiah, Powell, Barrow and Odie-Ali [Part I].

Our final area of interest was women's participation in group activity, the extent to which the groups to which they belong are involved in programmes centering on women, the extent to which leisure activities are shared with partners and women's assessment of the general situation of women in their country. Data of this nature, we felt, could be particularly useful to women's groups and to national machinery. In fact, the major finding that women tend not to join organisations has considerable implications for the programmes of these organisations [Clarke Part II]

This section addressed the theme of power and authority as it derives from the leadership training potential implied by membership of formal organisations; the theme of emotional support is also addressed as it relates to satisfaction derived from group solidarity, from other recreational activities and from perceptions of the current position of women. These issues are discussed by Roberta Clarke [Part II].

vi. Time Use

The team was ethically opposed to the standard techniques of time-use surveys which makes extraordinary demands on the time and privacy of the respondents. Such techniques assume that respondents have endless spare time to devote to the data gathering activities of researchers while at the same time saying that women's time is heavily burdened. Eventually, the team opted for a one-shot operation based on the interviewers' ability to obtain reasonable responses and their ability to record an assessment of the reliability of the responses. The objectives in this regard were threefold:

- to judge whether the technique was possible and/or useful in the region;
- to gain some notion of women's allocation of their time;
- to use the results as a basis for understanding how women define work.

We asked the women to detail all their activities sequentially and the time spent on each during the 24 hours preceding the interview; to identify activities which were not done yesterday but which are usually done and to give an indication of the intensity of these activities. Because of the length of the interview, we did not feel justified in pursuing in depth, such details as whether the activity was primary or secondary, which tasks were assisted by whom and in whose presence.

Our next question, 'Which of these activities would you describe as work?' was, for us, the main purpose of the time-use data.

The entire experiment was supplemented by interviewers' observations and recording of their impressions of the reliability of the data, by similar inputs from project researchers on the second round of interviews and in one particular sector study, that of unemployed women, where participant observations were used to match data given in the first round of interviews. Results of this experiment are discussed in Massiah, Barrow, Odie-Ali [Part I] and Clarke and Cummins (1982).

2. ORGANISING THE PROJECT

The issue of devising suitable research techniques related not only to questions of sampling, data collection and data analysis but also to the larger question of how the project should be administratively organised. The major administrative task was to create an atmosphere which would keep the commitment and the interests of the group alive for the duration of the project and to continually devise ways of ensuring a constant flow of their creative energy. At the same time, it was necessary to maintain effective control of a group which was geographically scattered, and variegated in training, disciplinary attachment, level of skills and experience.

i. Interdisciplinary Approach: From the outset it was agreed that the study should be interdisciplinary. At the beginning of the project we saw ourselves as a group of multidisciplinary researchers with training and experience in a range of disciplines which included sociology, anthropology, demography, Caribbean literature, and political science. Our hope was to develop how to change that group into an interdisciplinary one by the end of the project. The achievement of this objective was viewed as an ongoing process starting from the initial design and ending with the production of the final report. To effect this process, team members were expected to regard themselves as participating in a joint effort for which all were equally responsible. This philosophical approach set the stage, so to speak, for handling the many difficulties which the project encountered.

To build self confidence, specific efforts were made to ensure that researchers became exposed to similar work being conducted outside the region. All invitations to attend international meetings were accepted. These meetings served several purposes: they afforded an opportunity for project researchers to establish contact with colleagues outside the region and to promote the existence of the project and its conduct by nationals; they served to reduce the sense of isolation and uncertainty which existed in the early stages of the project and they provided an opportunity for personnel attending those meetings to prepare background papers for use by project staff (Durant-Gonzalez 1980, 1981; Massiah 1980a, 1980b, 1980c, 1982). The meetings also served to make available to the project, advice and support from persons working on similar projects in other regions of the world to whom project members would not normally have access.

The project itself hosted a planning workshop in September 1979, which was intended to design an agenda of work for Phase I, to formulate the methodologies for its execution and to prepare a programme for disseminating the results of the project. Workshop participants included the core group of WICP researchers, members of the UWI teaching staff, personnel from national and regional agencies involved with women's programmes and US-based researchers with experience of the Caribbean. This workshop marked the first attempt by the project to introduce intensive interdisciplinary activity involving both project and non-project personnel into the project (ISER 1979). The dynamic interchange experienced at that workshop was viewed as a critical starting point of the WICP interdisciplinary process.

Built into the WICP were a variety of techniques intended to maintain that dynamism. Particular emphasis was placed on local participation and the use of regional consultants where necessary. Overall coordination of the project was assigned to the administrative head of the ISER(EC). Tasks were organised on a campus basis at several levels, with each level having responsibility for specific tasks. Campus coordinators were responsible for coordinating the activities of the group of researchers on the relevant campus. This translated into direct supervision of the activities of junior staff, the organising of regular discussion groups and liaison with the regional coordinator. All levels of researchers were expected to be involved in the designing of data collection instruments, data analysis and report writing.

In order to reduce the effect of geographical and communication isolation, the regional coordinator made occasional visits to campus sites; research assistants made data collection visits to individual territories on behalf of the team; individual researchers visited other campus sites whenever possible. To deal with the problem of access to library material, a bibliography was prepared before the project by Massiah et. al. This was supplemented by the issuance of accessions bulletins of material arriving in the ISER(EC) library and by the introduction of a photocopying and book loan service to researchers. To maintain contact with relevant individuals and agencies, newsletters were issued periodically, and frequent personal contact was maintained with regional agencies, e.g., CARICOM Secretariat, Women and Development Unit (WAND), the Caribbean Women's Association (CARIWA) and with national machinery operating in project territories.

ii. Vehicle of Training: Training here was conceived as informal 'on-the-job' training of researchers by researchers and reflected a concern with sharing a learning experience at various levels. It involved participation of all members of the group in every stage of the project: learning about group dynamics, about leadership, about delegation of authority, about responsibility, about new and different approaches to an issue; in sum, about working together as a team. The various techniques employed were in tended to develop an ongoing process of interaction to overcome differences in personality, interests and disciplinary outlook and to build that commonality of interest necessary for the successful completion of the project.

iii. Multi-Media Dissemination: In keeping with its wish to sensitise as wide a public as possible, the project developed a comprehensive multimedia dissemination programme aimed at directing different aspects of the findings to different audiences. Extensive discussions both within and outside the UWI resulted in the implementation of the following programme:

1. National Workshops: These were intended for the territories in which fieldwork had been conducted and were directed at key technicians and relevant government departments. The aim was to present the findings and expose government personnel to a cadre of local women who now have experience in fieldwork with women on WID issues and together, to derive recommendations and suggestions for their implementation within ongoing development programmes.

2. Community Level Workshops: These workshops were intended to present the project findings to the women who were respondents. An illustrated brochure highlighting the basic findings and identifying reference persons/organisations in the territory was distributed.

3. Regional Conference: This was intended to bring policymakers, administrators of women's programmes and researchers together to assess the project, discuss its findings and identify ways of implementing recommended programmes and to advise on further activity. For the benefit of the academic community, a selection of those technical papers is presented in the present volume. Other

technical papers will be published in appropriate scholarly journals. Proceedings of the conference have already appeared in a more informal publication.

4. General Reader: This will be an illustrated general reader prepared in simple, readily understood language on the basis of the conference papers. Appropriate abstracts will be serialised in regional newspapers.

5. Video-Tape Recording: This concentrates on women's work in the region, focusing particularly on women in non-traditional job situations. This recording was shown at the conference.

6. Synchro-Slide Production: This focuses on the major findings of the project and is intended as a teaching guide particularly for groups interested in developing their own research. Copies have been distributed to national machinery throughout the region.

7. Papers from Phase I: These include a seven-volume series of papers based on available documentary data, a compilation of relevant statistical material and an annotated bibliography.

The particular structure of the dissemination programme arose because of a need to make the findings known to both academic and non-academic audiences and to do so in a language and format which would be most readily understood and acted upon. Underlying this was the concern to give back to the communities and respondents something of the achievements of the project. In this context, the national- and community-level workshops were a particularly useful vehicle for influencing and stimulating thought on a wide range of issues affecting women.

3. REFLECTIONS ON THE CONDUCT OF THE PROJECT

The WICP was a unique experience in regional, multidisciplinary research. The successful completion of comparable surveys in three territories, thirty-eight life histories in three territories and six sector studies in eight territories is in itself an achievement. To have done so within the time constraints set by contract agreements is even more remarkable. It is not common for surveys of this kind to be terminated without publication of results, casualties of the infelicities of both people and machines. That the WICP did not fall victim to such caprice is directly attributable to the tremendous team spirit which existed among the researchers and their determination to make a success of a project for which they bore the final responsibility. Within a very short time, the research team was moulded into a group whose enthusiasm, dedication, level of commitment and capacity for sheer hard work was unsurpassed.

The experience of planning and executing an undertaking such as WICP indicates that multi-territory surveys in the Caribbean are feasible and useful. However, a project of this size and nature encounters many problems only some of which can be anticipated. While particular care was taken to introduce a certain degree of flexibility, definitive limits were placed on this flexibility by the project's objectives and the particular constraints within which it was operating. Constraints were varied in nature, e.g. in the area of personnel. Crucial skills were either unavailable to the project or available only on a consultancy basis. We felt that the project needed a full-time economist for the entire project; a data-processing specialist, part-time initially, and full-time from some point during the fieldwork; a full-time media specialist for the final year; a historian and a social psychologist on a part-time basis throughout the project. In general, alternative arrangements were introduced to compensate for one or other deficiency, but none of the alternatives really approached the ideal we would have wished.

In the area of training, major emphasis was placed on on-the-job training consisting of project meetings, group sessions, individual attention and do-it-yourself activities. The constraints of time prevented the introduction of more formal seminar-type sessions at strategic points, e.g., at the outset of the project immediately before the interviewer training and prior to the report writing. This would have been a powerful addition to the battery of training techniques.

Another type of constraint related to the absence of strong, visible support from male colleagues or from male personnel in relevant government and non-government agencies. In some cases, male colleagues were unaware of the issues and unwilling to be informed. In other cases, though unaware, they were willing to enter into dialogue and even to agree that women's issues could and should constitute a legitimate area of scholarship. In yet other cases, tangible support was evident – in the form of contributed papers, technical advice and consultancy services. But in no case was there a willingness to join the project team. There was therefore some male support but this, while critical in several areas, remained largely invisible. A major disadvantage of this was that the project was perceived as a female segregated one which discouraged male participation. Another constraint, particularly in respect of male government personnel in key positions, was the sense of powerlessness felt by the group as they found themselves incapable of providing the assurance which respondents sought for the alleviation of their several problems. A major advantage was that it forced the group to look inward for the academic and other resources needed to carry the project to a successful conclusion.

An indirect constraint related to the effect of the public relations activities of the project. The central office was overwhelmed with requests from WID practitioners from within and outside the region, for information about the project and for data specific to their own programmes. The volume of these requests seemed to vindicate our original premise that a broad-based, comprehensive research project was urgently required in the region. Accordingly, considerable amounts of time had to be devoted to answering written requests, meeting people, addressing groups and participating in workshops in an effort to comply with the group's objective of bridging the gap between researchers and practitioners.

A specific word needs to be said about the role of the Project Coordinator. In an integrated, interdisciplinary project such as WICP, the important criteria for selecting this person should be competence in her disciplinary specialty, an understanding of women in development issues generally, and experience in survey work. More importantly, such an individual should have "a high degree of multi-disciplinary tolerance", being able to interact with all other disciplines represented in the team. Even where these criteria are satisfied, appropriate administrative ability and experience are critical to the efficient functioning of the joint effort.

Ideally, such a position should be full-time and should be accompanied by an assistant capable of assuming the role of Coordinator, when necessary. In this project, this ideal was not attained. The Coordinator was part-time and was required to function as an administrator without the benefit of an assistant coordinator, and also as a researcher with responsibility for a sector study, as general editor, teacher, counsellor, guide, public relations officer and campus coordinator, in addition to being responsible for the daily administration of the host institute. Even though duties/responsibilities were clearly specified, the sheer volume of work and the available time meant that inordinate demands were made and had to be made on the Coordinator.

Despite these constraints, the WICP has been able to achieve much in the context of its central objective, that of providing an adequate data base, the project has compiled a comprehensive data bank consisting of both quantitative and qualitative data which can provide a sound base on which to develop future research activities and perhaps even a women's studies programme in the two participating universities. In terms of its methodology objective, the project has provided the research community with an integrated package of data collection, data analysis and data dissemination techniques which have particular appeal in a region consisting of small, geographically separated territories with limited resources.

The WICP objective related to the development of policy guidelines was achieved, not only by the production of recommendations based on its findings but also by their presentation in a variety of formats which more readily demonstrate the relation of the findings to key policy issues and programmes. The wealth of data now available negates the claim of planners and policymakers that insufficient data exist on which to base plans or inform decisions. It also provides WID practitioners in the region with ready-made data inputs for their own programmes. Further, the data and their manner of dissemination have served to sensitise public officials to the relevant issues without being didactic or polemical.

An important indication of the extent to which the project achieved its training objective lies in the influence of the project on future activities of project researchers. One senior researcher is currently utilising material from the project as the basis of a Ph.D. dissertation for which she has registered at UWI, Mona. One Research Assistant has completed the graduate programme of the Department of Latin American Studies, University of Florida, on the basis of a study which attempts to fill one of the gaps the project was unable to address. Another went to York University. Another has joined the teaching staff of the University of Guyana as a Lecturer in Social Work, in which programme she has introduced a module on rural women. The project has provided researchers with an unforgettable experience of collaborative group research. It has helped them to develop a high level of female self-consciousness and it has produced a cadre of skilled personnel on whom governments and NGOs can now call. Comments from the evaluation reports reflect the range of benefits which researchers have received from participation in the project.

"...it has strengthened the friendships with colleagues across the. Campuses: this was a source of support to me as a lecturer..."

"...As my first job experience, the need for teamwork was especially heightened."

"...The wealth of knowledge about the rural women of my own country which I have now acquired – knowledge which I previously thought that I had, but which has since been proven false – and with this new knowledge I am better able to empathize with them...."

"...being involved in the training programme and supervision of interviewers...in coordinating fieldwork...has been an invaluable learning experience."

"...I have been strengthened in my conviction that the University can, in the role that it has been designed to perform – scholarship – be 'relevant' in the society."

Among the interviewers, the project has produced a group of local personnel who have become conscious of the position of women in their societies, who have gained skills in data collection in that regard and who are now committed to making a contribution to national life in that area. Their comments on the personal benefits achieved from the project are no less revealing than those of the researchers:

"The fieldwork has given me confidence in myself to do other research off a more complex nature" [Guyana].

"I asked myself questions I have never asked before" [St. Vincent].

"... it provided an insight into the problems encountered by women but which are not often related to other people [Barbados].

"... I have been motivated to continue studies in the area of women and development" [Antigua].

Among the respondents, the project provided an avenue for the expression of many problems and issues about which they had not thought before and which served to sensitise them to the plight of women in the region.

"Many of these questions I never gave thought to. You have really jammed my mind [Antigua].

"They brought back memories. I hope this would come in with something to make things better for women" [Barbados].

"I like to share things with people. It's no use you have ideas and keep them to yourself so I was glad for the opportunity to share my ideas" [St. Vincent].

Finally, among the general community it has served to raise the level of consciousness of women's needs and their problems and the possible solutions to those problems. More importantly, it has served to highlight the many positive and significant contributions which Caribbean women are making to their societies.

It is doubtful whether a single project could realistically be expected to produce more.

References

Anker, R., "Demographic Change and the Role of Women: A Research Programme in Developing Countries" in Anker, R., et al (eds.) *Women's Roles and Population Trends in the Third World*, London: Croom Helm, 1982

Brathwaite, L.E., "Sociology and Demographic Research in the British Caribbean". *SES* 6 (4), December 1957.

Clarke, Roberta, "Women's Organizations, Women's Interests" *SES* 35 (2), June1986.

Clarke, Roberta & Cummins, Diane, *Women in the Caribbean Project – St. Vincent Country Report*. Prepared for St. Vincent Workshop, Kingstown, St. Vincent, July 13, 1982.

Deere, Carmen Diane et al., "Class and Historical Analysis for the Study of Women and Economic Change" in Anker, R. et al (eds.) *Women Roles and Population Trends in the Third World*, London: Croom Helm, 1982.

Deere, Carmen Diane and Leon De Leal, Magdalena, "Measuring Rural Women's Work and Class Position", *Studies in Family Planning* 10 (11/12), 1979.

Durant-Gonzalez, Victoria, "Female Labour Force Participation: the Jamaican Case". Paper presented at Conference on the Impact of Development on Women in the Caribbean, University of Minnesota, St. Paul Campus, February 8–9, 1980.

———, "The Realm of Female Familial Responsibility in WICP Vol. II, *Women in the Family*, ISER, Cave Hill, Barbados, 1982.

———, "Women in the Caribbean Project and Female Self Consciousness". Paper presented at VI Annual Caribbean Studies Association Conference, St. Thomas, US Virgin Islands, May 27-31, 1981.

Foner, Nancy, *Status and Power in Rural Jamaica*, New York: Columbia University, Teachers College Press, 1973.

Graham, S. and Gordon, D., *The Stratification System and Occupational Mobility in Guyana*, Mona, Jamaica, ISER, UWI, 1977.

Greene, J.E., "Challenges and Responses in Social Science Research in the English-Speaking Caribbean *SES* 33 (1), March 1984.

Massiah, Joycelin, "Family Structure and the Status of Women in the Caribbean, with particular reference to women who head households". Paper presented at the International Meeting of Experts on Research on the Status of Women, Development and Population Trends, Evaluation and Prospects. Paris: UNESCO November 25-28, 1980a.

———, "Female Headed Households and Employment in the Caribbean". Paper presented to International Centre for Research on Women Workshop on Women Headed Households and Employment in the Third World, NGO Forum, World Conference on the UN Decade for Women, Copenhagen, July 14–24, 1980b.

———, "Indicators of Women in Development: A Preliminary Framework for the Caribbean". Paper presented to UNESCO meeting of Experts on The Indicators of the Extent of Women's Participation in Socio-Economic Development, Paris, UNESCO, April 21–24, 1980c.

———, "Manual for the Use of Socio-Economic Indicators of Women's Participation in Development". Paper prepared for UNESCO, Division for Socio-Economic Analysis, February 1982.

Odie-Ali, Stella, "Women in Agriculture: The Case of Guyana". *SES* Vol 35, No 2 1986.

Oppong, Christine, "A Synopsis of Seven Roles and Status of Women: An Outline of a Conceptual and Methodological Approach". ILO Population and Labour Policies Programme Working Paper No. 94, Geneva, September 1980.

Oppong, Christine and Church, K., "A Field Guide to Research on Seven Roles and Status of Women: Data Collection and Analysis Relevant to the Study of Work and Demographic Change". ILO Population and Labour Policies Programme, Working Paper No. 94, Geneva, 1980.

Roberts, G.W., *Fertility and Mating in Four West Indian Populations*. Kingston: ISER, UWI, 1975.

Roberts, G.W. and Sinclair, Sonja, *Women in Jamaica: Patterns of Reproduction*. New York: KTO Press, 1978.

Smith, R.T., "Social Stratification in the Caribbean" in Plotnicov, L. and A. Tuden (eds.), *Essays in Comparative Social Stratification*. Pittsburgh: Pittsburgh University Press, 1970.

World Fertility Survey, *Guyana Fertility Survey*, 1975 *Country Report Vols. I and II*, Georgetown: Statistical Bureau, Ministry of Economic Development, 1978.

―――, *Jamaica Fertility Survey, 1975/76 – Country Report, Vols. I and II.* Kingston: Department of Statistics, 1979.

Notes

1. This approach was substantiated by work coming out of the ILO after the project started. See Anker (1982), Oppong (1980), Oppong & Church (1980).
2. One of the earliest pre-project activities was to develop a possible frame work and to assemble data for the derivation of such index in the Caribbean. However, it was soon apparent that although some potential indicators undoubtedly exist, appropriate data for an acceptable single index were simply not avail able. (Massiah - Indicators 1980c).
3. Two recent studies have developed a very similar approach. See Deere & Leal (1979), Deere et al (1982), Anker (1982).
4. Detailed socio-economic profiles of each of these territories are provided in the appendix to this volume Part I. [Note from editors: not included here - see original publication.]
5. Findings from each of these sector studies, except the one on Women in Public Life are presented in this volume. [Note from editors: not included here – see original publication.]
6. These papers have been produced in a seven-volume series entitled *Women in the Caribbean* Barbados ISER., UWI, 1982.
7. In Barbados, the 1980 Enumeration Districts were used; in St Vincent, the project was forced to rely on the 1970 Enumeration Districts and in Antigua, the sampling frame was provided by the Statistical Division of the Ministry of Planning.

10. Learning to be a Man*

Barry Chevannes

...

The objective of this work was to study at the community level in a number of Caribbean countries the socialization process, focusing on males. As will be explained presently, the methodologies adopted were qualitative. Specifically and within our short timeframe, the aim was to identify the processes and events through which Caribbean males were imbued with knowledge of the roles they were expected to play as boys and later as men; the process through which they acquired the status of manhood; and the concomitant attitudes and values shaping their conception of themselves and their relations with others, females and males. Because the study of one gender is offset against the other, it was envisaged that this study would also keep within its purview the socialization of females, insofar as it was necessary for our understanding of the males. Thus this was not intended to be a study of the socialization of children in general, but rather a study specifically of our males.

This objective encompassed a *how* and a *what*. We assumed, first, that there was a way, or ways, in which children were trained to be girls and boys, women and men. This could imply some methodology or system. If there were, we wanted to find out what these were. We assumed, secondly, that parents, adults and whoever were the agents of socialization had some fairly definite ideas about gender roles, which they would be seeking to impart. It was important also to get as clear a picture of these as possible.

Our decision to site our study within communities was determined by the methodologies we planned to adopt, namely a combination

---

* Reprinted with permission from *Learning to be a Man: Culture, Socialization and Gender Identity in Five Caribbean Communities*. Kingston: UWI Press, 2001, 5–13. Excerpted.

of ethnographic and animation techniques. To be able to observe the interaction between the sexes, on the one hand, and between adults and children, on the other, we saw communities as ideal locations. As *loci* of primary relationships, both in the sense of where families and other primary groups are located as well as in the sense of systems of face-to-face relationships, communities are also tied into the wider social system, through the school, the communications media and other secondary institutions. The community in this sense is a hub of interpersonal and formal relations.

All the decisions except identification of the communities were made jointly with UNICEF. Limiting the timeframe to only six months and the number of communities to six was determined primarily by the funding available. We felt that six months was the absolute minimum for any meaningful ethnographic work, though a year would have been better. And while the funds could permit longer field work in fewer communities, we felt it was important at this exploratory stage to get as wide a cross-cultural comparison as possible. The reader may judge whether we made an error of judgement. Jamaica was chosen for the acuity of its urban problems; Guyana for its ethnic polarization, which is sharper than in Trinidad, the only other anglophone country with a large Indian population. Determined to include one of the smaller countries, we settled on Dominica, as against any other Windward or Leeward island, primarily for funding reasons.

...

Decision on the types of communities to study was also made jointly with our sponsors. We both wished to ensure a rural-urban spread. That done, we were left on our own to identify the particular communities, which we did after extensive local consultation. Only five, however, form the basis of the present study; due to personal misfortune, no ethnographic data were available from the sixth, Williamsfield, an Afro-Guyanese "ghetto" in Georgetown, selected to provide a contrast with the Indo-Guyanese community of Overflow and the inner-city Jamaican community of Joetown. Two communities in the study are rural, one suburban, and two urban. The two rural ones are Grannitree in Jamaica and Overflow in Guyana, while the suburban one is Riverbreeze, a working-class community two kilometres from central Roseau, which was settled by people drawn from rural Dominica. The two distinctly urban communities in the study are Motown and Joetown in Kingston. Motown was founded after a major hurricane in 1951, while Joetown lies in that part of Kingston now called the "inner city", a term used to describe the extreme urban decay that is characteristic of similar urban communities across the world.

Research Methods

Our next step was the selection and training of the research team. As this depended very much on the research methodologies we decided to use, it is best to say a few words here. Each team was made up of one male ethnographer and an animation group of three persons, two animators, one male and one female, and a documentalist.

Ethnography is "the art and science of describing a group or culture" (Fetterman 1989:11). To be able to describe, one must first understand, that is to make sense and meaning out of what one observes and hears. To achieve this understanding, the ethnographer must cultivate the trust of the people he or she studies, as a way of getting them to impart knowledge about themselves which is accurate and not misleading. Building trust in a stranger is not accomplished overnight. To help, the ethnographer often relies on a "broker", someone already known to, and trusted by, the community or the group, and, once accepted, he or she adopts the method known as *participant-observation*, a term which "suggests that you are directly involved in community life, observing and talking with people as you learn from them their view of reality" (Agar 1980:114). Participant-observation has the additional advantage of reducing the stranger element which sometimes makes people perform for the observer rather than behave normally. Thus, apart from his or her own observations of what people do and say, the ethnographer asks questions of and converses with just about anyone, but primarily those he or she identifies as knowledgeable and reliable, the "key informants". The ethnographer sees the actions, interactions and products of people, enquires about their beliefs, opinions, attitudes and values, why they do the things they do, what is the meaning of their actions, words, gestures, and in this way tries to arrive at an understanding of the group being studied.

These observations and interviews provide the contents of the ethnographer's fieldnotes; which in turn provide the material on which his or her study is put together. Thus, on top of each ethnographer's observations and interviews comes the writing, the presentation of what the ethnographer understands about the community or culture to the unfamiliar, a process which inevitably involves interpretation. It is here that ethnography has come in for a great deal of introspection and criticism (see Clifford and Marcus 1986). As a text, the ethnographic work is inevitably selective of what it includes and excludes; thus what is presented as a factual portrayal of the way of life of a community is indeed "something made or fashioned" (Clifford 1986:6) by the writer -at best partial truths. As an interpreter of the unknown, the unfamiliar, the ethnographer is like Hermes, who, when he agreed to be "messenger of the gods, he promised Zeus not to lie. He did not promise to tell the whole truth" (Crapanzano 1986: 53).

I would have to agree that the profiles and analyses of the males and females whose residence, actions and interactions form the communities we studied are ultimately my own constructs, made even less representational by the fact that they have been reprocessed from the interpretations of our researchers. I have no quarrel with this perspective, insofar as it seeks to expose the inextricably subjective nature of any attempt to know the other and to dethrone the hubris of Western canons of epistemology where *the colonial other* is concerned. But as Comaroff and Comaroff (1992: 9) remind us, "Ethnography, in any case, does not speak *for* others, but *about* them. Neither imaginatively nor empirically can it ever 'capture' their reality." The fact that we can never know fully and absolutely does not mean that we cannot and therefore should not attempt to know anything at all.

Supplementing the ethnographic perspective are the data gathered by the animation team. Animation is a reflexive method widely used in development work which utilizes drama, games and other performance techniques to get participants to act out normative patterns of behaviour, to question them in discussion and formulate actions for change (see Kassam and Mustafa 1982; Barndt 1981; Slim and Thompson 1993). It was particularly useful in the work of Sistren Theatre Collective (1986) in raising the consciousness of women, and had recently been adopted by

Brown, Anderson and Chevannes (1993) in their research project among fathers in rural and urban Jamaica. The animation method begins with an "entire event", a play, or a series of dramatic skits, or a concert, at which the community is informed of the research project, and groups are organized to discuss particular issues and questions. These discussion groups are of two sorts: seed groups and core groups, the difference being that seed groups are formed first, and become core with consistency in attendance. Groups may be gender specific or mixed, or organized according to age. The animators' role, as in a focus group, is to lead but not to dominate the discussion, while the documentalist records the data, who says what, along with any relevant observations. Each meeting of the group goes through three phases, a warm-up phase aimed at breaking down inhibitions, the main phase spent exploring the issues, and a cooling-down phase which recalls the evening's conclusions and sets the next agenda. Later the team meets and prepares a summary of the proceedings, in addition to the verbatim notes.

Given our relatively short timeframe, we saw the use of both ethnography and animation as complementary. For the ethnography four students and one social scientist were recruited. For the one Dominican and three Jamaican communities the students were all graduates who had either taken a course or received training in qualitative research. The social scientist was a member of the Faculty of Social Sciences at the University of Guyana, who had himself conducted research using ethnographic methods. Of the ten animators, six were trained social work or dramatic arts graduates, the rest practising dramatists or teachers. The documentalists were drawn from the teaching profession.

A five-day orientation and training programme was then arranged for members of the research teams and the local coordinators, with members of a project advisory committee of academic experts that had been set up in attendance. Apart from the expected introduction of the project's aims and objectives, the researchers were exposed to the general issues by way of expert-led reviews of socialization literature and the problematic position of men in contemporary Caribbean society. One day was devoted to the ethnographic methodology and practice, one to animation techniques, and a third to the key questions for research.

In relation to this last, we formulated eight topics:

1. Gender preferences for offspring, by men and women; the reasons for them, and their practical implications.
2. Gender segregation in household labour, income-generation and leisure activities along children, adolescents and adults.
3. Gender role expectations and performance by men, as perceived and defined by men and by women.
4. Peer group socialization among children, adolescents and adults.
5. The meanings and expression of love, affection and emotional supports as they differ or are similar, for men and women.
6. The different bases (accorded by men and women) for respecting or rejecting men in society.
7. The behaviours that merit reward and punishment, the means of rewarding and punishing, and the differences in application with respect to gender.
8. The rights adults, adolescents and children perceive adolescents and children to have, at what stages of their development, and the gender differences with respect to these rights.

This being a qualitative research project and not a survey with its carefully designed and tested questionnaire, in which each subject is the anonymous respondent to the specific questions asked, our researchers, particularly those engaged in ethnographic data gathering, were instructed to maintain a degree of flexibility in deciding which of the above concerns to give priority to and when, as well as being "led" by our informants and the field experience.

Fieldnotes were to be written up as soon as possible after the particular engagement (for example, at the end of the day, or first thing in the mornings after activities of the night before), to reduce the loss of important details. These notes were to be turned in to the local coordinators and sent to us to be typed for easier analysis. The research period was to have lasted from February 1995 to July/August 1995.

It would have been a miracle if the project had gone as planned. As it turned out, problems developed in Guyana and Dominica which had serious impact on both the quality and quantity of the ethnographic data, resulting in personnel changes over which we were unable to exercise the kind of control we would have liked. And with time ticking away, we had to make the best of it. It was not until September-October that data gathering, which started late, was everywhere brought to an end.

But even without such unforeseen developments, there was bound to be a certain unevenness. In the quest for new knowledge, every social scientist needs the cooperation of people. Whereas in the survey method (the most widely used in quantitative social research) cooperation is premised on complete anonymity, in ethnography (the most extensively used in qualitative research) cooperation is personalized and based on trust, on the rapport the researcher is able to establish with the people he or she interacts with. The ethnographic field is therefore narrow in range but intended to be penetrating in depth, as the researcher seeks admittance into people's personal worlds of experience and meaning. Five teams of researchers working each in a different community will produce profiles of varying emphases and quality, for under the constraints of the short time frame some individuals will generate rapport more quickly than others, or display better skills in observation, interviewing, interpretation and writing. The result is an unevenness in the quality of the profiles.

In presenting the findings, the choice lay between a thematic and a community-based approach. I chose the latter so as not to lose the context of community, which plays a far greater role in shaping our males than is generally thought, and as I hope will become clear. The result is a profile of each community of social relations and culture within which the socialization of our children takes place, and sketches of the personalities and agents effecting that process. The order of presentation is from rural to urban, from Grannitree to Joetown, the general direction of internal migration. The final chapter highlights some of the themes running through the five communities.

References
Agar, M. H. *The Professional Stranger: An Informal Introduction to Ethnography.* New York: Academic Press, 1980.
Barndt, D. *"Just Getting There: Creating Visual Tools for Collective Analysis in Freirean Education Programmes for Migrant Women in Peru and Canada."* Toronto: International Council for Adult Education, 1981.
Brown, J., P. Anderson, and B. Chevannes. "Report on the Contribution of Caribbean Men to the Family." Unpublished paper, the Caribbean Child Development Centre, University of the West Indies, 1993.

Clifford, J. "Introduction: Partial Truths" In *Writing Culture: The Poetics and Politics of Ethnography*, edited by James Clifford and George Marcus. Berkeley: University of California Press, 1986.

Clifford, James, and George E Marcus, eds. *Writing Culture: The Poetics and Politics of Ethnography*. Berkeley: University of California Press, 1986.

Comaroff, J., and J. Comaroff. *Ethnography and the Historical Imagination*. Boulder: Westview Press, 1992.

Crapanzo, V. "Hermes' Dilemma: The Masking of Subversion in Ethnographic Description." In *Writing Culture: The Poetics and Politics of Ethnography* edited by James Clifford and George Marcus. Berkeley: University of California Press, 1986.

Fetterman, D. *Ethnography Step by Step*. Newbury Park: Sage Publications, 1989.

Kassam, Y., and K. Mustafa, eds. *Participatory Research: An Emerging Alternative Methodology in Social Science Research. Participatory Research Network Series No. 2*. New Delhi: Society for Participatory Research in Asia, 1982.

Planning Institute of Jamaica. *Economic and Social Survey of Jamaica, 1997* Kingston: PIOJ, 1998.

Slim, H., and P. Thompson. *Listening for a Change: Oral Testimony and Development*. London: Panos, 1993.

Sistren with Honor Ford Smith. *Lionheart Gal.* London: Women's Press, 1986.

UNDP United Nations Development Program. *Human Development Report 1993* Oxford University Press, 1993.

Witter, M. and C. Kirton. "The Informal Economy in Jamaica: Some Empirical Exercises." Unpublished paper, Institute of Social and Economic Research, University of the West Indies, Mona, 1990.

11. Gender Studies in Cuba: Methodological Approaches, 1974–2001*

Marta Núñez Sarmiento

I wrote this article to settle two debts. The first is to Cuban social scientists specializing in gender studies in Cuba, whose works are scattered all over domestic and foreign publications. It is a sort of an epistemological debt I owe these researchers because I think that their methodological approaches have been both serious and creative. The second debt is to social scientists from other countries who specialize in gender studies, because they are usually surprised when they read some of the works written by their Cuban colleagues. They have had access to many books and articles published by non-Cuban authors on Cuban women, but they know little about the reflections by Cuban scholars.

This article aims at organizing the Cuban gender studies jigsaw puzzle, emphasizing only its methodological approaches and its gender perspectives. I also try to describe the social and historical context prevailing in Cuba 15 or 20 years ago, to understand the moment when the majority of Cuban researchers started studying gender issues – mainly about women – and to explain why we started many years after our colleagues from Latin America, the United States, Canada, and Western Europe did so. In Cuba, there was no boom of social research on gender. I would prefer to describe what happened as a sort of a flow of studies in this direction, which we all slowly decided to join. The reasons for doing so are found at the macro social level as well as at the individual level due to the professional and emotional needs of the researchers.

Beginning in 1985, I focused my research on Cuban women in traditional and nontraditional jobs, as well as on images of women in the Cuban mass media. Since 1973, I have been teaching methodology and methods of sociological research at the University of Havana. The intersection of these subjects in research and teaching helped me to develop an in-depth

---

* Reprinted with permission from *Gender & Society* 17, no. 1 (Feb. 2003): 7–32.

interview for the researchers in my sample, asking them to focus on items concerning methodological approaches and methods that are linked to the gender perspectives they use in their studies.

Writing this article was a highly collaborative experience because the colleagues I interviewed changed the questions I posed and added others I had not imagined. It made us rethink methodological matters dealing with gender research and start dealing with others we had not previously thought about.

The appendix to this article lists the works on gender written by the researchers I interviewed, printed in a few Cuban journals, in many foreign publications, and in books or still unpublished.[1] The bulk of our studies were ready to go to press in the 1990s, in the midst of the Cuban crisis, when printing facilities were very limited and several publications were temporally closed. I respected the way in which each of the people listed their works. For the sake of brevity, I summarized these lists and included only five works from each researcher.

Before describing my interviews and methods, I want to clarify several important research issues. First, I focus on the methodological approaches used by these scholars to study gender relations. I did not study the contents of their works, although I am familiar with most of them. I see this as the next research step, and it is open to anyone who wishes to use the articles and books listed in the appendix. Second, I am not a specialist in gender theory and did not ask about theory during the interviews, nor did I focus on the difficulties in trying to apply the results of these studies. Third, I include only Cuban social scientists specializing in gender relations and living in Havana. I do not refer to the many colleagues dealing with gender relations outside the capital. I included colleagues from different disciplines and age groups: Most have specialized in gender issues, while others do not focus solely on these topics but pay attention to gender relations throughout their research. Finally, in preparing this article, I was inspired by the articles written during the second half of the 1990s by Cubans Mayda Alvarez (1995), Luisa Campuzano (1996), Nara Araújo (1996), Norma Vasallo (1995), and North American Carollee Bengelsdorf (1997), dealing with gender studies in Cuba.

---

1. Editors note: The appendix is not reproduced here but can be found in the original.

SAMPLE AND METHOD

From May to July of 2001, I interviewed 24 scholars. I intentionally selected the persons in my sample to include several disciplines and research topics, different sex and age groups and professionals working in academia, government, international institutions, and nongovernmental organizations. The key informants are among the most important specialists dealing with gender in Cuba. I have used this procedure repeatedly in other case studies that I have conducted during the past 15 years, and I always tend to apologize for not using a statistically representative sample. My sample is biased. I did not include some well-known scholars who strongly contributed to developing gender research and teaching in Cuba. I am thinking of Cuban professors and writers Graciela Pogolotti and Adelaida de Juan, Cuban journalist Mirta Rodríguez Calderón, Cuban psychologist and professor Patricia Ares, and North American anthropologist John Doumoulin. My interviewees mentioned their names, as well as those of Cuban writers Vicentina Antuña and Mirta Aguirre (also a poet), Dominican essay writer Camila Henríquez Ureña, and Argentine sociologist Isabel Larguía, who are no longer among us, but who taught in Cuban academia with a gender perspective. I believe there are strengths in working with intentional samples like the one used here.

Studies of this sort, which focus on the diverse ways in which scholars approach gender relations and the wide array of motives guiding them toward these topics, require deep professional and personal empathic relations between those who ask questions and those who answer them. These empathetic relations favor exchanges among equals rather than focusing on the well known. In my case, people in the sample followed the basic guidelines in my questionnaire but felt they could change some of the questions, cut out others, and include topics I had not considered. Eventually, I decided to become part of the sample, so that I exchanged my views with those I interviewed. I did so because they wanted to know my own answers and also because I felt the need to dissent from their opinions or to agree with them. I wanted to turn the in-depth interviews into actual dialogues to avoid problems that Bourdieu ([1973] 1987) identified long ago. He stated that sociological interviews usually do not favor the free flow of ideas for the interviewer controls the questionmaking process, leaving the interviewee to merely answer the questions. Therefore, information runs only in one way: from the respondent to the researcher guiding the interview, from the commanded to the person in command.

The guilt I felt for not following the rules of orthodox methodology vanished when several persons in the sample said that researchers must engage the rules of gender perspectives in the sense that they must understand their own subjectivities to explain the subjectivities of the persons they are studying. The issue is not one of denying my right to take part in the research process when using my own subjectivity. It is a matter of understanding our own ideologies from a scientific point of view, of controlling their inclusion throughout the research process, so that we are able to avoid imposing our own views of those persons we are investigating.

I asked the interviewees to focus on the social and personal settings in which they became involved in gender studies, the motivations leading them to do so, the most distinctive methodological traits composing their gender perspectives, the methods that they generally have used in the course of their research, and the non-Cuban authors who have influenced their studies. Finally, I asked them to summarize the ideas they would suggest to Cuban social scientists engaging in gender studies. This article organizes their analytical and critical thoughts on the ways they approach their topics, highlighting their methodological views.

I interviewed 20 women and 4 men. Their ages range from 23 to 65 years old: 3 of them are in their 20s, 1 is in her 30s, 6 are in their 40s, 7 are in their 50s, and 7 are in their 60s. There are 20 whites and 4 blacks. Occupationally, 6 are sociologists, 5 historians, 3 in arts and letters, 2 lawyers, 3 psychologists, 3 demographers, 1 biologist, and 1 psychiatrist. Fifteen are PhDs and 7 hold master's degrees, which they completed in Cuba, the former USSR, the former German Democratic Republic, Chile, Romania, Hungary, and Mexico. There are 12 full professors, 2 assistant professors, 3 full researchers, and 3 assistant researchers, which are the highest teaching and research ranks in Cuba.

Several of them hold decision-making posts: the director of the Center for Studies on Population and Development at the National Statistics Office of Cuba and also of the National Census of 2002, the editor-in-chief of the journal *Revolución y Cultura* and the head of the Women's Studies Program at the Casa de las Américas, the head of the Women's

Studies Center at the Federation of Cuban Women, the directors of the Women's Studies Programs of the University of Havana and of the Cátedra Gertrudis Gomez de Avellaneda, belonging to the Institute of Literature and Linguistics. Other specialists in the sample head or have headed departments and research teams at the university and centers belonging to the Academy of Sciences.

The interviewees deal with the following topics within gender relations and basically concentrate on women: the history of Cuba in the nineteenth and twentieth centuries (families, black female slaves, and women underground and guerrilla fighters during the 1950s); the role of women in history, culture, and the shaping of Cuban identity during the nineteenth and twentieth centuries, emphasizing the way they were represented in literature, history, political documents, and all types of texts; women in population and development studies in Cuba; gender and empowerment; women and race; traditional and non-traditional women's jobs; images of women and men in mass media; rural women; homosexuals; female prostitution in the nineteenth century and today; women and health, health policies, and reproductive health; middle-aged women; women, generations, and youth; women in comparative and family law; and differences related to gender in the life standards of people suffering stigmatized illnesses (e.g., HIV, tuberculosis, and leprosy).

They work at the University of Havana; in institutes of the Ministry of Sciences, Technology and the Environment; at the National Office of Statistics; in the Casa de las Américas; at the journal *Revolución y Cultura*; at the University of Medical Sciences; at the Ministry of Culture; in the United Nations Fund for Population Activities Havana field office; and in the Federation of Cuban Women. In reporting my results, I do not use pseudonyms. Indeed, I have the scholars' permission to use their names.

THE SOCIAL AND PERSONAL CONTEXT FOR CUBAN RESEARCHERS IN THE 1980s AND 1990s

The majority of the researchers in this sample started focusing their studies on gender relations, mainly on women, in the middle of the 1980s or early in the 1990s. Therefore, I decided to reconstruct the social and personal conditions of that period to help the reader understand why they decided to begin dealing with gender-related topics.

The three researchers, who were younger than 30, became familiar with gender topics in the course of their undergraduate studies during the 1990s. This explains why they wrote their bachelor's and master's degrees theses on gender relations. They began dealing with these themes at a younger age than the rest of my informants and with a wider gender-sensitive culture around them.

In the midst of the 1970s, the three demographers and the sociologist who taught demography were the first specialists in the sample to acknowledge the differences revealed in statistical data when using the variable *sex*. But they started using a gender approach only at the beginning or middle of the 1980s. Next came the specialists who, early in the 1980s, wanted to study women in Cuban literature of the nineteenth and twentieth centuries. The rest started investigating gender relations during the second half of the 1980s or early in the 1990s.

I cannot explain yet why the process of entering the field of gender studies evolved this way. It may have had to do with the professions of the scholars in my sample. What were the social contexts related to women when gender studies began developing in Cuba, and what were the personal settings of the researchers? Cuban women's social and economic development became evident around 1985–1986. Women composed 38 percent of the labor force and 56 percent of all professional and technical workers in the state civil sector (*Anuario Estadístico de Cuba 1986* 1987, 199). Increased female representation in education was visible, with 52 percent of all university graduates and 54 percent of upper-secondary-level graduates being women (*Anuario Estadístico de Cuba* 1986 1987, 521–22). Indeed, women workers had higher educational levels than men in the same jobs.

At the political level, the rectification process, which expanded from late 1984 until 1988–1989, was aimed at correcting sex discrimination, especially that suffered by women workers. This was one of the reasons for the massive construction of nurseries, houses, and new schools. In 1986, the Third Congress of the Communist Party of Cuba declared the need to promote women, blacks, and youth to decision-making positions.

The Fourth Congress of the Federation of Cuban Women in 1985 evidenced the rise of women's participation in all spheres of life. This organization urged Cuban specialists (women and men) to attend international events where they could compare the situation of Cuban women with those of women in other countries. Such events included the preparatory meeting of Latin American and Caribbean representatives for the United Nations Conference in Nairobi on the Decade of Women (in Havana in 1984), the international meeting of Women on the Foreign Debt (in Havana in 1985), and the United Nations Conference for the Decade of Women (in Nairobi in 1985).

The presence of Cuban scholars at international conferences on women grew beginning in 1985. Through the Federation of Cuban Women, Cuba was represented in the meetings of the Convention for the Elimination of all Forms of Exploitation on Women at the United Nations headquarters in New York. In the course of these and other meetings, Cuban delegates were able to give and get feedback regarding the implementation of social policies benefiting women in Cuba. Cuban scholars dialogued with their colleagues from Latin American, American, Canadian, and Western European universities and became acquainted with their women's studies programs. They were attracted by the feminist trends of thought aimed at unveiling and explaining inequalities between men and women, especially questions related to the feminization of poverty. At the same time, the United Nations Fund for Population Activities promoted studies on population and development, underlining the need to use sociological approaches to analyzing demographic data.

The Federation of Cuban Women coordinated social research programs on Cuban women with Cuban and foreign scholars. These investigations mobilized a revival of sociological research in Cuba, not only in reference to women. For example, in 1987, a study of women workers was carried out at the Celia Sánchez Manduley textile factory in Santiago de Cuba; another study was carried out between 1986 and 1989 by American anthropologist Helen Safa (1989) and the Federation of Cuban Women in the Ariguanabo textile factory, 40 kilometers southwest of Havana; and a third comparative study was carried out from 1987 to 1988 on women's employment in five countries of the Americas. Participants in the 1988 National Seminar on the Implementation of the Nairobi Strategies for Women in Cuba (held in Havana) developed multidisciplinary reflections on the situation of Cuban women.

In 1991, Cuban scholars and the Federation of Cuban Women jointly created the Women Studies Program at the University of Havana as well as women and family programs in other Cuban universities. The federation created houses for women and the family at municipal levels and the Center for Research on Women of the Federation of Cuban Women. Casa de las Américas, the Cuban Union for Artists and Writers, the Institute of Literature and Linguistics, and the Union of Cuban Journalists created permanent spaces to discuss gender matters among Cuban and foreign specialists. Since 1986, scientific conferences organized by Cuban universities and the Academy of Sciences have created working groups to discuss gender issues, and these are usually the most attended sessions.

In Cuba's crisis of the 1990s, the so-called special period, the basic role played by Cuban women was acknowledged, thanks to the creative ways in which they implemented strategies to survive and to live with very few resources. Nonetheless, differences between men and women openly appeared in terms of access to empowerment and youth-related issues. Prostitution reappeared, and although it had new traits in comparison to other periods of Cuban history, it worried and still worries Cuban citizens.

Social scientists in my sample lived throughout all these experiences inside Cuba, and they studied them, having difficulty balancing matters of involvement and detachment. During the second half of the 1980s and the beginning of the 1990s, the specialists I interviewed had fully developed their personal and professional lives. (Of course, this excludes the three younger specialists.) As professionals, they had defended their doctoral dissertations or were preparing to do so. Many of them had already completed their master's degrees. They were full or assistant professors and/or researchers, which are the highest-ranking categories in Cuban academia. They had accomplished a considerable amount of research in their specialized topics. From these positions, they engaged in gender studies. They were capable of selecting matters in which they were definitely interested and which they could connect to their previous research. They were, therefore, able to open a permanent process of feedback between feminist knowledge and the outcomes of knowledge in which they were specialized, such as the methodology of social research, the social history of Cuba, comparative and family law, or relations among rural workers.

Having read the curriculum vitae of the scholars in this sample, I can state that during the past 15 years, they have developed a very wide array of contacts on gender issues with colleagues around the world. They have discussed papers at conferences, joined organizing committees for international scientific events, taught in foreign universities, joined international multidisciplinary research teams, received scholarships from outstanding scientific agencies, and worked as experts for the United Nations and other international agencies. Between the middle of the 1980s and through the early 1990s, these scholars had fully matured. They had raised children, had changed their marital status or stayed with their original partner, and had lost their parents or were taking care of them. They had lived through processes that made them make constant decisions. Engaging feminism and/or gender studies was one of them.

I have more to do in order to work out the intertwining of these three levels – what happens at the level of society as a whole, in their professional environments, and their personal lives – not to mention what is happening at the global level concerning gender studies. All this would enable me to explain more comprehensively and sociologically how each of these levels has placed its stamp on the research process of these Cuban scholars. The reader should also consider the fact that feminist trends were stigmatized in Cuba for many years, and prejudices toward them still persist. It is necessary to consider these facts in analyzing why we in gender studies engaged so late compared to our colleagues from other countries.

DISTINCTIVE TRAITS OF CUBAN RESEARCHERS' GENDER PERSPECTIVE

Practically all the scholars interviewed confessed that during their research process, they do not spend much time defining what a gender approach means, either in terms of theory or methodology. Some admitted that they had never defined this concept. This does not mean that they lack methodological or theoretical knowledge in terms of gender. They are well read on gender issues and well trained in observational techniques. They are widely experienced in deciding how they are going to approach their subjects, to collect the required information, to organize their own database, and to infer knowledge from them. Therefore, when I asked them to define their gender perspectives, their answers were very rich.

Before indicating the ways in which they specifically defined gender perspectives, let me underscore that practically everyone started using a gender approach in their research intuitively. This was even true for those who began studying gender relations in the 1990s. Some wanted to bring out matters concerning women who were marginalized, concealed, invisible, or discriminated against. For example, Luisa Campuzano, Susana Montero, and Mirta Yáñez studied women in Cuban literature during the nineteenth and the twentieth centuries to help redefine the history of literature and the way women perceived this process. As early as the 1970s, Juan Carlos Alfonso, Sonia Catasús, Alfonso Farnós, and Niurka Pérez noted interesting differences coming out of their demographic data when controlling for the variable *sex*, although then they lacked a gender approach. Others suffered at the end of their research, for they acknowledged losing precious information because they had omitted gender-related topics. This happened to María Isabel Domínguez at the end of the 1980s when she was studying generations and youth. She confessed, "I felt terribly upset, because for five years of research I had gathered loads of information, which I couldn't fully work out, because I hadn't used a gender approach from the beginning."

Once the scholars engaged the gender perspective in a scientifically conscious way, they kept enriching its definition. I have grouped their widely ranging definitions of gender perspectives into five components. First, everyone agrees on abroad definition of this concept: to approach society understanding that men and women not only have biological sex but that societies assign them different roles. Some of the specialists proposed revising the dichotomous definition of gender, which allows only for the masculine and the feminine. This is biased by societies that are based on patriarchal culture, and therefore, a scientific definition of gender ought to include homosexuals who may follow neither set of norms. The majority also differentiated among sex, gender, and sexual orientation. Luis Robledo believes that

> while studying everyday lives among homosexuals, I found out that sexual orientations are not directly related to the traditional gender identities they assume or are given by society. For example, men working as dancers or beauticians are easily labeled by Cubans as gays.

Almost all scholars felt that identifying gender perspectives only with women was a limited view. All of the specialists believe it is time to study men, too. For example, according to Juan Carlos Alfonso, a researcher gains knowledge when analyzing the impact of men and women's behaviors in the divorce process Usually, women decide to divorce and get through the process quickly, while men encounter divorce with fears.

Second, the respondents agreed that the use of a gender perspective is a scientific imperative for all the social sciences. Without it, it is impossible to understand either social processes in Cuban history or contemporary events. The scientific significance of this perspective lies in its promoting the use of a historical perspective to understand contemporary phenomena. Consequently, those of us who studied survival strategies developed by Cuban women during the crisis of the 1990s had to acknowledge the survival abilities and the sense of creativity that are part of Cuban culture, inherited mainly from African slaves and their offspring. Digna Castañeda's article on women slaves' working conditions in colonial Cuba contributed to understanding this heritage.

The gender perspective also helps one understand the subjectivities both of those who are studied and of the researchers. Many of the specialists in the sample admitted that they stopped feeling guilty and uncomfortable for having incorporated their own subjectivities and emotions in the course of their studies. It is not a matter of denying one's own or others' ideologies, for it is impossible to do so, but to be capable of understanding how they operate in each person's everyday research activities. Those who study violence because, to some extent, they were subject to it have to pull out of their subjectivities all feelings and emotions linked to their own violent experiences to attain the difficult balance between involvement and detachment. This is the only way to produce valuable reflections from life experiences of one's own. Whenever you practice these rationalizing procedures concerning subjectivities, all persons involved in the research process will be able to participate in it in a creative way that will enhance everyone's self-esteem.

There is another scientific quality in the gender perspective: It admonishes us to admit differences in society and to study them, take others into account, and promote constant comparisons. This approach analyses general and global levels of society as well as the individual level. The gender approach is an inclusive one for it underscores the need to understand gender as linked to all other structures of a given society:

class, generation, political concepts, and ideological concepts, among others. These scholars see the gender perspective as a Marxist perspective, for it implies a feminist commitment to pursue social justice for all and not only for women. In the words of Luisa Campuzano, "It is Marxist because it is engaged in the feminization of equality and criticizes those trends of thought that allow only one-sided flows of equity, for example, trends which do not acknowledge differences in their aspirations for equity." Susana Montero considers that "the gender approach is a nondogmatic one since it does not accept fixed or established truths. It promotes discussing and questioning everything and affirms its dislike for any imposition of power towards researchers' thoughts."

Third, the scholars concurred that a gender perspective has to do with politics and power. It helps to understand the structures of inequalities between men and women by revealing sexist traits in political decision-making, along with social and legal policymaking and their actualization in everyday life. It helps to disentangle the network of repressions and power, at the societal and personal levels, and consequently paves the way toward equity. Luisa Campuzano believes that the gender perspective is more a political than a methodological one. It means that each person has been affected by ideological schemes linked to given societies. She and other researchers think that it is also a political and revolutionary position as it seeks to unveil the hidden structures that explain the ways people think and act to help change them for new and more just attitudes.

Fourth, according to the social scientists I interviewed, the gender perspective is a methodological concept with multiple definitions for the reality it focuses on is ontologically diverse. In addition, when you approach society with a gender perspective, you do it with different views, according to your profession and your personal life experiences. It is a definition opened to new knowledge that will be gathered in the future, and consequently, it undergoes a constant process of construction. It is a nondogmatic conception.

Finally, these researchers feel that people using the gender approach must assume it as part of their identities, in the same way they accept their race and their birthplace. Mirta Yañez said she had to incorporate it "as one of my essences." Specialists feel that you have to practice it in your daily personal and professional lives. You cannot study women's employment and the double shift and then accept a sexist division of labor at home. Consequently, scholars using gender approaches must practice ethics that represent the goals of justice and equality. They take full responsibility for those research processes dealing with gender, which begin by studying gender relations and end up by analyzing society as a whole.

MOTIVATIONS FOR STUDYING GENDER ISSUES

The main incentive that led all my respondents toward gender studies was their goal of attaining social justice and erasing discrimination toward women and also toward homosexuals. Practically all of them sense that there is a need to study men in order to understand their role in the social and individual networks that have marginalized women and homosexuals. They also want to unearth the social, spiritual, and physical problems suffered by men, caused by the roles that society assigned them. The desire to struggle against the nobodyness assigned to women in many levels of society flourished based on discrimination experienced by several of the women over the course of their lives. Historians Gladys Marel García, Sonnia Moro, and Elvira Díaz Vallina, who fought in the underground movement against Batista in the 1950s, were compelled to prove that they were as good as the men they fought with. Two other graduates from arts and letters were annoyed by the lack of information on Cuban literature written by women and by the low representation of women in literary anthologies and on prize juries. Several women acknowledged that they were motivated to join gender studies by their feminist involvement. According to Luisa Campuzano, it is their broad conception of feminism, an inclusive one, that respects differences and pursues an understanding of equality that does not erase the differences between genders.

The second motivation to focus on gender topics was the need to create a comprehensive scientific approach to society. They were experienced scholars in their fields of knowledge who, at a certain point in their careers, admitted the need to include a gender view in their scientific approach in order to understand society both globally and individually. Historian María del Carmen Barcia used the gender perspective in her studies of the role of Cuban families in Cuban social history of the twentieth century. Digna Castañeda worked with it when she studied the role of women slaves in the labor force during the nineteenth century in Cuba and the Caribbean. Lawyer and sociologist Olga Mesa applied the gender approach in her studies of comparative law to understand why, although there is legal equality for men and women in Cuba today, many subtle and even open inequalities persist.

According to these scholars, one of the basic scientific traits of a gender approach is that it does much more than merely diagnose: it searches for diversities they can compare to find commonalities, and it helps them attain a comprehensive understanding of society without leaving out individualities. Therefore, all researchers using this perspective start focusing on gender matters and end up by studying the social environment as a whole. In the 1970s, sociologist and demographer Juan Carlos Alfonso became acquainted with a huge amount of social and demographic information in the Department of Demography where he started working. He admitted that all the data analyses had been impeccably calculated, but they lacked "sociological imagination." He began noting the gender differences that arose when he analyzed the data using the variable *sex*. "Imagine what happened when I used the gender approach many years later." As a way to explain this idea, he referred to the rich information one can infer when one analyzes fertility not just as an issue concerning women. You have to understand the social and economic settings where women and their partners are living and you have to question how men's behaviors affect the reproductive process.

When Cuban organizations started publishing statistical data on women, many of the researchers in the sample were interested in explaining the different behaviors among men and women. They mentioned the volumes *Mujeres en cifras* (Women in Numbers) (1975), *La población de Cuba* (The Population of Cuba) (1976), the *Statistical Yearbooks on Cuba* (which stopped being published in the 1990s due to the crisis), and the recent *Statistical Profile of the Cuban Woman in the Threshold of the XX.I Century* (1999). They also referred to other publications edited by the Federation of Cuban Women beginning in the mid-1970s, with data on women.

Specialists also began using a gender approach because of its usefulness in pointing out small, omitted, and forgotten things of everyday life and understanding their meaning in society. One case concerns women agricultural workers in the town of Guanimar, whom I studied in 1992. They used jokes to challenge their male coworkers, hammering on their sexual impotence. Men usually were unable to defend themselves against these jokes, and they always retreated. I inferred that this could be a way in which women workers used their power. In another example, in her book *Reyita*, Daysi Rubiera (1997) told the story of her mother, a black woman born of slave parents. Using the method of life history and paying attention to the most insignificant details of Reyita's life, the author embodied the intricate network of gender, class, and race in Cuba in the first half of the twentieth century.

The youngest specialists I interviewed, who started studying gender in the 1990s, were motivated to transcend the limits of research on women to be able to focus on men and homosexuals. They wanted to dig more deeply into the differences among sex, gender, and sexual orientation and to elaborate on the hypothesis that says that patriarchal cultures constructed the men-women dichotomy, leaving out homosexuals. They were willing to unveil the misconception that homosexuality is a social pathology. This is why Gryska Miñoso studied differences in criteria on the quality of life among HIV patients and why Luis Robledo wrote his master's degree thesis on homosexuals in Cuba.

During the 1990s, specialists in the sample started studying gender relations or continued doing so, thanks to their participation in discussions carried out by several multidisciplinary groups among Cuban women. They usually invited foreign specialists. For example, there have been workshops organized by the Women's Studies Program at the University of Havana, Casa de las Américas, the Federation of Cuban Women and its Fe del Valle school, the Union of Writers and Artists of Cuba, the Union of Cuban Journalists, the Martin Luther King Jr. Center, the program Gertrudis Gómez de Avellaneda of the Institute of Literature and Linguistics, and Magin (a Cuban nongovernmental organization of mass media specialists). As a result, reading foreign authors who specialize in gender matters and getting to know them personally has been a third and permanent source of motivation to develop gender studies. My informants mentioned the fact that they have learned much from working together with foreign specialists in Cuba or abroad. Throughout these exchanges, both parties benefited. They referred to the Mexican scholar Elena Urrutia and her Interdisciplinary Program for Gender Studies at El Colegio de Mexico; to the Brazilian sociologist Mary García Castro and the American anthropologist Helen Safa, who headed the Ariguanabo textile factory research project on women; to the American economist Carmen Diana Deere and Colombian economist Magdalena León de Leal for their studies with rural working women; to Dominican sociologist Magaly Pineda; and to anthropologists Dolores Juliano and Verena Stolke from Barcelona. Several respondents began studying gender topics because they were asked by Cuban organizations to help them do so. Once they started, they could not stop. Only one of these specialists was already a feminist when she was invited; the rest engaged feminism later.

IMPORTANT NON-CUBAN SCHOOLS OF THOUGHT AND METHODOLOGIES

One important question I asked was which are the non-Cuban schools of thought and authors, especially focused on methods and methodology that have influenced you the most? Which are the methods you primarily use?

At the end of the eighteenth century, Don José Agustín Caballero recommended that intellectuals in Cuba practice an "eclectic approach." He urged his students to extract knowledge from all readings and experiences that could help them understand their realities, wherever they came from. All these scholars have widely practiced electivism. They named it a nondogmatic approach, illustrated electivism, and also referred to it as the infinite capacity to absorb all wisdom that contributes to understanding reality in an intelligent and committed way. These specialists studied Marxism in the course of their careers, their master's degree programs, and their doctorates, and they have used it to implement their methodological perspectives. They became acquainted with the Soviet Marxist handbooks but preferred to draw out methodological hints from the works of the classics and contemporary Marxist authors. A solid academic education plus all the vital experiences she attained living in Cuba and working as a professional led Mirta Yañez to exclaim, "I practice Marxism with a historical and logical perspective, from Havana, and from my perspective as a middle-aged woman who is always trying to keep her condition as a science fiction writer."

All members of the sample favor constructing their own information and reflecting on it, for the purpose of drawing their own conclusions. Historian María del Carmen Barcia writes social history or historical sociology following recommendations she derived from the works of Charles and Louise Tilly. She analyses data she has personally collected and opposes those who use ideas written by others, later adding a theoretical framework also picked up from other authors.

In matters concerning methods, practically all researchers I interviewed claimed to use both quantitative and qualitative methods but favored the use of the latter. They use sociodemographic information to understand the social and historical settings where the persons they study live. They compare statistical data concerning people in their samples with macro sociodemographic information to be able to locate similar and different traits in their behaviors, leading them to draw conclusions, for example, the age of women when they have their first child, the type of family they live in, their marital status, and race. These researchers combine quantitative and qualitative methods for the purpose of identifying people they study in demographic terms, mainly to measure their quality of life.

They privilege qualitative methods for two reasons: First, to analyze the subjectivities of people, as well as other facets of their lives, when questions contained in surveys are unable to disclose this. Second, qualitative methods are cheaper in terms of material and human resources, at least in Cuba. The crisis of the 1990s drastically cut down the possibilities of printing questionnaires and mobilizing huge numbers of interviewers.

The specific qualitative methods used vary according to the researchers' professions. Historians use procedures of historical anthropology and of micro history. While studying families in the nineteenth century, María del Carmen Barcia applied methods of "formal and informal sociability" worked out by Maurice Agulhon (1983). Formal sociability methods study the associations constituted through contracts, while informal sociability refers to the integration of networks, including families, individuals, and civil society, and links between the public and private spheres. She also mentioned James Casey (1990), whose works define families by their internal coherence, their capability of permanence, and their ability to be open to external environments. Casey broke the home-family link widely used by demographers. Many of them also refer to Michael Foucault's methods for analyzing the diverse and unseen levels of empowerment not included in the political sphere. They always analyze documentary sources and secondary ones. When they study contemporary history, oral history allows historians to explore subjectivities of the persons they are interviewing. This is a procedure that requires empathy among researchers and their research participants. Niurka Pérez, who lived with a Nicaraguan family for one month, declared.

> It also permits everyone involved in the research process to uncover their affections, and it is a method which facilitates the need of people to be heard. When used properly, it is difficult to find persons who are not willing to talk.

The researchers I interviewed are familiar with the methodological aspects of work by other scholars including Mexicans Eugenia Meyer and Marcela Lagarde and with those of American sociologist Marietta Morrissey and historian Rebecca Scott.

Scholars specializing in women in literature approach literary texts focusing on their contents and the social and historical environments where they were produced. They also consider the intertextual and intratextual relations, as well as the biography of the authors they study. They privilege reading and gaining experiences from those foreign authors who practice a critical social view and who analyze race, gender, and class. They mentioned North American and European scholars bell hooks (writer), Jean Franco (literary critic and former president of the Latin American Studies Association), Mary Louise Pratt (literary critic and Latin Americanist), Julia Kristeva (whose literary criticism focused on semiotic theory), Elaine Showalter (feminist critic and literature scholar), and Latin American authors Silvia Molloy (Argentine literary critic), Elena Urrutia (Mexican gender scholar), Aralia López (essay writer and professor), Marlyse Meyer (writer), and Rosario Ferré (Puerto Rican author). They also referred to Italian Luisa Murano and the philosophers of the Diotima group from Verona.

Susana Montero has used idiothematic analysis *(análisis idiotemático)* to search for the diverse expressions arising from women and men as readers. She submitted literary texts written by women to male and female readers and found out how differently they interpreted those texts according to their gender. For example, men saw historical perspectives, myths, and elements of continuity in them. Women brought out the semantics of denial, the intentions of breaking with traditional feminine discourses, and the purpose of denying social rules.

Sociologists and anthropologists use participant observation because it reveals even the smallest significant behaviors of men and women. It also helps researchers become involved in the social process they are observing. These scholars feel that investigations must start with observation methods because it is a way to become acquainted with those parts of society they are studying. These methods are useful in designing research projects because they enrich the visions of social scientists and they help decide on the appropriate sample. For example, in the exploratory phase of his research on homosexuals, sociologist Luis Robledo visited several gay groups in Havana until he decided which of them he would invite to participate in discussion groups. In studies carried out by Niurka Pérez with women agricultural workers and peasants in rural communities, by Gryska Miñoso with HIV patients, and by María Isabel Domínguez in her studies of young women, observation methods served to decide which groups would be given questionnaires, which would do in-depth interviews, and finally, which people might be the subjects of life histories. Sociologists, economists, and anthropologists in the sample have read North American sociologist Maria Patricia Fernández-Kelly, anthropologist Helen Safa, economist Carmen Diana Deere (the latter also are past presidents of the Latin American Studies Association), Colombian economist Magdalena León de Leal, and Brazilian María Aparecida Morais to become acquainted with the use of observation methods.

Researchers who have practiced observation techniques with their equals or people similar to themselves (gays, professional women, middle-aged women) admit that it has been easier to develop empathetic links with these persons. But they are conscious of the risk of committing themselves to these persons, as well as the danger of developing transference and countertransference. Both mistakes could block their vision and limit their capability to observe how others behave. Indepth interviews provided them with information that people transmit only when they trust their interviewers. Therefore, they became acquainted with such traits as sexual behaviors and problems arising from relations between subordinates or with topics of violence. They mentioned learning in-depth interview techniques from authors such as Brazilian sociologist Mary Garcia Castro, Cuban-American Yolanda Prieto, and American anthropologist Helen Safa.

The sociologists and anthropologists I studied also have used group interviews, discussion groups, and techniques related to popular education. They use them to complement other methods of collecting information, to submit final reports, and to give feedback to persons who have been studied, including the conclusions and the recommendations of the research. Ana Violeta Castañeda said that these methods "contribute to the research/action and participation processes, for they favor an open flow of reflections, where participants speak from their realities. Their subjectivities can be analyzed and, with this new knowledge, they can transform their environments." Among the sources they have consulted for these methods are texts produced by the Research Center for Women's Action, headed by Magaly Pineda in the Dominican Republic, and the Center for Women's Studies in Chile and the works of Brazilian educator Pablo Freire.

Sociologists have used content analysis to reveal the images of women transmitted by Cuban mass media and to unveil the new needs and values related to gender that are present in Cuban ideology today. This was the main method used in studies on images of men and women in the lyrics of the traditional and the new *trova* (songs) and images of women in tourist advertising developed by Cubans. The foreign authors most often consulted were Michelle and Armand Mattelart and Maureen Honey.

Specialists in the sample also are acquainted with the life history method developed or honed by Oscar Lewis, Elena Poniatowska, Elsa Chaney, and Arlie Hochschild, but they have not used it very much. The only sociologist who has published a work based on life history is Niurka Pérez (1986), titled *El hogar de Ana* (Ana's Home).

CONCLUSIONS: METHODOLOGICAL SUGGESTIONS FOR SPECIALISTS ENGAGING IN GENDER STUDIES

I would like to conclude with several methodological suggestions that these researchers had for others interested in gender studies. They indicated that whoever decides to study gender relations must consider gender a relational category that expresses hierarchical cultural attributes of one sex in relation to the other. They must not forget this approach when they analyze the history of cultural relations in terms of power and domination at the societal and individual levels. One must study feminism in its widest conceptualization and not reduce it to the faulty interpretation of the female gender as the superior one. Gender includes both men and women, and we have to look at both. It is necessary to scientifically view men and to study their attitudes in the process of manipulating power mechanisms and the traumas they have suffered by playing these roles. This does not mean that women's studies are over. The fact is that there are more studies on women than on men. And many of the recommendations coming out of these studies aimed at equity cannot be implemented until there is enough scientific knowledge on the role of men in the social patterns used to dominate women. The new studies on men, gays, lesbians, and transsexuals should relate their findings to those available in research on Cuban women.

These scholars also said they practice epistemological vigilance, which means not imposing their own ideologies on those they are studying, to facilitate the flow of respondents' ideas. One must confer leading roles to all persons being studied, even those who play minor roles. Researchers look for meaning in unnoticed events of everyday life, like those performed by the marginalized and the forgotten. This is also important when you are studying history, and it curbs the predominance of the researcher's voice. In contemporary studies, you must practice participative research/action whenever possible.

The researchers felt they should try to control the power they impose on their respondents throughout an investigation. Specialists admit that when they interview people and observe them, they actually invite them to, and make them, unveil parts of their lives that interest the researcher and that are usually very intimate. On the other hand, investigators never share their own experiences.

These scholars believe in multiple methods. One should learn from everything that helps one understand gender relations: literature, lyrics of songs, and the messages contained in mass media. For example, one must be able to disentangle the most sexist manifestations conveyed in texts and images to learn what they mean and how they have been constructed. It is very useful and revealing to learn from negative experiences.

All the researchers said they must practice intuition in matters of gender, but within a process led by their skills, which are highly trained in gender issues. Specialists must be familiar with theoretical and epistemological works on gender relations and must also read research reports. They must know the social settings in which each of these works was written. By doing so, they will be able to decide how these methods can be applied in each specific social setting and how they can be used to produce comparative studies to explain gender relations. They have to know the life experiences, the historical and current facts surrounding issues that they are studying, and only afterwards can they analyze them using theory. This is the only way to avoid imposing straitjackets on society, to avoid submitting social relations we are studying to theories that cannot explain them.

These scholars noted that a gender perspective is valuable in analyzing economic, political, and ideological relations in society. It is impossible to study any matter concerning social behavior without a gender perspective. One has to understand gender linked to social and historical structures, linked to class, race, and generations. Therefore, one must transcend the description of what men and women do. Researchers have to rise beyond the limits of how they think of themselves to be able to understand how each of them constructs his or her truths in specific social systems.

Scholars studying gender relations cannot use a double standard. They must believe in what they are studying, and they must be able to change their most intimate conceptions and attitudes to approach their studies in an honest, genuine, and legitimate way. To commit themselves to the gender approach in their professional and personal lives means to passionately dedicate themselves to changing people's lives, policies, cultural productions, and all scopes of life. These researchers feel that they cannot be pleased just with publishing their works; they have to do everything possible to apply the recommendations of their research to the way they and others think and act. They must fight all sorts of repression toward their works and be activists.

Throughout the investigation process, they must be creative, from designing the study to concluding with recommendations.

They must pay more attention to epistemological traits in Cuban gender research, concerning questions such as research/action and participative approaches; comparative studies; case studies and macro-social structures, multidisciplinary, interdisciplinary, and transdisciplinary trends; and involvement and detachment. It would be useful to analyze the Cuban distinctive methodological traits coming out from the Marxist training of all researchers dealing with gender studies.

Finally, a general observation: The fact that the majority of researchers in Cuba started focusing on gender in the midst of the 1980s meant that they did so once already solidly positioned in academia and living in a society where gender relations dramatically changed. This enabled them to learn from the 1960 to 1980 histories of feminist movements in Latin America, the United States, Western Europe, and Canada and to study the huge existing gender studies literature. Therefore, they could close the gap of almost two decades that had passed since their colleagues in other countries started dealing with gender topics. I suggest future analyses focus on the history of feminist thought in Cuba prior to 1959, especially on the characteristics of research done on gender. This would link the delay in the beginning of women's studies to the ways in which feminism was stigmatized up to the middle of the 1980s.

...

References
Agulhon, Maurice. 1983. *La ville de /'age industriel*. Paris: Editions du Seuil.
Alvarez, Mayda. 1995.*Las mujeres cubanas: Problemas de estudio* (Cuban women: Problems of study).*Temas* 1.
Anuario Estadistico de Cuba 1986. 1987. Havana, Cuba: Comite Estatal de Estadfsticas
Araujo, Nara. 1996. *Otras viajeras del Caribe* (Other Caribbean women travelers). *Temas* 5.
Bengelsdorf, Carollee. 1997. *Terreno en debate: la mujer en Cuba: Unensayo bibliogrtifico* (Debatable terrain: Women in Cuba A bibliographic essay). *Temas* 9 (January–March).
Bourdieu, Pierre. [1973] 1987. A opinilio publica nao existe (Public opinion does not exist). In *Critica metodol6gica, investigafiiO social e enquete operaria*, edited by Michel Thiollent. Sao Paulo, Brazil: Editora Polis.
Campuzano, Luisa. 1996. *Ser cubanas y no morir en el intento* (To be Cuban women and not die in the process). *Temas* 5.
Casey, James. 1990. *Historia de la Familia*. Madrid, Spain: Espasa Calpe.
La Población de Cuba (The population of Cuba). 1976. Havana, Cuba: Center for Demographic Studies of the University of Havana.
Mujeres in Cifras (Women in numbers). 1975. Havana: Federation of Cuban Women.
Pérez, Niurka. 1986. *El Hogar de Ana*. Havana, Cuba: Editorial de Ciencias Sociales.
Rubiera, Daysi. 1997. *Reyita*. Havana, Cuba: Word Data y Prolibro.
Safa, Helen. 1989. Women, industrialization, and the federation of Cuban women. Working paper no.133, Kellogs Institute.

Statistical profile of the Cuban woman in the threshold of the XX/ century. 1999. Havana, Cuba: National Office of Statistics.
Statistical yearbooks on Cuba. 1987. Havana, Cuba: Comite Estatal de Estadfsticas.
Vasallo, Norma. 1995. Evolución del tema mujer en Cuba (Evolution of the woman). *Revista Cubana de Psicología* 12 (1–2).

12. Feminist and Quantitative: Measuring the Extent of Domestic Violence in Georgetown, Guyana*

Linda Peake

Introduction

The title of this article alludes to an almost impossible association in Anglo-American Geography; feminist researchers cannot be assumed to conduct quantitative research. Should this even be a matter for concern? Many geographers trained in the Quantitative Revolution period of Geography now avoid a quantitative approach, regardless of their theoretical stance. Methodological approaches, as much as theoretical ones, enjoy their hour in the spotlight, going in and out of fashion with the rise and fall of analytical trends. But in Anglo-American Geography quantitative techniques have never come back in fashion, their association with positivism tainting them beyond redemption. In this paper I attempt to show how these techniques can be decoupled from such a damaging association so that being feminist and quantitative is not only possible but desirable too.

My musings on this issue began during my six-year stint as the Managing Editor of *Gender, Place and Culture: Journal of Feminist Geography*. During this period I oversaw the publication of over 150 articles (as well as reading many more that did not make it through the review stage). Apart from six of these that constituted a set of theme papers on GIS and feminist geography they were all, bar one, based on qualitative research. In addition, over the last sixteen years I have supervised over 30 MA and PhD students in both Geography and Women's Studies, not one of whom has used quantitative methods in their analyses. I raise these figures because I am genuinely concerned that Anglo-American feminist geographers are producing a new generation of students for whom the question "can

---

* Reprinted with permission from *Treballs de la Societat Catalana de Geografia* Issue 66 (2006): 133–48. Excerpted.

feminist research be quantitative?" is irrelevant, simply because they do not have the ability to conduct quantitative research. Many of the papers in *Gender, Place and Culture* are written by senior scholars who were students during the days when Geography was going through its Quantitative Revolution. So, while they have the ability to conduct quantitative research but have chosen not to, the younger authors in the journal most probably did not have this choice; they have either not been given the opportunity to learn how to do quantitative research or they have shied away from it. There are serious political and academic consequences to such moves that I explore here.

The first point I address is how feminist researchers came to disavow the use of quantitative techniques. There is a somewhat lengthy and I would argue fallacious debate in Women's Studies about the nature of feminist research and whether feminist quantitative research is indeed an oxymoron. Feminist geographers have added little to this debate, but some significant points have been raised that deserve further discussion. In particular, I hope to show that it is possible to uncouple quantitative techniques from masculinist versions of positivism, a coupling that "is historically produced and is not necessary or inevitable" (Lawson 1995, p. 451). To illustrate how a critical approach that incorporates feminist practices when using quantitative methods of analysis is possible, I then turn to an examination of a research project I conducted with the Guyanese women's organisation Red Thread on a topic that does not lend itself easily to quantification, namely the nature and extent of domestic violence in Georgetown, Guyana. I conclude by discussing some of the consequences for feminist knowledge production of feminist geographers engaging with quantitative analyses.

Can Quantitative Methods Be Feminist?

In a set of papers addressing quantitative feminist research in Geography published in *The Professional Geographer* in 1995, Sarah McLafferty claims that the central critiques against the use of quantitative methods by feminists are, "Quantitative methods claims of objectivity and their assumed legitimacy; problems of measurement and definition; and the fact that the methods break the living connections between researchers and the subjects of that research" (McLafferty 1995, p. 436). I now turn to address each of these three concerns.

Claims of Objectivity and Legitimacy

The arguments against the use of quantitative techniques are well rehearsed in feminist literature, the most common objection to them being cast at an epistemological level; namely the association of quantitative research with positivism, its claim that science is value neutral and the resultant objectivity of statistical techniques (Harding 1986). It was positivists concern with being able to observe and the counting of observations as the basis on which experiments could be conducted that led to a reliance on quantitative techniques. Hence, claims of the objectivity and legitimacy of quantitative methods arise from them being the techniques used to implement the 'scientific method' associated with positivism, the philosophy of knowledge that undergirded the rise of the sciences in Europe in the nineteenth century. Table 1 outlines the main differences between feminists and positivists in terms of what knowledge is considered legitimate and how it is produced.

Table 1: Defining Legitimate Knowledge for Positivist and Feminist Philosophies of Knowledge

POSITIVISM	FEMINISM
Scientific knowledge derives from the Enlightenment and is based on factual evidence of what can be observed, i.e., it is based on knowledge of objects. It is what Maria Mies refers to as 'contemplative, uninvolved spectator knowledge' or what Donna Haraway refers to as the 'god-trick', or the 'view from nowhere'.	Knowledge is always partial and situated based on experiential, emotional, and subjective values, and developed through praxis.
	Knowledge production includes analyses of how the researchers' identity, experience and theoretical framework shape the research agenda, data analysis and findings.
Knowledge production is a rational undertaking by qualified scientists that aims to specify connections between ideas (scientific theories), experience (what our senses – especially observation – and experiments tell us) and reality (what actually exists).	Knowledge is anti-foundational, i.e., there is no external truth waiting to be discovered. The only possible bases for truth claims lie within communally created history, tradition and culture through dialogic, co-operative debate, i.e., producing knowledge is less an issue of observing objects than of negotiation within an epistemic community.
	Knowing other people is central to the production of human subjectivity.

What Table 1 reveals is that rather than a "quantitative versus qualitative" divide, it is the beliefs about what comprises knowledge and how it is constituted that divides positivists and feminists. It is, moreover, increasingly being recognized within the discipline of Women's Studies that feminist debates about the unsuitability of quantitative methods for feminist purposes are less about these techniques of inquiry being incompatible with feminist research and more with attempts by academic feminists to 'professionalise' their discipline by claiming its own distinctive epistemological approach to knowledge production, one that was least likely to mimic the objectivist, value-neutral epistemological positions adopted in mainstream scientific approaches. As the feminist sociologist Annie Oakley states:

> "Feminism needed a research method, a distinct methodology, in order to occupy a distinctive place in the academy and acquire social status and moral legitimacy. Opposition to 'traditional' research methods as much as innovation of alternative ones provided an organizing platform for feminist scholarship…and the whole contention of positivism and realism as inherently anti-feminist" (Oakley 1998, p. 716).

In other words, the association of quantitative techniques with masculinist views of science has been socially and historically constituted and is itself an ideological position.

A related point is that many academic feminists concerns with explicating a feminist approach to knowledge production have focused solely on questions of epistemology and it is these that have come to define the parameters of debates about the theoretical grounding of research, largely replacing the feminist link between praxis and knowledge production.

Problems of Measurement and Definition

Emphasising the unsuitability of a positivist approach to knowledge production has led to a voluminous literature on feminist methodology. Although exploring a range of issues this body of work is largely constitutive of that which has narrowed down its focus to viewing positivism as synonymous with quantification. Hence the simplistic view that it is the differences between quantitative and qualitative approaches that is of importance and that only qualitative methods can be considered suitable for feminist research: quantitative research is "objective, irrelevant and superficial" while qualitative research is "subjective, relevant and descriptive" (Jayaratne and Stewart 1991, p. 94). There are numerous problems with such a characterisation not least of which is that it erases the similarities between them: "For example, quantitative methods rely on considerable subjective interpretation, and qualitative methods necessarily entail considerable objectification" (Lawson 1995, p. 451). Both methods produce sets of data that require the subjective constituting of boundaries and as such both have problems, albeit different types, of measurement and definition. Although all data, regardless of whether they are quantitative or qualitative, are representations, the quantitative approach of employing numbers to represent women has been deemed unacceptable and the qualitative approach of using women's words acceptable (although the final choice of which words are used is at the discretion of the researcher and not that of the speaker). This understanding of quantitative research, however, jars with the understanding that all data are representations and need to be understood as such.

Breaking the Connections between Researchers and Subjects?

Quantitative research has also been accused of 'breaking the connections between researchers and subjects' thus denying the reality that quantitative methods or counting can be compatible with research that examines contextualized relations. Quantitative research can be conducted in domains other than that of a positivist top-down setting of research priorities, with a separation of expert knowers from those at the bottom of hierarchies of power. What is at stake is not the use of quantification but the ways in which research participants are treated and the care with which researchers attempt to represent their lived experiences, and how they use this knowledge to change lives (Stanley and Wise 1983). It follows that feminist research should be based not on an *a priori* understanding that only qualitative methods can be deemed suitable, but rather that a feminist methodology meets the following criteria:

1. that it can yield knowledge that is reliable, effective, and oppressive neither to women not to other socially marginalized or other disempowered people;

2. that it honours feminists' commitments to taking women's experiences seriously;
3. that it addresses differences between women while retaining a capacity to draw general, even law-like conclusions, but conclusions that derive from specific historical and geographical contexts and not a generalized notion of women.

It is with these criteria in mind that I now turn to a case study of a feminist research project that makes extensive use of quantitative methods while situating itself within a context that takes these criteria as their starting point.

...

The Research Project methods

Having established a Research Team in Red Thread in the early 1990s that had conducted research on a range of topics, the organisation was well equipped to conduct a largescale research project on the extent and nature of domestic violence.[1]

Training the Research team

Two months were spent training the eight members of the Research Team in research techniques including basic skills in literacy and computing. Most time was devoted to an introduction to concepts and skills in research methodologies including participant observation, experiments, archival research, and survey research. Survey research training included learning about survey design, random and non-random sampling, questionnaire construction, in-depth interviews and interview techniques. Training was also given in transcribing interviews, coding of questionnaires, transferring data from questionnaires to coding sheets and transferring data from coding sheets into the SPSSx software programme.

Designing the Survey

In order to conduct research that would investigate the *extent* of the violence experienced by Guyanese women we needed to conduct a survey (as opposed, for example, to focus group or interviews with specifically chosen women). This purpose required a representative sample, i.e., one that would reflect variations existing in the population from which it was taken. This is probably best achieved by taking a random sample because a basic principle of random sampling is that a sample will be representative of the population from which it is taken if all members of the population have an equal chance of being selected. Thus, a random sample (also referred to as a probability sample) refers to the way in which each unit in the sample population is chosen, i.e., each unit has an equal choice of selection and can only be chosen once. In other words, the definition of randomness refers to the mode of selection of sample units and not to the resultant sample.

The study population, i.e., the aggregate of elements from which the sample is selected was the adult population of the country. However, lack of time and financial resources prevented us from conducting a simple random sample that would have involved interviewing women in every region of the country. It was necessary therefore to restrict the sample to Greater Georgetown where 41 per cent of all residents live (Government of Guyana 1998). The elements (i.e., those units about which information is collected and which provides the basis of the analysis) in this case were adult women over the age of 18 years in Georgetown. A list of all adult women over the age of 18, known as the sampling frame (i.e., the list of sampling units from which the sample is selected) was available, namely the 1997 Electoral Register. The Electoral Register lists the names and addresses of men and women of the age of eighteen and over. While we could have drawn new lists to contain only women this would have been an extremely time-consuming task. Hence, our use of the register was based on the underlying assumption that it contained equal numbers of women and men. The high percentage of women who were not available for interview (approximately 40 per cent) because they had moved from the address listed for them does give rise to some concern about the degree of bias this could have introduced into the survey. It is also indicative of the acute housing problem in Georgetown and could not have been avoided. Bias was minimized, however, by selecting the sample randomly and by achieving an extremely high response rate of the women interviewed of over 90 per cent. We are convinced that it was the expertise of Red Thread members, in being able to allay women's fears about answering questions, which resulted in such a high response rate.

In order to compensate for the large geographical area to be covered and make the most efficient use of resources a simple random sample was not chosen. We needed to adopt a sampling design that would concentrate the fieldwork and save time, labour and money. Hence, we adopted multi-stage cluster sampling with stratification. This meant that rather than taking a random sample of all women in all areas of Georgetown that only certain areas (or clusters) were selected (randomly). The first stage clusters (or Primary Sampling Units, PSUs) were the 62 electoral subdivisions of Greater Georgetown. These PSUs were stratified by social class into middle-class and working-class strata. The designation of an area as working class or middle class was determined through discussions with the Research Team and other Red Thread members. While there was much agreement on the designation of the majority of the areas we acknowledge that this is a subjective exercise and acts only as a rough proxy for the variable of social class.

One immediate problem we faced with our choice of PSUs was their differing population size. Whenever the clusters to be sampled are of greatly differing sizes the standard procedure is to use a modified sampling design called probability proportionate to size (PPS). Therefore, because of the unequal population sizes in each electoral subdivision, each PSU was selected with probability proportional to size (PPS). For example, if one PSU has twice the population of another one then it was given twice the chance of being selected. The same number of women could then be selected from each of the chosen PSUs with the overall probability of selection of any woman being the same (remembering that a random sample is defined as one in which each element has the same chance of selection). A sample of the Secondary Sample Units i.e., individual adult women, within each PSU, was then taken (without stratification).

The Interviews

In drawing up the questionnaires, team members drew on their own experiences to discuss the themes we wanted to address. The wording of questions was also altered to fit in with the Guyanese vernacular. Time was spent ensuring that the women could interview in a way that would inspire trust. This involved them being very familiar with the questionnaire so that awkward silences did not disrupt the flow of conversation. No member of the Team was allowed to go beyond this stage to conduct survey interviews until she had the ability to do so. Although this involved considerable time, it was only through such intensive 'quality control' measures that an acceptable level of proficiency could be assured. When sufficient practice interviews had been conducted to ensure that all Team members had acquired a high level of expertise they were further tested through the use of small pilot surveys of ten women each.

At the time of the survey the political crisis in the country meant there were often street demonstrations and riots and the fear, for many, of being attacked was palpable. As a result there were several days when the women in the Research Team did not feel safe to go into certain areas of the city to work. In addition, our decision that the women would work in pairs instead of singly in order to provide a safer context in which to work, obviously increased the length of time it took to complete the survey and three months were spent in the field in Georgetown. Each respondent was interviewed by two Red Thread interviewers in interviews lasting on average for 90 minutes and ranging from fifteen minutes to just over two hours. Each woman on the list was contacted on at least four separate occasions, at different times of day, before a participant on the substitute list replaced her. As mentioned, we believe the high response rate of over 90 per cent owed much to the professional training of the Team members and the close attention paid to quality control. At the end of each day's work, when the Research Team had finished their interviews, each questionnaire was checked over. This was a very time-consuming exercise but was considered vital to maintaining quality control and ensuring that any observations the interviewers had about the area they were working in or their comments on participants could be recorded immediately. It was also at these daily debriefing sessions that decisions were made as to whether a participant would be a good candidate for the focus group discussions that also formed an integral part of this research project.

Analysis of Data on Domestic Violence

The major findings are listed in Table 2. These reveal that regardless of class or race, domestic violence is a prevalent feature in many women's lives. Nearly 80 per cent said domestic violence is very common in Guyana. Over one in four women currently in a relationship were experiencing violence and one in three women knew of someone else experiencing violence. And as surveys in many countries have shown, of

Table 2: Main Findings on Domestic Violence Survey

Aspects of Violence	Findings
Perception of Violence	Nearly four out of every five respondents perceived violence in the family to be very common in Guyana (76.8%).
Definition of Domestic Violence	With regards to the kinds of behaviours that the respondents defined as domestic violence everyday physically violent behaviour such as fighting, beating, or hitting, was recognised by 83 per cent of respondents. Moreover, 50 per cent of the respondents also defined domestic violence as verbally abusive behaviour such as curses, threats, and humiliation.
Experience of Violence as a Child	Over 84 per cent said that they had experienced physical abuse such as licks, slaps, beating. In approximately eight out of ten cases of childhood abuse it was the respondent's mother or other female relative who had administered this abuse. However, for sexual abuse it was invariably male relatives who were responsible.
Knowledge of Violence Experience of Domestic Violence in Current Relationship	Over one in three of the respondents knew someone currently experiencing domestic violence (35.5%). There were 237 respondents (65.8%) currently involved in a relationship or union of some kind. Of these 27.7% (or one in four) had experienced physical abuse; 26.3% (or one in four) had undergone verbal abuse; and 12.7% (one in eight) had suffered sexual violence.
Violence in the Community Women's Responses to Violence	The majority of respondents felt safe as a woman in their own neighbourhoods (81.3%). Most of the women who had experienced domestic violence with their current partner said that they had not done reported their case to the police (78.9%), indicating that only one in five cases of domestic violence is reported.
Women's Knowledge and Use of Services	The majority of women, or more than 65 per cent, had no knowledge of the Domestic Act (67.5%). Of the women who did have some knowledge of the Act, only a few (15.3%, or one in eight) knew what the Act provided for.
Attitudes and Behavioural Practices Relating to Violence Against Children	The majority of all women in the survey felt that children should be punished in some form (70.0%). When the women who agreed that children should be punished were asked about how children should be punished, the most common response was hitting, slapping, and/or lashing. Out of all the respondents hitting was seen as the most agreed upon form of punishment by nearly a third (30.8%). A slightly smaller percentage believed privileges should be withdrawn (26.2%) or that children should be grounded (18.1%). Approximately three in four (72.2%) women with children said they disciplined them by means of physical violence.

those experiencing violence only 40 per cent had sought help of some sort and of these only one in five had gone to the police. Unsurprisingly, over 65 per cent of all women interviewed had no knowledge of the Domestic Violence Act. Yet, while it was women who were experiencing violence perpetuated by men, it was women who were responsible for administering violence towards their children. Over 70 per cent of all women with children admitted hitting their children and over 80 per cent have experienced physical abuse such as slaps and beating as a child.

In 80 per cent of these cases it was the women's mother or other female relative who administered this abuse. Our analysis of the data thus led us to address women's entanglement in violence and define domestic violence as any act, including the threat of acts, committed by a person with whom the victim has or had a conjugal, love or sexual relationship, or a relationship of dependence, which impairs the life, body, psychological well-being or liberty of a woman and/or children.

While the vast majority of abuse between women and men is perpetuated by men we argue that the power relations involved in violence are complex, multiple and contradictory, rather than fixed and predictable. Just like men, women do not live outside patriarchal ideology and practice, and some perpetuate violence against people they are likely to have control over such as children and elderly people. Hence, we argue domestic abuse has a common basis in the playing out of relations of authority and control over other people's bodies.

Conclusion

Karen de Souza, co-ordinator, Red Thread: *'Many decisions about our lives are taken from figures and we don't know where these figures come from and we should be able to control this'*.

I started this paper by referencing the divide between those who do quantitative research and those who choose not to, pointing out the potentially larger divide between those who do not and those who *cannot*. But is this divide only a feature of the Anglo-American academy? It is not often replicated in the South where geographic research in the academy and by non-governmental organisations is often quantitative and where funding and policy decisions are usually made on the basis of quantified data. The avenues open to obtain funding to do research in the South are dominated by international institutional agencies such as the United Nations and the Inter-American Bank for Development. Research projects are concerned with accountability and the ability to measure results, which often require quantitative research. Hence, I argue, a desire by Anglo-American feminist geographers to refrain from using quantitative methods is not an innocent one. It is partially from a cocooning in the academy as opposed to engagement in activism that they have refrained from asking certain questions and have allowed epistemology to take the place of praxis. This has certainly led to an ignorance of the need for certain types of data by women in the South. Feminists who can conduct only qualitative research are limited to asking only certain types of questions, those for which qualitative methods are appropriate; they can ask, for example, about the nature of domestic violence but not about its extent.

Our aim in conducting quantitative research in Red Thread has been to find out more about the nature and extent of domestic violence. Red Thread has used the results of this research not only to help women interviewees who were experiencing domestic violence but also to use the data generated to apply for monies to conduct educational work on eliminating violence against women and against children. The research experience gained has also led to the Research Team being employed by other agencies. It has also been about what Vicky Lawson calls the 'politics of counting' (Lawson 1995), becoming aware of the ways in which women can become 'data literate' in that they can understand what data sources are available, how data come to be collected and how they are translated into statistics, which often purport to portray aspects of their own social lives, as well as the deficiencies of such data, (as the quotation above from Karen de Souza reveals). Our aim was also to prove to funding agencies that women who often had no schooling beyond primary level could work together to produce reliable and valid data. Indeed, it is their very positionality, their already situated knowledge of women's everyday lives in Georgetown that has allowed women in Red Thread to collect such high quality data. Engaging in these research projects has also allowed us to discuss such questions as: why are only certain data collected and why the data are organised into particular categories. Not only do these questions expose the political nature of the process of the production of social statistics about women and also the ways in which quantitative techniques can powerfully reveal lived oppression, they also reveal assumptions about the valuing of women.

The implication for Anglo-American feminist geographers is that there needs to be much greater flexibility over questions of suitable feminist methods; the recognition that no method is inherently feminist and that all data are representations are useful starting points. Finally, for those feminist geographers concerned with the social construction of knowledge there also needs to be a re-emphasizing of the links between activism, social change and research as opposed to a focus primarily on questions of feminist epistemology and the diversionary debate over quantitative versus qualitative research.

Notes

1. For the results of other research projects conducted by Red thread see Peake (1998), Peake and Trotz (1999, 2001), Trotz and Peake (1999, 2000, 2001). For information on Red Thread see Andaiye (2004), de Souza and Peake (2009) and Peake (1993, 1996).

References

Andaiye et al. [on behalf of Red Thread Women's Development Programme]. 2004. *You Talking 'bout everyday story': An Exploratory Study on Trafficking in Persons in Guyana*. Georgetown: International Office on Migration.

Bunch, C. 1990. Women's Rights as Human Rights: Toward a Revision of Human Rights. *Human Rights Quarterly* 12:486–98.

de Souza, K., and L. Peake. 2009. Feminist Academic and Activist Praxis in Service of the Transnational. In *Towards a Transnational Feminist Praxis*, ed. R. Nagar and A. Swarr. Minneapolis, MN: University of Minnesota Press.

Government of Guyana. 1998. *1990–1991: Population and Housing Census of the Commonwealth Caribbean. National Census Report Guyana*. Georgetown, Guyana: CARICOM.

Harding, S. 1986. *The Science Question in Feminism*. Ithaca, NY: Cornell University Press.

Jayaratne, T., A. Stewart. 1991. Quantitative and Qualitative Methods in the Social Sciences: Current Feminist Issues and Practical Strategies. In *Beyond Methodology: Feminist Scholarship as Lived Research*, ed. M.M. Fonow and J.A. Cook, 85–106. Bloomington, IN: Indiana University Press.

Lawson, V. 1995. The Politics of Difference: Examining the Quantitative/Qualitative Dualism in Post-Structuralist Feminist Research. *The Professional Geographer* 47, no. 4:449–57.

McClafferty, S. 1995. Counting for Women. *The Professional Geographer* 47, no. 4:436–41.

Moser, C., and L. Peake. 1996. Seeing the Invisible: Women, Gender and Urban Development. In *Urban Research in Developing Countries Volume 4: Thematic Issues*, ed. R. Stren, 279–347. Toronto: Centre for Urban and Community Studies, University of Toronto.

Oakley, A. 1998. Gender, Methodology and People's Ways of Knowing: Some Problems with Feminism and the Paradigm Debate in Social Science. *Sociology* 32, no. 4:707–31.

Peake, L. 1993. The Development and Role of Women's Political Organisations in Guyana. In *Women and Change in the Caribbean*, ed. J. Momsen, 109–31. London: Macmillan. Reprinted in *Engendering Caribbean History: Cross-cultural Perspectives: A Reader*, ed. V. Shepherd. Kingston, Jamaica: Ian Randle Publishers, 2008.

Peake, L. 1996. From Social Bases to Subjectivities: The Case of Red Thread in Guyana. In *Global Cities – Local Places: Issues in Urban Sustainability*, ed. D. Bell, R. Keil and G. Wekerle, 147–54. Toronto: Black Rose Books.

Peake, L. 1998. Living in Poverty in Linden, Guyana in the 1990s: Bauxite, the 'Development of Poverty' and Household Coping Mechanisms. In *Resource Sustainability and Caribbean Development*, ed. D. McGregor, 171–94. Kingston, Jamaica: University of the West Indies Press.

Peake, L., and A. Trotz. 1999. *Gender, Ethnicity and Place: Women and Identities in Guyana*. London: Routledge.

———. 2001. Feminism and Feminist Issues in the South. In *Companion to Development Studies*, ed. V. Desai and R. Potter, 334–37. London: Arnold.

Profitt, N. J. 1994. Resisting Violence against Women in Central America: The Experience of a Feminist Collective. *Canadian Social Work Review* 11 no. 1:103–15.

Trotz, A., and L. Peake. 1999 (on behalf of Red Thread). 'Givin' lil bit for lil bit': Women and Sex Work in Guyana. In *Sun, Sex and Gold: Tourism and Sex Work in the Caribbean*, ed. K. Kempadoo, 263–90. Boulder, CO: Rowman and Littlefield.

———. 2000. Work, Family and Organising: An Overview of the Emergence of the Economic, Social and Political Roles of Women in British Guiana. *Caribbean Journal of Social and Economic Studies* 49, no. 4:189–222.

———. 2001. Work, Family and Organising: An Overview of the Contemporary Economic, Social and Political Roles of Women in Guyana. *Caribbean Journal of Social and Economic Studies* 50, no. 2:67–102.

13. Interdisciplinary Feminist Research, Environment, and Community: The Nariva Swamp Case Study

Rhoda Reddock and Grace Sirju-Charran

This chapter draws on the research experience and findings of a multidisciplinary, multi-method study of a 'wetland of international importance', The Nariva Swamp in Trinidad and Tobago. It addresses a number of theoretical and methodological questions related to the study of gender and the environment. The research questions were organized around the sub-themes of livelihoods, sustainability, equity, and governance and addressed themes such as (1) the history of state policy over the twentieth century; (2) household and community governance; (3) the impact of natural resource use on sustainability of the ecosystem; and (4) socio-economic, culture, and community relations of the inhabitants, all using a gender analysis for two communities located in the swamp, Kernahan and Cascadoux.

The Nariva Swamp was selected over other areas due to the national conflicts and contestations taking place at that time regarding the use of the area and its resources. There is a history of activities with deleterious effects on the environment, such as logging, large-scale rice cultivation, over-fishing, and now seismic oil exploration. The scale of human pressures and dependency on the land has made it an area of acute interest at a local, national, and international level and an example of the conflicts between the state and farmers' concerns with food security, and the imperatives of ecological security which may appear less immediate. In 1992, it was declared a site of international ecological importance under the Ramsar Convention, and in 1993 it was placed on the Montreux Record which lists wetlands whose ecological character is threatened.

This research was considered particularly groundbreaking in that it aimed to incorporate gender analysis into an interdisciplinary study of a contested ecosystem. This innovative and experimental project sought to examine the socio-economic, cultural, political, and ecological factors impacting upon the sustainable use of the Nariva Swamp. Further, it was anticipated that this research could provide a gender-sensitive database of material, which would ensure that policy initiatives emanating would empower women and the communities in general. This could be achieved by sensitizing them to the biophysical environment and the impact of their use of its resources; to produce research material that integrated a gender analysis into an interdisciplinary framework and finally, to thoroughly evaluate 'the scientific method' as understood and practised by natural and physical scientists as a tool for researching environmental situations.

The research study comprised four principal components. The first was designed to develop a gender analysis of this ecosystem, examining how its natural resources were utilized differently by men, women, children, and youth of both sexes and subsequently to use this information to develop proposals for sustainable use. The second component involved the exploration of power relations and governance within the households, the community, and at national levels, with a particular focus on the historical perspective. This component focused on the history of state policy in the Swamp over the last century, tracing the changing policy approaches of colonial and post-colonial governments and the process contributing to its current status. The third component focused on household and community-level governance issues and the economic, gender, socio-economic, and other differentials. This component enabled researchers to grasp the manner in which the local administrative and control structures functioned in order to develop a community, despite the precarious natural, political, economic and social environment. The fourth component integrated material on gendered social relations within households and the wider community, economic configurations, and cultural practices of the women and men living in the swamp and their location within and relationship to the bio-physical environment.[1]

Research Methodology

This study went beyond many of the development-oriented women/gender and environment studies carried out in other parts of the world. For one, it was conceived as an interdisciplinary study, which would bring together a number of academic disciplines that do not normally work together. In particular, it raised issues about 'the scientific method' and the debates around it. One question raised was whether what we were trying to do was to introduce a new variant/approach to the scientific method or whether there was only one scientific method in which case this research could be perceived as non-scientific. As noted by Lélé and Norgaard:

> What starts out in the pure sciences as only a problem of subjective choice of taxonomies or models burgeons into the issue of the value-laden nature of natural science when working on phenomena of social relevance. But most natural scientists have been brought up on the notion that science is value neutral. This belief proves to be a barrier both to working across disciplines and to doing good science (Lélé and Norgaard 2005, 969).

One final concern driving the research exercise was a commitment to empowering the women of these communities and exploring possibilities for facilitating gender consciousness and heightened sensitivity to the biophysical environment within the community and in policy prescriptions.

The overall research was conducted in each of the 78 households of Kernahan and the 33 households of Cascadoux, and spanned almost one year. A team of four young researchers – economist, ecologist, agricultural scientist, and political scientist/gender studies scholar (three female and one male) carried out the field research. Two project coordinators, a sociologist and gender studies scholar, and a plant biochemist coordinated the overall study. Interestingly, an animal scientist carried out the historical study of state policy in the Swamp over the twentieth century.

The methodological philosophy adopted was one aimed at establishing strong interpersonal connections with the members of the communities, hence, avoiding the patterns of the rapid rural appraisals, which have more commonly been used in the region. Methods of gathering and validating data were drawn from both the natural and social sciences (and were influenced by feminist methodological concerns). Hence, they involved the application of both qualitative and quantitative methods and participatory approaches. Qualitative techniques employed included participant observation, transect walks, historical and social mapping, direct observation, semi-structured interviews, focus groups, oral narratives, genealogies, and archival research on secondary data. The quantitative methods comprised the use of questionnaires, water and soil testing, and the collection and analysis of demographic data.

Central to the epistemological framework of this project was a critique of traditional scientific methods of accumulating data. Approaches characteristic of Participatory Rural Appraisal (PRA) methods were used as they provided an alternative to traditional methods used in environmental research. In addition to integrating and empowering the communities, this approach permitted members of a community to create their own representations of their realities and their relationships to the environment. PRA is a structured methodology that perceives community participation in the research process as essential. Moreover, it seeks to gain multiple perspectives, recognizing that local knowledge is as important as academic knowledge. It provides a forum for interactive learning and the sharing of knowledge as well as giving voice to members of the community. This was combined with ethnographic observation techniques and sustained interaction with community members.

The expansion of traditional PRA methods to include feminist epistemological concerns and ethnographic techniques emerged from the recognition of the limitations of this approach. As noted by Ilan Kapoor (2002,104), although starting from a premise of participation and theorizing from the bottom up, by privileging the existing structures, this approach may be less successful in addressing issues of power, hierarchy, and even participation; its very point of departure.

To accumulate material, the researchers lived within close proximity to the communities for a period of approximately nine months. They were able to develop strong connections with the villagers, through various means, such as sharing daily tasks, having informal discussions and 'liming'.[2] It was envisaged that such activities would build a sense of trust between the researchers and the villagers and result in a more comprehensive understanding of their existence and links with the environment.

More challenging, however, were the efforts to integrate gender into the research exercise. The researchers, trained in a mainstream scholarship that excluded gender analysis and was antagonistic to interdisciplinarity, felt ambivalent at times, or even resentful of the challenges to their existing worldview. Researcher Sharda Durbal, trained in agricultural science and environmental science describes this below:

> Permeating the entire research process was my difficulty in grappling with the concepts of gender, ethnography, PRA and the methods to

be utilised in such a study. The need to collect data and incorporate it into a framework for analysis ...posed a particular problem for me, particularly as I came from a science background. Cook and Fonow (1986) appropriately describe (sic) this problem as follows: 'we have been trained to think in terms of a positivist schema which equates the term methodology with specific techniques for gathering and analysing information.'... I had no prior understanding or knowledge of the ethnographic process or the use of reflexive accounts in the documentation of the research process. Methodology was a key issue for me as I worked in fear of my results being considered superficial by a life science body. My readings and discussions with various people however allowed me the freedom to better understand why and how to use and work with the methods that were being introduced to me (Durbal 2000, 19).

The mapping techniques used, drew heavily on information from villagers as well as observations in the field. They generated data on the history and development of the communities with respect to changes over time, the use of the natural resources, and decision-making processes between men and women. Some of these maps included: gendered resource maps, seasonal charts, and historical maps. These were useful tools for fieldworkers, as local people often have a deeper knowledge of their surroundings and awareness of the subtle changes over time, and these maps produced by the community members were local conceptualizations and representations of space based on peoples' lived experiences, reinforcing Sletto's argument that maps are now being re-read as ideological representations of the social contexts and interests of their creators (Sletto, 2002, 390). These maps encouraged the villagers to think reflexively about their position and role within the environment. In the words of researcher Sharda Durbal:

Mapping exercises were done with individuals and groups of different ages, sex and number of years lived in the communities. Villagers were asked to describe the development of the communities, the plant and animal life, the people, the use of resources and the changes in the area over different periods of time. These methods also assisted in creating greater awareness within the community of the importance and benefits of wetlands, as they were able to see from their own descriptions and drawings the change in the use and availability of resources over time and how this has affected livelihoods and the environment in which they live...Maps drawn by women served as a reminder of the first families to settle in the area, whereas men's maps showed the vastness and dense nature of the forest at that time (Durbal 2000, 12).

The use of questionnaires was seen as complementary to ethnographic and other qualitative techniques. Indeed, many of the observations and informal discussions with villagers supported the questionnaire responses. Yet a major contradiction of the use of PRA methods proved to be the gendered limitations placed on women in these communities. It was easier to access male participation in the collective research activity with community members than female participation. This was due mainly to the sanctions on mobility for women as well as their heavy responsibilities for housework, childcare, and subsistence agriculture (gardening). This experience supports the contention of Kapoor who pointed to the coercion and intimidation that prevented free and equal deliberations in PRA exercises (Kapoor 2002).

The use of Geographical Information Systems (GIS) was also integrated into this approach, particularly in the research on Gender and Natural Resource Use. This technique generated land-use maps, including gender-differentiated spatial-use maps of the area and their changes over time. Nature and transect walks[3] through the community and adjacent areas, accompanied by biologists, provided an opportunity for the villagers to identify the species around as well as determine which of these resources were used by the community, how they were used, and by whom. Data on the history of the area, medicinal plants, cultural practices, and use of resources were recorded. It gave the researchers and younger villagers an opportunity to learn from the older members about the natural and social history of the area and the behaviours of plants and animals in the natural environment.

Many findings were further substantiated through direct and participant observation by the researchers. The constant presence of the researchers in the villages aided this process of verification or refutation. Although no claims of empowerment can be made for this exercise, the approach used also involved sensitizing villagers on a range of ecologically related issues. Educational workshops were organized, for example, on the importance of wetlands, and on bush fire prevention and women of the community were taken on field trips.

In relation to the empowerment component of the research, there were many issues which emerged. On the one hand, as noted in the Composite Report:

> We were faced with the task of facilitating, mobilising and organising in a community divided by religion, class and physical location. Family networks, age and gender also contributed to the difficulty of these tasks. Existing community groups provided an opportunity to more easily organise youth for eco-tourism activities. However, these groups were not really active.

It was acknowledged that even such methods as PRA are not without their limitations.

Ultimately, the data belong to the researcher, and very rarely are truly collaborative efforts achieved. *Give Back Sessions* can be instrumental in reversing this sense of exploitation and lack of ownership by the people being researched. Additionally, the researchers realized that collecting data about the villagers' personal lives was problematic, as their time was precious and few were keen to have such information published and potentially made public knowledge. Hence, issues of ethics arose during and after the research period as villagers objected to some of the information presented in one of the reports as community members could be easily identified. In that instance, the team had to undertake to withdraw the documents and have them re-written; not in a way that sacrificed substance but one which protected their identities.

The researchers were reflexive about their experiences in the field, recognizing that their own gendered identity and social class and cultural assumptions heavily influenced the research data collected. For example, it was noted that the male researcher was considered more accessible to the men, especially when discussing illegal activities, such as cultivating marijuana and trading arms. Conversely, female villagers were reluctant to speak openly with the male researcher unless their spouses were present which, in turn, altered the content of the conversations.

THE CASE STUDY

Robert K. Yin (1984) defines the Case Study Research Method as 'an empirical inquiry that investigates a contemporary phenomenon (issue or problem) within its real-life context when the boundaries between the phenomenon and the context are not clearly evident.' In contrast to the Scientific Method and statistical surveys which use large samples and follow a rigid protocol to examine a limited number of variables, case study methods involve 'an in-depth, longitudinal examination of a single instance or event: a case.' While the Case Study is typically used to carry out qualitative descriptive research on an individual or group of similar individuals, it does not preclude quantitative methods which could form part of the 'multiple sources of evidence.' This latter allows for the process of triangulation of the data which takes into account alternative perspectives and explanations in order to minimize the limitations of a single study and hence achieve greater accuracy.

The case study approach that had largely been used for law, medicine, and business studies proved to be useful in determining the success of community-based prevention programmes and seemed to be a viable option for the study of Gender and Environmental Sustainability in the Nariva Swamp. Previously documented research on this protected wetland area was disciplinary in nature, e.g., the biological specimens present in the swamp were documented by Peter Bacon et al. (1979), and a sociological analysis of the Kernahan community was reported on by Sletto (2002). Several reports on environmental sustainability projects led to the widespread recognition that scientific and other quantitative research methods which are inflexible in their requirements, provided data which were inadequate and could not be easily transferred into policy and actions. By using a case study approach, it was possible to gather data based on a gendered and interdisciplinary examination of the historical, socio-economic, cultural, political, and ecological factors affecting the sustainable use of Nariva Swamp, beginning with an exploratory phase which led to description and some explanation of the findings to guide policymaking.

The unit of analysis was the Nariva Swamp in which the communities of Kernahan and Cascadoux were selected for study. Each community was treated as an individual entity in order to arrive at a comprehensive understanding of the ways in which men and women use and relate to the natural environment in their setting, without attempting to treat them as replicas in the study. Although the project was initially conceived to carry out the research in three other communities with some degree of similarities but each having their particular uniqueness, the financial resources and trained researchers required were not available. It was, therefore, decided to limit the study to an in-depth analysis of these two communities.

However, the data obtained in both studies could be analysed based on the theoretical propositions espoused in the literature on gender and environmental sustainability, and empirical patterns could be compared with those predicted, using reasoning from specific to more general terms (inductive method). In addition, comparisons could be made between both communities and explanations given for similarities and differences observed.

Data on each of the communities were gathered using a variety of sources and methods in order to obtain as complete a picture as possible. These included documents and archival records (history); open-ended, focused, and structured interviews (social sciences); direct observation (ethnography); and bio-physical artefacts (life sciences). Examples of the latter include collecting data on the flora and fauna using a transect walk and determination of the soil and water quality in the swamp. Tools for gender analysis (e.g., evaluation of the sexual division of labour, ownership, and control of resources, resource use, decision-making) as well as tools used in participatory methodology (e.g., focus group, resource mapping, key informants, story-telling) were included as far as was feasible in each of the methods employed. All attempts were made to cross-check the data from the multiple sources of evidence (four researchers and multi-method data gathering) using the processes of triangulation and reflection. Triangulation is a method in Trigonometry and Geometry used by navigators, surveyors, and mapmakers to accurately determine the distances between three points. The term was adopted in social science research to describe using multiple sources of evidence to more accurately determine complex human behaviours and in qualitative research as a way to improve the validity and credibility of the findings. It removes the bias and shortcomings inherent in a single-observer; single-method, single-theory approach. In this study, triangulation was achieved in two ways: (i) by having at least two and in some instances all four researchers obtain data on the same social phenomenon (e.g., spatial mapping and use of the resources) and (ii) by using different methods (e.g., observation; focus group, key informant) to obtain the same data. Reflection on the data was achieved by allowing the researchers to individually analyse and interpret the data collected before sharing with the others, in order to arrive at a consensus on the findings.

A further exercise in triangulation was carried out in that the draft report was presented orally to the community and copies made available for their perusal and comments in preparation for a further meeting at which corrections were made, until a consensus was reached. Following this, the conclusions were drawn and the report document finalized.

The case study was suitable since the behaviours being researched were not homogeneous and routine and, therefore, not amenable solely to research methods that use statistical analyses. In order to achieve as complete an understanding as possible on the roles of men and women in their environment, the interplay among all the variables examined was attempted in the analysis. It involved descriptions of the sexual division of labour, gendered responsibilities, and expectations, understanding how these were arrived at in that particular community and explaining how such analysis could influence policy and actions to promote sustainable use of a protected environment. This also required an overlay of interpretation of community values, their gender ideologies, motives, cultural norms, mores, and attitudes all through a gendered lens.

Not only did the case study approach allow for the collection of both quantitative and qualitative data using several methods and sources of evidence, which could be 'triangulated', it also facilitated a multidisciplinary team of researchers to carry out an interdisciplinary study which had gender as its focus. The challenge of becoming immersed in the community was addressed at various levels. The initial introduction to the community was made by a senior biologist who was well-known and respected in the community. This was followed up with community training using an international facilitator who was an expert practitioner in community-based resource management. Further community meetings at which refreshments were provided were held by the researchers in order to build trust among the members.

GENDER ANALYSIS

Gender analysis involves disaggregation of quantitative and qualitative data by gender in order to highlight the different experiences and power relations and the impacts of learned behaviours of men and women. It seeks to understand how these differences shape and are shaped by structural (demographic, economic, legal, spatial, institutional), cultural and religious factors.

It was important to obtain gender-disaggregated data in this research in order to produce gender-sensitive policies, since it was well-documented at this stage that earlier community-based projects which were carried out without regard for gender had failed in the implementation stage. It was important to have participation of both men and women in all of the research activities.

A number of gender analysis frameworks now exist in the literature. Most of them incorporate the following: an activity profile during which data on *who* does *what* or the 'Sexual Division of Labour' is gathered. It records what men, women, children (boys and girls), and even the elderly do and when and where these activities take place. The *'what'* normally includes all aspects of work – the productive, reproductive, and community. Differences related to ethnicity, class, location (rural/urban), and age should also be documented.

The second layer involves identifying 'who has what' that is who has access to and control of the resources (land, capital, equipment) and services (labour, credit, and decision-making) and the benefits derived from this. The trends observed in stages 1 and 2 are analysed based on the socio-economic context, and are then considered in planning projects or developing policies which are more likely to be effective and equitable.

SCIENTIFIC METHOD

Steps in the scientific method include the observation and description of phenomenon, formulating a hypothesis to explain the phenomenon, designing, and performing experimental tests which would either support or refute the hypothesis and reporting the results for scrutiny of the methods used and the results obtained. The results could be replicated and the hypothesis used to predict the results of further similar tests.

Water and soil quality tests were performed on the water found in the channels and soil samples taken from selected areas in Kernahan. It was hypothesized that the lack of a sewerage system as well as the use of agrochemicals would have compromised both water and soil quality and thus affected the population of Cascadoux and other river dwelling organisms. This was also responsible for rashes and other health problems observed particularly among the children. The experimental tests were carried out using established scientific procedures with appropriate controls and duplications.

While similar results would be expected if these experiments were repeated in another laboratory using the water and soil samples collected, if they were to be repeated using samples taken at a different time or at a different site in the same ecosystem, some variation is to be expected, since these results would be affected by seasonal variations in weather as well as land and water use. The requirement of the scientific method to be predictive also could not be satisfied in this instance.

HISTORICAL METHOD

Historical methods involve collecting data from primary and secondary sources to create a narrative which explains a hypothesis or adds new knowledge in a particular area. During the last three decades of the twentieth century, social history has grown in importance, removing the prior dominance of archival-based history of important people and events. Social history has focused on the lives of ordinary people and everyday events which, in the past, would not have been considered significant. It also involves the use of methods such as the oral history interview, genealogies, analysis of visual documentation, etc., in addition to the analysis of documents and archival material.

In constructing the narrative on the origins of Kernahan and Cascadoux communities, the primary and secondary sources of evidence included historical documents, newspaper reports, and 'historical' mapping of the land space (constructing spatial maps) using focus groups. This latter engaged the community, particularly its elders, to draw pictures of the area at specific time periods, e.g., when they first inhabited the space followed by other maps at different times, noting the significant event which caused the changes (e.g., women moving in; destruction by a hurricane, etc.). This was juxtaposed with the history of governance systems in these communities by tracing the changes in state policy during the same time period. 'Oral histories' were used to triangulate this data. This method involving interviews from different classes, age groups, ethnicities, sexes, etc., would be useful in documenting the history of any community in the Caribbean.

The data gathered using different methods were segmented according to the issues being researched, e.g., the change in agricultural crops being produced; changes in land use patterns and population growth during the period of its settlement. Data from both communities (Cascadoux which was settled much earlier and Kernahan) were compared and an account of the analysis and conclusions were documented in the report. Although there is software available to assist in qualitative data analysis, e.g., NVivo8 and QSR, these were not accessible and hence were not utilized in this study.

PARTICIPATORY RURAL APPRAISAL METHODS (PRA)

PRA methods were used as they provided an alternative to traditional methods used in environmental research. In addition to integrating and empowering the communities, this approach permitted members of a community to create their own representations of their realities and their relationships to the environment. PRA is a structured methodology that developed out of the RRA – Rapid Rural Appraisal methods in response to the critiques of that method. This approach, usually associated with the work of Robert Chambers (1994), perceives community participation in the research process as essential. Moreover, it seeks to gain multiple perspectives, recognizing that local knowledge is equally important as academic knowledge. It provides a forum for interactive learning and the sharing of knowledge as well as giving voice to members of the community. PRA has developed a number of characteristic techniques drawn from other methodological approaches and include – semi-structured interviewing; focus groups; preference ranking; mapping and modelling; seasonal and historical diagrams; trend lines, institutional diagrams; wealth ranking. While some of the methods are similar to the ethnographic methods the main difference is the need for community participation.

The main PRA techniques used in this study were informal group discussions, in-depth and key informants' interviews, resource access profiles, gender-based needs assessment, gendered and community mapping exercises, and transect walks. Attempts at wealth ranking failed due to resistance by the villagers to have this information documented, although proxy markers of wealth (e.g., type of house, ownership of television, car, etc.) could have been attempted to ascertain how wealth is accumulated in the community.

The tools used were mainly qualitative and, therefore, the analysis followed the norm used in analysing such data, i.e., segmenting based on the phenomenon being examined; using the multiple sources of data for triangulation and arriving at a consensus report with conclusions; and recommendations for policy and action, from the findings.

A two-week training and orientation programme for the researchers and community members was organized in the community at the start of the research process. This was facilitated by an expert in PRA who trained the researchers and carried out workshops with up to 100 villagers.

This was critical for the success of the PRA approach. It was difficult, however, to maintain this level of community participation due to time constraints of villagers, especially women who were normally quite busy and experienced gender constraints on their mobility. There was greatest participation by young men as even young women were constrained by domestic responsibilities.

The expansion of traditional PRA methods to include feminist epistemological concerns and ethnographic techniques emerged from the recognition of the limitations of this approach in being able to mobilize women and the marginalized and hence their voices and concerns. As noted by Ilan Kapoor (2002, 104), although PRA starts from a premise of participation and theorizing from the bottom up, it often privileged the existing structures. This approach turned out, in some instances, to be less successful in addressing issues of power, hierarchy, and even participation – its very point of departure. In our study, a major contradiction of the use of PRA methods proved to be the gendered limitations placed on women in these communities. It was easier to access male participation in the collective research activity with community members than female participation. This was due mainly to the sanctions on mobility for women as well their heavy responsibilities for housework, childcare, and subsistence agriculture (gardening). This experience supports the contention of Kapoor who pointed to the coercion and intimidation that prevented free and equal deliberations in PRA exercises (Kapoor 2002).

Another issue which emerges with PRA has to do with the benefits derived by community members for their participation. While policy-related research can point to possible changes in the future, this is not always possible for academic researchers. In this study, the research team sought to give back to the community some benefits for the use of their time. Although some members would have preferred more tangible results like employment or money, the community benefited through a greater understanding of the ecosystem and their role as its custodians. The women in the community – young and old – were provided with alternative models of womanhood through their observation of the young women researchers who challenged gender stereotypes through their education and in conducting this research as well as other professional activities in which they were involved.

The literacy level of these Caribbean communities is sufficient to allow them to participate fully in research. This became evident when we received their feedback on the draft report one week after they had received it.

ETHNOGRAPHIC METHODS

This method is derived principally from anthropology and involves studying people and their activities, operating in their natural environment in order to understand the world or community from the point of view of those who inhabit it. The researcher(s) immerse themselves in the community in order to understand the culture and gather data from within through questioning, listening, watching, talking, participating, etc., and not only to describe but to analyse how this social organization is accomplished, understood, and achieved by the social actors.

As mentioned earlier, the field researchers in this study comprised three females and one male, each from a different disciplinary background viz. agriculture, biology, gender studies/political science and economics. While housing accommodation in the communities was desirable, this was unavailable and the researchers were therefore housed close to the community for a period of nine months, which allowed them to spend all day until late evening in the community. They had to overcome a great deal of scepticism and mistrust from community members engendered as a result of a number of issues. The community had already experienced a number of studies conducted by researchers from which they had experienced little benefit; some members were involved in illegal activities and may have been wary of being discovered and reported on; in addition, their ability to remain in the swamp to eke out their livelihoods was under threat from the state since they were 'squatters', and environmental NGOs were reporting on the unsustainable way in which the resources were being used. The researchers, however, were able to negotiate their entry and to build trust among the members of both communities by holding workshops which emphasized the ways in which the community could benefit through their empowerment as participants in the research. An important first task was the mounting of a facilitator's workshop to train 12 community members to conduct participatory research (PR), and this was followed by a community workshop at which the trained facilitators assisted community members in conducting the PR activities.

The methods employed included direct and participant observation, in-depth interviews, focus group discussions; community mapping, key informants' interviews (oral histories, trend lines) and informal conversations ('liming'). While tape-recording of the data is sometimes used in ethnography, in this particular case, the principal method used was to record all observations in a fieldwork diary at the end of each day. This was seen as less intrusive and less inhibiting by the researchers. These were all qualitative methods which were analysed as appropriate for each tool used.

Most observations were overt, and could be critiqued as being 'contaminated' since the research subjects were aware that they were being studied; however, this avoided the ethical concerns of collecting data covertly. In spite of the financial (limited budget) and time constraints (nine months), the researchers were able to produce 'thick descriptions'. This was facilitated by the researchers' commitment and their decision to spend most of the budgeted time in the field at the expense of returning to home-based libraries and discussions with the research co-coordinators, a feature which did compromise the data analysis during the report writing stage. A further limitation of ethnographic methods is that the data could be 'shaped' by the researchers' own cultural location; however, this was minimized in this study through the multidisciplinary nature of the research team as opposed to the norm of a single individual doing anthropological studies, as well as by sharing the data with members of the community, which contributed to the final editing of the research report. The most significant outcome of this approach, however, was that it enabled the voices of a range of community members – women, men, girls and boys of diverse economic status and physical location in the community – to be heard. It was clear that in order to achieve sustainable use of the resources in Caribbean countries, community participation was essential.

MAPPING EXERCISES

The mapping techniques used, drew heavily on information from villagers as well as observations in the field. They aided in the generation of data on the history and development of the communities with respect to changes over time, the use of the natural resources and decision-making processes between men and women. This approach provided another layer of data to add to data obtained using traditional historical methods which does not involve the community's participation.

Some of these maps included gendered resource maps, seasonal charts, and historical maps. These were useful tools for fieldworkers, as local people often have a deeper knowledge of their surroundings and awareness of the subtle changes over time. These maps produced with the community members were local conceptualizations and representations of space based on peoples' lived experiences, reinforcing Björn Sletto's argument that maps are now being re-read as ideological representations of the social contexts and interests of their creators (Sletto 2002, 390).

Although wealth-ranking is usually one of the features of social mapping, in this study there was great reluctance from the community to declare the source and quantity of earnings. However, maps were constructed to position other indicators of well-being, e.g., schools, places of worship, water supply, sources of fish, as well as the location of leaders and other skilled persons. These maps (social mapping) encouraged the villagers to think reflexively about their position and role within the environment. It could assist in avoiding duplication and encourage collaboration among members of the community.

GEOGRAPHIC INFORMATION SYSTEMS

According to gis.com 'A geographic information system (GIS) integrates hardware, software, and data for capturing, managing, analyzing, and displaying all forms of geographically referenced information'. The use of geographical information systems (GIS) was also used in this research study, particularly to document gender and natural resource use and the spatial organization of the ecosystem. One of the researchers worked closely with an expert to generate land-use maps including gender-differentiated spatial-use maps of the area and their changes over time.

Data from aerial photographs taken in 1942, 1980, and 1994 were digitized, and the G.I.S. software, Arc Info., Digital Automation Kit, and Arc View were used to produce land maps. These were infused with data obtained from men's and women's focus groups discussions on land and resource use to produce 'gender resource maps'. This method was useful as it integrated both quantitative and qualitative research data into a visual representation.

TRANSECT WALK

A transect walk according to one source 'is essentially a walk over the transect of an area to observe and document the similarities and differences of socio-economic and bio-physical features'. It is usually used in areas where there is spatial diversity (http://portals.wi.wur.nl/ppme/?page=1143). It is one of the tools used in PRA to observe and document the bio-physical and socio-economic features of the study site. Ecologists also use transects to document the populations of plants and animals in an ecosystem. (See http://pcs.aed.org/manuals/cafs/handbook/sessions10-12.pdf.)[4]

In this study, a transect line was selected in the Kernahan community which traversed the representative micro-ecosystems (swamp land; dry land (fallow and cultivated). Observations and documentation of the flora and fauna were carried out by a team comprising a botanist, an entomologist/zoologist, elders in the community familiar with the biological resources as well as youth of the community who aspired to become tour guides and environmental custodians. The data gathered were compiled into a list which included the scientific and common names of the biological organisms observed as well as the common names and local uses of these resources. It provided an opportunity for the villagers to identify the species and determine which of these resources were used by the community, how they were used, and by whom. Data on the history of the area, medicinal plants, cultural practices, and use of natural resources was recorded and some of this was used to construct a resource map. In addition to providing data for the study, this method gave the researchers and younger villagers an opportunity to learn from the older members about the natural and social history of the area and the behaviours of plants and animals in the natural environment and to identify whether any specie had become extinct or were requiring conservation measures. Although both women and men participated there were usually more men for reasons mentioned earlier. These were some of the more popular activities and both researchers and community members learned a great deal. This method lends itself to easy replication in other parts of the Caribbean. It was interesting to experience the adaptation of this tool, used by ecologists, to gather sociological data which enhanced purely natural scientific data (e.g., plant and animal abundance).

Conclusion and Discussion

The research methods used were successful to varying degrees. Some were more successful than others. For example, the researchers could not live in the communities due to unavailability of accommodation. As a result, they lived close by and visited daily. Residence within the community may have facilitated a deeper understanding of those aspects of life not easily observed during the day. They could also have observed with greater insight, the dynamics of the sexual division of labour and household power relations. Additionally, the two lead investigators came from two different disciplinary frames – one from the natural sciences and the other from the social sciences resulting in continuous debates throughout the study on a number of conceptual issues. This may have been a bit confusing for the field researchers.

The inclusion of a significant component of reflexivity in the full research report, therefore, allowed these issues to be reflected on and provided useful learning for future researchers. At the time the research was being conducted, the Nariva Swamp was very much a contested wetland and the community members mainly squatters. The presence of researchers in the community was viewed with suspicion by some villagers. This was so even though the researchers were introduced to the community by a senior biologist who had earned their respect; community meetings were organized to explain the research to the community in the early stages and community based exercises were carried out. These suspicions were allayed to some extent by community give-back sessions where the information was returned to the community and with time as community members became more familiar with the researchers.

If this study were to be replicated, every effort should be made to have the researchers live in the community as this would increase access to female community members and give greater insight on life experiences as a whole. In addition, the researchers may need greater preparation and clearer guidelines to successfully carry out inter and multidisciplinary work. The male researcher was responsible for the research on household and community governance. In his reflections he noted his difficulties in speaking with women without their spouse's presence which affected the data collection process. In similar vein, the female researchers examining the socio-economic, cultural, and gender analysis found that they were unable to access male community members, e.g., in the 'rum shop', which was the place where men frequently congregated and spoke freely. Clearly, gender was a factor in the social and spatial organization of the community. This affected the research exercise itself and this should be considered in research design. Finally, this kind of ethnographic and participatory research requires sustained interaction. In the planning stages, we had to convince scholars in the natural sciences of the need for such a long research period in the field. In replicating this study this extended research period should be maintained or even extended.

References

Academy for Educational Development, Population Communication Services. 2002. Session 10: Transect Walks and Observation. In *Empowering Communities: Participatory Techniques for Community-based Programme Development*, Vol. 2, Participant Handbook. Washington, DC. http://pcs.aed.org/manuals/cafs/handbook/sessions10-12.pdf.

Bacon, P., J.S. Kenny, M.E. Alkins, S.N. Mootoosingh, S.N., Ramcharan and G.B.S. Seebaran. 1979. Studies on the Biological Resources of Nariva Swamp, Trinidad. Occasional Paper No. 4, Zoology Department, University of the West Indies, St. Augustine.

Chambers, Robert. 1994. The Origins and Practice of Participatory Rural Appraisal. *World Development* 22, no. 7:953–69.

Kapoor, Ilan. 2002. The Devil's in the Theory: A Critical Assessment of Robert Chambers' Work on Participatory Development. *Third World Quarterly* 23, no. 1:101–17.

Yin, Robert. K. 1984. *Case Study Research: Design and Methods*. Newbury Park, CA: Sage.

Lélé, Sharachchandra, and Richard B. Norgaard. 2005. Practising Interdisciplinarity. *Bioscience* 55, Issue 11 (November): 967–75.

Sletto, Bjorn. 2002. Producing Space(s), Representing Landscapes: Maps and Resource Conflicts in Trinidad. *Cultural Geographies* 9:389–420.

Research Project Reports

Basdeo, Rishi. 2000. Community Level Governance in Kernahan and Cascadoux: A Gender Analysis. Research Report, Centre for Gender and Development Studies, The University of the West Indies, St Augustine.

Centre for Gender and Development Studies. 2001. The Nariva Swamp: A Gendered Case Study, with special reference to Kernahan and Cascadoux, Composite Report, The University of the West Indies, St Augustine.

Cross, Nicola and Gabrielle Hosein. 2000. Socio-Economic, Cultural and Gender Analysis of Kernahan and Cascadoux, Research Report, Centre for Gender and Development Studies, The University of the West Indies, St Augustine.

Durbal, Sharda. 2000. Gender and Natural Resource Use in Kernahan and Cascadoux, Research Report, Centre for Gender and Development Studies, The University of the West Indies, St Augustine.

Lans, Cheryl. 2000. State Policy and Governance in the Nariva Swamp: A Historical and Gender Analysis, Research Report, Centre for Gender and Development Studies, The University of the West Indies, St Augustine.

Notes

1. The project encompassed four areas of research study, from which the following reports were produced: 'Gender and Natural Resource Use in Kernahan and Cascadoux'; 'State Policy and Governance in the Nariva Swamp: A Historical and Gender Analysis'; 'Community Level Governance in Kernahan and Cascadoux'; and finally, 'Socio-Economic, Cultural and Gender Analysis of Kernahan and Cascadoux'. In addition to these, a composite report was prepared in January 2001.
2. Liming – passing the time, hanging out with others, socializing.
3. Transect Walk – A transect walk is a systematic walk along a defined path (transect) across the community/project area together with the local people to explore specific ecological or environmental conditions by observing, asking, listening, looking, and producing a transect diagram. A tool for describing and showing the location and distribution of resources, features, landscape, and main land uses along a given transect, https://www.google.tt/?gfe_rd=cr&ei=AvYpV520A9aK-gWqsbLYCw&gws_rd=ssl#q=transect+walk.
4. These two websites initially viewed around 2007–08 are no longer available.

Sexualities Research

14. No Tide, No Tamara/Not Today, Not Tomorrow*

Gloria Wekker

Misi Juliette Cummings's Life History

...

How do I tell the story of Misi Juliette Cummings's life, a life that spanned almost the entire twentieth century, 1907 through 1998? It is clear that the narrative that unfolds in these pages is a story that we, in a very real sense, crafted together, and thus I am as present in these pages as she is. In seeking the truth in between the participant-observer and the informant, I do not play the "God trick." I cannot hide myself behind the role of an invisible and omniscient third-person narrator (Haraway 1991). Having finally tapped into Juliette's seemingly endless source of stories about women she had sexually connected with, I teasingly remarked one day: "Luku, Juliette, a gers' ef' ala sani den umasma hen du, in' a ten dati, a ben de fu didon makandra" /Look, Juliette, it looks like the only thing women in the olden days did was to lie down together. She was indignant: that was not true at all. I was the only one who wanted to know everything about her life and hear her stories. On the most obvious level, then, Juliette and I crafted this narrative together. No one had ever asked her in such a sustained way about her life, her friends, how she made a living, what she expected from and enjoyed in male and female sexual partners, or about her children. Inspired by my ceaseless questions, events that had become shrouded in the mists of time came to light again for her.

On yet another level, this narrative is a coproduction, a segment of the lives of each of us that was crossed. In that sense I want to

---

* Reprinted with permission from *The Politics of Passion: Women's Sexual Culture in the Afro-Surinamese Diaspora*. Columbia University Press 2006, 3-54. Excerpted.

acknowledge the ways in which our, both mine and Juliette's, erotic subjectivity were crucial in its forging. My positionality as an Afro-Surinamese anthropologist who loves women was vital in helping me gather thick information about her and other Afro-Surinamese women's sexuality. In the past decade the debate has been opened on the powerful vantage point that acknowledgment of the erotic subjectivity of the ethnographer affords. Instead of the ideal agent of value-free, objective knowledge, which "requires a notion of the self as a fortress that must be defended against polluting influences from its social surroundings" (Harding 1991:158), fieldwork by an ethnographer who starts from the premise of equality and who acknowledges difference yields less biased, more valuable and sensitive data.

If in participant observation it is the person of the researcher, which serves as the most central and sensitive instrument of research, it behooves us to be transparent, accountable and reflexive about the different modalities in which the self engages with others. Acknowledgment of sexual subjectivity should not be misread as a license for an unbridled, honorless exploitation of the Other on a more intimate level than has thus far generally been acknowledged. I am suggesting that methodology provides information about the various ways in which one locates oneself- psychologically, socially, linguistically, geographically, epistemologically, and sexually – to be exposed to experience in a culture (Wekker 1998). This position entails a fundamentally different relationship between the researcher and the people with whom she works than traditionally has been envisioned. I work from an inverted model, which starts with a simple but rather fundamental acknowledgment: but for the grace, patience, and interests of the people involved, there would be little research. Both researcher and the people involved are subjects, active agents with their own en1otions and agendas. Moreover, all knowledge is gained at the intersections of race, gender, class, and sexual locations; thus, "all scientific knowledge is always, in every respect, socially situated...neither knowers nor the knowledge they produce are or could be impartial, disinterested, value-free, Archimedean" (Harding 1991: 11). There is not *one*, optimal position from which to do research; the positions are as varied as we are. At the very least we must own and acknowledge our locations, and there is no good reason to exclude sexual locations from our work, either as an a priori or a posteriori excision.

So, by way of preliminary answer to the question I posed at the beginning of this chapter: I will tell Juliette's story as faithfully as she told it to me, and the process of her telling me her stories, embedded as it was in an atmosphere of being mutually attracted to each other, is a part of this narrative as well, with all the joys and difficulties our positions entailed.

I want to ask this question in a second sense: how do I tell Miss Juliette's life history, and the sexual stories of other Creole working-class women, in light of a dominant Euro-American history of representing Black women's sexuality as excessive, insatiable, the epitome of animal lust, and always already pathological? How do I avoid staging a latter day Sarah Baartman show, with Juliette as the traveling spectacle this time? In this second sense, as well, I feel implicated. The question has preoccupied me in the many years since I first embarked on this project. Ultimately, the only pertinent answer is that I expressly call attention to the history of dominant representations of black female sexuality in order that this deeply racialized, lethal imagery can be deconstructed. By now it has become commonplace to say that sexuality is gendered and classed – and I will discuss these interconnections elaborately in the course of this text – but the imbrication and foundational inscription of sexuality with "race" is still something that can be overlooked, in many studies, without too many serious consequences. Thus not only black sexualities suffer from these inscriptions, white and other ethnicized and racialized sexualities are also constructed by various inscriptions, resulting in differential positions regarding appropriate and "normal" sexuality and corporeality. In lending my pen to Creole working-class women who speak in their own words about their sexualities, I hope to contribute to that deconstruction.

On Oral History

> *To tell a story is to take arms against the threat of time, to resist time, or to harness time. The telling of a story preserves the teller from oblivion; the story builds the identity of the teller and the legacy which she leaves for the future* (Portelli 2001:59).

Juliette was a gifted storyteller, who obviously enjoyed being my center of attention over an extended period of nineteen months and incidentally also after the first period of my fieldwork when I returned to Suriname or when she came to visit her children, including me, in the Netherlands. The point in her life cycle at which she told me her stories, in 1990–1991, was significant. She had a lot of time, because she did not have any children that she was responsible for and she did not have to work anymore. She accommodated her life, no more or less, to mine. In addition, she still was very sharp and remembered minute details of events that had happened seventy years earlier. When I last was with her, in 1997, she could not tell me those stories any more, although she vividly remembered our time together. The length of the period in which I interviewed her resulted in my hearing several stories repeatedly as well as different versions of one story, e.g., she told me two versions of the first time she had sex. As rapport grew and she trusted me more, she gave me more details and her stories started to include quite intimate details.

Juliette did not tell me her life history chronologically; one day she preferred to tell me ado/proverbs and sing songs; another day something propelled her to recount an event in her life or to give me an interpretation of the characters of her children. Yet I have chosen to reconstruct her life mainly, but not exclusively, chronologically because that has seemed the most accessible form to me. Oral historian Alessandro Portelli notes that when the narrator herself does not perceive one particular event or epoch as a key event or pivot in her life, that is to say, when she sees her entire life as meaningful, then that makes it easier to take chronology as the organizing factor (2001:66).

Sometimes the story wanted to be told differently, however, jumped ahead of itself. As I reconstructed her life, I have encountered problems dating events. Often I have had to estimate her age in the context of public events or the length of intimate relationships. Like her, I used the ages of her children or grandchildren, or other significant events like World War II, as signposts.

In interviewing Juliette about her life, I have worked on the assumption that I was dealing with verbal artifacts (stories) shaped by Juliette's self-perception, by the encounter with me as the interviewer, and by my perception and interpretation of Juliette and her words (Portelli 2001). It should thus be clear that oral history as an ethnographic practice cannot lay claim to the impossible dream of attaining the absolute "truth" of a life or of history. Since Juliette's telling of her life is part of her life, what we have is something that may not be the truth, but it is something otherwise invaluable: her interpretations of her experiences. These are coloured in the light of what she perceived me to be interested in. I have no doubt that with a different interviewer, interested in other themes, she would have come up with other stories. The question to be contemplated is not "what is the relation *between* life and story," but far more interesting, rather, "what is the place of the story *within* the life" (Portelli 2001)? How does she construct the story in order to project a particular persona? What are the characteristics of that persona? What is important for her to bring across?

In order to answer those questions, it is necessary to introduce another way of analyzing Juliette's story. In addition to the chronological or horizontal mode, which narrators may or may not pay attention to in their narration, they often use three different vertical levels to organize the narrative of their life: a personal, a collective, and a national and global level. Portelli describes these levels as follows:

> *Personal:* private and family life; the life cycle of births, marriages, jobs, children, and deaths; and personal involvement in the two other levels. Space referent: the home.
>
> *Collective:* the life of the community, the neighborhood, and the workplace; strikes, natural catastrophes, and rituals; and collective participation in "institutional" episodes. Space referent: the town, the neighborhood, and the workplace.
>
> *Institutional:* the sphere of politics, government, parties, unions and elections; the national and international historical context; and ideology. Space referent: the nation and the world (Portelli 2001:70).

...

Power and the "Erotic Equation in Fieldwork"

> *My informants are not just interesting cases. Over the years many have become friends of mine...I fully recognize this common affinity and use it to understand my informants better, to engage in discourses with them, and, through these dialogues, to develop my own insights into their culture and personality...I am one with them, yet not one of them* (Obeyesekere 1981:11).
>
> *The field researcher, therefore, has an objective stake in equality, as a condition for a less distorted communication and a less biased collection of data* (Portelli 2001: 31).

Not nearly enough has been written about the psychological underpinnings of "the erotic equation in fieldwork" (Newton 2000), either from the point of view of the anthropologist, much less from that of the "informant." I will assume that the days and the gendered dangers of being labeled a "field groupie," committing professional suicide, are long gone. Or, worse, that my relationship with Juliette would be considered as taking advantage of a poor, lonely, older woman. I believe it is important that we continue a frank conversation about the erotic subjectivity of the ethnographer who is doing fieldwork. I was confronting a psychologically extremely potent mixture of loneliness, being without the context of family and friends, of dependency, my "normal" persona of a professional erased or simply not relevant (Kondo 1992), at times, being very different from the women around me, feeling reduced to somewhat childlike status, and at others being like one of them, gratitude for being seen by another person, even if Juliette's gaze only included particular aspects of myself. Admittedly, these were aspects of self that I had not been interpellated by before, such as Juliette reading me as being carried by Amerindian spirits, meaning that she saw me as warm-hearted and friendly; yet she also saw me as extremely argumentative always taking things too seriously, thinking too much, "full of tricks"; not having proper mati manners, not showing respect at the right moments and in the required ways. At times I was aware that I eroticized Juliette's knowledge. Interestingly, the relationship between Juliette and me reminded me in some ways of a relationship between a client, me, and a very special and wise therapist. When new knowledge is part of the stuff that eroticism is made of, then Juliette provided me with plenty. My appreciation for and excitement about the knowledge I was acquiring of the way the world functioned, my development of cultural, linguistic, and religious insights and skills, knowledge of her and myself, was considerable. The setting, very accepting and very loving, in which it was possible to say, ask, and share everything and in which I had the feeling she saw me in by-and-large favorable ways, worked toward that perception too. Knowing Juliette renewed me, it shed new light on me in ways that I had not known before. My research was an adventure that taught me not only about a sexual culture but also about myself. Our encounter was a mutual benevolent sighting; we liked each other and each of us came to see the other as a gift, a very unexpected one. All these ingredients resulted in fertile conditions for me to connect erotically with her.

Not nearly enough has been written yet either about the differential power aspect in a same-sexed erotic relationship between an "informant" and an anthropologist (but see Whitehead and Conaway 1986; Kulick and Willson 1995; Lewin and Leap 1996; Newton 2000). At the time it was important to me not to be the initiator of the relationship. For mostly ageist reasons I never imagined Juliette as a possible sexual partner or that she had erotic interests in me. Had I been the initiator, it would have been hard to sort out my motivations, whether I was doing it to get better data – which would have been unacceptable to me – or because I was "simply" and genuinely attracted to Juliette. Ironically, although the end result ostensibly is the same, I note the different positioning of Ralph Bolton (1996), who made an intentional decision to use male same-sex sexual encounters as a form of data collection in the field of sexual practices in the time of the HIV/AIDS plague. I am less concerned with ethical aspects of his methodology, although he generally does not seem to address power dynamics and imbalances sufficiently and he unproblematically assumes that a sexual encounter will carry the same weight and meaning for his sex partners. More interesting in these configurations are the gendered positions a gay male and a lesbian anthropologist occupy in the field of sexuality, which underscore that gayness and lesbianism, within Euro-American contexts, are not symmetrical positions, that we need to be far more attentive to such differences, and that one of the ways to uncover them is precisely through being transparent about our sexual positionings.

During my research I was not consistently aware that, while I was ostentatiously learning about the construction of her sexuality, I was also and simultaneously learning about my own. Many insights came afterward as I was reading through my extensive field notes. There is a rich field of oppositions in the ways in which she and I constructed desire and acted on it; whereas for her an age difference of more than forty years did not play a role, for me this difference was – initially and also in the long run – largely prohibitive. In my diary at the end of July 1990 I noted:

> This morning, when I came out of the shower, I passed Juliette in the kitchen and, laughing loudly, pleased with herself, she cupped my

breasts with both hands. To her grandson Raymond, visiting from the Netherlands with his wife and sitting in the living room, she exclaimed: "Mi fas' en bobi, yere!"/I touched her breasts, you hear! I was somewhat taken aback and said: Ee-eeh!?! She said: "M' e kon grani kaba, mi pikin s'sa, na granisma kan du den san' disi"/I have grown old already, little sister, it's older women's prerogative to do this.

I took her gesture for what she said it was and thought it rather charming. In hindsight, I have come to interpret it as Juliette already expressing her sexual interest in me. This gesture could have gone unnoticed to Raymond and his white Dutch wife Rita, who was appreciably older than him, since they were in the living room and Juliette and I were in the kitchen. But Juliette expressly called their attention to it. Coupled with her clear pleasure in her own audacity, she was not only playing and flirting with me, but she was also showing herself as a sexual persona to her grandson. There was a naughty and ingenious touch to this gesture: in the first place, she seemed to be signifying a well known odo to him: "M' e owru, ma mi n' e kowru"/ I may be old, but I am not cold. Raymond, who was about my age, responded by chuckling, which I read as his applauding his grandmother. Thus, in this reading, she was showing off to him: look, I am much older than you, but I am still capable of flirting with a woman of your age, while you have a much older woman. The second reading I offer of the gesture is that it is ingenious because it remains ambiguous whether a sexual overture is being made or not. It *is* true that older women may teasingly touch younger girls' budding breasts, but I could not possibly be counted in that age category. I felt her gesture as a sexual overture, and she implicitly conceded that it might be sexual, but that did not matter anyway. Since she was old already, it was her prerogative to do so, implicitly pointing me to the privileged position of older women in Creole culture. I later regarded this as a key signifier in how she conceived of our relationship.

In my diary of August 1990 I jotted down the following thoughts, struck by the directness of Juliette's sexual overtures, which contrasted with my own, until then largely implicit, standards in this matter.

> How is it possible that in a culture that has been called so "roundabout," e.g., by Herskovits in his diary at the Schomburg (1928), I am being propositioned so directly? Her way of courting me is so incredibly

direct, according to my standards. No double entendres here – maybe they are lost on me? But I do not think so; the objective is sex. No vanilla sex is intended, no cuddling and stuff; she wants sex, genital sex.

On the one hand, it is sort of embarrassing that our flirting and teasing got so out of hand. On the other, incredibly funny, rich, true to life. I have to admit that I do like the thought that she finds me attractive and that I get the old mati treatment. But am I really drawn to her?

What am I to do? I don't think having sex is a very good idea, I want to remain her daughter rather than become her mati. How would we continue to live together, if things do not work out? I am not prepared to move out, look for another place to live, and lose her, the worst scenario.

With Juliette as the initiator, I, having ended the relationship with Carmelita by then, but socialized into the notion that being sexually intimate with "an informant" was certainly not the thing to do, kept on hesitating for a while, going back and forth, trying in my diary to come to clarity about the nature of my feelings for her, struggling with my ageism. I sometimes hoped that her desire would dissipate, that it would vanish as silently as it had come, and that things would return to being warm and unproblematically mother-daughterish. Sometimes I enjoyed her ardency, making the knot of contradictory emotions even more inextricable. I have no doubt that I sent contradictory messages. I thought she was attractive and I liked flirting with her, but I did not want to pay the price that was apparently attached to a relationship. I was living on her premises and I had her and my house to lose if things did not work out. Moreover, I had reasons to believe that my freedom to go and come as I pleased would be seriously jeopardized – specifically, that she would object to my sleeping with someone else. Having had multiple simultaneous relationships in the past, this was not an academic issue. I had socialized, during the seventies and eighties, in mainly white lesbian circles in Amsterdam that put premiums on individuality and on inventing and living models of relating in which monogamy and possessiveness were avoided (Wekker 1993, 1998). Jealousy was just not cool, and one would not want to be caught at it. I was quite competent at performing in these modes. At a later stage the Eurocentric model of lesbian relating had become tiresome to me: "equality" along several dimensions, age, education, income, and status, was deemed important, with ethnicity playing a more problematical part, and one's lesbian "identity" inescapably meant sexual incarceration with only women. But I knew experientially no other models. From the late eighties on, I mainly had relationships with black women, but that did not necessarily guarantee different models of relating, largely correlating with how long a partner had lived in the Netherlands and whether she had mainly dwelt in white or black circles. Nor was I really prepared to change my ways when someone wanted another, monogamic, way of relating to each other.

My ways of handling the situation with Juliette, stalling, explaining why I did not think it was a good idea, interrogating her about what would change if I did sleep with her, negotiating with her, did not make much impression on her. She had made up her mind that she wanted me and was not about to take no for an answer. As I came to understand her perspective in due course, the fact that she, as the older woman, was propositioning me made it something I could almost not refuse. There was no ambiguity in Juliette's answer when I queried about the sustainability of my love of freedom: "I mus' denk' m' e law"/You must think that I am crazy.

Oral historian Alessandro Portelli reminds us of the importance of thinking through the roles of equality and difference in field research. The two concepts, equality and difference, are related:

> Only equality prepares us to accept difference in terms other than hierarchy and subordination; on the other hand, without difference there is no equality only sameness, which is a much less worthwhile ideal. Only equality makes the interview credible, but only difference makes it relevant. Fieldwork is meaningful as the encounter of two subjects who recognize each other as subjects, and therefore separate, and seek to build their equality upon their difference in order to work together (Portelli 2001:43).

How can these notions of equality and difference be unpacked in the encounter of Juliette and me? And, more specifically, did our landscapes of equality and difference, as we would have described them to ourselves or to a sympathetic outsider, look the same? Putting the matter in the latter terms already points to a fundamental point of difference in the domain of the formation of our subjectivities. While I would have welcomed the occasion to piece myself together by laying out my understanding of the relationship to a trusted outsider, who came along later in the person of

Delani, Juliette would never have directly or fully described the relationship to someone else. She might have dropped hints about it to her peers, as she did with Raymond and Rita and other family members, on occasion, and she might have listened to others jokingly allude to it, but she would never have openly discussed the ins and outs of the relationship. Writing about our relationship now means that I am engaging in a practice that is foreign and not necessarily congenial to her. Even though we agreed that her life was worth telling, and she was very supportive of my writing a book about mati, it was understood that I would only write about our relationship after her death (Wekker 1998). In seeking the truth of the relationship from her point of view, it might seem as if I am ventriloquizing her. I base myself upon my descriptions of her behavior and utterances, as they are recorded in my field diaries. The extent to which I manage to describe the relationship as it appeared to her, and describe it with integrity, is also the extent to which I have come to understand the world from her point of view. The encounter between Juliette and me, in this land in-between, is open to aesthetic and moral judgment (McCarthy Brown 1991).

It might be easy to assume that I had more power than Juliette in the relationship. In many respects and contrary to what the few descriptions of sexual relationships between (white) male anthropologists and informants of color have told us, Juliette on balance had more power than I. As Creole women, although I was a "prodigal daughter," we were on a level playing field in our negotiations with respect to the intersection of gender and ethnicity. My unpracticed eye put us within the same range of light skin colors, but her insiders' eye did not fail to notice several shades of color between us. This signified differently in her universe than it did in mine: since I had not grown up in Suriname, I did not automatically make connections between lighter skin color and class status. On several occasions it became clear to me that part of her pride in showing me off had to do with the combination of my age and my lighter skin color. Our class situation as measured by income was not radically different, neither she needing me financially nor the other way around. We both had income in foreign currency, the most desired financial modality; she received her most important means of living from her children in the Netherlands, while I had two consecutive U.S. scholarships. Certain elements of my middle-class status, e.g., being a PhD candidate – which to me was very meaningful – were virtually erased in her universe; my professional accomplishments simply were not visible and thus did not mean much to her. She did like the poem "Creole Women", which I wrote in March 1990,[1] and she was proud when, shortly after, it was published in one the national dailies, *De Ware Tijd*.

Other possibilities that my class position, in conjunction with my nationality, might and did entail in my interactions with others, e.g., entry into the Netherlands by acting as someone's guarantor or even the possibility of Dutch citizenship by being in a relationship with her/him, simply were not relevant in my relationship with Juliette. She had her children to ease her entry into the Netherlands whenever she wanted to visit and, at her age, had no need whatsoever for the Dutch nationality. The intersection between class and nation did not carry significance in our case.

Besides being meaningful as regards skin color, class, in its lived reality, was accentuated for us both at different moments. I already mentioned the occasions when I accompanied her to the doctor and protested against the treatment that was deemed appropriate for someone of her class. She became strangely mute in middle-class environments, where working-class people are often treated with disrespect. However much I liked my house and the neighborhood where we lived, I did occasionally experience the need to be away from the noise – with different kinds of music coming from four corners – the crowding and the basic living conditions. Sometimes, when the chance presented itself, I stayed in the homes of middle-class friends, who were traveling, and twice Juliette and I spent a weekend in a luxurious hotel. In the environments where I was most at ease she was least at ease, and the other way around was true too; where she blended in, e.g., in our neighborhood, at Winti Prey, and at parties, I was initially uncertain as to the proper behavior. At the hotel we would sit on the terrace by the swimming pool, on a Sunday afternoon, drinking high tea. I enjoyed our outing immensely, while she was mostly silent. I realized that she enjoyed being with me, but not necessarily the location where I took her. People of her class background, which was evident by her traditional working-class Creole attire, had never been welcomed at the hotel before. When we got home she would not fail to tell our next-door neighbor, however, where we had been that weekend.

In the end, it was culture and age that played out most in her favor in the balance of equality and difference between us. She was the expert in a culture, a politics of passion, that I wanted to understand. Moreover, she was older and thus within a Creole context where respect is due to older people, especially women, she was "always right." By the end of October I accepted her standing invitation to "lie down with her." I was enamored of the deeply cultural explanation she had given me of her feelings for me, how her yeye/ her "soul" had taken to mine and had clearly recognized the *Inyi Winti/* the Amerindian spirits that were carrying me. These were the same Winti carrying her. Interestingly, at other times, she used a biological discourse to explain her feelings. She supposed that the blood-building injections and pills the doctor had been giving her for her spleen had given her blood more strength and had made her feel alive again: after all, she was not made out of wood.

In *Death Without Weeping: The Violence of Everyday Life in Brazil* Nancy Scheper-Hughes writes about the strong connection poor Brazilians make in their autoethnography between poverty and sex. Sexual vitality is the only thing that reminds them that they are not dead. She movingly describes an old woman, a bag of bones, her infected foot doused in iodine, dancing sexily and suggestively with a young boy (1992: 164–165). Poverty and hunger have not been as endemic and systemic in Suriname as in Brazil's Nordeste, and thus the Surinamese configuration, although in some respects reminiscent of the Brazilian, is not the same. I have understood Juliette's zest for life and sex within the context of a culture that grasps sexuality as an extraordinary joyful and healthy aspect of life, possibly a feature of the West African "grammatical behavioral principles" (Mintz and Price 1992 [1976]) in the domain of sexual subjectivity, the expression of which does not need to end in an advanced stage in life. This is in stark opposition to the representation of asexuality that predominantly characterizes older Euro-Americans, with all its limitations and loss of pleasure. The latter representation works toward limiting sex to that venerated stage of life, youth, and is in need of as much explanation as the Afro-Surinamese modality.

Juliette was extraordinarily frank with me in discussing her feelings and behavior and to the extent that I have come to understand the mati work and Creole working-class culture, I owe it largely to her. Our relationship was complex, multilayered, by no means easy, or to be taken for granted. I felt a mixture of love, gratitude, and sometimes transferred anger toward her as a dominant, demanding mother and a jealous lover. She was my most important informant, collaborator, commiserator, supporter, friend, mother substitute. She saw me as a child with Surinamese roots, her little sister, who did not know the first thing about the culture and who badly needed educating in terms of the language and culturally appropriate manners. Juliette's openness toward me was a mirror of my attitude toward her and it certainly helped that in my life, too, mostly women have been the "apples of my eye." We often exchanged information and I would tell her as much from my side of the world as she would tell me about hers. I discussed different theories about the mati work with her, e.g., that some people who had studied the phenomenon thought that women engaged in it because of the absence of men. She responded with a tyuri, sucking her teeth. I told her about developments with regard to homosexuality on the African continent; that the leaders of some African nations held whites responsible for spreading homosexuality. Her concise comment: "No wan bakra ben leri mi, mi pikin s'sa"'/no white person has taught me, my little sister. We shared our stories about the women who had been important in our lives and laughed till we cried about ourselves and the women who had broken our hearts: cathartic sessions for us both. Juliette would repeatedly sigh: "a mati wroko na wan law sani"/the mati work can drive you crazy. And after an exchange about different techniques of having sex, she summed it up: "baya, ala sortu nay de"/my word, there is all kinds of screwing. I told her my coming out story and how my father, at first, had not liked my being a lesbian at all. I explained to her that, where I came from, to be a woman who loves women had long been disparaged and brought feelings of shame and hiding. Such feelings were unthinkable in Mis' Juliette's universe; she had never heard of anything of that kind. "Sortu, syen? Meisje, un kon mit' a wroko dya. A no un' mek' en"/What do you mean, shame? Girl, we found the mati work when we got here. It was not us who invented it. It was one of the early markers of her radically different value structure and the formation of her sexual subjectivity.

...

Epilogue

I was no good at the rules of her game and she did not see any honor in mine.
(Gloria)

The multifaceted relationship I developed with Misi Juliette has been pivotal in my understanding of the mati work. In my diary of March 1991 I wrote:

> I stayed home today to get all kinds of things done, but can't say I was very productive. Have mainly been chatting with Juliette. We talked about how it will be when I move back to L.A. again in July. It made me very sad and she noticed it and said that I should not cry. She is so beautiful and wise. I do feel utterly safe with her and when, as last night, she is sitting with me and chatting a mile a minute, while I am working on my paper, my whole heart melts for her and I find myself wishing and expressing to her that she was forty-five years old again. She said that if we would have been the same age, we would have stayed together all of our lives. I told her that I love her as my mother, and that that is really not a bad thing, because it will last forever. We have become family. She said that she knew that, but that she loves me more than I love her, since I am her last mati. After me she will take no other lover and she knows that I will.

But times were not always so edenic. In fact, in hindsight I learned most intensely on occasions of conflict and misunderstanding, moments when my ideas and values as a Europe-centered lesbian sharply clashed with her mati world. Inadvertently I caused wounds and a cultural crisis by my, in her eyes, unspeakable behavior. Shortly before I wrote the above entry, I met Delani McDonald, a thirty-eight-year-old schoolteacher, and I thought that it would be possible to openly have a relationship with her, because I had now defined my relationship with Juliette as family. Although I suspected that it would be no simple matter, I still believed that as long as I was clear about my feelings, and if I took care to keep on spending considerable time with Juliette, it would have been possible. My attitude baffled and scandalized Juliette, and this she made clear in no uncertain terms.

In Juliette's view I was still her last mati, her little "chicken," whom she spoiled mercilessly, but in return for which she demanded absolute fidelity. And if she could not have absolute fidelity, she wanted me to hide artfully my other liaison from her. Delani was not to come to my house or to parties and events that Juliette and I attended. Delani's attempts to be on good terms with Juliette, by sending over a bouquet of flowers and fruit on her birthday, were met with flat refusal: the flowers were immediately thrown in the trash can. Unfortunately, there were some *lemki*/little limes,[2] in the basket, which Juliettte read as a sure sign of Delanis bad faith: her wish for the relationship between Juliette and me to go sour.

My job, the prescribed way of placating Juliette, was to make her feel that my eyes were on her only, whatever it took. I could not do that. Her jealousy drove me crazy, my "roving eye" made her furious, wanting to beat me up, although she was so tiny and fragile. I was no good at the rules of her game and she did not see any honor in mine. She always thought that I really knew better, that I was willfully violating mati codes. For my part, I was desperately groping to make her see my view of the situation. She exposed me, on several occasions, for behaving callously and selfishly toward her, of behaving like a man – the ultimate putdown – when I thought I was merely being my own autonomous self, putting a lot of store in a situated and, under the circumstances, myopic version of being "transparent and honest." I often thought of Adrienne Rich's words in her noteworthy essay "Women and Honor: Some Notes on Lying:"

> An honorable human relationship – that is, one in which two people have the right to use the word "love" – is a process, delicate, violent, often terrifying to both persons involved, a process of refining the truths they can tell each other...And so we must take seriously the question of truthfulness between women, truthfulness among women...so that lying (described as *discretion*) becomes an easy way to avoid conflict or complication? Can it become a strategy so ingrained that it is used even with close friends and lovers (1979:188–190)?

These insights were of little help, indeed counterproductive, in my situation. Juliette and I shared some important aspects and values of a same-sexed universe, but others we decidedly did not.

I became sharply aware that we both inhabited a *specific* same-sexed sexual space. Not only did I thus learn about her world, I also came to see characteristic aspects of my own construction of sexuality. Knowledge about the proper ways to embark upon and to end a relationship, which I so took for granted, is deeply culturally inflected. There can be no doubt that "same-sexual activities in distant cultural settings are not transparently comparable to such relationships at home" (Lewin 2002:114). It was in the domain of how to end a relationship that I fell most seriously short of Juliette's norms because, according to her, I gave *Delani ede na tap' en/* placed Delani above her. I had humiliated Juliette. Juliette reproached me with never having formally ended the relationship with her, after which I could have had sex with Delani and then returned to Juliette. She preferred to see Delani as an incidental sexual interest and continued to treat me as her mati, because I had not followed the culturally prescribed way to end the relationship: *mi no ben bedank en/*had not "thanked" her, temporarily ended the relationship. She felt very strongly about the fact that she had been there first, before Delani; since I had not ended the relationship with her, it was still going on, as far as she was concerned.

I preferred to blur the fact that my sexual relationship with Juliette had ended. I did not want to have sex with her anymore, but, apart from that, I did not want to end or change my relationship with her at all I wanted two simultaneous relationships, with her and with Delani. In a typically boundary-blurring mode, however, I did not want to openly state that. It was too painful to tell her that the sexual part of our relationship had ended.

Further intercultural puzzles were presented by the cultural markers that indicate one is in a relationship with another woman, by the different modalities in which one can relate to another woman, the proper ways to deal with one's mati – which, to me, seemed oppressive, violent, and insincere, at times – or about the best techniques to have sex with a woman; all this I learned and all this was different from the knowledge I possessed. My relationship with Juliette confronted me with my ageism, my preconception that an octogenarian would not be interested in sex, would not be jealous, would willingly and wholeheartedly give me the space I wanted. I also came to see that my preferred configuration of autonomy, transparency, and sexual freedom was, from the perspective of the mati work, highly situated, individualistic, self-centered, and really untenable.

In the end, Juliette, Delani, and I were, not without struggle, able to come to terms and to live with ourselves and each other. I learned a bit of *kor'kori/sweet-talking*, humoring her; she, being always right, stated that she did not have to learn or change anything. When I behaved in a decent and respectful mati way, that is, kept Delani out of her sight as much as possible, she was quite pleased. But gradually she indulged me by consenting to Delani's more frequent presence. Again, food played a symbolical role in the process of rapprochement between Juliette and Delani. While for months Juliette refused to feed Delani when she came to visit me, she eventually would give her food, too, although naturally she would not serve her.

Juliette made sure that there was enough food on my plate so that I could share it with Delani. Sleeping arrangements were another issue when the three of us were together, either in Paramaribo or later in Amsterdam. Invariably I slept in Juliette's bed, giving her *ede na tap' Delani/*honoring her above Delani *Ik ben een gouden munt* was launched in September 1994. So were her sons and daughters and several of her grandchildren, living in the Netherlands, who have become my family. She always reminded me in telephone conversations that I had left Suriname just in time and that it was because of her that I did not end up dead, by getting myself in deep trouble with *den wenke/*the girls, through my lousy mati manners. I never quite measured up, in that respect, to her standards.

I last saw Juliette in December 1997 in Paramaribo, when she was already ill and weakened, small as a twelve year old in her pink housecoat. Her face resembled a Benin death mask. I sat and lay in bed with her, feeding her okra soup, chatting, laughing, and reminiscing about the days we had lived together. When Mama Matsi called me two months later to say that Juliette had passed, just days before her ninety-first birthday, I arranged ads on the Surinamese Kankantri radio station in Amsterdam, listing myself as her daughter, and I observed mourning rites, as she had taught me to do them properly.

Back in the United States or in the Netherlands, when people have asked me: "What did you actually do during your research period?" I have been able to truthfully and simply say: I lived. I lived with gusto, with passion, with curiosity, meaningfully connected with illuminated parts of myself and with significant others. I could not wait to begin every new day, never having been as productive before: coauthoring a book and writing several articles besides doing the research. I sometimes wondered whether this was real: one of the happiest periods in my life and being funded to live it. Comparing this fieldwork experience with a previous one in France, I know that the intensity of my feelings in Suriname was and is deeply connected to my bringing my whole self into the situation: my Creole, woman-loving self met its karma. In the encounter of my selves with various other significant selves, I have received some lasting gifts. The (self-) knowledge I gained through my connection to Juliette has become part of the universe I inhabit. One of the legacies Juliette has left me is that she has given me a glimpse of how mati of her generation spoke with each other; moreover, by becoming fluent in Sranan Tonga under her guidance, she has bequeathed their speech to me. She has enlarged my *bere/* my matrikin by giving her family to me. Simultaneously, she has given me to her family: we attend each other's *bigi yari/* crown birthdays; I dance at their Winti Prey for the *kabra/* the ancestor spirits of the family, thus for Juliette. As my family, they come to my book launches and they attended my oration, when I accepted the IIAV chair[3] at the University of Utrecht. Juliette gave me the most exquisite and intimate gift: understanding the lived reality and the beauty of the mati work, its sociocentricity, its passion, its longevity, and its survival wisdom.

Notes
1. The poem is printed in the preface and acknowledgments [of the book] and I have dedicated it to Juliette.
2. Citrus aurantifolia (Rutaceile). (Sordam and Eersel 1989).
3. The IIAV is the International Information Center and Archives for the Women's Movement, in Amsterdam, which took the initiative for the chair in gender and ethnicity that I have held at the University of Utrecht since 2001.

References
Bolton, Ralph. "Coming Home: The Journey of a Gay Ethnographer in the Years of the Plague." In *Out in the Field: Reflections of Lesbian and Gay Anthropologists*, edited by Ellen Lewin and William Leap, 147–68. Urbana and Chicago: University of Illinois Press, 1996.

Haraway, Donna. *Simians, Cyborgs, and Women: The Reinvention of Nature.* London: Free Association Books, 1991.

Harding, Sandra. *Whose Science? Whose Knowledge? Thinking from Women's Lives.* Ithaca, NY: Cornell University Press, 1991.

Kulick, Don, and Margaret Wilson, eds. *Taboo: Sex, Identity and Erotic Subjectivity in Anthropological Fieldwork.* edited by New York, Routledge, 1995.

Lewin, Ellen "Another Unhappy Marriage? Feminist Anthropology and Lesbian/Gay Studies." In *Out in Theory: The Emergence of Lesbian and Gay Anthropology.* Ellen *Lewin and William L. Leap, Eds*, edited by Ellen Lewin and William Leap, 110–27. Urbana and Chicago: University of Illinois Press, 2002.

Lewin, Ellen, and William L Leap, eds. *Out in the Field: Reflections of Lesbian and Gay Anthropologists.* Urbana and Chicago: University of Illinois Press, 1996.

McCarthy Brown, Karen. *Mama Lola: A Vodou Priestess in Brooklyn.* Vol. 4, Berekely: University of California Press, 2011.

Newton, Esther. *Margaret Mead Made Me Gay: Personal Essays, Public Ideas.* Durham: Duke University Press, 2000.

Portelli, Alessandro. *Death of Luigi Trastulli and Other Stories, The: Form and Meaning in Oral History.* New York: Suny Press, 2010.

Price, Richard, and Sidney W Mintz. *The Birth of African-American Culture.* Boston: Beacon, 1992 [1976].

Rich, Adrienne. *On Lies, Secrets, and Silence: Selected Prose 1966–1978.* London: Virago, 1979.

Wekker, Gloria. "Of Sex and Silences: Methodological Considerations on Sex Research in Paramaribo, Suriname." *Thamyris - Mythmaking from Past to Present* 5, no.1. (1998).

Wekker, Gloria. "Mati-Ism and Black Lesbianism: Two Idealtypical Constructions of Female Homosexuality in Black Communities of the Diaspora". *Journal of Homosexuality* 24, no. 3/4 (1993).

Whitehead, Tony Larry, and Mary Ellen Conaway, eds. *Self, Sex, and Gender in Cross-Cultural Fieldwork.* Urbana and Chicago: University of Illinois Press, 1986.

15. Embodied Theories: Local Knowledge(s), Community Organizing, and Feminist Methodologies in Caribbean Sexuality Studies*

Angelique V. Nixon and Rosamond S. King

Introduction

This collaborative project outlines and addresses the significance of feminist methodologies in Caribbean sexuality studies through embodied theories that encompass the importance of community organizing and attention to the local. We will identify various theories and languages that offer insights into the experiences and multiplicities of identity in terms of gender and sexuality and their intersections with race, class and religion. This project troubles the divide between academia and community, and demonstrates the myriad ways our theorizing can bridge this gap. We consider feminist theories at the core of feminist methodologies; hence, we offer the concept of embodied theories as a feminist methodology that privileges the local, community organizing and different forms of knowledge. As writers and scholars, we will engage the work we both have done with the Caribbean International Resource Network (Caribbean IRN) in terms of marginalized populations, oral histories, digital archives, and local, regional, and diaspora community organizing. We wonder, like our colleagues, "How can we deploy power creatively and consciously in the service of radical justice? And how effective are these strategies for bringing about individual and social change?" (Rodriguez 2003, 46) We assume all research activity – what we read, choose to study, and write about, and what and how we publish and teach – is political. We also assume that researchers strive to be not only ethical and responsible to their own ideas, but also to the people or material that is being studied. Therefore, we prioritize the local and

---

* Reprinted with permission from *Caribbean Review of Gender Studies* Issue 7 (December 2013).

community needs and different ways of knowing, particularly with regard to the study of Caribbean sexuality inside the region. This essay itself utilizes some of the same methods it proposes. One principal example of this is its collaborative nature: two humanities scholars present this essay, both of us committed to interdisciplinary research and active in creative, community, and analytical work beyond the academy, and both of us engaged as diasporic researchers and writers. While we do not wish to perpetuate "the mistaken notion that only one kind of justice work could lead to freedom," we put forward the following ideas as one set of ways to approach Caribbean sexualities research, one possible way to freedom (Alexander 2005, 281).

The Role of the Diasporic Researcher

Places such as New York City, Montreal and Miami are real and legitimate Caribbean sites because of population and cultural presence, as well as long histories of migration and transnational flows. Nevertheless, the role of the diasporic researcher is more fraught than many of us often admit.[1] We identify as Caribbean (with or without an additional, hyphenated marker), and yet we spend the majority of our time outside of the region. This physical distance does not always mean we know less about the region than those who live there, but it does mean that we know *differently*. Diasporic researchers should acknowledge those differences, which can lead to particular perspectives and insights. This type of acknowledgement can also spur the diasporic researcher to consult local archives and to collaborate with local scholars, community-based researchers and other experts in meaningful ways. At the same time, location outside of the region means that we often have more access to resources. The greater access to resources means a greater responsibility to try to share resources and results within the regions – an important part of the methodologies we propose in this essay. In other words, as Caribbean diasporic researchers and writers, we acknowledge our subject positions within our research and theories as fundamental to what we define as embodied theories that affirm the place of local knowledge(s) and community organizing. These concepts are evident in Caribbean feminist theorizing and practice – attention to the local and regional. But how do these feminist methodologies translate into Caribbean sexuality studies? What is the relationship between Caribbean feminism, feminist practice, and sexuality studies?

Significance of Feminist Methodologies in Caribbean Sexuality Studies

Caribbean sexuality studies have in many ways emerged through the established field of Caribbean feminist theory. Feminist methodologies in Caribbean studies necessarily assert the importance of focusing on regional and local histories/herstories in practice and theory. As Patricia Mohammed asserts in her article "Indigenous Feminist Theorising in the Caribbean", "feminism as an expression of sexual equality must be itself historically located, despite the global discourse which feeds its growth" (Mohammed 1998, 7). Therefore, as we engage the significance of feminist methodologies in Caribbean sexuality studies, we must consider and define some of the practices of feminism in the Caribbean. The Caribbean feminist movement and women's organizing for sexual equality can be seen in part through the publications by the Institute for Gender and Development Studies (IGDS) at The University of the West Indies (in Jamaica, Trinidad and Barbados). Significant collections from these centres include *Gender in Caribbean Development* (1991), *Stories in Caribbean Feminism* (1998), *Gendered Realities: Essays in Caribbean Feminist Thought* (2002), *Gender in the 21st Century: Caribbean Perspectives, Visions and Possibilities* (2004) and more recently with the new journal *Caribbean Review of Gender Studies*. Caribbean feminism and community organizing can also be seen more explicitly through organizations such as CAFRA (Caribbean Association for Feminist Research and Action) and CODE RED for Gender Justice.

CAFRA positions itself as an organization committed to fighting oppression: it "is a regional network of feminists, individual researchers, activists, and women's organizations that define feminist politics as a matter of both consciousness and action. We are committed to understanding the relationship between the oppression of women and other forms of oppression in the society, and we are working actively for change."[2] CAFRA frames feminism within the Caribbean context as being both consciousness and action, that is, engaged praxis – and feminist politics are grounded in the practical and intersectional analysis of oppression. However, in practice, sociopolitical issues in the Caribbean (as with much of the Global South) concerning women tend to be addressed through the topic of "gender and development" or through women's organizations that may or may not support feminist consciousness. But CAFRA, along with other activist groups, is committed to feminist praxis *and* feminist thought within the region, building solidarity and connections that embrace different Caribbean women's experiences. They fulfil their mission through various conferences, community workshops, publications, political actions, and community organizing, establishing cross-cultural and regional relationships. Further and more recently, the vibrant online and social media presence of the feminist activist collective CODE RED for Gender Justice has expanded the work of CAFRA through insightful and engaging conversations about gender and sexuality issues in the region.[3] Graduate students at IGDS, at Cave Hill in Barbados, formed this collective, which has grown to include Caribbean feminists around the region and diaspora. They have engaged in a number of exciting activities and projects, including annual symposiums, workshops, and online campaigns; they also initiated the young feminist network called CatchAFyah. CODE RED uses a variety of approaches in its work that reflects the dynamic work of feminist activists, organizers, and scholars inside and outside the region. Hence, we can understand the work of Caribbean feminist academics and organizers with an intersectional multidisciplinary praxis whose methodologies are deeply invested in local actions and what we would argue are (local) embodied theories.

Caribbean feminist scholars also engage the practice of feminism grounded in the local even as they theorize about and debate definitions of Caribbean feminism and reveal its distance from Western notions of feminism. The special issue of *Feminist Review* in the summer of 1998 titled "Rethinking Caribbean Difference," edited by Mohammed, represents an overview of activism and scholarship in Caribbean feminism. This issue includes articles by prominent Caribbean scholars who do work on gender, feminism, and women's issues in the Caribbean, among them Rhoda Reddock, Hilary McD. Beckles, Bridget Brereton, Linden Lewis, and Eudine Barriteau; they cover the region while also discussing the specifics of Puerto Rico, the Netherlands Antilles, Haiti,

Jamaica, Trinidad, Barbados and Cuba. Mohammed's much cited "Towards Indigenous Feminist Theorising in the Caribbean" is a seminal essay that seeks to define feminism and feminist theory in the region through engagement with the politics of history and the complexity of Caribbean identity. She begins by explaining the region's (and by extension the field of Caribbean studies') necessary preoccupation with the past and ethnic identity as rooted in the sordid and brutal history of colonialism, which disrupted and eradicated much of the cultural memory of the indigenous Amerindian population and African peoples (Mohammed 1998, 7). In considering how ethnicity has political appeal that elides gender and sexual difference, Mohammed asserts the following:

> Recognizing the different ways in which men and women within any cultural group experience enslavement, indentureship, or migration is integral to understanding ethnic identity. The psychological scars of emasculation or defeminization caused by such uprooting are not skin deep and have residual effects on gender relations and gender struggles within a society far beyond the periods of disruption (1998, 8).

In other words, she argues that the construction of masculinity and femininity during colonization continues to affect present relationships for all races and classes of people in the Caribbean. Thus, feminism in the Caribbean has been engaged with these constructions of "manhood" and "womanhood" while being affected by the struggle for gender equality in the larger global discourse. Mohammed's project then seeks to theorize and interrogate gender identities inside the region, while deconstructing difference in an effort to support a feminist movement that is historically progressive and committed to changing consciousness, policies and programmes. Mohammed's redefining of feminism is firmly grounded in Caribbean gendered experiences and histories while also reflecting a liberatory approach to the struggle of ending systems of oppression and domination.

An overview of feminist methodologies can provide us with a sense of how these resonate for the study of Caribbean sexualities. It is important to trace these relationships and investigations of gender, in part because they offer us a glimpse into both the silences and possibilities around the study of sexualities, same-sex desire, and sexual minorities in the region. The present collaborative project seeks to respond to the following question:

how do feminist methodologies address issues of gender identity and sexuality, or do they? On the one hand, to be grounded in the local we must affirm the place of indigenous theorizing of feminist methods; on the other hand, if these grounded theories do not account for historically overlooked silences or possibilities, then we must borrow from other theoretical traditions or look more deeply at a range of Caribbean epistemologies. It is perhaps in this looking harder, or rather looking differently, that we will discover what we are calling "embodied theories" for the study of Caribbean sexualities. These theories can be grounded in feminist methodologies that utilize both social science and humanities approaches. Furthermore, they ought to engage the everyday experiences of sexual minorities, and offer tools and ways of examining sexualities (including same-sex desire) in the realm of culture and cultural production, where we may find multiple ways of knowing. In addition, feminist methodologies that are useful for Caribbean sexuality studies must incorporate not only specific local historical contexts, but also the intersections of race, class and religion with gender and sexuality.

Women of colour feminists have offered many theoretical and practical spaces for the understanding and analysis of these intersections, through the framework known as intersectionality. Chandra Mohanty asserts that there is a need for feminist analysis to recognize not only the importance of rewriting history, but also that such "practice of remembering and rewriting leads to the formation of politicized consciousness and self- identity" (2003, 78). Similarly, in "Age, Race, Class, and Sex: Women Redefining Difference," Audre Lorde argues that members of marginalized groups must create new patterns of understanding difference in order to build coalitions and fight against racism, sexism, ageism, heterosexism and elitism (1984, 115). Lorde explains that we must be wary of ignoring and misnaming difference; thus, within the struggle for revolutionary change and liberation, we must define ourselves outside oppressive structures. For example, people who are marginalized must take charge of knowledge production – we must do the work of redefining ourselves, asserting subjectivity and resisting dominant and oppressive structures. Lorde's work exemplifies intersectionality and offers a pragmatic framework in which to organize around difference and against violence.

More specifically in her essay "Sexism: An American Disease in Blackface," Lorde discusses the multiple forms of violence that affect black communities in US, specifically forms that emerge from sexism, racism and homophobia. She argues that until we see those interconnections and build a consciousness and dialogue about them, "the continued blindness between us can only serve the oppressive system within which we live" (Lorde 1984, 64). While the context for the essay is the US, her analysis is useful for other communities of colour and postcolonial societies. In particular, her words resonate as we think about the Caribbean context and the intersections of race, gender, class and sexuality. The Caribbean still exhibits "the systematic devaluation" and economic, political and social marginalization of black women and other women of colour. Lorde argues that we cannot accept some forms of violence and condemn others. In other words, we cannot fight against domestic violence and sexual abuse and do nothing about homophobia. Lorde's work exemplifies the practical workings of feminist theories and methodologies that take into account the body and lived experiences.

Key Aspects of Embodied Theories

The acknowledgement of one's own location is a fundamental aspect of embodied theories, an approach that is particularly relevant in sexuality studies, which are necessarily preoccupied with bodies. An embodied theory is a theory that does not ignore the reality of bodies – either of the people being studied or of those doing the analysis. We too often, for instance, talk about sex without any mention of pleasure, as is clear in the heavily used term "MSM (men who have sex with men)," which privileges global north epistemologies, HIV/AIDS work, and the international non-governmental funding complex over local language and ways of knowing. Embodied theories pay particular attention to the material reality of the body – how the body's need for sustenance and safety can drive the decisions of everyone in every sector of a society. Most scholars are accustomed to discussing gender and sexuality together and in relationship to particular social groups, but not necessarily in conjunction with other factors. If we examine sexuality without attention to colour, race, class, rural, or urban location and other aspects of identity, then we are quite literally not considering the *whole* person, and these omissions will diminish our research and its results.

This attention to the material body also needs to be applied in some degree to scholars ourselves. We should ask ourselves: What is the physical location of my body? How does the body I live in affect my perception of Caribbean sexualities? And for those who engage in fieldwork, how do my apparent colour, phenotype, and gender affect my interaction with subjects? The authors of this essay are often struck by how gleefully some white, North American scholars describe how they decided to study the Caribbean after a vacation, after experiencing carnival, or after sleeping with a Caribbean person. But these experiences are rarely included in their publications. Other scholars, though, do address this issue, some including autoethnography in their scholarship, as Carlos Decena and Gloria Wekker do. Wekker argues "if you are transparent about the ways in which you position yourself, including the sexual positions you occupy, then you produce better knowledge" (2009, 3). By proposing the importance of embodied theories, we encourage the production of knowledge that reveals and takes into account the material body. Yet such work should also account for the emotional body – that of ourselves as diasporic researchers and those of the people we are studying, writing about, and theorizing around. Embodied theories inherently suggest an embrace of the material *and* emotional body, and an acknowledgement of what that means for both the (diasporic) researcher and the subjects of study.

It would be naïve, however, not to point out that such disclosures can more negatively affect junior scholars and those who are women, and/or people of colour, and/or not heterosexual, and/or not located in the global north. But even if scholars choose not to disclose intimate knowledge of their bodies, we can still be aware of how that information affects our methods and analyses. And we must at least consider the ramifications of absenting the researcher's body from the written record when often our bodies are implicated during every stage of research (i.e., what we study, how we study, why we study and how we write). We must also acknowledge that our research can have an impact not only on our own bodies, but also on the bodies of our subjects. In many ways, incorporating these considerations is a more honest approach to the work we do – avoiding the supposed but never achieved "objective" gaze that too often is or is assumed to be European, white and male. This essay builds on the archive of feminist postcolonial theories and methodologies that have proposed and incorporated such practices.

Another aspect of embodied theories is taking different kinds of theories and discourses seriously. As Omise'eke Natasha Tinsley suggests, "while it is of paramount importance that we have theorists who engage with, deconstruct, and reconstruct now canonical cultural and gender theory, a real restructuring of postcolonial and sexuality studies will only take place when the academy *listens to other kinds of theorists*" (2010, 28). There is much work still to be done regarding how folk wisdom, subaltern cultures, and Caribbean traditions understand, describe and theorize sexuality. Given that Caribbean cultures have survived slavery, indentureship, colonialism (in its original, as well as post and neo forms), globalization, and cultural imperialism, surely these "subordinated knowledges" are worth considering as legitimate epistemologies (Alexander 2005, 7). By treating methodologies as "conscious engagements with knowledge production," we can expand the content of our knowledge while also making it more reflective of the Caribbean region (Rodriguez 2003, 161). In other words, we can understand this kind of knowledge production in conjunction with an awareness of the body and of local and regional contexts. As was mentioned briefly at the start of this essay, sexuality scholars (with the general exception of psychologists) are far more likely to describe and analyse what our bodies do rather than how we feel. Careful attention to feelings and the body can help researchers avoid one-dimensional portraits of Caribbean people and phenomena that often portray people as victims of circumstance who cannot feel pleasure, and/or as exotic others who are always ready or available for sex and pleasure.

Theorizing and accounting for the Caribbean sexual subject, including sexual minorities, must also factor in the ways in which colonialism, neocolonialism, globalization, tourism, and cultural appropriation affect conceptions and understandings of self and sexuality. Kamala Kempadoo argues in her book *Sexing the Caribbean* that we must begin to explore the complexity of Caribbean sexuality by coming to terms with its diversity: She proposes that: "We need a different lens for thinking about Caribbean sexuality—that we cannot simply view it as a fabrication of the European mind and imagination, or dismiss it as colonial discourses or metaphors, but need also to view hypersexuality as a lived reality that pulses through the Caribbean body" (2004, 1). If we take seriously Kempadoo's argument here, then we must account for the body, for pleasure, for lived experience, for what is happening on the ground and in between/among actual people. We must account for the daily and "embodied sexual practices, identities, knowledges, and strategies of resistance of the colonized and postcolonial subject without lapsing into notions of an essential native sexuality" (2). Kempadoo proposes that "colonial and neocolonial ideas about the region have combined with West African, East Indian, Amerindian, and other non-Western traditions and legacies," which have created a variety of sexual arrangements and practices that comprise Caribbean sexuality (2). These include multiple partnering, serial monogamy, informal polygamy, same-sex and bisexual relationships, and various types of transactional sexual relationships. The Caribbean sexual landscape consists of complicated and non-normative relationships and different sexual expressions that often contradict the national consciousness of much of the region, and the accompanying dominant (mostly) Christian conservative and pious conceptions of the region that are often posited as the Caribbean way. The region is (simply put) wrapped up in a politics of respectability, not only through dominant religions but also through the remnants of colonial structures of social and cultural norms.

Kempadoo acknowledges that dominant constructions of sexuality (of course) exist across the region, and she asserts hypersexuality and heteropatriarchy as two defining concepts of Caribbean-ness. Hypersexuality is a concept that explains the representation and framing of the region as overly sexual (i.e., paradise, exotic, primitive, other, etc.), and heteropatriarchy describes the privileging of male experiences within the dominant heterosexual structure, which delegitimizes women as well as non-normative sexualities and genders. "In this structure (heteropatriarchy), coupled with a discourse of hypersexuality, lesbians, gays, trangenders, prostitutes, and other 'sexual deviants' are cast not only as oversexed Caribbean subjects but as outlaws and noncitizens" (2). Nevertheless, Caribbean sexual minorities – sometimes named as lesbian, gay, bisexual, transgendered, or queer and other so-called sexual deviants – live and exist in the region. And if one pays particular attention to the community organizing within the region, we can begin to see the ways that people have challenged normative relationships, fought for change, and written their "outlaw selves" into citizenship.

The Issue of Language

When the issue of language(s) is raised in Caribbean studies, the obvious concern is the monolingual nature of most of our work. This reality reflects the difficulty of attending to the many similarities and the many differences among territories speaking variants of Spanish, English, French, and the oft-forgotten Dutch. The thoughtful work of scholars such as Omise'eke Natasha Tinsley and Kamala Kempadoo serve as models of multilingual research and analysis of Caribbean sexualities. In addition to this serious issue, there are other language concerns particular to Caribbean sexuality studies. Foremost among them is not to take seemingly benign terms – such as *woman*, *man*, and *prostitution* – for granted. Much work has been done, from Sojourner Truth to Toni Cade Bambara and Judith Butler, and specifically in Caribbean studies by Tinsley, to question the term "woman" and how it functions in relationship to people of different races, classes, and times.[4] Reading and citing this body of work, and taking the questioning of "basic" and "obvious" terms seriously will enrich analysis. Similarly, we should avoid the use of "victim language," language that makes people into objects rather than subjects. Examples of problematic language include "victims of AIDS," and "victims of sexual abuse;" alternatives include "people with AIDS" and "survivors of sexual abuse." This kind of attention to language is directly linked to our desire to affirm individual agency and acknowledge people's humanity and feelings as complex beings.

Furthermore, researchers must know the origins and context of terms. A clear example is the use of queer, LGBT and MSM to refer to people who use very different terms to define themselves. At best, such labels are inaccurate; at worst, they enact an epistemic violence upon Caribbean subjects by denying their own agency to name and define (or not name *or* define) themselves and/or their behaviour. While the use of terms such as *gay* and *prostitution* may seem to make sense, they actually invoke particular places, histories and circumstances. It is important to consider how people name themselves and describe their own behaviour, as well as expressions found in regionally specific language. If researchers insist on using terms such as *gay* and *prostitution* rather than less geopolitically based – and potentially more accurate – terms such as *sexual minority* and *sex work*, then we must acknowledge the histories of those terms and explain why they are appropriate. Similarly, when we use local Caribbean terms, we must do so accurately, consistently, and in appropriate contexts. Simple translations (e.g., masisi=faggot, friending=prostitution, pato=queer, mati=lesbian, or manroyal=dyke[5]) are far less useful than detailed explanations of how and when a particular term is used. Lawrence La Fountain-Stokes' use and transformation of the term *loca* is a good example of appropriate, creative, and analytical employment of a local term. Loca in Spanish literally means "mad woman," but in the Puerto Rican context loca "in its slang derivation, means queer, perhaps something akin to queen" that can have both derogatory and endearing connotations generally used to describe feminine men (La Fountain- Stokes 2011).

Just as we advocate for the inclusion and analysis of different types of theories, we should also have a more expansive attitude toward language. For instance, use of language of and about the sacred is, in non-theological academia, in its nascent stage.[6] Similarly, the "language" of cultural products such as music, carnival, sport, and child-rearing practices "provide important insights that may not be gleaned from statistical data," which can be even more useful when such data are not available (La Fountain-Stokes 2009, xiii). Additionally, the collection and study of oral histories/herstories within Caribbean sexuality studies offers additional ways of knowing and understanding the landscape of sexuality in the region and its diaspora.

Disseminating Research

How and where we scholars disseminate our research has a direct effect on the field of Caribbean studies, which depends, as does any academic field, on researchers reading, responding to and building on each other's work. A variety of scholarly formats beyond the printed, peer-reviewed journal now exist, even though that format remains the standard for tenure decisions in North American colleges and universities. As two untenured faculty members, we are deeply empathetic to this situation (as we both work towards tenure). And yet we remain convinced that publishing beyond the traditional route is more a sense of responsibility than option, and can contribute to both community building and activism, while coexisting with various tenure requirements.

A number of Caribbean-oriented, peer-reviewed journals exist, including *Small Axe*, the *Journal of West Indian Literature*, the *Journal of Caribbean Literatures* and *Sargasso*. There are also several electronic, peer-reviewed journals, including, the *Caribbean Review of Gender Studies*. These are respected journals that publish cutting-edge work. Other publishing options include non-academic venues such as blogs, Caribbean newspapers and online resources such as the Caribbean IRN's online collection. While some of these publications are less likely to be considered strong contributions to a tenure dossier, many have readerships that are broader than those of academic journals and reach a different audience. Both the prestige-conscious and those who lack job security should consider publishing their work in a peer-reviewed print journal, and then publishing a shorter, longer or slightly differently focused essay in another venue. If interviews have been conducted as part of the research, these can be published separately. As scholars and creative writers, we have pursued all these avenues. We have also sent PDFs of published papers directly to Caribbean colleagues and community groups in an effort to make our research more accessible within the region.

We must begin broadening the academy's notion of "important" publications, and begin "valorising diverse publications as valid sites for the dissemination of knowledge," even as we continue to publish beyond its boundaries (Parés et al. 2007). Asking libraries to subscribe to Caribbean-based journals (and to buy books from UWI Press, Ian Randle Publishers, and other Caribbean-based publishing houses), engaging colleagues about the quality of electronic journals and extolling these publications when writing recommendations or tenure evaluations for junior colleagues are all ways that we can change the academy from within. In addition, we urge emerging scholars to consider non-print venues, such as radio interviews and talks to a variety of audiences, especially beyond the university. Further, we can ask conferences to webcast lectures and panels so that they are more accessible to people in the region. As Juana María Rodríguez reminds us, "Discursive spaces need not be institutional, however;

the chatroom, the bar, the street corner, the computer screen also serve to define subjects and construct knowledge practices" (Rodriguez 2003, 6). The issue of dissemination is vital, because one way research can benefit Caribbean communities is by *reaching and engaging* those communities as equals; this is a key way to take seriously the lives and experiences we are writing about and studying. This issue is connected to how scholars interact with and how our work affects Caribbean communities.

Obviously, the question of whether information benefits Caribbean communities depends both on the research and the researcher. The clear solution is to ask people in the relevant communities. Though this may not be as easy as it sounds, it is not particularly difficult. Communication with non-academic stakeholders of our work (and academics in different regions) can take place at every stage of the research process, from conceptualization to analysis to publication. Such communication might consist of asking activists what research questions they would like answered or asking stakeholders to comment on publication drafts. "Benefit" also has a broad range of meanings. Benefit can be the legitimization of an identity, strategy, or organization. It can also mean physical materials, data, information technology, and/or labor provided to a community. Traditions of engaged scholarship provide a number of similar approaches to conducting research in a respectful, responsible and responsive manner, rather than "hit and run" work that benefits the scholar's career but is not made available to any non-academic community. In other words, research, data, oral histories/herstories, collected archives, and interviews ought to be readily accessible to the community they are about and from.

Local Knowledges and Community Organizing

We must turn to the realities of Caribbean sexual minority community organizing to investigate and interrogate the possibilities and successes of how diasporic researchers make "selves" and bodies legible, written, and known. A vital question, then, is how are these embodied theories that we have described above working in practice – and what are the related challenges, successes and strategies? Furthermore, it is important to ask how the successes of Caribbean sexual minority organizing affect the academic research and methodologies of Caribbean sexuality studies. We argue in this project that like-minded researchers seek answers and tools for analysis, with specific attention to the work being done in the region. We also argue that it is through local scholarly and non-scholarly knowledges, community organizing, and embodied theories that we can transform the limited discourses around sex and sexuality for Caribbean people generally and sexual minorities particularly.

This attention to the local and to the realities of sexual minority organizing in the region has led to important interrogations of different kinds of homophobias and explanations of how homophobia works in different communities across the region. Such work was brought together though the first "Caribbean Sexualities Gathering" in Kingston, Jamaica, in June 2009, sponsored by the Caribbean International Resource Network (IRN), which connects academic and community-based researchers, artists, and activists around the Caribbean and in the diaspora in areas related to diverse sexualities and genders.[7]

The Caribbean IRN brought together over 30 scholars, artists, writers, and activists from around the region, representing more than ten Caribbean countries, as well as several of the local and regional Caribbean sexual minority advocacy organizations – including SASOD, CAISO, J-FLAG, FOKO Curacao, among others.[8] The gathering consisted of a panel discussion at the Caribbean Studies Association (CSA) conference, a five-hour workshop, and a closing reception; during these events, we communed, networked and collaborated. Some of the highlights included intense dialogues about the many issues affecting sexual minorities in the region, and shared specifics in different countries. We also talked about sexual minority communities in the region and how to deal with homophobia and the struggle for sexual and gender equality. We discussed the need to theorize about different kinds of homophobia and the need to recognize and discuss how vibrant sexual minority communities can exist alongside intense homophobia. We talked about different ways of "being out," concerns about safety, and the privilege of visibility. We discussed allies, the support of families and creating new kinds of families. We brainstormed about how to create safe spaces for sexual minorities and gender non-conforming people. We formulated ideas about how to use academic and creative work as forms of activism. We discussed possible collaborations among researchers, community organizers, and creative producers – and how some of us blur the lines among these distinctions.[9]

Out of this network and regional building in 2009, and our work with the Caribbean IRN and other organizations, several projects have emerged that blur the lines between academia and community. These projects are grounded in the local and reflect embodied theories in their creation and production, including various oral history projects and the building of a digital archive housed through the open access Digital Library of the Caribbean at www.dloc.com/icirn, comprising three collections so far – a general collection of materials from newspaper articles to academic papers, the Jamaica Gay Freedom Movement Archives, and the Rainbow Alliance of the Bahamas Archives. Furthermore, we published an online, open access collection in June 2012 called *Theorising Homophobias in the Caribbean: Complexities of Place, Desire and Belonging*, at caribbeanhomophobias.org. This is a multimedia collection of activist reports, creative writing, critical essays, film, interviews, and performance and visual art that defines and reflects on the complexities of homophobias in the Caribbean, while also expanding awareness about Caribbean sexual minority lives, experiences and activism in the region and its diaspora. This collection is unique in its creation and production because of its accessibility, multimedia format and the collaborative work among activists, scholars, artists, writers, and community-based organizations and researchers inside and outside the region. The concept of embodied theories is at the centre of this collection as it pays careful attention to and privileges local and regional knowledge production and community organizing. The Caribbean IRN has also initiated a collaborative intervention in the realm of academia through the annual Caribbean Studies Association (CSA) conference. At the last three CSA conferences, the focus and networking of people involved in the Caribbean IRN and regional sexual minority organizations have strengthened both academic and community knowledge production and building. At these conferences, we have seen the numbers of panels and discussions about sexuality grow, as well as the participation by openly sexual minority Caribbean people – scholars, graduate students, activists, and community workers. We challenged the heteronormative and heterosexist dynamics of the conference space. We opened spaces and forums to discuss strategies to confront homophobia, while building coalitions and theorizing/

researching Caribbean Sexuality Studies. We also started the dialogue and organizing within CSA to form the first Caribbean Sexualities Working Group, and many of us through local, regional and diasporic networks are sustaining this work. Moreover, the Caribbean IRN collaborated with the Institute for Gender and Development Studies at UWI St Augustine and CAISO to offer a unique short course on Critical Sexuality Studies in July 2013, which included a series of public events.[10] The authors have focused here on our own work with the Caribbean IRN because it spans both academic and non-academic realms, and because we are intimately familiar with it. Of course, many individuals and organizations, including CAFRA, SASOD, Pink House, Red Thread, CAISO, Sevovie, Caribbean HIV/AIDS Partnership, CODE RED for Gender Justice, CatchAFyah Network, and CariFLAGS are doing important work around Caribbean sexualities.

Some of the challenges Caribbean communities continue to face include the politics of respectability, failures to openly discuss sex and sexuality, religious fundamentalism, cultural norms, legacies of colonialism, the ways in which homosexuality is framed as a white or Euro-American disease, and emergent forms of imperialism and neocolonialism. Moreover, the symptoms of homophobia sometimes emerge in violent ways through institutions and culture – for instance in music (particularly dancehall, which when labelled "murder music" becomes the scapegoat for all things homophobic, whereas other Caribbean music is rarely discussed), HIV/AIDS work, human rights discourse, foreign funding, silence and stigma of HIV/AIDS and sex work, and the push/pull of migration. However, the local and regional engagement with these serious issues must be highlighted, analysed and engaged to achieve a more complete understanding of Caribbean sexualities and lived experiences of sexual minorities. Therefore, anti-violence work and sexual minority community organizing must be connected to locally rooted conversations and frameworks about social change and social justice – and they must account for intersectionality and the relationships among various kinds of violence (e.g., patriarchal violence contributes to homophobic violence).

The successes of this kind of work are reflected in the work of campaigns in the region through Caribbean advocacy organizations such as SASOD (Guyana), CAISO (Trinidad and Tobago), J-FLAG (Jamaica),

CariFLAGS (Regional), Sevovie (Haiti) and PinkHouse (Curaçao), among others. These organizations and networks have built and are building coalitions and reflecting the praxis we have outlined here through existing coalitions that expand political campaigns to include sexual minority concerns, the hosting of political education workshops and community dialogues on gender, sexuality, homophobia, violence, community building, and Caribbean history, all the while providing and sustaining safe spaces for sexual minorities, sex workers and others in the region. Caribbean sexuality studies must take praxis, itself an embodied theory, seriously in its scholarship. Meanwhile, those of us in academia outside the region (diasporic researchers) who are deeply engaged with and tied to this work must continue working to make the research, data and scholarship more available and more easily accessible for activists, community workers, teachers, artists, writers, and institutions in the Caribbean. In this way, we can strive to truly connect with each other and create community among scholars, researchers, writers, activists, community workers, activists, and artists.

Conducting research that is respectful of and responsive to the communities we study, that acknowledges the spatial as well as intellectual location of the scholar, that acknowledges the materiality and affect of the body, may seem to be an onerous task, especially when one is also encouraged to take different languages and ways of knowing seriously, and to distribute one's research broadly. In truth, though, many of us scholars want our work to be responsive and to be widely read and understood. Our work is typically not simple or easy, even without these considerations, and we know that the better our scholarship is, the more it can benefit our communities in and beyond the academy. We encourage our fellow scholars "not [to] be ashamed of finding pleasure in our work," and to find that pleasure in an expansive worldview represented, in part, in the methodological approaches suggested here (Rodriguez 2003, 161).

Notes
1. Carole Boyce Davies and Rinaldo Walcott are two notable exceptions.
2. The Caribbean Association for Feminist Research and Action, www.cafra.org.
3. CODE RED for Gender Justice. http://redforgender.wordpress.com.
4. For more info, see Sojourner Truth's "Aint I A Woman," Toni Cade Bambara's essay "On the Issue of Roles," and Judith Butler's *Gender*

Trouble, more work needs to be done to unpack the term "man" in relationship to the Caribbean, though the collections *The Culture of Gender and Sexuality in the Caribbean* by Linden Lewis and *Learning to Be a Man: Culture, Socialization, and Gender Identity in Five Caribbean Communities* by Barry Chevannes are major interventions.
5. For descriptions of these terms, see Lescot and Magloire's film *Of Men and Gods*, Kamala Kempadoo's *Sun, Sex, and Gold*, Lawrence La Fountain Stokes' article, "Queer Ducks, Puerto Rican Patos and Jewish American Seygelekh: Birds and the Cultural Representation of Homosexuality," Gloria Wekker's *Politics of Passion*, and Makeda Silvera "Man Royals and Sodomites."
6. See Jacqui Alexander and Elizabeth Paravisini for explorations of the sacred.
7. The IRN is housed at the Centre for Lesbian and Gay Studies at the City University of New York, funded through the Ford Foundation, and located on the Web at http://www.irnweb.org.
8. The authors of this paper were co-organizers of this event. Organisations represented included Coalition Advocating for Inclusion of Sexual Orientation in Trinidad (CAISO), FOKO Curacao, Jamaican
9. Forum for All Sexuals, Gays and Lesbians (J-FLAG), Society Against Sexual Orientation Discrimination in Guyana (SASOD).
10. The full report is available online through the Digital Library of the Caribbean, Caribbean IRN Collection: http://dloc.com/AA00000022/00001. For more info about the Critical Sexuality Studies course, see the Caribbean IRN website: http://www.irnweb.org/projects/advanced-sexuality-studies-course.

References

Alexander, M. Jacqui. 2005. *Pedagogies of Crossing: Meditations on Feminism, Sexual Politics, Memory, and the Sacred*. Durham: Duke University Press.

Caribbean IRN. June 2012. *Theorising Homophobias in the Caribbean: Complexities of Place, Desire, and Belonging*. Multimedia Collection. http://www.caribbeanhomophobias.org.

Kempadoo, Kamala. 2004. *Sexing the Caribbean: Gender, Race, and Sexual Labour*. New York: Routledge.

La Fountain-Stokes, Lawrence. 2009. *Queer Ricans: Cultures and Sexualities in the Diaspora*. Minneapolis: University of Minnesota Press.

———. 2002. *Trans-locas: Migration, Homosexuality, and Transvestism in Recent Puerto Rican Performance*, ed. Freddie Mercado, Javier Cardona, Eduardo Alegría, Jorge Merced, Arthur Avilés. New Brunswick: Centre for the Critical Analysis of Contemporary Culture, Rutgers University.

Lorde, Audre. 1984. Age, Race, Class, and Sex: Women Redefining Difference. In *Sister Outsider*, 115. Berkeley: Crossing Press.

———. 1984. Sexism: An American disease in Blackface. In *Sister Outsider*, 64. Berkeley: Crossing Press.

Mohammed, Patricia. 1998. Indigenous Feminist Theorising in the Caribbean. *Feminist Review* 59: 7.

Mohanty, Chandra Talpade. 2003. *Feminism without Borders: Decolonising Theory, Practicing Solidarity.* Durham: Duke University Press.
Parés, Luis Aponte, Jossianna Arroyo, Elizabeth Crespo Kebler, Lawrence La Fountain- Stokes, and Frances Negrón Muntaner. 2007. Introduction. *CENTRO Journal* 19:1, 12.
Rodríguez, Juana María. 2003. *Queer Latinidad: Identity Practices, Discursive Spaces.* New York: New York University Press.
Tinsley, Omise'eke Natasha. 2010. *Thiefing Sugar: Eroticism between Women in Caribbean Literature.* Durham: Duke University Press.
Wekker, Gloria. 2009. Politics and Passion: A Conversation with Gloria Wekker. Interview by Andil Gosine, *Caribbean Review of Gender Studies* 3. http://sta.uwi.edu/crgs/november2009/journals/CRGS%20Wekker.pdf.

16. Researching Caribbean Sexual Labour

Kamala Kempadoo

Introduction

Sexual labour, especially in the global South, was until the late 1990s, an under-theorized and under-researched subject, one that was rarely a topic of academic study. At most it was cast by Western feminists as an oppressive patriarchal institution for women, with 'prostituted women' in the global South represented as the quintessential victims. My research over the years helped reconceptualize prostitution as sexual labour, foregrounding the conditions, experiences, and perspectives of Caribbean and other 'Third World' or 'global South' women and making visible complex interactions of structure and agency that shape the global sex trade and women's participation in it.

In the following, I present the methodology I utilized for researching sexual labour, which was grounded in a social praxeological approach that enabled an intersectional and transnational feminist theorizing of the sex trade as well as critical study of discourses of human trafficking. Here, the focus is on research related to the Caribbean, tracing it through a chronological and somewhat circuitous route during the period from 1991 to 2010. The research began in Amsterdam, followed leads that produced a study of racialized sexual labour in Curaçao in the Caribbean, went global with a primary focus on sex work in Asia, Africa and the Americas, then returned to the Caribbean region for a more careful exploration of sexual labour in its entanglements with tourism, HIV and transactionality. Through this trajectory, I discuss the specific methods I employed for studying a subject that is mostly hidden and often taboo, touching on some of the possibilities and challenges that were faced along the way as well as some of the theoretical and substantive outcomes. Above all, this chapter represents a methodology that has sought to make the marginal and the marginalized visible, through the study of everyday social practices.

Social Praxis

When living and studying in Amsterdam in the 1980s, three distinct activities converged to focus my attention on sexual labour: a) I was engaged with a sociological analysis of Black women's work in the Netherlands, which required me to think about the nexus of race, gender, migration and labour; b) I lived on the border of and regularly traversed the Red Light district, where I became aware of an overrepresentation of women of colour sex workers from Latin America and the Caribbean, Sub-Saharan Africa, and Southeast Asia, especially in the massage parlours and sex clubs; and c) I helped organize meetings of non-European migrant exotic dancers in my role as coordinator of Flamboyant – a Black and Migrant women's resource centre in Amsterdam. From this convergence, I deduced that the labour of Brown and Black strippers, prostitutes, masseurs, dancers, etc., had received barely any attention from scholars, feminists, or even the prostitutes' rights movement while, with an emerging international discourse about 'human trafficking', their migrations, activities, and status were becoming the subject of a discourse about violence against women.

From a Black feminist activist-scholarly framework, I set out to try to understand why such large numbers of racialized (migrant) women were engaged in the Dutch sex trade and to investigate what this meant to them. Given that some work had already started on women from Southeast Asia, I followed the route women from the Caribbean and Latin America took to get to the Amsterdam district, landing on the departure point in the Caribbean island of Curaçao, which, as a part of the Dutch Kingdom with a colonial status, enabled relatively easy movement from the region to the Netherlands. It was there that I was able to investigate the questions further. However, the matters were complex, as Curaçao hosted a large, state-controlled brothel *Campo Alegre* that allowed foreign women from around the region to legally work there under specific conditions, yet little research existed on either the workings of the brothel or of the women's movement to the island or to Amsterdam. I settled then on trying to understand the situation in Curaçao, what sex work meant to the women, and the ways that migration, gender, and economics were implicated. As a migrant woman of colour of Caribbean descent, from an unconventional family that taught me to think outside the box, who had often been labelled and identified as a 'loose woman', and who had for several years worked in informal, domestic, and other marginalized work, I identified with many aspects of the women's lives, even while I had never taken up sex work formally. I was in a classic insider/outsider position, which, I quickly came to realize, brought several advantages as a researcher as well as a distance from the sex trade, and positioned me squarely as a sex workers' rights activist/scholar and sex worker ally.

My research was initially framed through a critical social studies perspective that seeks to address the continual sociological question about the intersection of structure and agency – that meeting point between the macro and micro – which has been identified as a theory of praxis or 'social praxeology' (e.g., see Bourdieu 1977 and Wacquant 1992). I employed then an approach that examines the dialectical relationship between underlying structures of social life and the immediate, lived experience of agents, and the ways that the dialectic both reproduces and transforms the structures. Informed by an historical materialist reading in which social life is conceptualized as emerging from material relations and conditions and from the existence of 'real' human beings and the intercourse between and among them, my approach was from the start, deeply inspired by the work of scholars such as Walter Rodney, C. L. R. James, and Frantz Fanon, which critically examines in tandem the workings of a racialized political economy on a global scale and resistances and struggles for liberation and freedom from colonialism and imperialism by working Caribbean and Black people. Contemporary Caribbean social theorists who have continued the James/Rodney/Fanon legacy in Caribbean studies, but also complicate their analyses through taking up gender and conditions of postcoloniality in the Caribbean (such as Rhoda Reddock, Patricia Mohammed, Jacqui Alexander, and Carole Boyce Davies) have also, from early on, been important sources of inspiration. The approach has further been informed by a wider feminism, and particularly that which in the 1990s was identified as 'Third World feminism' and which today is more readily named 'transnational feminism', drawing from material-feminist traditions that centre the examination of gender relations but, as Chandra Talpade Mohanty, and Himani Bannerji make clear, are lodged in the study of oppositional struggles to and consciousness of hegemonic regimes shaped by colonialism, capitalism, race, class, and gender.[1]

This methodology aims to make visible the perspectives, experiences, and conditions of those who stand on the underside of relations of power and involves a 'bottom up' or inductive approach that produces grounded theory. And while I had been trained in both quantitative and qualitative sociological methods and techniques, as well as in cultural anthropology, the methods I decided on were guided by the topic of inquiry. Sexual relations and sexual labour, given their 'private' and often clandestine nature, steered me towards an almost exclusive use of qualitative methods, involving forms of participant observation, semi-structured interviewing, document analysis, and participatory action. I have continued to rely on this methodology and set of methods throughout my research on sex work and sexual labour, expanding them over the years with analyses of texts, media reports, legislation, and policy. Always at the heart of my approach, have been the lives and experiences of highly marginalized, Black and Brown migrant women.

From the Dutch Sex Trade to Global Sex Work, 1991-97

The research in Curaçao started in earnest in 1991 as my doctoral study and analysed legalized prostitution under Dutch colonialism.[2] The three-year study, based on the above described methodology, involved primary analysis of historical and archival documents, in-depth interviews with 46 participants in the Curaçaon sex industry, including registered sex workers, brothel owners, police officials, medical practitioners and clients; sustained periods of observations; and secondary analyses of earlier studies of prostitution in the Caribbean. Having visited the island several times prior to the official period of fieldwork, speaking Dutch – the official language of the island – armed with generalized knowledge of the Caribbean, and knowing several Dutch Antillians who over the years had become good friends, meant that I was quite familiar with the island and its culture, and could communicate quite comfortably. However, the places I wanted to go to learn more about the sex trade and meet sex workers were not always directly accessible. I barely knew the sex work areas of town, did not speak Spanish (the language of many sex workers on the island), and, in the case of the brothel *Campo Alegre*, was neither a client nor a registered sex worker, thus was barred as a 'local' woman from entry. In addition, I was not comfortable wandering into bars and 'snacks' in unfamiliar territory, knowing that identifying myself as a researcher would not get me far. Soliciting friends' company to visit the districts, brothels and bars was also difficult – most women I knew deliberately distanced themselves from anything to do with prostitution and were loath to be seen in certain places out of fear of being associated with prostitution or read as a 'whore'. It was after all, a small island-society, hard to move around incognito if you were a resident, and people talked easily about things or people 'out of place'. Not surprisingly, a politics of respectability was adhered to closely by middle-class and elite women, including most of my feminist friends. Colonialism had, after all, defined Black and Brown women's sexuality as inherently deviant, lascivious, sinful, and out of control, and many women sought to gain respectability through distancing themselves from such interpretations, even while that meant ignoring or denigrating women in the sex trade. Yet, I persevered, strategically using my insider/outsiderness as a way to side-step societal conventions, defying the politics of respectability, and relying on a sole feminist friend and a few men to help me in the research process. I felt bold and empowered, pleased to push my own sexual and gender boundaries as well as those of existing feminist research on prostitution, while striving to make visible a hidden population. The snow-ball method worked well. Through my key informants I gained official access to police records dating back to 1949 about sex work on the island, was able to enter the brothel both at night and day to observe activities and to interview the brothel managers and on-duty nurses, and, with the help of a Spanish-speaking social worker, held interviews with a number of the brothel sex workers.

This initial research in Curaçao, while opening up whole new areas for me, personally and research-wise, simultaneously revealed the paucity of contemporary academic, including feminist, knowledge on the subject, both for the Caribbean and other global South countries. My key findings, that women consciously and deliberately migrated from around the region to Curaçao and defined what they did in the brothel as 'work', seemed to contradict or complicate the then dominant feminist social theories and everyday conceptions of prostitution and the sex trade. As well, the representation of a particular 'erotic-exotic' category of women as the sex worker in Curaçao raised questions about the role of race in configuring sexual relations, practices and desires. The trends suggested, first, that not only was prostitution not simply an activity forced upon women and girls but rather, in most instances, a voluntary activity of adult women considered to be work or labour; and second, that sexual labour was not only gendered in a particular way but was also racialized – white and light-skinned Black women were the most highly desired and valued in sex work, while dark-skinned Black women worked the most dangerous and lowly paid sectors of the sex trade. The trends were, however, very localized and hardly generalizable. I needed to know more, to get a bigger picture in order to understand what my research in Curaçao was pointing to.

My interest in deepening the insights prompted me to investigate the subject of sex work more generally and led to a post-doctoral research project between 1995 and 1997 about global definitions of sex work. It emerged out of a collaboration with two sex worker rights' activists – Licia Brussa and Jo Doezema – in Amsterdam, and involved communications and interviews with sex workers and other sex worker rights' activists around the world, secondary analyses of documents, participant observations in various conferences and meetings on prostitution and sex work, study of research and policy documents on sexual labour, and visits to sex worker organizations, brothels, red-light districts and other sex work sites, with an emphasis on situations in global South countries. Through contact with the Maxi Linder sex workers' organization in Suriname, I was also able to expand and deepen my own understandings of sexual labour in the Caribbean context. From all this activity, I co-produced the book, *Global Sex Workers: Rights, Resistance and Redefinition*, which contributed to the small body of feminist work that at that time was engaged with redefining prostitution as sexual labour (see, Kempadoo and Doezema 1998). It was the first sustained effort to place global South sex workers – women, men and trans – and their definitions, experiences and voices, at the centre of the debate, covering countries such as Malaysia, India, Thailand, Japan, South Africa, Ghana, Senegal, Brazil, Mexico, and Cuba, offering a counterpoint to the discourse on sex work that was becoming globally hegemonic through the prostitute's right movements located in Western Europe and North America.

The Caribbean Sex Trade Project, 1995-99[3]

Alongside my engagement with the Global Sex Workers book project, I began discussions with other Latin American and Caribbean feminists about the extent to which 'sex tourism' was embedded in Caribbean societies and the rapidity and ease with which it was spreading in Cuba. We realized that this new development was not isolated from a sex trade that had existed in the region for several centuries or from international racialized and gendered divisions of labour and power and the new recolonizations that were occurring through globalization. Nevertheless, it was not until Gladys Acosta Vargas, who at the time was attached to the Instituto Latinoamericano de Servicios Legales Alternativos (ILSA) in Bogota, Colombia, Elena Diaz, director of the Facultad Latinoamericana de Ciencias Sociales Program (FLACSO) at the University of Havana, Cuba, and I met in late 1995 to address the issue, that an initiative was taken to conduct a collaborative region-wide research project on the sex trade in the Caribbean. Our hopes, from the beginning of the project, were to document the contemporary sex trade, to stimulate regional attention from policymakers and activists for the subject, and to encourage Caribbean feminist analyses of prostitution.

We conceptualized a research project that would be a collaborative, interactive effort that, rather than employ a top-down approach to the production of knowledge about sex work, would develop from an exchange between and among feminists who were already engaged, or seeking to be engaged, with the subject – as sex workers, researchers and/or activists. Very quickly the Caribbean Association for Feminist Research and Action (CAFRA) joined the project, and a coordinating team, comprising Cynthia Mellon of ILSA, Jacqueline Burgess of CAFRA and myself refined the project concept, raised the necessary funds from international agencies and sources, and managed the project.

To accomplish our objectives of developing grounded research on Caribbean sex work, we outlined a general framework for the project and invited research proposals that could form the substance of the project. Our focus was on identifying and working with feminist Caribbeanists who could combine research with some forms of activism and public consciousness-raising around the subject of prostitution, and who were interested in breaking down hierarchies and divides between 'the researcher' and 'researched', and the sex worker and non-sex worker. Understanding prostitutes and other sex workers to be one set of actors in the sex trade – as providers of sexual labour – yet a social group whose lives and voices had commonly been dismissed or ignored, we were emphatic from the outset of the project that the perceptions and experiences of this population needed to be centre stage.

The coordinating team selected and sponsored eight research proposals that shared its general approach and concerns. With a restriction that we placed on the number of countries that could participate in the study, the location also acted as a criterion in the selection process (one study per country was to be chosen), enabling us to gather as broad a basis for comparison and elaboration as possible. The project design led to case studies in the eight Caribbean territories of Belize, Barbados, the Dominican Republic, Guyana, Jamaica, the Netherlands Antilles, Suriname, and the Colombian Caribbean coastal city of Cartagena, with participation by three organizations – the Stichting Maxi Linder Association for sex workers in Suriname, the Center for Gender and Development Studies at the University of the West Indies in Jamaica, and the Red Thread Women's Development Program in Guyana – and 13 researchers who were attached to these organizations as well as to universities in the US, Canada, and Britain. Fieldwork was conducted during 1997–98, culminating in a two-day conference in Kingston, Jamaica, in July 1998 at which the project participants and other researchers and representatives from sex workers' and non-governmental organizations presented their work and ideas. Papers by Julia O'Connell Davidson and Jacqueline Sanchez Taylor on their research among sex tourists in the Dominican Republic, by Beverley Mullings on tourism in Jamaica and Nadine Fernandez on race and tourism in Cuba, complemented the project work so well, sharing the framework and goals of the project research, that these were later included in the book in which the case studies were published.[4]

Ultimately, the studies all fell loosely within a framework that viewed prostitution as a form of sexual labour that was shaped and transformed by a variety of gendered, economic, and racialized relations of power – a generalized orientation that was reflected in the work of others (for e.g., see Truong 1990; O'Connell Davidson 1996; Chapkis 1997; Kempadoo and Doezema 1998; Lim 1998). However, this was not necessarily the starting point for all the project researchers. Indeed, it was through the research process itself, from listening to, observing and interacting with women and men who worked in the sex sector (very few of whom were associated with sex workers or women's organizations), that such an understanding of sex work developed. The results thus constituted notions about the Caribbean sex trade that were not theoretically or politically derived but, instead, lodged in everyday realities and practices. Sex work emerged through these studies as a sexual-economic exchange in which the persons providing the sexual labour did so with multiple partners while publicly acknowledging their participation in this exchange. This definition of sex work rested not simply on a concrete action and a set of relations, but as much upon the meanings and interpretations of the act by the persons providing sexual labour.

The researchers employed a number of qualitative research methods, often relying on a combination of two or more, among them observations, in-depth interviews, life histories, and focus group sessions. The study in Suriname was an extension of out-reach work undertaken by the Maxi Linder sex workers' association, involving prior experience with research on the Surinamese sex trade and researchers who were also sex workers and/or peer-educators. It was structured as part of the organization's efforts to gain new knowledge about sex work practices in the country (particularly around issues of safe sex), and to make contact with sex workers who had, to that date, no knowledge of, or access to, the organization's support programmes. In the other seven case studies, the issue of gaining trust among sex workers was critical. Rapport had to be established and confidentiality ensured before work could begin. In some cases, such as in Colombia and the Dominican Republic, local sex workers' organizations and/or peer educators facilitated the process by providing information about sex work sites and practices. In the case of Belize, the Ministry of Health that was engaged in AIDS prevention work among sex workers was an important vehicle. In some instances, however, officials acted as gatekeepers, attempting to censor the information collected and to control the researchers' movements. That prostitution was by and large an illegal activity yet lined the pockets of many a business person, police officer or government official (apart from providing pleasure to many Caribbean men) meant that probes and investigations by, in particular feminist, researchers into the field could be viewed as a challenge to state or male complicity in the sex trade. Care and caution was thus needed on the part of the researcher or teams to avoid placing themselves in a situation where they could be perceived as a threat by the authorities or where their investigations would harm sex workers.

From discussions throughout the project and at the conclusion of the fieldwork period, the positionality of the researcher was considered important to the construction of knowledge about sex work in the region. In particular, ideas and specific biases held by researchers regarding female sexual agency were areas for reflection and discussion. Relations of power between the researcher and researched around 'race' and ethnicity, nationality, class, and gender were also interrogated during the research process, in some studies more explicitly and extensively than in others. In some cases, an unfamiliarity with sex work studies and practices meant that the researcher was confronted with an 'outsider' position in a way that she had not anticipated – being 'of the local culture' or of the same nationality or ethnicity was, she soon discovered, not a sufficient basis for gaining access to the sex trade. Other codes and sensibilities that derived from in-depth knowledge or prior experience with the trade of sex were required. Being in an outside position to the very specific local context, yet very familiar with Caribbean societies in general, sometimes, however, enabled the researcher to feel more comfortable with entering the arena, particularly because she was not hindered by knowledge of local taboos, dominant constraints on 'decent' feminine behaviour, or the possibility that a friend or relative might see her in a place of 'ill-repute'. In such a situation the researcher was able to extend the boundaries of her investigation in ways that might not have been possible had she been a part of the local community. A complete outsider position – of having no longstanding relationship with Caribbean culture and society or the sex trade – was, however, also a severe limitation on the cultural interpretations that a researcher could make, and this was particularly evident in one of the studies. The complexity in the researchers' positionality was a constant reminder of the significance of cultural identity in the research process, and of the importance of taking into account hierarchies, exploitations, appropriations as well as empowerment that shape the fieldwork encounter.

During the course of the project, a total of 191 sex workers – 170 women and 21 men – were interviewed in the eight countries. In addition,

20 clients – half of whom were women – were interviewed. These figures were not intended to be representative of the gendered composition of the sex working population or the clients in the Caribbean, but were a reflection of general assumptions that undergirded the project and underpinned the initial research proposals. The main concern was for the lives of, and conditions for, female sex workers, and rested on notions that the high degree of female participation in the global sex trade was due to the way in which feminine sexuality and labour had historically been controlled and organized to serve masculine and male interests. Nevertheless, we could not ignore the fact that in each country, men were also active in the trade. Only one case study, however, explicitly addressed this aspect, focusing on heterosexual male sex work and recognizing the need to theorize gender relations more broadly (male sex work for men as well as transgender sex workers are also a part of the Caribbean landscape, but were not the focus of any of the proposals submitted for consideration in the project). This particular case study later became important in helping to complicate the analysis we were making of sex work, and to probe meanings of female sex tourism. The overall project methodology helped to ensure that the research was locally situated, dependent upon specific cultural and national experiences and meanings of sex work, and was part of feminist discourses and practices in the region.

The project was designed to develop a substantive body of feminist work on the sex trade in the Caribbean, through collaborative research. It was a first trans-Caribbean effort to record and analyse details of sex work as defined by the people who provided sexual labour, and thus to provide new information and insights, carrying with it a number of implications for feminist theorizing. The variety of arrangements and working conditions, the diversity of people as both clients and sex workers, and the various perspectives that were described through the project indicated that sex work and prostitution relations were being produced and reconfigured not simply along the axis of gender, but also along those of ethnicity and 'race', nation, and class. In this respect the project confirmed ideas that had been advanced by such theorists as Thanh-Dam Truong, that feminist theory on sex work and prostitution needed to proceed with great care and attention to historical and contextual specificities, and not reduce itself to the production of grand, universalizing notions about prostitution as the quintessence of women's oppression, resting upon the assumption of a unified category of 'woman'. It also deepened insights I had gathered in my initial doctoral research in Curaçao. The careful empirical investigations thus contributed to reformulations and reconceptualizations in feminist discourse and practice about prostitution.

The ways in which sexual labour had to then been historically, culturally, and socially organized and how these specificities allowed for a multiplicity of sexualized and gendered categories, identities and dependencies needed, we argued, to be integral to theories of sex work. Indeed, the research moved us beyond essentialist notions of 'the prostitute' and 'the client' to remind us that these categories were not fixed, universal, or transhistorical, but subject to transformation and change in particular ways. The project also starkly illustrated the global repositioning that was occurring between postindustrial and postcolonial societies, where Black and Brown bodies remained sites for the construction of (white) North American and Western European power, wealth, and well-being. The research, thus, while providing many new details about constructions of sex work in contemporary Caribbean societies, also contributed a substantive basis for the re-examination of theories of prostitution and sex work and to feminist theorizing that paid attention to contradictory and multiple gendered positions and locations within globalized relations of power. It also led to going beyond or outside of a conceptualization of sexuality as an identity category, to an understanding of it as action, interaction and lived experience – which I defined as 'sexual praxis' (see also, Kempadoo 2004). This was especially relevant due to the silence around the marginalization of non-normative sexual behaviour and the 'private' and often clandestine nature of sexual relations and identities in the Caribbean region.

Policy-oriented Research on Caribbean Sex Work and HIV and AIDS – The 2000s

Having established over the years a methodology that had quite successfully examined sexual labour from the vantage point of those working within the sex trade, and having demonstrated an appreciation for sexual labour and women's sexual agency from a Caribbeanist perspective, my research was taken up not only by academics and activists, but increasingly within policymaking circles. I was invited to participate in Caribbean policy-oriented, development projects that focused on HIV and AIDS prevention and sexual health. In this work, despite the apparent top-down character of the projects and the quantitative mindset of epidemiologists, health researchers and policymakers, I stuck to the earlier methodology, insisting that qualitative research and a 'bottom-up' approach were vital for understanding sexual relations and cultures in the region.[5] This approach was accepted, especially for exploratory phases, and seen to be compatible with 'evidence-based' approaches. One project I undertook was to support the Pan Caribbean Partnership against HIV/AIDS (PANCAP) in its goal of understanding the ways in which sex work activities were organized, legislated, and defined throughout the region. Commissioned by PANCAP with a grant from the World Bank and conducted in collaboration with UNAIDS in the context of its work on the Regional Strategic Framework on HIV and AIDS, the task was to conduct a desk review of published literature and studies alongside an examination of laws on prostitution. Part of the research effort was guided by an earlier review of laws on prostitution and homosexuality in the English-speaking Caribbean by Tracy Robinson (2008), for the United Nations Women's Bureau (UNIFEM). The research was supplemented and deepened by information about laws on the Dutch and French-speaking territories and by further research on the English-speaking Caribbean through internet searches and email contact with persons in different countries. The empirical studies often confirmed and repeated, deepened and broadened the information and analyses from my earlier research projects, yet the review established that the full scope of the sex trade in the region had not been researched or documented, and that what had been produced was mainly inaccessible to the general public. Nevertheless, the data was analysed for several trends and the results were published by CARICOM as a policy-background document (see Kempadoo and Taitt 2009).

The second part of this work was carried out through empirical research during 2010 in 14 Caribbean Community (CARICOM) member states – Antigua and Barbuda, the Bahamas, Barbados, Belize, Dominica, Grenada, Guyana, Haiti, Jamaica, St Kitts and Nevis, St Lucia, St Vincent and the Grenadines, Suriname, and Trinidad and Tobago – to identify the common types of sex work and describe the main locations where sex work took place, the sexual services offered, and the kinds of populations that sex workers serviced. The overall objectives of the project were to analyse the sex industry in the context of national and regional socio-economic conditions and in relation to the HIV and AIDS epidemics; and to generate a broad definition of sex work and an analysis of the sex industry that could be used for the region as a whole and that would help to inform national and regional HIV programming, policy, and decision-making, and could influence current legal and public health debates. The project would pay attention to sexual-economic relations that were commercialized as well as those that were transactional. It was to be an exploration into the regional sex industry, in particular those areas of the industry and in those countries where little or no research or documentation had been carried out, and was intended to complement the earlier PANCAP/CARICOM study.

We set out to create a baseline of information and to develop a general conceptual apparatus and working definitions, all of which helped to prepare and guide the researchers as they went into the field. The researchers had been selected on the basis of their non-judgemental perspective on sex work, their availability to travel the region, and experience with research and writing about Caribbean sex work and sexuality. To prepare for the fieldwork interviews, we held an intensive workshop to elaborate the research design, construct research questionnaires, plan the field trips, and identify key informants. Key in all of these preparations was a methodology that held sex worker perspectives and knowledge as critical to understanding the Caribbean sex industry. The two researchers spent at least five working days holding interviews and making observations in each of the 14-member states, including additional visits to Bequia in the Grenadines, and to Nevis and Tobago, the sister islands of St Kitts and Trinidad, respectively. The interviews were semi-structured and open-ended, and were held with key informants from government institutions, non-governmental organizations (NGOs), international agencies, community organizations, and organized sex worker groups. Permission was sought for interviews with representatives of the national police forces and immigration services for all countries. All interviews were usually set up for one and a half hours, although they often lasted longer. The respondents were selected through a snowball method, on the basis of their reputation for having in-depth knowledge of the local sex industry. People seen as able only to speak about their own experience with sex work or about general gender issues were not initially approached for an interview as such interviews would deliver relatively few insights into the sex industry as a whole and were very time-consuming. In some countries few people could speak comprehensively about the sex industry and could only provide anecdotes. In other instances, a person's knowledge was too much to be contained in one interview. In all cases information was sought from other informants and/or in follow-up sessions by telephone, email or in person. 135 people were interviewed, including a range of sex workers. We were looking for trends, agreed upon and collective understandings, and insights and information that could be corroborated through multiple sources.

The research was to focus on HIV and AIDS but could not provide an estimate of the size or the scale of either the sex industry or the sex worker population in the 14 CARICOM member states, or the ways in which HIV and AIDS affected this population, as the data at the national levels was simply not available. However, it was the first study of its kind to try to assess the sex industry in the CARICOM region, and the data collected indicated certain trends that, for the most part, confirmed, or expanded findings from earlier research. A series of policy recommendations were made, which included further research into the role of the state and masculinity in organizing, profiting from, using, and benefiting from the regional sex trade and transactional sex, with attention to relations of power in transactional sexual relations and sex sectors; the creation of safe, sustainable income-generating possibilities that would not exclude sexuality, in order to adequately address working people's material needs and desires; and the destigmatization of sexual-economic transactions in their varied articulations and meanings. It reflected a sex worker rights perspective, one that was aimed at empowering those whose lives are often harmed by local and regional policies and laws deemed to protect public health. However, as with many policy-oriented pieces of research that are commissioned by governmental, UN and non-governmental agencies, the report was not made publicly available and continues to circulate in very restricted circles.[6] Nevertheless, it could be considered the first 'baseline' study of the Caribbean sex sector in the twenty-first century.

Conclusion

Conducting research on sexual labour for over twenty-five years has involved a 'bottom-up' approach that started from women's experiences in the Caribbean sex trade, went global, returned to the Caribbean, and involved collaboration with multiple actors, agencies, researchers and sex workers. It has produced new insights and theoretical formulations about sex work, including the notion of 'sexual praxis' and the significance of race in configuring sexual labour. Importantly, the research has relied upon carefully listening to and taking seriously the experiences and views of marginalized Black and Brown women, men and trans about the ways through which they make meaning of income-generating strategies, sexual labour, transnational sex, and sexualized international relations; about the harms, violence, and force they encounter in sex sectors; and about the hopes, dreams, and pleasures they derive from their sexual praxis. It has led to conclusions that transactional sex and prostitution can best be captured as two, but different, expressions of the way in which sexuality and economics are related – that they cannot be subsumed into one or the other, nor seen to exist on a continuum but rather that 'boopsing', 'escorting', 'whoring', 'tactical sex', 'romance tourism' or 'friends with benefits' are intertwined practices, some of which involve affect or passion, others that involve third parties and a high degree of organization, while other practices are independently organized often on irregular or occasional basis. Many of the activities service (white) Western racialized fantasies, desires and needs, and all (re)produce Black and Brown sexual praxis and, at times, support a resistive, hypersexualized Caribbean subjectivity.

The research has involved not only fieldwork but also the reading of scores of reports, studies and legal documents, which has allowed for the deciphering of hegemonic as well as counter hegemonic narratives about prostitution, HIV and AIDS, and migration for sex work, and for the unpacking of power dynamics that underpin Caribbean sexual labour. But above all, the methodology has enabled marginalized Caribbean women, with whom we have in common much more than we tend to think, to have a voice and a place in transnational feminism, Caribbean scholarship, and activism and policymaking. And while we can hardly claim to have moved the debate from margin to centre, Caribbean sexual praxis, sexuality, and sexual labour have become far less taboo than when I first started this research almost three decades ago. It is my hope that the methodology can continue to be refined, deepened, and extended in the future, and will continue to support the lives, praxes, and desires of Caribbean (sex) working people.

Notes

1. Mohanty argues that Third World Feminism is, in part, constituted through 'the common context of struggle against racist, sexist and imperialist structures' (1991, 7). Or as Bannerji writes: 'We non-white women who seek not only to express but to end our oppression need reliable knowledge which allows us to be actors in history. This knowledge cannot be produced in the context of ruling but only in conscious resistance to it. It must retain the integrity of our concrete subject positions within its very project and its present day method of investigation, in so far as it searches the history and social relations to trace the reasons for and forms of our oppression' (1992, 93).
2. This resulted in my doctoral dissertation 'Exotic Colonies: Caribbean Women in the Dutch Sex Trade,' University of Colourado, Boulder, 1994.
3. This section is a revised excerpt from my previously published essay, 'Freelancers, Temporary Wives and Beachboys'.
4. The initial CAFRA/ILSA/University of Colourado research report based on the eight case studies that was compiled by myself and Cynthia Mellon, 'The Caribbean Sex Trade', was later expanded and edited into the collection. *Sun, Sex and Gold: Tourism and Sex Work in the Caribbean.*
5. Apart from the projects described in the rest of the section, for PANCAP and UNAIDS, this included research for the United Nations Development Fund for Women (UNIFEM)-Caribbean Office on gender, sexuality and implications for HIV and AIDS (Kempadoo 2006), and the participation in the coordinating team of the IDRC/UNWomen project, 'Building Responsive Policy: Gender, Sexual Culture and HIV/AIDS in the Caribbean', which although not exclusively about sexual labour, addressed the subject in various ways: http://caribbean.unwomen.org/en/news-and-events/stories/2011/5/building-responsive-policy-gender-sexual-culture-and-hiv-and-aids-in-the-caribbean.
6. The final report '"Whoring", "Boopsing" and Other Business: A Situational Analysis of Sex Work and the Sex Industry in the CARICOM' (March 2010) was produced for the UNAIDS Caribbean Regional Support Team (UNAIDS CAR-RST), Port-of-Spain, Trinidad, and can be requested from that office or from this author.

References

Bannerji, Himani. 1992. But Who Speaks for Us? Experience and Agency in Conventional Feminist , Paradigms. In *Unsettling Relations: The University as a Site of Feminist Struggles*, ed. Himani Bannerji et al. Boston: South End Press.

Bourdieu, Pierre. 1977. *Outline of a Theory of Practice.* Cambridge: Cambridge University Press.
Chapkis, Wendy. 1997. *Live Sex Acts: Women Performing Erotic Labour.* New York: Routledge.
Kempadoo, Kamala, ed. 1999. *Sun, Sex, and Gold: Tourism and Sex Work in the Caribbean.* Lanham: Rowman and Littlefield.
———. 2001. Free-lancers, Temporary Wives and Beachboys: Researching Sex Work in the Caribbean. *Feminist Review* 67 (Spring): 39–63.
———. 2004. *Sexing the Caribbean: Gender, Race and Sexual Labour.* New York: Routledge.
———. 2009. Prostitution, Sex Work and Transactional Sex in the English, Dutch and French-Speaking Caribbean: A Literature Review of Definitions, Laws and Research. Final Report. PANCAP/CARICOM.
Kempadoo, Kamala, and Jo Doezema, eds. 1998. *Global Sex Workers: Rights, Resistance and Redefinition.* New York: Routledge.
Kempadoo, Kamala, Oonya Kempadoo, Althea Perkins, and Andy Taitt. 2010.*'Whoring', 'Boopsing', and Other Business: A Situational Analysis of Sex Work and the Sex Industry in the Caricom.* Port-of-Spain: UNAIDS Caribbean Regional Support Team.
Kempadoo, Kamala with Andy Taitt. 2006. Gender, Sexuality and Implications for HIV/AIDS in the Caribbean. A Review of Literature and Programmes. UNIFEM-Caribbean Office and IDRC-Ottawa.
Mohanty, Chandra Talpade. 1991. Cartographies of Struggle: Third World Women and the Politics of Feminism. In *Third World Women and the Politics of Feminism*, ed. Chandra Talpade Mohanty, Ann Russo, and Lourdes Torres. Bloomington: Indiana University Press.
Lim, Lin Leam, ed. 1998. *The Sex Sector: The Economic and Social Bases of Prostitution in Southeast Asia.* Geneva: International Labour Office.
O'Connell Davidson, Julia. 1996. Sex Tourism in Cuba. *Race and Class* 38 (July/September): 39–48.
Robinson, Tracy S. 2008. *A Legal Analysis of Sex Work in the Anglophone Caribbean.* Bridgetown: United Nations Development Fund for Women (UNIFEM).
Truong, Thanh Dam. 1990. *Sex, Money and Morality: The Political Economy of Prostitution and Tourism in South East Asia.* London: Zed Books.
Wacquant, Lois J.D. 1992. Toward a Social Praxeology: The Structure and Logic of Bourdieu's Sociology. In *An Invitation to Reflexive Sociology*, ed. Lois J. D. Wacquant. Chicago: University of Chicago Press.

17. Caribbean Sexualities and Ethnographic Research Methods

David A. B. Murray

Introduction

In this chapter, I discuss qualitative research methods for research projects focusing on sexuality, a broad and highly politicized subject of inquiry spanning multiple disciplines. I will primarily discuss *ethnographic* research methods that I have been trained in as an anthropologist and which have been helpful to me when conducting research with sexual and gender minority communities in the English- and French-speaking Caribbean. In this chapter, I will focus primarily on a research project which examined sexual diversity, sexual rights, and discrimination in Barbados in the early 2000s, resulting in the book *Flaming Souls: Homosexuality, Homophobia and Social Change in Barbados* (2012). There are many directions a conversation about social science research methods in sexuality studies could take, including the development of appropriate research questions, appropriate methodological frameworks to answer those questions, ethical dimensions of different research methods (particularly in relation to sensitive issues pertaining to sexual practices, values and beliefs), and the social impact of different methods on marginalized or vulnerable communities. In this chapter I will primarily focus on the application of ethnographic research methods to answer a set of questions pertaining to sexual diversity and discrimination in Barbados, why I found these methods to be productive in addressing these issues, and some of their challenges and limits in the Barbadian context.

I am trained as a sociocultural anthropologist specializing in issues of gender and sexuality, meaning I am interested in how gendered and sexual desires, practices, and beliefs are organized in particular social and cultural contexts, how they relate to other aspects of everyday life in these local contexts, and how these local contexts are connected to wider political and economic forces. Thinking about gender and sexuality in relation to local cultural and social contexts is of course not restricted to anthropologists, but a sociocultural anthropological perspective is often unique in that it emphasizes an ethnographic dimension of research in addition to other research methods found in numerous other disciplines like history, women's and gender studies, sociology, political science, and geography. As I shall outline below, ethnographic research is a productive method for developing analytical insights into human sexual practices, values, and attitudes, but it also comes with a set of challenges and limitations which must be considered before, during and after conducting research.

Ethnographic Research Methods

Research methods can be conceptualized as what is 'done', that is, the techniques of collecting data (interviews, questionnaires, focus groups, photographs, videos, observation, etc.) in order to answer research questions and/or test hypotheses. By contrast, methodologies are those sets of rules and procedures that guide the design of research to investigate phenomena or situations, part of which is a decision about what methods will be used and why. Methodology can be understood as the logic that links the project's theoretical, ontological, and epistemological objectives to the selection and deployment of these methods (Browne and Nash 2010, 10–11).

Ethnographic research is a qualitative research method (as opposed to quantitative research method)[1] that generally involves learning about social worlds by positioning the 'self' in relation to 'others' through shared lived experiences. Ethnographic research is a way of understanding social worlds through lived experiences and participation in daily activities and social contexts of everyday life of the group or community being studied. The ethnographer's goal is to describe and analyse connections between everyday practices, beliefs, and/or actions and wider domains of social life such as religion, gender, sexuality, economy, or the state. Ethnographic research methods are actually a collection of research methods chosen on the basis of the research project's objectives and/or the community/ topic being studied. However, a key component to all ethnographic research is fieldwork. Fieldwork is usually conducted by the ethnographer in the location(s) in which research participants live or spend a significant amount of time (e.g., online worlds), where the ethnographer engages in *participant observation* – sustained contact and communication with individuals and/or groups in face-to-face settings and/or via digital technologies. That is, the ethnographer obtains information through participating in and observing the 'everyday' life of a group of people…mundane, common actions, comments, and behaviours are considered to be important and worthy of extended ethnographic analysis.

Fieldwork generally requires long-term commitment, that is, a commitment to interact with people for an extended period of time (the amount of time can vary from several months to many years, depending on a variety of factors). While ethnography is a research method derived in relation to a research plan designed in dialogue with key theoretical and/or disciplinary debates, it is also inductive, that is, it is conducted in such a way that observations derived from long-term fieldwork with a particular group or community may produce explanatory theories rather than simply proving or disproving hypotheses derived from existing theories or models. Ethnographic research also has a dialogic quality in that it is conducted by the researcher whose interpretations and findings are tested and revised through ongoing dialogue with participants.

Queering Ethnographic Methods

Since the late 1990s, the rise of 'queer theory' has had a great impact in North American activist and academic circles. While there is a great deal of debate over the definition of 'queer' and there have been significant changes over the past 20 years in its meanings, the central notion of queer theory acknowledges the inherent multiplicity and fluidity of sexual subjectivities in human societies and seeks to reveal and challenge processes which normalize and homogenize particular arrangements of sexual and gender practices, relationships, and subjectivities (Browne and Nash 2010, 5). Queer theory thus challenges the normative social ordering of identities and subjectivities along the heterosexual/homosexual binary as well as the privileging of heterosexuality as 'natural' and homosexuality as its deviant and abhorrent 'other'. Its goal is to create a space that allows for multiple perspectives that recognize complex lives as they are lived and the various social, political, and economic positionings which manage or restrict or discipline those lives, as well as the agency or actions of individuals and groups towards those attempts to manage or discipline (Castell and Bryson

1998). However, it is important to recognize that much queer theorizing originated in the global North with its particular social, political and historical contexts. Queer theory's often uncritical or non-engagement with gendered and sexual politics and lives in other geographical locations potentially limits its cross-cultural or transnational usefulness, a highly relevant issue for the Caribbean region, which I will return to below.

With the emergence of queer theory as an interdisciplinary field of study, there have been a number of discussions about queer methods and methodologies, including the possibility of queer ethnographic methods. Queer ethnographic methods follow queer theory's principles in that a primary goal is to find ways to reveal the mundane, everyday contexts within which 'normal' forms of gender and sexuality are organized and performed, rendering their artifices and illusions evident (Castell and Bryson 2008). Queer ethnographic methods may be particularly helpful in unpacking what is 'taken for granted' in the everyday conversations, performances and activities of research subjects. In research deemed 'queer', ethnographic methods utilized are often (but not always or only) in relation to sexual/gender identities and practices located within anti-normative frameworks, and revealing complex worlds, identities, and practices that often reveal a much more dynamic and complex perspective of a particular society. This theoretical and methodological relationship can be found in numerous other interdisciplinary and emerging fields including feminist, gay/lesbian, antiracist, and postcolonial studies (Browne and Nash 2010; Buch and Staller 2007; Scharff 2008). However, as Michael Jackman notes, queer ethnographic methods are no different from 'traditional' ethnographic methods in that they face similar challenges and limitations of representation, authorial authority, and objectivity (2010, 116).

Ethnographic Research and Sexual Diversity in Barbados

My research in Barbados began with a simple question developed from my professional interest in better understanding how social science research on Caribbean sexualities had been theoretically framed and analysed, and a personal interest based on a relationship that I had with a Barbadian man and his fellow Barbadian friends who I met while I was a graduate student in Washington DC in the early 1990s. Most of this group would be identified in North America as 'gay men' although some of them told me that they didn't identify with the term 'gay', which I did not fully understand at that time, given my experiences growing up in a homogenous white middle-class suburban community in Canada and self-identifying as a gay man. Among these friends, there were lots of conversations about life in Barbados and how it was difficult for them, but at the same time they missed their homeland a great deal. My partner passed away from AIDS in 1994, but by that time I had come to know some of his family and friends who resided in Barbados, and I wanted to learn more about their beliefs and attitudes about same-sex sexualities. I also wanted to better understand what everyday life was like for men who are attracted to men in Barbados at a time when many Barbadians lived transnational lives (moving back and forth between North America and Europe), HIV was a major health crisis in the Caribbean, and there was also increasing talk about sexual rights for lesbian, gay, bisexual and transgender people around the globe.

My research questions were thus developed through a combination of personal and professional motivations, desires, and interests. The decision to make Barbados the field site for my research was derived from a set of friendships and a desire to stay connected to people who were close to my deceased partner. However, my questions pertaining to sexual minority identities, experiences and rights were derived from reading contemporary theoretical debates on sexuality alongside the relatively slim collection (at that time) of ethnographic research on non-heteronormative sexualities in the Caribbean. One of the interesting debates in anthropological studies of sexuality in the early 2000s was in relation to the usefulness and limits of sexual identity terminologies in cross-cultural contexts. As noted above, queer theory had emerged in the 1990s as a challenge to the relatively established field of 'lesbian and gay studies' (itself a challenge to prior discussions of homosexuality in the field of 'sexology'), moving away from essentialist sexual identity labels towards developing an analytical framework of the multiple ways through which normative sexualities regulated personal, social, and state lives while simultaneously calling for closer attention to diverse possibilities and combinations of sexual desires, identities, and politics.

As more scholars turned their attention to 'queer worlds' that were mostly located in Euro-American spaces (but see Cruz Malave and Manalansan 2002 as an early challenge to this tendency), I became increasingly interested in how (what some claimed to be) 'global' sexual identity terminologies and rights discourses were moving into and through Caribbean socio-sexual spaces. My first objective was to conduct a review of existing research on Caribbean sexualities, primarily exploring anthropological research on sexuality in the Caribbean: What were the framing questions in this body of research and what questions hadn't been asked? What were the disciplinary and theoretical orientations of the research and how were they useful or not? From my preliminary conversations with my partner's network of friends and family, it was clear that the transnational circulation of particular popular Euro-American sexual identity terms like 'gay' were having some sort of impact in Caribbean locales, but their meanings in these locales were not necessarily identical to their North American counterparts. In reviewing the existing research literature on Caribbean sexualities, I was deeply influenced by M. Jacqui Alexander's analysis connecting sexual politics to economic and political processes in the Bahamas and foregrounding the way in which the Bahamian nation state consolidated a form of neo-imperial heteropatriarchal power through its laws, economic policies, and transnational political-economic alliances (Alexander 2005). However, I could not find substantial research examining the transnational dimension or circulation of sexual minority terminologies and their uses in everyday Caribbean social worlds, much less any sustained argument about LGBT rights and/or forms of resistance.[2] Ethnographic analysis would, I hoped, help to uncover the tensions between variously constituted local discussions of same-sex identities and practices and globally circulating 'LGBT' discourses of identity and rights, thus providing a better understanding of these local/global encounters.

Cognizant of Kamala Kempadoo's (2004) important observation that efforts to address sexuality in the Caribbean are constantly in danger of reinscribing a discourse of negativity and hypersexuality on the bodies of people who have been historically oversexualized through colonial and racist discourses, I sought to employ research methods that would engage with relevant 'everyday' conversations taking place in a range of locations like people's homes, bars and night clubs, sexual minority support groups, and community organizations. In order to better understand how male same-sex relations, practices, and identities were framed, organized, and discussed in everyday contexts in Barbados, I developed a multi-pronged methodological framework, with fieldwork-based ethnographic analysis as the core method.

I began my research by conducting textual analysis of Barbadian newspaper articles and feedback media (letters to the editor columns, website commentaries, and radio call – in shows) focusing on same-sex issues. I noticed that papers like *The Nation* and *The Advocate* regularly contained articles and letters to the editor with strong opinions about sexual rights, homosexuality and HIV/AIDS, so I started to collect them and pay attention to how they would talk about these issues. I also became a fan of local radio phone-in shows like 'Down to Brass Tacks' where there would occasionally be interesting discussions between the host and callers about LGBT rights, public morality and changing socio-sexual attitudes in Barbados. Analysing common themes in newspaper texts, letters to the editor and phone-in shows helped me grasp how popular, mostly negative, attitudes and feelings about homosexuality and sexuality more generally were being articulated. Through this examination of one site of Barbadian public culture, I was able to observe how 'the homosexual' regularly operated as a seminal figure through which a complex array of local, national, and transnational social, political, and economic tensions were aligned, related, and defined (or redefined). I developed the argument that realignments of political and economic power on local and transnational scales were bringing about significant changes in the socio-economic fabric of life of many Bajans, resulting in what some observers claimed was a submissive, subordinated, or 'feminized' (defined through a heteropatriarchal lens) economy and nation-state. Thus I argued that by the late 1990s and early 2000s, a particular incarnation of the 'homosexual' had become the visible index of (dis)respectability, (im)morality, and social (in)stability in mainstream media and public discourses. This silent, spectral, yet ever-present sexual entity was the new 'pariah' amongst some individuals and groups who were unhappy with the current socio-economic and political situation of Barbados, and who were nostalgic for a return to a heteropatriarchal past.

However, I also came to recognize that these popular or public discourses tended to represent a particular perspective of mostly Christian-identified, heterosexual, older men and women that was considered acceptable or respectable in particular public spheres, but that this was not the only perspective on these issues in Barbados. As I wanted to find out more about what daily life was like for Barbadian sexual minorities, and I didn't hear or see their presence on radio phone in shows or in newspaper letters and articles, I therefore decided to meet and spend time with them in person. I was able to meet some research participants through my ex-partner's family contacts in a working-class neighbourhood of Bridgetown. I also reached out to the one public organization supporting sexual minorities at that time, UGLAAB (United Gays and Lesbians Against Aids in Barbados), whose leaders were very generous in allowing me to introduce my project to their members and sit in on their meetings.

'Face-to-face' or interactional meetings with research participants provide numerous methodological opportunities for the researcher: what is the best method for learning about sexual attitudes, identities, and practices in the encounter between researcher and research participant? One of the most common methods across the social sciences is 'interviewing', where the researcher sits down with the research participant or group of participants and asks them a series of questions about a particular topic. There are many interview styles or formats, and I decided to conduct oral history or life narrative interviews in which I would ask the interviewee to narrate to me their life story starting from childhood, with some guiding questions from me focusing on sexual experiences, identification, and discrimination. I found that oral history interviews were a good starting point for understanding the interplay between the individual and broader social and historical forces, or put in slightly different terms, the relationship between agency and social structure, that is, the ways in which different social, political, and economic forces shaped life trajectories and how individuals adapted to, resisted, or negotiated these forces.[3] From semi-structured oral history interviews with gay men/men who have sex with men in their 50s and older, I heard different self-identifications and opinions about sexual identity terms like 'gay' or 'queen' compared with men under 30. However, I did not fully understand the similarities and differences between these terms and the contexts in which they were utilized, and my attempts to get interviewees to further elaborate were generally not successful. Through the interviews, I also began to learn that experiences of sexual discrimination for people from poor or working-class families occurred more often than for those from middle-class families. Nevertheless, I found one-on-one oral history interviews had limitations inherent to their structure and format. Even though they were designed to be open-ended in subject matter and direction, they were still influenced by my research objectives and related questions, and could thus reflect issues that were of greater importance to me than to the participant. There was also the distinct possibility that interviewees might be self-censoring or editing comments to fit what they thought the interviewer would want to hear, particularly if the interviewer was from outside the community (which I was in terms of national, racial and, in some cases, generational affiliation; my institutional affiliation with a Canadian university may also have shaped responses) and they were asking about personal or sensitive topics like sexual practices and attitudes (see Yanos and Hopper 2008 for more discussion on self-censorship and interviewer bias).

Given the limitations with interviewing, I also employed participant observation techniques through multi-sited fieldwork, which means I spent time in the homes of various members of UGLAAB and my partner's family's Bridgetown neighbourhood, accompanying them on everyday tasks like shopping, going to the bank or hanging out with them at parties or bars in the evening. I also attended UGLAAB meetings and other public gatherings such as a series of town hall meetings organized by the National HIV/AIDS Commission on the topic of decriminalization of homosexuality and sex work. It was through spending time and hanging out with people in every day private, semi-public, and public contexts, that I was able to observe and learn about a number of different aspects of social life for sexual minorities in Barbados: First, I gradually became aware of the ways in which terms like 'queen' and 'gay' were used interchangeably, and how they indexed (for some) sexual orientation and gendered performances organized in ways that did not replicate mainstream white North American gender/sexual orientation binaries. Second, from everyday conversations and observations of interactions between people in informal contexts like homes, parties and just walking down the street, I learned to understand the importance of values like 'respectability' for queens and gay men, and how it formed central nodes through which relationships and social standing in the community were organized. Third, through long-term relationships with participants I learned about the importance of cell phones in creating and maintaining *intra*-Caribbean regional connections between sexual minority communities – in my original research plans, I did not have any questions about cell phone technologies at all, but over time I saw how important they were in initiating and maintaining local and long distance romantic and social relationships. I, therefore, learned through long term participant observation in the field that these objects needed to be made a central part of the analysis.

Thus it was through multi-sited fieldwork and participant observation, the key tools of the ethnographic method, that I was able to develop my core argument about sexual diversity and rights in Barbados: while sexual minority subjectivities and rights discourses in Barbados are immersed in, partially productive of, and partially produced through contemporary Euro-American gendered and sexual politics and identities (which are produced and circulated through mobile bodies of tourists, workers, lovers, relatives, communications technologies, and liberal democratic political and economic policies), these subjectivities and discourses are simultaneously produced through and in relation to local and regional gendered and sexual-identity politics. In other words, the ongoing influence of a colonized past (and its attendant gendered, classed, raced, and cultural hierarchies) combined with exposure to transnationally circulating sexual identities and rights discourses and diverse local interpretations of these discourses, produces multiple possible articulations of sexual subjectivities and rights in contemporary Barbados (Murray 2012).

Challenges of Ethnographic Research Methods

For sexuality researchers in the social sciences there are significant challenges in finding answers to questions about people's sexual practices or beliefs due to privacy issues and high levels of sensitivity around these topics. I have heard some researchers claim that the Caribbean is a particularly challenging region in which to conduct research on sexuality due to the 'conservative' values of its population. However, I would argue that such a claim makes problematic assumptions about the complex moral and ethical terrains of sexual practices and attitudes in this large, dispersed and socioculturally diverse region. To put it slightly differently: no matter what methodological model we adopt, there are always limitations to gaining a complete understanding of sexual practices, discourses, and values in any society. While I have thus far argued that ethnographic research methods may help to develop more nuanced understandings of everyday social worlds of sex and sexuality, and help us to better understand relationships between individual lives and wider socio-economic, cultural, and political forces, these methods are certainly not without substantial challenges, ranging from practical to ethical.

In terms of practice, ethnographic methods – fieldwork and participant observation in particular – can present a number of challenges in research focusing on sexuality. One might ask how the researcher can be a participant observer of sex! In fact, most ethnographic fieldwork-based research on sexuality is based on observing and listening carefully to how an individual, group, or different groups of people talk (or remain silent) about different aspects of sexual behaviour in different social contexts and/or in relation to various daily practices. Fieldwork may also be based on participation in and/or observation of different performances by the same individual (ritual, staged, artistic, bureaucratic, everyday) which may convey consistent or inconsistent, direct or indirect, messages about sexual attitudes and practices. What is of interest to many ethnographers of sexuality are the many ways in which sexual practices are made meaningful and valued, although the researcher must always be attentive to potential disjunctures between discourse and practice, that is, the difference between what people say and what they do, particularly when it comes to topics like sexuality. These disjunctures are particularly relevant in the Caribbean, where I have found that certain public and governmental discussions around sexual practices and activities are often constrained through a particular moral framework emphasizing respectable gendered and sexual assemblages, which may be highly distilled versions that are less complex than moral and ethical orientations manifested in personal or private lives and/or through informal social networks (family, friends, neighbourhoods). However, once again, the process of identifying and analysing these disjunctures in everyday conversations or performances can be challenging, particularly in relation to sensitive, problematic and/or taboo topics like homosexuality, gender variance and/or non-reproductive heterosexuality.

Another practical challenge for the ethnographer may arise in establishing relationships with members of marginalized sexual/gender communities. In societies where same-sex activities are criminalized and/

or negatively viewed in public domains, an ethnographer with no prior connections to these communities may find it difficult to find and establish a working relationship with people whose sexual orientation, practices and/or gender performances do not follow heteronormative expectations, and who may view an outsider with justifiable suspicion. In some cases, social media (Facebook, Twitter, cruising/dating apps) and the internet (blogs, human rights, and LGBT support group websites) now provide opportunities to establish connections, which can be the entrée to long-term fieldwork, however, one cannot assume all members of marginalized communities have equal access to digital technologies and/or want to have a connections with an LGBT or human rights organization. Therefore, in some cases, the ethnographer may need to seek out other avenues to establish contacts, such as meeting with community group leaders, local government and NGO agency staff who may work with members of these communities in other capacities (i.e., through poverty reduction, social welfare or health and well-being).[4] In other cases, spending time in public or semi-public spaces like bars, cafes, parks, or beaches where members of these communities are known to congregate may be an option for outreach and contact, although this carries potential personal safety risks for both researcher and research participant.[5] In Barbados, I benefited from family connections made through my partner and generous support from local leaders of UGLAAB who allowed me to participate in their meetings and social events, which provided the opportunity to meet and develop relationships with other group members.

Some ethnographers argue that it is preferable for the researcher and the participant to share similar identity traits, i.e., that a Barbadian, lesbian anthropologist will be able fit into, gain trust and produce more accurate findings about women who have sex with women in Barbados. This is often referred to as 'insider/outsider' positionality, and has generated significant debates over the pros and cons of researchers sharing or not sharing similar identifications (racial, gendered, sexual, religious, class) with research participants. Lazarus (2013) explores this debate in detail, highlighting issues of power differentials, trust, and vulnerability analysed by Caribbean feminist and queer researchers. Suffice to say this is not a Black and white issue (literally!), and that while a local Barbadian lesbian identified anthropologist may find it easier to access and work with a sexually marginalized community of women in Barbados than a straight white North American female anthropologist, other challenges, trust issues and/or possible self-censorship connected to socio-economic status differences, employment affiliation, family/kin connections, religious beliefs, and/or racialized typologies may arise. In my research in Barbados, my own positionality in relation to the people I worked with did not easily fall into the insider/outsider binary. While I was clearly an outsider through my national, racial and, in some cases, socio-economic status, my similar sexual orientation produced a limited degree of 'insider' status and trust with some research participants, but not others. While it is difficult for me to ascertain how these similar and different identifications may have created communication bridges or barriers, I think it safe to assume that a researcher with different gender, sexual, racial, national, and/or socio-economic identifications would have a distinctly different relationship with the same research participants which may produce different nuances and insights on similar topics.

Practical challenges arising from similarities and differences between the researcher's and participant's subject positions or ascribed identities are often also ethical challenges: All research methods involving human subjects have ethical dimensions: Obtaining information about any society or group is never a neutral process in that the process impacts everyone from the researcher to the people being studied to the people reading about the research. Issues of power and exploitation are thus always present in human research, and may be intensified when that group or community is marginalized, vulnerable, and/or structurally and historically disempowered. Ethnographic methods enact particular ethical dilemmas that arise in various and sometimes surprising ways when the researcher is recording information about a group or community through prolonged and intense daily interactions and observations.

One standard 'ethical' procedure in ethnographic research that is supposed to ensure the safety of participants and researchers is 'informed consent' from every participant involved in the research project – that is, the researcher is supposed to explain the research project, its methods, objectives and risks (or present potential participants with a document summarizing these points), ask research participants if it is acceptable to do such research, and, if approval is given (verbally or via signature), allow them to review what has been written (recorded or filmed) about them. For most researchers working in institutional environments like the university, hospital or science laboratory, consent forms are designed and regulated by these institutions (and often also by governmental bodies who fund them), which may render the process straightforward in terms of standard questions and expectations, but at the same time create complications through the assumption of 'one model fits all'. For example, my university's 'Human Participants Review Sub-Committee Protocol Form' has a question that asks, 'What, if any, are the risks to the participants (who consent to participate)'? In most ethnographic research projects where research participants' confidentiality and anonymity is enacted through the use of pseudonyms and redaction of any identifying information, the answer would be 'no risk'. However, this may overlook other types of risk that may not be generated by research interactions at the individual level but rather could be generated through the circulation of research results, creating risk for the community at large (for example, if the published research circulates through legal enforcement or hostile political networks). In ethnographic research, we need to continually reflect on what exactly is being consented to – in giving consent, are research participants fully aware of the implications of long-term participant observation? Are all conversations in all locations at any moment in time appropriate for the researcher to utilize as potential data? Is the researcher consenting to having their final analysis reviewed and possibly disapproved by research participants? Are research participants (or the researcher for that matter) fully aware of the potential effects of a written document circulating through academic, public and/or digital circuits? Ongoing discussions and debates over the ethical dimensions of ethnographic research have resulted in some methodologies that emphasize how research agendas must be derived from active and ongoing conversations with research participants, with objectives based on social justice principles that address social, political, and/or economic problems as defined by the research participants. This co-constructive approach to the production of knowledge is sometimes referred to as participatory action research (PAR).[6]

Additional ethical issues may arise in other aspects of ethnographic research, particularly in relation to long term fieldwork. For example, strong personal relationships between researchers and participants often develop on the basis of extended periods of time spent together, which can generate deep, nuanced, and complex insights into private and social worlds. However, challenges can arise from such close relationships – will deeper insight into the life of one participant result in analysis that prioritizes their perspective or experience over others? What happens if the researcher is in the midst of fieldwork and discovers that a person who they have come to respect and like is engaging in illegal or duplicitous behaviour that the researcher finds immoral? Finally, the obligations, responsibilities, and priorities of the ethnographer may change over time due to changes in their research participants' lives, thus requiring consistent critical reflection on research goals and objectives.

Conclusion

All forms of research involving human participants are fraught with practical and ethical problems, challenges, and tensions. In this chapter, I have endeavoured to explain why I employ ethnographic research methods when conducting research focusing on sexual minority communities in the Caribbean, and how these methods have helped me to answer questions about sexual and gender identities, rights, discrimination, and social change through their emphasis on long-term fieldwork (often in multiple locations) emphasizing participant-observation. I have found ethnographic research methods to be particularly adept at revealing the nuanced complexities of beliefs towards and attitudes about sexual orientation and gender identity in Caribbean societies, where the 'imperial debris' (Stoler 2008) of colonial histories of racial, sexual and gendered exploitation, and violence circulate within contemporary Caribbean communities impacted by global forces of neoliberal capitalism and its attendant political and ideological formations. Ethnographic research methods are adept at helping the researcher better understand linkages between everyday life – practices, conversations and performances – and the wider sociocultural, political, and economic forces that shape or are shaped by them. They also help the researcher move past what may be rehearsed or edited responses found in formal interviews, mainstream media representations and/or statements from those in leadership positions, therefore providing insight into complex personal and social worlds beyond the publicly normative. They may even generate glimpses into emergent, not-yet-fully-formed social worlds. However, like any other qualitative or quantitative research method, ethnographic research can never answer all our questions, and comes with its own set of practical and ethical challenges, such that it may not be the most appropriate methodological tool for every research project. Ethnographic research is a method that requires ongoing training, adaptability, flexibility, critical reflexivity, and dialogue with research participants, but its long-term investments and challenges may be particularly rewarding for researchers engaged in the important but challenging work of better understanding complex, changing Caribbean sexualities and genders and local and global forces shaping and shaped by them.

Notes

1. Qualitative research gathers information that is not in numerical form, and includes numerous methods ranging from interviews to participant observation. Qualitative data is typically descriptive and provides more nuanced analysis of particular individual or group worldviews. Quantitative research gathers data in numerical form which can be put into categories, or in rank order, or measured in units of measurement. This type of data can be used to construct graphs and tables of raw data and is often helpful in discovering broad patterns of similarities/differences across particular arrangements of groups categorized according to particular characteristics (gender, age, race, national identity, etc). See Bernard 2006 for a more detailed explanation.
2. This is not to discount important research on Caribbean sexualities such as Gloria Wekker's groundbreaking research on mati relationships among working-class women in Suriname, which explores local ethno-racial sexual identifications and practices that do not align with Euro-American gender/sexual terminologies and models (2006).
3. See Boyd 2008 for a more detailed analysis of oral history methods in queer/sexuality studies.
4. Throughout much of the Caribbean, sexual orientation and gender identity communities are often publicly visible under the aegis of HIV/AIDS prevention, education and treatment organizations, although this is changing, with more LGBTQ advocacy groups emerging over the past 10–20 years, including the Society Against Sexual Orientation Discrimination (Guyana), the Coalition Advocating for Inclusion of Sexual Orientation (Trinidad), the Jamaica Forum of Lesbians, All-Sexuals, and Gays, and Fundashon Orguyo Kòrsou (the FOKO Curaçao Pride Foundation (King 2016).
5. Note-taking (or the creation of field notes) in public spaces may also be a challenge. For more information on field notes, see Bernard 2006.
6. See McIntyre 2008 for an overview of PAR and Detamore 2010 for a more extended discussion of this issue in relation to sexuality research.

References

Alexander, Jacqui. 2007. *Pedagogies of Crossing: Meditations on Feminism Sexual Politics, Memory and the Sacred.* Durham, NC. Duke University Press.

Bernard, H. Russell. 2006. Fieldnotes: How to Take Them, Code Them, Manage Them. In *Research Methods in Anthropology*, 387–412. Lanham: AltaMira Press.

Boyd, Nan Alamilla. 2008. Who Is the Subject: Queer Theory Meets Oral History. *Journal of the History of Sexuality* 17, no. 2 (May).

Browne, Kath, and Catherine Nash, eds. 2010. *Queer Methods and Methodologies: Intersecting Queer Theories and Social Science Research.* Surrey: Taylor and Francis.

Buch, Elana, and Karen Staller. 2007. The Feminist Practice of Ethnography. In *Feminist Research Practice: A Primer*, ed. Sharlene Nage Hesse-Biber and Patricia Leavy, 187–222. Thousand Oaks: Sage.

Cruz-Malave, Arnoldo and Martin Manalansan, eds. 2002. *Queer Globalisations: Citizenship and the Afterlife of Colonialism.* New York: New York University Press.

deCastell, Suzanne, and Mary Bryson. 1998. Queer Ethnography: Identity, Authority, Narrativity, and a Geopolitics of Text. In *Inside the Academy and Out: Lesbian/Gay/Queer Studies and Social Action*, ed. J.L. Ristock and C.G. Taylor Toronto: University of Toronto Press.

Detamore, Mathias. 2010. Queer(y)ing the Ethics of Research Methods: Toward a Politics of Intimacy in Researcher/Researched Relations. In *Queer Methods and Methodologies*, ed. Kath Browne and Catherine Nash, 167–82. Surrey: Taylor and Francis.

Jackman, Michael. 2010. The Trouble with Fieldwork: Queering Methodologies. In *Queer Methods and Methodologies*, ed. Kath Browne and Catherine Nash, 113–28. Surrey: Taylor and Francis.

Kempadoo, Kamala. 2004. *Sexing the Caribbean: Gender, Race and Sexual Labor.* New York: Routledge.

King, Rosamund. 2016. The International Resource Network: A Hard-Won Success, an Uncertain Future. *WSQ: Women's Studies Quarterly* 44, nos. 3 and 4:296–300.

Lazarus, Latoya. 2013. Working with Marginalised and 'Hidden' Populations: Researchers Anxieties and Strategies for Doing Less Harmful Research. *CRGS*, no. 7: 1–22, ed. Kamala Kempadoo, Halimah DeShong, and Charmaine Crawford.

McIntyre, Alice. 2008. *Participatory Action Research.* Thousand Oaks: Sage.

Murray, David A.B. 2012. *Flaming Souls: Homosexuality, Homophobia and Social Change in Barbados.* Toronto: University of Toronto Press

Scharff, C.M. 2008. Doing Class: A Discursive and Ethnomethodological Approach. *Critical Discourse Studies* 5, no. 4:331–43.

Stoler, Anne. 2008. Imperial Debris: Reflections on Ruin and Ruination. *Cultural Anthropology* 23, no. 2:191–219.

Yanos, Philip, and Kim Hopper. 2008. On 'False, Collusive Objectification': Becoming Attuned to Self-Censorship, Performance and Interviewer Biases in Qualitative Interviewing. *International Journal of Social Research Methodologies* 11, no. 3:229–237.

Wekker, Gloria. 2006. *The Politics of Passion: Women's Sexual Culture in the Afro-Surinamese Diaspora*. New York: Columbia University Press.

18. Subjective Mapping: A Brief Introduction

Krystal Nandini Ghisyawan

When I first thought of using maps in my research into same-sex loving women's social and spatial relationships, I imagined the various geographic maps my data collection would yield and the understanding of the queer geographies of Trinidad and Tobago they would allow. The first mapping exercise I conducted met this expectation, with Jean drawing two images. One was of Trinidad, where she signalled the different spots she liked to lime, to hike and vacation, where she worked and lived. Her second map gave more detail of a part of Chaguanas near where she lived (figures 3 and 4). I expected my next interview to be similar, but the result, captured in figure 1, blasted all of my expectations. I was unsure of how to process and analyse what was being presented to me as a 'map' since it was not in the format I had anticipated or was prepared to work with at the time. Both women were responding to the same prompt: Draw a map of where you feel safe to express yourself regarding your sexuality. Yet they created visuals that were different in form and content. As the project continued and I gathered more maps (for a total of 20), the meaning of 'map' in this research endeavour developed.

Mapping is a central technique to the field of cartography, the study and process of map creation. Maps are used to represent the natural as well as the human world, and as a data collection tool can include 'the representation of an individual or group's cognitive map, hand sketched, and/or computer assisted, in drafting and labelling a map or adding to and labelling an already existing map' (Gieseking 2013). Participatory mapping methodologies aim to capture the organization of concepts, ideas or space, as perceived by individuals or groups. Participatory maps of many forms including cartographic maps, concept maps, mind/mental maps or mental sketch maps, have been employed as a form of data collection and representation in many scholarly fields, including planning, agriculture, epidemiology, international development, anthropology and sociology, education, and many more. Nesbit and Adesope (2006) estimate that more than 500 peer-reviewed articles just in the field of education, most published post-1997 have made substantial reference to applying concept or knowledge maps.

Nesbit and Adesope (2006) used the terms concept map, mind map, and knowledge map interchangeably, but there has been much debate about what these maps entail. Developed by Joseph Novak in the 1970s, concept maps were originally designed to assess how thoughts are organized and structured, through the labelling and linking of concepts pertaining to a theme, from which meaningful propositions and claims can be made. Concept maps are considered hierarchical and formal, while mind maps are less formal diagrams linking words, themes, or tasks, starting with a central idea and building outward. Data gathered from mind maps are unique to each individual, representing their personal style and understandings. Mind maps may include pictures, images, colours, and differentiated lines to enhance the associations represented in the map. Regardless of the definitional ambiguities, and the variations in form and content, considering these maps as graphic representations of knowledge is useful for looking at their shared theoretical foundations and utility in various fields of research.

The maps gathered in my research shared similarities with mental maps, concept maps, and the participatory maps of other social science research. Some maps resembled what is typically seen as geographic maps, depicting places on a road map, while others combined representations of various spaces into a collage, or were idealized or imagined scenes that captured their safe or unsafe spaces. Similar to mind maps, some representations included words, text, symbols. Each map was unique to the individual who created it, yet collectively the maps reflected general truths of the population being studied, while simultaneously breaking out of the constraints of language to express their material and emotional realities.

Critical geographers Rob Kitchin and Martin Dodge (2007) and Kitchin (2008) outlined the trajectory of ontological thinking about maps, tracking the changes in how maps have been conceptualized and critiqued by other scholars of space and geography. Kitchin (2008) outlined D. Wood and J. Fels (2008) critique of cartographic theorists Arthur Robinson and J.B. Harley, who thought of maps as objective truths and maps as social constructions, respectively. Despite this difference, both Robinson and Harley conceived of maps as having an inherent truth reflected in the content and subject of the map (Kitchin 2008).

Wood and Fels (2008) believed that the map itself held an ideological message through its construction, its design, the symbols used within it and the attached text and discourse, through which the map does not just represent the world, but (re)produces it. Kitchin and Dodge's (2007) analysis goes further, considering maps as always emergent and dynamic, changing in interpretation as ideologies change around and through them. They highlight mapping as a process based on practices or interactions within space, and not just seeing maps as fixed representations of space. Kitchin and Dodge stress the interpretive and mutable nature of maps, also context specific, and therefore not universal truths; maps, they argue, are partial truths based on the knowledge, impressions and inclinations of the person/s creating them.

The employment of maps as research tools in the social sciences utilizes this understanding of maps as subjective documents capable of reflecting unique and personalized data, while revealing power dynamics and general truths related to the situations captured in the maps. For this reason, in my research, I call these graphical representations 'subjective maps', and the process of creating them 'subjective mapping'. All maps are subjective, being dependent on the identities, perspectives, and purpose of the individual, group, or institution that produces it. The subjective maps in my research offer insight into how these social identities operate through and against hegemonic power; they demonstrate the power exerted on the individual from external sources, like family, religion, social class, legislation, and media, but also depict the women's claiming of space and agentive power. In other words, these women have produced maps of power.

Because of its potential to capture the voice of socially and politically marginalized groups in a complicated multilayered manner, I found subjective mapping to be novel, interesting and valuable for understanding the experiences of same-sex desiring women in the Caribbean. It attends to the unique experiences of the persons being studied, noting the nuances influenced by their intersecting identities of race, social class, education, age, gender expression, sexual orientation, and relationship status. Employing subjective mapping as an elicitation tool allowed flexibility in the interview context, as I could use it as an icebreaker for participants who needed to be drawn out of their protective shells. Presenting them with an array of drawing and colouring implements and allowing them to be free and creative in their use of images, words, shapes, and colours served as a catalyst to relax the participants, while gathering rich data. The method also centres on embodied knowledge or the knowledge gained from lived experience, treating it as valid, authentic, and important. In this chapter, I discuss subjective mapping as I have used it to study sexuality in the Caribbean, the cognitive logic behind its utility as a data collection tool, how it was utilized in interviews, and how these subjective maps were analysed.

Participatory Mapping and the Study of Sexuality

Participatory mapping methodologies are not new to Trinidad, having been employed by geographer Bjørn Ingmunn Sletto in 1998 to investigate land claims of Indo-Trinidadians in Kernahan village and compare it to the Penom peoples of southeastern Venezuela. Both groups were facing the potential loss of their land to national parks. Through mapping, Sletto uncovered the competing knowledges pertaining to nature, place, and people as constructed by regional and state political economies and by the peoples themselves. Sletto sought to 'consider the roles of memory, performance, and embodiment in participatory mapping, in part to draw attention to the negotiations of power, identities, and authenticities implicated in community-based productions of spatial representations' (2009, 444). He argued that participatory mapping is a counter-hegemonic activity.

In Sletto's work, it is apparent that power is operating here regarding the way land is used and governed. As it relates to sexuality, the lines of power are more obscure, especially due to the cultural silences around sexuality; non-normative forms of sexuality, in particular. As mentioned before, the maps produced by same-sex loving women in my research, are in their essence, maps of power, charting the hegemonic as well as the agentive paths of resistance, such as the claiming of space. Same-sex loving women's experiences have been shrouded in secrecy. Rosamond King (2014) refers to this experience as one of 'near invisibility' in the community through the active erasure of female same-sex desire in public records, creative writings and expressions, and embodiments in public spaces. While there has been some work in the arts and literature (Elwin 1997; Tinsley 2010;

King 2011 and 2015; Mootoo 1993, 1996 and 2008; Nixon 2016), there are fewer in the social sciences (Wekker 2006; Clemencia 1996; Ghisyawan 2014, 2015 and 2016) addressing the presence of same-sex loving women in the region. The silence is more acute for Indo-Caribbean women whose sexual experiences have been subject of fewer studies, and whose same-sex desires have not previously been addressed in scholarship but merely alluded to (Pragg 2012). My project adds to this list of work that seeks to uncover the hidden stories of same-sex loving women, demonstrating the acts of resistance in which they engage to challenge the threads of power that work to keep them hidden. The women's spatial presence, reflected in their maps, is the most direct challenge to their invisibility and erasure.

Participatory mapping practices have been used as data collection methodologies in sexuality studies by cultural geographer Gavin Brown (2001), anthropologist William Leap (2009) and sociologist Yvette Taylor (2007). Brown utilized the method to look at Tower Hamlets in London's East End and the ways in which the local gay population relate to the area, but used a cartographic road map as the base. He was not so much interested in how they would chart the terrain but how they perceived the spaces which they inhabited. As such, he provided participants with a road map of the boroughs and asked them to mark off places they felt were 'particularly "gay"', leaving the term open to interpretation. Brown recognized the biases of his research demographic, who were mainly white men about age thirty, and were not representative of the area's residents. Leap took this participatory mapping technique a step further by having the participants draw their own cartographic maps to represent gay spaces in Washington, DC, which, like Brown's study, demonstrated that these men's cognitive maps were not simply determined by their sexuality but also by their (objective and subjective) class position and their ethnicity. Leap's participants' maps also illustrated a kind of clustering of gay persons, which according to David J. Bell (1991) can be linked to ethnic clustering and similarities among the sample population.

Yvette Taylor's (2007) work looking at the intersections of sexualities, class, and geography, among mainly middle-class and working-class white lesbians in Glasgow, Manchester, and Edinburgh, UK, utilized this same research method, calling it 'emotional mapping'. Her maps most closely resemble those that came up in my research, as they included figures of homes, people and vehicles, words and scenes, instead of the roadmaps yielded in Leap's and Brown's respective works, and reflect the unique experiences and understandings of a space or concept.

In 'Sexualities, Sociologies and the Intersectional Potential of Two Qualitative Methodologies', Kendal Broad (2010) discusses mapping as a 'valuable strategy' for identifying how situated knowledges intersect with deconstructive knowledges, especially as it pertains to lesbian, gay, bisexual, transgender, and queer (LGBTQ) lives. In other words, mapping as a method can highlight the experiences specifically connected to particular identity categories, and thus be used to demonstrate LGBTQ subjectivities, while posing challenges to normative discourses and power-knowledges. Broad references A. E. Clark (2005) who outlines three mapping strategies sociologists can use when investigating how competing discourses are represented and get interpellated in various contexts. These three types of visual maps are situational maps, arena maps, and positional maps. Situational mapping is a tool for the researcher to analyse all the elements in a research situation and the relations among them, such as the space, objects, persons, props, etc. Arena mapping is a strategy to analyse the collective actors and how they are involved in ongoing discourse and negotiations. Finally, positional mapping is an analytic strategy for laying out the major discursive positions taken (or not) within a given situation. Each of these three mapping strategies involves drawing pictures and making lists of elements, discourses and positions in the situation of inquiry (Broad 2010). Situational maps, arena maps, and positional maps are not participatory maps but analytical tools for the researcher to assess a research context. By contrast, subjective maps generated by research participants contained this same type of data from the women's own perspectives, the actors, objects, places, and discourses at work in their lives. My analysis of the subjective maps created by the women (discussed in a later section of this chapter) entail an assessment of these features detailed by Broad (2010), including the objects and actors, the discourses present and how participants within a space engage with these discourses, as the women drew and articulated them.

The Cognitive Reasoning behind Mapping Techniques

The logic for how participatory mapping exercises work is grounded in how human beings think about their lives through archetypes and patterns that can be recognized and made intelligible (Butler 1999). Science writer and reporter Stephen S. Hall (2004, 15) describes this as orientating or 'crashing through the larger landscapes of memory and experience and knowledge, trying to get a fix on where we are in a multitude of landscapes that together compose the grander scheme of things.' Participants must draw on what sociological theorist Anthony Giddens (1986) calls discursive and practical consciousness in order to navigate this cognitive space and create these maps. Practical consciousness refers to the implicit use of unarticulated 'stocks of knowledge' to orient oneself, and understand situations and others' behaviours (Giddens 1986, 90). This is the learned behaviours and patterns about one's spatial and social relationships that have become instinctive or taken-for-granted. Discursive consciousness pertains to one's conscious engagement with their surroundings to be able to reason and rationalize one's own situation and behaviours (Giddens 1986, 91).

Giddens (1986) suggests daily interaction is mediated through the subconscious and conscious processing of these cognitive maps of memory, experience, and knowledge. People actively and passively gather, organize, and store data, retrieving and processing events, experiences, and information, giving meaning to them and using these meanings to build cognitive maps in their imagination. These cognitive understandings become the lenses through which new experiences are perceived and processed. Participatory mapping harnesses these 'stocks of knowledge' to express data in ways that are not bound by linguistic understandings of concepts.

Asking participants to create maps was an exercise in bringing together their practical and discursive consciousness and reproducing these discourses and relationships onto paper. Some participants took a minute to construct a whole representative image in their minds before putting it to paper, while others started with one icon or symbol and added to it as they travelled through the experiences collected in the mind. Although I interviewed 40 women for this project, only 20 opted to draw the maps, accepting the challenge of bringing together their seemingly unconnected life experiences into a symbolic composition representing their interpretations and understandings of these experiences. While in other applications of mapping there is focus on a single central theme, the mapping exercise I've employed sought to elucidate the interactions occurring at the meeting of sexuality, space, and safety for same-sex loving women. This combination of concepts pushed participants to engage in more complicated ways, often revealing other aspects of their social identities.

Employing Subjective Mapping as a Data Collection Tool

For my doctoral research, I interviewed 40 same-sex loving women and intended to do mapping exercises with them all. The research participants were of different (self-declared) ethnic backgrounds, including two Caucasian-Trinidadians, one Chinese-Trinidadian, 15 Afro-Trinidadians, 13 Indo-Trinidadians, and nine women of mixed descent. They all ranged from age 19 to 45, at the time of the interviews, and came from various urban and rural areas across Trinidad, including Diego Martin, Carenage, San Juan, St Augustine, Sangre Grande, Chaguanas, Princes Town, San Fernando, and Point Fortin. They also varied in religion and how they chose to sexually self-identify, some refusing to pick a label and others choosing more than one, including lesbian, bisexual, queer, pansexual, and fluid. The commonality amongst them was their same-sex desire and their engagement in sexual relationships with other women. They shared the experience of being female-bodied and attracted to other female bodies, while facing a society wherein this was illegal (Sexual Offences Act) and publicly shamed.

The women and I decided on an appropriate location for the interviews, some preferring public places like the Rituals coffee shop, others the privacy of an office or unused classroom, and mature women with private residences often chose to invite me to their homes for a more intimate atmosphere and more open sharing. The interviews began with the usual pleasantries, assurances of confidentiality, and the women's granting of consent to audio record the interviews (or not, in a few instances) and use their data. Our conversations began with the gathering of data related to the participants' name, age, employment, family information, and how they sexually self-identified. After chatting for several minutes, they were invited to do the mapping exercise. For more talkative interviewees, the exercise served to focus their attention when they were tempted to go off topic, while for less talkative interviewees, the exercise encouraged them to use another form of communication from which I could elicit more details. I laid out regular 8 x 11 printing paper, pencils, coloured pencils, crayons, and markers, and ask them to draw a map to answer the question, 'where do you feel safe to express yourself regarding your sexuality'. Twenty declined drawing maps citing their lack of artistic skill or simply not knowing what to draw, and preferred speaking about their safe spaces. Twenty others chose to draw graphic representations of their safe and/or unsafe spaces.

The most common response to the prompt was 'What do you mean by "map"?' I encouraged participants to bring their own interpretations of the term to their drawings. The other most common responses were 'what should I draw'? and 'where do I begin', moreso asking themselves than directing their questions to me. The opening part of the interview was geared towards having them think about their negotiations regarding their sexuality, asking about the areas of their lives where they were out and open about their sexuality or not. Based on how rapport was developing between us, I posed the prompt in slightly different ways. For example, with Nikita, I said, 'Part of the interview is a mapping or drawing exercise, where you draw out where you feel safe to be yourself, and express your sexuality.' With others, like Rachel and Anna, a couple who were interviewed together, I was more detailed. I said:

> Let's move on to the drawing part of the interview now. I have some coloured pencils here, a few coloured pens and markers, I don't know if you want these. So the drawing bit is a mapping exercise. You are essentially drawing a map but however you want to draw it, as an actual literal map, or something abstract is up to you. But what you try to represent is where you feel comfortable. What aspects of your life or what places you can go to feel comfortable being yourself, expressing yourself, etc., in terms of being lesbian, and where you are not comfortable.
>
> Rachel: Places where we feel comfortable or don't feel comfortable?
>
> Me: or where you feel safe
>
> (Interview, Rachel and Anna, 3 September 2013).

Some participants were already familiar with the research, having heard me present on it at a conference in early 2013, or by having been referred to the study by a friend who I had already interviewed. During Karen's interview, when I said, 'Ok now we doing the mapping exercise of where you feel safe,' she quickly asked, 'Can I just draw it?' She started drawing her map and describing it to me as she went along adding elements to it. Reagan also had prior knowledge of the mapping exercise but I still explained it further for her:

> The drawing exercise is about mapping. How do you envision space? The multiple spaces that you inhabit – where are you comfortable, where are you happy, where are you not happy… if you can encompass these things into one drawing…there's more paper if you need it… and as you saw in the video some people drew maps of Trinidad, and others were more abstract. It's up to you what you want to create. But basically, where do you feel safe, happy, comfortable or not. And tell me what you doing. You want pens? This one is a pencil (Interview with Reagan, 29 August 2013).

These introductions into the exercise are influential on what and how these women chose to create their maps. It was most apparent in Ariel's map (figure 2). I asked:

> Okay, do you mind if I occupy your hands now with the drawing. Same things that you've been telling me. I would like for you to draw a map of where you feel comfortable… not just with her (referring to her girlfriend that she was talking about), but where you feel comfortable to be yourself, to be open, however you want to phrase it and whatever you want to represent (Interview with Ariel, 28 August 2013).

After her hesitation and uncertainty, I elaborated:

> So where would you feel comfortable expressing your sexuality, that kinda thing. Try to focus on the queer identity part of it…but it's your map so do whatever the hell you want to do…I have some pencils, coloured pencils, coloured pens and markers here too if you want…You can draw and then talk, or just tell me what you are doing as you go along (Interview with Ariel, 28 August 2013).

When she was done, I asked why she drew this idealized landscape, and she said it was because I asked 'where would you feel comfortable', using that conditional term. She drew her ideal in order to reflect the limitations of her current reality, and depict her fantasies for the future.

The mental maps used by Jen Jack Gieseking (2013) requested women to describe their average day at college as it was when they attended, by picturing themselves making a trip across campus and documenting the sequence of people, places and events they would encounter. This encouraged them to place themselves in the situation, with questions being asked strategically to probe the women's memories, encourage them to label and annotate their maps as they spoke, and then pushed them to question their own recollection. I did not influence the maps' construction and appearance as directly. As I was not investigating a single space, participants were free to include whatever spaces they wanted to reflect in their maps, to pick their own mental route through their safe or unsafe spaces. Participants were encouraged to add to their maps as we discussed them if they felt the need to do so. The maps that were drafted in these interviews were varied in form including cartographic maps, landscapes or fantasy-scapes, pictures of scenes, and what I call 'organized geometric drawings', or the use of an abstract yet ordered design to represent spaces. The next section addresses steps taken in analysing these diverse and complicated documents.

Analysing Subjective Maps

As Gieseking (2013) notes, its development and analytics have been inconsistent. In their paper 'Where do we go from here', Gieseking provides 'an informed guide for the examining human-environment relationships through mental mapping', developed from a critical geographic perspective, 'i.e., geography that aims to develop theory, methodologies, and research to combat social exploitation and oppression while building upon major and minor economic, political, and social theories' (2013, 715). Gieseking drew upon literature in critical geography, as well as 32 mental maps and the interviews during which they were drafted, to detail 57 analytic components and techniques. Similarly, I drew on Gieseking's analytics while adding my own.

Gieseking grouped techniques (ways of mappings) and components (elements included in the maps) into four analytical categories, mechanics of method (MOM), drawing elements (DE), narratives of place (NOP) and personalization (P). Mechanics of method includes 'the traditional notions of how a map portrays a convincing representation of spatial reality, as well as participants' level of focus on and sense of success in that process', including sequence of the drawing and labels, the relation between map elements, and the mirroring of physical space. Gieseking used the term drawing elements (DE) to refer to 'core map elements' or how a map conveys knowledge, including the use of a legend or north arrow, the placement of elements, colours, borders, symbols and doodles. Narratives of place (NOP) connect the mapmakers' identities to physical space as experienced, remembered and imagined, as they articulate the built and natural environmental elements, landmarks, nodes, and paths. Personalization (P) are those elements of the map that reveal the personal experiences and emotions of participants. Gieseking gave the example of Kelly who justified beginning her map with the chapel, by saying she was a spiritual person.

Based on features from Gieseking's and my own unique maps, I devised a system of features and characteristics to look for in the maps. I have employed analytics taken from critical geography and critical cartography in my own analysis of the maps in my research. These I separated into five categories:

a. What is shown: Places, persons, objects depicted; built environmental elements and landmarks; physical/natural environmental elements; shapes, doodles, scratches; symbols; and what is being represented by the objects, persons and symbols depicted, what intangible concepts and discourses

b. Mapping tools: Shapes; colours; Key; North arrow; Centres and borders; Text and Style of labelling; Style of drawing buildings, people; Time taken; Use of entire paper; Scale; Orientation of drawing on paper

c. Type/Style of representation: Road map/mirror of standard map; abstract; scene; geometric design

d. The Mapping experience/exercise: Drawing anxiety; drawing skill; feelings about the mapping process; first drawn element; last drawn element

e. Subjectivities and Meanings, that is, from whose/what perspective is the drawing being done; what indicates their subjectivities, and social identities, their race or class or gender or education, etc; symbols; emotions; intimate spatial details, and personal meanings.

Additionally, I interrogated the temporal relevance of each space (when is it relevant to the mapmaker?, do they frequent the space and for what purpose?) and looked for clusters of meaning within and among the maps, questioning how the map elements are related to each other. For each map, I assessed what images were being used and what tangible and intangible things they represented, such as family or religion, as well as physical spaces. In order to know what the symbols and images used in the maps represented, I analysed them alongside the women's descriptions of what they drew. For instance, many of the maps feature simple line drawings of houses, which represented the physical space of the house, but also as a symbol of home, family, domesticity, and private space.

The maps were also grouped according to the type of image or map they were and compared against each other for similarities and differences, to get a better understanding of HOW women map spaces cognitively and visually, but also socially through lived experience. In this exercise of creative cartography, instead of a key as with a map in an atlas, these maps are interpreted through the intense narratives accompanying them. The producer of the map equips the reader with the tools needed to read the map as they intended, which suggests the chance of misreporting to preserve a certain image of self. As such, I have refrained from making any assumptions about what the maps portrayed, instead relying on the women who produced it to perform the work of translation. My interpretations are limited to particular patterns and iconographies repeated through the maps, and any unspoken connections between the women's maps, their stories, and the wider society. These analyses are the jumping off points for my theorizing about identity, space-making, queering, and queer decolonial praxis.

For Gieseking (2013), an important aspect of working with participatory mapping was watching the maps being created so as to analyse the steps taken. Other scholars suggest recording the map making on video to allow review and deeper analysis. In my research, making video recordings of the interviews was out of the question as most of the women were opposed to being visible, even positioning the camera to capture only their drawings. I relied on the audio recording of the interviews and close observations of the steps taken as the women drew their maps. I made notes detailing the order in which various aspects of the maps were added and what changes may have been made. Two of the maps were produced distantly, as those interviews were conducted over Facebook chat and Skype. I was unable to watch the map-making processes of these women, who preferred to draw the map and then share it with me. Neena drew her map by hand then sent a photo, while Stevie used Paint (a microsoft app) to make her map.

All data analysis was done using the original maps produced by the women. The 19 hand-drawn maps collected were recreated using Microsoft

Paint for clearer presentation, as scans and photos were still too unclear for the figures to be clearly reproduced in print or in digital publications. I tried to follow the lines as closely as possible and use similar lettering style as the mapmaker. Small scratches and erased lines were not included in the recreation, but are necessary parts of analysing the process of mapmaking, the organization of thought and knowledge. Also excluded in these reproductions were the real names of the participants where they had included it and replacing it with the pseudonym being used in the study. Showing the original maps would still entail editing them to block out any such identifying information. I have since been able to access better scans that offer a clearer picture (such as those included in this publication). Figure 3 below shows a section of the map drawn by one respondent, named Jean and the digitalized version of it. Differences can be seen in the gradient of the lines, style of text, placement of the north arrow, the checkmark beside the word 'Market', and the square labelled Fair & Square was accidentally overlooked. Figure 4 is the much clearer scan of the same map. With each new map, the utility of the maps and of mapping exercises in understanding the spatial organization of race, class, and power became increasingly apparent.

Learning from Maps

The subjective maps gathered in my research pointed out the spaces, the actors and the discourses at work in Trinidad, showing the power relationships at play in creating or denying spaces of belonging. They showed spaces along different scales, highlighting the intimate (the bedroom, the home, the mind) and the external (relationships, regional, and international linkages), the private and the public, allowing interrogation of the porous nature of these boundaries and of spaces deemed private and thus beyond interrogation/critique. The maps illumined how power works through space to govern the lives of same-sex loving women, and how the women's own space-making practices challenged the iterations of power in their lives.

Spatial representations yielded from the mapping exercise allowed for a discussion of the production of space – conceptions, perceptions, and spatial relationships that give particular meanings to a given space, and in turn influence social interactions. This means the maps themselves can give insight into how participants perceived their social world and social relationships. For instance, one mapper drew a church to represent religious upbringing, while simultaneously pointing to current anxiety around religious fanaticism, the ex-gay evangelical ministries, and her relationship with her Pentecostal mother. Her mother's religious fervour was a barrier in their relationship as it prevented an open and honest relationship between mother and daughter.

Another mapper, Jean (her map shown in figures 3 and 4) spoke of the racism and sexism she experienced in communities dominated by Indo-Trinidadian people, as a masculine-presenting same-sex loving woman with a mixed-race girlfriend. She referred to these places as 'coolie-villes', referencing the history of indentureship in Trinidad and alluding to the perceived narrow-mindedness and religious zeal of working-class Indo-Caribbean peoples (Ghisyawan 2014, 2015, and 2016). Jean did not pinpoint these places on her map, but she listed them by name. These were places she avoided, especially if accompanied by a lover. She had herself given up her religious upbringing and tried to distance herself from persons and communities that she felt held homophobic and bigoted ideas.

The maps showed themselves to be palimpsestic, layered with meaning and reaching across times, referencing the past through drawing on their past experiences, while narrating their current feelings of safety and belonging and sometimes even pointing to the future in the form of a hope or a fantasy, as with Ariel's map. They demonstrate the non-linearity of time in cognitive understandings of experience; events that share meaning and relevance get bridged and grouped together regardless of when they had occurred. While holding meanings that reach through time, the maps were also created at a fixed point, so capture the individual's experiences, meanings, and behaviours connected to a particular cultural, social, and political moment. Changes to their circumstances would result in changes in opinions and in how they chose to represent them.

Limitations of Subjective Mapping

Participatory mapping has limitations not dissimilar from other qualitative data collection methods in how it is influenced by mood, time, setting; in the tendencies of the participant to reveal or conceal only as much as they wish to, and to engage in impression management; and in its ability to give unique and specific detail while also pointing to more general truths.

The creation of subjective maps depends heavily on the mood and frame of mind of the person drawing it (Kitchin 2008). Kitchin (2008; Kitchin and Dodge 2007; Kitchin et al. 2013) refers to this dynamism in the shape, form and interpretation of maps as ontological insecurity. If administered at another time, the exercise can yield an entirely different map. One participant, Jane, abandoned her first map, and asked for us to meet again to continue the interview and for her to complete the exercise, but at our second meeting, she didn't even remember what she was trying to depict and started a new map. Both maps are pictured below (figure 5). The first map includes a double-decker bus and a glass closet. The bus was used to symbolize the time Jane spent attending University in London, the people she met there and the experiences she had. The glass closet contrasted the freedom of London to the vulnerability she felt in Trinidad. She described coming out to her family, the transnational influence of the returning gay Diaspora, and her other thoughts on gay politics and activism. In our second session, she spoke more directly to the construction of her second map and the places where she felt safe – a house in Blanchisseuse, another similar accommodation she had experienced in the island of Dominica, group retreats for gay youth while in England, and her own bedroom in the bottom right hand corner. In both maps we see a kind of citizenship and belonging that transcends the boundaries of Trinidad and Tobago. Jane's map demonstrates her engagement with multiple places and points in time, recruiting ideas from each space to construct a kind of idealized space.

The exercise was only administered once with the other participants. Repeating this exercise after some time with the same respondents would be a fascinating project, enabling a comparison of the women's changing ideas and perceptions, but also changes in political, social, and cultural contexts, like elections or legislative changes. For instance, on April 12, 2018, Trinidad and Tobago High Court Justice Devindra Rampersad ruled that sections 13 and 16 of the Sexual Offences Act, which criminalize consensual sexual contact between persons of the same-sex were unconstitutional, and amended the law's phrasing to account for consensual sexual conduct between adults. Mapping exercises would be a valuable way of assessing how these changes have influenced the space-making practices of same-sex loving women in Trinidad, their perceptions and experiences of safety and belonging.

Another limitation is the incompleteness of the maps; they are not total representations. They do not encompass everything that may answer the prompt being used to elicit the drawing. It is an important analytic point to observe what is included, what is left out, and why those choices were made. It is important to note which spaces were included in the drawing and what is their particular significance to the cartographer, or more pointedly, to their response to the prompt that was posed. The narrative must be taken in conjunction with the map itself, acting like a key to translate the map for the reader.

The Future of Subjective Mapping in Caribbean Sexuality Studies

According to James Corner, 'Maps are highly artificial and fallible constructions, virtual abstractions that possess great force in terms of how people see and act' (1999, 216). In other words, maps have power, be it the maps of territories produced through European colonial expansion, or the maps of nation demonstrating the movement of their borders, or the subjective maps of Trinidadian same-sex loving women. These maps all have power. They demonstrate how a space is understood and lived in, while also influencing the same. Participatory mapping practices place power into the hands of mappers to demonstrate their lived experience of space and discourse. Subjective mapping enhances this by allowing participants flexibility in how they chose to represent these spaces, discourses, and power dynamics that influence their day-to-day lived experience as same-sex loving women in Trinidad. Maps are unique documents, yet contain observable trends and shared features, facilitating a discussion of spaces of (un)belonging as experienced by my research participants, and the development of general truths pertaining to same-sex loving women's experiences.

In addition to its applications in scholarly research, subjective mapping can be gainfully employed in workshops and group discussions to explore other aspects of social identity and space-making. Many of the women who did the mapping exercise enjoyed the process, and felt it provided some release both creatively and emotionally. This was especially true for the women who drew their safe spaces, as they felt strengthened through thinking about the social and spatial relationships wherein they find support. Thus, maps can be used in a variety of situations, including as a therapeutic exercise.

The maps reveal aspects of the individuals' identities, their family lives and relationship statuses (shown through their representations of home, family, and partnerships), their religion (depicted through religious symbols), their social class and education (by the places they engage with). They reveal the ways in which sexuality (sexual behaviour, desires, and identities) become entangled with other social identities, and challenge the silences surrounding female same-sex desire in the Caribbean. Subjective mapping gave the women voice and agency to assert themselves, their presence, and their beliefs into the maps, and into scholarship. The study's greatest merit is its capturing of these silenced voices and the internalized discourses that otherwise keep these women silenced.

References

Bell, David J. 1991. Insignificant Others: Lesbian and Gay Geographies. *Area* 23, no. 4:323–29.

Broad, Kendal. 2010. Sexualities, Sociologies and the Intersectional Potential of Two Qualitative Methodologies. In *Theorising Intersectionality and Sexuality*, ed. Yvette Taylor, Sally Hines and Mark E. Casey, 193–211. New York: Palgrave Macmillan.

Brown, Gavin. 2001. Listening to Queer Maps of the City: Gay Men's Narratives of Pleasure and Danger in London's East End. *Oral History* 29, no. 1:48–61.

Butler, Judith. 1999. *Gender Trouble: Feminism and the Subversion of Identity*. New York: Routledge.

Clarke, A.E. 2005. *Situational Analysis: Grounded Theory after the Postmodern Turn*. Thousand Oaks: Sage Publications.

Clemencia, Joceline. 1996. Women Who Love Women in Curaçao: From 'Cachapera' to Open Throats: A Commentary in Collage. *Feminist Studies* 22, no. 1:81–88.

Corner, James. 1999. The Agency of Mapping: Speculation, Critique and Invention. In *Mappings*, ed. Denis Cosgrove. London: Reaktion.

Elwin, Rosamund, ed. 1997. *Tongues on Fire: Caribbean Lesbian lives and Stories*. Toronto: Women's Press.

Ghisyawan. Krystal. 2014. Geographies of Sexuality: Constructions of Space and Belonging. *Journal of the Department of Behavioural Sciences* 3, no. 1:28–43.

———. 2015. Queer(in) the Caribbean: The Trinidad experience. In *The Global Trajectories of Queerness: Rethinking Same-Sex Politics in the Global South*, ed. Sruti Bala and Ashley Tellis, 161–78. Amsterdam: Rodopi.

———. 2016. (Un)Settling the Politics of Identity and Sexuality among Indo-Trinidadian Same-sex Loving Women. *Indo-Caribbean Feminist Thought: Genealogies, Theories, Enactments*, ed. Lisa Outar and Gabrielle Hosein. London: Palgrave.
Giddens, Anthony. 1986. *The Constitution of Society: Outline of the Theory of Structuration.* Cambridge, UK: Polity Press.
Gieseking, J.J. 2013. Where We Go from Here: the Spatial Mental Mapping Method and Its Analytic Components for Social Science Data Gathering. *Qualitative Inquiry* 19, no. 9: 712–24.
Hall, Stephen. 2004. I, Mercator. In *You are Here: Personal Geographies and Other Maps of the Imagination*, ed. Katherine Harmond, 15–35. New York: Princeton Architectural Press.
King, Rosamond S. 2008. More Notes on the Invisibility of Caribbean Lesbians. *Our Caribbean: A Gathering of Lesbian and Gay Writing from the Antilles*, ed. Thomas Glave, 191–96. Durham: Duke University Press.
———. 2011. New Citizens, New Sexualities: Nineteenth-Century Jamettes. In *Sex and the Citizen: Interrogating the Caribbean*, ed. Faith Smith, 214–23. Charlottesville: University of Virginia Press.
———. 2014. *Island Bodies: Transgressive Sexualities in the Caribbean Imagination.* Gainesville, FL: University Press of Florida.
Kitchin Rob and Dodge Martin. 2007. Rethinking Maps. *Progress in Human Geography* 31, no. 3:331–44.
Kitchin, Rob. 2008. The Practices of Mapping. *Cartographica* 43, no. 3:211–15.
Kitchin Rob, Justin Gleeson and Martin Dodge. 2013. Unfolding Mapping Practices: A New Epistemology for Cartography. *Transactions of the Institute of British Geographers* 38: 480–96.
Leap, William. 2009. Professional Baseball, Urban Restructuring and (Changing) Gay Geographies in Washington, DC. In *Out in Public Reinventing Lesbian/Gay Anthropology in a Globalising World*, ed. Ellen Lewin and William L. Leap, 202–22. Oxford: Wiley-Blackwell.
Mootoo, Shani. 1993. *Out on Main Street.* Vancouver: Press Gang Publishers.
———. 1996. *Cereus Blooms at Night.* Vancouver: Press Gang Publishers.
———. 2008. *Valmiki's Daughter.* Toronto: House of Anansi Press.
Nixon, Angelique V. 2016. Seeing Difference: Visual Feminist Praxis, Identity, and Desire in Indo-Caribbean Women's Art and Knowledge. In *Indo-Caribbean Feminist Thought: Genealogies, Theories, Enactments*, ed. Lisa Outar and Gabrielle Hosein. London: Palgrave.
Sletto, Bjørn Ingmunn. 2009. 'We Drew What We Imagined': Participatory Mapping, Performance, and the Arts of Landscape Making. *Current Anthropology* 50, no. 4:443–76.
Tinsley, Omise'eke Natasha. 2010. *Thiefing Sugar: Eroticism Between Women in Caribbean Literature.* Durham: Duke University Press.
Wekker, Gloria. 2006. *The Politics of Passion: Women's Sexual Culture in the Afro-Surinamese Diaspora.* New York: Columbia University Press.

Wood, Denis. 2007. A Map is an Image Proclaiming Its Objective Neutrality: A Response to Denil. *Cartographic Perspectives* 56:4–16.

Wood, D., and J. Fels. 2008. *The Natures of Maps: Cartographic Constructions of the Natural World.* Chicago: University of Chicago Press.

Figures

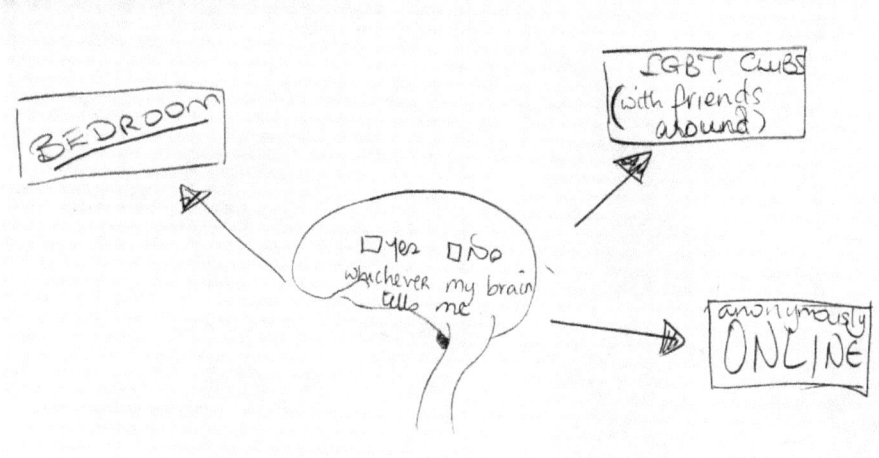

Figure 1: Scan of N'Dare's map.

Figure 2: Scan of Ariel's map (name removed).

346 Methodologies in Caribbean Research on Gender and Sexuality

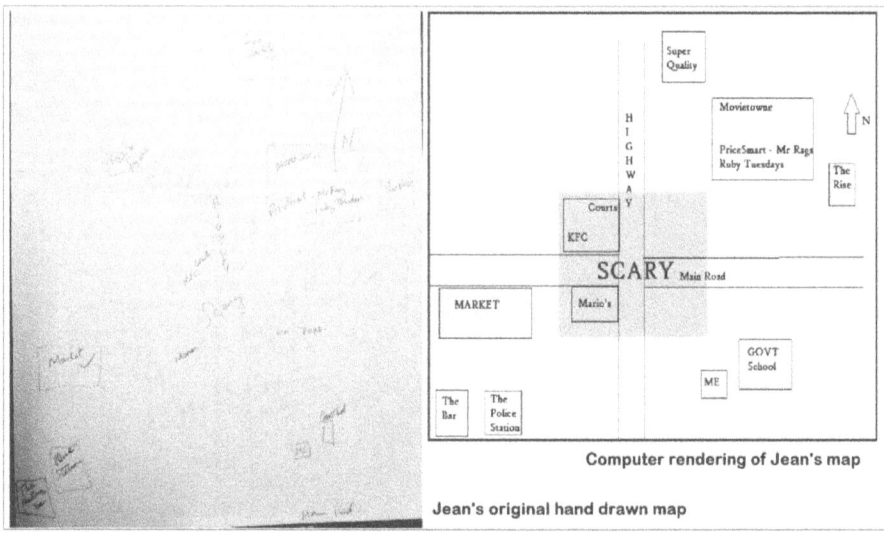

Figure 3: Photo of Jean's map alongside a digital reproduction.

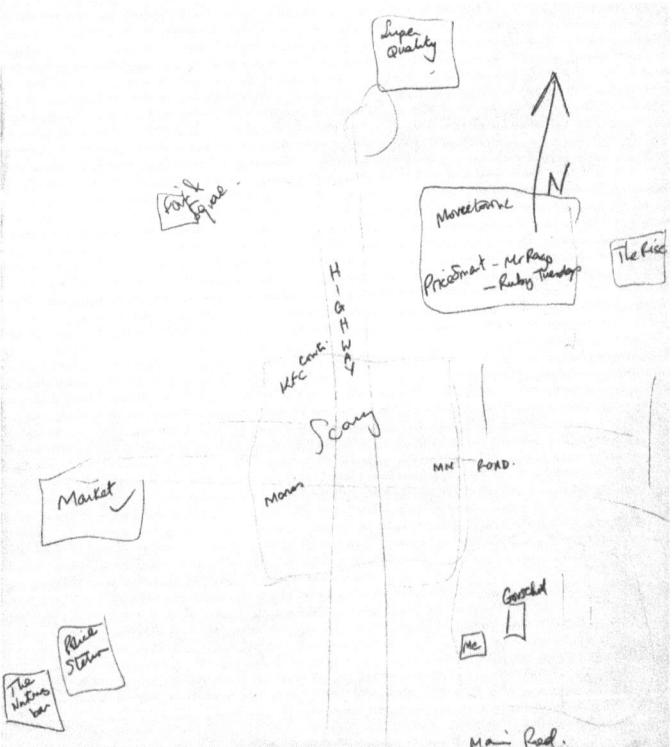

Figure 4: Scan of Jean's map of Chaguanas.

Subjective Mapping: A Brief Introduction

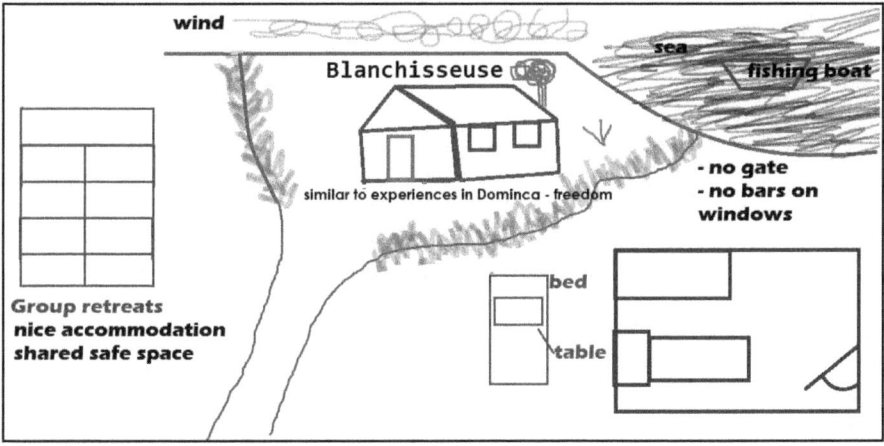

Figure 5: Jane's maps.

Researching the Visual and Cultural

19. Defining Women Subjects: Photographs in Trinidad (1860s–1960s)*

Roshini Kempadoo

Introduction

This article explores techniques and methods of the research process that are considered cornerstones to the analysis of colonial photographs of women. The first section, 'Researching photographs as embodied and partial knowledge', explores the articulation of the researchers' perspective and viewpoint; 'Postcolonial perspectives and visual representation of colonial women subjects' examines the importance of visual analysis framed within the present conjuncture of postcolonial discourse; 'Geo-political, historical and everyday contexts to photographic representations of women' recognises the importance of site-specific historical and cultural contexts to the analysis of photographs; and lastly 'Which photographs? Research choices – photographic genres and types' is concerned with family photography as a genre, which is inextricably linked to the representation of women subjects.

Discursively contained in the article are two case studies as examples of textual analysis that, along with the reproduction of other images, reveal their complex and rich significations of women associated with the history of colonial Trinidad.

Researching Photographs as Embodied and Partial Knowledge Production

Abstract from my **Notebook** *of a Return*[1]

> As a school child and teenager in Guyana and Trinidad in the 1960s and 1970s, I became familiar with the illustrations published in our history and geography schoolbooks depicting the European 'discovery' of the

---

* Reprinted with permission from *Caribbean Review of Gender Studies* Issue 7 (December 2013).

Caribbean from the 1400s. [The year] *1492 was the key date from which everything else and all knowledge about the Caribbean seemed to flow. The black and white reproductions[2] of woodcuts and engravings found in the schoolbooks were primary historic[al] references visualising the Caribbean. The illustrations were elaborate and fascinating for their detail and craftsmanship, whilst appearing grotesque and repelling for their content and depiction.*

It wasn't until the end of a secondary education in Guyana that I was introduced to the photographs of Indian indentured labourers featuring men standing in rows in the background, with significantly [fewer] women, usually squatting in front.[3]

In 2000, as a researcher in Port-of-Spain, Trinidad, I found two key texts for secondary education Caribbean history studies in Ishmael Khan & Son's bookshop on Henry Street, Port-of-Spain. The now familiar images (illustrations and photographs) of colonial Caribbean were reproduced, visualising both the 'discovery' of the Caribbean islands and 'life' under colonial rule. At the National Archives offices in St Vincent Street, I was referred to The Book of Trinidad (1992) in which the image types had been reproduced. This time, some of the illustrations were 'redrawn' or re-fashioned sketches of the previously described paintings, engravings and etchings.[4] *The following year in 2001, whilst researching the material and galleries of the National Museum and Gallery in Woodford Square, I came across more reproductions of the image types described – the pictorial history of the Caribbean as reproductions of the original woodcuts, engravings, paintings and photographs, mounted and framed on display in the museum's exhibition rooms.*

Referring to diary notes as a method of research is paramount to feminist approaches to visual analysis of photographs. It is through the research practice involving the autobiographical-personal notes and entries that we are able to make explicit our perspective and the position from which we speak; bring into consciousness the visual memories we evoke as we encounter each new photograph or image; contest the conventional rhetoric of history writing; and provide further insight into the ways in which we produce knowledge from photographs and other visual material. My research notes incorporate *but do not prioritise* a reflexive practice in researching photographs of Trinidad. By reflexive, I mean that I acknowledge and privilege an awareness of the visual material, whilst excavating and making known my relationship to the material. Photographs considered as *image types* place emphasis on the recurrent use of reproductions and emphasise the relationship between past pictorial conventions of illustrations and the iconic signs of photographs.[5] Here, I reflect a more visceral sense of how I encountered and recall historical imagery as someone from the Caribbean Diaspora. I recall imagery I have previously encountered and suggest the influence these have in considering the visual "tropes" of historical illustrations. I reflect on the contemporary reproduction of "image types" and how they give rise to questions of "authenticity" and "factual accuracy". And I note the distinctive visualising practices that were developed for picturing different Trinidadian ethnic populations as they became the majority citizens of Trinidad.

The embodied action of research, the journey and the subsequent notes the researcher makes are inextricably linked, therefore, to the personal perspectives and memories she brings. A familiarity, *a priori* knowledge and the memory of photographs that are *much like the ones we are researching* haunt the 'spectral' dimension of the material being researched. We are deeply familiar with conventions of signs and concepts *a priori* of the photograph we are looking at. There is historical memory of the photograph where '*presupposed*' and prior texts contribute to the question of its meaning and yet are not necessarily present in the photographs or imagery themselves.[6]

It necessarily involves an embodied awareness of the practice of research itself through a self-conscious and contested reflection on the materials and the places they are found in, such as the library, archive or family album. Autobiographical writing as diasporic 'memory-talk', to use Kuhn's term, determines a differentiated research process through which to consider such historical photographs/imagery. This is inherent to questioning the assumptions often made about archives and records – that authority somehow comes from the documents themselves. Narratives involving memory and autobiography, instead, come *from having been there*, as C. Steedman (1986, 2001), M. Hirsch and V. Smith (2002), S. Alexander (2010), A. Kuhn (2007), and others remind us.

Overtly acknowledging the process of research also means to declare a partial vision at any one time and incorporates what D. Haraway (2002) proposes as a 'situated' vision to the material. The adoption of an autoethnographic research practice[7] that includes multidimensional and yet always partial perspectives has been pioneered by feminist historians, scientists, anthropologists, and artists, including S. Ahmed (2000), N. N. Chen and T.T. Minh-ha (1994), C. Fusco (2008), Haraway (2002), Minh-ha

(1989), R. McGrath (2002, 2007), S. Pink (2001), C. Sandoval (2000), N. Seremetakis (1996) and A. L. Stoler (2002). Haraway continues, 'vision is *always* a question of the power to see...the split and contradictory self is the one who can interrogate positionings and be accountable...the topography of subjectivity is multidimensional; so therefore, is vision.' Those of us creating, engaging and researching visual projects, Haraway contends, have the responsibility of being consciously aware of the perspectives we adopt in dealing with the visual. This, I argue, is also particularly pertinent when considering colonial visual material and its association with racism, gender, privilege, fear, fantasy, and representation of the colonial subject.

Postcolonial Perspectives and Visual Representation of Colonial Women Subjects

Researching photographs as representations of the woman figure involves considering the material as inherent to the colonial project, particularly in relation to race and privilege. It also involves reflecting on the material in the Foucauldian sense of the present moment, that is, as a researcher familiar with contemporary postcolonial discourse and perspectives. We engage with colonial photography through the contemporary postcolonial prism including Fanon's seminal text on the psychological state of the black man; Sandoval's writings on feminism and oppression; Said's concept of Orientalism; Spivak's proposition of the subaltern; Gilroy's configuration of the black Atlantic; and Hall's writings on difference. It is from this knowledge we are able to consider retrospectively how photographs portray the colonial woman plantation worker.

Postcolonial and contemporaneous approaches to exploring photographs – individually and collectively – are of primary importance to exploring the representation of women in colonial photography. This necessarily involves observing all things about the photograph, its context of production and reception – including the way the researcher encounters the collection in the archive – exploring the taxonomy of the photographic collection and closely researching the content, contexts and aesthetics of each photograph and of each photograph in relation to the next.

Of primary importance is that images are not only about how they look, but how they are looked at. Consideration can, therefore, be given to the women subjects in the photograph as well as to who is doing the looking. Representations of her visually uphold racial and gender difference as recurring tropes and markers of difference. Franz Fanon's seminal text (1986) *Black Skin, White Masks*, originally published in 1952, is significant in conceptualising the psychology between racism, colonialism, and the scopic drive. Writers continue to critique and expand on notions of race, its relationship to colonialism, and the scopic drive of the European that 'fixes' and objectifies the racialised Other.[8] H. K. Bhabha (1990) proposes that this fixity and objectifying firmly embed the stereotyping process, suggesting the look as being particularly charged when it crosses the colour line because of its association with the regulation of sexual activity between black and white.

As a colonial process, photography contributed to the operation of repeatedly representing the colonial subject as primitive, childlike, mentally deficient, and sexually charged or in need of civilising. Photography as a visualising technology for colonialism, I argue, partially fulfilled the (white) male psychic need to consign visually the black body to a safer preserve. Research methods for textual analysis of colonial photographs of women, therefore, involve a 'reading' of the image as a form of representation of the colonial subject and acknowledge the active process and fetish involved in the 'gaze' embedded in photography. Photography as a signifying system involves what V. Burgin describes as a scene (the photograph) and the '*gaze of the spectator*' or 'a viewing subject' (Burgin 1982, 146).

Analysis of women in colonial photographs also allows us to consider the construction of masculinity and, in particular, to acknowledge the predominance of the male gaze in determining the meaning of images of women. It is widely acknowledged that men historically (if not contemporaneously) have controlled the production of images. The scopic drive is typically considered to be a masculine one embedded with an entitlement to look at women, whilst women also watch themselves being looked at, as L. Mulvey (1996) and others have explored. This visualisation or objectivisation of women is, therefore, a consequence of the male colonial gaze. As McGrath describes, photography is most often embedded with a 'heterosexual visual economy' in which the 'woman's body...excites the hand and eye' (McGrath 2002, 1). D. Willis and C. Williams (2002) also argue that the colonial traveller journeying to the colonies found that an 'element in the picture-making process was undoubtedly the titillation of the photographers themselves, who were at least temporarily freed from the moral restrictions of their Western cultures' (Willis and Williams 2002, 19–21), and who were exacerbated by a sense of liberation and *risqué*. Feminist historians, art critics, media and photography theorists – including M. Allouha (1987), R. Espinet (1993), McGrath (2002), Minh-ha (1989), Mohammed (1998), R. Reddock (1985, 1987,1994, 1998), V. Shepherd, B. Brereton and B. Bailey (1995, V. Shepherd (2002), D. Willis (2010), J. Williamson (1984), and L. Young (1996) – have thoroughly explored the complex and recurring tropes deployed to signify or represent the woman figure, whether in popular culture, literature, or photography. Young perceptively comments that 'although black women were seen as "not-male," they were not seen as women in the same sense that white women were. Since slavery, African females had been seen as at once women – inasmuch as they were sexualised, reproductive, and subordinate – and not-women, that is not pure, not feminine, not fragile but strong and sexually knowing and available' (Young 1996, 64).

The photographs representing women from the 1860s to the 1960s, found in Trinidad, mostly functioned and were purposed as colonial documentation, visual confirmation of what happened and what was there, imputing a currency of "truth" and unequivocal evidence to the events and records of the period. Their credibility, legitimacy, and value is assured through the archive and collection process that we find them in, whether these are collections found in official archives or personal collections. As photographs were most often taken by those in positions of authority, with the financial and ideological interest and power to envision the colony (colonial administration, landowning families, travelling photographers), they are embued with the convention of historicising images as seemingly objective and transparent – a window through which to look.

From our present perspective, we are mindful of the original function and purpose of the photographs taken in the period: They may have been commissioned as evidence of an example of 'good' colonial governance, or privately commissioned by plantation owners to signify and represent their wealth in the colonies, or merely taken by travel photographers as postcards to encourage tourism and exploration of colonial landscapes, or to sell as portraits to families who could afford it. Photographic technologies contributed to the visual perception and clear distinction between the colonised and the coloniser. Methodology for visual analysis, therefore, necessarily involves seeking the origins of production, who commissioned the photograph, who took the photograph, to what end were they taken, as well as prioritising and noting gender-specific influences involved in the creating and staging of the photographs.

The exploration of photographic technologies, the development of photographic conventions and how they influenced the portrayal of colonial women subjects are invariably also important as methods for analysis. The early and rapid development of photography technologies from the 1850s to 1930s meant photography emerged as a significant part of a European visual economy with a compulsion to order and a desire to dominate world populations alongside those considered the 'enemy within'. The European visual economy or visualising science, during this period, scrutinised in forensic detail the habits and physiognomy of all others but the 'normalised' European male figure.

Under the guise of advancing medical knowledge, discovering the empire and its races or policing the state, photography was put to work in envisioning women, non-European races, those considered abnormal mentally or physically, and those considered a danger to social order. Critics and writers researching photographic collections from the 1850s onwards – at a time when photography emerged as a commercial and popular medium – have established a photography discourse of collections *in relation to* conceiving photography as social acts. Most notably, these include A. Sekula (1986) on Bertillon and Galton's work of exploring social deviance and scientific policing; J. Tagg (1988) on prison and police archives; J. Taylor (1994) on the Kodak phenomenon; Willis and Williams (2002) on the black female body in a range of photographic archival material; McGrath (2002) on medical images of women from the archives in Scotland; Thompson (2006) on exploring photographs from tourist campaigns in Jamaica and the Bahamas between the 1890s and 1930s; G. Rose's (2010) writings on family photography in public and domestic spaces; and T. Campt's (2012) consideration of archive photographs of the African Diaspora in Europe.

These writers explore the ways in which photographic techniques and conventions helped determine their societal function. In approaching the photographs, much consideration is given to how the photographs are received, who they were made for (whether as police records, photographs associated with tourism and travelling, or medical visualisation) and who would have seen them at the time.

Case Study 1 explores an image found in the National Museum of Trinidad and Tobago archives.

Illustration 1: Anon. (unknown). *Untitled (Standing on either side)*[9]
Laser copy: Port-of-Spain, The National Museum and Art Gallery
of Trinidad and Tobago.

Geopolitical, Historical, and Everyday Contexts to Photographic Representations of Women

As in the case study analysis referred to earlier, methods for analysing photographic representations of women involve researching the historical contextual narratives from which emerge the visual depiction or the *mise en scène* of the photograph. Visual representations of place, people and events are better understood as set within historical contexts from which cultural identities and perspectives emerge and are set within the topology and terrain of specific locations, often involving scenes from the vernacular and everyday. The portrayal of women during this period is conceived in the case study as associated with everyday plantation space, whether the location is the domesticated space of the plantation house or the field. We are mindful, for example, of plantation labour systems during this period as creating and sustaining gendered divisions of labour, devastating familial relationships, and instituting racial hierarchies.

The geopolitical history of Trinidad, like many ex-British colonial Caribbean islands, is constituted from a history of plantation economies and colonial rule and, as such, has both common and highly distinctive historical narratives that might be associated with the island. Analysis of photographs of early colonial Trinidad with its majority population of mostly ex-plantation workers is further complicated by a unique history inextricably linked to the plantation labour system. That history includes a smaller percentage of slaves making up the overall Trinidad population than in other British colonial Caribbean islands; a noticeable percentage of 'coloured' and 'black freedmen' and various changes in colonial rule involving Spain, France and Britain;[10] an indentureship (and British) labour system as a substitute form of labour after slavery that brought a significant Indian population from Calcutta and Madras;[11] an ever-changing mixed economy

Illustration 2: Kempadoo, Roshini. (2006) "Mrs Procope's family photographs". Port-of-Spain.

that transformed the dependency on cultivating sugar to include coffee, cocoa and citrus trade; a rapid urbanisation and industrialisation of the country's economy due to Trinidad's natural resources of petroleum (crude oil, natural gas, petrochemicals)[12] in the San Fernando area, southwest of the island; and the island's being perceived by the US as a strategic military base located close to the Americas. Wider historical contexts pertaining to Trinidad's history may be drawn from closely examining the detail of photographs for stylistic conventions associated with colonial woman subjects, including dress code, composition of the photograph, posture, the 'gaze back' from subject to photographer/viewer, and *mise en scène*. The photographic depiction of informal historical detail of the everyday provides exciting visual clues with which to research the wider particular history of the island and its women populations.

Which Photographs? Research Choices – Photographic Genres and Types

> Photographs taken in everyday life, snapshots in particular, rebelled against all of those photographic practices that reinscribed colonial ways of looking and capturing the images of the black 'other'...these snapshots gave us a way to see ourselves, a sense of how we looked when we were not 'wearing the mask'"...hooks, b. (1994, 50–51).

Photographic genres and types of photography chosen for the research process are crucial to expanding a visual analysis that explores women represented in colonial Trinidad. Where are representations of colonial women to be found? What genre might they be associated with and what were their purpose and function at the time they were created?

Case Study 2 Explores a Portrait from a High Street Photographic Studio.

Finding photographs representing women requires deep and forensic research that includes informal and formal archives.[13] Colonial photographs are most often visually dominated by the European men as owners/colonisers of the island, whilst the postcolonial visual trope has emerged from the image and narrative of the liberated male ex-slave as an independent and free citizen. Photographs of women from the majority population of ex-colonial workers of Trinidad end up supportive and subservient to these twin visual narratives. Family album collections

**Illustration 3: Anon. (unknown). 'Untitled 3'.
Photograph: Port-of-Spain: Mr. Dalla Costa, Film Processors Ltd.**

and high street portraits as informal archives are important and fruitful sources for photographs depicting women in opposition to and in dialogue with official national history. There is a long genealogy of feminist writers and photographers, including A. Azoulay (2008), J. Spence and P. Holland (1991), M. Hirsch (2012), Kuhn (2002), M. Langford (2008), Rose (2010), Stoler (2002), Thompson (2006) and Willis (2005). They have explored the relationship between domestic or family photography as a genre and its value and importance as a genre to visualising women.

In an analysis, then, of the domestic image that may include portraiture and self-portraits, documentation of social occasions and events, including weddings and other civil ceremonies such as graduations or birthday celebrations, snapshots and family archives of earlier generations, we may be able to focus on women's presence in photography. We can also pay further attention to other aspects that are symptomatic of this type of photography and its conventions, including the examination of gendered postures, questions of intimacy and displays of power, power relationships between photographer and the photographed, questions of civic duty and responsibility, as spectators exploring the photographs, and the inherent relationship between maintaining familial togetherness and the mobility of photographs (Rose 2010).

Formal portraits that are created as valuable family documentation are mostly curated and managed by women. The portrait found in Mr Costa's collection is symptomatic of a genre and photographic type that extends the way in which women had photographs taken of themselves. In engaging with different genres of photography – in this case the portrait – the researcher is able to examine and explore a differently negotiated envisioning practice.

Conclusion

The 1860s–1960s saw photography emerge from Europe that was within what G. Batchen suggests was the 'peculiarly modern arrangement of knowledges', (Batchen 1997, 186) and what Young describes as a 'compulsion to order and construct taxonomies' (Young 1996, 48). Researching and analysing different kinds of colonial photographs including high street portraits; family snapshots; formal social portraits; and other local photographers' contributions become important counterpoints to the long history of envisioning women in the colony. As photography became popular and more readily available by the 1920s onwards, we are able to find photographs that reflect an emergent consciousness of liberation and citizenship. As women historians have pieced together the presence and action by women in colonial documentation, so too, the researcher is able to find alternative visual practices where women were able to partially or fully determine and control their own image.

A 'postcolonial perspective' and research process for exploring Trinidadian (or Caribbean) women subjects in photography, therefore, necessarily must take into consideration photography's purpose and function as inherent to colonialism. Postcolonial perspectives of colonialism include geopolitical explorations specific to the locale of Trinidad; photographic and archive theories of visualisation, typification, and visual tropes; feminist approaches to research and knowledge; and acknowledgement of embodied and partial perspectives. Analysis of women subjects in photographs of colonial Trinidad emerges from reading against the grain (Stoler 2009) of the photographic archive in order to envision these women's presence in history.

Photographs have been reproduced with the kind permission of The National Museum and Art Gallery of Trinidad and Tobago and Mr Dalla Costa, Film Processors, Port of Spain.

References

Ahmed, S. 2000. *Strange Encounters: Embodied Others in Post-coloniality*. London and New York: Routledge.
Alexander, S. 2010. Memory Talk: London Childhoods. In *Memory: Histories, Theories, Debates*, ed. B. Schwarz and S. Radstone, 235–45. New York: Fordham University Press.
Alloula, M. 1987. *The Colonial Harem*. Manchester: Manchester University Press.
Azoulay, A. 2008. *The Civil Contract of Photography*. New York: Zone Books.
Batchen, G. 1997. *Burning with Desire: The Conception of Photography*. Boston, Mass: MIT Press.
Baxandall. 1988. *Painting and Experience in Fifteenth-century Italy: A Primer in the Social History of Pictorial Style*. Oxford: Oxford University Press.
Bhabha, H.K. 1990. The Other Question: Difference, Discrimination and the Discourse of Colonialism. In *Out There: Marginalisation and Contemporary Cultures*, ed. R. Fergson, M. Gever, T.T. Minha-ha and C. West. New York and Cambridge, Mass: The New Museum of Contemporary Art and MIT Press.
———. 1994. *The Location of Culture*. London and New York: Routledge.
Birbalsingh, F. 1993. *Indo-Caribbean Resistance*. Toronto: TSAR Publications.
Brereton, B. 1979. *Race Relations in Colonial Trinidad 1870–1900*. Cambridge, UK: Cambridge University Press.
Brereton, B., and G. Besson. 1992. *The Book of Trinidad*. Port-of-Spain: Paria Publishing Company.
Burgin, V. 1982. Looking at Photographs. In *Thinking Photography*, ed. V. Burgin, 142–153. London/New Jersey: The Macmillan Press/Humanities Press International.

Campt, T. 2012. *Image Matters: Archive, Photography, and the African Diaspora in Europe.* Durham: Duke University Press.

Césaire, A. 1995. *Notebook of a Return to My Native Land.* Tarset: Bloodaxe Books.

Chen, N.N., and T.T. Min-ha. 1994. Speaking Nearby. In *Visualizing Theory: Selected Essays from V.A.R. 1990–1994*, ed. Lucien Taylor, 433–51. New York and London: Routledge.

Cudjoe, Selwyn. R. *Narrating the Nation: Naming the Land.* Accessed August 18, 2004, http://www.triniview.com/narrating.htm.

Dabydeen, D., and Samaroo, B. 1987. *India in the Caribbean.* London: Hansib Publications.

———. 1996. *Across the Dark Water: Ethnicity and Indian Identity in the Caribbean.* London: Macmillan Caribbean.

Enwezor, O. 1997. Reframing the Black Subject. In *Catalogue for 2nd Johannesburg Biennale, Trade Routes: History and Geography*, ed. O. Enwezor. South Africa: Johannesburg Biennale.

Espinet, R. 1993. Representation and the Indo-Caribbean woman in Trinidad and Tobago. In *Indo-Caribbean Resistance*, ed. F. Birbalsingh, 42–61. Toronto: TSAR Publications.

Fanon, F. 1986. *Black Skin, White Masks.* London: Pluto Press.

Ferguson, R., M. Gever, T.T. Minh-ha and C. West. 1990. *Out There: Marginalisation and Contemporary Cultures.* New York and Boston Mass: The New Museum of Contemporary Art and MIT Press.

Fusco, C. 2008. Framing Whiteness: *Emisférica: Race and Its Others* 5, no. 2:1–4, http://hemisphericinstitute.org/hemi/en/e-misferica-52.

Gilman, S. 1985. *Difference and Pathology: Stereotypes of Sexuality, Race and Madness.* Ithaca and London: Cornell University Press.

Hall, S. 1989. Cultural Identity and Cinematic Representations. *Framework: Third Scenario: Theory and the Politics Of Location*, no. 36:68–81.

Haraway, D. 2002. The Persistence of Vision. In *The Visual Culture Reader*, 2nd ed., ed. N. Mirzoeff, 677–84. London: Routledge.

Hirsch, M. 2012. *Family Frames: Photography, Narrative and Postmemory.* Cambridge, Mass. and London: Harvard University Press.

Hirsch, M., and V. Smith. 2002. Feminism and Cultural Memory: An Introduction. *Signs* 28, no. 1:1–19.

hooks, b. 1994. In Our Glory: Photography and Black Life. In *Picturing Us: African American Identity in Photography*, ed. D. Willis, 43–54. New York: The New Press.

Kuhn, A. 2002. *Family Secrets: Acts of Memory and Imagination.* London: Verso Books. Kuhn, A. Photography and Cultural Memory: A Methodological Exploration. *Visual Studies* 22, no. 3:283–92.

Langford, M. 2008. *Suspended Conversations: The Afterlife of Memory in Photographic Albums.* Montreal: McGill-Queen's University Press.

Light, A. 1991. *Forever England: Femininity, Literature and Conservatism between the Wars.* London and New York: Routledge.

Lister, M., and L. Wells. 2001. Seeing beyond Belief: Cultural Studies as an Approach to Analysing the Visual. In *Handbook of Visual Analysis*, ed. T. Van Leeuwen and C. Jewitt. London: Sage.

McGrath, R. 2002. *Seeing Her Sex: Medical Archives and the Female Body.* Manchester and New York: Manchester University Press.

———. 2007. History Read Backward: Memory Migration and the Photographic Archive. In *Projecting Migration*, ed. A. Grossman and A. O'Brien, 36–52. London: Wallflower Press.

Minh-ha, T.T. 1989. *Woman, Native, Other: Writing, Postcoloniality and Feminism.* Bloomington: Indiana University Press.

Mohammed, P. 1998. Editorial. *Feminist Review* 1, no. 59:1–4.

———. 2004. Gendering the Caribbean Picturesque. Paper presented at The Gender and Visuality Conference, University of Western Cape, Cape Town, August.

———. 2009. *Imaging the Caribbean: Culture and Visual Translation.* Oxford: Macmillan.

Mulvey, L. 1996. *Fetishism and Curiosity.* Bloomington and London: Indiana University Press and British Film Institute.

NYPL, Digital Gallery. *The Book of Trinidad*, ed. T.B. Jackson. (Accessed 12 March, 2007).,http://digitalgallery.nypl.org/nypldigital/dgkeysearchdetail. cfm?trg=1&strucID=5 77982&imageID=1229412&parent_id=440047& word=&snum=&s=&notword=&d=&c= &f=&sScope=&sLevel=&sLabe l=&total=34&num=0&imgs=12&pNum=&pos=1.

Pink, S. 2001. *Doing Visual Ethnography: Images, Media and Representation in Research.* London: Sage.

Pinney, C. 1997. *Camera Indica: The Social Life of Indian Photographs.* Chicago and London: The University of Chicago Press and Reaktion Books.

Powell, R. 1997. Re/Birth of a Nation. In *Rhapsodies in Black: Art of the Harlem Renaissance*, ed. R.J Powell and D.A. Bailey, 14–33. London and Berkeley: Hayward Gallery, Institute of International Visual Arts, and University of California Press.

Pratt, M. L. 1991. Arts of the Contact Zone. *Profession: Modern Language Association* :33–40.

Reddock, R. 1985. Women and Slavery in the Caribbean: A Feminist Perspective. *Latin American Perspectives* 12, no. 1:63–80.

———. 1987. The Women in Revolt. In *The Trinidad Labour Riots of 1937: Perspectives 50 Years Later*, ed. R Thomas, 233–64. St Augustine, Trinidad: Extra-Mural Studies Unit, The University of the West Indies.

———. 1994. *Women and Labour in Trinidad and Tobago: A History.* London: Zed Books.

———. 1998. The Indentureship Experience: Indian Women in Trinidad and Tobago 1845–1917. In *Women Plantation Workers: International Experiences*, ed. S. Jain and R. Reddock, Oxford and New York: Berg.

Rose, G. 2010. *Doing Family Photography: The Domestic, the Public and the Politics of Sentiment.* Farnham: Ashgate.

Russell, C. 1999. Experimental Ethnography. Durham and London: Duke University Press.

Samaroo, B. 1995. The First Ship – The Fath Al Razak. In *In celebration of One Hundred And Fifty Years of Indian Contribution to Trinidad and Tobago*, ed. B. Samaroo,

K. Haraksingh, G. Besson, D. Quentrall-Thomas and K Ramchand. UK: Historical Publications Ltd.

Sandoval, C. 2000. *Methodology of the Oppressed.* Minneapolis: University of Minnesota.

Sekula, A. 1981. The Traffic in Photographs. *Art Journal: Photography and the Scholar/Critic* 41:15–25.

———. 1986. The Body and the Archive. *October* 39:3–64.

Seremetakis, N. 1996. The Memory of the Senses, part I: Marks of the Transitory. In *The Senses Still: Perception and Memory as Material Culture in Modernity,* ed. N. Seremetakis, 1–18. Chicago: University of Chicago Press.

Shepherd, V. 2002. 'Petticoat rebellion'?: The Black Woman's Body and Voice in the Struggles for Freedom in Colonial Jamaica. In *In the Shadow of the Plantation: Caribbean History and Legacy,* ed. A. O. Thompson, 17–39. Kingston, Jamaica: Ian Randle Publishers.

Shepherd, V., B. Brereton and B. Bailey. 1995. *Engendering History: Caribbean Women in Historical Perspective.* New York: St Martin's Press.

Smith, S.M. 2004. *Photography on the Colour Line: W. E. B. Du Bois, Race, and Visual Culture.* Raleigh: Duke University Press.

Spence, J., and P. Holland. 1991. *Family Snaps: The Meanings of Domestic Photography.* London: Virago.

Steedman, C. 1986. *Landscape for a Good Woman.* London: Virago.

———. 2001. *Dust: The Archive and Cultural History.* Manchester: Manchester University Press.

Stoler, A. L. 2002. *Carnal Knowledge and Imperial Power: Race and the Intimate in Colonial Rule.* Berkeley: University of California Press.

———. 2009. *Along the Archival Grain: Epistemic Anxieties and Colonial Common Sense.* Princeton: Princeton University Press.

Tagg, J. 1988. *The Burden of Representation: Essays on Photographies and Histories.* Minneapolis: University of Minnesota Press.

Taylor, J. 1994. *A Dream of England: Landscape, Photography, and the Tourist's Imagination.* Manchester: Manchester University Press.

Thompson, K.A. 2006. *An Eye for the Tropics: Tourism, Photography, and Framing the Caribbean Picturesque.* Durham: Duke University Press.

Tinker, H. 1974. *A New System of Slavery: The Export of Indian Labour Overseas 1830–1920.* London: Institute of Race Relations.

Vergès, F. 1997. Creole Skin, Black Mask: Fanon and Disavowal. *Critical Inquiry* 23, no. 3:578–95.

———. 1999. *Monsters and Revolutionaries: Colonial Family Romance and Métissage.* Raleigh and London: Duke University Press.

Williamson, J. 1984. *Decoding Advertisements: Ideology and Meaning in Advertising.* London: Marion Boyars.

Willis, D. 2005. *Family, History, and Memory: Recording African-American Life.* New York: Hylas Publishing.

———. 2010. *Black Venus 2010: They Called her 'Hottentot'.* Philadelphia: Temple University Press.

Willis, D., and C. Williams 2002. *The Black Female Body: A Photographic History.* Philadelphia: Temple University Press.

Wilton, A. 1992. *The Swagger Portrait: Grand Manner Portraiture in Britain from Van Dyck to Augustus John, 1630–1930.* London: Tate Publishing.

Young, L. 1996. *Fear of the Dark: 'Race', Gender and Sexuality in the Cinema.* New York and London: Routledge.

Notes

1. The subtitle refers to my research notes and makes reference to Aimé Césaire's *Notebook of a Return to My Native Land*, first published in 1939.
2. Notable early illustrators, painters, and engravers of Caribbean and American events included Théordore de Bry (1528–98); Agostino Brunias (1730–96); and Antonio de Herrera (1601–15). These have also been referred to in Patricia Mohammed's publication in 2009 entitled *Imaging The Caribbean: Culture and Visual Translation.* De Bry and de Herrera, ironically, did not travel to the 'New World' but relied on accounts and journals from the explorers to make interpretations about the voyages and details of what were found there. While the reproductions in the school texts mostly appeared in black and white, many of the originals were in colour, particularly the oil paintings of the later period.
3. Several Caribbean scholars, including Dabydeen and Samaroo (1987, 1996), Birbalsingh (1993) and Tinker (1974), have written extensively about the Indian indentured system in Trinidad and British Guiana. This includes details of the first ships carrying indentured labourers, the *Whitby*, which sailed from Port Calcutta to British Guiana on January 13, 1838, and the *Fatel Razack*, which left Kolkata on 16 February 1845 and landed in the Gulf of Paria, Trinidad, on May 30, 1845.
4. The redrawn reproductions of etchings and engravings in Brereton and Besson's text *The Book of Trinidad* (1992) are credited to Shim. The book of some 424 pages contains an extensive number of black and white, and sepia-toned reproductions of photographs, illustrations, maps and written accounts, with an average of at least two reproductions per page. The title makes reference to a previous publication of the same name that was an album of photographs of Trinidad produced in 1904 and edited by T.B. Jackson. A digital edition of Jackson's book is available online as part of the NYPL Digital Gallery of the Schomburg Centre for Research in Black Culture, New York Libraries Division. See *The Book of Trinidad*, edited by T. B. Jackson, NYPL Digital Gallery (2004–07). [Internet database] New York: Available from <http://digitalgallery.nypl.org/nypldigital/dgkeysearchdetail.cfm?trg=1&strucID=577982&imageID=12294 12&parent_id=440047&word=&snum=&s=&notword=&d=&c=&f=&sScope=&sLevel=&sLabel=&total=34& num=0&imgs=12&pNum=&pos=1>(Accessed 12 March 2007).
5. Lister and Wells' (2001) writing is helpful in considering the notion of image typification and its close relationship to the signification of photography. Referencing Baxandall's analysis (1988) of a fifteenth- century woodcut, they trace the way meaning is attributed to a pictorial image in which 'a certain kind of mark has been matched (and agreed by all who can understand the convention...) with a certain kind of object or quality of objects in the real world' (Lister and Wells 2001, 72). This is the way that the concept of a

(pictorial) convention 'is extended to that of a 'code'– an extended system of signs which operates like a language' (Lister and Wells 2001, 73).
6. We are deeply familiar with conventions of signs and concepts *a priori* of the photograph we are looking at. Burgin introduces the term 'complex "intertextuality"' to refer to the condition of the photograph that 'engages discourse beyond itself' where *'presupposed* and prior texts that are very much taken for granted contribute to the question of its meaning and yet are not necessarily present in the photograph itself (Burgin 1982, 144).
7. For further information on autoethnography as a concept in approaching research, *see* Pratt (1991) and Russell (1999).
8. Among such works on stereotyping and the notions of race as they relate to literature and visual culture are *Difference and Pathology: Stereotypes of Sexuality, Race and Madness*, by S. Gilman (1985). *Fear of the Dark: 'Race', Gender and Sexuality in the Cinema*, by. L. Young (1996). 'Reframing the Black subject', by O. Enwezor (1997), in *Trade Routes: History and Geography*, the catalogue for the 2nd Johannesburg Biennale; 'The Other Question: Difference, Discrimination and the Discourse of Colonialism', by H.K. Bhabha in *Out There: Marginalisation and Contemporary Cultures* (1990), edited by R. Gever Ferguson, T.T. Minh-ha, and C. West; F. Vergès' 'Creole Skin, Black Mask: Fanon and Disavowal', *Critical Inquiry* 23, no. 3 (1997): 578–95 and *Monsters and Revolutionaries: Colonial Family Romance and Métissage* (1999).
9. This is a title I provided to describe the photograph. The original found in the gallery was a laser copy. There was no original to refer to, no title, no date or any contextual documentation such as an index card.
10. Coloureds (also known in French as *gens de couleur* or *affranchis*) and black freedmen were colonial categories or a process of 'racial accounting' that was used by the British. The first term referred to the population of mixed race who may or may not have been enslaved, the second referred to those of African descent who had acquired manumission or were free from bondage.
11. Indian indentured labourers soon dominated the plantation labour force in Trinidad. As Brereton notes, by 1872 'they constituted 75.3 per cent of the total sugar estate labour force; in 1895 the proportion had reached 87 per cent' (Brereton 1979, 178).
12. Trinidad's industrial base now accounts for some 40 per cent of its GDP. These statistics are based on figures available for 2002/2003 and 2005 from the International Energy Agency: Data Services. See OECD/IEA. (2006). *Share of Total Primary Energy Supply in 2004: Trinidad and Tobago.* <http://www.iea.org/Textbase/stats/country results.asp?COUNTRY_CODE=TT&Submit=Submit> (Accessed 10 February 2007). And OECD/IEA. (2006). *Evolution of Total Production of Energy from 1971 to 2004: Trinidad and Tobago.* [Internet] <http://www.iea.org/Textbase/stats/countryresults.asp?COUNTRY_CODE=TT&Submit=Submit> (Accessed 20 February 2007).
13. I conceive of formal visual archive material as characterised by qualities that include photographs owned and administered by local, national, or

regional institutions; photographs constituted officially and that have a system of access to professional researchers and, in some cases, the general public; and photographic collections conserved by professional archivists, including curators, official administrators and librarians. Informal visual archive material is defined as photographs owned, administered and conserved by private companies or individuals whose access, publishing and use are subject to individual discretion and corporate decisions.

20. Feminist Witnessing: Creating Visual Media through Ethnographic Research

Deborah A. Thomas

Several Caribbeanists have discussed the ways the region has been represented visually, from the initial classification as 'natural' landscape, 'untouched' by the human labour early colonial observers erased from view to the more recent visual tropes of hypersexuality and glorified violence (Sheller 2002; Thompson 2006). Fewer researchers have engaged visual culture methodologically; that is, despite a long history of ethnographic film within the discipline of anthropology, social scientists, and humanists have only recently become critical producers of images as well as analysts of them. Yet contemporary developments in technology, including inexpensive cameras, editing software, and internet platforms for sharing work have made new representational techniques widely available and familiar, especially to younger generations now moving into academia. Researchers are experimenting with visual and performative representations of their work, and this trend will surely accelerate as the technology develops further, as people who are comfortable with that technology become faculty members, and as broader conversations continue regarding the forms higher education research will take in the humanities and social sciences. I argue in this essay that visual ethnography constitutes a feminist methodology not only in relation to potential subject matter, but also because it is necessarily interdisciplinary and unavoidably collaborative – with the people who are at the centre of the research; with other scholars and specialists in a number of fields; with community-based groups and organizations; and potentially with the broader governmental and non-governmental infrastructures the research addresses. Using two visual ethnography projects in which I have been involved as anchoring cases, I discuss the processes and collaborations we developed, as well as the feminist analytics and strategies we mobilized.

Archives and Counter-archives

Beginning in 2007 and continuing to today, I have been involved in two projects that have been oriented toward creating archives of state violence. The first dealt with state violence against Rastafari, and one particular event in 1963, now euphemistically called the Coral Gardens 'incident'. As a result of an ongoing land dispute near the community of Coral Gardens close to Montego Bay, the government, security forces and civilians were part of a massive round up of Rastafari across western Jamaica. Hundreds of brethren were jailed, beaten and tortured, and an unknown number were killed. This 'incident' was the basis of the 2011 documentary film I made with John Jackson and Junior 'Gabu' Wedderburn, called *Bad Friday: Rastafari after Coral Gardens*. The second project, and the one that currently consumes my time and energy, concerns the state of emergency in West Kingston in May 2010 that was declared to apprehend Christopher 'Dudus' Coke – leader of the Shower Posse and 'don' of the Tivoli Gardens community[1] – who had been ordered for extradition to the US on charges related to drug- and gun-trafficking. This 'incursion', as it is called, is the basis for 'Tivoli Stories', a multimedia installation and social memory project I worked on with Junior, again, and psychologist Deanne Bell. 'Tivoli Stories' was designed to provide a platform through which participating Tivoli Gardens and neighbouring community members could recount their experiences during May and June 2010, and name and publicly memorialize loved ones they lost. In both these projects, representing violence (and particularly state violence) audiovisually (and *publically*) has raised questions about the ways different moments of exceptional violence are connected through ongoing forms of structural and symbolic violence, about the different truths variously located members of a community are willing and able to acknowledge and examine, and about the potential for repair or transformative justice. And they have both resulted in the development of a collection of material that had previously been unavailable.

Some might claim that what I am talking about is not 'archival' work per se, but is instead counter-archival. Indeed, many literary scholars and historians have viewed 'the archives' themselves as sites of violence – violence against women, people of colour, and others excluded from formal recognition within the stories of nation-building official archives are designed to tell. Feminists and critical diaspora scholars have thus worked from fragments, attempting, in different ways, to reconstruct the lives of those who were or would be slaves, those who were considered not fully human, those whose lives had been actively silenced (Trouillot 1995), to glean insight into their aspirations, their imaginations, and their day-to-day movements by putting together a mention in a diary here, or a list in a log there. Saidiya Hartman has struggled with the ethics of this process on various levels. What does it mean, she asks, to tell the stories of those who were slaves without privileging the narratives of the institutions of slavery? How can we write about those whose death is foretold as a counter-history, a practice of freedom? 'How,' she writes, 'does one revisit the scene of subjection without replicating the grammar of violence?' (2008, 4). And, perhaps most telling – how do we tell these stories without giving in to our own longings – for agency, solidarity, human connection? For Hartman, 'straining against the limits of the archive' (2008, 11) requires the sober recognition of the impossibility of narrative as a form to represent the lives of captives. For those working on slavery in the Americas and elsewhere, this is painstaking work. However, for those of us working in contemporary ethnographic time, other questions emerge that have to do with the limits of the counter archive – what Anthony Bogues would call a 'dread history' (2003) – and how we produce and represent these.

Diana Taylor has argued that counter archives constitute a repertoire, a collection of embodied acts of memory that opposes official records, the usually text-based archives the state itself collects. For Taylor, repertoires include 'performances, gestures, orality, movement, dance, singing – in short all those acts usually thought of as ephemeral, nonreproducible knowledge' (2003, 20). They produce and reproduce knowledge through participation, and the knowledge they transmit are themselves transformed as a result of the context of their production. While the camera would appear to fix these processes of knowledge production in time and space, as I will outline below, the production of visual archives actually troubles these temporal and spatial certainties. Instead, repertoires of narratives become 'products' through which to reflect collectively, and in this way they not only mediate the relationships between the individual and the social, but also move forward and backward in time as well as in and out of space. Many scholars of Latin American contexts, particularly during the Civil Wars and counterinsurgency battles of the 1970s and 1980s, championed narratives insofar as they formed a genre of testimonial. These testimonials were used not only to produce the possibility of writing the self (Mbembe 2002), but also to generate political solidarities, especially within a North American context in which citizens could protest their own government's involvement in these wars. However, Veena Das (2007), writing of the post-1984 anti-Sikh riots in India has suggested that we look equally closely at silence as we do telling. Within the context Das examines, the absence of testimony seems to create the possibility of repair in the everyday, where public 'telling', such as that which happens during Truth and Reconciliation Commissions, might lead to public reawakenings of trauma without any repair.

In both cases I discuss here, producing visual archives as a scholarly methodology has also been a form of witnessing, but one that we might characterize as quiet, a form that sits somewhere between the testimonial impetus of earlier Latin American human rights work and the explicit commitment to silence over public 'truth' telling. I argue that reading visual archives closely and producing them complexly encourages us to ask more pointed questions about what is at stake in the production of presences where there have been absences, and about the broader geopolitical and epistemological dimensions of this production. I believe that this kind of process has the potential to catalyse new possibilities for seeing connections previously unexamined and for re-ordering our ontological taken-for-grandeds, like time and space, politics and justice. In this way, visual archives of state violence can shift the politics of reparations away from discretely local and legally verifiable events and toward the long and slow processes undermining our ability to forge social and political community together. They can also urge us to be more sceptical about nationalist narratives of perfectibility, whereby we triumph over past prejudices and injustices through a force of will and commitment to moral right, instead encouraging us to train our vision more pointedly to the transnational geopolitical spheres that have constituted the frame of reference for other social movements and that infuse the social and political worlds of postcolonial Caribbeans. At the same time, witnessing – through the creation of visual archives – can help us to focus on the everyday ways people innovate life without constantly projecting today's struggle into a future redemption. And finally, because witnessing is the modality through which people insert politics into everyday meaning making, this kind of archive can help us to see and hear differently; it can cultivate a sense of mutual recognition that not only exposes complicity but also demands collective accountability.

CORAL GARDENS

'Rastas on rampage in MoBay – 8 persons killed.' So screamed the headline of Jamaica's daily afternoon paper, the *Star*, on April 11, 1963. Two days later the *Daily Gleaner* led their news coverage with four articles under the heading '8 killed after attack on gas station. Two policemen, three Ras Tafarians among the dead.' And by 10:00 am on that fateful Holy Thursday morning, RJR (then Radio Jamaica and the Re-Diffusion Network, now Radio Jamaica) reported the following: 'Three people are now known to have died in this morning's uprising by Rastafarians in Montego Bay.' For those who today understand Rastafarians as primarily advocating a philosophy of universalism (the 'One Love' Bob Marley sang about), and even for those who prefer to foreground Rastafari's ideological roots in Black supremacy and pan-Africanism and its more general Black nationalist stance, news of a 'rampage' or an 'uprising' by Rastafarians would seem uncharacteristic. But during that immediate post-independence period in Jamaica, fear and disdain were the attitudes most commonly directed toward Rastafarians, not only by those in the middle and upper classes, but also by many working-class Jamaicans. This means that events that were primarily local in scope generated national attention and concern.

The prime minister at the time – Sir Alexander Bustamante – flew to Montego Bay, Jamaica's second city, accompanied by the Commissioner of Police, the top command of the Jamaica Defence Force, the Security Chief, two Ministers of Government, and several police from the headquarters in Kingston. Once in Montego Bay, Bustamante mobilized police forces from St James, as well as those from the neighbouring parishes of Hanover, Trelawny, and Westmoreland, to join with civilians in the roundup of Rastafarians. Ultimately, because of the actions of five 'bearded' individuals who were motivated by an ongoing land dispute, over 150 Rastafarians were arrested, jailed, beaten and tortured. In addition to three of those five who were involved in the attacks on the gas station, a nearby motel, and an estate manager's home, an unknown number of Rastafarians died as a result of these tortures, and many more were permanently scarred. Since the 1990s, a group of Rastafari in Western Jamaica has kept a public vigil commemorating this 'Bad Friday', and in 2007, this vigil was folded into the yearlong schedule of events designed to commemorate the bicentenary of the abolition of the slave trade. At these commemorations, elder Rastafari offer testimony about their experiences, asking that the government make a formal apology to the Rasta community and that it consider reparations of some sort.

I had first learned about the Coral Gardens 'incident' as a graduate student in the mid-1990s when I read the book *Violence and Politics in Jamaica, 1960–1970* by Terry Lacey (1977). Lacey discusses Coral Gardens briefly as one among several incidents that provoked Jamaicans to believe that Rastafari as a whole were ready to violently revolt against the Jamaican state, thereby justifying an oppressive security policy. Wendell Bell and his student James Mau, American sociologists who conducted research in Jamaica during the 1960s, also briefly mention the events that transpired near Coral Gardens in order to demonstrate that middle- and upper-class Jamaicans have consistently viewed the Jamaican 'masses' as hostile, menacing, and ready to revolt at any moment (1964). Rex Nettleford treats the Coral Gardens 'incident' somewhat more substantially in his classic *Mirror, Mirror: Identity, Race, and Protest in Jamaica* in order to show how Rasta became associated in the minds of the Jamaican middle class public with crime and violence (1970). He, like Lacey and Bell, argues that the government's response to the events at the gas station and beyond amounted to an 'overkill' resulting from 'a pathological fear of violence' from particular sectors of the population (1970, 83). However, the official archive of what happened at Coral Gardens is slim, so when I saw the notice in the *Gleaner* about the 2007 commemoration and its links to the events related to the bicentenary of the abolition of the slave trade, I decided to attend to see if I could get a more grassroots sense of what happened to trigger the events at Coral Gardens, and to find out more about the injustices that took place afterwards.

I travelled with my friend Junior Wedderburn, a musician and Rastafarian from Portland, Jamaica who migrated to the US some 27 years before. During the plane ride, he confessed that though he and the older Rastafari who mentored him were no strangers to harassment at the hands of the police and other agents of the state, he had never heard about Coral

Gardens or about the suffering of the elders there in 1963. In part, he felt that this was the result of the particularly uneasy structural position of families like his when he was growing up. Working-class Black people throughout Jamaica who were reading or hearing about what happened at Coral Gardens would likely have felt sympathy for the Rastafari, he argued, because of a sense that the government's actions were motivated at least in part by a desire to undermine the development of Black pride. However, because at the time Rasta and Black pride were so intertwined, and because Rasta was seen by people like his parents as a fearful thing – even though they themselves had been influenced in the development of their own Black pride by movements like Marcus Garvey's – they would not have wanted to discuss the incident for fear of driving their own children toward Rasta. We were both eager, therefore, to hear the stories, to try to find out 'what really happened' on that fateful 'Bad Friday', and to learn what kind of reparations were being envisioned.

At the Coral Gardens commemoration, we were fortunate to meet a few elders who were willing to talk with us about their experiences, and we listened with them to the testimonies on stage. The actual events of that Holy Thursday are not popularly known, and at the commemoration they are usually related merely as a way to introduce the main story of Coral Gardens, which is not the event but the aftermath – the government roundup and criminalization of Rastafari.

Elders' testimonies about their experiences of this aftermath tended to frame it as an epic war between the forces of good and evil. Here, it was not only the police but also those civilians mobilized by the police who become 'Roman soldiers' – those representatives of a pagan society, also indexed by Rastas as 'Babylon',[2] who bullied Christians and were thus destined to fall. Like Christ, Rastafari were persecuted and betrayed by those they knew, subjected to extraordinary physical harm both directly and indirectly. The injustices done were rendered bureaucratic through the most inconsequential pedestrian resolutions – a fine levied here, a petty charge there. Nevertheless, at the annual commemoration, there were no victims among these elders, only resurrected soldiers. There, the elders' testimonies created an archive through which memory forged and instantiated the community's histories and social relations; inspired younger Rastafari; solidified the bonds of sociality within and between

Rasta communities; strengthened elders' positions as revered 'ancients'; *and* generated debate about future paths based on the aspects of the archives that are emphasized at any given moment.³ The stories themselves became performances, familiar phrasings were repeated, the rhythmic crafting of particular cadences were punctuated by rhetorical flourishes. 'Rasta suffer bad, bad,' they shouted, and the public memorializing became a generative force. Rasta, they asserted with pride, once persecuted and maligned, is now the symbol through which Jamaica is most recognized all across the world. Job persevered, and his fortunes were restored.

When we attended this commemoration, I was in the middle of writing a book about violence. I felt it might be compelling to think through the Coral Gardens events as a way to discuss state violence against Rastafari in terms of its connections to more general patterns of political violence in Jamaica. Toward this end, I asked one of the elders if he would retrace his steps with me, to show me as we walked along the landscape what exactly had happened to him during the days following Holy Thursday 1963. To my great surprise, he asked whether it wouldn't be more effective to do that on film. 'Of course,' I said, and thus began our odyssey as documentarians.

Junior, John Jackson, and I set about tracking down elders with the help of the late Junior 'Ista J' Manning, Ras Simba from Trelawny, and others. We interviewed them on camera about how they came to the Rasta faith, what happened to them as a result of Coral Gardens, and how they envisioned justice. As we worked on the film, we developed written agreements both with the individuals we interviewed, and with broader bodies of Rastafarians who had been involved in the struggle for intellectual copyright protection, among other things. We searched for archival footage of the era, and for other experts who could speak about the long-term effects of the events at Coral Gardens as well as more general efforts toward reparations. And on Friday 21 April 2011, the anniversary of Bad Friday, we showed the film at the annual commemoration to a rapt audience. Since then, the documentary had its official premiere at the Bob Marley Museum in Kingston, and has screened at film festivals internationally, and on college campuses across North America and the West Indies.

As much as possible when screening the film, we also conduct post-screening discussions. Within these spaces, we have watched as Jamaican audience members who migrated to diasporic locales like Toronto discuss, often for the first time in front of their children, what they remember of Coral Gardens and Rastafari during that earlier period, thereby creating new inter-generational forms of knowledge and reflection. Rastafari throughout Jamaica and in diaspora have tended to receive *Bad Friday* as *their* story, even if they were not yet born in 1963; and Rastafari in other parts of the Caribbean have used the film as a springboard to discuss their own experiences of persecution at the hands of the state. In South Africa, the post-screening conversations served as a platform for participants to elaborate the historical and contemporary similarities between postcolonial Jamaica (and the Caribbean more generally) and post-apartheid South Africa, and to share their strategies for ameliorating the effects of long-term state violence.

During post-screening discussions, we have also regularly been faced with questions about gender, as the majority of those narrating their experiences in the film are men. This has generated insightful discussions about the ways particular historical phenomena have affected men and women differently, and how the experiences of men and women in relation to historical events are therefore perceived differently. This should remind us of Fiona Ross's (2004) insightful study of the South African Truth and Reconciliation Commission, during which women were asked about their suffering vis-à-vis the experiences of the men in their lives, rather than as the result of their own political activism, because they were not seen by the Commission as political actors unto themselves. In this case those who were rounded up by civilians and police were – with one exception – men.[4] The one woman who appears prominently in *Bad Friday* – Empress Enid Steele – tells how she 'saved' her husband from the state's brutality, and then prematurely gave birth to their child who perished within a week. In other words, her individual actions were geared toward protecting her 'King Man', but her subsequent suffering, for Rastafari, also represented a loss to the whole of the community.

Questions about gender have also allowed us to talk about how we strove to include women's voices and feminist analytic frames in other ways. For example, we chose women to develop the meta-narrative as well as some key aspects of the music; and we decided that the elders would tell the story of what happened during and after the events at Coral Gardens without a legitimating omniscient 'talking head' narrator. This has resulted in some discrepancies between narrators, but for us these gaps allow us as producers to challenge audiences' need for a neat and fully legible accounting of events that were, at any rate, experienced as non-linear at the time. Indeed, most of the Rastafari who were rounded up did not know until they were in prison together (and sometimes even later than that) why they were being persecuted. This was largely because they were not from the immediate area of the land dispute and therefore had no contemporary understanding of the causality chain for what they were going through. For us, presenting accounts of events that sometimes seem to be contradictory – and presenting the police officer's account as just one perspective among many – reflects a feminist epistemological commitment regarding the authority of voice, and we have attempted to enact this even in the absence of a range of women interlocutors.

The post-screening discussions, therefore, have been incredibly rich and generative for us, and have shown us that the meanings of the film and its narratives also shift and transform as they become part of broader dialogues. More materially, the Public Defender's office in Jamaica has begun to pursue a reparations case based on the 'incident'. His representatives have travelled to the western parishes to take sworn testimony from elders and witnesses, and they have also gathered corroborating evidence from the dusty boxes of records in police stations and jails. Additionally, the western extension campus of the University of the West Indies in Montego Bay subsequently developed a digital archive of Coral Gardens that includes our interviews as well as testimonies from additional police and civilians who were part of or witnessed the events of that week; and the Institute of Jamaica incorporated our interviews into their recent exhibit on Rastafari. In other words, an event that was all but lost to public consciousness has within the past five years become part of the national terrain.

In part this is because the position of Rastafari vis-à-vis the Jamaican state is much changed since the early 1960s. In the early years Rastafari marked the limits of citizenship in independent Jamaica. They were seen as a threat to the consolidation of the new nation because they did not accept the authority of the Jamaican political leadership (instead seeing Africa as 'home'); they did not subscribe to capitalist economic and social development models; and they attempted to turn the normalized hierarchies of colour and class on their heads through both linguistic and ideological reconstruction. Now, Jamaica is known all over the world because of Rastafari and reggae music, and though some Rastafari maintain an opposition to political participation, newer organized groups have sought to create relationships with the state in order to advocate for their interests *within* the Jamaican polity via both local and transnational institutional fora. The scale of Rastafari's impact and critical intervention, therefore, both locally and transnationally, has intensified to the extent that elements of the community's language, worldview, and day-to-day practice have become part of the nation's performance of itself. It is Rastafari, in other words, that is largely responsible for the growth of Black pride and consciousness in Jamaica among all classes, and that has put Jamaica on the map globally, and particularly throughout the postcolonial world.

Coral Gardens has also been able to capture sympathetic public attention because we are now over 50 years on from the incident – most of the police who were directly involved have either passed on or 'repented' in one way or another; and while some of the families who were influential in the persecution of Rastafari in that area at that time are still active in the community, the general will of the population has changed. What I mean to say is that it has been possible to create this archive now because while the question of racial equality remains open-ended, significant transformations have occurred globally that no longer render Rastafari a threat to citizenship and nationalist integrity. This is not as obviously the case when we turn our lens to Tivoli Gardens.

Tivoli Gardens

On Monday, May 24, 2010, Jamaican police and military forces launched 'Operation King West', entering the community of Tivoli Gardens in West Kingston under a limited state of emergency in search of Christopher Coke. By the end of the week, Coke had not yet been found and at least 73 civilians had been killed. Despite the immediate activities of various civil society organizations such as Jamaicans for Justice and the Jamaican Civil Society Coalition, it took almost three years for the Office of the Public Defender to submit an interim report to Parliament regarding the conduct of the security forces. The Report called for a Commission of Enquiry into the conduct of the security forces during the operation, which took place between December 2014 and March 2016. This commission made a number of recommendations, including a public apology and compensation for many who lost loved ones or property, but many community members still feel they haven't been fully heard.

Beginning in early 2013, therefore, Junior, Deanne and I carried community residents into a studio where we shot still photographs and recorded their narratives. These narratives form the backbone of an installation partially organized as a triptych, with the three screens presenting a mixture of archival stills, video, and audio footage of the community, radio and television reports on the days in question, and other related material, such as the video footage from the US surveillance drone that was positioned over West Kingston on May 24.[5] Junior again composed music and created soundscapes to accompany the visual environment, and both the images and the sound move – literally – from screen to screen as suggested by the content. We sought to contextualize the narratives within a broader story – which we tell wholly through archival footage – that links together the development of political nationalism in Jamaica, US intervention throughout the region, and the drug and arms trades. The triptych is meant to suggest an altar space, drawing from its origination in early modern Christian art but transformed by the Afro-Jamaican context to evoke Revivalism, the African-derived religious practice most common to West Kingston communities as they were forming in the 1950s (a practice that was extensively researched by Edward Seaga as part of his MA thesis in Anthropology at Harvard University, work that forged the relationships he was later able to draw upon in his political career). The revival altar space also opens an opportunity to memorialize the dead and connect them to other ancestors, as well as to those who remain in the earthly world.

While *Bad Friday* had us traipsing throughout the hills to film Rastafari elders in their home spaces, 'Tivoli Stories' has us removing West Kingston residents to a studio outside their community. We have done this as part of an effort to challenge the hegemonies of visual representation in urban Caribbean spaces. For planters, travel writers, and later tourism promoters, the region has been both 'picturesque' and 'playground', 'virgin' and 'peopled', 'seductive' and 'sensational' – and all of these are terms that emerge from and reproduce gendered stereotypes.[6] These binaries reflect something of the tension between what Nicholas Mirzoeff has called 'visuality' and 'the right to look' (2011). Within his formulation, visuality develops as imperial history; it is a weapon for authority and a means of subjection to that authority. The 'right to look', on the other hand, challenges this authority and the individualism and surveillance that enable it. Our own visual work has been oriented toward challenging the expectations embedded in Mirzhoeff's reading of visuality, in this case toward creating a different kind of archive of Tivoli Gardens than that which is more generally publicly available (on YouTube, for example).

What I am referencing here is the fact that most visual representations of garrison communities – those downtown Kingston communities characterized by homogenous voting practices and a leadership structure that connects local dons to members of parliament – highlight the sensationalist dimensions of poverty and political violence, becoming a kind of 'ghetto porn'. This has had two important effects, the first of which is that the violence that occurs in these communities is seen as episodic and culturally derived rather than the result of structural and institutionalized political decisions over time. The second, related, effect is that most Kingstonians (and Jamaicans more generally) who do not live in downtown garrisons have a difficult time imagining people who do as being fully human and therefore possessing either individual and collective rights, or an imagination of an alternative future. Indeed, a phrase we commonly hear in the process of telling others in Jamaica about what we are doing, even those who have a long history of political progressivism, has been 'there are no innocents in Tivoli'. For those articulating this sentiment, the actions of the security forces during the May 2010 incursion were legitimate and necessary, not examples of extrajudicial violence. As a response to this hegemony of visual expectations, we chose to photograph those individuals who agreed to be visually represented against a stark white background. We did this in order to encourage audience members to focus on their words and their faces, to attempt to generate the mutual recognition Mirzoeff sees as essential to the 'right to look', and to the realization of its claims to political subjectivity.

The narratives community members shared tell us not only about what they experienced (which in most cases challenges official narratives about 'what happened'). They also tell us about three related aspects of their lives, and more broadly, about life in contemporary Jamaica. They say something about the everyday conditions of structural and symbolic violence that lay the foundation for the periodic eruptions of exceptional violence (and about how these are expressed through gender and status); they tell us about how extreme violence also produces the experience of time compression, which provides some windows onto the entanglements that undergird forms of structural violence; and they give us a sense of the extent to which people are able to imagine, or imagine themselves enacting, alternative political futures.

For example, young men's stories of being removed from their homes, tied to other men and ordered from place to place under terror of the gun tend to reflect the structural violence of the garrison system whereby all male youth are seen as criminals or potential criminals, and young men's options are limited to either 'legitimate' work that they can obtain through their links to a don (because these opportunities are typically generated through state contracts that flow to the community from the MP through the don), 'illegitimate' activist work for the don himself, or through self-employment, like driving a taxi or running a shop (employment that is also nevertheless typically mediated in some way by the local authority of the don). I make these points not to demonize garrison dons, but to suggest that their *leadership* is exploited by elected politicians, and therefore by a broader political system that since its inception with universal adult suffrage in 1944 has tolerated a parallel political structure. This structure has allowed elected representatives to avoid responsibility for both partisan political violence and involvement in illicit international trades in drugs and arms, and has created the illusion that we are not all complicit in these patterns. These are points also made by Anthony Harriott (2008), who argues that not only is there a partnership between those engaged in informal and illicit criminal networks and politicians, but also that 'sections of the Jamaican middle-class are a core part of the criminal-political linkage on both the PNP and JLP sides of the political divide,' and therefore have a stake in, and a responsibility for, the maintenance of the status quo (Harriott cited in Lewis 2012, 49).

What at first seems *surprising* about some of these men's narratives – though upon further reflections seems obvious – are the connections they describe having with various sectors of social and political life outside their community. One young man, for example, told us that beyond regular visits from his baby-mother and his son, what kept him afloat (materially and emotionally) during his period of 'exile' from Tivoli Gardens was the Japanese expatriate community in Kingston; because he was a 'selector' for a sound system, he had Japanese friends who looked out for him during and after the state of emergency. His everyday, then, included transnational networks of young Japanese men and women who travelled to Jamaica to participate in the very popular cultural practices that are often derided locally, both by those committed to a particular notion of respectable citizenship, *and* by those professing a more Marxist point of view and who therefore see popular cultural practices as distracting to the larger project of socio-political liberation. Yet participation in the spheres of popular culture and other forms of cultural production, while central to several men's broader strategies of negotiation and healing, individually and collectively, also indexes a gendered structural dynamic that invites us to question who has links to the world beyond the garrison, how these links are developed and elaborated, and how this world is strategically mobilized in different ways by women and men.

Indeed, what has been clear in many of the women's narratives of the state of emergency is that women rely on men, principally baby fathers but also sons and brothers, as breadwinners, and their sudden absence (or the sudden inability to attract them) renders their situations intensely precarious. Of course, feminist researchers have argued these points for decades, and what we are confirming with this archive is that the loss of men in the community is not only, and sometimes not even primarily, reckoned through affective expressions but also reflected through a complex intertwining of emotional and financial mourning and lamentation, which reminds us that one of the structural realities for women within poor communities in Jamaica is that their ability to attract a man is never merely about love and desire.

The narratives of these community residents also tell us something about structural variation within garrison communities, communities that are most regularly discussed as if they are homogenous. This kind of variation, as well as the ties community members maintain to other communities both within Kingston and throughout the country, challenge the flattening that happens within both policy-oriented and popular discourse. Why is this important? Policymaking pivots on the idea that these are monolithic 'communities' defined by a cultural 'orientation' that is unassimilable to the normative mainstream. In Jamaica, this orientation is articulated through the discursive framework of a 'culture of violence' one that is seen to have emerged as the result of historical experiences of slavery, colonialism and clientalistic partisan politics.[7] In the US, on the other hand, it is usually expressed in relation to a so-called 'culture of poverty',[8] there the result of de-industrialization and Black middle-class flight from inner cities (Wilson 1987). In both cases, the purported cultural difference is seen to reflect a lack of social ties to the world beyond the ghetto or the garrison. John Jackson (2001) has shown us that within the US context, it is decidedly not the case that inner city African-Americans live in a cordoned off world; instead they negotiate their own marginalized position vis-à-vis affective and material ties to other classed experiences, networks and forms of sociability. Similarly, in Jamaica, it has long been shown that urban dwellers maintain important ties to both rural areas and transnational sociocultural spheres through the circulation of food, children, and capital. A politics that rests upon a monolithic, homogenous view of garrison residents, therefore, is impoverished and ultimately ineffective because it misses people's already-existing intimate networks and therefore compresses them spatially.

Another form of compression is evident throughout the narratives we have been recording, and this is a form that exposes the complex connections among global political economy, cultural practice, and psychic internalities not as context or history but as producing alternative temporal realities. Here, the past lives in the present but not through linear causality or cyclical repetition. Instead, what the narratives show us is that time – during exceptional moments – is experienced as 'out of joint' (Derrida 1994) not just because it is multi-directional, nor merely because it reflects the multiple entanglements and palimpsests (Alexander 2005) of events and experiences that, as they layer on top of each other, create the conditions for the haunting of the present. What this archive shows, instead, is that the kinds of 'bare life' that are produced through and within exceptional moments suspends the possibility of both linear and cyclical time, and time becomes experienced instead as simultaneous – all killings bleed into each other, all become parts of one immediate story. An approach to temporality that takes seriously this sense of simultaneity – what physicists would call quantum entanglement, or what neurologists would see as non-unitary versions of time – would rescue it from the hegemony of liberalism (and its political teleologies of progressive time), and would untether it from popular and scientific notions of evolution. Understanding the experience of time in exceptional moments as multiple and simultaneous instead opens alternative analytic spaces – feminist relational epistemologies – within which we more clearly see the entanglements that matter in the world. The entanglements I am speaking of here have to do with the international trades in drugs and arms, the emergence and strengthening of the geopolitical dominance of the US throughout the twentieth century, patron-clientelistic political relations, corruption and racial and gendered motivated disenfranchisement.

Incidentally, while gender has been an obvious analytic tool in our production and use of the narratives we have been collecting, explicit discussions of race seem absent from them, and therefore from the broader context in which they are developed and told. However, if we look more closely raciality remains an organizing principle for the experiences community members have shared.[9] For instance, one young man shared a story about the police forcing him and others to dance and sing as if they were at *passa passa*.[10] As we were recording him, I cringed at this point because what immediately came to mind were the images of slaves during the Middle Passage being brought up from the ship's hold to dance and drum for traders concerned with keeping them fit in order to garner a good price at their New World ports of embarcation. Or consider how one woman, a lifelong resident of Tivoli Gardens whose sister was one of two women killed during the incursion, answered our question about what she thought of the impending Commission of Enquiry. She stated that an Enquiry could not possibly compensate people for lives lost or provide comfort in the long process of mourning, and then added, in passing, that she herself went to a grief seminar where she mentioned that she took comfort in the police killing of Mr Keith Clarke in an uptown community after the beginning of the state of emergency. This was because, 'if it never happen outside of Tivoli Garden, nobody wouldn't believe' that the security forces were capable of killing citizens in this manner.

Keith Clarke was an upper St Andrew businessman (accountant) and brother of former PNP minister Claude Clarke, who was killed on May 27, 2010 by the security forces in front of his wife and daughter in the middle of the night. Clarke, who was shot 21 times (16 in the back, suggesting automatic gunfire), was thought to be harbouring Coke, with whom he had close ties and who also had ties to another prominent businessman who lived nearby. There was intense public uproar over Clarke's murder, happening as it did to a member of a prominent family in a wealthy 'uptown' neighbourhood. In July 2012, the Director of Public Prosecutions ruled that three soldiers would be tried for Clarke's murder. The trial date was postponed several times, yet the family has sued the government for $18 million (about US$160,000) in special damages. By comparison, former Public Defender Earl Witter's Interim Report on the 2010 State of Emergency was not released until April 2013 (Witter 2013), and the Enquiry – which had been opposed by many prominent persons, including the former JLP Prime Minister – began in December 2014.[11] For this woman, it was important that the police and military would have acted 'uptown' in the same manner in which they did 'downtown', in order to give people a taste, as it were, of what it is like to live everyday with the distinctions that have structured Jamaica's socio-political worlds. That these distinctions are no longer reckoned strictly along colour lines but instead are mobilized in relation to education, occupation, area of residence, participation in certain forms of cultural practice, and notions of respectability do not mean that they are not still apprehended and experienced as racialized.

Finally, and only very briefly, let me mention one of the most striking patterns within the narratives we have been archiving, and this is the fact that with only one exception, community members do not say Christopher Coke's name. They refer to him as 'that man', 'the man they were looking for', and 'the one they wanted to extradite'. Now, it is important to remember that the context in which we are developing aural and visual archives with Tivoli Gardens Community members is one that is still very much in the thick of things. This is evident through the clear parameters we have been given (by community members themselves, who have been negotiating dual power structures – that of the state and that of the Coke family). There are parameters for what can and cannot be asked and what community residents should or should not say (or what we were asked to edit out if they do), in order for everybody (including ourselves) to remain safe. By this logic, saying his name out loud positions one as a loyalist, potentially disrespecting other Coke family members who are currently struggling for power within the community. We might think of this in relation to the sorts of projects and processes that, like certain other histories, resist archivization (Ellis 2015).

But we feel that this phenomenon is also related to a broader structural issue within garrison communities that has to do with a narrowing of political imagination; when we first began recording community members' narratives, they seemed unable to envision different political futures. When we asked them what they thought could and should happen to change their situations, beyond the Commission of Enquiry (about which most community members were sceptical), they seemed unable to articulate any kind of transformative programme, instead leaving it obliquely up to the next generation. This was not striking because we wanted them to have an emancipatory political vision, or because we were looking for them to be the vanguard of 'resistance'. It is striking because it constituted the single biggest difference between the archive we created about the Coral Gardens 'incident' and this one. Those Rastafari elders who were humiliated and tortured by police and civilians in April 1963 could find strength in a worldview that positioned them as already possessing the tools of their own freedom – physically and psychologically – as part of a redemptive transnational struggle against racial degradation and white imperial supremacy. The political and spiritual worlds of the garrison, on the other hand, are considerably more circumscribed, despite some community members' transnational family networks and most Jamaicans' access to all things American. What we have been trying to think through is how the complex calculus between loyalty and benefits (both financial and juridical) seems to have generated a socio-political sphere in which imagination beyond the localities of the here and now is exceedingly difficult.

Conclusion

What the visual archives I have participated in generating illuminate are the entanglements that produce both the exclusions perpetuated through liberal rule, and the strategies through which these exclusions are reproduced. We were not striving for closure or a clear blow-by-blow accounting of events and blame, but were instead seeking to be attuned to the non-monumental, unspectacular world of the everyday, even as this world was being illuminated in the aftermath of spectacularly violent events. This kind of an emphasis on what the routine and unmelodramatic repetitions of daily life (Das 2007; Taylor 2003), also informs many of the scholars interpreting photographic documentation within intimate, quotidian spheres (Campt 2017), as well as the body of scholarship on intimacy and the everyday, or what Kathleen Stewart terms 'ordinary affects' (2007). It is a perspective that exposes what Beth Povinelli has deemed the 'ordinary, chronic, and cruddy' nature of suffering, as well as the ways these forms of suffering constitute the common sense of other people's 'good life' (2011, 4), and in doing so it forces us also to address the geography of complicity and accountability. This is why, for me, the narratives of trauma and state violence we have generated are best envisioned as a form of archival repair. Open-ended and profoundly experiential, they shed light not only on the present of the 'event', but also on the simmering foundation of its priors and on the potentialities of its posts. In other words, assembling archives of violence has the power to produce an affective transformation by 'presencing' the historical political economy of institutionalized marginalization while at the same time cracking a window through which we might recognize each other and collaborate to build a common future.

Notes

1. 'Don' is the term used in Jamaica to denote the local leader – often connected to the international trades in arms and drugs – of what are locally known as garrison communities. Garrisons are homogenous voting communities in downtown Kingston where state benefits flow to the community from the Member of Parliament through the don, who then guarantees votes and election-era party activism.
2. In *The Promised Key*, Leonard Howell (2007[1935]) introduces 'Babylon' as another name for Rome.
3. On the shifts in practice and consciousness from the late 1980s and the new centrality of international 'trods', see Homiak 1990, 1999. For the critical role of Rastafari in youth pedagogy, see Niaah 2005.
4. There was one woman who was arrested with her husband, but she died during the 1990s and we were unable therefore to interview her. We also heard recorded testimony from another woman about what she experienced, but she had also passed on by the time we began work on the film.
5. This installation opened at the Penn Museum in November 2017, and will remain on view until December 2019.
6. See Sheller 2002; Thompson 2006.
7. Thomas 2011; Patterson 1967, Gray 1991, 2004.
8. Lewis 1965, but see Stack 1974 for a critique of this position.
9. Nicole Fleetwood and Alessandra Raengo have both written about the question of the ontology of race vis-à-vis visuality in asking what it means to see blackness. Their discussions inform my brief points here (Fleetwood 2011; Raengo 2013).

10. Before the 'incursion', an internationally known and attended weekly street dance.
11. According to Witter's report, however, 1,295 complaints from 688 West Kingston complainants were documented, and he quantified their claims at $110,806,705.00 (about US$981,000); payouts had already been made in the amount of 92,100,000 (about US$816,000) by the Ministry of Labour and Social Security at the insistence of the Social Development Commission, and this amount includes $4,327,000 (about US$39,000) to assistant with the funeral expenses of 46 of the deceased.

References

Alexander, M. Jacqui. 2005. *Pedagogies of Crossing: Meditations on Feminism, Sexual Politics, Memory and the Sacred.* Durham, NC: Duke University Press.
Bell, Wendell. 1964. *Jamaican Leaders: Political Attitudes in a New Nation.* Berkeley: University of California Press.
Bogues, Anthony. 2003. *Black Heretics, Black Prophets: Radical Political Intellectuals.* New York: Routledge.
Campt, Tina M. 2017. *Listening to Images.* Durham, NC: Duke University Press.
Das, Veena. 2007. *Life and Words: Violence and the Descent into the Ordinary.* Berkeley: University of California Press.
Derrida, Jacques. 1994. *Spectres of Marx: The State of the Debt, the Work of Mourning, and the New International.* New York: Routledge.
Ellis, Nadia. 2015. *Territories of the Soul: Queered Belonging in the Black Diaspora.* Durham, NC: Duke University Press.
Fleetwood, Nicole. 2011. *Troubling Vision: Performance, Visuality and Blackness.* Chicago: University of Chicago Press.
Gray, Obika. 1991. *Radicalism and Social Change in Jamaica, 1960–1972.* Knoxville: University of Texas Press.
———. 2004. *Demeaned but Empowered: The Social Power of the Urban Poor in Jamaica.* Kingston: University of the West Indies Press.
Harriott, Anthony. 2008. *Organised Crime and Politics in Jamaica: Breaking the Nexus.* Kingston: Canoe Press.
Hartman, Saidiya. 2008. Venus in Two Acts. *Small Axe* 12, no. 2: 1–14.
Homiak, John P. 1990. From Yard to Nation: Rastafari and the Politics of Eldership at Home and Abroad. In *Ay Bobo: African-Caribbean Religions*, ed. Manfred Kremser, 49–76. Vienna: Institut Für Völkerkunde der Universität Wien.
———. 1999. Movements of Jah People: From Soundscapes to Mediascape. In *Religion, Diaspora, and Cultural Identity: A Reader in the Anglophone Caribbean*, ed. John W. Pulis, 87–123. London: Gordon and Breach Publishers.
Jackson, John. 2001. *Harlemworld: Doing Race and Class in Contemporary America.* Chicago: University of Chicago Press.
Lacey, Terry. 1977. *Violence and Politics in Jamaica, 1960–1970: Internal Security in a Developing Country.* Totowa, NJ: Frank Cass and Company.
Lewis, Oscar. 1965. *La Vida: A Puerto Rican Family in the Culture of Poverty – San Juan and New York.* New York: Random House.

Lewis, Rupert. 2012. Party Politics in Jamaica and the Extradition of Christopher 'Dudus' Coke. *Global South* 6, no. 1:38–54.
Maragh, G. G. (Leonard Howell). 2007[1935]. *The Promised Key.* N.p.: Forgotten Books.
Mbembe, Achille. 2002. African Modes of Self Writing. *Public Culture* 14, no. 1:239–73.
Mirzoeff, Nicholas. 2011. *The Right to Look: A Counterhistory of Visuality.* Durham, NC: Duke University Press.
Nettleford, Rex. 1970. *Mirror, Mirror: Identity, Race and Protest in Jamaica.* Kingston: William Collins and Sangster Ltd.
Niaah, Jalani. 2005. Sensitive Scholarship: A Review of Rastafari Literature(s). *Caribbean Quarterly* 51, no. 3–4:11–34.
Patterson, Orlando. 1967. *The Sociology of Slavery: An Analysis of the Origins, Development, and Structure of Negro Slave Society in Jamaica.* Vancouver: Fairleigh Dickinson University Press.
Povinelli, Elizabeth. 2011. *Economies of Abandonment: Social Belonging and Endurance.* Durham, NC: Duke University Press.
Raengo, Alessandra. 2013. *On the Sleeve of the Visual: Race as Face Value.* Hanover, NH: Dartmouth University Press.
Report of the Commission of Enquiry, Appointed to Enquire into Events which Occurred in Western Kingston and Related Areas in May 2010. June 2016. Government of Jamaica.
Ross, Fiona. 2003. *Bearing Witness: Women and the Truth and Reconciliation Commission in South Africa.* London: Pluto Press.
Sheller, Mimi. 2002. *Consuming the Caribbean: From Arawaks to Zombies.* New York: Routledge.
Stack, Carol. 1974. *All Our Kin: Strategies for Survival in a Black Community.* New York: Basic Books.
Stewart, Kathleen. 2007. *Ordinary Affects.* Durham, NC: Duke University Press.
Taylor, Diana. 2003. *The Archive and the Repertoire: Performing Cultural Memory in the Americas.* Durham, NC: Duke University Press.
Thomas, Deborah A. 2011. *Exceptional Violence: Embodied Citizenship in Transnational Jamaica.* Durham, NC: Duke University Press.
Thompson, Krista. 2006. *An Eye for the Tropics: Tourism, Photography, and Framing the Caribbean Picturesque.* Durham, NC: Duke University Press.
Trouillot, Michel Rolph. 1995. *Silencing the Past: Power and the Production of History.* Boston: Beacon.
Wilson, William Julius. 1987. *The Truly Disadvantaged: The Inner City, the Underclass, and Public Policy.* Chicago: University of Chicago Press.
Witter, Errol. 2013. Public Defender in his Interim Report to Parliament (Concerning Investigations into the Conduct of the Security Forces during the State of Emergency Declared May, 2010).

21. Decoding the Image as Method for Researching Culture

Patricia Mohammed

All images, whether printed, painted, sketched, digitized or sculpted contain, apart from the image maker's imaginative originality, precise visual codes. Some of these codes are consistent with the conventions of the format and methods used in making the image; others are more generic to reading pictures. Some of these codes are culturally specific but in the matter of images there are many shared visual codes that are being presented. If we apply an historical lens when reading images, we can also read not just laterally but horizontally to understand how visual codes take root and are challenged or elaborated over time. The value of learning to read the image is that we have another prism through which we may understand the intricate processes by which society, perception and identity are continuously being managed, and how in doing so the maker of images has the power to perpetuate hierarchies of beauty and morality as an embodiment of aesthetics. The stereotypes of gender, class and race – the unholy trinity that defines the social structure – may be revealed through the careful and informed reading of the image along with other subterranean ideas that might only surface through a visual rather than primarily textual rendition. A good example of the latter might be to consider one of the well-known and often cited images produced by William Blake.

Blake had begun his training as an artist apprenticed to an engraver and such was his skill at copying other artist's work through this method of reproduction, that he became commercially successful at his trade. However, Blake's talent was not to lie in his reproduction of other artists' vision but in the uniqueness of his own. While many of Blake's celebrated drawings and sketches are imaginative and visionary, this one bore the stamp of the literal. It records faithfully Stedman's account from observation. Stedman described the event in order to *inspire the most unfeeling reader with horror and resentment...a beautiful Samboe girl of about eighteen, tied up by both arms to a tree, as naked as she came into the world, and lacerated in such a shocking manner by the whips of two negro-drivers, that she was from her neck to her ancles literally dyed over with blood. It was after she had received two hundred lashes that I perceived her, with her head hanging downwards, a most affecting spectacle...Upon investigating the cause of this matchless barbarity, I was credibly informed, that her only crime consisted in firmly refusing to submit to the loathsome embraces of her detestable executioner. Prompted by his jealousy and revenge, he called this the punishment of disobedience, and she was thus flead alive* (Campbell Fine Art, 2009).

Figure 1: 'Flagellation of a Female Samboe Slave' William Blake c. 1791

Engraving with etching by William Blake, as published in *Narrative, of a Five Years' Expedition, Against the Revolted Negroes of Surinam*, by Captain J.G. Stedman (J.Johnson & J.Edwards, London, 1796).

It was thought that the brutality of the treatment of enslaved Africans described in Stedman's book influenced William Blake's views on slavery. Blake had been working on the engravings for this book during the year 1791 and later went on to express his own anti-slavery position in *Visions of the daughters of Albion* of 1793, a body of work that is subversive for its themes of sex and oppression. In addition, Blake adapted figures which he had used in the Suriname engravings for the illustrations to his famous *America*, also of that year. In 2007 Blake was selected by various galleries in Britain to represent the artist who had presented daring ideas of freedom and equality from the eighteenth century onwards and who had influenced the sentiments against slavery (Cumming 2007). His work needs therefore to be understood in context. He was both a poet and an illustrator and the blended forms of expression that he then selected in a pre-photography period to emotively connect to the viewer complemented each other. His drawings remain central in the visual discourses around slavery and equality to this day. Once the context of the production of the image, the format and the perspective of the image maker is recognized, the drawing itself becomes a historical passage in the text of slavery. The clothed gentlemen represent those with power, over both the whipped and the whippers themselves who are reduced to diminutive characters at the background. The tree is as significant as the female slave in this engraving. In Britain, death by hanging was the principal form of capital punishment from Anglo-Saxon times and a tree was the earliest form of gallows. This offered both a spectacle for morbid onlookers as well as a lesson to deter those who would commit crimes. The tree therefore becomes a visual signifier of conventions of brutality that Blake confronted in this image.

Clichés have to be dispensed with when we decipher the image. If a 'picture tells a thousand words', what do we need to extract from the messages encoded in the pen, paintbrush or light angles of the camera, from the props that balance the composition, from the traditions that guide or inspire the maker of the image and from the constraints or possibilities afforded by the materials selected by the artist? That we are blessed with vision does not necessarily mean we are also gifted with the natural power to pick up the clues in an image or to even comprehend the image as data. I have realized over the years of working with different formats of image making, including film, that there are vast differences in the way in which each individual approaches an image. It might be a colour that appeals and summons up a memory, or an object that takes their fancy. Some might have a narrative approach, looking at the story being told, rather than critically engaging with the medium that is chosen to tell this story. All of these are legitimate ways of reading an image. The main thing is that one must be predisposed to learning to look at the image, not unlike the way that we also learn to interpret the layers of a text. There are references within an image to past conventions that like any research must be appreciated to grasp the visual morse code that is being transmitted.

In the reading of Caribbean images in particular, the postcolonial construction of identity and place in the world has most influenced our understanding of Caribbean culture in past and present processes of globalization. The invention of the region from 'discovery' to 'independence', the currency by which nations negotiate with each other, and by which people negotiate privileges within, are all manifested in the visual products of culture. As James Ryan comments in *Picturing Empire* (1997), visual definition was a key way in which the Empire was 'fashioned, maintained and extended…imperialism involved not only territorial acquisition, political ambition and economic interests, but also cultural formations, attitudes, beliefs and practices.' Mimi Scheller (2003) underscores the innocent indulgence in the pleasures of thoughtless consumption of this region over many centuries as a result of its history of colonial exploitation. Krista Thompson in *An Eye for the Tropics* (2006, 392) demonstrates from an evaluation of the aesthetics of the tropicalized images of Jamaica and the Bahamas through western eyes, how such representations created to project an image to the outside world, altered everyday life on the islands themselves, producing stereotypes which were expected of the outsider as representations of self, a tendency particularly evident in the tourism industry of dance performance and tourist art and craft.

Thus a visual text has its own grammar and references that can be marshalled to decode the image. In an examination of the visual text we are engaged in the process of decrypting the inherent or unintended meanings of the image-maker. How might contemporary visual interpretations unfold hidden passages and textures of the past that have not come to light, and equally how may we, the scholars in gender, history or art, guard against reinforcing the selfsame stereotypes in the present by encoding other meanings? What is to be gained from enhancing our visual intelligence? This then becomes part of the challenge in engaging in the deconstruction of visual text.

The idea of reading gendered messages from the image emerged initially from a search for the data of gender in history. I found that gender recurred or surfaced in history as metaphor rather than as concrete causality, fact or even subject worthy of analysis. The visual recorders of events or landscapes, while not possessing the gender consciousness that has currency today, were by no means indifferent to the people whom they encountered. The possibility of examining the meaning of gender through painting, for instance, occurred to me many years ago when I looked at an exhibition of Agostino Brunias's paintings on loan to the Barbados Museum, many of which contained images of men and women. 'These pictures of...faces are small miracles, like stills snipped from a lost film of the past. Although they seem to speak in a whisper they are revolutionary. They teach a new and radical way of seeing.' (Graham-Dixon 1996, 63).[1] To demonstrate this epiphanic moment of recognition let me employ one of these paintings to illustrate the point.

Works of art create fictions (or may be crafted from fiction) from which visual metaphors are fashioned. In reading pictures of the Caribbean in the absence of a cohesive literature on visual iconography or visual semantics, the methods I apply are varied. Visual perception which amounts to visual thinking requires connecting dots between sight data and textual references, employing a set of correspondences that the images bring to mind. This is conjoined with the intention in reading the image. In relation to this image, I am interested in the concepts of beauty as these emerged as both racialized and gendered in the eighteenth century and simultaneously, how the picturesqueness of the Caribbean was being constructed. The significance of Caribbean new world culture is its complete interlocution with philosophies, fictions, religions, languages and other art conventions of the old worlds of Europe, Africa and Asia from which populations of the Caribbean were drawn. To decode these we must continue to treat such visual texts, building on theoretical insights from Mikhail Bakhtin's[2] method of reading, as a dialogic work that carries on a continual conversation with its source.

Figure 2: Agostino Brunias: *A Negro Festival in the Island of St Vincent.* Lithograph of Original Oil on Canvas, (painted between 1773 and 1796).

Source: Print Courtesy National Library of Jamaica

As a point of entry one can begin with what was once accepted as the ideal of beauty in the West. Amelia Jones (2002, 218) argues that:

> In the history of Western art and the most dominant kinds of aesthetic judgement, the naked white female body has long been staged as the most consistent (if contentious and highly charged) trope of aesthetic beauty as exemplified by Edmund Burke's *A Philosophical Inquiry into the Origin of our Ideas of the Sublime and the Beautiful*... (and in) bestsellers such as Kenneth Clark's book *The Nude: A Study of Ideal Art*...the female nude is understood to articulate fully 'the alchemic powers of art' to transform through beauty.

The region's picturesqueness and beauty begins with a series of binary oppositions – a presentation of the female and counter-point male body and the elements of a landscape and climate that allowed for freedoms of bared flesh all year round. The comparative beauty found in the nakedness of the white and Black female is underplayed in the polite painting that is introduced in Figure 2, although several other paintings by Agostino Brunias do, in fact, play on this theme of clothed versus nakedness of femininity (see Figure 3 as one example). Dancing bodies, and opposing Black and white couples, form one of the earliest constructs of the picturesque gendered images in the Caribbean. Figure 2, a painting by Agostino Brunias entitled 'A Negro Festival in the Island of St Vincent' was executed between 1773 and 1796. Brunias was an Italian-born and both Italian- and British-trained painter who was retained as a 'court artist' by Sir William Young on the latter's appointment as first Governor of Dominica. Brunias is also the first European painter in the region that we know of to have painted *en plein air* (in front of the subject), in the islands. The majority of the previous works we have of the period of early colonization from the fifteenth to the eighteenth centuries, including maps and sketches, suggest imaginary or reported scenes executed by sailors, explorers, artists, tradesmen, planters, and government officials from Europe.

In this oil painting, the viewer stands as if in the foreground, onlookers, joining the spectators in the background of the scene. Two dancing couples dominate the canvas. We barely observe the two men, although the contrast between them is immediate, as is that between the two fore-grounded women and the male drummer at the left forefront whose beat inspires the motion of the dancers. There is a comparison being made between the white and Black women who are placed centre stage on this dance floor. Formal compositions of painting in general and image making in particular usually draw the viewer's attention to focal point through the placement of the objects and precision of light flows on the surface and the activity and angles that send our eyes in the desired direction. That we are drawn primarily to the two women and to the comparison between them is not accidental. Their head and shoulder positions are replicated, possibly derived from the working method of the artist who sketched from one model and then varied the composition by juxtaposing bodies in changed settings, adjusting minor features such as height and skin colour, costumes and activity. In this painting the lighter-skinned woman is taller, more elegantly dressed as conveyed in the trimmings of her hat, the graceful folds of her dress fabric. To her left, the darker-skinned woman is shorter and wears brighter island colours as contrasted against the pastel whites of the other, and more than likely barefooted like her partner, although her feet are not visible in the image. The unshod Black dancers compared to the shod male and female already signifies a primary marker of difference in status, wealth and assumed level of 'civilization' according to the hierarchical codes of culture. All the other characters are reduced proportionately in size so that ultimately, the fair-skinned couple is the tallest, and their facial features most prominent in this composition. It is as if they are the surveyed, the focus of both the artist as well as have the attention of the crowd and thus ourselves, the viewers outside of the picture plane. Are the white couple, the planter and his wife, who through *noblesse oblige* join in this festival, the first image of white tourists slumming with the natives?

The opposition of Black and white, of highbrow and low culture is sustained by the cheerier colours of the workers as opposed to softer tones of the European, of carefree dancing under warm tropical skies, where dancers are refreshed by tropical fruit from sugary plantations. All of these had already by the eighteenth century come to signify pleasures available in the Caribbean. Brunias's paintings were being exhibited in London and sold to planters of the region and other collectors in Europe who were captured by the difference these paintings represented of landscapes with temperate vegetation and 'native' scenes. Here the dance setting, though consistent with the folksy fairground or outdoor maypole dancers of Europe, are nonetheless geographically identified through the prominent palm or coconut tree that signified these climes: the adjacent fields and outdoor setting is tropical and admits to the warmth of the day or the night, for the painter is neither specific about the 'festival' or the time, except that the shortened shadows cast by the dancer suggest an overhead source of light and the sunlit skies in the distance denotes a day-lit sky. The female fruit-seller to the right of the dancers with her array of pineapple and other tropical fruit, the shirtless drummer on the left whose gaze can be followed to rest on the white couple, all lead to a set of metaphors that Brunias's paintings begin to set up as gendered, racialized and class differences that populate the Caribbean picturesque. We do not have a glimpse of huts occupied by the enslaved population, and although this is painted during the system of slavery, the 'natives' here are obviously well fed and enjoying themselves.

These unproblematic representations of power dynamics and relations of race, class, and gender are a constant set of references that we have come to read from paintings by Agostino Brunias. That the artist selected such compositions and subject matter may be derived from his classical training in Italy where a structured composition would feature perspective, depth, and some imaginative contribution to the content. It was thought that Brunias often grafted details, figures and even whole groups from one composition to another, even when they purported to represent different communities from separate islands.[3] This must be coupled with the artist's idiosyncratic preoccupation and interest in the new lands leading him to depict a sentimentalized narrative of what he encountered. It may be that he was commissioned to depict such interpretations of the colonies by his patrons who needed to demonstrate the harmonies of race relations in the Caribbean despite the bad press of slavery. It might also be construed that he encountered such events in which master and enslaved enjoyed the festivities occasioned by harvests or other ritual traditions. By this time abolitionist propaganda had already sounded the knell that would eventually bring the slave trade to an end. We can only surmise. Brunias was himself obviously captured by the space and, not unlike the twentieth century cliché of the anthropologist who goes 'native', he elected to return to the region after he and Sir William Young were repatriated to Britain, continuing to live for the rest of his life in the island of Dominica[4] where he is said to be buried.

In many of Brunias's paintings, Black bodies are configured in poses of serving or deference as is again seen in Figures 3 *The Barbados Mulatto Girl*, and 4 *The West India Serving Girl*. In Figure 4, Brunias has placed the Black woman as a servant to the mulatto and white. Although she is the subject of this painting and positioned centrally on the canvas, the lightest-skinned woman imperceptibly invites the first enquiring gaze. The flattened features of the serving girl do not allow us to examine her feelings or emotions in this narrative other than as the present yet invisible character, not unlike the roles held by many Blacks in early North American films. Our eyes turn to the right of the painting, to the woman who thus represents the top of the hierarchy. She occupies the most illuminated space of the canvas where her expression and posture are most clearly discernible. One of the reasons that the artist was able to depict white bodies and faces with more accuracy is that oil paints and colour skin pigments had not yet mastered the colour harmonies to create illusions of depth that did justice to dark-skinned persons. Thus in many paintings from the fifteenth century onwards apart from their secondary status generally within the scene being depicted, the features and skin colours of Blacks were generally not as well defined.[5]

Figure 3: *The Barbados Mulatto Girl*, **Agostino Brunias.**

Source: Print Courtesy The National Library of Jamaica.

Figure 4: *The West India Serving Woman,* Agostino Brunias.

Source: A print courtesy The National Library of Jamaica.

Slightly lower and to the left of the canvas's plane in Figure 4, the mulatto woman represents the second tier, her head tie is shorter, less elaborate, her seated position is less confident and assured. She is in a servile position, arrested in a moment of readiness to uproot herself, not in a relaxed space with an equal counterpart. She does not need the accoutrement of a fan to deal with the weather as she is supposed to have been acclimatized through birth. Her face is in profile, again a device of painting tradition to identify the secondary importance of the character in the narrative of the painting. The black skin colour of the serving woman by contrast appears to absorb physical form. This more featureless representation, one can argue, also serves to diminish the multiple roles which Black women performed as workers, mothers, wives, and as equally desired sexual partners. The majority of Brunias's paintings are poetic/romantic/expressive examples of social differentiation on the West Indian population, encouraging the popular lure and allure which the Caribbean held, as a space of innocence, simplicity, fertility, and abundance.

If white and Black women and men were demographically more present and thus more represented in images, Asian women of Indian, Chinese, and Indonesian descent remained virtually absent until the nineteenth century when these migrant populations arrived. But by the later nineteenth and early twentieth century, the improvements in travel, postal services and photography had allowed new and cheaper ways in which the picturesque could be defined in postcards and in illustrated travel books. The bejewelled East Indian female was concocted as an 'exotic' other, the woman protected within the patrilocal family and decorated with the family jewels as this illustrated wealth and well being in one example shown in Figure 5. In the midst of this deliberately composed scene, a young child crawls in

Figure 5: Hand Coloured Postcard Trinidad, East Indian Women, circa 1890.

Courtesy J. Chin Aleong, Trinidad.

the forefront near the feet of the woman to the far left, barely visible but serving as a reminder of the substantive roles that these women occupied as mother and homemaker. Such images were accompanied by a fairly extensive literature which both deconstructs the stereotype of East Indian women as well as inscribes East Indian femininity as the victim of a strident and violent masculinity.[6] Many other images of Indian women and men were to emerge in the landscape to offset the earlier stereotypes that surfaced as iconic, just as those of white and Black women laid down by Brunias established the primary visual font from which Black and white femininities would be configured.

Iconography and the Elements of a Visual Grammar

The decoder of images must be armed with a visual grammar, the structural rules that inform the reading of the image as well as the language that conveys the feeling, emotions and meanings that these signify. In reading the image one must learn to both recognize and unpack the iconic. One expects to see in the Caribbean coconut trees, trunks elegantly curved by the wind and swaying palm leaves, on a beach front. But string a hammock across two coconut trunks, place a young female in scanty beachwear, heighten the colours of the sea to a sparkling ultramarine and put this on a cable television advertisement to the strains of Bob Marley's 'One Love' and it transports an iconic message of the Caribbean as a place of sun, sand, sea and, of course, the unstated hedonistic sensuality which all such visual messages convey. It is not that this reading of the pleasurable or desirable Caribbean is untrue, but rather that they have come to denote an assemblage of iconic images of a once-leisured colonial existence, the presumed early sexual heathenism/hedonism of the region, the obvious attractions of sun over snow, heat over cold, and the transportation of the idea of heaven through a reflected blue of a clear sky unfettered by threatening gray clouds.

'While, by definition, all art history translates the visual into the verbal, the iconographic approach consciously sought to conceptualize pictures as encoded texts to be deciphered by those cognizant of the culture as a whole in which they were produced,' an approach systematically formulated by Erwin Panofsky. Panofsky distinguished between the former use, as simple resonance or what it signifies or reminds one of, to iconography in the narrower sense expanded to a more complex meaning, that of the 'identification of conventional, consciously inscribed symbols, say a lamb signifying Christ'. This must also be separated from iconology, a deeper probe 'excavating an intrinsic meaning of the work of art by ascertaining those underlying principles which reveal the basic attitude of a nation, a period, a class, a religious or philosophical persuasion' (Cosgrove and Daniels, 1988, 2), although again these ideas are clearly not absent when we explore iconographic resonances in the creation of a visual grammar. For instance, in the iconography of Christian motifs how and why did the lamb come to signify Christ? Who or what shapes the meaning of the icon needs also to be considered, not just that it exists as a universalized meaning. For instance, if we look at Figure 6 without the caption we might wonder where this is located, and which century?

What other visual grammars does it possess other than place and time. I have used this image (figure 6) to pursue the iconography of the hammock in *Imaging the Caribbean: Culture and Visual Translation* (Mohammed 2010), looking at the origins of the word hammaca which was one of the objects drawn by Gonzalo Fernandez de Oviedo in his *Natural History of the West Indies* published in 1526. Oviedo marvelled at the materials in which it was made and its functional use as a portable bed for indigenous migrant groups in the region. Yet the transposition of this word in our current vocabulary denotes a mental picture association with leisure and relaxation.

Figure 6: Two Women Seated in Hammock in Trinidad, circa 2003.

Photo by Author.

Clearly there are fundamental rules that apply in reading images. What is the format or type of image, who produced it, and under what circumstances was it produced? Was it commissioned for a particular reason or the independent work of an artist? What social or political imperatives would still influence the artist, and depending on the period in which the work is executed, what styles influence the image? It is important to establish the provenance of an image so that we do not take details out of context either temporally or spatially. Is the image a particularly historicized or politicized one, and what is the purpose of reading the image? What are the materials used and how has the image-maker manipulated or employed the form to achieve an effect? When a selection of images is being read against the other, why were these images chosen and what is the purpose of the critical examination of the selection? What information does this confer to the viewer and what is the location of the viewer in reading the image? Are they within the discipline and situated or belong to the same geographical space from which it was produced?

There are other very fundamental considerations in reading images and using them in printed or published material, the latter is, in fact, currently one of the most problematic of the issues that the user confronts. Is the image copyright restricted and what permissions are required? From whom must permission be sought? The tedious, although admittedly legitimate question of access and copyright permissions, is something that every researcher needs to verify before use.

Finally, what is the partiality and positioning of the reader of the image? One of the first concerns that academic disciplines used to positivist methods raise is that the viewer is always subjective. The assumption is that reading an image also relies on affect or our emotional response to the painting or image. While this may have posed a major problem two or even one decade ago, the sheer proliferation of the image in both moving and still forms, the revolution in digital technologies that is transforming perception of reality in accelerated time, has forced the academy to make sense of this visual world. The contemporary emergence of *affect* as a legitimate perspective through which we can better understand the social world provides good underpinning support for the individual perspectives that any reader brings to an image. It is precisely the idiosyncratic difference based on visual sensibilities, disciplinary training or passionate involvement with the subject over another that gives rise to the new passages in an ongoing narrative of discovering truths and transforming knowledge, the ultimate goal of the scholarly effort.

Notes

1. This discovery was captured in an early paper, 'Image and Icononography in Evolution of Identity,' in *New Caribbean Thought: A Reader*, ed. Brian Meeks and Folke Lindahl (Jamaica: University of the West Indies Press, 2001), 232–64.
2. Mikhail Bakhtin, a Russian philosopher whose work complicated the reading of fiction and presented complex deconstructive methods for a critical literary discourse. See, for example, Mikhail Bakhtin, *The Dialogic Discourse: Four Essays* (Austin: University of Texas Press, 1981).
3. Martin Myrone Agostino Brunias Dancing Scene in the West Indies 1764–96, September 2013, https://www.tate.org.uk/art/artworks/brunias-dancing-scene-in-the-west-indies-t13869.
4. Much of the information on Brunias's life is owed to the research by scholar and historian from Dominica, Lennox Honeychurch.
5. See, for example, https://www.huffingtonpost.com/entry/prussian-blue-colour-art_us_563bbd85e4b0307f2cac9ccd.
6. See, for example, Brinda J. Mehta, *Diasporic Dis(locations): Indo-Caribbean Women Writers Negotiate the Kala Pani* (Kingston: University of the West Indies Press, 2000).

References

Blake, William. 1793. *Visions of the Daughters of Albion.* https://ebooks.adelaide.edu.au/b/blake/william/visions-of-the-daughters-of-albion/Campbell Fine Art 2009-2018. http://www.campbell-fine-art.com/items.php?id=720.

Cosgrove, Denis, and Stephen Daniels. 1988. *The Iconography of Landscape, Essays on the Symbolic Representation, Design and Use of Past Environments.* Cambridge: Cambridge University Press.

Cumming, Laura. 2007. http://www.theguardian.com/artanddesign/2007/apr/15/art.williamblake.

Fernandez de Oviedo, Gonzalo. 1596. *Natural History of the West Indies.* https://www.biodiversitylibrary.org/bibliography/8045#/summary.

Graham-Dixon, Andrew. 1996. *A History of British Art.* London: BBC Books.

Jones, Amelia. 2002. Every Man Knows Where and How Beauty Gives Him Pleasure: Beauty Discourse and the Logic of Aesthetics. In *Aesthetics in a Multicultural Age*, ed. Emory Elliot, Louis Freitas Caton and Jeffrey Rhyne, 218. Oxford and New York: Oxford University Press.

Mohammed, Patricia. 2002. *Gender Negotiations among Indians in Trinidad, 1917-1947.* Basingstoke: Palgrave Macmillan.

———. 2010. *Imaging the Caribbean: Culture and Visual Translation.* Basingstoke: Palgrave Macmillan.

Panofsky, Erwin. 1989. Introduction. In *The Iconography of Landscape: Essays on the Symbolic Representation, Design and Use of Past Environments*, ed. Denis Cosgrove and Stephen Daniels. Cambridge: Cambridge University Press.

Panofsky, Erwin. 1939. *Studies in Iconology: Humanistic Themes in the Art of the Renaissance*. Oxford: Oxford University Press.
Ryan, James. 1997. *Picturing Empire: Photography and the Visualisation of the British Empire*. Chicago and London: The University of Chicago Press.
Scheller, Mimi. 2003. *Consuming the Caribbean: From Arawaks to Zombies*. London: Routledge.
Thompson, Krista. 2006. *An Eye for the Tropics: Tourism, Photography, and Framing the Caribbean Picturesque*, 392. Durham, NC and London: Duke University Press.
Yudice, George. 2003. *The Expediency of Culture: Uses of Culture in the Global Era*. Durham, NC and London: Duke University Press.

Methods for Analysing Talk and Text

22. Reconceptualizing Voice: The Role of Matrifocality in Shaping Theories and Caribbean Voices*

Michelle V. Rowley

...

Voicing Sameness/Voicing Difference: The Articulations of Agency

I use the term "voicing" to refer to the varying, articulated levels of consciousness and alienation, action and inaction which categories of Caribbean women experience. The term "voicing" stems from a need to reflect women's lived realities within our theoretical frames; it is a response to the challenge issued by Joycelin Massiah that women "speak for themselves, name their experiences and make their own connections" (Massiah, cited in Senior 1991). "Voicing" itself is significant, as a form of speech that is in the present continuous and therefore representing ongoing activity. The term possesses a subject that can, has been, and will voice. Finding the subject of this speech, however, presents us with the dilemma of the subject that has no name, again highlighting the need for a speaking "matrifolk" subject.

The act of voicing is one that also challenges dichotomous representations, in that it prompts the recognition that women's voices are not locked within social, ethnic, classist or ideological groups but that there is a continuous pendulum between discord and harmony, exclusion and inclusion. Voicing as an act of naming and representation is also a distinctly political and agentive process. Naming, and in this sense to name a matrifocal category, is a decidedly limited approach to politics, yet, it is not one that should be too readily dismissed, as it is through processes of naming that we are able to solicit attention to a range of different positionalities. Naming invokes but ought not to be coterminous

---

* Reprinted with permission from *Gendered Realities: Essays in Caribbean Feminist Thought*, ed. Patricia Mohammed. Kingston: UWI Press, 2002, 22–43. Excerpted and revised.

with agency. It is through naming that we have clues, *and only clues*, about why an individual may choose to act or not. Further, it is through practices of naming that we can point to modes of harm. To name therefore, simultaneously locks and unlocks possibilities for the subject who is named. It is through naming that we can mark what has been consolidated over time as abject and point to the practices that have informed such consolidations. It is through naming that we can challenge these consolidations.

I am not suggesting that we can invoke the exercise of agency simply by the process of naming. I am drawing on Kamala Viswesaran's (1994) discussion on agency as performance, where she notes that while speech is important to the exercise of agency, the capacity to speak cannot be reducible to agency. This highlights the need to be constantly cognizant not only of what is said, but of the locales in which speech occurs. How does the interview process itself become a combined narrative of speech, whose silences, continuities and discontinuities are not only part of the interviewee's ability to construct and present versions of self, but simultaneously a reaction to a number of impacting, normalizing and countervailing discursive realities? In this context, therefore, how do we identify the agentive moment? Do we merely examine the text of the talk? What do we do with the experience of the text? Since respondents rarely, if ever, make the pronouncement "... and oh, I was exercising agency here!", the location of agency and interpretations of representation is the point that brings the hierarchical dimension of research sharply into focus, despite claims that attest to egalitarianism and democratic interactions.[1] In addition, because the exercise of agency is not coterminous to a freewheeling, autonomous subject, how then do we also locate the text of the matrifolk within the frame of the "unsaid" and "already said" intertextuality of all discursive interactions (Foucault 1972: 25)?

Historicizing the Matrifocal "Already Said"

Both the voiced and the silenced experiences of the matrifolk are crucial elements in historicizing the construction of the matrifocal identity and the embodiment of these discursive antecedents. By way of a quick overview, matrifocality needs first to be understood as an interaction with a colonial slave ideology, characterized by the pursuit of capital and the perpetuation of patriarchy. For example, historians such as Michael Craton (1991: 228) have observed that the "'myth of matrifocality' stems from the planters' emphasis on motherhood because of their need to perpetuate slavery through the female line and their vain wish to breed rather than buy new slaves by granting slave mothers relatively easier conditions." At this point, issues of production reflected a seemingly coterminous relationship with issues of reproduction.

Similarly, the period of wage labour showed a continuum of women being placed in a socially and financially disadvantaged position. So evident was the shift in labour that J. Momsen (in a contemporary description of postemancipation changes in 1841) observed in 1838 that "mothers of families have retired from the field, to duties of the home" (cited in Momsen 1993). The difficult economic environment within which matrifocality was to exist as a result of unfavourable labour shifts was made even more difficult socially and politically by the sentiments of the Moyne Commission report.[2] In this regard, economic burden was even further intensified by the social "unacceptability" of the female single-headed family form. The report notes that where there was no father

> the whole financial responsibility [would] fall on the mother ... In such circumstances cases of extreme poverty are inevitable, for the standard of living must be lower than it would be in a family group where even if both parents were not employed, more money would be available since the wages of men are normally higher than those given to women. (p.40)

Rather than upgrade the structural and institutional needs available to matrifocal, single-headed family forms, the report, in dismissing the need for women to find gainful employment, advocated instead that girls were "to be companions for husbands" and would therefore need an adequate education for the achievement of such.

The adversarial construction of matrifocality in the Caribbean has in many ways impacted negatively upon women and their self-conceptualization. I draw on Barriteau's (1992: 7) assessment of the Women in the Caribbean Project Report conducted between 1979 and 1983. Here she states:

> Women emerge as economically vulnerable and insecure (Powell 1986; Barrow 1986); display alarming levels of female self-contempt (Clarke 1986); doubt their abilities to be effective leaders (Clarke 1986); and defer decision-making to their male counterparts (Odie-

Ali 1986) ... "They recognise that they must accept male domination and a male dependent role" (Anderson 1986: 311).

This assessment is not homogeneous nor a universal position – as Barriteau herself notes – as Caribbean women were also found to have a strong sense of equity in relation to their male counterparts.

In addition to this constellation of sociohistorical discourses, there has been a decidedly misogynistic trend that has impacted forcibly on the formation of education policy in the Caribbean. It is in this vein that Errol Miller observes that

> [t] he matrifocal family and kinship institutions *characteristic of lower strata groups* in Caribbean society are neither African survivals nor merely the legacy of new world slavery. These matrifocal forms are the product of domination/subordination has [sic] been contested by men in Caribbean society and the liberation of Caribbean women in an *unintended consequence of this contest between men.* (Miller 1988; emphasis mine)

Miller's reading of matrifocality as "female liberation" is here a monolithic denial of the class, gender and ethnic differentials that operate in subject formation. Miller's assertion does not take cognizance of the fact that figuratively, matrifocality in the context of the Caribbean is much like an obstacle race being run on a course filled with weakening communal networks, decreasing social and state support services, low wages, inadequate workers' representation and working conditions for many of the matrifolk who work in low-income, feminized occupations (such as domestic workers and free zone employees).

Third, Miller needs to adopt a more sophisticated position on notions of power. What he refers to as the "promotion" of women does not automatically carry with it commensurate and proportional measures of power to act and effect change. The assumption that matrifocality exists primarily because of patriarchal contestations among men denies the fact that matrifocal forms are constructed within the dynamics of gendered inter- and intra-group relations, with institutional, ideological and social forces which are challenged and supported by both men and women. The perpetuation of these forms cannot be seen as an unintended consequence of intramale contestation. This denies the complex – and sometimes contradictory – interrelatedness of gender relations and the construction of our gendered identities.

Voicing as Bridge between Theory and Method

Nuancing the contradictory subtleties of matrifocality requires that we seek to identify variables of difference and to recognize that these variables can only be informed by asking new questions, alongside asking the old questions differently. Further to this is the need to bridge the gap that exists between the conceptual and operational, the experiential and material. I argue here that the tool that bridges these spaces is the *talk* of the narrative. In this assertion I am not making a purely linguistic turn, but rather suggesting that language becomes the means by which we can explore experience (Polkinghorne 1988: 22). My use of language is two-tiered, in that at one level I am referring to the performance of the talk, while at another, I refer to the content and intertextuality of the talk, to the multiple discursive elements that constitute *talk*.

The performance of talk is both an individual and collective activity. Equally important, however, is the social site of production as it conditions the content of the talk. On one end of the spectrum that sees talk as social discourse is David Edward's argument that

> [t]elling stories is discursive action doing discursive business. This certainly emerges when studying research interviews, but those essentially work against interaction considerations, because they tend to substitute, for the ordinary occasions on which stories might be told, got-up occasions for set-piece performances for interview. It is better to collect samples of natural talk, where possible, if we want to see how talk performs interactional work other than informing researchers who are interested in narratives, in family relations, in violence or social attitudes, or whatever (Edwards 1996).

While the moment of talk is also a moment of co-construction, as well as being socially derived, the problematic assumption here is that we can actually identify something that constitutes "natural talk" or "unnatural talk". Admittedly, there may be differently produced talk in different sites of production, but it is questionable whether one talk can be seen as more legitimate or authentic than another. The interpretive moment should be guided by the context and situation of the talk, but not as means to produce notions of authenticity.

Similarly, talk not only projects experience, but also provides a vista into the impact that historically constituted discourses (as well as contemporary constructions and interactions) have on subject formation.

Talk therefore enacts historical discursive formations (Scott 1992: 36). How do we then approach the talk in such a way that we are able to capture the experience; the collective, multiple and historical constructions of impacting discourses; and the interaction between these discourses and the individual? One means of approaching talk to achieve these aims is to look at the narrator's positioning in the talk. Does the narrator position herself as victim, perpetrator and so on? Second, how does the narrator position herself in relation to her audience/interviewer (for example, is there an attempt to convince or ally herself with the interviewer)? Third, what is the narrator's position in relation to other discursive realities intertwined in the local production of talk (for example, racism, sexism, and so on) (Bamberg 1988)?

...

Forging Caribbean Feminist Theory

A distinctive feminist body of literature in the Caribbean has mushroomed, challenging dominant structures and their inability to adequately engage with definitions of otherness. Significantly, this growing body of work has questioned notions of economics and development (Mohammed and Shepherd 1988; Hart 1986; Leo-Rhynie, Bailey and Barrow 1997); social history (Reddock 1984); anthropology and structures of class and ethnicity (Senior 1991). While these publications have successfully posed a challenge to broader paradigmatic concerns, there has also been a parallel feminist challenge which has allowed Caribbean women "to speak for themselves" (Massiah, cited in Senior 1991).

The potential for indigenous Caribbean feminist theorizing is limitless. At the point at which women are able to speak for themselves, to name their experiences, positions of difference will be articulated. Only at these points of difference can we accurately identify those variables that make for a distinctly Caribbean sense of feminist theory. Theoretically, therefore, the question that we must ask ourselves is: what are the variables which reflect an experiential difference between Caribbean women and women who occupy other geographical, political, economic, social and ideological spaces? Matrifocality represents only one such area of concern.

References

Bamberg, Michael. 1997. Is There Anything behind Discourse? Narrative and the Local Accomplishments of Identities. Paper presented at ISTP conference, Berlin, April.

Barriteau, Eudine. 1992. The Construct of a Postmodern Feminist Theory for Caribbean Social Science Research. *Social and Economic Studies* 41, no. 2.

Beckles, Hillary. 1989. *Natural Rebels: A Social History of Enslaved Black Women in Barbados*. London: Zed Books.

Borland, Kathrine. 1991. 'That's Not What I Said': Interpretative Conflict in Oral Narrative Research. In *Women's Words: The Feminist Practices of Oral History*, ed. S.B. Gluck and D. Patai. New York: Routledge.

Brathwaite, Edward Kamau. 1975. Caribbean Man in Space and Time. *Savacou* 11 and 12.

Craton, Michael. 1978. *Searching for the Invisible Man: Slaves and Plantation Life in Jamaica*. Cambridge, Mass.: Harvard University Press.

———. 1991. Changing Patterns of Slave Families in the British West Indies. In *Caribbean Slave Society and Economy*, ed. H. Beckles and V. Shepherd. Kingston, Jamaica: Ian Randle Publishers.

Devault, Marjorie. 1990. Talking and Listening from Women's Standpoint: Feminist Strategies for Interviewing and Analysis. *Social Problems* 37, no 1: 96–116.

ECLAC/CDCC (Economic Commission for Latin America and the Caribbean/Caribbean Development and Cooperation Committee). 1996. Poverty Eradication and Female-Headed Households (FHH) in the Caribbean. Paper prepared for the Caribbean Ministerial Meeting on the Eradication of Poverty, Port of Spain, Trinidad, October 28–November 1.

Edwards, David. 1996. *Discourse and Cognition*. London: Sage

Fairclough, Norman. 1992. *Discourse and Social Change*. Cambridge: Polity Press

Foucault, Michel. 1972. *The Archaeology of Knowledge and the Discourse on Language*. New York: Pantheon Books.

Harding, Sandra. 1992. *The Instability of the Analytical Categories of Feminist Theory: Knowing Women, Feminism and Knowledge*. London: Blackwell.

Hart, Richard, ed. 1986. *Women and the Sexual Division of Labour in the Caribbean*. Mona, Jamaica: Institute of Social and Economic Research, University of the West Indies.

Leo-Rhynie, Elsa, Barbara Bailey and Christine Barrow, eds. 1997. *Gender: A Caribbean Multi-Disciplinary Perspective*. Kingston, Jamaica: Ian Randle Publishers.

Lincoln, Yvonna S. 1997. Self, Subject, Audience, Text: Living at the Edge, Writing in the Margins. In *Representation and the Text: Reframing the Narrative Voice*, ed. William G. Tierney and Yvonna S. Lincoln. New York: State University of New York Press.

Mathurin, Lucille. 1986. *Women Field Workers in Jamaica during Slavery*. Mona, Jamaica: Department of History, University of the West Indies.

Miller, Errol. 1988. The Rise of Matriarchy in the Caribbean. *Caribbean Quarterly* 34, nos. 3 and 4.

Mohammed, Patricia. 1988. The Caribbean Family Revisited. In *Gender in Caribbean Development*, ed. P. Mohammed and C. Shepherd. St Augustine, Trinidad: Women and Development Studies Project, University of the West Indies.

Momsen, Janet. 1993. Gender Roles in Caribbean Agricultural Labour. In *Caribbean Freedom, Economy and Society from Emancipation to the Present*, ed. H. Beckles and V. Shepherd. Kingston, Jamaica: Ian Randle Publishers.

Morrisey, Marietta. 1991. Women's Work, Family Formation and Reproduction among Caribbean Slaves.' In *Caribbean Slave Society and Economy*, ed. Beckles and V. Shepherd. Kingston, Jamaica: Ian Randle Publishers.

Polkinghorne, Donald E. 1988. *Narrative Knowing and the Human Sciences*. New York: State University of New York Press.

Powell, Dorian. 1975. Caribbean Women and Their Response to Familial Experiences. *Social and Economic Studies* 35, no. 2.

Reddock, Rhoda E. 1994. *Women, Labour and Politics in Trinidad and Tobago: A History*. Kingston, Jamaica: Ian Randle Publishers.

Scott, Joan. 1992. Experience. In *Feminists Theorise the Political*, ed. J. Butler and J. Scott. New York: Routledge.

Senior, Olive. 1991. *Working Miracles: Women's Lives in the English-Speaking Caribbean*. Kingston, Jamaica: Ian Randle Publishers.

Smith, R.T. 1988. *Kinship and Class in the West Indies: A Genealogical Study of Jamaica and Guyana*. Cambridge: Cambridge University Press.

———. 1996. *The Matrifocal Family: Power, Pluralism, and Politics*. London: Routledge.

Spivak, Gayatri. 1992. The Politics of Translation. In *Destabilising Theory: Contemporary Feminist Debates*, ed. Michele Barret and Anne Phillips. Stanford, Calif.: Stanford University Press.

Viswesaran, Kamala. 1994. *Fictions of Feminist Ethnography*. Minneapolis: University of Minnesota Press.

West India Royal Commission. 1945. *West India Royal Commission Report, 1938–39 (Moyne Report)*. London: His Majesty's Stationery Office.

Notes

1. An interesting discussion of this relationship can be found in Borland's "'That's Not What I Said': Interpretive Conflict in Oral Narrative Research," which deals with the problems of interpretation and appropriation of the text, as well as the designation of agency in text. She observes that "Lest we as feminist scholars, unreflectively appropriate the words of our mothers for our own uses, we must attend to the multiple and sometimes conflicting meanings generated by our framing or contextualizing of their oral narratives in new ways" (1991: 73).
2. The West India Royal Commission Report arose out of the 1930s labour disturbances in the Caribbean.

23. Studying Religious Mobilizations in the Anglophone Caribbean: A Feminist Critical Reading of Discourse[1]

Latoya Lazarus

Introduction and Overview

In 2009, I embarked on a research project that was aimed at understanding how conservative and evangelical Christians were engaging in public debates, and thus contributing to knowledge production, on matters relating to gender, sexuality, human rights, and citizenship in Jamaica. At that time, the primary aim was to examine the ways in which these groups were seeking to shape various discussions and produce discourses about such issues as the decriminalization of 'buggery' (sometimes loosely referred to as the decriminalization of homosexuality) as well as about what constituted sexual and reproductive rights both within the media (that is, the print media, internet, social and broadcast media) and the legal system (particularly in processes of constitutional reform and the review of the abortion legislation). This research asked a number of questions, including, how are these gender and sexuality-related issues linked, directly and indirectly, to wider concerns over human rights, public (national/cultural) morality/values, and 'postcolonial' citizenship? Additionally, in moving beyond the scope of the two specific processes of law reforms, the research also asked: what are the more general ways in which Christianity intertwines with the society at large, through participating in and informing discussions around these issues?

This largely exploratory and analytical research, from its conceptualization, to analysis and composition, also included a methodological journey into feminist methodologies – theories and analyses or 'accounts of [how] research should proceed' (Harding 1987, 2). Specifically, I have drawn upon more than one feminist methodology, in the end, adopting, what I am calling, a 'Caribbean feminist standpoint', with elements of social constructionism in my analysis of how knowledge gets constructed and embedded in 'truths'. Feminist standpoint theory emerged in the mid 1970s and early 1980s, notably in the works of Sandra Harding and Patricia Hill Collins (1986), as an alternative to traditional androcentric methods of scientific research (Harding 2004). As a theoretical and methodological device it has generated much debate and at other times seemed to have been eclipsed by a number of other approaches, such as Black and decolonial/anticolonial feminist analyses, which have both shaped and been informed by Caribbean research. Arguably, however, these latter approaches may be seen as contributing to the development of standpoint theory, in that, they are very much dedicated to providing alternatives to androcentric knowledge, but using this primary principle have gone a step further in also challenging and creating knowledge alternative to white, Western constructions.

A combined approach to research is not at all unusual, as feminists in general, draw upon multiple methods that allow them to approach a research interest from their dominant epistemological standpoint or worldview. Indeed, although there are divergences between feminist methodologies, they share several crucial commonalities in terms of concerns and visions about doing research, which makes it possible, as I have done, to combine approaches (see Lazarus 2012; 2013a, 2013b). As I have noted elsewhere, 'feminist methodologies in general and Caribbean feminist methodologies in particular include: (1) recognizing that there is no one 'Truth', but rather, that knowledge is based on individual's locations, positionality and situatedness; (2) increasing awareness of differences; (3) identifying and seeking to address a range of methodological issues that draw attention to the working of differential power within research contexts; and (4) viewing research as empowering' (see also Massiah 1986; Lazarus 2013a; Lazarus 2013b, 85–86).

Fast track to 2017, I am still on this research and methodological journey, as I go about observing and analysing the public mobilizations of conservative and evangelical Christian groups in Jamaica and across the Anglophone Caribbean in general. My intent in this ongoing research is twofold. First, to understand and track these forms of religious mobilizations in the region, especially as they seek to shape matters relating to sexuality, gender, human rights, and citizenship. And second, to draw attention to new and already existing concerns about Caribbean sociocultural development and the role and politicization of religion, and Christianity in particular. Simply put, I seek to investigate the continuous power of religion (and particularly certain conservative manifestations of Christianity) in shaping body and identity politics; and more broadly, its involvement in public life, including in aspects of community and national development around the aforementioned matters.

In undertaking this research, over the years I have utilized a number of techniques, most notably semi-structured (open-ended) interviews with key informants, observations of relevant events and the analysis of primary and secondary data (written, oral and visual texts). These traditional qualitative methods or 'techniques for gathering evidences' (Harding 1987, 2) are in keeping with feminist methodological approaches to doing research; specifically, research that is sensitive to various forms of power imbalances, including discursive ones and that which recognizes differences as well as the possibility for multiple truths based on individual's locations, positionality and situated-ness. Moreover, this particular mixed or multi-methods approach was adopted because it provides (1) the opportunity to analyse written as well as spoken words, (2) to ask questions that would complement the analysis of the pre-existing texts and (3) to interact with persons with first-hand experiences or who have informed knowledge about the issues being discussed, thus allowing for a more comprehensive understanding of the types of mobilizations that are taking place, the issues that are being tackled and the types of messages that are being presented as well as contested. Combining research techniques is, of course, not unusual; rather, increasingly more feminists are recognizing the benefits in multi-method research or 'triangulation', namely, compensating for the weakness or gaps in one method 'by the counter-balancing strengths' (Jick 1979, 604 quoted in Jayaratne and Stewart 1991, 91) of the other. In this research, as will be discussed in reference to specific examples, the adopted research techniques have been implemented in a variety of ways, sometimes sequentially, sporadically and, at times, simultaneously. Critically, this research is particularly interested in the ways dominant discourses are reproduced, challenged and transmitted within and outside of social movements by social actors with set agendas and ideological positions. Consequently, I engage in the critical readings and interpretations of a variety of written texts, visual representations and speeches in an array of contexts (i.e., settings, locations, times and interactions). To this end, the broader aim is to provide insight into the ways in which social actors and symbolic elites, including conservative and evangelical actors, produce, legitimate as well as seek 'access to or control over' the text and context of public discourse (van Dijk 2015, 470) on the aforementioned issues.

It is also crucial to emphasize here that the specific contexts and focus of the research also shape the ways in which these qualitative techniques are implemented. Specifically, studying sexuality and religion within the 'postcolonial' Anglophone Caribbean means confronting various taboos, which shape the types of questions that can be asked, the voices that can be accessed and the activities that are easily observed, hence the need to always be aware of and seek to infer from the unstated and the implicit in analysis. It also means analysing complex and ambiguous types and relations of power that structures discourses and attitudes towards sexuality and religion, which further highlights the need to see power in a more nuanced light, where it is not always explicit or coming from sources of formal authority. Moreover, in this particular research context, implementing a form of feminist critical discourse analysis was seen as a natural choice, as much of the critical engagement with sexuality and religion has traditionally emerged out of various Caribbean feminist theorizations (see, for example, Alexander 1991, 2005; Barrow 1995). These theorizations greatly influenced how I read, coded and interpreted written and spoken words, with particular attention paid to the ideological, geographical, social and economical contexts in which discourse and power operate. In summation then, the context and subject matter of the research shaped my decision to examine not only the linguistic aspects of talk and texts but also the non-linguistic features, including the extra-textual context.

In what follows, I first discuss what is meant by discourse and the justifications for paying critical attention to it in scholarly interrogations of knowledge production and the differential workings of power within society. Second, I discuss discourse analysis as an analytic practice and provide a conceptualization of what I am calling feminist critical discourse analysis. Third and finally, I provide insight into the actual data collection and critical discourse analysis processes, with an emphasis on the period 2009–12 where I focused on understanding how conservative and evangelical Christians were engaging in public debates and contributing to knowledge production, on matters relating to gender, sexuality, human rights, and citizenship in Jamaica.

Discourse as an Area of Study

Discourses are more than the production of meanings; rather, they 'constitute the "nature" of the body, unconscious and conscious mind and emotional life of the subjects they seek to govern' (Weedon 1987, 108). Stuart Hall summarizes as follows:

> Discourses are ways of referring to or constructing knowledge about a particular topic of practice: a cluster (or formation) of ideas, images and practices, which provide ways of talking about forms of knowledge and conduct associated with a particular topic, social activity or institutional site in society. These *discursive formations*, as they are known, define what is and is not appropriate in our formulations of, and our practices in relation to, a particular subject or site of social activity; what knowledge is considered useful, relevant and "true" in that context; and what sorts of persons or "subjects" embody its characteristics. 'Discursive' has become the general term used to refer to any approach in which meaning, representation and culture are considered to be constitutive ([1997] 2003, 6).

Discourse thus encompasses ideological engagements as well as referring to a type of social action or practice that constitutes subjectivities, societies and cultures (see Fairclough and Wodak 1997; van Dijk 2015). As such, discourse can be seen as 'not simply an isolated textual or dialogic structure. Rather it is a complex communicative event that also embodies a social context, featuring participants (and their properties) as well as production and reception processes' (van Dijk 1988, 2).

Examining discourse, as Michel Foucault argues, is thus a means of analysing 'how human beings understand themselves in our culture and how our knowledge about 'the social, the embodied individual and shared meaning' comes to be produced in different periods" (quoted in Hall [1997] 2003, 43). Accordingly, I am also interested in analysing discourses because I believe that existing and emerging discourses have a tremendous impact on an individual's life and social interactions. Indeed, analysis of discourses may reveal the various relations of ruling and dominance that are woven within them, which shape and are in turn informed by various material, social and institutional structures and locations. For discourse not only refers to ways of producing knowledge, but also to the 'power relations which inhere in such knowledge and the relations between them' (ibid.; see also Lazar 2007, 142). At the heart of critical research on discourse, therefore, is a focus on the ways in which social power abuse, inequality and bias are 'enacted, reproduced, legitimated and resisted by text and talk in the social and political context' (van Dijk 2015, 466).

Similar to other feminist scholars, I too am drawing on some aspects of a Foucauldian understanding of discourse (though not his actual methods of analysis), which emphasizes that discourse is not simply 'the property of individual actors but is itself a "practice" that is structured and... has real effects' (Ferguson 1994, 18 quoted in Naples 2003,10). Indeed, discourses not only reveal particular groups' interests, but they also determine what can be known and is considered possible to achieve and implement through, for example, legal reforms. I am therefore least concerned with the biases of individuals, but rather, in

> the assumptions generated by "ways of life" and generated in discursive frameworks, conceptual schemes, and epistemes, within which entire dominant groups tend to think about nature and social relations, and to use such frameworks to structure social relations for the rest of us... (Harding 2008, 334).

Moreover, what I most appreciate in Foucault's theoretical perspective on discourse is the importance placed on understanding 'regimes of truths' or the relation between knowledge and material and discursive workings of 'power'. In *Power/Knowledge*, he argues that,

> Truth isn't outside power.... Truth is a thing of this world; it is produced only by virtue of multiple forms of constraint. And it induces regular effects of power. Each society has its regime of truth, its 'general politics' of truth; that is, the types of discourse which it accepts and makes function as true, the mechanisms and instances which enable one to distinguish true and false statements, the means by which each is sanctioned... the status of those who are charged with saying what counts as true (Foucault 1990, 131 quoted in Hall [1997] 2003, 49).

Prior to that, in the *History of Sexuality: An Introduction, Volume 1*, Foucault explains how power-knowledge-pleasure sustain the discourse on human sexuality in the western part of the world through various periods in its history. To uncover these regimes of truth he proposes undertaking a version of critical discourse analysis, arguing that,

> The central issue, then (at least in the first instance), is not to determine whether one says yes or no to sex, whether one formulates prohibitions or permissions, whether one asserts its importance

or denies its effects, or whether one refines the words one uses to designate it; but to account for the fact that it is spoken about, to discover who does the speaking, the positions and viewpoints from which they speak, the institutions which prompt people to speak about it and which store and distribute the things that are said. What is at issue, briefly, is the over-all "discursive fact," the way in which sex is "put into discourse." Hence, too, my concern will be to locate the forms of power, the channels it takes, and the discourses it permeates in order to reach the most tenuous and individual modes of behaviour, the paths that give it access to the rare or scarcely perceivable forms of desire, how it penetrates and controls everyday pleasure – all this entailing effects that may be those of refusal, blockage, and invalidation, but also incitement and intensification: in short, the "polymorphous techniques of power." And finally, the essential aim will not be to determine whether these discursive productions and these effects of power lead one to formulate the truth about sex, or on the contrary falsehoods designed to conceal that truth, but rather to bring out the "will to knowledge" that serves as both their support and their instrument (Foucault [1978] 1990, 11–12).

Simply put, there is a possibility to observe the relationship between discursive formations about a subject and other social processes, but also these discursive formations work within and, in turn, reinforce power relations. Moreover, Foucault's articulation here provides a possible framework or an approach for actually doing Critical Discourse Analysis (CDA); specifically, one that interrogates how a subject is put into discourse, the forms and relations of power that are utilized in crafting knowledge and in turn sustaining power.

Moving from *Critical Discourse Analysis* to a *Feminist Critical Discourse Analysis*

Although I draw on some important aspects of Foucault's theorization, and, like Norman Fairclough and Teun A. van Dijk, acknowledge his great influence on discourse analysis in general, his approach, however, does not completely suit my research goals of actually analysing how and what is being said in various texts (from government reports to newspaper articles), visual representations and dialogue or in the very act of talking. Foucault focuses on the 'non-linguistic analyses of statements, more precisely, with developing a strategic model (a 'theory of practice', if one wishes) that could account for discourse, knowledge, truth, and relations of power simultaneously' (Foucault 2003 quoted in Blommaert 2005, 241). In other words, the focus is on structures or 'the rules which "govern" bodies of texts and utterances' (Fairclough 2003, 123); instead of placing emphasis on the detailed analysis of texts or simply, on the detail of text or of 'real instances of people doing or saying or writing things', (Fairclough 1992, 57). As such, '[…] in the major analyses, the dominant impression [of Foucault's analysis of discourse and power] is one of people being helplessly subjected to immovable systems of power' (ibid.).[2] That is, whilst Foucault 'certainly insists that power necessarily entails resistance…he gives the impression that resistance is generally constrained by power and poses no threat' (ibid.). This view of power does not appear to make room for the occurrences of processes of social change and/or agency, which though not always fully achieved remain a significant focus in feminist methodologies.

In this research I therefore adopted a more nuanced view of power, which highlights its multifaceted nature and the fact that it is 'not always exercised in obviously abusive ways by dominant groups', (van Dijk 2015, 469), or easily pinpointed in a given interaction. Equally, it is rarely ever absolute, that is, 'Groups may more or less control other groups, or only control them in specific situations or social domains'; and, 'dominated groups may more or less resist, accept, condone, collude or comply with, or legitimate such power, and even find it "natural"' (van Dijk 2015, 469). Indeed, in this study, critical analyses of interview data, varied media sources and existing scholarship on sexuality and gender within the region revealed the ways in which certain dominant/privileged heteropatriarchal and conservative Christian discourses on morality, respectability, and 'appropriate' gender and sexual performances are reproduced, circulated and normalized (or legitimized) in an array of national spaces in Anglophone Caribbean countries such as Jamaica. Nevertheless, there are also implicit and explicit resistances to these constructs; the engagement by sexual and women's rights activists in national dialogues around issues relating to sexual and reproductive rights speaks to this resistance. Similarly, there are complex and, at times, ambiguous responses within the public to the discourses that are transmitted by conservative and evangelical Christians (and like-minded individuals). Such complexities are also evident in the ways in which dominant international discourses on gender, sexuality, and human rights 'are [strategically] interpreted, resisted and/or transformed' (Murray 2012, 18) within the local setting by people who approach these from multiple subjective and collective, including religious, lenses. All this highlights how access and control over certain forms of public discourse (inclusive of text, visual displays, talk and the context in which these unfold) may act as a power resource for enacting social control. However, as discussed below, this is by no means an uncomplicated process, as it involves competing players and institutions vying for access to and control of discursive spaces, as well as a constant negotiation of contexts and the inevitable resistance alluded to above (van Dijk 2015).

Feminist Critical Discourse Analysis

Somewhat in keeping with these interconnected definitions of discourse and the justifications for its analysis, Michelle M. Lazar (2007), for example, makes the case for specifically doing and studying 'feminist critical discourse analysis' (feminist CDA). The aim of feminist CDA would therefore be to,

> show up the complex, subtle, and sometimes not so subtle, ways in which frequently taken-for-granted gendered assumptions and hegemonic power relations are discursively produced, sustained, negotiated, and challenged in different contexts and communities. Such an interest is not merely an academic de-construction of texts and talk for its own sake, but comes from an acknowledgement that the issues dealt with (in view of effecting social change) have material and phenomenological consequences for groups of women and men in specific communities (Lazar 2007,142).

Naturally, feminist CDA, both in its thematic focus and analytic execution bears many similarities to CDA, especially as proposed by van Dijk. This is especially unsurprising considering that CDA has itself been greatly influenced by feminist approaches in women's studies (see van Dijk 1991; Lazar 2007). This is made apparent in CDA's general properties:

> It focuses primarily on *social problems* and *political issues* rather than the mere study of discourse structures outside their social and political contexts.
>
> This critical analysis of social problems is usually *multidisciplinary*.
>
> Rather than merely *describe* discourse structures, it tries to *explain* them in terms of properties of social interaction and especially social structure.

More specifically, CDA focuses on the ways discourse structure, enact, confirm, legitimate, reproduce, or challenge relations of *power abuse (dominance)* in society (van Dijk 2015, 467, emphasis in the original).

As with CDA, feminist CDA is therefore an 'overtly political stance and is concerned with analysis of various forms of social inequality and injustices' (Lazar 2007, 142) that unfold in an array of socio-political contexts and discourses with a commitment to social transformation or change. However, as pointed out by Lazar, feminist CDA is not only guided by the general principles of CDA, but unapologetically and openly acknowledges the benefits and influences of feminist principles and insights to critical analysis and transformation. In this research a concern over ongoing coloniality, which manifests in such things as talk, text, relationships, and attitudes towards sex, gender, spirituality, and sexuality, was analysed as an important factor informing social inequalities and injustices within the region. I therefore engaged in a form of anti-colonial feminist CDA.

In practice, feminist CDA seeks to transcend the divide between work that focuses on social theory (the more traditionally inspired Foucauldian approach) and work that exclusively pays detailed attention to the linguistic features of text (Fairclough 2003). In so doing, it adopts an interdisciplinary approach that pays attention, on the one hand, to critical analysis of the use and structure of language and varied texts within particular contexts. On the other, it recognizes the importance of feminist epistemological and methodological perspectives in guiding the interpretative and explanatory assessment of discourse (both texts and contexts). In my execution of feminist CDA, Caribbean and de/anticolonial feminist analyses were particularly crucial in guiding the interpretative and explanatory processes.

In sum, the actual execution of feminist CDA includes examining the various discursive framings (language, visual images, gestures and practices) that are being deployed by various actors in an array of contexts (inclusive of spaces, forums, time, locations, and types of interactions), which forms knowledge about the relevant issues at hand. It also involves deconstructing the particular embedded, taken-for-granted ideas and meanings in order to reveal (with the aim of addressing) not 'truths' per se, but rather, various relations of power and the ways in which these constitute our subjectivities and group relations; indeed, the 'regimes of truth' that constitute gender and sexuality and govern social life. Throughout, it aims to remain aware of the diversities between people as well as the complexities in their experiences and in the workings of power. As Lazar puts it, feminist CDA thus seeks to offer a diagnosis-through-discourse of societal power relations:

> Based on close empirical analysis, the data in feminist CDA include contextualised instances of spoken and written language along with other forms of semiosis such as visual images, layout, gestures, and actions in texts and talk. While the analysis includes overtly expressed meanings in communication, it is also attentive to less obvious, nuanced, implicit meanings to get at the subtle and complex renderings of ideological assumptions and power relations in contemporary modern societies (2007, 151).

Feminist CDA shares similarities and parallels with other feminist approaches to discourse analysis, namely feminist poststructuralist discourse analysis (FPDA), in that both approaches, as Judith Baxter suggests, have one common key principle that is the idea that all subjectivities are discursively constructed. Arguably, both approaches are committed to some kind of social transformation and, as such, are political. Initially, I had some scepticism during the research design stage of this project about supporting a 'political agenda', as doing so seemed to entail 'taking sides' across the very polarization of discourse and ideology that I was seeking to analyse. Eventually, however, it became apparent that the project was not only aimed at tracking and analysing the discourses being deployed by certain religious groups, but also sought to assess their impact on how citizenship and human rights were being imagined, interpreted, and constructed to the detriment of those who are often largely already marginalized and made vulnerable because of their gender, sexuality, colour, nationality, location, religion, and class. To this extent, a political positioning was strongly implicit in the terms of reference of the project as they came to be defined, thereby justifying a methodological approach that openly acknowledged such a positioning.

However, these two feminist approaches have some divergence, worth emphasizing here because of their significance in shaping what I consider to be a feminist critical discourse analysis. First, FPDA believes in complexities rather than polarization, the assertion being that whilst feminist CDA, at times, polarizes subjects into a binary category of the powerful and powerless (despite its emphasis on extra-textual context),

FPDA recognizes that people's subjectivities and experiences are 'complex, shifting and multiply located. It suggests that the ceaseless interaction of competing discourses means that speakers will continuously fluctuate between subject positions on a matrix of powerfulness and powerlessness' (Baxter n.d., 3). In conceptualizing my research, there was considerable appeal in this urge to nuance and preference for spectra over dichotomies: despite the avowedly emancipatory aims of this research, I actively sought to investigate the complexities in discourses and people's experiences, rather than accept or reify an already existing dichotomized vision of Jamaica or Caribbean societies in general. As such, through the analysis of various types of texts emerging from an array of contexts, I was able to observe differences, ambiguities, and contradictions in people's attitudes, ideological perspectives, and approaches to issues relating to sexualities, gender, and rights. Equally, a refusal to see the world in polarized ways meant that I was able to pinpoint, in my analysis the complexities in the workings of power, recognizing, as Baxter puts it, that someone can be powerless in one interaction and not in another, or simultaneously, 'being powerful or powerless in different ways at the same moment in time' (ibid.). However, the adoption of this perspective, I argue, does not diverge much from feminist CDA, as feminist CDA focuses on the ways in which the construct of gender intersects with other socially constructed categories of social identities such as sexuality, 'race', colour, religion, socio-economic class, geographical location, and nationality in informing people's experiences and relations to power (Lazar 2007). As such, it opens itself to seeing the complexities in people's experiences and subjectivities, even as it does not shy away from identifying clear instances of disempowerment (whose consequences are political) where it finds them.

Secondly and finally, FPDA also diverges from feminist CDA in that the former tends to adopt an anti-materialist perspective, where the view is that realities are always discursively constructed. In contrast, feminist CDA assumes 'discourse to work dialectically (Fairclough and Wodak, 1997) in so far as the discursive event is shaped by, and thereby continuously reconstructs, "real" or "material" events, situations or structures' (quoted in Baxter n.d., 4). For this research, I adopted the more materialist approach put forward by feminist CDA.

Execution of Feminist CDA in Social Research Analysing Written Texts, Speeches, and Visual Presentations

In what follows, I provide a brief description of the ways in which I implemented feminist discourse analysis as an analytic strategy in the above mentioned research project, focusing here on work that was done between 2009 and 2012. During this period, I analysed an array of discursive framings, inclusive of written text, images, and spoken words, to shed light on conservative and evangelical engagements with issues relating to homosexuality, the decriminalization of 'buggery' and abortion and more broadly, the interpretation of sexual and reproductive rights. These engagements were unfolding in an array of sociocultural contexts (legal and political forums, parliamentary reports, mass and social media, blogs, websites, public rallies, and conferences). I reviewed, for example, relevant legal documents, such as the 1962 and amended 2011 Jamaica Constitution as well as the *Offences against the Person Act* and the 2007 *Abortion Policy Review Advisory Group Final Report*. Overall, I analysed approximately:

- 41 local and international blog posts.
- Nine Jamaican government reports (including laws).
- 28 non-governmental reports and other types of documents (such as submissions to the government of Jamaica in regards to issues of sexual orientation and abortion).
- 35 online news reports from websites and 28 newspaper articles from outside Jamaica, including six from non-Caribbean sources.
- 243 articles from local newspapers, 164 of which were from the *Jamaica Gleaner* and 72 from the *Jamaica Observer*.
- Eight television talk shows, seven of which were aired on local television networks.

Analysis of multiple sources allows for an opportunity to formulate more comprehensive views, to assess areas of similarities and divergences, conflict, and contradictions. It also allows for the opportunity to examine discourses not as isolated practices but rather as 'historically founded, socially constitutive and always interwoven' (Wodak 2001, 9 quoted in Baxter n.d., 3).

Furthermore, ongoing analyses of various media materials was particularly beneficial to this research because the media space was, and remains, a popular site where both dominant and alternative discourses and meanings on these issues were being transmitted, legitimated, contested, and reaffirmed. Through this medium, one also gets insights into ongoing struggles between competing groups for access to and control over dominant cultural spaces and discourses about gender, sexuality, human rights, and citizenship. Since news and communications media generate a constant flow of discourse, they also allow diachronic analysis of discourses as they evolve over time in the course of the research period.

Undoubtedly, certain media sources function, more than others, 'to reinforce normative meanings and values' (Hall ([1997] 2003, 353) in the types of product or text that they produce and distribute. They therefore sustain, through their discursive formations, a regime of truth on such issues as 'Christian perspectives', homosexuality, abortion and human rights, which is not based on any absolute unchanging knowledge or 'Truth' per se, but on certain dominant constructions that are accepted and treated as 'true' and are thus 'true' in that they come to have real effects, even if they have never been conclusively proven (Hall [1997] 2003, 49). For example, there are those who make the claim that a comparison between Jamaica's two leading newspapers, the *Observer* and the *Gleaner*, will reveal that the latter is the more progressive in terms of its reporting on such issues as homosexuality, a sentiment that was commonly expressed following the publication of an editorial titled 'End Discrimination Towards Gays Now' in the newspaper on April 1, 2011.[3] Of course, one would have to undertake a rigorous analysis of these two newspapers in order to conclude that this is, in fact, the case. Nonetheless, similar critiques have also been voiced by some Christians, who accuse the mainstream print media for predominantly focusing on more conservative and fundamentalist Christian opinions on the issues at hand, to the detriment of more moderate positions (*Jamaica Gleaner*, December 25, 2011). These are arguably dominant opinions within the broader sociocultural context of Jamaica, as arguably they reflect the views held by a large number of people within the society (Perkins 2016; Lazarus 2013a).

These observations provided insights into the ways in which power imbalances reproduce themselves within the society, through the deployment of discourses that are circulated within mainstream national spaces, including in news reports, editorials, and prime time television programmings. Specifically, the publishing decisions of the mainstream print and broadcast media speak to the ways in which powerful institutions may seek to control not only 'specific knowledge and opinions' but also 'the generic knowledge, attitudes, and ideologies shared by whole groups or all citizens' (van Dijk 2015, 472). In fact, through this research it became apparent that more marginalized groups, such as atheists, as well as sexual rights activists, utilized social media platforms more than the mainstream media spaces. However, the value of using newer media, namely internet-based information and communication technologies, is naturally not lost on conservative and evangelical players who also seek to transmit ideological positions and comments that may not always garner consistent and extensive coverage in traditional spaces: thus, internet platforms such as Twitter and Facebook 'not only provide alternative spaces to the traditional media' but also the opportunity to voice counter-hegemonic or radical views as well as to 'access a transnational audience and to share resources' (Lazarus 2015, 129).

A comprehensive focus on the struggle over the control of discourse also involves an examination of various groups' strategic framings and ability to mobilize support as well as on the contextual influences on interpretations. According to van Dijk, 'Discursive control of specific situation models and shared generic social representations such as sociocultural knowledge as well as group attitudes and ideologies depend not only on the persuasive structures of text and talk but also on the contextual conditions' (2015, 473). That is, in undertaking a critical analysis, the researcher may assess whether the speakers are seen as 'authoritative, trustworthy, or credible sources' (ibid.). Moreover, are the recipients essentially obliged by context to accept the presented views or do they have access to alternative comprehensive views (van Dijk 2015)? Equally, do the presented materials resonate within the specific context in which they are being transmitted, that is, is there any evidence to support them and are they consistent or do they bear any similarities with broader cultural myths? In this research, it was found that conservative and evangelical Christians were oftentimes able to gain discursive control within a number of national mainstream spaces and forums because the speakers were seen as highly credible (being lawyers, doctors, and, of course, members of the clergy). They framed their messages in ways that were largely consistent with the pre-existing beliefs, anxieties, attitudes, and ideologies of many citizens, including lawmakers and parliamentarians. Additionally, the general public was not provided with the same level of comprehensive public alternative discourses on issues relating to sexual and reproductive rights, abortion, and homosexuality.

A number of steps were taken in an effort to carry out an in-depth analysis of the selected materials. First, for each source I identified the following: the names of author(s), the date it was drafted and published, the various issues that it takes up, the context in which it was produced, the purpose and intended audience, the types of languages used in discussing the issues and the connections being made, implicitly and/or explicitly about these issues. Second, I kept track of various author(s) or contributors to particular debates, identifying, for example, the number of times specific issues were raised by certain bloggers or columnists. I was thus able to begin identifying not only important issues around gender and sexuality that were being taken up, especially within the local media sources, but also certain individual and/or organizational voices that contributed to and played important roles in these debates. As a result of these initial observations, as well as my ongoing discussions (some informally and others in the context of interview) with more knowledgeable persons on the broader topics of sexuality, policy, and law within the Caribbean, I narrowed my archival search to focus in on specific voices and themes related to the foci of the research. Additionally, I was also guided to and, at times, given other useful materials during the interviewing process. Steps one and two were thus continuously repeated in these later stages of my discourse analysis. Thirdly, in moving beyond these primary descriptive linguistic analytical methods, I also looked at the ideological, political, and theoretical underpinnings in people's talk and texts, which shape the nuanced ways wherein matters such as sex, sexuality, gender, marriage, reproduction, morality, citizenship/nationhood, and human rights are understood and discussed. This approach to critical discourse analysis is based on the premise, as Fairclough argues, that two of the effects of texts are meaning-making and ideological effects, that is, the 'effects of texts in inculcating and sustaining or changing ideologies' (2003, 9). Consequently, textual analysis needs to consider 'bodies of texts in terms of effects on power relations' (ibid.). In the analysis of special reports considering issues of constitutional reform and/or the legalization of abortion, I was able to observe the anxieties by various players around the effects of including certain clauses and even wording into proposed legal documents. This relays their beliefs in the power of text, specifically, that such inclusion, from example of the word 'sexual orientation' would change the intent of the document but also open avenues for real life sociocultural change relating to the decriminalization of buggery and the legalization of same-sex marriage.

Interviews as Spoken Texts for Critical Analysis

In addition to tracking and analysing the above-mentioned written texts, speeches and visual presentations, between the months of February to June 2012, I visited Jamaica with the primary purpose of conducting interviews.[4] The purpose of these interviews was to address the gap in the academic literature and analysed material in regards to whether, for example: (1) people believe churches have an influence on public opinion and the course of the (public and legal) debates about sexuality; (2) what should be the role of public morality in defining criminal offences and justifying restrictions on personal conduct; (3) should the criminal law be used to enforce public morality; (4) who should define morality; (5) what should be the relationship between the 'Church' and state, and (6) what are the perceived threats against both institutions in light of increasing sexual activism in Jamaica and the region in general? Towards exploration of these questions, I decided to undertake in-depth, semi-structured, open-ended interviews, a method which is commonly used by many feminist researchers.[5] Many feminists, in general, see interviewing, as a potentially empowering method, for if one avoids the androcentricism of positivist, masculine research, interviews can serve the purpose of giving voices to people and subjects that have been traditionally marginalized or silenced in research. The issue of different styles of speech and their perceived legitimacy as conveyors of testimony is drawn sharply into focus in this regard. For instance, Marjorie DeVault (1999) argues that the researcher should not dismiss the utterances and various speech habits of certain groups as simply trivial. Instead, these particular usages of language and style of communication may reveal useful information about individuals and communities. In paying close attention to my respondents' use of language, I was able to learn more about their feelings and orientations towards certain issues. For example, the ways in which some church leaders made a distinction between 'wayward' churches and 'historical' ones highlighted the differences between and even within Christian communities and alliances, as well as the need certain denominations felt to be treated as separate entities. In addition, the pauses and tendency of some persons to provide lengthy elaborations or explanations illustrated in most cases the perceived high degree of sensitivity of the issue being discussed, respondents' complex and even ambiguous positions as well as their deliberate efforts not to be misunderstood (or misrepresented).

In-depth, open-ended questions or semi-structured interviews in particular are especially desirable for many feminist researchers, as they create the atmosphere of a dialogue where respondents get to share their experiences and knowledge and the researcher can follow up on issues that are being raised and take cues from what is being said to ask additional questions that may be of more relevance to that particular individual, community or context. Indeed, feminists researchers such as Dorothy Smith (1987) and Kamala Kempadoo (2001) suggest that in this process of dialoguing and paying close attention to what is being said and, in some cases, asked for, researchers may learn more about what issues or problems are important to the respondents and the extended community, which may eventually shape and guide the research in the next stages. This kind of supplementary collaboration by the subjects, of course, also requires a degree of flexibility in shaping the research parameters, which may not be ideal for some researchers or contexts (where research has been explicitly commissioned, for example). However, my own purposes permitted such flexibility to a degree and I thus aimed to listen to and take cues from respondents in order to produce a nuanced account. For example, I entered each interview setting, as Evelyn Blackwood (1995) and Tuhiwai Smith (1999) encourage, by disclosing information about the project and what the data would be used for, as well as about myself, to build rapport based on shared experiences as well as differences.

Respondents were then encouraged to ask questions of their own, which, as Rosalind Edwards (1990) states, not only builds rapport but also minimizes the visible division between the researcher and the respondent and the possible feelings of personal invasion. In exercising this right, several respondents made recommendations on such things as the issues that were more pertinent to them as individuals as well as members of a particular community. In fact, although I had, on at least three occasions, pretested the questionnaire guide and refined it accordingly, after the first three official interviews, the semi-structured open-ended questionnaire that was constructed to guide the interviews was further re-worked to include previously absent issues, such as the challenges facing churches in their efforts to educate congregations and publics on matters of sexuality. Ultimately, I conducted ten interviews with knowledgeable and active players in the public debates about sexuality and its related issues.[6] These interviews, like the various other primary sources that were critically analysed, covered a number of issues relating to sexuality, abortion, HIV and AIDS, human rights, legal and constitutional reform, as well as the mobilization, role, challenges, and failures of churches within the society.

Importantly, the information obtained from written as well as visual texts and speeches helped to shape the interview processes and vice versa. For example, based on the prior knowledge garnered from the available literature and particularly the analysis of various key print documents and non-print media sources, I compiled a list of most desirable respondents. This version of the key informant sample involves the researcher recruiting one or a few individuals 'to act as guides to a culture' (Tongco 2007, 147). Ideally, these 'key informants are observant, reflective members of the community of interest who know much about the culture and are both able and willing to share their knowledge' (ibid.), as well as 'recommend useful potential candidates for study (snowball sampling)' (Marshall 1996, 523).[7] For example, through two knowledgeable, well-situated individuals who consented for the study, I gained access to additional materials for analysis, some of which were not easily available or known to me. Also, I was able to contact others with more knowledge and experience in the areas of interests. This latter technique (snowballing) is considered appropriate in situations that do not allow for the kinds of probability samples that are commonly used in large-scale quantitative surveys. Likewise, this technique was useful for my own research, as it would otherwise have proved difficult to find (as an insider/returnee/outsider) a range of persons with knowledge and experience who were willing to participate in the study. Specifically, I initially had some difficulties finding church leaders who had nuanced opinions about sexuality-related issues, particularly in matters around homosexuality and abortion; that is, most of the persons, particularly the Christian leaders and individuals, who were initially contacted, had similar conservative views on these issues. These were a natural starting point, as some of these respondents' opinions were regularly reported in the local newspapers and blogs as well as in the various documents summarizing deliberations over the matters of constitutional reform and the review of abortion laws. Whilst there may have been some amount of bias in terms of whose opinions the media and bloggers chose to focus on, I nevertheless, contacted (through email or telephone) some of these individuals, particularly those whose names were also mentioned by other respondents, including the two key informants. However, through my key informants I was able to make other useful connections, thus enriching my data collection and more importantly, my understanding of the complexity of the research area.

Factors Shaping the Interpretation and Analysis Process

The interviews as well as most of the other written texts were analysed using QSR NVivo, a qualitative analysis software tool.[8] According to Elaine Welsh,

> Using software in the data analysis process has been thought by some to add rigour to qualitative research (Richards and Richards 1991). One way in which such accuracy could be achieved is by using the search facility in NVivo, which is seen by the product designers as one of its main assets facilitating interrogation of the data. This is certainly true when the data are searched in terms of attributes, for example, how many women from the Labour party self-identified as feminist? Clearly, carrying out such a search electronically will yield more reliable results than doing it manually simply because human error is ruled out. This kind of interrogation of data is important in terms of gaining an overall impression of the data, which has not been unduly influenced by particularly memorable accounts (2002, 7).

However, the reliance on this software may be somewhat more difficult if one desires, as in the case of conducting this form of critical discourse analysis, a more in-depth interrogation of texts (Ibid.). Consequently, even though I used NVivo as an organizing tool, I still had to manually go through each uploaded interview and other data sources in order to analyse the different ways things are expressed as well as the underlying ideologies and themes, rather than simply focusing on concepts and phrases.

Put differently, I actively decided on the ways in which to code my data. I selected codes based firstly on key terms or topics, such as 'abortion'; secondly, on what was being expressed or rather the meanings that were being transmitted, for example 'abortion as killing' and thirdly, the possible ideological underpinnings: Christian conservatism, heteropatriarchal, liberal feminism worldview, or a combination. Because of the complexities in language use, no two persons will necessarily use the same words even when they are naming and describing the same thing. As such, I had to analyse for the nuanced ways in which persons, based an array of factors, use language, and draw on an ideological framework. Although this may be less ideal for some researchers who are wary of human error(s), manual coding of the data was in this research nevertheless essential so as to highlight the subtle nuances that would have been missed without the informed and organizing vision of the human researcher. I was thus able to extrapolate a number of recurring, and somewhat interconnected, themes pointing up various ideological and political perspectives, many of which feed into the broader more far-reaching dominant heteropatriarchal discourse that Caribbean scholars of sexuality and gender, have identified within the region. Jacqui Alexander draws on Lynda Hart's concept of heteropatriarchy to explain the ways in which postcolonial Caribbean states use laws and various other techniques to police and regulate sexualities and performances of gender, thus subsequently ranking citizens into class of 'good, loyal reproducing heterosexual citizens' and 'a subordinated, marginalized class of noncitizen who, by virtue of choice and perversion, choose not to do so' (Alexander 2005, 46). This ranking of citizens reveals the working of heteropatriarchy, which includes the twin processes of heterosexualization and patriarchy, as the dominant organizing principle within the Caribbean region. Though Alexander focuses predominantly on the violence of Caribbean states in foreclosing on same-sex desires, the concept is also useful for making sense of the construction and disciplining of gender and sexuality, more broadly, by non-state actors and institutions, such as the church. In so much as heteropatriarchy refers to a structuring principle that signals the distinction and relatedness between the ways in which gender and sexuality are socially, legally and politically organised within our societies: "It privileges heterosexual, promiscuous masculinity [and heterosexual men's overall "experiences, definitions and perceptions of sexuality"] and subordinates feminine sexuality, normalising relations of power that are intolerant of and, oppressive toward sexual desires and practices that are outside of or oppose the dominant sexual and gender regimes (Kempadoo 2004, 9 quoted in Lazarus 2013a, 27).

While the heteropatriarchal discourse appears to remain dominant, there were, however, competing perspectives that highlight gray areas that do not seem to readily support or at first sight have anything to do with this particular discourse. However, based on my analysis, these gray areas often constitute contradictions within this discourse (especially where various contradictory ideas exists alongside each other) as well as outright challenges to it (usually in the form of people adopting new world views that call into question the dominant discourse's relevance and overall validity). Consider as an example the following statement made by a well known clergy man in Jamaica:

> People are still strongly, for whatever reasons, informed or uninformed, people have an emotional aversion to homosexuality, especially male homosexuality. (Pause) I think we have gone to the extreme, in terms, of treating them as if they are not persons. I have argued from the pulpit and from my radio programme on Love FM that nobody who sustains a negative view about homosexuality, as people as persons, can continue to consistently claim to be a Christian. You have to modify those views. They are people created by God and in the image of God and they are entitled to respect, irrespective of what they are doing. It is just like murderers are entitled to respect, they are killing people and that's not nice, but they are still people and we must respect as such. So, the agitation and the bad language and the foul language that we use at homosexuals, I don't support that as a Christian leader. And I don't think that we should ever think of lifting a hand to throw a stone or any implement at a homosexual because of their lifestyle. So many of the people in Church are doing other sins, which are just as heinous, the social gossipers are causing cancer in the Church in terms of relationships, but nobody treats them like sinners, they should be talked to too. They should be counselled to change their ways, try to respect them as persons. All behaviours are not equal and therefore some behaviour must be outlawed as immoral, abnormal, not proper, [and] not fitting for a particular society, because I think

it is a safe philosophical principle any behaviour that I countenance for myself I should be able to universalise for everybody and see what result would resound in the society. Will it help the common good or would it harm the common good? (in discussion with the author, April 3, 2011)

On the surface, one could quickly summise that the clergyman's statement simply reflects and in turn reinforces a heteropatriarchal discourse, in that he describes and supports steps to label certain sexual practices (namely 'homosexual ones') as 'immoral', 'abnormal', and 'dangerous', solely on the basis that they do not adhere to what is seen as 'natural' sexual practices and identities nor are inline with his interpretation of God's will; his involvement in debates unfolding within the wider society at the time of this interview also allows one to draw this conclusion. At the same time, however, we see certain contradictions in his speech, which seem to undermine, or at least complicate, certain heteropatriarchal principles. Namely, he vocalizes a rejection and condemnation of physical and verbal violence towards 'homosexuals', thus evincing conversance with other worldviews, such as appeals to a certain notion of rights and, of course, tolerance. Tolerance, however, does not disrupt heteropatriarchy (see Lazarus 2013a).

The ideological, political, and theoretical underpinnings of texts were obviously not always overtly visible, but rather, at times, emerged in subtle and even, as suggested, quite contradictory ways. Identifying and naming these more subtle ideological, political, and theoretical perspectives thus required some amount of judgment on the part of the researcher; such subjectivity may call into question the reliability of the analysis. However, to offset this possible shortcoming I used the existing academic literature, interview conversations, other more informal dialogues with knowledgeable individuals and, of course, close attention to the various debates (who is saying what and why) as well as the sheer breadth of the material analysed to guide (and support) my interpretations.

Nevertheless, one must also come to terms with the reality that critical discourse analysis or any form of textual analysis 'is also inevitably selective: in any analysis, we choose to ask certain questions about social events and texts, and not other possible questions' (Fairclough 2003, 14). Indeed, there is 'no such thing as an "objective" analysis of a text', even when the goal is simply to describe 'what is "there" in the text without being 'biased' by the subjectivity of the analyst' (ibid.). As Fairclough stresses, 'our ability to know what is "there" is inevitably limited and partial. And the questions we ask necessarily arise from particular motivations which go beyond what is "there"' (2003, 15). It is therefore natural that in this research, the questions I chose to ask, the phenomena I observed and the kinds of interpretations that I eventually formed were in large part influenced, as stated before, by a worldview inspired by feminisms. Part of this influence included a commitment to engaging in the ongoing practice of critical reflexivity, including self-reflexivity. This entails reflecting on the ways in which my own situated position, as a Caribbean insider/outsider/returnee, influenced the analysis process, specifically my access to resources, my navigation and understanding of the different contexts in which certain discourses were being circulated and, likewise, the arrived at meanings or interpretations of events and texts (see Lazarus 2013a, 2013b). Critical reflexivity thus entails an awareness of my role as an active player in the co-production of knowledge that emerged from the interviews and from the very practice of critical analysis. As Kim England (1994) puts it, this means recognizing that I am an instrument in my own research.

Ongoing reflexivity also extends to a continuous consideration of the importance of contexts in discourse formation and circulation. Also, it involves 'questioning the values and assumptions made by discourse analysis' (Baxter n.d., 2). Additionally, this process also includes a recognition of the partiality of what I could garner from a research that predominantly relied on discourse analysis of various types of texts, especially when the context of some of these were not always fully known. Though I conducted interviews to compensate for this limitation, it was also important to recognize that my key respondents, due also to their situated positions, only had partial knowledge of the broader sociocultural phenomena under investigation. I thus approached the interviews as an opportunity to engage also with knowledgeable persons who were not only sharing their experiences but also through our interaction, co-constructing knowledge about particular issues (some of these voices are often overlooked in the existing academic scholarship on Caribbean people's sexualities). The co-construction involved respondents and me sharing first- and second-hand experiences as well as personal thoughts and wider ideological viewpoints. This kind of interaction had an implication for the types of questions I asked and the ways in which I asked them (as well as on the ways in which I went about analysing non-interview textual materials). However, I had to accept that in the end I was in charge of the final analysis, with, of course, an accepted responsibility to represent my voice as well as that of my respondents.

Still, I had concerns about appropriation and misrepresentation of texts and people's opinions, but also an overwhelming sense that I had to, as England (1994) recommends, take responsibility for the research. Part of this responsibility was accepting my own active role in the research process. Thus, whilst it is crucial not to misrepresent or appropriate others' voices and texts in my analysis and authorship of this study, I also believed, like many feminist scholars, that I should not cede my interpretative authority. As such, my interpretations often existed alongside those of my interview respondents and others whose contributions to the debates are taken under consideration. One notable way in which this is evident is the use of direct quotes, as Anne Opie (2008) recommends, as well as the presentation, where applicable, of research subjects' alternative and even counter-interpretation and/or analysis of the issues. In so doing, the aim was to provide spaces '[...] in a discourse analysis for the coexistence of distinctively different voices and accounts, such as those of the research participants...' (Baxter n.d., 5), which adds layers to one's analysis. I again drew on and married elements of FPDA to my practice of CDA. This marrying of the approaches was crucial in my attempt to incorporate the voices of others in my critical analysis without, as England cautions, 'colonising them in a manner that reinforces patterns of domination' (1994, 242). Additionally, it is my attempt to move beyond the polarization that CDA and feminist CDA have been accused of reproducing, instead providing a more complex analysis of the social world, which includes dealing with differences and various nuances in the analysis, whilst at the same time striving to retain a degree of explicit political self-positioning and advocacy.

Conclusion

Critical discourse analysis is not a unified field of discourse analysis; rather, as exemplified in this paper with the emphasis on a feminist CDA, it is a multidisciplinary analytic strategy drawing on diverse epistemological and methodological perspectives (see also Baxter n.d.). A feminist critical discourse analysis as illustrated in this paper incorporates principles associated with CDA and feminists theoretical and methodological perspectives. As such, on the one hand it highlights the benefits of critically analysing discourses as a means of understanding the ways in which power plays out in knowledge construction in various forms of interactions, which shapes people's subjectivities and differential experiences. On the other, it explicitly emphasizes the usefulness of feminists' perspectives in guiding interpretations and the actual execution of the critical discourse analysis.

It was also, at times, useful to draw upon other approaches to discourse analysis, namely FPDA in the aforementioned research project. This combination was not seen as problematic, as the two feminist approaches share some commonality, including their incorporation of reflexivity into the research process. Moreover, a FPDA approach was beneficial because of its explicit emphasis on recognizing the complexities in people's subjectivities, relations and the workings of power. This theoretical underpinning informed the ways in which I interacted with interview respondents, but also the ways in which I read and interpreted various texts. Thus, I did not shy away from including in the analysis the various differences, contradictions and ambiguities that emerged from interview interactions and from the analysis of selected primary and secondary texts. These added tremendous value to the final research product and opened up other questions for ongoing research. For example, are non-conservative and non-fundamentalist Christian groups and leaders seeking to shape public national discussions around sexuality, gender, human rights and citizenship within the region? And, how do they support and/or challenge the conservative and fundamentalist discourses that remain dominant with certain public arenas in the Jamaican society? Although FPDA was, at times, useful, I ultimately identified more with the principles of feminist CDA, especially its unapologetic embracement of doing research that contributes to a feminist 'political agenda', even as I highlight complexities and differences and call into question (and shy away from producing) grand narratives.

My execution of a version of feminist CDA thus involved an in-depth analysis of various types of texts. By marrying a number of approaches to CDA, generally, and feminist CDA, I sought to investigate not only the structures or rules that govern what can be said and known, but also the actual linguistic features, content and meanings of particular texts and discourses. Importantly, I was interested in analysing what was being said and done by 'real' people in specific contexts. I examined what was being presented on the surface, but also the ideological underpinnings, which were not always easily apparent. In doing all this, I sought to show the following: the connections between various discourses; the power of discourses to shape people's subjectivities, experiences, and relations to each other; and, also the ways in which various discourses get reproduced, circulated, and, of course, challenged, all the time contending with and seeking to minimize my own limitations and biases throughout the research process.

Notes

1. This chapter is a critical reflection on conducting feminist critical discourse analysis of data collected as part of doctoral research on religion and sexuality in the Jamaica/Caribbean.
2. Fairclough (1992) acknowledges that Foucault does, in fact, pay some attention to textual analysis, through the concept of 'discursive practice.' However, 'he introduces this in a confusing way, as "rules" which underlie actual practice.' Thus, Foucault's focus, it would seem, tends to be more on "structures" to account 'for what can and does actually happen' (Fairclough 1992, 57). Consequently, Fairclough notes that, '[t]he questionable assumption is that one can extrapolate from structure to practice, that one can arrive at conclusions about practice without directly analyzing real instances of it, including texts' (ibid., 57–58).
3. Larry Chang, a prominent rights activist, responded, in the comments section of that editorial, by saying,

    "Thank you, *Gleaner*. That is the strongest position you have taken to date in protection of the rights of sexual minorities since the time in the '70s when you published my first letter on the subject and when you could only print the word gay in quotation marks. Kudos to Dane Lewis for bravely continuing the struggle. The evolution of Jamaican social consciousness is slow and painful but there is hope" (quoted in *Jamaica Gleaner*, April 1, 2011).

4. Initially, I sought to conduct at least fifteen interviews, however, this did not come to fruition and in the end I interviewed ten respondents. Other attempts to contact alternative respondents also failed, as these individuals did not respond to email and telephone requests; a few suggested that they heard about the study from colleagues but had nothing new to contribute.
5. The selected persons met at least two of the following conditions: (1) they actively participated in the public discussions (in the media and/or legal forums) about constitutional reform and/or the review of the country's abortion laws; (2) they entered these discussions as interested citizens or as representatives of an organization (whether a church, a governing body of

churches, other faith-based institutions, women's as well as sexual rights groups); (3) they participated in broader discussions or work around other sexuality-related matters (such as HIV and AIDS, sexual rights activism or research matters relating to sexuality) within the country and/or region as a whole; and (4) they were either self-identified Christians, or knew, based on their participation in the various activities and/or interactions with others who had first-hand knowledge, of the ways in which Christian groups and individuals shape sexual politics and ongoing debates around sexuality in Jamaica and/or the Anglophone Caribbean in general.

6. Ma. Dolores C. Tongco states that

> there is no cap on how many informants should make up a purposive sample, as long as the needed information is obtained...Seidler (1974) [for example] studied different sample sizes of informants selected purposively and found that at least five informants were needed for the data to be reliable. It is important to lessen bias within the sampling population and to have some idea of the variation in the data. If unbiased informants are scarce, finding informants that are biased in both ways allows for finding the middle ground and cancelling out extreme biases during data interpretation (2007, 152).

7. Snowballing may be distinguished from judgement or purposive sampling in that the latter 'does not necessarily use the sources of an informant as an informant as well' (Bernard 2002 quoted in Tongco 2007, 125).

8. A few sources, for example, television talk show interviews, were only analysed manually.

References

Alexander, Jacqui M. 2005. *Pedagogies of Crossing: Meditations on feminism, Sexual Politics, Memory, and the Sacred*. Durham and London: Duke University Press.

———. 1991. Redrafting Morality: The Postcolonial State and the Sexual Offences Bill of Trinidad and Tobago. In *Third World Women and the Politics of Feminism*, edited by C.T. Mohanty, A. Russo and L. Torres, 133–42. Bloomington, IN: Indiana University Press.

Barrow, Christine. 1995. 'Living in Sin': Church and Common-Law Union in Barbados. *The Journal of Caribbean History* 29, no. 2:47–70.

Baxter, Judith. n.d. Feminist Post-Structuralist Discourse Analysis – A New Theoretical and Methodological Approach? Retrieved September 2013. https://research.aston.ac.uk/portal/files/216277/Feminist_Post.pdf.

Blackwood, Evelyn. 1995. Falling in Love with An-Other Lesbian: Reflections on Identity in Fieldwork. In *Taboo: Sex, Identity and Erotic Subjectivity in Anthropological Fieldwork*, ed. D. Kulick, and M. Wilson, 51–73. New York: Routledge.

Blommaert, Jan. 2005. *Discourse: Key Topics in Sociolinguistics*. Cambridge, U.K.: Cambridge University Press.

Collins, Patricia Hill. 1986. Learning from the Outsider Within: The Sociological Significance of Black Feminist Thought. *Social Problems* 33, no. 6:514–32. Retrieved April 02, 2018 (URL: http://www.jstor.org/stable/800672)

DeVault, Marjorie L. 1999. *Liberating Method: Feminism and Social Research.* Philadelphia: Temple University Press.
Edwards, Rosalind. 1990. Connecting Method and Epistemology: A White Woman Interviewing Black Women. *Women's Studies International Forum* 13, no. 5:477–90. doi10.1016/0277-5395(90)90100-C.
England, Kim, V.L. 1994. Getting Personal: Reflexivity, Positionality, and Feminist Research. *The Professional Geographer* 46, no. 1:241–56. Retrieved June 10, 2017. http://www.praxis-epress.org/CGR/18-England.pdf.
Fairclough, Norman. 2003. *Analysing Discourse: Textual Analysis for Social Research.* London and New York: Routedge, Taylor and Francis Group.
———. 1992. *Discourse and Social Change.* Cambridge, U.K.: Polity Press.
Fairclough, Norman and Ruth Wodak. 1997. Critical Discourse Analysis. In *Discourse as Social Interaction: Discourse Studies: A Multidisciplinary Introduction*, vol. 2, ed. T. A. van Dijk, 258–84. Thousand Oaks, CA: Sage Publications.
Foucault, Michel. [1976] 1990. *The History of Sexuality: An Introduction.* Vol. 1. Trans. Hurley. Reprint, New York: Vintage Books.
Hall, Stuart, ed. [1997] 2003. *Representation: Cultural Representations and Signifying Practices.* Reprint, London, Thousand Oaks, CA, New Delhi: Sage Publications.
Harding, Sandra, ed. 1987. *Feminism and Methodology: Social Science Issues.* Bloomington, IN: Indiana University Press.
———, ed. 2004. *The Feminist Standpoint Reader: Intellectual and Political Controversies.* New York and Great Britain: Routledge.
———. 2008. Borderlands Epistemologies. In *Just Methods: An Interdisciplinary Feminist Reader*, ed. A. M. Jaggar, 331–41. Boulder, CO; London: Paradigm Publishers.
Jamaica Gleaner. 2011. Editorial – End Discrimination Towards Gays Now. April 01. Retrieved November 03, 2011. http://jamaica-gleaner.com/gleaner/20110401/ cleisure/cleisure1.html.
Jayaratne, Toby Epstein, and Stewart, Abigail J. 1991. Quantitative and Qualitative Methods in the Social Sciences: Current Feminist Issues and Practical Strategies. In *Beyond Methodology: Feminist Scholarship as Lived Research*, ed. Mary M. Fonow and Judith A. Cook, 85–106. Bloomington, IN: Indiana Press.
Kempadoo, Kamala. 2001. Freelancers, Temporary Wives and Beach-Boys: Researching Sex Work in the Caribbean. *Feminist Review* 67:39–62.
———. 2004. *Sexing the Caribbean: Gender, Race and Sexual Labor.* New York: Routledge.
Lazar, Michelle M. 2007. Feminist Critical Discourse Analysis: Articulating a Feminist Discourse Praxis. *Critical Discourse Studies* 4, no. 2:141–64. doi:10.1080/17405900701464816.
Lazarus, Latoya. 2015. Sexual Citizenship and Conservative Christian Mobilisation in Jamaica. *Journal of Eastern Caribbean Studies* 40, no. 1:109–40.
———.2013a. The Church and the Law: Examining the Role of Christianity in Shaping Sexual Politics in Jamaica. PhD diss., York University.
———. 2013b. Working with Marginalised and 'Hidden' Populations: Researchers' Anxieties and Strategies for Doing Less Harmful Research. *Caribbean*

Review of Gender Studies 13:1–2, ed. Kamala Kempadoo, Halimah DeShong, and Charmaine Crawford.

Marshall, Martin N. 1996. Sampling for Qualitative Research. *Family Practice* 13:522–25. Retrieved December 28, 2012. http://fampra.oxfordjournals.org.

Massiah, Joycelin. June 1986. Women in the Caribbean Project: An Overview. *Social and Economic Studies* 35, no. 2:1–29.

Murray, David A. B. 2012. *Flaming Souls: Homosexuality, Homophobia, and Social Change in Barbados.* Toronto, Buffalo, London: University of Toronto Press.

Naples, Nancy. 2003. *Feminism & Method: Ethnography, Discourse Analysis, & Activist Research.* New York and London: Routledge.

Opie, Anne. 2008. Qualitative Research, Appropriation of the 'Other' and Empowerment. In *Just Methods: An Interdisciplinary Feminist Reader*, ed. A. M. Jaggar, 362–73. Boulder, CO; London: Paradigm Publishers.

Perkins, Anna Kasafi. 2016. More than Words: Evangelicals, the Rhetoric of Battle and the fight Over Gay Rights in the Caribbean. *Journal of Eastern Caribbean Studies* 41, no. 1:13–46.

Smith, Dorothy. 1987. *The Everyday World as Problematic.* Boston, MA: Northeastern University Press.

Smith, Linda T. 1999. *Decolonising Methodology: Research and Indigenous People.* London: New York: Zed Books.

Tongco, Dolores C. 2007. Purposive Sampling as a Tool for Informant Selection. *Ethnobotany Research & Applications* 5:147–58. Retrieved September 22, 2012. http://www.ethnobotanyjournal.org.

van Dijk, Teun A. 2015. Critical Discourse Analysis. In *The Handbook of Discourse Analysis, Second Edition*, ed. D. Tannen, H.E. Hamilton and D. Schiffrin, 466–85. John Wiley & Sons.

———. 1991. Editorial: Discourse Analysis with a Cause. *The Semiotic Review of Books* 2: 1–2.

———. 1988. *News Analysis: Case Studies of International and National News in the Press.* Hillsdale, NJ: Lawrence Erlbaum.

Weedon, Chris. 1987. *Feminist Practice and Poststructuralist Theory.* London: Blackwell.

Welsh, Elaine. 2002. Dealing with Data: Using NVivo in the Qualitative Data Analysis Process. *Forum: Qualitative Social Research* 3, no. 2 Art. 26:1–12. Retrieved December 12, 2012. http://www.qualitative-research.net/index.php/fqs/article/view/865/1880.

24. Caribbean/Anticolonial Feminist Methods for Analysing Talk and Text in Research on Gender-Based Violence

Halimah A. F. DeShong

Introduction

The inter- and multi-disciplinary work on gender and sexuality in the Caribbean, conducted largely by feminist researchers, has provided a range of conceptual and analytical tools for reading data produced as talk, text, images, and actions. For example, working with still images in the form of paintings and photographs, Patricia Mohammed (2009) and Roshini Kempadoo (2013a, 2013b) provide methods for reading visual cultural artefacts. This work calls attention to a need to decode colonial images in ways that account for the political and social context out of which they were created (Mohammed 2009), acknowledging photography's purpose and function as inherent to the colonial project (Kempadoo 2013a, 2013b). Preparing audio-recorded interviews (a source of data widely utilized in Caribbean feminist research) involves converting identity and identity relations into text, as well as navigating 'intersecting and cross-sectional identities' (Rowley 2002, 23). While reading/analysing/writing about data is inextricably linked to the philosophical and, by extension, epistemic investments in the production of any study, the insights offered by Mohammed, Kempadoo, and Rowley point to a method through which aural, textual, and visual data should be read across multiple and overlapping levels, simultaneously.

My own analysis of qualitative data, emerging from talk and text on gender-based violence, centres on a commitment to exposing the materiality of discourse/narratives/storying. Analytical techniques taken up in the study of violence ought to expose the material/discursive effects of talk and text, or how such data 'mark the flesh of the individual' (Rowley 2002, 26). Moreover, such work involves erecting histories and geographies of violence, specific to the making of the Caribbean. In this chapter, I present a methodology for reading talk and text on gender-based violence (specifically that which occurs in Caribbean heterosexual unions), grounded in Caribbean/anticolonial feminist research praxis.

While, in this chapter, I isolate data analysis from other aspects of research and research design, the processes by which knowledge is generated in any study are interlinked. Elsewhere, I have discussed what it means to engage feminist methodological approaches in conducting interviews on intimate partner violence in the Caribbean (DeShong 2013). In many ways, this chapter builds on that earlier conversation about Caribbean feminist approaches to research as consciously engaged in the process of producing situated knowledge. The focus here on how data can be read is inspired by my experience of teaching feminist research methodologies to graduate students and their desire to see more explicit discussions of data analysis processes and approaches in Caribbean feminist methodology literature. Their challenge has forced me to begin the process of consciously collecting my own thinking about and methods for reading data based on talk and text on violence and intimacy.

Situating the Study of Violence and Intimacy in the Caribbean

It is well documented and widely cited that a major problem in Caribbean societies is the so-called rising levels of violence and violent crimes. State-produced statistics on crime are often used as the basis upon which to conclude that the Caribbean is more violent now than ever before. My personal preoccupation has to do with how we might challenge the dominance of reductionist explanations in which violence gets coded as an effect of interpersonal conflict and/or 'cultural peculiarities' within the Caribbean. The coding and counting of specific manifestations of violence through surveys and official statistics, produced by various arms of the state, as well as media coverage on some of the most gruesome murders, provide the basis upon which claims about rising levels of physical harm in the region are made. This distortion of violence in Caribbean societies masks the creation of the Caribbean itself; a process and set of practices enacted through the most heinous attempts at cultural erasure and the use of brute force. Physical violence as a perpetual feature of life in the region, occurs as part of larger mechanisms of regulation, surveillance, and control that are themselves violent processes. Franz Fanon (2008), M. Jacqui Alexander (2005), Hilary Beckles (2013 and 2016), Deborah Thomas (2011), Sylvia Wynter (2003), Mimi Sheller (2012), and several other Caribbean intellectuals, as well as the intellectual work performed across various social movements, provide the conceptual tools for locating violence in the region at the intersection of race, gender, class, sexuality, and ability; and as embedded within histories dominated by colonial relations power. Indeed, Thomas urges us to think about violence, not as a consequence of culture but as 'an effect of class formation, a process that is immanently racialized and gendered' (2011, 4). While this move signals an important shift in the starting point away from violence as culture to one in which we attend to its structural and institutional contexts, I propose that we think about violence as those mechanisms of power enacted to maintain particular racial categorizations at the time of the emergence of European colonialism; out of which a coloniality of gender (Lugones 2010 and 2016) and gendered violence emerges. Omi'seke Natasha Tinsely reminds us that we occupy 'a Caribbean landscape that was never a natural topos but one constructed for colonial purposes' and that it was under such conditions that the cane field became 'a site for sexual violence and exploited labour' (2010, 3).

Women's and feminist organizing on gender-based violence have generated some of the most productive analyses of how a history of structural and institutionalized inequalities creates the conditions under which women, children, and persons who do not conform to normative gender identity expression are made most vulnerable to gender-based harms. In short, gender and sexuality operate in ways that make these groups vulnerable to experiencing violence. Significant legislative and policy shifts aimed at addressing gender-based violence have occurred across countries in the Caribbean. While these shifts in legislation and policy were largely due to feminist activism in the region, they lack the critical interventions about colonialism and gendered violence made by Caribbean and other global South feminists.

Official statistics on homicide perpetrated against an intimate partner in the Caribbean (as well as in other parts of the world) reveal a pattern in which the victims of these crimes are overwhelmingly women killed by a male partner. Explanations of violence mobilized in interviews on intimate partner violence are often saturated with a colonial gender logic

(DeShong 2018). As part of my on-going research on scripting violence in the Caribbean, I examine how the narration of GBV betray broader socio-historical and sociocultural investments. More recently, my approach to reading violence, particularly intimate partner violence (IPV), has explicitly engaged Caribbean and other anticolonial feminist frames of analysis. Such violence is understood as multi-layered and multiply produced. Based on this conceptualization of IPV and GBV, I have deployed aspects of narrative and discourse analysis to operationalize a method for reading IPV based on text translated from interview talk, those contained in media scripts and state-generated case files of violent crimes involving IPV. This approach is outlined in the foregoing. For the purpose of this chapter, I focus on reading data generated from qualitative, one-on-one in-depth interviews.

The Politics of Reading as Epistemic Practice

In my early writings on IPV in the Caribbean, I performed focused discourse analysis of interview text as my main approach for understanding how women and men draw on socially available explanations in accounting for violence (DeShong 2011, 2014 and 2015). In all three publications cited here, I provide a synopsis of how feminist poststructuralist discourse analysis (FPDA) was deployed as both conceptual and analytical tool. In these writings and (more expansively) in my doctoral thesis, I make a case for this approach as attentive to both the textual and intertextual context inherent in explanations of violence, and, more specifically, the gendered relations of power inherent in the storying of violence.

The approach applied at that time was informed by discourse analysis (DA) and it centred on the notion that language structures/mediates reality. Feminist poststructuralism was endorsed as a framework for assessing the gendered relations of power inherent in language (Weedon 1997). As an analytical tool, a specific version of DA was identified as compatible with a feminist-poststructuralist framework (Baxter 2003; Gavey 1997), for the examination of language as the main unit of analysis. The approach to DA utilized then involved a particular reading of texts by focusing on how 'speakers draw from culturally available explanatory frameworks to construct the objects about which they speak and an array of subject positions' (Avdi 2005, 498). The concern then was with what language is used for (Brown and Yule 1983); and how talk and texts are used to perform action (Potter 2003).

DA, itself, is an umbrella term for a range of methodologies for reading text drawn from a variety of theoretical traditions and from a range of disciplines. Critical Discourse Analysis and Feminist Critical Discourse Analysis, Discursive Psychology, Foucauldian Discourse Analysis and FPDA are examples of the different forms of DA defined in the methodological literature. What they share in common, according to Gill, 'is a rejection of the realist notion that language is simply a neutral means of reflecting or describing the world, and a conviction to the central importance of discourse in constructing social life' (2000, 172). In these approaches dialogue is a primary condition of the production of discourse (Abrams 1999; Bakhtin 1994; Mills 2004). What can be gleaned from the several disciplinary perspectives on discourse is that it refers to 'groupings of utterances or sentences, statements which are enacted within a social context, which are determined by a social context and which contribute to the way that social context continues its existence' (Mills 2004, 10). Discourses are named as dialogically produced and maintained, and as such should not be regarded in isolation. It involves the study of situated meanings produced in talk and text (Sunderland and Litosseliti 2002). These meanings are said to be negotiated between people in a discursive context or through social interaction.

Though FPDA was meant to capture specificity in narratives of IPV as gendered in my early work, a number of epistemic, conceptual, and methodological tensions emerged. There was insufficient emphasis on such violence as enfleshed, institutional, and structural in reading personal accounts of violence through the prism of FPDA. In other words, the materiality of IPV was often not made explicit. The embodied, racialized history of gender was also insufficiently reckoned with in this early work. While some of the tools for reading talk and text, drawn from DA, remain useful in my later work, a shift away from the conceptual focus on FPDA as the prism through which to read IPV, developed. In many ways, the tensions between my anticolonial feminist politics and the methods for reading and conceptualizing literary, and aural and textual data, cultivated in the university classroom, was confronted as I developed a larger archive of data, and made a conscious decision to historically locate my analysis. If we regard reading/analysing data as epistemic practice – the outcome of which shapes the kind of knowledge generated – then we must constantly interrogate not only our philosophical grounding, but also the conceptual and analytical devices we use, as feminists working from/in/on the Caribbean, for how they might inhere the very arrangements we seek to displace. This reflection provided a basis from which I began to shift my conceptual and analytical approach to the study of IPV.

Caribbean/Anticolonial Feminist Textual Analysis for Reading Data on Intimate Partner Violence

Caribbean and other global South feminists have always been critical of the centrality of the man/woman binary in Western feminist frameworks. In particular, the theoretical works of Sylvia Wynter (2003), Maria Lugones (2010 and 2016), and Xhercis Méndez (2015) reveal how the invention of race with the emergence of settler colonialism in North, Central and South America, and the Caribbean calls on us to centre the human/non-human distinction in feminist thought and analysis. Several scholars working in this tradition, define their approach as decolonial/anticolonial feminist methodology/praxis. They acknowledge that gender never travels away from a colonial/modern system, and its attendant logic.

Michelle Rowley (2002) has argued that researchers must make sense of articulations of self in talk and text that do not reproduce dichotomies but instead captures the intertextuality and embodiment of discourse. Cautious of the effects of adopting a purely linguistic approach, Rowley outlines the strength of doing textual readings, in which the material effects of experience and talk are at the centre of the analysis. I place Michelle Rowley, Roshini Kempadoo, and Patricia Mohammed's approaches to reading text and images within anticolonial feminist analyses that centre the materiality of textual and visual data within Caribbean historical relations of power. Applied to the study of violence, IPV, in particular, is revealed as an effect of challenges to a dichotomous and hierarchical gender order. By displacing the focus on the man/woman distinction so pervasive in much of Northern feminist analyses, a decolonial/anticolonial feminist approach exposes these narratives of IPV as imbued with harmful and overlapping assumptions about race, class, gender, and sexuality (DeShong 2018). For example, mobilizng a colonialist gendered logic, men who use violence often narrate themselves as victims of women's irrationality and disobedience. They mobilize the very logic engaged to organize Caribbean society into free and unfree, labour and capital/capitalist under colonial rule – in ways that defied the binary man/woman gendered logic to which they remain attached. Put differently, these explanations and rationalisations of violence often feature a binary gendered logic produced in colonial societies that were organised largely along racial/ised categories. This way of reading data grew out of a need to revisit how 'gender' is deployed as analytical tool in keeping with anti/decolonial feminist politics and praxis.

In my earlier work I argued that:

> Given the lack of focus on the socio-political and socio-historical context within which Caribbean gender systems are created and sustained in the research on IPV, frameworks that centre the production of gender and its attendant relations of power, in explanations of violence, predominate in Caribbean research (DeShong 2018, 124).

Though usefully pointing to the salience of gendered scripts, actions, beliefs, and institutions in undergirding the practice of violence, this work ought to interrogate the coloniality of gender and account for the 'dehumanizing and racializing work that [it] performed' (Mendez 2015, 49). This move should not be read as an attempt to eliminate 'gender' as one of several Caribbean feminist analytical devices, but to deploy the concept in ways that recognizes that it does not operate away from a colonial/modern logic of race and racialization. To this end, I have proposed that:

> Rather than thinking about the colonial/modern logic of race and racialization as intersecting other social relations of power such as class, sexuality and ability (as is often the case in reductionist (mis) applications of black feminist scholarship on intersectionality) the theoretical import of a decolonial feminist analysis is its focus on how race and racialization organize social relations in an attempt to produce normative bodies/citizens and systems of power. In other words, race and racialization overdetermines the production of gender, (hetero)sexuality, class domination and citizenship in post-colony societies (DeShong 2018, 124).

This shift in vantage point for conducting textual analysis on IPV in the Caribbean can be observed in how women from different racialized and classed positions are interpolated within and across the nation-state. Both African American and Afro-Caribbean working-class women are often positioned outside a white Anglo-American gendered logic based on the man/woman binary in discussions of IPV (See the works of Danns and Parsad 1987; Brice-Baker 1994; O'Neal and Beckman 2017, for examples of this). Danns and Parsad's early observation that Afro-Guyanese women are regarded as fighting with their partners, while Indo-Guyanese women are cited as experiencing violence against women, is one such example of how engaging the state through its agents in law enforcement and social welfare disturb dichotomous and hierarchal assumptions of gender, based on the man/woman binary. These distinctive subject positions created for Indo- and Afro-Caribbean women, perform equally troubling and racist harm against both groups of women. Similarly, constructions of African-American and Afro-Caribbean women in the US are imbued with notions of Black women as strong, emasculating matriarchs, responsible for causing the violence they report (Brice-Baker 1994). Thus, 'it becomes even more urgent to assess gender as a system and as a set of racialised practices bequeathed us when considering the state and social response to IPV in the Caribbean' (DeShong 2018, 125).

So what does this vantage point offer by way of performing concrete analyses on qualitative data produced about IPV? To recap, I perform and propose a reading of qualitative data on IPV in the Caribbean that does the following:

1. Locates narratives of violence and intimacy within broader understandings of violence in Caribbean society. Such violence is cited as epistemic, structural, institutional, interpersonal, felt/embodied/enfleshed, and strategic. IPV narratives are read within situated histories and geographies of violence.
2. Reconfigures gender analysis, so central to the feminist literature on IPV, as explicitly anticolonial/decolonial to account for the specific context out of which gender systems and logics emerge in the region.
3. Mobilizes specific techniques for reading text and performing intertextual analysis to capture the material/discursive effects of textual data on gendered violence, as well as its antecedents.

The selection of a set of techniques for reading text is intimately tied to the research questions posed, as well as the philosophical and conceptual orientation of the study. This is also the case as it relates to data collection, and the overall research design. I have found the selection of techniques, drawn from both narrative and discourse analysis particularly useful, when performing textual analysis, guided by the three concerns outlined above.

Rather than centre discourse and narrative analysis as that which drives the generation of knowledge about IPV in the Caribbean, an iterative process of moving between insights drawn from the data itself and the politics of a Caribbean anticolonial/decolonial feminist reading of talk and text are prioritized. In short, even as the methodological literature provides several approaches to reading qualitative data based on text and talk, approaches taken up in any study should emerge out of a set of philosophical, conceptual, and methodological concerns specific to that research.

Both narrative and discourse analysis trace how individuals and institutions erect and arrange stories. Both approaches are concerned with the production of meaning in language. Narrative analysis emphasizes what *stories* accomplish in a given situation, while the techniques drawn from discourse analysis emphasize the actions performed and meanings produced in language. Storying of events and experiences are prioritized in the former. There is overlap in how both narrative and discourse analysis emphasize the ways in which experiences and events are constructed, however, in discourse analysis there is, indeed, greater emphasis on intertextuality or rather how a speaker or text draw on existing ways of framing and producing meaning.

There exists the possibility for conceptual slippages in my simultaneous reference to the production of narratives and discourses in accounts of IPV, given the varied theoretical lineage within and across both approaches. However, this is mitigated by my more recent practical view of both types of analyses as providing a set of techniques through which to foreground a Caribbean anticolonial/decolonial feminist reading of IPV. The shared focus on how talk is organised provides a set of practical methods for systematising data analysis.

A narrative, according to Catherine Kohler Riessman (2003), can mean a person's entire life story as articulated in interviews, documents, or observations; stories based on characters, setting and plot; and it might also signify long sections of talk or extended accounts over one or several interviews. Discourses are ways of defining the world, in which speakers/writers re/produce/resist existing frames of reference. They reveal the operation of power. In the production of discourses, speakers/writers often position themselves and others. Particularly useful is how both approaches regard narratives and discourses as refracting, rather than mirroring actual events and experiences.

To summarise, my own method of reading text entails a focus on:

1. How talk and text are organized;
2. Navigating across the narrative structuring of accounts, and the identification and interpretation of the discourses mobilised as individuals story violence.
3. The dialogic production of talk and text in the context of the interview;
4. The actions performed as stories about violence are created and the material effects of producing specific explanations for violence; and
5. The broader assumptions embedded in speech.

This method for analysing talk and text is even more specific when the subject and speaker are considered. The experience of conducting over 50 interviews with Vincentian police officers, prosecutors, lawyers, counsellors, activists, officials within the state gender machinery, survivors/victims and perpetrators, and analysing the data generated fosters the development of additional tools for reading and conceptualizing IPV. Although, the focus here is on reading interview data, the broader project includes case files, print media, popular culture, policy documents, and legislation. When the analysis is performed across these multiple sources/types of data, the storying of IPV often inheres harmful and overlapping assumptions about gender, race, class, and sexuality, even in instances where agents of the state explore/propose forms of remediation. The structure, content, and strategies used to frame accounts of IPV demonstrate widespread endorsement of what has been described here as the colonial logic of gender. Consequently, the very strategies created to address violence often reinforce the rationalizations and ideologies associated with its enactment in intimate relationships. In other words, the analysis of these sources of data through anticolonial/decolonial feminist lenses exposes how IPV is overwhelmingly produced (across these various sites) as an effect of challenges to this specific gendered logic. In short, the approach for reading these data simultaneously engages a specific set of techniques, a conceptual approach grounded in anticolonial/decolonial feminist research praxis and a knowledge-base on IPV generated over a number of years of working in the field.

To illustrate the application of this approach, I use an example of analysis drawn from a previously published paper on the subject. The extract comes from an interview with a Vincentian woman on her experience of IPV. Below, I provide both the extract and my reading of our conversation at this stage of the interview:

> *Int.:* In terms of housework, how did you'll get along deciding how you would share the chores?
>
> *Chantal:* Me. He's not sharing. He doesn't want to do anything. He just wants to sit down whole day watching TV or on the phone whole day with women. If he goes out and comes back and doesn't meet food he would want to lash you.
>
> Chantal's account is indicative of men's attempt to sustain particular arrangements of power in violent intimate relationships. There is an expectation of women's domesticity. In spite of the historical participation of large groups of Caribbean women in the public paid labour force…there remains the tendency to situate these women within British colonialist middle-class values of femininity bequeathed by a history of colonialism in the Anglophone Caribbean. This explains men's expectation of their evening meal upon arrival. These examples emphasise unequal relations of power between men and women in the context of intimate relationships and the family. Colonialist discourses on gender are used to justify violence against women who, in men's view, fail to satisfy the ideals of domesticity. These discourses are also used to blame women for men's use of violence (DeShong 2018, 136–37).

In the above reading, I situate the exchange with Chantal within histories of violence, that is, the violence of a colonialist gendered logic. Chantal signals this logic when she mentions the violent consequence of a failure to acquiesce to regulations around domesticity. It is equally important to identify how she responds to my supposition that household chores may have been shared. The sharpness and brevity of her response are clues to her disapproval of her partner's lack of participation. It is in reading both the narrative structure of her response, alongside its intertextual content that a picture of her discomfort with this colonist gendered logic emerges. The organization, dialogic production of meaning, localized and intertextual content, the actions performed in speech, and the assumptions embedded in talk and text are read simultaneously in performing this specific form of analysis.

Performing analysis of interview data, particularly with men who have perpetrated violence, emphasizes how individuals are invested in presenting particular versions of themselves in the interview. A consistent feature of interviews with men is a tendency to externalize violence, define violence as disembodied acts (becoming someone or something else), present themselves as essentially non-violent, minimize their actions, deploy the use of the passive voice as a strategy to distance themselves from the use of violence, and engage in strategic silences (DeShong 2017 and 2018). It is through a simultaneous reading of the narrative structure and organization of the content of men's talk that I was able to decode the actions performed and the possible purpose of producing their narratives in specific ways. The operationalization of and consciousness about methods for reading data must be cultivated over time. Working iteratively, I was able to develop a means through which to read meanings of men's silences and men's overall strategic self-presentation.

Conclusion

Over the years of conducting qualitative research on gendered violence using mostly, but not exclusively, in-depth one-one-one interviews as sources of data, I have applied two main approaches to textual analysis – discourse and narrative analysis. My orientation to deploying techniques of data analysis from both approaches have shifted with time. In the earlier work, while recognizing and accounting for the intertextuality of talk and text, the analysis was not sufficiently anchored in histories of violence in the region. Performing data analysis for qualitative research on gender-based violence in the Caribbean requires a robust conceptualization of both gender and violence as produced out of specific historical and social context. The material effects of specific ways of storying violence and the extent to which they inhere colonialist gendered logic have become fundamental to my approach to reading and writing about violence and intimacy. The tools offered within narrative and discourse analysis provide useful ways in which to systematise methods of data analysis driven by decolonial/ anticolonial feminist politics. My analysis has focused on the historically and socially situated ways in which text and talk are organized/structured, used to perform specific actions and to achieve specific effects, mobilized to generate particular subject positions, and produced inter-textually and materially.

References

Abrams, M.H. 1999. *A Glossary of Literary Terms*. 7th ed. Fort Worth: Harcourt Brace Publishers.

Alexander, M. Jacqui. 2005. *Pedagogies of Crossing: Meditations on Feminism, Sexual Politics, Memory, and the Sacred*. Duke University Press.

Avdi, Evrinomy. 2005. Negotiating a Pathological Identity in the Clinical Dialogue: Discourse Analysis of a Family Therapy. *Psychology and Psychotherapy: Theory, Research and Practice* 78:493–511.

Bakhtin, Mikhail. 1994. *The Bakhtin Reader*, ed. Pam Morris. London: Arnold.

Baxter, Judith. 2007. *Positioning Gender in Discourse: A Feminist Methodology*. Houndmills: Palgrave Macmillan.

Beckles, Hilary. 2013. *Britain's Black Debt: Reparations for Slavery and Native Genocide*. Jamaica, West Indies: University of West Indies Press.

———. 2016. *The First Black Slave Society: Britain's 'Barbarity Time' in Barbados, 1636–1876*. Kingston: University of the West Indies Press.

Brice-Baker, Janet R. 1994. Domestic violence in African-American and African-Caribbean Families. *Journal of Social Distress and the Homeless* 3, no. 1:23–38.

Brown, Gillian, and George Yule. 1983. *Discourse Analysis*. Cambridge: Cambridge University Press.

Danns, G.K., and Parsad, B.S. 1989. 'Domestic Violence in the Caribbean: A Guyana Case Study.' Georgetown: Women's Studies Unit, University of Guyana.

DeShong, Halimah A.F. 2018. The Language of Violence in the Caribbean: A Decolonial Feminist Analysis. In *Caribbean Crime & Criminal Justice: Impacts of Post-Colonialism and Gender on Crime*, ed. Corin Bailey and Katharina J. Joosen, 123–38. London: Routledge.

———. 2017. 'The Will to Forget': Silences and Minimisations in Men's Talk on Violence. *Journal of Eastern Caribbean Studies* 42, no. 3.

———. 2015) Policing femininity, Affirming Masculinity: Relationship Violence, Control and Spatial Limitation. *Journal of Gender Studies* 24, no. 1: 85–103.

———. 2014. Gendered Discourses of Romantic love/ing and Violence. In *Doing Gender, Doing Love: Interdisciplinary Voices*, ed. S. Petrella, 103–22. Oxford: Inter-Disciplinary Press.

———. 2011. Gender, Sexuality and Sexual Violence: A Feminist Analysis of Vincentian Women's Experiences in Violent Heterosexual Relationships. *Journal of Eastern Caribbean Studies* 36, no. 2:65–96.

———. 2013. Feminist Reflexive Interviewing: Researching Violence against Women in St Vincent and the Grenadines. Special Issue on Caribbean Feminist Research Methods for Gender and Sexuality Studies, *Caribbean Review of Gender Studies*, Iss.7:1–24.

Fanon, Frantz. 2008. *Black Skin, White Masks*. New York: Grove Press.

Gavey, Nicola. 1997. Feminist Poststructuralism and Discourse Analysis. In *Toward a New Psychology of Gender: A Reader*, ed. Mary M. Gergen and Sara N. Davis, 49–64. New York: Routledge.

Gill, Rosalind. 2000. Discourse Analysis. In *Qualitative Researching with Text, Image and Sound*, ed. Martin W. Bauer and George Gaskell, 173–190. London: Sage Publications.

Kempadoo, Roshini. 2013a. Gazing Outward and Looking Back: Configuring Caribbean Visual Culture. *Small Axe: A Caribbean Journal of Criticism* 41: 136–53.

———. 2013b. Women Subjects: Photographs in Trinidad (1860s–1960s). *Caribbean Review of Gender Studies* 7:1–16.

Lugones, Maria. 2016. The Coloniality of Gender. In *The Palgrave Handbook of Gender and Development*, ed. W. Harcourt, 13–33. Houndsmill: Palgrave Macmillan.

Lugones, Maria. 2010. Toward a Decolonial Feminism. *Hypatia* 25, no. 4:742–59.

Méndez, X. 2015. Notes Toward a Decolonial Feminist Methodology: Revisiting the Race/Gender Matrix. *Transcripts* 5:41–59.

Mills, Sarah. 2004. *Discourse*. London: Routledge.

Mohammed, Patricia. 2009. *Imaging the Caribbean: Culture and Visual Translation*. Macmillan.

O'Neal, N., and L. Beckman. 2017. Intersections of Race, Ethnicity and Gender: Reframing Knowledge Surrounding Barriers to Social Services Among Latina Intimate Partner Victims. *Violence against Women* 23, no. 5 2017:643–65.

Potter, Jonathan. 2003. Discourse Analysis and Discursive Psychology. *Qualitative Research in Psychology: Expanding Perspectives in Methodology and Design*, ed. P.M. Camic, J.E. Rhodes and L. Yardley, 1–30. Washington: American Psychology Association.

Riessman, Catherine Kohler. 2003. Performing Identities in Illness Narrative: Masculinity and Multiple Sclerosis. *Qualitative Research* 3, no. 1:5–33.

Sheller, Mimi. 2012. *Citizenship from Below: Erotic Agency and Caribbean Freedom*. Duke University Press.

Sunderland, Jane, and Lia Litosseliti. 2002. Gender Identity and Discourse Analysis: Theoretical and Empirical Considerations. In *Gender Identity and Discourse Analysis*, ed. Jane Sunderland and Lia Litosseliti, 3–39. Amsterdam: John Benjamins Publishing Company.

Thomas, Deborah A. 2011. *Exceptional Violence: Embodied Citizenship in Transnational Jamaica*. Durham, NC: Duke University Press.

Tinsley, Omi'seke Natasha. 2010. *Thiefing Sugar: Eroticism between Women in Caribbean Literature*. Duke University Press.

Weedon, Chris. 1998. *Feminist Practice & Poststructuralist Theory*. 2nd ed. Oxford: Blackwell Publishers.

Wynter, Sylvia. 2003. Unsettling the Coloniality of Being/Power/Truth Freedom: Towards the Human, After Man, its Overrepresentation – An Argument. *CR: The New Centennial Review* 3, no. 3:257–37.

Reflections on Positionality: Lessons from the Field

25. Toward a Native Anthropology: Methodological Notes on the Study of Successful Caribbean Women by an Insider*

Nesha Z. Haniff

This account of the research methods used in a study of Caribbean women by a Caribbean woman is an exercise in native anthropology. It begins with my discovery that research about women from the Third World, such as myself, failed in its depiction of us. The account, using my study as an example, suggests how the traditional social science paradigm must be adapted to the Third World circumstance. It concludes with the warning that the native anthropologist, the insider, must be ideologically conscious during her study else her research becomes co-opted.

The Start

I mark my own awareness of the women's issue to the time I was embarking on my master's degree in public health. In deciding on which area I should focus, I perused journals in many fields. I was partial to international health and my reading gravitated to this area. It was 1975, International Women's Year, and there were many articles about women in the Third World. Reading about these women was in a way reading about myself and about the women who surrounded me as a child. The literature said that these women were abject, that they were oppressed, that they were victims, and that they were ill, uneducated, and pregnant from the first day of menstruation until menopause. The following excerpts are from the journal Ceres, volume 8, 1975:

> She contributes her physical and biological energy to the work unit, is fed and clothed in return, but her identity as an autonomous being remains suppressed. She works but does not act (p. 30).

> The man controls the home and is the absolute master of the wife and children. She accepts this situation with complete passivity (p. 48)

---

* Reprinted with permission from *Anthropology and Humanism Quarterly* 10. 4 (1985),107-113.

> She weaves, embroiders, sews, spins, dyes, makes pottery and baskets. She also cooks, washes and looks after her children and her husband. Humble and unselfish, she is totally subject to the man's authority (p. 48).
>
> To be underfed, ill, uneducated and pregnant from the first day of menstruation until menopause is the usual lot of woman in the Arab world and in certain rural areas of Southeast Asia (p. 50).
>
> Forsaken, these women cannot help perpetuating a corrosive social pattern of idleness and inefficiency (p. 50).

I could not accept this picture. It was not that these things were untrue; they were simply incomplete. To me the women were not oppressed, they were powerful; they were not weak, they were strong; and they were not abject, they were assertive. Why was it that a science aimed at discovering truth was not discovering what I and others felt and saw when it was writing about us? The literature subliminally correlated low status with low self-concept. Delmos Jones captured the idea well:

> Current literature is filled with discussions concerning Black self-image, and the conclusions are that in general Blacks have a more negative self-image than whites. First of all, there is some resentment over having one's own group described in this manner, although as a scientist, one must allow for the possibility that the findings are indeed correct. But as a skeptic, one can also consider the possibility that there may be something in the situation that other people are missing. For example, when I looked at my own experience of relating to other Blacks within a Black social context, I could not see the general conclusion of a negative self-image as being consistent with these experiences (Jones 1970, 252).

If the women were in an abject condition, did it follow that they themselves became abject? If one went to the poorest, most oppressed women, would this low-status translate into a low self-concept? I was able to test this hypothesis in a study of the relationship between status and self-concept among Muslim women who lived on the streets in Delhi, India, in hovels made of flour bags, plastic, paper, or cardboard. I found that these low status women had high self-esteem. When men were near, the women concealed themselves. Only when I spoke to them alone or in the company of other women and only when they saw me as a Muslim woman did they reveal themselves. This research illustrated that the perception of the researcher as an insider was crucial to the openness with which the women spoke.

Having this experience, I then embarked on my research on successful Caribbean women. At home, in the Caribbean, since my knowledge was native born, I would have greater freedom with the population and I could take bigger risks with the research methods and design. Clearly, the traditional methods of research could only get at the surface of what I wanted to investigate; clearly, too, as an anthropologist returning to her culture, I had to heed Fanon's warning:

> At the very moment when the native intellectual is anxiously trying to create a cultural work, he fails to recognize that he is utilizing techniques and language which are borrowed from the stranger in his country. He contents himself with stamping these instruments with a hallmark which he wishes to be national, but which is sharply reminiscent of exoticism. The native intellectual who comes back to his people by way of achievements behaves in fact like a foreigner (Fanon 1963, 223).

The Research Paradigm in Social Science

The overall paradigm of standard social science research and discovery is:

a. problem definition,

b. hypotheses formation,

c. and data collection.

It is necessary that all the conditions to disprove the hypotheses are met. If the conditions are not met, the research is not truly "empirical" and therefore there are many questions about the "truth" or "reliability" of the research.

I was constantly struck by the fact that social existence is disordered, ambiguous, and humanly messy; yet, we try to make sense of the social world with methods that are conspicuously unable to take account of that messiness and that appear stainless, sanitized, and hopelessly inappropriate in comparison to the subject matter (Bottomley 1978, 221).

In no way am I arguing for the rejection of the standard paradigm and the logical empiricist mode of research, nor is it my intention to take on the past hundred years of scientizing the social sciences. This has been historically and repeatedly done. It is not a new argument that if social science persists in mimicking physical science, it will remain unable to get beneath the surface (Becker 1971; Berlin 1980).

We on the contrary must feel our way back into this tradition by first showing the difficulties that result from the application of the modern concept of method to the human sciences. Let us therefore consider how this tradition became impoverished and the claim to truth of the knowledge of modern sciences came to be measured by a standard foreign to it, namely, the methodological thinking of modern science (Gadamer 1975, 23).

The debate has raged on for over a hundred years, and the limitations of traditional social science have been well documented (Bell and Encel 1978; Kuhn 1969). Despite this, the standard scientific paradigm remains entrenched. We are now in the eye of a paradigm crisis. Of the many reasons for the crisis, the two most salient are:

1. The rise of consciousness among Third World scholars. They are aware that the current social science paradigm presents their reality superficially (Jones 1970, Mamak 1978), and
2. The women's movement. The movement has documented the exclusion of women in almost every field.

Social science ideas and literature have been both "eurocentric" and male dominated. Consequently, to resolve the crisis, the current paradigm must be altered to include the reality of the Third World and of women.

So long as the tools a paradigm supplies continue to prove capable of solving problems it defines, science moves fastest and penetrates most deeply through confident employment of these tools. The reason is clear. As in manufacture so in science—retooling strategy is an extravagance to be saved for the occasion that demands it. The significance of crises is the indication they provide that an occasion for retooling has arrived (Kuhn 1969, 76).

The following is a delineation of the retooling taken to adapt the standard paradigm to the reality of successful women in the Caribbean.

Problem Definition

At one point in the history of ideas, a man of learning had only to be that—show that he knew, that he had read, and that he had thought. With increasing technological advances knowledge came to be associated with action and change. Because he contributed to practical solutions, the scientist was elevated. As a result, we have two rather false divisions in knowledge: the old view that knowledge must be for its own sake; the other that knowledge must be useful. The social sciences, while attempting to hold on to their classical tradition, have, at the same time, been trying to mimic the physical sciences. The result is that many dissertations and pieces of research are done in the name of utility while they are in the genre of knowledge for its own sake. Given this context, the native researcher must ask herself the following questions:

1. Will the definition of the problem contribute to ideas or utility;
2. Will this contribution solve any of the problems affecting my people;
3. Will this contribution generate ideas relevant to my people or relevant to the western system of generating knowledge?
4. Given the context of knowledge acquisition, is it possible for me to generate knowledge that is in fact my own?

Because I feel strongly that developing countries cannot afford knowledge for its own sake, I designed my study so that it met two needs. One was the need to profile outstanding women in the English-speaking Caribbean, and the other was the need to contribute to the scholarly pursuit, to the generation of ideas as they affect the Third World. In an environment where a new consciousness about women was emerging and where stereotypes were being eroded, there was a need to understand what contributed to those women who have made it, women who are successful. As history books and most of what was read in the region did not include women, profiles of successful women could be compiled for a social studies high school textbook to be used throughout the region. These women may be held up as role models to younger men and women and may be examples of women's achievement. The Inter-American Foundation approved and financed the project, which was based in the Women and Development Unit of the Extra-Mural Department of the University of the West Indies. The countries to be included in the project were Antigua, Barbados, Belize, Dominica, Guyana, Jamaica, Montserrat, St. Kitts, St. Vincent, St. Lucia, and Trinidad and Tobago.

The problem that I faced was: Who were the successful women and what was the measure of their success? The traditionally defined success model was a male, because those who were deemed successful worked as president, executive, chairman, and so on of their professions. In addition, all the studies of successful women have been of literate women as opposed to illiterate women (Adams 1979, Bachtold and Werner 1970, Barnett and Baruch 1978, Choksey 1980, Helson 1971, Hennig and Jardim 1976, Knudsin 1974, Lagemann 1974, Mednick, et al. 1975, Berberian 1977, Segal 1981, Flexman 1981). Success, therefore, because of its association with literacy, which has been historically the right of the European male, also took on a eurocentric and male interpretation. These studies invariably associated success with "professional." The literature that did include women who were not "literate" but who were outstanding usually referred to those whose life and works had reached epic and heroic proportions (e.g., Harriet Tubman. See Raven and Weir 1981, Marlow 1981). In sum, successful women were those who were literate professionals or those who were heroic and had acquired sainthood status.

An educated native attempting to do research at home, unless she heeded Fanon's warning, would be tempted to employ a similar definition of success.

The Caribbean is essentially a working-class population and those who are in the professions are not representative of the entire successful population. Being conscious that the traditional success model would have excluded many successful Caribbean women and would, therefore, be inappropriate for the region, I attempted to define success in a cross-class, cross-occupation framework. Each country was to have two women profiled, one visible and one "invisible" (twenty-four in all). Because I saw research as a social act, this was a profoundly important, ideological decision that had implications for the redefinition of my own scholarship. The redefinition meant that women would be selected not only from such occupations as executive, artist, politician, and business woman, but also from such jobs as market vendor, cane-cutter, and farmer.

My criteria for success follows:

The visible woman:

1. known by most people in her country,

2. recognized as having made a significant contribution by her peers or fellow countrymen, and;

3. successful by her own efforts and not through marriage or family connections.

The successful invisible woman:
1. known by her peers in her field of activity,
2. achieved goals that she set for herself, and
3. met these goals on her own rather than through someone else's initiative.

Hypotheses Formation

Having defined the problem and what was meant by success in the study, my next step was to set up the hypotheses. Part of the standard research paradigm is that the literature be reviewed and the hypotheses set. If hypotheses come from the literature, then all that the research can possibly do is expand or add to that literature. How could you "discover" anything if the parameters for that discovery were already present? In addition, this hypothesizing also makes no sense for studies relevant to women in the Third World. How could we create hypotheses to investigate these populations if the populations are excluded or, if included, derogated? The point is that the hypotheses that we use are not really ours. Not only are the hypotheses not ours, they are tautological. We have proved that five and five make ten because we already have agreed what five is. Because the previous literature said that parent and role models were important to successful women, I asked women about these models. Perhaps I should have asked them about the scenes they saw every day on the streets they walked, or if they saw themselves as beautiful or ugly, or if they had their own beds.

The debate on the limitations of hypotheses formation is not new. Some have argued that despite its prominent position in the social science paradigm, the procedure for formation is greatly flawed (see Medawar 1967).

Initially, from the literature on successful women I had generated two general hypotheses. The study had only begun, however, when I added two additional ones generated by the women themselves. The four overall hypotheses were:

A. From the literature
   1. Role models, particularly male ones, are important in the lives of successful women, and

2. Successful women have a high self-concept;
B. From the women
1. A high feminist consciousness is important in explaining the women's success, and
2. Religion is another important factor in explaining women's success.

The variable of a high feminist consciousness, which I had encountered before on the Muslim women's project, was articulated by the Caribbean women in a variety of ways, but the religion variable was expressed clearly and unequivocally. In the final analysis, while there were, of course, differences, most of the women corroborated the hypotheses of the importance of feminist consciousness and religion. Almost all of the women supported the hypothesis that successful women have a high self-concept; however, an equal number stressed the importance of a female, rather than a male, role model.

Having formulated the hypotheses, I next had to devise an empirical technique to select both the visible and invisible successful women.

The selection of the visible women was easy. They were not simply successful, but outstanding; their contributions were so striking that only the very biased would take issue with their selection. Nonetheless the choice of women had to be made on reliable criteria. As the project was based in the Women and Development Unit of the University of the West Indies, the field staff of the Unit was consulted regarding the compilation of the list of visible Caribbean women and the contribution and the visibility of each person named was discussed.

The more difficult process of finding invisible women was accomplished with the assistance of the Women and Development Unit. Because the Women and Development Unit was a regional organization in the business of women for a few years, it had developed contacts and relationships with community organizations. These organizations were asked to consider who were the prominent women in their community. The response to these requests was quite positive. Usually a committee was set up, and the committee would come up with a list of five women. The final choice of the women, visible and invisible, was made by me. At this point I needed verification by a method that did not use categories, or field workers, or community organization contacts. The simplest method was to ask people within the country or the community itself. This method is known as a reputational survey.

The reputational survey (Hunter 1953, D'Antonio and Erickson 1962) was first used by Hunter in his study of community power structure in Atlanta. He made a list of possible leaders that he presented to six "judges."

> Persons who had lived in the community for some years and who had a knowledge of community affairs were provided with three lists and asked to select from each one {and rank in} order of importance ten persons of influence (Hunter 1953, 265).

Hunter found a high degree of agreement among the judges about who the top leaders were in the four fields. Various critics have condemned the method for its subjectivity, but Freeman replies,

> What [its defenders ask] but a lifelong involvement in the activities of a community could possibly yield sophisticated answers to the question "who are the leaders?" The reputational approach then assumes the possibility of locating some individuals who unquestionably meet the criteria of community leadership, and who in turn will be able to name others not so visible to the outside observer (Freeman et al. 1968, 191).

Agreeing with Freeman, I, nonetheless, had to adapt the technique to the circumstance of my study. It was conducted verbally rather than in written form. While written questions were appropriate when asking peers of the visible women, as they were all educated and would handle such a schedule with ease, written questions were completely inappropriate in eliciting verification from market women or rural women. Handing these women, a questionnaire would not only intimidate them but tax their functional level of literacy. When interacting with community people about the "invisible women," I asked all questions in dialect. In the community I selected four or five people (mostly women) who had lived in the village for a long time or who knew many people there. Some I simply picked at random. Because the candidates for visible women were few in each country and indeed often there was only one choice, the visible women who were finally chosen appeared consistently in the top three of everyone's list.

This accounts for the selection of the women. The native researcher must choose the traditional methodology technique most applicable to her research, in this case the reputational survey method. The important thing is to choose and to adapt so as to create methods most relevant to the Third World.

Data Collection

The issue of data collection is one of meaning, yet who can really get at the meaning? Native anthropology explores the role of the native researcher and concerns itself more with meaning than with measurement. By a Native Anthropology, I mean a set of theories based on non-western precepts and assumptions in the same sense that modern Anthropology is based on and has supported western beliefs and values (Jones 1970, 251).

In the past, the term native anthropology was used by anthropologists trained in western science who were studying a foreign culture and wanted the "native's view." They had to train a native who could best interpret native life from within. Materials collected by the trained native had

> the unmeasurable advantage of trustworthiness, authenticity revealing precisely the elusive intimate thoughts and sentiments of the native who spontaneously reveals himself in these outpourings. This attitude strangely implies that Native Anthropologists are seen as potential "tools" to be used to provide important information to the "real" white male anthropologists (Jones 1970, 252).

This legitimacy of the insider view is critical to the conduct of investigation by the native in her home (Gwaltney 1981; Hymnes 1972; Jones 1970). The insider can immediately interpret the cues in an interview. Because she knows the rules, she can minimize class differences. I could make sexual jokes with the women whom I interviewed that would immediately put them at ease; I could tease them on a variety of topics because we shared the same norms.

Native research cannot be delegated. Although other natives can do it, the field fortunately has not developed to such an extent that there is the big, chief native researcher, and the little, graduate native researchers. This will probably happen, but for it to occur, there must be large sums of money, which native scholars currently do not have, unless large foundations donate big grants. In quantitative social science research, where this is frequently the case, often the spokesperson for the research (the big chief) has never conducted any interviews and relies on reports from fieldworkers. In conducting interviews there is a whole world of knowledge that is not voiced but that adds to the researcher's grasp and credibility.

> ...no concatenation of concepts will give one an understanding of a man, a work of art, of what is conveyed by gestures, symbols, verbal

and non-verbal, of the style, the spiritual essence of a human being, a moment, a culture...(Berlin 1979, 7).

It is my view that the native researcher must conduct the research herself. The reasons are not only her store of verbal and non-verbal knowledge, but the affordability of such research. The costly infrastructure that large-scale research requires often puts such research out of the reach of most Third World scholars. Our economies simply cannot afford it. Therefore, to work within our economies and to limit ideological and economic dependence, the researcher must do the research herself. By so doing she sets up a structure in which many of the layers between the people and the researcher are eliminated. Of course, a native researcher who is not conscious of her work and who is "utilizing techniques and language borrowed from the stranger" will defeat the whole purpose of the exercise.

Native anthropology, anthropology done by the native insider, then, was the most useful procedure for the data collection process in this study because it legitimizes the role of the insider. It is small research rather than big research, and it demands that the researcher conduct research in a manner consistent with the culture, values, norms, and ideas not only of the women being studied but also of the investigator herself.

To collect data, that is, to interview my fellow natives about their success, I drew upon phenomenology. Here is one description of phenomenology.

> Phenomenology and the objective consciousness reside in dialogal interwovenness within our thematic universe. We must acknowledge the force of phenomenology as a weapon of social change. For its task to unveil reality, to demythicize the second order constructs of social science and penetrate to the essence of our social phenomena (Suransky 1980, 177).

I drew from phenomenology the idea of dialogic research and how that type of interviewing differs from that associated with the traditional paradigm. According to social science

> It is not enough for the scientist to understand the world of meaning of his informants. If he is to secure valid data via the structured interview, respondents must be soothed into answering questions in the proper fashion (Sjoberg and Nett 1968, 210).

The standard interview, then, is basically a mechanical instrument for data collection and a special form of communication in which one person asks questions and another gives the answers (Oakley 1981, 36–37; for additional examples see Goode and Hatt 1952; Sellitz et al. 1965; Moser 1958).

Contrasting this paradigm, Freire argues for dialogal research.

> Dialogal research demands that the researcher be dialogally conversant with subjects at some phase of the research. But dialogue takes place among persons on equal levels, without the divisiveness of social or professional stratification. Dialogical research dispenses with researchers and subjects, it takes place among co-researchers (Colaizzi 1978, 69, on Freire 1970).

For the native researcher this process was a requirement because she had a decided advantage. Dialogal research argues that you must dialogue. It does not, however, tell you how to dialogue. How can you have dialogue if you do not know how to dialogue and what the dialogue is? Here, the native anthropologist has the decided advantage. As an insider, she knows the dialogue and how to dialogue. I did legitimately attempt to make the women I interviewed my co-researchers, and they responded by telling their lives in such a manner as to reveal correlations that I would not have thought of.

Even though I was an anthropologist, I was also a native. I quote one of the women I interviewed:

> But how come you been away so long and you aren't have no American twang? I said well she must be been away so long she forget we eh. And you sound like you never left a day, just like you never been away.

Conclusion

This exploration into native anthropology has looked at the methods used in conducting research with Caribbean women by a Caribbean woman. Its premise is that the standard social science paradigm is inadequate to study these women because of the historical exclusion of the Third World and of women in the generation of present-day social science knowledge. Each step of the research was examined:

1. Problem definition. The research defined the problem so that the results would have relevance both to the need in the region to profile successful women, both visible and "invisible," and the need to generate ideas pertinent to the Third World.

2. Hypotheses formation. Two hypotheses were based on previous studies of successful women and stressed the importance of role models and the presence of a high self-concept among successful women. Two additional hypotheses were generated by the women themselves, my co-researchers, and stressed the importance of a feminist consciousness and religion in the lives of outstanding women. Having formed these hypotheses, I adapted the reputational survey method to assist in the selection of women to interview.

3. Data collection. Drawing upon phenomenology, I collected data in interviews that employed a dialogue format. In this format, in contrast to the standard social science format in which one person asks and the other responds, the researcher has a dialogue with her co-researchers.

In native anthropology, the anthropologist, herself an insider, does the research. This decreases the distance, both ideologically and socially, between the researcher and the researched and so encourages the exposure of indigenous ideas. It also necessitates working within the cultural and economic context of home. It is small research as opposed to big research. The native researcher presumes that her people have explanations and logical reasons for their reality; consequently, research is an act both of discovery and verification. There is a consciousness that the current social science paradigms are geared for measurement, and that the realities of such studies are the realities only of that which is measurable. The native anthropologist employs a method that treats the population of the study as co-researchers.

This essay does not define insider or native. To do so could cause much debate and dissension. Insider and native are not easily definable because an insider may be of more detriment than an outsider and a native more foreign than a foreigner. Often western ideas gain credibility as universal ideas because we (the natives) have learnt and applied them so well at home. In this sense we continue our own ideological domination. The domination is so pervasive that perhaps it is unreasonable to expect that a critical perspective on research methods can make any serious dents. Yet we must try. I leave native and insider to be placed under the category of those who are conscious of the difficulties in generating Third World ideas and those who are sensitive and open toward and both love and respect the people they study. An outsider must understand that despite her own sensitivity, her outsider status will limit her research. It is only when we are perceived and accepted as an insider that we can truly understand the meaning of the lives we study. An insider or native must take this status seriously. Its methodological implications are profound, for it is this group who can either do the most harm or the most good. It is up to us to "begin the history of mankind all over again" (Fanon 1963).

References

Adams, J. 1979. *Women on Top: Success Patterns and Personal Growth.* New York: Hawthorn Books.

Ahmed, Wajihuddin. 1975. The Husband is the Employer. *Ceres* 8(2): 28–31.

Bachtold, L.M., and E.E. Werner. 1970. Personality Profiles of Gifted Psychologists. *American Psychologist* (April): 234–243.

Barnett, Rosalind C., and Grace K. Baruch. 1978. *The Competent Woman.* New York: Halsted Press.

Becker, Ernest. 1971. *The Lost Science of Man.* New York: Braziller.

Bell, Colin, and S. Encel. 1978. *Inside the Whale.* Australia: Pergamon Press.

Berberian, Rose Marie. 1977. A Study of the Bases of Success of Professional Women in a Predominantly Male University. PhD diss., University of Michigan.

Berlin, Isiah. 1980. *Against the Current.* New York: Viking Press.

Bottomley, Bill. 1978. Words, Deeds and Postgraduate Research. In *Inside the Whale.* See Bell and Encel 1978.

Choksey, Linda. 1980. Elderly Women of Achievement. PhD diss., University of Michigan.

Colaizzi, Paul F. 1978. Psychological Research as the Phenomenologist Views It. In *Existential-phenomenological Alternatives for Psychology*, ed. Ronald S. Valle and Mark King. New York: Oxford University Press.

D'Antonio, Williams V., and Eugene C. Erickson. 1962. The Reputational Technique as a Measure of Community Power. *American Journal of Sociological Review* 27 (June 1962):362–376.

Fanon, Frantz. 1963. *The Wretched of the Earth.* New York: Grove Press.

Flexman, Nancy Ann. 1980. Women of Enterprise: A Study of Success and Failure Incidents from Self-Employed Women. PhD diss., University of Illinois at Champaign-Urbana.

Freeman, Linton C., Thomas Fararo, Warner Bloomberg, Jr., and Morris H. Sunshine. 1962. Locating Leaders in Local Communities: A Comparison of Some Alternative Approaches. In *The Search for Community*, ed. Willis D. Howley and Frederick M. Wirt. Englewood-Cliffs, New Jersey: Prentice-Hall.

Freire, Paolo. 1972. *Pedagogy of the Oppressed.* New York: Herder and Herder.
Gadamer, Hans-Georg. 1975. *Truth and Method.* New York: Continuum.
Goode, W. J., and P.K.Hatt. 1952. *Methods in Social Research.* New York: McGraw Hill.
Gwaltney, John. 1981. *Drylongso.* New York: Vintage Books.
Helson, R. 1971. Women Mathematicians and the Creative Personality. *Journal of Consulting and Clinical Psychology* 36:210–220.
Hennig, M., and A. Jardim. 1976. *The Managerial Woman.* New York: Doubleday.
Hunter, Floyd. 1953. *Community Power Structure.* Chapel Hill: University of North Carolina Press.
Hymes, Dell, ed. 1972. *Reinventing Anthropology.* New York: Pantheon.
Jones, Delmos J. 1970. Towards a Native Anthropology. *Human Organisation* 29(4):251–258.
Knudsin, Ruth, ed. 1974. *Women and Success.* New York: William Arrow.
Kuhn, Thomas. 1970. *The Structure of Scientific Revolutions.* Chicago: University of Chicago Press.
Lagemann, Ellen Condliffe. 1974. *A Generation of Women.* Cambridge, Mass.: Harvard University Press.
Marlow, Joan. 1979. *The Great Women.* New York: Galahad Books.
Mamak, A.F. 1978. Nationalism, Race, Class Consciousness, and Social Research in Bougainville Island, Papua, New Guinea. In *Inside the Whale.* See Bell and Encel, 164–181.
Medawar, P.B. 1967. *The Art of the Soluble.* London: Mitheun.
Mednick, Tamara Martha, Sandra Schwartz Tangri, and Lois Wladis Hoffman, ed. 1979. *Women of Achievement.* New York: John Wiley.
Oakley, Ann. 1981. Interviewing Women: A Contradiction in Terms. In *Doing Feminist Research*, ed. Helen Roberts. London: Routledge and Kegan Paul.
Moser, C. A. 1958. *Survey Methods in Sociological Investigation.* London: Heinemann.
Presvelou, Clio. 1975. The Invisible Woman. *Ceres* 8(2):50–54.
Raven, Susan, and Alison Weir. 1980. *Women of Achievement: Thirty-five Centuries of History.* New York: Harmony Books. Segal, Judith. 1981. Profiles of Successful Women Working in Non-traditional Occupations with Special Reference to Their Androgynous Characteristics. PhD diss., The Fielding Institute.
Sjobert, G., and R. Nett. 1968. *A Methodology for Social Research.* New York: Harper and Row.
Suransky, Valerie. 1970. Phenomenology: An Alternative Research Paradigm and a Force for Social Change. *Journal of the British Society for Phenomenology* 11(2).
Torricelli, Graciela D. 1975. Engulfed in Myths. *Ceres* 8(2):46–50.

26. Anthropological Research Methods for the Study of Black Women in the Caribbean*

A. Lynn Bolles

Historically, the methods of anthropological research have tended to separate that discipline from the other social sciences. First, in anthropological research, one usually incorporates the technique of participant observation. Second, in anthropological field work, one participates and observes. Often, the inquiring anthropologist is not the social equal of the subjects. In addition, "the field," more than likely, is located in the Third World, or among poor peoples of color. The relationships between the anthropologist and the folk "of the field," during the research period and afterwards, when the investigator has returned to her or his home, have been the topic of concern for many, but not for all. Those who question the traditional model of inquiry have created alternative research methods in anthropology, methods based primarily on notions of equality. Equal emphasis is placed on both the kind of relationship established between the researcher and the folk, and the nature of the results derived from that field work experience. My purpose is to discuss one of these nontraditional methodological approaches in anthropology and to show how it has been used in research on working-class women in urban Jamaica.

The discipline of anthropology has had the dubious honor of being called "the child of imperialism." Established in the late nineteenth century, during the height of social Darwinism, anthropology has been used to serve the colonization efforts of the British, to document the U.S. government's maintenance of Native American reservations, and to romanticize the exotica of black America.

---

* Reprinted with permission from *Women in Africa and the African Diaspora*. Eds. Rosalyn Terborg-Penn and Andrea Benton Rushing. Howard University Press, 1987/9, 43-54. Excerpted.

Despite its less than constructive history, however, anthropology has the ability to serve as a positive social force for advancing equality among people. This capacity is based on its nature. Unlike some other disciplines, anthropology luxuriates in its eclectic manner. That is, anthropology has taken so much from the humanities, social sciences, and natural sciences that some aspect of its perspective can be attractive to all and of value to many. Anthropology's point of view is at once holistic, comparative, particularistic, and general. Its approach is founded on a historical-evolutionary model that takes contemporary situations and attempts to view them as just one moment in the human journey. Individual anthropologists describe and analyze the scenes before them in a variety of forms that are based on the four classic areas of anthropological study: archeological, physical, linguistic, and social-cultural. However, the anthropologist always returns to some concept of culture, which provides *the* social arena in which all else occurs. Culture is the crux of the discipline and the methods one employs to illustrate culture as a phenomenon are diverse.[1]

How, then, can we use anthropological perspective to its best and avoid the perpetuation of the sort of scientific imperialism reminiscent of the colonial and neocolonial, state-interventionist past? How can we establish what anthropologist John Gwaltney calls "native anthropology," equal relations that are on many levels between researcher and respondent (community or culture) and that are based on mutual respect? Further, how can we apply the tenets of "responsible, equitable" research in our study of black women? And, given the contemporary setting for the majority of women of African descent, especially in the societies of the Americas, we speak of those who are the least powerful of the powerless. Finally, to offer an additional aspect to this query, when the intruding anthropologist is a member of one black American culture, what challenges arise in her study of black women of another black culture?

My responses to these questions are organized into three sections. The first addresses some methodological questions – some operational, others more ethical in nature. The second describes my own work in Jamaica as an example of how one uses native anthropology, or responsible research, in praxis. And the third offers a discussion of other approaches to the study of blacks in the Caribbean for comparison and as food for thought.

Methodology

Anthropologist's training in research methods eventually leads them to choose between becoming creative by designing alternative or remaining traditional by following the standard fare. A variety of factors influence which methodological path students follow, inducing their educational situation, i.e., their graduate school and the faculty under whom they study. Regardless of these variables, for the most part, anthropologists learn research methods by reading and analyzing "classic" ethnographic literature, the descriptive account of a specific people's or group's way of life, focused primarily on preliterate folk of color during the first half of the twentieth century. Of course, it was that body of "classic" ethnography that provided the basis for anthropology's tag "child of imperialism." Gwaltney reminds us that

> ...traditional Euro-American anthropology has failed to produce ethnographers who are capable of assessing black American culture in terms other than romantic...We have traditionally been misrepresented by standard social science.[2]

But during the period of social upheaval in the 1960s, a series of articles called for the reassessment of anthropology as a discipline, a review of its methods of inquiry, and a review of its relations among folk in the field.[3] Many of these energies focused on black cultures in the Americas, since it was at home that the obvious harm had been done by anthropology under the rubric "culture of poverty." Also included under that heading were studies such as *Soulside* and similar examples of street-corner exotica, which, owing to the misguided perceptions of their various authors, effectively obfuscated the totality of U.S. black culture.[4] Delmos Jones, Charles Valentine, and Charles and Betty Lou Valentine called for the rectification of this misportrayal of black American culture, in perspective, method, and practice.[5]

Valentine argues that "special care must be taken that studies [of Afro-America] not be used by the establishment to perpetuate the status quo."[6] Any research on black people, carried out by blacks or whites, even of the highest quality and with the best intentions, might be used as a tool to oppress and control the people being studied with better efficiency and to an even greater extent than previously possible. He also reminded us that anthropologists' responsibilities must encompass the method of data collection, of publication, and of the researchers' attitude. In addition, anthropologists must be concerned about who will use the information. Various conditions necessitate that anthropologists or researchers exercise this principled responsibility in their work. Policy decisions were promoted by inappropriate techniques and a specific ideological set of baggage, whereby abused women were contributors to the salvation of their families, men and children. The price of irresponsibility becomes obvious when we acknowledge, for example, that the culture of poverty concept abused black people, particularly black women. Studies that embraced this concept overwhelmingly attributed the decay, deprivation, and composite social ills associated with urban ghetto life to these women. Their men were depicted as emasculated, their children as latchkey offspring running in the streets – their sons were dope addicts; their daughters were sexually indiscriminate – and their households as pathologically disorganized. Finally, such studies concluded that the culture of poverty was transmitted transgenerationally; that is, it was passed on from mother to children, and so on. Thus, the effect was that the victims were ultimately blamed for their own situation, although they were scarcely in any position to refute the allegations of the culture-of-poverty enthusiasts, since they happened to be the least powerful among the powerless—impoverished black women.[7] These women could only *wish* to be able to earn the fifty-nine cents for every dollar a man earned. The low-paying, dead-end jobs that most U.S. black women held did not exemplify the "work of liberation" envisioned by the 1960s and 1970s activists of the women's movement, whose goals were self-awareness and financial independence.

In the Caribbean, specifically in Jamaica, the situation was somewhat similar, with studies on household organization of poor and working-class families receiving the bulk of attention from social scientists.[8] The major concern of these studies was to explain why there were so many variations in Jamaican household structure and why there was such a high incidence of female-headed households. Considerably less attention was devoted to the various roles that women played in those societies, aside from their fertility patterns and mating habits. The rate of illegitimacy and the high number of female-headed households were seen as problematic; that factors like these revealed the resourcefulness of women, which enabled them, as well as men and children, to function, somehow, under adverse social and economic circumstances, seems to have been lost on these researchers. Therefore, the underlying difficulties associated with the poor black mothers, poor black fathers, and poor black children depicted in these studies were attributed to a great extent, to systems of inequality that were based on color and class, rather than to other interconnected factors.

Sensitivity to the forms of publication and the kinds of persons and organizations given access to materials gathered must be considered an important aspect of conducting responsible social research. The importance of how and where to make the material accessible should be underscored, and these features must be built into the research agenda. In particular, there should be a sense of accountability toward communities, groups, and individuals of the study. When anthropologists achieve this sense, they implant a certain degree of safeguard, so that situations that give rise to statements like those of Gwaltney's respondents can be avoided:

> Since I don't see myself or most people I know in most things I read about black people, I can't be bothered with that.
>
> Harriet Jones
>
> I think this anthropology is just another way to call me a nigger.
>
> Othaman Sullivan[9]

Finally, researchers should not shield themselves behind the veil of "scientific objectivity" in reneging on their responsibilities toward the folk under study. "Establishment anthropologists," as Valentine calls them, tend to play "treacherous verbal games with stereotypes," and they rely on the humanist issues they address to shield them from the effects of their lack of an ethical stance.[10] However, irresponsibility may invite more than the moral indignation of the group under study. Researchers are beginning to learn that nowadays, not only can the people of the field read and write, but also they can take legal action. We find that the Navajo Indians, for instance, screen prospective researchers' proposals and will not grant entry into their communities when they find that the work being proposed has already been done. The Navajo even provide bibliographies to support their denial of entry decisions.

Anthropologists must exercise particular care in conducting research among "native" folk—using Gwaltney's translation of Fanon—the subordinate, dark, and poor. And this especially should be observed when the folk are female. Formerly, the intruding imperialist, powerful stranger (social scientist) expected simply to draw from a data bank of giving, powerless people. Now, the guidelines of native anthropology, or responsible research, provide an opportunity for exchange, increased accuracy, mutual respect, and the sharing of civic responsibility between the researcher and the folk under study. Not only will anthropologists' cross-cultural comparisons of the role and status of women of the diaspora be beneficial, but also the kinds of material generated will more likely be significant to black women and their activities. This is the kind of perspective that formed the basis of my field work research in Jamaica.

Female Industrial Workers in Kingston, Jamaica

There were three underlying premises for my work in Jamaica: (1) the material would be useful to appropriate policy makers; (2) the research would involve areas already on the agendas of appropriate organizations; and (3) the outcome of the research would, in some manner, positively affect those under study.[11] Elsewhere, I have documented the pluses and minuses of being a black American woman carrying out research among folk similar to, but distinct from her own people.[12] Issues of nationality, ethnicity, education, and class came into play during the field work. The manner in which these biases and stereotypes were overcome had much to do with my method of inquiry—native anthropology. Moreover, since native anthropology has much in common with many aspects of core black American culture, I intensely acted out my own cultural perspective to gain that of another. Tenets of core black culture include, for those not familiar with the concept, a notion of setting the story straight, common courtesy, reciprocity, intracommunal style and status (which had to be learned Jamaican style), and a sense of nationhood, which I expanded to a sense of common ancestry and the diaspora.

The most important set of relations was found among those with whom I shared the most, and whose instructions I held in high esteem. These individuals included, first, the personal friends who schooled me in Jamaican customs and manners prior to my entry into working-class neighborhoods; and second, those urban working-class women and their household members whose lives formed the basis of my research, as well as some of whose friendships I earned and still value. The following discussion will illustrate how native anthropology worked for me in the field.

My research focused on female factory workers who were employed in typical "female industries"—garment, food processing, and canning manufacturing. The goal was to see how industrial employment affected these women's productive and reproductive (in the broadest social sense) activities, along with their household organization. To gain more information from various industrial subsectors, I visited different factories, contacted those who might be interested in helping me out, and then worked out topics for further discussion.

I entered an underwear factory in downtown Kingston. The firm is owned by a local Chinese-Jamaican family. The working conditions were the poorest I had ever seen—hot, and full of lint and overworked women. I was introduced by the trade union officer as a "lady from the States who is doing a study for her doctorate." I knew I was in serious trouble as the glares of disgust nearly paralyzed me. I began to explain what I was doing and why, that in our efforts (mine and the trade unions', in this instance) to gain maternity leave with pay and better wages for women workers, their help in the study would be directly beneficial to them. I explained how they would have to help by answering sets of questions that would show how their wages were spread too thin and that would reveal the magnitude of their responsibilities. Since men generally did not recognize or care to know these facts, and since it was they, especially "big men" (members of Parliament) who made policy, males needed to be provided with all the facts to support what we already knew to be true about working mothers.

Some women walked away, while others started talking among themselves. I started speaking louder and faster. Finally, one woman began to deride me—how could I, a fine American woman with everything, come to tell them anything—I didn't know what work was. I was a soft, American so-and-so! This assessment received much applause, and soon others joined in, telling me where I should go and what I could do with myself once I got there. I realized that if I didn't respond in kind all would be lost.

To begin with, I gave a fiery rebuke (in my best Jamaican patois) to the woman who had spoken first. Then I pointed out to all of them that here I stood, a black American woman, where no Jamaican woman from campus (meaning University of the West Indies—read: Jamaican middle class) would dare come. I said to them, "Listen, there is a way to try to gain what you have been struggling for, and you cuss me off because you think all Americans are stupid. Well, if this is how Jamaican women act, then I could say the same about you. You think all Americans are soft—well, the white man tells us all what to do, and hard work has never been absent from any black woman's life, here or in the States." I concluded my soliloquy, now with a captive audience, by saying, "You are black women, and so am I. I was lucky enough to get an education to do something to help others. You try to send your children to school would you want them to get such a hard time if they were in my shoes? You are who you are, and I am who I am. But, together, we can do one thing which might help us all." After responses of a series of begrudging "all right's" and a more positive "she all right, da Yankee gal," I left the factory floor, promising to return the next day to talk only with those interested. And I did.

The point being here is that it was hard work to gain the respect of these black working women. They have become accustomed to having their opinions abused under similar research situations. Reciprocity also was crucial in that I had much to learn from them, and I gave of myself by showing interest, by supplying information, and by offering gratuities that they could appreciate personally—such as laundry detergent, which was scarce in the supermarkets. Our mutual plight of being black women struck a chord, and when I admitted my own vulnerability, it became another way to reach a commonality across class lines.

When the research was finished, and copies of the promised material were made available to designated agencies and organizations, the women studied and other interested parties were shocked. No one could remember the last time a researcher from abroad had ever followed through with his or her promises. The working-class women most actively involved in the study particularly appreciated my description of their working conditions on the job and at home. One woman commented that she had not realized how much she did in one day, and she felt more tired than she had before, after reading about her own daily routine, but her work had to be done.

The data I collected on working-class women's opinions on maternity leave issues were made available to the Jamaica Women's Bureau. That branch of the government aided the successful battle that put into law maternity leave with pay. Whether or not my research was instrumental in the case presented before the Parliament is not known; however, the information was there if they needed it. Other data on rank-and-file trade union membership served as the basis of a three-year, regional project on women in labor organizations. The project was sponsored by the Trade Union Education Institute and international agencies.

Overall, my research method was not unique. But in contrast with other methods—the type that these women and governmental agencies were all too familiar with—I placed emphasis on the individuals under study, rather than on the research itself. I did not set out with a precise research topic that I must find at whatever cost to anyone involved. Instead, the eclecticism of anthropology allowed me to study my general interests—black women, urban life, and economic systems—together as a cohesive unit. Additionally, the tenets of core black culture and native anthropology made it possible for me to achieve the three goals I set forth for myself and my work.

CONCLUSION

In contrast to my solo Caribbean field work situation, I would like to discuss some of the key points of what I consider to be one of the most exhaustive, exciting, extensive pieces of research focusing on the contemporary lives and issues of women of the African diaspora. In this way, I will demonstrate how some of the same principles of native anthropology and social science research discussed here were applied on a very large scale.

Perhaps one of the most significant projects undertaken within the English-speaking Caribbean was the multidisciplinary Women in the Caribbean Project (WICP). A three-year (1979–1982) endeavor, the WICP was directed by Joycelin Massiah, then director of the Institute of Social and Economic Research, Eastern Caribbean (ISER, EC), at the University of the West Indies, Cave Hill, Barbados. Research was carried out almost exclusively by women scholars from the three campuses of the University of the West Indies (UWI): Mona, Cave Hill, and St. Augustine; from the University of Guyana, the School of Continuing Studies (then known as the Extra Mural Centers); and from small social-welfare agencies in the countries targeted for investigation: Barbados, Guyana, St. Vincent,

Antigua, and Jamaica. WICP goals were to establish, in the English-speaking region, a data base for teaching, research, and planning purposes, and to develop guidelines for a cohesive social policy that recognized the needs of women and drew on their skills and talents for program planning and execution. The magnitude and importance of the WICP was heightened by its multilevel and interpersonal methodologies, and by the large number of women participants—approximately, 1,526.[13]

The multilevel method warrants further explanation. Integrated into an overall method were standard sociological, structured survey sample and anthropological, unstructured, in-depth interviewing techniques. In-country workshops; junior and senior women research teams; questionnaires; follow-up, in-depth studies; community social service inventories; and training of interviewers and supervisory staff were all provided for in the detailed research design implemented in the field work. In addition, special preparation was made for the interviewers initially entering the field, as an attempt to prevent inhospitable situations from arising. Whether or not all the research was conducted in the systematic nonhierarchical manner indicated in the methodology is not known. The point is, however, that a grand-scale research project attempted to follow such a plan.

The WICP made history on three counts. First, because of it, a major contribution was made to cross-cultural research efforts on women and specifically on women of African descent. Second, in its research design, the WICP attempted to combine a statistical profile on the lives of Caribbean women with a commonsense understanding of their day-to-day lives. Third, the WICP brought together the minds and expertise of feminist and women-centered women scholars who worked on the campuses and in the agencies of the region. The collective process of the project made it possible for the inauguration of Gender and Development Studies at UWI as an academic field of scholarly concentration.[14] The WICP also recognized the bridges that women scholars and activists cross between their academic and community work.

Results of the WICP are found in four formats: a video prepared by CARIMAC (Mass Communication Program at the University of the West Indies Mona); a double issue of *Social and Economic Studies* 35, no. 2 and 3 (1986); the in-house publications of the Institute of Social and Economic Research (EC), Cave Hill, Barbados; and the book *Working Miracles: Women's Lives in the English-Speaking Caribbean* by Olive Senior.

In the "Foreword" of the volume, Joycelin Massiah, who is the driving force behind the WICP, introduces Olive Senior as a leading Jamaican fiction writer, editor, and journalist and as the author of *Working Miracles*. Senior produced a beautifully written text- jargon-free and comprehensible to all. The way it frames the repartee between the women and the interviewers makes both the readers and Senior become bystanders listening to these dialogues. When the moment seems right, Senior uses literature, music, history, and government documents alongside the responses of the women. The limits of the book are seen in the area of social science of women, especially for those who waited patiently for the results of the WICP to be published.

Working Miracles and other works by feminist scholars and creative writers, delivers an important message about women's lives in the English-speaking Caribbean scholarship.[15] Major contributions are being made to the study of the complex lives of women in the Caribbean, to the cross-cultural study of women of African (and Indian) descent, and to the better understanding of the bases of Caribbean women-centered and feminist activism.

Notes

1. In this paper, the term *culture* is employed in accord with Sidney Mintz's definition of the subject. That is, culture is a historically developed form through which members of a group relate to one another. It is a resource for human action, choices, materials, behavior, self-perception, and world view. Culture is used to confirm, reinforce, maintain, change, or deny arrangements of status, power, and identity. See Mintz, "Forward," *Afro-American Anthropology: Contemporary Perspectives*, ed. Norman E. Whitten Jr. and John Szwed (New York: Free Press, 1970), 1–16.

2. Gwaltney's seminal work, *Drylongso*, is a collection of personal narratives gathered from a group of "core black culture" participants in northern New Jersey. It stands as a prime example of creative, alternative, and equitable anthropological research. The sources of data were found as an outcome of folk seminars that were held in such varied locations as churches and taverns. "Good talk" often inspired good food, which was prepared by a participant who shared Gwaltney's aim of "setting the story straight" about most black Americans—drylongso—ordinary people. Participants also donated indispensable personal documents, life histories, and other valuable commodities, including their time, because they, too, wanted to contribute truth-building about black American culture. Gwaltney's name is the only non-fictionalized name to appear in the volume, to protect those who gave so earnestly. The narratives

appear as they were taped, with Gwaltney organizing them by theme. *Drylongso: A Self-Portrait of Black America* (New York: Random House, 1981), xxii.
3. Dell Hymes, ed., *Reinventing Anthropology* (New York: Random House, 1974).
4. Ulf Hannerz, *Soulside: Inquiries into Ghetto Life* (New York: Columbia University Press, 1969).
5. Charles A. Valentine and Betty Lou Valentine, " Making the Scene, Digging the Action, and Telling It Like It Is: Anthropologists at Work in a Dark Ghetto," in Whitten and Szwed, *Afro-American Anthropology*, 403–18; Charles Valentine, *Black Studies and Anthropology: Scholarly and Political Interest in Afro-American Culture* (Addison-Weley Modular, no. 15, 19 72); Betty Lou Valentine, *Hustling and Other Hard Work: Life Styles in the Ghetto* (New York: Free Press, 1978); and Delmos Jones, " Towards a Native Anthropology," *Human Organisation* 28 (1970): 251–59
6. C. Valentine, *Black Studies and Anthropology*, 45.
7. Elizabeth Higginbotham, "Two Representative Issues in Contemporary Sociological Work on Black Women," in *All the Women Are White, But Some of Us Are Brave*, ed. Gloria T. Hull, Patricia Bell Scott and Barbara Smith (Old Westbury, N.Y.: Feminist Press, 198 1), 93–98.
8. Frances Henry and Pamela Wilson, "The Status of Women in Caribbean Societies: An Overview of Their Social, Economic, and Sexual Roles," *Social and Economic Studies* 24 (1975): 165–98; A. Lynn Bolles, *My Mother Who Fathered Me and Others: Gender and Kinship in the English-Speaking Caribbean* (East Lansing, Mich.: Michigan State University, Women and International Development Series, no. 175, 1988).
9. Gwaltney, *Drylongso*, xix.
10. Charles A. and Betty Lou Valentine, "Making the Scene," in Whitten and Szwed, *Afro-American Anthropology*.
11. Faye V. Harrison, ed., *Decolonizing Anthropology: Moving Further Toward an Anthropology for Liberation* (Washington, D.C.: American Anthropological Association, 1991).
12. A. Lynn Bolles, *Sister Jamaica: A Study of Women, Work and Households in Kingston* (Lanham, Md.: University Press of America, 1996). The research referred to here was conducted in Jamaica, 1978–1979. It was funded by National Institute of Mental Health National Research Service Award (1F31MHO7997-01) and a predoctoral fellowship from the Inter-American Foundation. One hundred twenty-seven female factory workers and their households were the focus of the work.

I made initial contact with these women at their places of work through their trade union officers. After a degree of mutual trust was established, about a dozen women extended invitations for home visitations. Hence, only those interested enough in the project participated on a level beyond completing an interview schedule. The schedule covered household composition, domestic organization, economic responsibilities, work histories, and opinion questions on topical issues of the day, e.g., maternity leave with pay. I made observations at the factories and at the homes of those who invited me to visit.

During the eighteen-month research period, the social, economic, and political situation in Jamaica was tense, and I am indebted to all of those women for their time, patience, and kindness. In addition, other social and economic materials were gathered from libraries, government ministries, and newspaper archives. Factory managers, trade unionists, and faculty members from the University of the West Indies, Mona, were interviewed.

13. A. Lynn Bolles, "Of Mules and Yankee Gals," *Anthropology and Humanism Quarterly* 10, no. 4 (1985): 114–19.
14. Olive Senior, *Working Miracles: Women's Lives in the English-Speaking Caribbean* (Bloomington, Ind.: Indiana University Press, 1991).
15. Patricia Mohammed and Catherine Shephard, *Gender in Caribbean Development* (Mona, Jamaica; St. Augustine, Trinidad and Tobago; and Cave Hill, Barbados: University of the West Indies, Women and Development Studies, 1988).

27. Downtown Ladies: Informal Commercial Importers, a Haitian Anthropologist, and Self-making in Jamaica*

Gina A. Ulysse

...

Reflexive Political Economy

When I began my research on Jamaican Informal Commercial Importers (ICIs) in 1992, I was interested in development and political economy (narrowly defined). ICIs were an exciting and relevant topic, where development is concerned. They were predominantly females, often of working and lower-class lineage, who participate in the "informal" economy and circumnavigate state-imposed restrictions, social marginalization, and civil society's disdain. In some cases, many not only succeeded but thrived; hence, they were a prime subject for contemporary research. With more data collection over a seven-year period, I came to understand them as both economic agents who now possessed and manipulated what Nesha Haniff refers to as the hegemonic U.S. dollar, as well as social actors engaged in battles to claim places and spaces in Kingston that they have been historically denied. I could not divide or split these two perspectives, as each informed the other. The articulation of the dialectic between these two positions was fueled by their individual family's history, though always within an even broader social and historical context.

The process of coming to this explication, however, was a tumultuous one that forced me to consider and unpack the multiple tensions that emerged as I grappled with issues concerning feminist epistemologies, research methods, and the politics of representation. I confronted these

---

* Reprinted with permission from Gina A. Ulysse, *Downtown Ladies: Informal Commercial Importers, a Haitian Anthropologist, and Self-Making in Jamaica*. Chicago: University of Chicago Press, 2007, 9-11, 119-131.

questions, as the realities I sought to document required that I cross and transcend disciplinary boundaries to gain a deeper understanding of traders who persistently strived to occupy and go through the cracks of global capitalism. It was after extensive field research that I came to understand the multiple ways that their self-making practices are nuanced responses to the daily-lived impact of global fluctuations. By self-making, I mean the various ways ICIs shape their gendered and racial/color identities through choices that affect how they view themselves and how others perceive them. ICIs' choices are linked and informed by time and place within the context of both Jamaica's broader racial/spatial cartography as well as the island's place within the world. Central to my approach is a reflexive stance that extends beyond representation to delve into material conditions. This perspective also engages the symbolic aspects of social position and location as well as the moral economy of authority and power (Thomas 2001). This reflexive political economy is practiced by the ICIs featured in this study. I elaborate on this concept in chapter 6.

For now, let me note that the reflexive political economy of both the researched and the researcher involves numerous factors and is grounded in a sense of personal history, or what Austin-Broos refers to as heritable identity (1994). This forms the basis of traders' self-perception and self-making practices as related to their place in local national and global dynamics. In our numerous conversations, ICIs in this study were constantly reflecting on their children or their parents as indicators of their place. This reflection was central to decision making; it was their motive. They kept one eye on the past and another on the future. In that sense, not only are they people with histories (Wolf 1982), but they also operate their businesses aware of the implications of their various historical connections. In 1992, when I asked two young ICIs why they were in the business, their answer was quite revealing: "because I want to have a house in the hills, too," one said. The awareness that they have been denied is precisely what drives many of them to wish and work for a big house. Most importantly, they seek to have one because others do, so why shouldn't they? It is that same reflection that influences their consumption patterns and where they invest their capital. For many, these constant evaluations reveal how they consider the multiple levels of constraints they confront in the world in which they operate. The limits that determine the course of their activities and lives are still best articulated by the old Marxian adage that man makes history, though not exactly as he chooses.

To consider ICIs' situation from a historical perspective, in their local setting, and to gain greater knowledge of the field that they maneuver, I converse mainly with Jamaican producers of intellectual and popular discourses. Thus, often North American theorists and scientists are eschewed in favor of regional scholars whose concern mirrors discussion in the North or even preceded the publications of North American and European scholars. My aim is twofold: to persist in pluralizing the native, and to frame ICIs within their broader history, particularly as they know and understand it. In *Global Transformations: Anthropology and the Modern World*, Trouillot makes a strong case for engaging locally produced scholarship. He notes, "anthropology has produced not only peoples without history, but peoples without historicity" (2003:136). He elaborates further and explains how contempt for local scholarly discourse often viewed as elitist only allows anthropologists to erase the knowledge that societies produce about themselves. In so doing, he argues, we not only homogenize the native, but also treat her as a noninterlocutor. To this end, I actively engage in dialogue primarily with local scholars. I also interact with the broader internationally produced scholarship that seeks to explicate Jamaican or thematically related conditions. The placement of this work at the center of these discussions has the potential to be illuminating in complex ways.

...

Field Methods: Cross-Dressing-Across-Class

In 1993, unbeknownst to me, in certain circles, I was on the verge of social self-termination. I had failed to perform class, that is, to wear the locally recognized symbols that would properly signal my socioeconomic position. Without this mediation, my class identity was fixed by my skin color and its concomitant stigma. Hence, I was placed on the lower rungs of the social ladder, particularly in those spaces that were more rigidly policed by social gatekeepers. Yet my North American-accented English, foreign mode of dress, and overall demeanor were inconsistent with the class position I assumed, working-class, and the one that was ascribed to me, upper middle-class. Living where I did in Papine, yet dressing as I did, I was a walking contradiction.

In January 1994, I had a conversation with Trouillot in which we discussed the dilemma of black anthropologists and the point at which they enter the field. He recounted his experiences in Dominica, where he conducted his dissertation fieldwork. He spoke of the difficulties he faced in getting appointments with ministers for his research. He noted that he would arrive at the ministries dressed in accord with the weather and proceeded to wait in line to see these officials. While waiting, he wittingly observed twelve French, ten Americans, and three British students, casually dressed, who would proceed up the stairs to the offices of the male ministers who were "unavailable" to him. Once he ceased cross-dressing-across-class and changed his clothing to a formal three-piece suit, those ministers were no longer occupied.

Similarly, I was in another country in the region where members of the black middle class habitually display their economic status, often ostentatiously, depending on the aesthetic in order to be ascribed a position and to be treated with basic respect. Trouillot had cautioned me to enter the field from the top and not from the bottom. Then I would reaffirm my class position based upon my education and source of income. The fact is that I am a dark-skinned, single female who looked even younger than she was in a region that valued status and its myriad manifestations. Entering at the top would have facilitated my research and helped me mediate the multiple intersections that I embodied. Indeed, race, color, class, gender, marital status, and generational stratifications, which are indices of station in the region, also determine the larger context within which one's research occurs. This was confirmed when I returned to Jamaica in 1994. Patricia Anderson, a sociologist at the Mona campus of the University of the West Indies (UWI) questioned me about how I presented myself during that first trip.[1] In her final analysis, she exposed me to the consequences of the disjunctures in my self-making practices. Through her, I learned that as I dressed down or cross-dressed-across-class, my mediations of capital were invisible. She concluded that for locals, I simply blurred too many boundaries, which rendered me totally out of place. Both Trouillot's and my experience attest that the blurring of boundaries has its dangers for blacks.

Given the experiences recounted above, I prepared for the final phase of fieldwork in 1995 adamant about minimizing any visible inconsistencies.

Knowing that skin color must be mediated with the "appropriate" class markers, I specifically requested funding (which I did not receive) for status symbols on several of my field research grant applications. I wanted to document the fact that as a dark-skinned female in Jamaica, my negotiation processes differed from those of others with more privilege. I entered the field racially stigmatized without the political or social luxury ascribed to whiteness. Indeed, as discussed earlier, whiteness is property. The cultural capital (education and elite university affiliation) and symbols that I did possess were invisible markers, and hence had limited value. In addition, though I am a native of sorts, individuals often localized me. I was expected to "know better" and, as a result, to act accordingly. This perception of me was specific to context. It revealed the spatial organization that underlies social relations. In other words, it depended on whom I was with and where we were.

After weeks of sun worshipping, my skin became quite dark. I was often addressed as local, especially when accompanied by whites, who were automatically perceived as tourists or foreigners. This occurred constantly, especially during my study-abroad programs in 1992 and 1993. In uptown and downtown Kingston, Port Antonio, and on the north coast, waiters and others in tourist areas addressed me as the local tour guide of white North American colleagues. Once at Coronation Market in Kingston, street vendors approached me, asking me to entice my white Jamaican friends to purchase their wares from them. These examples not only highlight the pitfalls of my failure to visibly assert my socioeconomic status, but they also indicate how the visibility and invisibility of various forms of capital operate in conjunction with cross-class and -color fraternization. I return to this issue in the final chapter. Hence, my request for certain items was an early attempt to engage in what I call a reflexive political economy in praxis. My goal was to forecast the influence of the researcher's socioeconomic position on different aspects of the project and to point to anthropology's normative notions of the "researcher," "the field," and "methods" (Harrison 1991b, Gupta and Ferguson 1997) in order to unpack some of the intersecting gender, class, and racial codes embedded therein.

These biased concepts unquestionably perpetuate race and class privilege by ignoring and even exploiting existing baseline inequalities on the ground in the field. In the Caribbean and elsewhere in the black diaspora, white skin has been upheld across racial lines as the ultimate status symbol, allowing individuals a range of privileges including gender and class. Most will have access to resources and the advantage of flaunting ignorance of social expectations with little to no consequences. Without a doubt, these are different for a black female depending on her shade. In the region, particularly among the middle and lower classes, white anthropologists are ascribed immediate social status and power regardless of presentation. Generally, reflexivity is not a common practice among Caribbean ethnographers. While anthropologists of color tend to cross the boundary, their white counterparts working in cultural settings where color/race matters rarely (with the exception of Goldstein 2003) reflect on how their whiteness operates in the field.[2] White anthropologists may be ridiculed for their foolishness (disregard of social order), but they are often forgiven for not adhering to these social norms. The socioeconomic status of white anthropologists and their abilities are doubted differently, if at all, as Edwidge Danticat noted "their skin itself is their three-piece suit."

In addition, as I indicated above, native anthropologists in these circumstances not only must adhere to social norms, but are often also expected by subjects to be more responsible and ethical. There may be a gender component to this. To diversify black anthropologists, let me note that individual positioning and choices ultimately determine the character of researchers' relationships with subjects and how these are ultimately presented textually.[3] For those who practice more engaged research, the negotiations differ. Racial and color proximity when working among one's "skinfolk," to use Zora Neale Hurston's term (1979), sometimes heightens the possible dangers of anonymity that could make data gathering in certain contexts improbable.[4] Initially, I had tremendous difficulty getting access to certain high-ranking government officials on my own. I am certain that the work I carried out with Metropolitan Parks and Markets (MPM) would have been virtually impossible had it not been for my upper-class networks. This inevitably highlights the class-based access that I had as an outsider compared to the more restricted resources of the marginal masses.

In 1995, prior to leaving to pursue my fieldwork, I purchased power.[5] These material and symbolic items included silver jewelry with lapis lazuli and Giorgio Armani designer glasses that were clearly "foreign" and costly. The clothing included numerous tailored pieces (especially for the interviews with upper-class government officials) and simple skirts and pants, as well as other items that symbolically affirmed a stable middle-class position. These objects, carefully chosen, comprised a particular classed aesthetic. I observed and respected certain gendered rules and brought back a rather stylish "ladies" wardrobe, several pairs of highheeled shoes, perfume, make-up, etc. Similar to the colored and black females who sought symbols to assert their denied femininity during slavery, these items allowed me to perform class and mediate the ways that blackness has been stigmatized. I also brought a pair of Adidas loafers for those long days when living in Kingston became unbearable, as they did in 1993. Indeed, performing the lady entails high heels, which require a presence and comportment that could become taxing over time. Instead of renting in Papine, I sought housing in a middle-class neighborhood. I lived in the New Kingston area, halfway between the university and downtown, in a studio that gave me physical comfort and a sense of safety. My choices were reflexive consumption practices meant to present a mediated self to counter the myriad manifestations of class and color stigma.

At the arcades downtown, I wore long floral skirts and linen shirts or blouses that covered my arms. I tied my head with a scarf. This got me the respect of the older men and the socially conscious younger men (who dubbed me their African Princess or Roots Lady).[6] Simultaneously, this mode of dress annoyed several of the ICIs who thought I must be soft (spineless) because I hid my body under all those clothes; I did not accentuate it like many of them do. Both of these responses suggest a sexualized construction of the black female based upon the lady/woman binary discussed in chapter 1. Yet I was never referred to as a woman by either of these two groups. While ladies may accentuate their bodies, they do not cover their figures. Such practices are associated with religious observances. It is precisely this affinity that the ICIs were objecting to. When I wore anything that revealed even my calves, I dreaded going downtown, especially to my primary field site, where numerous young men worked and lingered around the arcade posing. They would grab me, demanding that I talk with them because "dem like me." I would have to assert myself by performing tuffness in a manner I resented. In chapter 5, I examine the embodiment of a corporeal shield as a necessary component of self-making among those who work or live downtown.

To complicate matters, the UVA [United Vendors Association] was managed by two older Rastafari who were not pleased when I tried to dress in accordance with the tropical weather. They objected when I wore pants or anything that showed any skin and when I continued to get my hair cut very low. Their disdain for my cropped, rebel hairstyle stemmed from Rastafari doctrine, which honors one's locks as a crown of glory and prohibits the cutting of one's hair. They wanted me to become a Rasta, especially since they felt I showed a lot of potential: I often openly expressed my politics, and my research wardrobe consisted of long skirts and louses, which reflected a Rastafari aesthetic.

Sometimes I conformed to these gendered self-making sensibilities. This conventionality highlighted the complexities of the multiplicity of gendered identities that are the result of class and color crossings. Sometimes, I tied my head with a scarf and went downtown, which meant I had to decide to not go to certain places uptown such as the bank, the supermarket, the university, or the cafe, where this accessory was usually frowned upon because of its class code. Historically, the head-tie or tie-head (scarf) is an accessory, a marker of working-class status in the English-speaking Caribbean (Robertson 1995:113). More recently it has been associated with certain social or religious groups (popular with Rastafari and Pentecostals among others). Headscarves are visible uptown among more Afrocentric and black nationalist middle-class females, especially in various African cloths. Like any other ethnic-identified accessory, this headdress has different significance for black or brown, Chinese. Indian, or white females. The darker the skin, the more this accoutrement necessitates the "appropriate" jewelry and clothing to mediate an unquestionable middle-class and/or uptown identity. When I did wear head-ties, several of the ICIs I knew expressed their disapproval: "You like dem Rastas too much." They were very concerned that I was getting too close to the dreads. For these black females of working-class or lower-class lineages who do not possess the social and cultural capital that I do, visible mediations of color and class codes are even more crucial. Their constant warning regarding my proximity to Rastafari also signified their own recognition of this association as a form of class suicide. My devaluation would inevitably impact them, as my questionable class position would lessen the status they derived from my research interest in them.

These issues made me increasingly conscious of the symbolic politics of the ethnographer's identities, especially with regard to the limits and problems of how, through appearance and embodiment, one navigates the racialized spatial orders of field sites. These issues are brought under analysis here to give greater consideration to what Enuna Tarlo (1994) refers to as the problem of what to wear. I wish to complicate this question even further by emphasizing another aspect. Where does one go because of what one is wearing? The visibility of clothing renders dressing a significant component of class performance and negotiations. As a result a dressing method is required. My tendency was to rebel by cross-dressing-across-class.

Like gender cross-dressing, which disrupts the social categories of male and female, cross-dressing-across-class confounds socioeconomic orders.[7] Whereas the former has long been considered an anomaly, Marjorie Garber (1992) has argued that transvestism is an uncanny intervention that represents a space of anxiety about fixed and changing identities and throws into question gender norms. She locates transvestism "at the juncture of 'class' and 'gender,' and increasingly through its agency gender and class were revealed to be commutable, if not equivalent. To transgress one set of boundaries was to call into question the inviolability of both, and of the set of social codes—already under attack—by which such categories were policed and maintained" (1992:32). In that sense she argues, the transvestite (also a trompe l'oeil) represents not just a category crisis, but a "crisis of category" itself. Indeed, cross-dressers offer a performance of the performance. By this I mean that they are performing a gender that they are seeing performed. Their aesthetics, which also fall in between categories help to illuminate some of the manifestations of my cross-dressing-across-class. More specifically, how did I collapse class? Where did I fit in this ordered world? As I show below, nothing highlights the social construction of both gender and class more than when this performance is exaggerated. As a result of my dressing methods, I also represented a crisis in category as I stood at the intersections of the crossroads of class, color, gender, sexuality, and nationality constantly in flux because of my ability to manipulate different types of capital. Indeed, I disrupted existing hierarchies. I caused class trouble as I confounded various codes and their concomitant historical ideals.

Sometimes I simply did not adhere to local class and gendered expectations. I wore what I would on a college campus in Ann Arbor to try to maintain some sense of equilibrium. By not always conforming, I did not lose myself as Kondo (1990) did and found some solace in the process of living against the culture. During these times, my senses were more acute. Reactions to me were evidence of my disruption of class and color codes. Nevertheless, I was not always aware of the basis of my cultural faux pas. Did wearing Doc Martens with faded jeans and a kente wrap cause a stir at the National Dance Theatre Company performance lobby because they were pitchy-patchy,[8] to use local vernacular? Indeed, these items were respectively symbolic of dancehall, punk, arid Afrocentricity. I was forced to figure out what caused the reaction (the frowns, glares, stares, and even whispers). Was it the untidy aesthetic? Was it the mixed capital signs? Was it how these intersected with my color and/or perceived class? Regardless, my "inappropriate" performance created a disorder. To appropriate Butler, it was causing class as opposed to gender trouble. My "playful disruption" of the categories reinforced their severity (Butler 1990). While my performance went against the norm, it did force me to see and experience Jamaica from a range of classed perspectives. However, all of these occurrences differed depending on context. While the disruptions varied, responses to them were consistent. Without a doubt, they were systematically specific.

These reactions reveal that the "native" position ascribed to me in Ann Arbor certainly did not translate smoothly to Kingston. As a result of my appearance, my ability to immerse myself in the field or "go native," as they say, was inhibited or compromised by the fact that I am simultaneously a regional native and local outsider as well as an ethnographer. This forced me out of place, which inevitably had methodological implications. The numerous sites where fieldwork was conducted required that I shift among multiple positions at various times in different spaces that emphasized the incongruities in the intersections of gender, race, color, class, sexuality, nationality, and generation. In other words, I was actively code switching. My corporeal performances were determined by my context. They depended on who my interlocutors were, where I was, and what I wanted to find out.

Alter(ed)native Ethnographer

Given the persistence of these discontinuities in my interactions, eventually I began to use them as a research tool. Through a process of trial and error, I sought to research informal commercial importers and the broader environment that created them. Knowing the difficulty that both local and foreign researchers have in collecting data from ICIs, I considered several methodological approaches. In terms of participant-observation, I briefly considered becoming an informal importer for a year to gain firsthand experience of the trade. This option and others were challenging on multiple levels. Foremost, in becoming an ICI, I would be perpetuating the belief that ethnographic authority can be gained only by becoming an insider – that is, that insider privilege is an actual condition of nativeness and that knowledge gained in this fashion is superior to others.[9] Furthermore, given the overt and subtle nuances of Jamaican self-making practices, there are raced, classed, and gendered obstacles that limited the possibility of my partaking in all parts of this process.[10] Going native in my case, as a black female, where the majority of the population is also black, becomes a rather complex endeavor. There is no native, but a plurality of locals in different colors, classes, genders, and gendered identities. The question remained, if I were to follow my training, which of these would I be? Which type of native could I become, given that there are different classes and multiple shades or color gradations of natives?

Despite my color, my middle-class position set me apart from the working-class individuals in the arcades. As I stress above, and will discuss in greater detail in subsequent chapters, my complex positioning at times limited the extent of my participation. As my interest was in documenting and analyzing the experiences of ICIs of a particular social location and economic position, I could not fully participate as one of them.[11] Had I become an ICI, the knowledge gained would, in fact, be inconsistent with what I sought to learn. My actual experience would be based upon responses to the incongruity between who I am and who others perceive me to be. I could have abided by my social position, but that would have hindered different aspects of the data-gathering process unless I attempted to pass by performing yet another class identity. I could have chosen to alter my speech, mannerisms, and presentation and sold goods on the street or in an arcade like a working-class ICI. Taking on another identity would soon make me even more suspect and would highlight yet another ethical problem, my real motive for conducting the research.[12]

Undoubtedly, the traders would likely perceive this approach as a mockery of their reality, since the majority of them did not have my options. Most ICIs enter this occupation to survive and gain respect. I would be viewed as yet another researcher who sought their knowledge entirely for personal gain. Given the copious research projects undertaken in the Greater Kingston Metropolitan area, the general consensus regarding researchers is that they do not reciprocate. This is reconfirmed every time I return to Kingston and mention my respondents by name. Individuals are surprised that I maintain contact with traders. Local scholars are even more distrusted by traders, as they often consult for the state.[13] Another popular opinion among locals is that the data collected is for the U.S. government. To address this concern, I explained that dissertations are public documents that I could not control, though I would choose what would be included in this work. I had been encouraged by my mentors to find ways to give something back to the traders and the UVA. Throughout fieldwork and beyond, I became active in the UVA. I attended meetings and, on occasion, even spoke on their behalf. Hence as a participant-observer, I used a methodological approach, which at times entailed conscious interactions and interventions.

My decisions were informed by my purpose in undertaking this project. I sought to diagnose the basis of social inequality in Jamaica and to interpret the various causes of its persistence in order to understand how these can be redressed. From that perspective, while I remained troubled by the category "native," I was dedicated to the activist component of the native anthropology project first outlined by Delmos Jones (1970). More specifically, Jones wrote, "I am an intrinsic part of the social situation that I am attempting to study. As part of that situation, I must also be part of an attempt to forge a solution" (1970: 255). As I stated earlier, my decision to enter the discipline was politically motivated and is tied to my commitment to Haiti. I shared Jones's ideals and believed that solutions could be found by going beyond Geertz's native's point of view (1976). I wanted to engage all of the natives (informal commercial importers, government officials, and local and regional scholars who have been formulating theories of their condition, as well as popular commentators and other organic intellectuals) to the extent that this was possible.[14] Given that native voices are often limited in anthropological texts, engaging locally produced scholarship and organic intellectuals entailed embarking on a more politically engaged anthropology that must extend the parameters of ethnography to include the very context of its production, which facilitated disavowal of such knowledge.

Building on the Du Boisian legacy of work and praxis in anthropology, Faye Harrison suggests that ethnographers turn their heightened and intensified different sensibilities, visions and understandings into a useful research instrument (1991b). From this place of multiple consciousnesses, she argues the researcher can play a strategic role in the struggle to decolonize anthropology and the imperialist project from which the discipline arose. While I worked in Jamaica, my logic and intuition were "rooted in some combination and interpenetration of national, racial, sexual, and class oppressions," as Harrison describes it (1991b:90). This awareness did not disappear when I returned to Michigan. I was living, working, and conducting my work in Anzaldua's borderlands (1987); the margins that I occupied were constantly shifting. This space, bell hooks suggests, can be used strategically to develop a critical black voice and to build feminist solidarity for political work (1990).

When I cross-dressed-across-class or performed class against culture, my senses and sensibilities about self-making and social relations in Jamaica were quite heightened. This in turn fostered greater understanding of the environment in which I conducted my research, as well as the socioeconomic and political economy of the ethnographic project itself. In addition, my performance highlighted how the research process is an embodied endeavor, one in which lived and felt experience, through all the senses, is integral to both the data collection process and the knowledge produced (Stoller 1989, Weismantel 2001). For U.S.-based black feminist anthropologists, acknowledgment of this relationship between knowledge and experience has been somewhat limiting. By this I mean that those who focus on such concerns are often constrained to reproduce hegemonic (or tenurable) ethnographies if they are interested in professional advancement within the discipline. Thus, work on epistemological questions is often addressed in separate articles that reflect upon fieldwork experiences.[15] Regardless of this choice, as Bolles has aptly argued, in the citation game that propels careers, black feminist anthropologists remain the least cited, especially by white feminists who tend to regard their work mostly as experiential

(2001). In "New Voices of Diversity, Academic Relations of Production, and the Free Market," Harrison takes this point even further. She contends that theoretical contributions of black feminists are continuously erased through consistent devaluation of writing that does not reinforce disciplinary hegemony. These exchanges, she asserts, are symptomatic of the division of labor within academic relations of production (1999). Black feminist anthropologists occupy a position as "outsiders-within" the discipline (Hill-Collins [1991) 2000). Unsurprisingly, as a result, historically, many have turned to other disciplines and/or to the arts to extend the full range of their expression (Harrison and Harrison 1999). In general, such works have been neglected and brought under the rubric of humanism, or adopted altogether by other disciplines.[16] In part, because of what Catherine Lutz calls the gender of theory (1995), reflections on the intersections of embodied knowledge are still relegated to the margins, outside of dominant discourses. When the object of reflection is race and class within the academy, and the larger politics that shape intellectual production, such discussions are treated as trivial, and not ethnographic. The panoptic lens extends only so far when the self is the object of the gaze.

As Bruce Knauft stresses, disregard for the cultural politics within anthropology is duplicitous. It neglects the fact that the academy in general, and anthropology, also has its own culture. The representation of cultural contestation is not simply a concern for the field among the people we study. Hegemonies (of voice and perspectives) are maintained by disciplinary practices as well (1996:250-252). I use a reflexive voice to consider the interconnections between aspects of fieldwork often hidden in conventional ethnographies as well as the broader political environment in which ethnographies are made.

Indeed, as Ruth Behar asserts, reflexivity is susceptible to the charge that it is simply self-serving and superficial. This, she argues, "stems from an unwillingness to even consider the possibility that a personal voice can lead the reader to the enormous sea of serious social issues" (1996:22). This, I argue, extends to reflections on the discipline as well. For black feminist anthropologists, the implications of this dismissal are even shoddier.[17] According to Narayan (1995), native anthropologists do face a particular dilemma (as both products and subjects of the discipline), which they must maneuver and that also constrains them. Kath Weston (1997a) puts it quite simply:

> social relations inside and outside of the profession pull her [the native ethnographer] toward the poles of her assigned identity, denying her the option of representing herself as a complex, integrated, compound figure. Instead of writing as "I, Native Ethnographer" – or some equally compound subject position – she ends up positioned as either "I, Native," or "I, Ethnographer." The nuance of the two as they are bound up together is lost. (1997a:171)

To retrieve this complex voice, I use auto-ethnography to reject on my interactions and relations with subjects and the dynamic power that binds us. As Irma McClaurin notes, "auto-ethnography is simultaneously autobiographical and communal, as the self encounters the collective" (2001b:69). The above reflexive moments make explicit the connections between the immersed subject (I, native) and the purported detached observer (I, ethnographer). It also begins to forge the intimacy Anzaldua (1987) suggested. With the particularities of how my Haitian nationality played out in Jamaica, I have revealed some of the complexities inherent in the category of the native.

As I stated in the introduction, my goal is to pluralize the native. I have done so by interweaving a tale out of various auto-ethnographic reflections. First, by pointing to the reasons for the ICIs' expectations of me (as a group that has been overstudied), and mine of them, I have revealed that we shared time, space, and place. Second, as a regional native and local outsider, I occupied a state of displacement on the border, as Haitian national and U.S. resident, that informed my interactions with diverse groups of locals.[18] Third, I was initially oblivious of the gendered components of the articulation of class and color codes. My disregard was most evident in my early dressing methods, which revealed my class performances to be incongruous in ways that symbolized class trouble or what I call socioeconomic disorder. Later, I will show how my use of codes notably diverges from that of most ICIs due to our different social positions. Through these observations, I seek to de-essentialize black female subjectivity to show divisions based on class, color, age, and nationality. Whether I was with higglers, ICIs, government officials, scholars, and others on the street, at the arcade, on buses, in taxis, at the university, or at the supermarket, I constantly crossed shifting class and color lines. My crossing required performances that informed aspects of the various methodological approaches used in this project. At times, the boundaries between native and ethnographer were obscure. The lines were blurred as the categories I embody necessitated conciliations of class and color codes that have both historical and contemporary referents. Thus, these mediations compelled my temporal crossings at various times in ways quite different from the ICIs whom I studied.

Notes

1. She asked where I grew up, where I went to school, my family background, why I talk like I do (as I did not speak like an African American), among other questions. At the end of this conversation, she informed me that in 1993, I behaved neither like a black American nor like a West Indian.
2. See, for example, Browne 2004, Freeman 2000, Stolzoff 2000, Smith 2001. In her monograph, Lisa Douglass (1992) reflected on some of her negotiations and constant policing by the white elites who were the subjects of her dissertation. I especially thank Melissa Johnson (Belize) and Kate Ramsey (Haiti) (both white females) for their frank and extensive discussions with me about their fieldwork experiences while working in the region.
3. Contemporary black reflexive anthropologists are few and far between and are commonly females. In the past, black female anthropologists who blurred different genres of writing, such as Zora Neale Hurston and Katherine Dunham, were relegated to the humanities because of the interdisciplinary aspects of their projects.
4. Black feminist anthropologists have used their "native" status in many complex ways. Kimberly Simmonds (2001) and Karla Slocum (2001) took different approaches to their fieldwork, deploying their identities in culturally specific ways to reveal the heterogeneity of this category.
5. Anthropologist Elizabeth Chin (2001) deconstructs the practice of purchasing power. In her monograph, she provides a complex reading of black kids' patterns of consumption and argues for structural understanding of pragmatic mediations of stigma in a wealthy society such as the United States.
6. These nicknames are important as they point to yet another characterization of black femininity. Even in my low hair phase, I was still referred to in those terms. I believe they were given to me precisely because of my penchant for long skirts and natural fabrics, etc. My aesthetic was the antithesis of the downtown/dancehall enthusiast, but I also did not conform to the conventional middleclass lady's code. I was also often asked by men who did not know me if I was Christian. These classifications, I argue, stemmed from a recognition that I chose to identify with the Jamaican masses. In "Ethnography as Politics," Faye V. Harrison discusses various aspects of her dissertation fieldwork experience in downtown Kingston during the 1980s. In terms of gender dynamics, our experiences varied

as her light skin color complicated her story to show the persistence and rupture of gendered class and color codes. In addition to being sexualized in a different way, she was "labeled 'white' or 'brown' — or sometimes 'red' — viewed as representative of 'Babylon,' the Rastafarian designation for Black Jamaicans domestic and foreign oppressors." (1997a:99).

7. This is a rampant practice among anthropologists in the field. Cross-dressing-across-class is also common in the U.S., especially on some college campuses, where students do not dress up. The University of Michigan, a state university located in a town with a liberal past is generally more relaxed in terms of appearance than Williams College, a private liberal arts college, or Howard University, a historically black college. Self-presentation practices at these institutions vary according to the demographics.

8. The term pitchy-patchy is a reference to the costume worn at the Jonkonnu Festival that was made of scraps and patches of fabric strategically sewn together. The costume was made of various cloths including burlap from the sugar and flour sacks from abroad as well as locally produced fabrics (Nettleford 1995). This term is analogous to Claude Levi-Strauss's "bricolage" (1966) and Jean-Francois Lyotard's "pastiche" ([1979] 1984).

9. Like di Leonardo (1991) and Haraway (1991), who argue that at the level of ethnography, no one can claim privileged access to knowledge, I believe that this process and the information acquired through it is situated knowledge.

10. I believe that within the Caribbean context, fieldwork methods are not as limiting for men. They can go native in ways that women cannot because certain aspects of female life are bound by constructions of class-specific gendered identities (such as lady and woman with qualifiers such as good and bad), which are premised upon the occupation of certain localities, that is. "inside" as opposed to "outside" or private as opposed to public.

11. Besides, the notion of the participation of the participant-observer is one-sided. "Participant" implies some sort of contribution and reciprocity. In the field, participation is on the researcher's terms. She/he is always on the receiving end. She/he is being taught how to participate by the subject (Nesha Haniff personal communication).

12. I would have had to pretend to be someone I am not, which is disrespectful to the traders because the pretense denies them knowledge and agency. As Haniff continually reminded me, respect is integral to conscious and responsible research. My motive was already an issue, especially with the UVA and several traders who thought I was in the CIA. In the downtown context that kind of suspicion is potentially dangerous because it is linked to greater concerns and different interests in the traffic of contraband, as well as local and national sovereignty and security. Another more plausible option would be for me to become a middle-class ICI.

13. ICIs and their organizations have been rather suspicious, since several studies conducted by researchers have been used to inform government policies that were detrimental to this group. See, for example, Le Franc 1989, Taylor 1988.

14. Despite a history of competition, my goal from the onset was to engage Jamaican and other Caribbean scholars in conversation. Trouillot rightly argues that the native has never been a full interlocutor in anthropological projects. Indeed, ethnographers tend to dismiss local scholarship as elitist, while engaging with Western scholarship as authoritative. In so doing, ethnographers determine which of the natives belong to the savage slot (Trouillot 2003).
15. See, for example, Williams (1991), Bolles (1985), McClaurin (2001b), Harrison (1991b).
16. See Baker (1998) on Du Bois and Harrison (1999) on Drake.
17. Irma McClaurin (2001b) recently asserted that indigenous and marginal voices have once again been banished to the margins with the exception of the token few. Lynn Bolles (2001) and Faye V. Harrison (1999) make a similar argument.
18. See, for example, Appadurai (1991), Basch, Glick-Schiller, and Blanc (1994).

References

Anzaldúa, Gloria. *Borderlands: La Frontera*. Vol. 3: Aunt Lute San Francisco, 1987.

Appadurai, Arjun. ""Global Ethnoscapes: Notes and Queries for a Transformational Anthropology." In *Recapturing Anthropology*, edited by Richard Fox. Sante Fe: School of American Research Press., 1991.

Austin-Broos, Diane J. "Race/Class: Jamaica's Discourse of Heritable Identity." *NWIG: New West Indian Guide / Nieuwe West-Indische Gids* 68, no. 3/4 (1994): 213-33.

Baker, Lee D. *From Savage to Negro: Anthropology and the Construction of Race, 1896-1954*. Berkeley: University of California Press, 1998.

Basch, Linda, Nina Glick Schiller, and Christina Szanton Blanc. *Nations Unbound: Transnational Projects, Postcolonial Predicaments, and Deterritorialized Nation-States*. New York: Gordon and Breach, 1994.

Bolles, Lynn. "Of Mules and Yankee Gals: Stuggling with Stereotypes in the Field." *Anthropology and Humanism Quarterly* 10, no. 4 (1985): 114-19.

Browne, Katharine. *Creole Economics: Caribbean Cunning under the French Flag*. Austin: University of Texas Press, 2004.

Chin, Elizabeth. *Purchasing Power: Black Kids and American Consumer Culture*. Minneapolis: University of Minnesota Press, 2001.

Di Leonardo, Micaela. "Introduction: Gender, Culture, and Political Economy: Feminist Anthropology in Historical Perspective." In *Gender at the Crossroads of Knowledge: Feminist Anthropology in the Postmodern Era*, edited by Micaela Di Leonardo. Berkeley: University of California Press, 1991.

Douglass, Lisa. *The Power of Sentiment: Love, Hierarchy and the Jamaican Family Elite*. Boulder: Westview Press, 1992.

Freeman, Carla. *High Tech and High Heels in the Global Economy: Women, Work, and Pink-Collar Identities in the Caribbean*. Durham: Duke University Press, 2000.

Garber, Marjorie. *Vested Interests: Cross-Dressing and Cultural Anxiety*. New York: Routledge, 1992.

Geertz, Clifford. "'From the Native's Point of View'": On the Nature of Anthropological Understanding." In *The Meaning of Anthropology*, edited by K. Basso and H. Selby. 26-45. Albuquerque: University of New Mexico Press, 1974.

Gupta, Akhil, and James Ferguson. "Discipline and Practice: 'The Field' as Site, Method, and Location in Anthropology." In *Anthropological Locations: Boundaries and Grounds of a Field Science*, edited by Akhil Gupta and James Ferguson. 1-47. Berkeley: University of California Press, 1997.

Haraway, Donna. "Situated Knowledges: The Science Question in Feminism and the Privilege of Partial Perspective." In *Simians, Cyborgs, and Women: The Reinvention of Nature*, edited by Donna Haraway. New York: Routledge, 1991.

Harrison, Faye V. "New Voices of Diversity, Academic Relations of Production, and the Free Market." In *Transforming Academia: Challenges and Opportunities for an Engaged Anthropology*, edited by Linda Basch, Lucie Wood Saunders, Jagna Wojcicka Sharff and James Peacock. 72-85. Washington D.C.: American Antrhopological Association 1999.

Harrison, Faye Venetia. *Decolonizing Anthropology Moving Further toward an Anthropology for Liberation*. American Anthropological Association. 1991.

Hill Collins, Patricia. *Black Feminist Thought: Knowledge, Consciousness, and the Politics of Empowerment* [in English]. Routledge Classics. Routledge, 1991. 357.

Jones, Delmos J. "Towards a Native Anthropology." *Human Organization* 29, no. 4 (1970): 251-59.

Kondo, Dorinne K. *Crafting Selves: Power, Gender, and Discourses of Identity in a Japanese Workplace*. Chicago: University of Chicago Press, 2009.

Le Franc, Elsie. "Petty Trading and Labour Mobility: Higglers in the Kingston Metropolitan Area." In *Women and the Sexual Division of Labour in the Caribbean, Kingston, Consortium School of Social Sciences*, edited by Keith Hart. Kingston: Consortium Graduate School, 1989.

Lutz, Catherine. "The Gender of Theory." In *Women Writing Culture*, edited by Ruth Behar and Deborah A. Gordon. Berkeley: University of California Press, 1995.

Lyotard, Jean-François. "The Postmodern Condition: A Report on Knowledge." Minneapolis: University of Minnesota Press, 1984.

McClaurin, Irma. "Theorizing a Black Feminist Self in Anthropology: Toward an Autoethnographic Approach." In *Black Feminist Anthropology: Theory, Politics, Praxis, and Poetics*, edited by Irma McClaurin. 49-76. New Brunswick: Rutgers University Press, 2001.

Narayan, Kirin. "How Native Is a 'Native' Anthropologist?" *American Anthropologist* 95, no. 3 (1993): 671-86.

Nettleford, Rex. "Fancy Dress and the Roots of Culture: From Jonkunnu to Dancehall." *Gleaner*, July 18 1985.

Simmonds, Kimberly. "A Passion for Sameness: Encountering a Black Feminist Self in Fieldwork in the Dominican Republic." In *Black Feminist Anthropology: Theory, Politics, Praxis, and Poetics*, edited by Irma McClaurin. New Brunswick: Rutgers University Press, 2001.

Slocum, Karla. "Negotiating Identity and Black Feminist Politics in Caribbean Research." In *Black Feminist Anthropology: Theory, Politics, Praxis, and Poetics*, edited by Irma McClaurin. New Brunswick: Rutgers University Press, 2001.

Smith, Jennie Marcelle. *When the Hands Are Many: Community Organization and Social Change in Rural Haiti*. Ithaca: Cornell University Press, 2001.

Stoller, Paul. *The Taste of Ethnographic Things: The Senses in Anthropology*. Phladelphia: University of Pennsylvania Press, 1989.

Stolzoff, Norman C. *Wake the Town and Tell the People: Dancehall Culture in Jamaica*. Philadelphia: Duke University Press, 2000.

Strauss, Claude Levi. *The Savage Mind*. Chicago: University of Chicago Chicago, IL, 1966.

Taylor, Alicia. "Women Traders in Jamaica the Informal Commercial Importers." Port of Spain, Trinidad: Economic Commission for Latin America and the Caribbean, 1988.

Trouillot, Michel-Rolph. *Global Transformations: Anthropology and the Modern World*. Springer, 2016.

Weismantel, Mary. *Cholas and Pishtacos: Stories of Race and Sex in the Andes*. Chicago: University of Chicago Press, 2001.

Weston, Kath. "The Virtual Anthropologist." In *Anthropological Locations: Boundaries and Grounds of a Field Science*, edited by Akhil Gupta and James Ferguson. 163-84. Berkeley: Univesity of California Press, 1997.

Williams, Brackette. *Stains on My Name, War in My Veins: Guyana and the Politics of Cultural Struggle*. Durham: Duke University Press, 1991.

28. "Insider" Experiences and Ethnographic Knowledge: Reflections from Trinidad and Tobago*

Gabrielle Hosein

This collection of essays is meant to be a good read for scholars new to fieldwork as well as those doing anthropological research in the Caribbean. It primarily situates fieldwork "overseas" and furthers the historical accessibility of an "outsider" gaze of the region, while noting how problematic this can be. This chapter adds to a panoramic view of ethnographic encounters in the Caribbean by speaking from "home." In relation to the anthropological literature on the region, few studies suggest how "difference" is mediated by anthropologists working *and* living in the Anglophone Caribbean (Mahabir 1989; Chevannes 2001; Tafari Ama 2002; Carnegie 2002; Hope 2006). This means that Caribbean students, Caribbeanists and anthropologists working "at home" anywhere in the world have little to turn to from the region for comparative insights on aspects of reflexivity, writing, identity, power and politics.

Keeping this in mind, I look reflexively at my own experiences as a PhD student, doing an ethnography of politics and governance from July 2003 to September 2004, in the southern city of San Fernando in Trinidad.[1] My goal is to contribute to how Caribbean scholars living at home experience and theorize doing research in their own country. Although as a Trinidadian I could be considered an insider, I show how being unmarried, female, Indian, middle-class, from a Muslim family and a student from northern Trinidad mediated my relationship to the "field" and those in it, marked a range of boundaries, and intersected my methodology.

Ethnographic method pays attention to women's and men's actual lives in order to plumb the informal logic in their interpretation of rules, habits and practices. This is because anthropology is committed

---

* Reprinted with permission from *Fieldwork Identities in the Caribbean*, ed. Erin B. Taylor. Caribbean Studies Press, 2010, 27–53.

to observing and understanding political, economic and social life from the perspective of participation and its consequences, not just from its form (Willis and Trondman 2002). My study delved into the relationships and practices that most mattered to ordinary women and men. It sought greater insight about the ways that these explained participation in different forms of authority and their relationships with the state. Participant-observation in natural settings provided a picture of everyday actions, experience and problematic moments as they occurred in people's lives, and allowed me to better grasp the meanings that women and men attached to them (Denzin and Lincoln 1994, 2).

I didn't start fieldwork with a clear research question or even a hypothesis. I had abandoned the one in my proposal as soon as I set foot in the field.[2] I therefore began by asking somewhat vaguely about life in San Fernando, how women and men lived, what they liked or didn't like; what they thought had changed, how they felt about it, and what their needs, aspirations and difficulties were. This kind of grounded theory approach sought to discover "theories, concepts, hypotheses, propositions directly from the data, rather than from a priori assumptions, other research or existing theoretical frameworks" (Taylor and Bogdan 1984, 126). The methodology opened up areas I would never have thought of if I were doing only interviews or asking structured questions.

As I waited for taxis, bought vegetables, listened to business transactions, attended women's meetings or just sat with fishermen at the waterfront, people's appropriation of authority and its meanings stood out. By moving out of my class, gender and geographical location, I was able to detail aspects of power often disconnected from some of Trinidad and Tobago's most marginalized groups and the surprising ways ordinary women and men govern normative order. In this way, I came to understand public life through the forms of power and meaning associated with family, law, elections, leadership, artistry and God. I also learned to see the taken-for-granted anew.

Reflexivity

All knowledge is subjectively based, partial and limited. Insiders and outsiders access different information and confidences (Tixier y Vigil and Elsasser 1976). Unspoken emotional understanding, years of association through growing up in a setting, pre-existing identities defined by kinship, and familiarity with traditional expectations all shape the experience of researchers working at home. In addition, researchers choose identities and people choose identities for them. What is most important is to acknowledge the hybridity of native anthropologists and the moments when they are also outsiders, the ways that their academic writing can marginalize others, and the need for genuine contribution to theories based on more than Western precepts and assumptions (Narayan 1993, 677; Madison 2005).

In the latter part of the 20th century, anthropologists began to systematically reflect on the ethical, interpersonal and political issues involved in conducting ethnography. These decades also witnessed an explosion of feminist and anthropological reflections about insider experiences in fieldwork. Writing by insiders has primarily highlighted their mixed feelings and experiences during fieldwork (Kondo 1986; Ladner 1987; Abu-Lughod 1988, 1991; Lal 1996; Matsumoto 1996; Ribbins and Edwards 1998; Mutua and Swadener 2004; Geller and Stockett 2006). In fact, many of these "indigenous" researchers felt they fit in several places at once in the insider-outsider binary because of their class, cultural, rural/urban backgrounds, language differences and Western university schooling. Often, this led to complex issues of trust, honesty, reciprocity and representation in the research process.

Others, such as Kirin Narayan, rejected the insider-outsider dichotomy, and argued that factors such as gender, class, sexual orientation, ethnicity and duration of contact may "outweigh the cultural identity we associate with insider-outsider status" (1993, 672). Narayan, Hill-Collins (1990) and others have also debated the significance of belonging to the distinctive worlds of academia and everyday life, noting the ways that power is wielded through both fieldwork and writing, and greater possibilities for shared understanding (Wolf 1996, 13-14).

The issue is one of understanding how to reflect on doing anthropology at home and how to be honest about the bicultural nature of being both regular folk and academic researchers. In an introduction that highlights the dilemmas of turning home into field in Jamaica, Donna Hope calls this duality a "sacred insanity" (2006, xii). Far more scholarship is needed, so that Caribbean students can share and learn how to straddle the nexus between being Caribbean and creating knowledge. By being "explicit about the operation of power within the actual process of researching and representing people" (Alldred 1998, 162), this literature would show how schooling, religion, gender or experience informs knowledge gathered.

Interrogating this involves thinking in terms of multiple perspectives and mobile subjectivities (Wolf 1996, 14). It aims for what Narayan (1993, 672) calls an "enactment of hybridity" in writing. However, reflexive thinking means more than looking at the implications of identities. It also means a "concrete and nitty-gritty" attention to "where, how and why particular decisions are made at particular stages" in the production of knowledge (Mauthner and Doucet 1998, 138). It is about seeing the subjectivity of the researcher as part of what is produced (Stanley 1987). We take part in community life as we study it (Kottak 2005, 27). In this context, it is especially important for scholars doing ethnography at home to interrogate how issues of trust, difference and representation shape their experience and their approach to knowledge.

Findings from the Field

Paying attention to the concrete and nitty-gritty moments, this section explores the following issues: positionality, by looking at experiences of finding a place to live and developing rapport and trust; reciprocity, by focusing on forming relationships and making research bargains; and finally, aspects of knowledge in terms of leaving the field to write and ethically writing up the work. Usually, choice of field site should be justified by questions arising out of scholarly literature. Yet, I decided to do research in San Fernando because I knew southern Trinidad very little and felt that a national scholar needed wider familiarity than I had with the island. As Altorki and El Solh noted over 20 years ago, although disciplinary trends may influence the choice of topic, a researcher's "indigenous status" shapes motivations, questions and entry (1988, 10).

I arrived in San Fernando on the day of local government elections and spent the first day in the constituency offices of the two main political parties in the country. The ethnicized nature of Trinidad and Tobago party politics meant that my ethnicity was as significant to my participation as my student status and age. At both offices, I knew someone who enabled me to enter the space. The first was a student, Catherine, who I knew from the University of the West Indies. My second contact was with the MP for San

Fernando West, who knew my family and whom I knew from her tenure as a Minister in the government.

One day, Catherine took me to meet the market vendor who sold tomatoes and whom she felt epitomized what she called mutuality, or the ways Trinidadians have of working things through together. This vendor and her neighbors in the market became aunties whom I went back to talk to many times about life and work in San Fernando. The Community Environmental Protection and Enhancement Programme (CEPEP) worker, Jennifer, whom I met on the first day in the People's National Movement (PNM) Constituency Office, got her roadside gang foreman to introduce me to people on the Railway Line.[3] For months, I would go down to the wharf and market, and start conversations with people there about the day, the news, my study or what I was learning about San Fernando.

The *mas* camp[4], suggested to me by another friend from San Fernando, was much easier to enter because strangers are constantly coming to the camp to get a costume or to help make costumes in the Carnival season. Within the first two weeks, I was helping almost every day.

Finally, my cousin, with whom I stayed for the first months, introduced me to the president of the mosque. He and another politician I already knew called me to help when the organization's election campaign began. During the leadup to the election, I began to regularly attend campaign and women's group meetings. I negotiated each of the four settings differently. From the beginning, the value, status, meaning and power attached to different identities shaped my entries and my relationships.

Identities and Intersectionalities

A key challenge was to work out who I was supposed to be while doing fieldwork. My supervisor told me that I should get out of the spaces I always moved in, do things that I ordinarily wouldn't do and experience Trinidad afresh: if I didn't usually go to church, or mosque, or temple, or drink in a rum shop, or play football on a Sunday, I should. To some extent, I did this and it opened my eyes to a variety of sites and practices I would not have known otherwise. However, I struggled with my own sense of authenticity in these encounters. Mascarenhas-Keyes (1987, 182-3) writes about the "dramaturgical exercise" of being a "multiple" native as her way of negotiating access. She wore different shoes, hairstyles, ornaments and other accessories when meeting different groups of people, dressing as they did and even pretending to share their views. I worried that this was disingenuous. I did not want to pretend to an insider belonging that I did not have, among people I felt I would know in later years and in other contexts on a small island.

I didn't believe in Islam, though it is my family's religion and has shaped our cultural practices. Perhaps, this closeness is why, despite the entry it would have given me with the community, I couldn't pretend that I was a practicing Muslim and felt I had to honestly represent who I was in my interactions in the mosque. Drinking alcohol provided another example. A number of male scholars and San Fernandians told me I had to go drinking with people in order to really gain entrance and trust. However, I didn't like bars, alcohol, getting drunk and conversations with drunken people (though I had many). My inability to be someone else for the sake of my fieldwork hindered my ability to cross my outsider status in different settings.

My desire to be the kind of anthropologist texts described competed with the ways I set boundaries on the demands ethnography placed on my life. This was evident in my search for the ideal family written about in anthropology texts. For the first three months, I lived with my mother's cousin for the five days of each week that I stayed in the city, even though he had initially agreed to my staying for three weeks only. I stayed because I couldn't find a suitable host family.

My father's brother, an Islamic scholar, also lived in San Fernando, but would not have been comfortable with the amount of time I spent on the wharf, with my Carnival activities in the mas camp nor with the fact that I left every Saturday evening to go to the apartment in North Trinidad where I lived in a common-law union with my non-Islamic, non-Indian boyfriend. During these months, I searched using my contacts with family members, CEPEP workers and even elites, but had no luck. No one, including my own family, understood the idea of living with an unrelated family. Unlike a student "from foreign," I was expected to draw on suitable family of my own.

I had been living on my own for several years by the time I began fieldwork. I had an income, complete independence and, while I lacked the benefits of being situated within a family, I also lacked any demands or responsibilities to others besides flatmates. In truth, I didn't really want to live with a strange family or, for that matter, my family. The ethnographic literature argues that living with a family provides access to communities and networks of family members of different ages as well as safety, comfort and feelings of belonging. The literature by insiders seems to especially romanticize family life. Yet, in this instance, it seemed easier to live alone and not have to negotiate the expectations of others.

Eventually, I moved into a family house, though one without a family. My Islamic uncle asked a family from the San Fernando Jamaat if I could stay in their father's house while he was sick and living with them, and the house was empty. It was perfect because I lived alone, had lots of time to work quietly, and saw Pappy and his family whenever they came. The experience of searching for a family highlighted the significance of being an indigenous researcher, living without any clear separation between one's life and the field. It also highlighted the significance of trying to do participant-observation as a Trinidadian. Many assumed that, after a few weeks, there was not much else that a local needed to (or could) learn from a space like the market or the wharf. People understood that I wanted to do interviews, but if I already knew about life in Trinidad, why did I need to be looking to get a sense of local habits? Was I simply minding people's business (Mascarenhas-Keyes 1987, 186)?

This wasn't the only way that insider knowledge was both expected of me and used to understand my activities. Women and men on the wharf found it strange that I chose the mosque for my research even though I wasn't a practicing Muslim. Mosque members were scandalized that I played mas in a skimpy costume. Women in the market worried about the time I spent on the wharf and my safety there, and the family running the mas camp especially didn't want me to live with the CEPEP worker who offered.

Elites kept their distance because I was a stranger below their class who might collect sensitive information and threaten their safety. They often quizzed me about who my parents were and their occupations, who funded my research and what I planned to do after and who we knew in common. Yet they remained guarded and looked askance at the amount of time I spent with vendors, fishermen and squatters. Reflecting on how much finding a family, friend or school connection to her mattered to her informants, Donna Young aptly observed, "It both made me less suspect and bound me more closely to acceptable codes of behaviour" (2005, 208).

My attempts at crossing difference, as a young, unmarried, middle-class Indian girl, were constantly commented upon and managed, especially in the first months. As Mascarenhas-Keyes (1987, 187) describes of her own experience,

> Anthropologists continually invite diverse comments as natives try to make sense of their behaviour. More so than the Outsider, I became an enduring topic of village comment precisely because I was a native who, by my activities, was constantly challenging multiple norms and values....Women anthropologists...have noted that the behaviour of a female fieldworker is more closely scrutinized than that of a male... my absence from the home and widespread research contact with men provoked numerous snide remarks and jokes from all sectors of the society (1987, 187).

Women I interviewed were also guarded about their husbands, and this too made it hard to adopt a family. Once, for example, I had contacted an Indo-Trinidadian CEPEP contractor whose workers lived on the wharf and whom I had met several times. I called him to book an interview and on the appointed time, a Friday at lunchtime, I called again to say that I was on my way. His wife, an Indo-Trinidadian whom I had also met before, answered and yelled at me for calling her house. I explained that I was calling about doing an interview, but she hung up on me. I felt that a young foreign woman, associated with transience, lack of familiarity and status, would have been less threatening. As a young local woman, it seemed more possible that I would choose to "share" a wealthy man or could be more easily available for a sustained relationship on the side.

Later, at the wharf, I went to their *roti*[5] shop to explain why I was calling and to tell her again about what I was researching. She was unconvinced and yelled some more. The contractor stood around, red-faced, muttering about how his wife wouldn't let him have conversations with anybody. Of course, all his workers heard about this scene from the few who were hanging around when it happened. They all thought it was an especially spicy story as it enabled them to gossip about their boss's infidelities, how he treats his wife and what this most recent outburst meant.

For me, it highlighted the pitfalls of male privilege in Trinidad, the significance of men's unfaithfulness, and the risks of doing research as a young, unmarried woman who needs to interact with men as well as women. I was afraid that this powerful couple would block my access to other contractors and otherwise hinder my work. I was also shaken by the ways that my neutral student and researcher identities were uncomfortably sexualized.

After this incident, I tried more to appear like a daughter figure around older women and to further highlight my identity as a student and researcher. I relied more on women with power in their settings to legitimize my interaction with a space. A friendly foreman, a woman, sent me to talk to people she recommended. The few women in the market with whom I became good friends helped point to others. In the mosque, the women were like aunties, even giving me books and scarves so that I could participate more.

Being a woman also enabled me to have discussions with other women about their gendered experiences. On the wharf, I could talk about issues of fathering and male providers with women struggling to make enough income or do all the household chores. In the market, the women talked about domestic violence and experiences of adultery, and in the mosque, they often talked about their responsibilities at home and how many things "the men" didn't understand. In this way, I drew on gender, age, fictive kinship and educational aspects of my identity to draw greater protection in fieldwork encounters. If I had been male, it would have been much easier to access men's perspectives. However, male privilege may have prevented me from exploring women's realities to such an extent.

My extra efforts to make women mother or auntie figures and to interact with men as fathers or uncles were strategies that I did not employ in other aspects of my life. Fieldwork itself required me to choose identities associated with respectability and a need for protection to counter the reputation that could result from being a friendly and adventurous unmarried adult woman willing to transgress class, gender and ethnic categories in developing relations with others. This tactic meant that one man later commented that he thought I was "only interviewing ladies."

I made a point of telling men that I wasn't interested in the complications of any relationships while I should be focusing on school and I deflected attempts to flirt with me. From the beginning, I dressed in loose jeans, sneakers and tshirts, wore no jewelry or makeup in the field, covered my head and arms in the mosque, and was very conscious of how I interacted with men. Sometimes, I would purposely tell people that I had a boyfriend, drawing on my union status to navigate distrust among women and men that I met.

In these ways, my positionality was central to ways that I gained entry, established trust, developed relationships, managed the demands of respectability and kept safe in masculinized spaces such as streets, taxis, bars, the mosque and the mas camp. Being a middle-class Indo-Trinidadian woman meant that I brought class power that helped to establish my student status and "respectability" (Hosein 2004) in my encounters with squatters, vendors and mas makers, as well as with state bureaucrats and party activists.

I also drew a range of reactions to the cross-class and inter-ethnic relations that I developed, such as with Afro-Trinidadian fishermen. Certainly, Indo-Trinidadians in the mas camp, market and mosque more easily treated me as a daughter, making perceptions of our shared race, culture and religion significant. My ethnicity was also a factor in a context where the field is politicized by party politics, and my political loyalty was certainly something that people wondered about, especially CEPEP bosses and URP personnel.[6]

My class became especially significant when a key informant began asking me regularly for money. She was very poor and struggling to support two sons in school, and a daughter with four children, on her CEPEP income. She would ask me and others for money for basic purchases. I wanted to help her out and I would give her a few dollars whenever she asked. Then she began asking for larger sums of money and it became very difficult for me to manage the relationship. The mas camp people knew her and said to stop giving her money and even others on the wharf began to disapprove of how easy I was to hustle.

People lost respect because I was not adequately streetwise. They expect such naivete of foreigners and tourists, but as a Trinidadian, I was expected to know how much and when it was appropriate to give and when it was appropriate to say no. I never successfully resolved the relationship, and I don't feel that I ended it well. I eventually stopped going to visit her and when I went back to look for her after a number of months, she had moved and the wooden house she had been renting had been torn down. This relationship taught me much about how difficult it can be to manage class privilege and to be truly committed to reciprocity with those who help so much in the field. It also highlighted the ways that respect can be gained and lost among different groups of women and men.

Class also worked against me when trying to access the elites. They were suspicious and uncomfortable with making their private networks available to another Trinidadian. Rotary Club members, for example, told me they were reticent about talking about their influence and that much of their influence is exercised over the phone or in small private social gatherings. While not owning a car meant that I could identify with people in the mas camp or Railway Line who had to walk to places and take taxis, elites more often took this as a sign of my outsider status. I could hardly find a site where I could regularly meet them in a social setting or make observations among groups. While elites understood interviewing, participant-observation felt too inquisitive and potentially threatening. Like Zora Neale Hurston many decades ago, I often wondered if someone truly other would have been given more leeway in terms of ethnographically "poking and prying with purpose" (Hurston 1942: 174).

San Fernando's elites have grown up together and form tight cliques linked by area of residence, business partnerships, secondary schooling, political involvement and charitable associations. Many simply didn't want to have a strange young woman hanging around. Older men and women were friendly, but some older women less so. Younger women and men that I met were indifferent. A few let me interview them but spent much of the interview asserting their status and class. They rarely gathered in public spaces and when they did, I found no gatekeeper to introduce me.

Truthfully, some of this was my fault as well. I was uncomfortable among the rich and elite in San Fernando, and often felt that I simply didn't have the energy to break into a clique. Interviews were difficult as I didn't know what to ask or what I was looking for in this group. Even if truth is only ever partial, I felt a chapter based solely on interviews (about what I wasn't sure) could not compare to the other settings where data were gathered through a combination of methods, including sustained participant-observation, interviews and photos.

The few interviews that I did focused on the historical and contemporary importance of family in San Fernando, the possible continuing influence of political and business elites, and the difference gender and generation have made to the experience of being in an important family. Yet, I felt I was never really getting at their values and practices, and I didn't know what the right questions were. I decided to abandon looking for the ways that elites exercise political and state influence.

Insider scholars are differently located in relation to trust, family, participant-observation and positionality because their familiarity can both help and prevent access; reciprocity obligations may be taken more seriously, and researchers and participants may continue to know each other long after the research has ended. These considerations inform decisions at every stage of fieldwork. They also help explain why researchers choose particular identities and why some are chosen for them. Although my age, student status, class, gender, and religious and family connections enabled access to people and privileged power in specific interactions, women and men of all occupations and backgrounds exercised power in their own ways. This determined where and how I could use ethnographic methods, ways my identities were understood and research bargains I was allowed to make.

Negotiating Knowledge

Research bargains rely on acceptance, trust and reciprocity. While a researcher tries to get to know and understand a setting, others are also responding to their impressions of her and the work she is doing. I gained trust over months of visiting and getting to know women and men in the market, mas camp and mosque and on the Railway Line. I also always answered questions that people asked me about myself and shared stories about relationships, contraception and family life with women to whom I talked. Women and men got to know me, and I grew familiar with their concerns and even their fears about what I would write.

People constantly tested me and reminded me about how protective they felt about their lives and stories. One day in the first weeks of fieldwork on the wharf, a dealer whom I had seen pulling drugs out from under a house came up and asked me how old I was, what I was doing and what it was I was writing about the wharf. Bandleaders in the mas camp didn't want their business and leadership practices misrepresented, and leaders in the mosque made extra effort to clarify why governance is gendered when they felt that I was misinterpreting women's participation in the election. Market vendors were keenly concerned that their illegal roadside trade not be depicted as criminality, but as making an honest dollar. People know from reading newspapers that the truth others present about them is often biased and partial. Yet, all the groups were also interested in, and at times even proud of, getting their perspective and story represented.

Although people would stop and tell me about things "to put in the book" and ask if I was including them, others became worried whenever I began making notes while talking to them. The first months of fieldwork, I almost never wrote notes in front of people, but waited until I got home or had left the area. Early on, I realized that people were uncomfortable being taped and I learned to take quick notes of key points to remember or sometimes would ask if I could write something down. By the time I started semi-structured interviews, almost a year had passed and people felt far more comfortable with me writing down their responses. Months passed before I began taking pictures. Some, especially men, wanted their picture taken whereas others didn't or wanted to be paid for a photograph. Women usually didn't mind having their photo taken, though it sometimes made them shy. Perceptions of the power and status of a book showed a variety of fears regarding appearing in print.

By visiting often, helping out where needed, being explicit about the methodology and research process, and updating women and men at each site about my research, I was able to manage knowledge and reciprocity during fieldwork. Market vendors and people on the wharf especially liked that I visited regularly, spending time chatting and joking. One woman on the wharf said, "I like how you get to understand this place, not forcing people to answer questions, observing and getting to know us." I was explicit that I wanted to spend a lot of time getting to know people before asking lots of questions, and certainly before using any surveys or questionnaires. I also frequently asked for advice on themes and issues to explore, and women and men to interview.

It took about four months of wandering around to begin to see the intersection between formal structures and informal links among individuals and groups, as well as the ways that women's and men's needs, educational attainment, economic situation, and family and community life shaped their views. To collect more systematic participant-observation data, I left the field for a month, roughly coded my fieldwork notes and began to decide on emerging themes. After about eight months, I repeated this process in order to develop questionnaires and begin semi-structured interviews.

When I sought permission from market vendors for interviews, I didn't tell them that I was interested in their talk on illegal roadside selling and their negotiations with police as it was these very practices that were sensitive to talk about. Similarly, I told Railway Line residents that I wanted to interview them about family life and about their experience of working for CEPEP and URP. I didn't tell them that I was interested in patronage relations among workers and party activists in case they also thought this should not be discussed. As the election in the mosque was contentious, it was easier to say that I was interested in women's and men's opinions rather than in the gendered nature of men's power. Similarly, when I requested interviews with state officials, I asked to generally discuss their approaches to Carnival state strategies for welfare provision or the laws regarding roadside selling rather than saying that I was interested in forms and practices of state authority. Asking about family, livelihood, God and culture enabled these more sensitive questions to be answered. This anthropological strategy illustrates common problematic moments in ethnographic research (Metcalfe 2002).

Unacknowledged power is particularly relevant for the writing-up stage in the research process "in which the other is inscribed within, and explained by, the power of the ethnographer's language" (Ribbens and Edwards 1998, 153). Feminist researchers have attempted to deal with this by sharing results, co-authoring texts with research participants (Billson 1991; Mbilinyi 1989) and increasingly acknowledging that texts are "constructed" domains of truth and "serious fictions" (Clifford 1988, 10; Geiger 1990, 178). Other researchers have tried sharing their interview transcripts for participants' corrections or suggestions, but this has not always left participants feeling empowered (Boreland 1991, 70).

Given the anthropological tradition of protecting the identity of communities and individuals, ethical dilemmas about representation arose from my desire to openly document the history of the mas camp and the mosque. My own fears that they wouldn't like what I wrote and that they might feel misrepresented meant that I refrained from some of my observations. I wanted to be able to return to these sites long after the dissertation was finished and to maintain relationships. Hsiung (1996) and Zavella (1996) have similarly noted that shared positionality may make it difficult for a researcher to critically "air the dirty laundry." The private network of community, family and friendship ties, and accompanying duties and obligations, often tangle with the public role of researcher. This informs decisions about what point to represent, what stories to leave submerged and what kinds of information to expose to outsiders.

After writing up and finishing a draft of the thesis, I gave copies to members of each of the four communities for their comments and suggestions. I continued to visit them every few months and, in the mas camp, I went to help out on the weekends leading up to Carnival. I did this in order to continue to have a relationship with the people in these communities, but also to be open and honest about the partiality of my understanding.

Conclusion

Bell hooks (1993b, 78) has written that a researcher's "biography, politics and relationships become part of the fabric of the field." Reflexivity therefore calls for the researcher's personal account of the politics of the research process, the quality of relations between researcher and research participants and the centering of authority in interpreting and writing.

This essay has reflected on aspects of deciding on a topic and site, defining and entering the field, managing money, taking notes and writing up. These are all key to participant observation. I've attempted to show how living in another part of the country and with a host family, and taking on religious or class customs not one's own highlight the intricacies of building trust, using connections, negotiating power and ensuring reciprocity. My personal experiences became the basis for conversations about the aspirations, difficulties, relationships and politics of market vendors and religious leaders, and the ways these women and men differently experienced a small, shared urban space

Particularly among Anglophone Caribbean scholars, there needs to be far more awareness of how we embark on research at home. This is not just a concern with good research, but a political commitment to "enacting hybridity" (Narayan 1993). Documenting our shifting identifications is part of interrogating the taken-for-granted and highlighting the politics and power relations of belonging to a range of communities, including academic ones. It is about treating methodological positions, methods and fieldwork experiences as research findings and knowledge. This occurs too little among Caribbean scholars because it is hard to demarcate participation in community and nation from scholarly interest, and because of unstated assumptions about who we are when we do research at home. Yet, reflexive openness can exemplify what relations actually constitute the field in the Caribbean, and can better prepare those entering to interrogate the production of ethnographies in action.

Notes

1. Fifty-six kilometres from the capital Port of Spain, San Fernando is Trinidad's second city. 18 km sq., the city has its own pre-Columbian, colonial and postcolonial story lacing through the larger history of the twin-island Republic of Trinidad and Tobago. By the end of the 19th century, and following the abolition of African slavery in 1834, Indians, Chinese, Syrians, Portuguese and others had been brought to the colony as laborers or migrated as traders. Census data published in 2002 give the total population of Trinidad and Tobago as 1,262,400 and Trinidad as 1,208,282. San Fernando's population is now 55,419 (28,325 women and 27,094 men), and is larger than Port of Spain's by just over 6,000 persons (CSO 2000). The city comprises about 4% of the nation. Nationally, the population is self designated as 37.5% African, 40% Indian and 20.5% mixed. Less than one percent identify as white, Chinese or other.
2. I had originally planned to examine the practice and meanings of democracy in Trinidad. However, as soon as I moved to San Fernando, I decided that this didn't dig deeply enough into the political implications of everyday values and, more simply, wasn't a word that ordinary people were overly concerned with in their daily lives.
3. He did this by telling everyone, most of who knew it wasn't true, that I was his girlfriend so they should make sure I got help and was kept safe!
4. *Mas makers* are women and men who prepare costumes for their Carnival "band" or group of costumed masqueraders. They work out of a building or shed known as a *mas* camp.
5. A *roti* comprises flat bread wrapped around meat or vegetables
6. The nation-wide Unemployment Relief Programme (URP) aims to provide temporary work to those finding it hard to secure paid employment. The Community Environmental Protection and Enhancement Programme (CEPEP), established in 2002, is intended to be more than short-term employment relief. It aims to "clean and beautify the environment, provide employment for unskilled and semi-skilled workers and develop a cadre of micro-entrepreneurship and new business." Both URP and CEPEP are widely considered to be patronage-related programs.

References

Abu-Lughod, L. 1988. Fieldwork of a dutiful daughter. In S. Altorki, & C. Fawzi El-Solh (eds.), *Arab women in the field: Studying your own society.* Syracuse: Syracuse University Press.

Abu-Lughod, L. 1991. Writing against culture. In R. Fox (ed.), *Recapturing anthropology* (pp. 137-162). Santa Fe: School of American Research.
Alldred, P. 1998. Ethnography and discourse analysis: Dilemmas in representing the voices of children. In J. Ribbins, & R. Edwards (eds.), *Feminist dilemmas in qualitative research: Public knowledge and private lives* (pp. 147-170). London: Sage Publications.
Altorki, S. 1988. At home in the field. In S. Altorki, & C. Fawzi ElSolh (eds.), *Arab women in the field: Studying your own society* (pp. 25-48). Syracuse: Syracuse University Press.
Billson, J. 1991. The progressive verification method: Toward a feminist methodology for studying women cross-culturally. *Women Studies International Forum*, 14 (3), 201-15.
Borland, K. 1991. 'That's not what I said': Interpretive conflict in oral narrative research. In S. Berger Gluck, & D. Patai (eds.), *Women words: the feminist practice of oral history* (pp. 63-76). New York: Routledge.
Carnegie, C. 2002. *Postnationalism prefigured: Caribbean borderlands*. New Brunswick, NJ: Rutgers University Press.
Chevannes, B. 2001. *Learning to be a man: Culture, socialisation and gender identity in five Caribbean communities*. Barbados: University of the West Indies Press.
Cooper, C. 2004. *Sound clash: Jamaican dancehall culture at large*. New York: Palgrave-Macmillan.
Clifford, J. 1988. *The predicament of culture: Twentieth century ethnography, literature, and art*. Cambridge: Harvard University Press.
Denzin, N., & Lincoln, Y. (eds.). 1994. *Handbook of qualitative research*. Thousand Oaks, CA: Sage Publications Ltd.
Geiger, S. 1990. What's so feminist about women's oral history? *Journal of Women History* 2 (1), 169-182.
Geller, P., & Stockett, M. (eds.). 2006. *Feminist anthropology: Past, present, and future*. Philadelphia: University of Pennsylvania Press.
Hill-Collins, P. 1990. *Black feminist thought*. London: Routledge, Chapman and Hall, Inc.
Hosein, G. 2004. "Gender, generation and negotiation: Adolescence and young Indo-Trinidadian women's identities in the late 20" century. Unpublished master's thesis, The University of the West Indies, St. Augustine.
Hsiung, P-C. 1996. Between bosses and workers: The dilemmas of a keen observer and a vocal feminist. In D.L. Wolf (ed.), *Feminist dilemmas in fieldwork* (pp. 122-137). Boulder, CO: Westview Press.
hooks, b. 1993. *Sisters of the yam: Black women and self recovery*. Cambridge: South End Press Classics Series.
Kondo, D. 1986. Dissolution and reconstruction of self: Implications for anthropological epistemology. *Cultural Anthropology* 1(1), 74-88.
Kottak, P. 2005. *Mirror for humanity: A concise introduction to cultural anthropology*. Boston: McGraw Higher Education.
Ladner, J. 1987. Introduction to tomorrow's tomorrow: The black woman. In S. Harding (ed.), *Feminism and Methodology* (pp.74-83). Bloomington, I.N.: Indiana University Press.

Lal, J. 1996. Situating locations: The politics of self, identity, and "other" in living and writing text. In D.L. Wolf (ed.), *Feminist dilemmas in fieldwork* (pp. 185-214). Boulder, CO: Westview Press.

Madison, S.D. 2005. *Critical ethnography: Methods, ethics and performance.* Thousand Oaks, CA: SAGE.

Mahabir, N.K. 1989. The collection, transliteration, translation, classification and critical analysis of East Indian folk songs of the West Indies. Unpublished doctoral dissertation, The University of the West Indies, St. Augustine.

Mascarenhas-Keyes, S. 1987. The native anthropologist: Constraints and strategies in research. In A. Jackson (ed.), *Anthropology at home* (pp. 180-195). London, New York: Tavistock Publications.

Mauthner, N. & Doucet, A. 1998. Reflections on a voice-centred relational method: Analysing maternal and domestic voices. In J. Ribbins, & R. Edwards (eds), *Feminist dilemmas in qualitative research: Public knowledge and private lives* (pp. 119- 146). London: Sage Publications.

Matsumoto, V. 1996. Reflections on oral history: Research in a Japanese American community. In D.L Wolf (ed.), *Feminist dilemmas in fieldwork* (pp. 160-169). Boulder, CO: Westview Press.

Mauthner, M. 1998. Bringing silent voices into a public discourse: researching accounts of sister relationships. In J. Ribbins & R. Edwards (eds.), *Feminist dilemmas in qualitative research: Public knowledge and private lives* (pp. 39-57). London: Sage Publications.

Mbilinyi, M. 1989. 'I'd have been a man': Politics and the labour process in producing personal narratives. In The Personal Narratives Group (ed.), *Interpreting women's lives: Feminist theory and personal narratives* (pp. 204-227). Bloomington: Indiana University Press.

Metcalf, P. 2002. *They lie, we lie: Getting on with anthropology.* London and New York: Routledge.

Mutua, K. & Swadener, B.B. (eds.). 2004. *Decolonizing research in cross-cultural contexts: Critical personal narratives.* New York: State University of New York Press.

Narayan, Kirin. 1993. How native is a "native" anthropologist? *American Anthropologist, New Series* 95 (3), 671-686.

Ribbins, J. & Edwards, R. (eds.). 1998. *Feminist dilemmas in qualitative research: Public knowledge and private lives.* London: Sage Publications.

Stanley, L. 1987. Biography as microscope or kaleidoscope?: The case of "power, in Hannah Cullwick's relationship with Arthur Munby. *Women Studies International Forum* 10 (1), 19-37.

Taylor, S. and Bogdan, R. 1984. *Introduction to qualitative research methods.* Chichester: John Wiley.

Tixier y Vigil, Y. & Elsasser, N. 1976. The effects of the ethnicity of the interviewer on conversation: A study of Chicana women. In B.L. DuBois & I. Crouch (eds.), *Sociology of the language of American women.* San Antonio, TX: Trinity University Press.

Willis, P. & Trondman, M. 2002. Manifesto for ethnography. *Cultural Studies – Critical Methodologies* 2 (3), 394-402.

Wolf, D.L. (ed.). 1996. *Feminist dilemmas in fieldwork.* Boulder, CO: Westview Press.
Young, D. 2005. Writing against the native point of view. In A. Meneley, & D. Young (eds.), *Auto-ethnographies: The anthropology of academic practices* (pp. 203-215). Ontario, Canada: Broadview Press.
Zavella, P. 1996. Feminist insider dilemmas: Constructing ethnic identity with Chicana informants. In D.L. Wolf (ed.), *Feminist dilemmas in fieldwork* (pp. 138-159). Boulder, CO: Westview Press.

29. 'You is One of We': Positionality in the Field

Tami Navarro

In September 2008, I boarded an airplane bound for St Croix, the largest of the three islands that comprise the American territory, the US Virgin Islands (USVI). As only one American city offered direct flights to the island, I found myself in a terminal of the sprawling Miami airport. Among throngs of would-be tourists clad in floral patterns and straw hats at the surrounding points of departure, I sat at a lonely gate, kept company by a handful of my fellow passengers on their way to St Croix. For me, this trip was a homecoming, of sorts: born and raised on the island, I had left to attend college, and later graduate school, on the US mainland. Since then, I had made innumerable trips back – to visit family and friends, to take much-needed breaks from graduate study, and to conduct preliminary research. Two years into my PhD programme, I had changed my project from one I was mildly curious about to one about which I could not stop thinking, and so I was on my way to St Croix to begin an ethnographic engagement with an economic development programme that was having drastic financial, political, and cultural effects on the lives of Crucians. Despite these many trips, I felt this one to be different: I had been awarded a competitive fellowship to conduct 12 months of fieldwork in my chosen field site of St Croix. Before boarding my plane, I thought much about the combination of 'going home' and 'conducting fieldwork'. Fortunately for me, the discipline in which I was being trained, anthropology, has a rich history of 'native' anthropologists who have long been exploring the limits – and possibilities – of this ambivalent positioning (not least of whom was Zora Neale Hurston, whose ethnographic work *Mules and Men* I clutched tightly in my carry-on bag).

My anthropological training had already taught me the crucial importance of self-reflexivity on the part of the researcher if there is to be any hope of presenting a comprehensive ethnographic account (this same training had also shown me that a complete reproduction or telling of one's experience in 'the field' is, by definition, impossible). Given this, I knew it would be impossible for me to tell this story of the EDC programme without telling the story of St Croix and its previous attempts at economic stimulation. That is, I could not engage with this development initiative without inserting myself first as a girl, and then a woman, whose memories and worldview were completely tethered to that island. At the end of what ultimately became 16 months of fieldwork, I was forced to grapple with the 'back door' access I had to informants on the island as a 'native' Crucian, born and raised on St Croix. This admission of my complicated position is meant as a gesture towards disclosure and honesty – yet it obscures nearly as much as it reveals: What does it mean to label a lifelong friend an 'informant'? Did these 'subjects' remain 'informants' on joint family vacations? During late-night phone calls? Or, when they were completely unable to understand me as anything other than a fellow Crucian, necessarily opposed to the 'others' brought to 'our' island by a development programme?

These divisions between 'self' and 'other', 'researcher' and 'informant', and even – with the combination of new technologies like social networking websites with longstanding anthropological realities like the determination of some informants to demand favours long after the conclusion of formal fieldwork – 'then' and 'now' become, if not completely indistinct, increasingly faint. Certainly these questions are not new. Anthropologists have grappled with them since the birth of the discipline – but perhaps no amount of training, of reading the accounts of others, is sufficient preparation for the mix of calculatedly professional and intensely personal experiences that characterize fieldwork. In my new role as a funded anthropologist, I planned to engage with this island and its people through the lens of my discipline – making, as it were, the familiar strange. My engagement with my mostly vacant boarding area was an early moment of this lens-switching from 'Crucian' to 'anthropologist': I had long been aware that significantly fewer tourists visited St Croix than other islands in the region, including its fellow US Virgin Islands, St Thomas, and St John. However, when I later looked up statistics of visitors to the island, the vastness of this difference became clear, as the combined port of call for St Thomas/St John received 685 cruise ships in 2008, while St Croix welcomed just two.[1] A comparison of commercial flights landing on these islands confirmed this uneven distribution, as the same period saw 10,503 commercial flights arriving on St Thomas/St John, but only 1,333 landing on St Croix[2]. This disparity was to serve as context for my project, as St Thomas and St John have both fared well in the global tourist market, while St Croix has struggled for decades with finding ways to attract and generate capital.

In light of St Croix's long-struggling economy, it had – along with many islands across the region – turned to neoliberal development as a model of economic stimulation. This shift in development thinking produced the Economic Development Commission (EDC) programme, an initiative launched in the USVI through an agreement between local politicians and the US federal government, designed to stimulate the economy of these US-owned islands by offering finance companies willing to relocate to the island staggering tax cuts of up to 90 per cent. In addition to opening offices on St Croix, companies were required to support local charitable organizations and hire Crucian employees as staffers. I was drawn to this project, in large part, by the frequent complaints I heard from many Crucians that EDC companies were saving vast sums of money – thus increasing their wealth – while circumventing the requirements around hiring and spending.

I realized that in order to engage with this programme, my methodology would necessarily include spending time at EDC companies with the Crucians selected to work in this sector. Thus, my primary ethnographic engagement took place through two unpaid EDC 'internships' I performed simultaneously over the course of 11 weeks at businesses receiving EDC benefits, the St Croix Fund and Stanford Financial. Of these companies, one was significantly larger and seemed to serve, for many Crucians, as a shorthand for the anxieties surrounding this offshore banking programme that had brought vast amounts of capital[3] – and its (white) handlers to the island. During the period of my fieldwork, rumours swirled around this company, Stanford Financial, with some claiming that the arrival of its proprietor Allan Stanford on St Croix came as a result of his being forced to leave Antigua by that country's government, while others objected to his penchant for purchasing vast tracts of land, adding to the growing problems of real estate availability and soaring property taxes on the island.[4] Given these suspicions, it did not come as a complete surprise, then, when I received a phone call from an informant-friend after the end of my fieldwork, informing me that Stanford Financial had been raided by the US federal government and that Allan Stanford himself was being charged with fraud (charges on which he was found guilty, and for which he is today serving a 110-year prison sentence). All of this was, of course, unknown to me at the time. What I *did* know was that EDC companies seemed to have a very particular profile they sought for their employees – a pattern I first began to notice when more and more of my former classmates and friends were offered positions in the EDC sector, despite their frequent lack of experience or training in either finance or economics.

This hiring profile, which favoured young, unmarried Crucian women from backgrounds of relative privilege, provided me particular access to these employees, as I had either grown up or attended high school with many of these would-be EDC workers. While I was hopeful that these existing connections with potential informants would facilitate my access to the EDC sector, I was more broadly interested in the paradigm shift that enabled the creation of the EDC programme, given the long history of the feminization of labour and the contemporary neoliberal emphasis on the figure of 'the girl' as the necessary agent of community change (e.g., Murphy 2013). In the case of the EDC programme, this gendered preference manifested in the frequent hiring of young women who were most often in their 20s – a group of female workers who became known as 'EDC girls'. In keeping with patterns in the Caribbean and beyond in which service labour – including financial services – has become feminized, the EDC preference for these 'girls' recalls the overwhelming number of female service workers in the industrialization period as well as the continued dependence of the tourism industry on the labour of young women.

Grounded in current and pressing questions regarding gender and neoliberal development, my research also engaged and built upon work that demonstrates how contemporary processes produce new dynamics of subject formation (Clarke and Thomas 2006; Freeman 2000; Hall 1997; Holt 2000; Khan 2004; Thomas 2004; Yelvington 1995). My work greatly benefited from the fact that gender has long been one of the primary units of analysis in Caribbeanist research, and scholarship on women and labour in the region has been particularly rich (Abraham-Van der Mark 1983; Anderson 1986; Barrow 1995; Barrow 1998; Bolles 1983; Ellis 2003; Kempadoo 2004; Leo-Rhynie 1997; Mohammed 2002; Mohammed and Shepherd 1988; Momsen 1993; Yelvington 1995). For instance, scholars have long noted the feminization of labour during industrialization – yet while women were preferred employees in factories, their labour was devalued, as women were not considered serious members of the workforce. Rather, they were presumed to be supported by their fathers, working only to earn 'pin money' for themselves (Enloe 1989). With the shift toward information and financial management, young women have remained desirable employees, although the logic for this preference has changed: in the current moment, women are understood as 'stable' employees, workers who will report for duty without fail as a result of familial and financial obligations.

As a springboard for conceptualizing the role of female EDC employees, I turned to Carla Freeman's (2000) scholarship on 'pink collar identities', in which she suggests a re-feminization of the labour process with the turn toward service industries, resulting in an upward repositioning of (some) women within local status hierarchies. Building on these insights, I sought to examine how young, US-educated female EDC employees could be positioned as both beneficiaries and victims of the current neoliberal moment, and what this might mean for socio-economic and political organization in St Croix and beyond.

As I had hoped, my pre-existing relationships with EDC hopefuls (and later, employees), allowed me access to this sector, resulting in the unpaid internships that enabled me to work alongside female EDC employees. At the outset of these internships, I was unsure what, exactly, my days would entail. While my interviews at both St Croix Fund and Stanford Financial had gone well, I was left wondering what role I would perform. During my first week at Stanford Financial, my time was largely spent going through orientation, a process that mostly involved watching informational videos on the company and its history and getting introduced around the office. My tasks included researching possible investments and evaluating financial trends in order to assess the likely success of various investment strategies. Given Stanford's penchant for purchasing real estate, there were a growing number of offices during the period of my fieldwork, but the particular Stanford office at which I worked housed 11 other employees, seven of whom were local women of colour. Of these, six fit the standard profile of 'EDC girls': relatively young (in their 20s or 30s) and educated on the US mainland.[5] What was unique about this company and its employees vis-à-vis the EDC programme as a whole was the styling of these workers – a difference that was a matter of degree, rather than of type. If 'EDC girls' were seen on the island as set-apart and somehow 'different' from their fellow Virgin Islanders, the local women employed at Stanford were seen as the epitome of that difference. Stanford's great wealth, the excitement surrounding his arrival on St Croix, and the company's strict dress code that made no concessions to the unforgiving Caribbean heat – an issue that was particularly relevant during summer, the period of my internship – made Stanford and his employees central topics of discussion on the island among both supporters and critics. Given the workplace dress of slacks or skirts, blazers, closed-toe shoes, and stockings for women (a requirement that was unspoken, yet strictly observed in the office), the aesthetics surrounding the women working at Stanford marked them as different. Beyond these wardrobe concerns, there were other aspects of the behaviour and expectations surrounding Stanford workers that marked them as somehow set apart from the local community: Shortly after I began my internship a new 'concierge' was hired. Larissa, a darker-skinned local woman in her early 20s, did not relax her hair and generally wore a ponytail at work. A few weeks after she began working in the office, we were chatting when she repeatedly asked me for my advice and opinion on whether or not she should get the curls in her hair loosened by getting a chemical treatment called a texturizer. When I asked her why she was concerned about this issue, she said that it was just something she had been thinking about, and that she had wanted to have 'nicer' – that is, looser – curls. Certainly, Larissa's decisions concerning hairstyle and texture are matters of personal choice. However, given her recent employment at this high-profile organization, a company foremost in a sector widely suspected of having unspoken hiring preferences that favour lighter-skinned local young women, I wondered about the connection between Larissa's workplace and her sudden concern with looking 'appropriate'. Further, the literature on Black women's hair and notions of beauty and respectability, including Ingrid Banks (2000), Ginetta Candelario (2007), and Lanita Jacobs-Huey

(2006) points to the significance of hairstyles beyond aesthetics.[6] In addition to concerns about dress and hair there was another marker that I noticed immediately about the Stanford employees with whom I worked. Of the 12 workers in my office, only two were unmarried (one of whom was engaged and got married shortly after my internship ended). This fact is of note, as the 2000 Census[7] shows that 41.7 per cent of women in the Virgin Islands have never been married. This privileging of marriage among Stanford employees against the norms of the island further set these workers apart from much of the Virgin Islands community. Moreover, the high percentage of married employees at Stanford is striking for the region and hints at employer preferences for 'classed' behaviour among its workforce. The relationship between marriage, class and respectability in the Caribbean has been theorized by scholars, including foundational work by T.S. Simey (1946), Fernanado Henriques (1953), R.T. Smith (1996), M.G. Smith (1965) and Edith Clarke (1957).[8] Writing in the Jamaican context, R.T. Smith's concept of the 'dual marriage system' was pivotal in theorizing marriage and class, as he analysed the practice of upper-class white men marrying white women – while keeping lower-class Black women as concubines. During the colonial period, the British in Jamaica abhorred such practices as serial monogamy and 'visiting unions', yet these were – and remained – extremely common, despite British efforts to increase 'low' marriage rates through state-sponsored programmes such as the Mass Marriage Movement.[9] What is more, such relationships remain common in Jamaica today: Writing in 1997 on the patriarchal influence colonial ideology has on present-day gender Laws in Jamaica, Suzanne LaFont and Deborah Pruitt write, 'serial monogamy is the norm, and most [lower-class] women have children with more than one partner' (LaFont and Pruitt 1997, 216). Thus, the disproportionately high number of married Crucians employed at Stanford seemed more than simply a coincidence, but rather a reflection on the classed and behavioural expectations projected by the company.

    The discourse of respectability which outlines 'appropriate' behaviour as determined by race, colour, class, and gender (Wilson 1973; Enloe 1989; Alexander 1997; Douglass 1992; McClintock 1995; Austin-Broos 1997) is rooted in ideals of white femininity (and its approximation by women of colour). This discourse, in large part, governed the behavioural expectations of EDC girls, as they were expected to dress modestly and attend 'appropriate' cultural events, such as jazz concerts, crafts fairs, and film screenings. In this awkward positioning, 'EDC girls' are subject to new expectations based on their employment within the EDC sector, yet they remain subject to long-standing local gendered and generational expectations in the wider community.

During the period of my fieldwork, I found that I was also expected to behave in ways that were recognizable as 'respectable'. In addition to my duties as an anthropologist-intern and the 'deep hanging out' (Geertz 1998) of fieldwork, I also needed to attend to quotidian tasks, including buying groceries, doing laundry and finding an apartment. This last, seemingly-mundane task made clear the degree to which gendered expectations and notions of respectability related to my presence in 'the field'. As I searched for a rental unit, ruling out many neighbourhoods as too expensive on my fieldwork stipend, and other areas as simply too far or secluded for my needs, I was frequently met with curious stares and concerned questions such as 'you have family here? Why such a pretty young girl like you looking to rent?' The desire for a space of my own was seen as unusual to the point of suspicious. This experience of being positioned as a young unmarried woman in need of familial protection – or at the very least, surveillance – brought the politics of respectability to the fore. What I experienced in that moment were gendered expectations that cast a long shadow on the daily lives of EDC girls.

Once settled into my apartment and well into my EDC 'internships', I more frequently experienced the pressures of these behavioural expectations, from both within and outside the EDC sector. For instance, during the island's 2008 Carnival season, I rose early to participate in that morning's J'ouvert. As the early-morning street party wound its way through town, it passed an EDC office where I saw three suit-clad female workers standing outside, taking in the scene. When I went over to say hello, surprise – and disapproval – clearly registered on their faces, with one woman saying to me: 'Is that you? What are YOU doing in the J'ouvert?' For these women, my decision to participate in early-morning drinking and dancing in the street to calypso music along with hundreds of scantily-clad revellers was a serious miscalculation of the limits of behaviour for ambivalently positioned EDC girls, a transgression of feminine ideals of respectability and 'appropriate' behaviour.

In addition to the gendered expectations that shaped many of my experiences in the field, I continued to grapple with my multiple commitments: to my discipline, to my project, and to St Croix and its people. With regard to this final set of commitments, I found myself in frequent conversation with my interlocutors, many of whom were unable or unwilling to make distinctions between my longtime role as their friend and my newer position as a researcher. In these conversations, I did not always have the final say, and my attempts to complicate my relationship to the community of Crucians were sometimes rejected by those I interviewed or with whom I worked. The title of this essay is drawn from one such ethnographically rich encounter during which I was unwillingly folded into the 'we' that (presumably) represented the local community. During the time of my fieldwork, there were many objections to the EDC programme, both general and specific. Of these, one of the most pronounced were concerns over the EDC hiring practices that were seen as discriminatory – preferences that produced the category of 'EDC girl'. One evening, after a long day of attempting to decipher financial projections in my role as EDC intern, I sat in a dimly lit restaurant, rehashing the events of the day with a friend who was filling in as the bartender that night. Overhearing our conversation, Tyrone, a waiter who had not long ago finished his shift, shouted, 'I hope you study how they discriminate against we!' Stunned, I mumbled something about 'studying all aspects' and 'remaining impartial'. As I thought about his comment later, however, I realized that the 'we' Tyrone invoked is complicated – and entirely unsteady – as this false binary of us/them is constantly shifting and complicated by the presence of many 'Others', including recently-arrived mainland Americans, Caribbean immigrants, a decades-old community of white Americans, and social scientists like myself, who were attempting to nuance this too-easy division.

Long after the conclusion of formal fieldwork, the assigning of pseudonyms, and the cataloguing of life events, it remains unclear to me how seriously my friend-informants took my protestations that I was neither fully an 'insider' or an 'outsider' and that this division was itself a slippery and dangerous slope toward determining who 'really' belongs. While I had the authority to assign names and privilege some events over others, in the end, I am unsure of my success in occupying – in the minds of my friends and informants – the position of researcher, and wonder if I always remained 'one of we'.

References

Abraham-Van der Mark, Eva E. 1983. The Impact of Industrialisation on Women: A Caribbean Case. In *Women, Men and the International Division of Labor*, ed. June Nash and Maria Fernandez-Kelly.Albany: SUNY Press.

Alexander, M. Jacqui, and Chandra Talpade Mohanty, eds. 1997. *Feminist Genealogies, Colonial Legacies, Democratic Futures.* New York: Routledge.

Anderson, Patricia. 1986. Conclusion: Women in the Caribbean. *Social and Economic Studies* 35, no. 2:291–324.

Austin-Broos-Diane. 1997. *Jamaica Genesis: Religion and the Politics of Moral Orders.* Chicago: University of Chicago Press.

Banks, Ingrid. 2000. *Hair Matters: Beauty, Power, and Black Women's Consciousness.* New York: New York University Press.

Barrow, Christine. 1998. *Caribbean Portraits: Essays on Gender Ideologies and Identities.* Kingston: Ian Randle Publishers.

Barrow, Eudine. 1995. Postmodernist Feminist Theorizing and Development Policy Practice in the Anglophone Caribbean: The Barbados Case. In Marian *Feminism/Postmodernism/Development*, ed. H. Marchand and Jane Parpart. New York: Routledge.

Bolles, Lynn. 1983. Kitchens Hit by Priorities: Employed Working Class JamaicanWomen Confront the IMF. In *Women, Men, and the International Division of Labor*, ed. June Nash and M.P. Fernandez-Kelly. Albany: SUNY Press.

Candelario, Ginetta. 2007. *Black Behind the Ears: Dominican Racial Identity from Museums to Beauty Shops.* Durham: Duke University Press.

Clarke, Edith. 1957. *My Mother Who Fathered Me: A Study of the Family in Three Selected Communities in Jamaica.* London: G. Allen & Unwin.

Clarke, Kamari, and Deborah Thomas, eds. 2006. *Globalisation and Race: Transformations in the Cultural Production of Blackness.* Durham: Duke University Press.

Douglass, Lisa. 1992. *Politics of Sentiment: Love, Hierarchy, and the Jamaican Family Elite.* Boulder, Colorado: Westview Press.

Ellis, Pat. 2003. *Women, Gender, and Development in the Caribbean: Reflections and Projections.* London: Zed Books.

Enloe, Cynthia. 1989. *Bananas, Beaches and Bases: Making Feminist Sense of International Politics.* Berkeley: University of California Press.

Freeman, Carla. 2000. *High Tech and High Heels in the Global Economy: Women, Work, and Pink-Collar Identities in the Caribbean.* Durham: Duke University Press.

Geertz, Clifford. 1998. Deep Hanging Out. *The New York Review of Books.* October 2.

Hall, Stuart. 1997. Old and New Identities, Old and New Ethnicities. In *Culture, Globalisation, and the World-System: Contemporary Conditions for the Representation of Identity*, ed. Anthony King. Minneapolis: University of Minnesota Press.

Henriques, Fernando. 1953. *Family and Color in Jamaica.* London: Eyre & Spottiswoode.

Holt, Thomas. 2000. *The Problem of Race in the Twenty-First Century*. Cambridge, MA: Harvard University Press.

Jacobs-Huey, Lanita. 2006. *From the Kitchen to the Parlor: Language and Becoming in African American Women's Hair Care*. New York: Oxford University Press

Kempadoo, Kamala. 2004. *Sexing the Caribbean: Gender, Race, and Sexual Labor*. London: Routledge.

Khan, Aisha. 2001. Journey to the Centre of the Earth: The Caribbean as Master Symbol. *Cultural Anthropology* 16, no. 3:271–302.

LaFont Suzanne and Deborah Pruitt. 1997. The Colonial Legacy: Gendered Laws in Jamaica. In *Daughters of Caliban*, ed. Consuelo L. Springfield. Bloomington: Indiana University Press.

Leo-Rhynie, Elsa. 1997. Class, Race, and Gender Issues in Child Rearing in the Caribbean. In *Caribbean Families: Diversity Among Ethnic Groups*, ed. Roopnarine, Jaipaul and Janet Brown. London: Ablex.

Lett, Christine. 2004. Gov't to Weather Expected EDC Storm. *St Croix Avis*, October 13.

Lohr, Lynda. 2008. Municipal Government Hot Topic at Constitutional Convention Meeting. *St Croix Source*, March 12.

McClintock, Anne. 1995. *Imperial Leather: Race, Gender and Sexuality in the Colonial Contest*. Routledge: Great Britain.

Mohammed, Patricia, and Catherine Shepherd, eds. 1988. Gender in Caribbean Development: Papers presented at the Inaugural Seminar of the University of the West Indies, Women and Development Studies Project. Centre for Gender and Development Studies, University of the West Indies, Kingston, Jamaica.

Momsen, Janet. 1991. *Women and Development in the Third World*. New York: Routledge.

Murphy, Michelle. 2013. The Girl: Mergers of Feminism and Finance in Neoliberal Times. *Scholar and Feminist Online* 11(1-2).

Simey, T.S. 1946. *Welfare & Planning in the West Indies*. Oxford: The Clarendon Press.

Smith, M.G. 1965. *The Plural Society in the British West Indies*. Berkeley: University of California Press.

Smith, R.T. 1996. *The Matrifocal Family: Power, Pluralism, and Politics*. New York: Routledge.

Thomas, Deborah A. 2004. *Modern Blackness: Nationalism, Globalisation, and the Politics of Culture in Jamaica*. Durham: Duke University Press.

Wilson, Peter. 1973. *Crab Antics: The Social Anthropology of English-Speaking Negro Societies of the Caribbean*. New Haven: Yale University Press.

Yelvington, Kevin. 1995. *Producing Power: Ethnicity, Gender, and Class in a Caribbean Workplace*. Philadelphia: Temple University Press.

Notes

1. 'Cruise Ship Calls', *US Virgin Islands Bureau of Economic Research*.
2. 'Major Carrier Direct Flight Seats,' *US Virgin Islands Bureau of Economic Research*.

3. Estimates place the amount of capital brought into the US Virgin Islands economy by the EDC programme at $100 million dollars (Lett 2004).
4. Describing the impact of these property tax increases, a 2008 article in the St Croix Source notes that 'in some cases St John property owners face tax bills six to ten times higher than their previous bill' (Lohr 2008).
5. One woman, Ellen, was in her late 40s and had not been educated in the States.
6. In her work on Jamaica, Ulysse (2007) writes, 'for dark skinned females of the middle class, colour is mediated through observance of the culture of femininity and dress. One of the ultimate symbols of ladyhood is her well-groomed hair. At the time my hair was permed or 'colonized'– a term I used much to the shock of the females I encountered. [Shortly after cutting] my hair to a low Afro, a female hairdresser asked me if was going to 'texturize' the new 'fro, that is soften it with more chemicals. Yet I had cut off the hair precisely to get rid of all the chemicals' (Ulysse 2007, 117).
7. Data from http://www.census.gov/Press-Release/www/2002/usvistatelevel.pdf.
8. See also Douglass (1992).
9. Clarke (1957) describes the Mass Marriage Movement in Jamaica as 'an attempt to halt th[e] presumed spread of 'promiscuity'...In 1944–45, Lady Huggins, wife of the then governor of Jamaica, launched an islandwide campaign to marry of consensually cohabitating couples and any others whose mating status and relations seemed to warrant this. This Mass Marriage Movement was initiated in response to the Royal Commission's demand for 'an organised campaign against the social, moral, and economic evils of promiscuity.' However, being based on ignorance of Jamaican folk society and family life, the movement was equally misconceived in its methods and goals, and proved unsuccessful. At its greatest impact the movement lifted the Jamaican marriage rate from 4.44 per thousand to 5.82 in 1946. By 1951 the marriage rate and the correlated illegitimacy ratio among annual births had reverted to their earlier level. By 1955, 'the Mass Marriage Movement had petered out" (Clarke 1956, xxiii).

Printed in the USA
CPSIA information can be obtained
at www.ICGtesting.com
LVHW020936051224
798157LV00009B/12